A Study Book for the NEBOSH National Diploma

in Occupational Health and Safety Practice

Workplace and Work Equipment Safety

Professional Membership (Grad IOSH)

Holders of the National Diploma may apply for Graduate membership (Grad IOSH) of the Institution of Occupational Safety and Health (IOSH), and on completion of a programme of Continual Professional Development (CPD) may apply for Chartered Safety and Health Practitioner status as a Chartered Member of IOSH (CMIOSH).
Chartered Member status reflects the competence demanded of professionals in health and safety management or leadership positions.

RMS Publishing Limited
Suite 3, Victoria House
Lower High Street
Stourbridge
DY8 1TA

© ACT Associates Limited.
First Published May 2005.
Second Edition August 2006.
Second Edition (Revised and Updated) October 2007.
Third Edition June 2008.
Third Edition March 2008 (reprint).
Third Edition July 2010 (reprint).
Fourth Edition September 2011.
Fourth Edition March 2012 (reprint).
Fourth Edition February 2013 (reprint).

All rights reserved. No part of this publication may be stored in a retrieval system, reproduced, or transmitted in any form or by any means, electronic, mechanical, photocopying, recording or otherwise without either the prior written permission of the Publishers.

This book may not be lent, resold, hired out or otherwise disposed of by way of trade in any form or binding or cover other than that in which it is published, without the prior consent of the Publishers.

Whilst every effort is made to ensure the completeness and accuracy of the information contained herein, RMS can bear no liability for any omission or error.

Cover design by Graham Scriven.
Printed and bound in Great Britain by CPI Antony Rowe.

Crown Copyright material is reproduced with the permission of the Controller of HMSO and the Queen's Printer for Scotland.

ISBN-13: 978-1-906674-10-6

Editor's Notes

Diagrams and photographs

This 4th Edition has been thoroughly revised, reformatted and updated and provides an excellent reference for those looking to undertake a career as a health and safety practitioner. We have taken particular care to support the text with a significant number of photographs and schematics. The photographs have been selected to be illustrative of both good and bad working practices and should always be considered in context with supporting text. I am sure that students will find this a useful aid when trying to relate their background and experience to the broad based NEBOSH National Diploma syllabus. They will give an important insight into some of the technical areas of the syllabus for those who may not have a strong technical background.

Where diagrams/text extracts are known to be drawn from other publications, a clear source reference is shown and RMS wishes to emphasise that reproduction of such diagrams/text extracts within the Study Book is for educational purposes only and the original copyright has not been infringed.

Legal requirements

Legislation is referred to in context in the various elements that comprise the study book. This reflects the interest of the NEBOSH National Diploma syllabus and requirements to study new/amended legislation under the rule from NEBOSH that it has to have been in force for six months before it becomes examinable. In addition, the essential points of legislation relevant to this Unit of the Diploma syllabus are contained in the section of the study book under Relevant Statutory Provisions.

Case law, as specified by the NEBOSH National Diploma syllabus, is referred to in the Workplace and Work Equipment Safety Study Book. It is important to note that these cases are examined in the NEBOSH National Diploma. Additional cases may be referred to in the same element. Though they are not referred to specifically in the syllabus it is useful to be aware of them as they have an influence on the workplace and showing knowledge of them at time of examination may emphasise a greater depth of understanding of the topic. Further information on other significant cases can be found in the other two RMS Publishing Study Books in the series for the NEBOSH National Diploma.

Syllabus

Each element of the Study Book has an element overview that sets out the learning outcomes, the contents, the relevant statutory provisions and any connected sources of reference. The Study Book reflects the order and content of the NEBOSH National Diploma syllabus and in this way the student can be confident that the Study Book reflects the themes of the syllabus. In addition, the syllabus, and therefore this study book, is structured in a very useful way; focusing on hazards, their control and core management of health and safety principles which would be useful as reference for any health and safety practitioner.

National Vocational Qualification

We are confident that those working to national vocational qualifications in occupational health and safety will find this Study Book a useful companion. For students working towards the S/NVQ Level 5 in Occupational Health and Safety Practice they will find a good correlation between the scope of the Study Book series for NEBOSH National Diploma and the domain knowledge needs at that level.

Higher Level Qualifications

The structure, level and content of this study book is appropriate for those involved in study of health and safety at university level. The NEBOSH National Diploma is recognised by IOSH as fulfilling the academic requirements for Chartered Membership (CMIOSH) conferring the official title of Chartered Safety and Health Practitioner. It is also accepted by the International Institute of Risk and Safety Management (IIRSM) as meeting their requirements for full membership (MIIRSM).

Relationship to other RMS Study Books

This study book content is built on the foundation knowledge contained in the RMS Publishing Study Books for Certificate level and should be read in conjunction with them, in particular the study book for the NEBOSH National General Certificate in Occupational Health and Safety.

Acknowledgements

Managing Editor: Ian Coombes

Member of the Safety Groups UK (SGUK) Management Committee. Former NEBOSH examiner, NEBOSH Director, member of NEBOSH Council, member of the IOSH Professional Committee and Chair of the IOSH Initial Professional Development Committee.

RMS Publishing wishes to acknowledge the following contributors and thank them for their assistance in the preparation of the Unit C Study Book for the NEBOSH National Diploma: Janice McTiernan, Barrie Newell, Geoff Littley, Peter Brookbank, Tony Cheesman, Nick Attwood, Kris James and Design and Development Co-ordinator Julie Skett.

Publications available from RMS:

Publication	Edition	ISBN
A Study Book for the NEBOSH National General in Occupational Health and Safety	Sixth	978-1-906674-07-6
A Study Book for the NEBOSH National Certificate in Construction Safety and Health	Third	978-1-906674-15-1
A Study Book for the NEBOSH Certificate in Fire Safety and Risk Management	Third	978-1-906674-05-2
A Study Book for the NEBOSH National Certificate in Environmental Management	Second	978-1-906674-16-8
A Study Book for the NEBOSH Certificate in the Management of Health and Well-being	First	978-1-906674-14-4
A Study Book for the International Certificate in Oil and Gas	First	978-1-906674-19-9
A Study Book for the NEBOSH International General Certificate	Second	978-1-906674-17-5
Study Books for the NEBOSH National Diploma in Occupational Safety and Health:		
■ (Unit A) Managing health and safety	Fourth	978-1-906674-08-3
■ (Unit B) Hazardous agents in the workplace	Fourth	978-1-906674-09-0
■ (Unit C) Workplace and work equipment safety	Fourth	978-1-906674-10-6
Study Books for the NEBOSH International Diploma in Occupational Safety and Health:		
■ (Unit IA) International management of health and safety	First	978-1-906674-11-3
■ (Unit IB) International control of hazardous agents in the workplace	First	978-1-906674-12-0
■ (Unit IC) International workplace and work equipment safety	First	978-1-906674-13-7
Controlling skin exposure (BOHS)	First	978-1-906674-00-7

Contents

UNIT C: WORKPLACE AND WORK EQUIPMENT SAFETY

ELEMENT	TITLE	PAGE NO.
Element 1:	General workplace issues	1
Element 2:	Principles of fire and explosion	33
Element 3:	Workplace fire risk assessment	69
Element 4:	Storage, handling and processing of dangerous substances	119
Element 5:	Work equipment (general)	153
Element 6:	Work equipment (workplace machinery)	177
Element 7:	Work equipment (mobile, lifting and access)	249
Element 8:	Electrical safety and Electricity at Work Regulations 1989	281
Element 9:	Construction hazards and controls	313
Element 10:	Workplace transport and driving for work	347
Element 11:	Pressure system hazards and controls	365
Relevant statutory provisions		389
Index		439

Figure List (including tables and quotes)

Figure Ref *Title and Source* Page No.

Element C1

Ref	Title and Source	Page
C1-1	Slip resistance surface on steps. *Source: RMS.*	4
C1-2	Anti-slip flooring. *Source: RMS.*	4
C1-3	Pendulum coefficient of friction tester. *Source: HSE/HSL.*	5
C1-4	Slip potential classification PTV. *Source: HSE/HSL.*	5
C1-5	Roughness measuring instrument. *Source: Taylor Hobson.*	5
C1-6	Slip potential classification, roughness. *Source: HSE/HSL.*	6
C1-7	Slip assessment tool. *Source: HSE.*	6
C1-8	Roughness suitable for contaminants of different viscosity. *Source: HSE/HSL.*	6
C1-9	Coefficient of friction of different materials. *Source: Roy Beardmore.*	6
C1-10	Hydrodynamic effect. *Source: CIRIA.*	7
C1-11	Housekeeping in office. *Source: RMS.*	8
C1-12	Housekeeping in garage. *Source: RMS.*	8
C1-13	Categories of safety signs. *Source: RMS.*	10
C1-14	Warning, Mandatory and prohibition. *Source: RMS.*	10
C1-15	Warning and safe condition. *Source: RMS.*	10
C1-16	Prohibition signs. *Source: RMS.*	11
C1-17	Warning and mandatory sign. *Source: RMS.*	11
C1-18	Mandatory sign. *Source: RMS.*	11
C1-19	Safe condition sign. *Source: RMS.*	11
C1-20	Hazard identification - obstruction. *Source: RMS.*	11
C1-21	Hazard identification - restricted width. *Source: RMS.*	11
C1-22	Codes for verbal signals. *Source: Health and Safety (Safety Signs and Safety Signals) Regulations (SSSR) 1996.*	12
C1-23	Hand signals. *Source: Health and Safety (Safety Signs and Safety Signals) Regulations (SSSR) 1996.*	13
C1-24	Confined space - definition. *Source: CSR 1997.*	14
C1-25	Confined space - chamber. *Source: RMS.*	15
C1-26	Confined space - sewer. *Source: RMS.*	15
C1-27	Confined space - tank. *Source: RMS.*	15
C1-28	Confined space - open tank. *Source: RMS.*	15
C1-29	Example PTW certificate (confined spaces). *Source: HSE Guidance note on permits to work.*	18
C1-30	Explosive atmosphere. *Source: HSE Guidance INDG370.*	20
C1-31	Ladder hoop. *Source: RMS.*	27
C1-32	Roof ladder and guard rails. *Source: RMG.*	27
C1-33	Mobile elevated work platform "Cherry Picker". *RMS.*	28
C1-34	Two people lifting heavy object. *Source: RMS.*	31
C1-35	Heavy electricity generator. *Source: RMS*	31

Element C2

Ref	Title and Source	Page
C2-1	Densities of flammable gases/vapours. *Source: RMS/Multiple.*	36
C2-2	Flammable/explosive limits gases/vapours. *Source: RMS/Multiple.*	37
C2-3	Critical temperature examples. *Source: FST.*	37
C2-4	Critical pressure examples. *Source: FST.*	37
C2-5	Maximum explosion pressures. *Source: FST.*	38
C2-6	Explosion pressure curves for hexane/air mixtures in vessels of different sizes. *Source: Ambiguous.*	38
C2-7	Suppressed explosion curve for a hexane/air mixture in a one gallon vessel. *Source: Ambiguous.*	38
C2-8	The fire triangle. *Source: CorelDraw! 5.0 Clipart.*	38
C2-9	Stages of combustion. *Source: RMS.*	41
C2-10	Effects of particle size of sugar on explosion indices. *Source: Explosion Testing Ltd.*	42
C2-11	Buncefield Oil Terminal. *Source: Chiltern Air Support.*	43
C2-12	Buncefield: Tank 912 indicated by the arrow. *Source: Chiltern Air Support.*	43
C2-13	Catastrophic bund wall failure at pipe penetrations. *Source: www.buncefieldinvestigation.gov.uk.*	44
C2-14	Loss of sealant between penetrating pipe and bund wall. *Source: www.buncefieldinvestigation.gov.uk.*	44
C2-15	Effects of trees and shrubbery on unconfined vapour explosion. *Source: Explosion Mechanism Advisory Group.*	44
C2-16	Likelihood of detonation arising from the unconfined vapour explosion. *Source: Explosion Mechanism Advisory Group.*	45
C2-17	Overpressure effects of an explosion. *Source: Explosion Mechanism Advisory Group.*	45
C2-18	Plan of area around 60 still base showing path of the jet flame. *Source: HSE report on the fatal fire at Hickson and Welch Ltd..*	48
C2-19	Mechanism of a dust explosion. *Source: IOP Publishing.*	50
C2-20	Overall assessment of dust explosibility. *Source: RMS.*	51
C2-21	West bucket elevator tower; silos 3, 2, and 1; and south packing building destroyed by the sugar dust explosions and fires. *Source: U.S. Chemical Safety and Hazard Investigation (CSHI) Report No. 2008-05-I-GA September 2009.*	53
C2-22	Inadequate housekeeping, heavy dust accumulation on conduit and spilled sugar on the floor (Imperial Sugar photo 1990). *Source: U.S. Chemical Safety and Hazard Investigation (CSHI) Report No. 2008-05-I-GA September 2009.*	53
C2-23	Non-dust rated and rated electrical devices in the silo tunnel. *Source: CSHI report.*	53
C2-24	Properties of steel and aluminium beams. *Source: FST.*	54
C2-25	Material classifications. *Source: FST.*	56
C2-26	Wall lining test results. *Source: Building Research Establishment.*	56
C2-27	Insulated core panel (sandwich panel). *Source: HM Government, Fire Safety Guide - 1.*	56
C2-28	Sandwich panel (insulated core panel). *Source: FST.*	56
C2-29	Collapse of upper floors. *Source: www.911myths.com.*	59
C2-30	Important dimensions of rotary valves used as chokes. *Source: HSG103*	61
C2-31	The use of a screw conveyor as an explosion choke. *Source: HSG103*	61
C2-32	Minimum separation for flammable liquids. *Source: HSE, HSG51.*	62

© RMS

C2-33	General layout of external store for flammable liquids. *Source: HSE, HSG51.*	63
C2-34	Work area storage - flammable liquids. *Source: HSG51.*	63
C2-35	Explosion suppression. *Source: FST.*	66
C2-36	Piper Alpha extract. *Source: Extract from Lord Cullen's report into the Piper Alpha disaster.*	66

Element C3

C3-1	Summary and indictable offences. *Source: Part 4 of the Regulatory Reform (Fire Safety) Order (RRFSO) 2005.*	73
C3-2	Risk assessment record example. *Source: RMS.*	81
C3-3	Fire detection equipment. *Source: FST.*	85
C3-4	Fire detection and warning system. *Source: Fire Safety Risk Assessment - Guide 1 - Office and Shops/RMS.*	87
C3-5	Smoke detector. *Source: RMS.*	89
C3-6	Manual call point. *Source: RMS.*	89
C3-7	Classification of fires. *Source: Rivington design/FST.*	90
C3-8	Fusible soldered strut - operating temperatures for sprinkler heads. *Source: FST*	95
C3-9	Quartzoid bulb sprinkler head. *Source: www.bintouqfire.com.*	95
C3-10	Quartzoid bulb type - operating temperatures for sprinkler heads. *Source: FST.*	95
C3-11	Quartzoid bulb operation sequence. *Source: COMPCO Fire Systems.*	95
C3-12	Cylinders for flood system. *Source: AFE.*	97
C3-13	Colour coded panels recommended for manufactures to use by BS 7863. *Source: FST.*	100
C3-14	Various fire extinguishing media. *Source: FST.*	100
C3-15	Summary matrix - fire extinguishers. *Source: FST.*	100
C3-16	Fire extinguishers in relation to their fire ratings. *Source: FST.*	101
C3-17	Maximum area of a class B fire. (Demonstration examples only, this is not a comprehensive list). *Source: FST.*	101
C3-18	Maximum area of Class B fire. *Source: BS 5306, part 8.*	101
C3-19	Summary matrix - extinguishing media. *Source: FST.*	102
C3-20	Minimum duration of discharge - extinguisher. *Source: FST.*	102
C3-21	Extinguisher well sited on escape route. *Source: FST.*	103
C3-22	Incorrectly sited plant. *Source: FST.*	103
C3-23	Extinguisher intervals of discharge. *Source: BS 5306, part 3.*	104
C3-24	Definition of means of escape. *Source: Fire safety risk assessment - a guide for offices.*	105
C3-25	Floor space factors[1]. *Source: Approved Document B (2000 Edition incorporating 2000 and 2002 amendments).*	106
C3-26	Exits - 45° rule. *Source: FST.*	107
C3-27	Known fire risks. *Source: FST.*	108
C3-28	Definition of travel distances. *Source: Fire Safety Risk Assessment - Guide 1 - Office and Shops.*	108
C3-29	Fire resistance rating symbols. *Source: www.mawwfire.gov.uk.*	109
C3-30	Self contained luminaire. *Source: RMS.*	110
C3-31	Directional arrows. *Source: BS 5449.*	112
C3-32	Poorly signed fire escape. *Source: FST.*	112
C3-33	Assembly point. *Source: RMS.*	113
C3-34	Needs of disabled people. *Source: BS 5588.*	116
C3-35	'Evac+chair'. *Source: FST.*	116

Element C4

C4-1	Heat production/volume. *Source: RMS.*	121
C4-2	Heat production/removal. *Source: HSG 143.*	124
C4-3	Top and side view of a processing batch reactor agitation components. *Source: RMS.*	124
C4-4	Spring loaded pressure relief valve. *Source: Motherwell Tank Protection UK.*	125
C4-5	Flameless vent IQR System™. *Source: BSandB Pressure Safety Management.*	125
C4-6	Spinning disc reactor. *Source: www.theengineer.co.uk Clive Whitbourn.*	126
C4-7	Oscillatory baffled reactor. *Source: www.theengineer.co.uk Clive Whitbourn.*	126
C4-8	Printed circuit heat exchangers. *Source: www.theengineer.co.uk Clive Whitbourn.*	126
C4-9	Definition - dangerous substances. *Source: DSEAR 2002.*	127
C4-10	Definition - dangerous substances. *Source: CHIP 2009.*	127
C4-11	Warning sign - explosive atmospheres. *Source: DSEAR 2002.*	127
C4-12	Storage of dangerous substances in drums. *Source: HSE, HSG 135.*	130
C4-13	Safety cabinet for flammable liquids. *Source: ARCO.*	131
C4-14	Storage of flammable liquids in a workroom. *Source: HSE.*	131
C4-15	Storage in racks. *Source: HSG71 Chemical warehousing.*	132
C4-16	Chemical drum storage. *Source: HSG71 Chemical warehousing.*	132
C4-17	Goods receipt area. *Source: HSG71 Chemical warehousing.*	132
C4-18	Hot air heating system. *Source: HSG71 Chemical warehousing.*	132
C4-19	Concrete bund. *Source: Safeguard Europe Ltd.*	133
C4-20	Brick bund. *Source: Safeguard Europe Ltd.*	133
C4-21	Flammable liquid filling and transfer. *Source: HSG143.*	134
C4-22	Labelled pipelines. *Source: HSG 143.*	136
C4-23	Dispensing containers. *Source: HSE, HSG140.*	136
C4-24	Waste solvent collection. *Source: HSE, HSG140.*	137
C4-25	Zone 1 - Metal footplate common earth potential when changing flammable chemicals. *Source: HSG143.*	138
C4-26	Examples of hazard labels and hazard characteristics with guidance for transport crews. *Source: UNECE.*	139
C4-27	HIN - Hazard identification number (kemler code) - does not require a telephone number. *Source: RMS.*	140
C4-28	Index of protection ratings. *Source: RMS.*	142
C4-29	Electrical equipment housing held closed with string. *Source: HSE.*	143
C4-30	Examples of ATEX marking and certification codes for dusts, gases and vapours. *Source: Wolf.*	143
C4-31	Apparatus for use in potentially explosive atmospheres. *Source: RMS.*	145
C4-32	Temperature classification limits. *Source: RMS.*	145
C4-33	"The term disaster". *Source: Chambers dictionary.*	145
C4-34	"The term disaster". *Source: Oxford dictionary.*	145
C4-35	Dangerous substances thresholds. *Source: RMS.*	148

© RMS

Element C5

C5-1	Anthropometric data for small openings. *Source: Ambiguous.*	160
C5-2	Reaching through openings. *Source: BS EN ISO 13857:2008.*	161
C5-3	Low risk of a friction or abrasion hazard. *Source: BS EN 13857.*	161
C5-4	High risk of a friction or abrasion hazard. *Source: BS EN 13857.*	162
C5-5	Reach distance/barrier. *Source: Proctor Bros Ltd.*	162
C5-6	Different maintenance management techniques. *Source: HSC Approved code of practice for PUWER 1998.*	170
C5-7	Examples of maintenance management strategies. *Source: RMS.*	170
C5-8	Equipment inspection. *Source: RMS.*	172
C5-9	Regulations 19 of PUWER 1998. *Source: Provision and Use of Work Equipment Regulations (PUWER) 1998.*	173
C5-10	Competence v supervision. *Source: RMS.*	175

Element C6

C6-1	Application of training to principles of safety integration. *Source: EC Enterprise and Industry Guide to Machinery Directive.*	181
C6-2	Risk assessment. *Source: Rockwell Automation.*	184
C6-3	CE Mark. *Source: Department of Business Innovation and Skills.*	184
C6-4	Essential health and safety requirements checklist. *Source: SMSR 2008/RMS.*	187
C6-5	Conformity assessments applicable to different types of machinery. *Source: SMSR 2008/RMS.*	189
C6-6	Procedures for conformity. *Source: Department of Business Innovation and Skills.*	190
C6-7	Overview procedure for the machinery directive. *Source: Rockwell Automation.*	191
C6-8	Planetary chart - A B and C standards. *Source: RMS.*	192
C6-9	Categories of machine posing special hazards. *Source: Supply of Machinery (Safety) Regulations (SMSR) 2008.*	193
C6-10	EC declaration of conformity. *Source: RMS.*	195
C6-11	EC declaration of incorporation. *Source: RMS.*	195
C6-12	Belt sander. *Source: Clarke International.*	197
C6-13	Example of a CNC machine. *Source: cncmachine-details.info.*	198
C6-14	Machinery hazards. *Source: RMS.*	198
C6-15	Bench cross-cut circular saw. *Source: RMS.*	199
C6-16	Shear. *Source: RMS.*	199
C6-17	Entanglement in chuck of pedestal drill. *Source: RMS.*	199
C6-18	Abrasive wheel. *Source: RMS.*	199
C6-19	Tension. *Source: RMS.*	201
C6-20	Compression. *Source: RMS.*	201
C6-21	Shear stress. *Source: RMS.*	202
C6-22	A tensile test-piece. *Source: Ambiguous.*	202
C6-23	Tensile stress-strain curve. *Source: Ambiguous.*	203
C6-24	Stress-strain curve for iron and glass. *Source: Ambiguous.*	203
C6-25	Properties of some metallic solids. *Source: Ambiguous.*	203
C6-26	Properties of some non-metallic solids. *Source: Ambiguous.*	203
C6-27	Metal fatigue. *Source: RMS.*	204
C6-28	Tensile stress and ductile failure. *Source: Ambiguous.*	204
C6-29	Tensile stress and brittle failure. *Source: Ambiguous.*	205
C6-30	Tensile stress and brittle failure. *Source: Ambiguous.*	205
C6-31	Scaffold standard. *Source: RMS.*	205
C6-32	Galvanic series in sea water. *Source: 14 Bimetallic Corrosion, Dept. of Industry in association with the Institution of Corrosion, Science and Technology. Courtesy of International Nickel Limited.*	206
C6-33	Corrosion of galvanised iron pipe. *Source: 14 Bimetallic Corrosion, Dept. of Industry in association with the Institution of Corrosion, Science and Technology.*	206
C6-34	Crane failure at Brent Cross. *Source: HSE Report on Brent Cross Crane Failure.*	208
C6-35	General layout of shaft hoist and tunnel. *Source: The hoist accident at Littlebrook 'D' Power Station, HSE Books.*	210
C6-36	Failure modes. *Source: RMS.*	215
C6-37	Fixed enclosing guard constructed of wire mesh and angle section preventing access to transmission machinery. *Source: BS PD 5304.*	220
C6-38	Fixed distance guard fitted to a press brake. *Source: BS PD 5304.*	221
C6-39	Interlocking guard for positive clutch power press. *Source: BS PD 5304.*	222
C6-40	Schematic representation of power and control interlocking. *Source: Ambiguous.*	222
C6-41	Probable effect of a failure to danger. *Source: RMS.*	223
C6-42	Interlocking system. *Source: Paper D (S Tech); Q5; June 1996 Previous NEBOSH Diploma.*	224
C6-43	Two position switches operating in opposite modes, mounted side by side, each actuated by its own cam mounted on the guard hinge. *Source: BS PD 5304.*	224
C6-44	Captive key switch. *Source: BS PD 5304.*	225
C6-45	Key Exchange Box system. *Source: Castell Safety.*	225
C6-46	Practical application of the trapped-key control system. *Source: BS PD 5304.*	226
C6-47	Automatic guard for a power press. *Source: BS PD 5304.*	226
C6-48	Trip device for drilling machines. *Source: BS PD 5304.*	227
C6-49	Pressure sensitive mat safeguarding the clamping and bending jaws of an automatic horizontal tube bender. *Source: BS PD 5304.*	227
C6-50	Photoelectric safety system used as a presence sensing device inside distance guards fitted around a robot served pressure die casting machine. *Source: HSG 129 Health and Safety in Engineering Workshops.*	228
C6-51	Hydraulic press brake using photoelectric safety system. *Source: HSG 129 Health and Safety in Engineering Workshops.*	229
C6-52	Adjustable guard for a radial or pedestal drilling machine. *Source: BS PD 5304.*	229
C6-53	Self-adjusting guard arrangement for snipper cross-cutting sawing machine. *Source: BS PD 5304.*	230
C6-54	Two-hand control device. *Source: BS PD 5304.*	230
C6-55	Physical isolation of valve. *Source: RMS.*	233
C6-56	Multiple (padlock) lock off device. *Source: RMS.*	233
C6-57	Practical application of ergonomic principles to machine design. *Source: Guide to the Machinery Directive.*	239
C6-58	System. *Source: RMS.*	239
C6-59	Series system. *Source: RMS.*	241
C6-60	Parallel system. *Source: RMS.*	241
C6-61	Three components in parallel. *Source: RMS.*	242

C6-62	The reliability of a mixed system (series and parallel). *Source: RMS.*	242
C6-63	Mixed system. *Source: RMS.*	243
C6-64	Examples of errors. *Source: RMS.*	243
C6-65	Diverse system. *Source: RMS.*	246
C6-66	Error rates for a control room. *Source: RMS.*	248

Element C7

C7-1	Counterbalance lift truck. *Source: HSE, HSG6 - Safety in working with lift trucks.*	251
C7-2	Reach lift truck. *Source: HSE, HSG6 - Safety in working with lift trucks.*	251
C7-3	Rough-terrain lift trucks. *Source: RMS.*	252
C7-4	Rough-terrain lift trucks. *Source: RMS.*	252
C7-5	Telescopic handler. *Source: Ambiguous.*	252
C7-6	Side loading trucks. *Source: Ambiguous.*	252
C7-7	Pedestrian controlled trucks. *Source: HSE, HSG6 - Safety in working with lift trucks.*	252
C7-8	Agricultural tractor. *Source: Massey Ferguson.*	253
C7-9	Mobile storage system moving robots. *Source: Kiva Systems.*	253
C7-10	Remotely controlled narrow isle storage and retrieval systems. *Source: SSI Schafer.*	254
C7-11	Overturning of lift truck. *Source: HSE, HSG6 - Safety in working with lift trucks.*	254
C7-12	Overbalancing of lift truck. *Source: HSE, HSG6 - Safety in working with lift trucks.*	255
C7-13	Use of working platform on fork lift truck. *Source: HSE.*	259
C7-14	Other attachments used on fork lift trucks. *Source: Contact Attachments Ltd.*	260
C7-15	Roll bar and seat restraint. *Source: RMS.*	261
C7-16	Risk of Falling materials. *Source: RMS.*	261
C7-17	Comparison between Fresnel lens (1) and normal lens (2). *Source: Pko.*	262
C7-18	Mobile crane. *Source: Liebherr.*	264
C7-19	Tower crane. *Source: Construction Industry Publications Ltd for the Building Employers Confederation.*	264
C7-20	Overhead cranes. *Source: Columbus McKinnon Corp.*	264
C7-21	Mobile person hoist. *Source: Arjo.*	265
C7-22	Ceiling person hoist. *Source: Dolphin Midlands.*	265
C7-23	Construction tower platform hoist. *Source: RMS.*	265
C7-24	Gin wheel. *Source: HSE Guidance Note PM28; Working Platforms on Fork Lift Trucks.*	266
C7-25	Construction platform hoist. *Source: HSE, HSG150.*	267
C7-26	Scissor lift. *Source: HSG150, HSE.*	267
C7-27	Vehicle lift. *Source: RMS.*	268
C7-28	Vehicle lift. *Source: RMS.*	268
C7-29	Mobile elevated work platform (MEWP). *Source: RMS.*	268
C7-30	Use of harness with a MEWP. *Source: HSG150.*	268
C7-31	Marking of accessories. *Source: RMS.*	271
C7-32	Mobile hoist for lifting people. *Source: RMS.*	271
C7-33	Lifting operations. *Source: RMS.*	271
C7-34	Lifting operations. *Source: RMS.*	271
C7-35	Danger zone - crane and fixed item. *Source: RMS.*	272
C7-36	Siting and stability. *Source: RMS.*	272
C7-37	Stability of cranes (Hand-drawn). *Source: RMS.*	273
C7-38	Siting and stability. *Source: RMS.*	273
C7-39	Regulation 4 of PUWER 1998. *Source: Provision and Use of Work Equipment Regulations (PUWER) 1998.*	274
C7-40	Single-leg sling. *Source: Ambiguous.*	274
C7-41	Typical wire rope construction 6 x 19 (6 strands with 19 wires in each strand). *Source: Ambiguous.*	274
C7-42	Types of chain sling. *Source: Ambiguous.*	275
C7-43	Fibre rope sling. *Source: Lincsafe.*	276
C7-44	Fibre rope sling. *Source: RMS.*	276
C7-45	Eyebolts. *Source: Ambiguous.*	276
C7-46	Case or drum sling. *Source: Ambiguous.*	276
C7-47	Hook with safety latch. *Source: Corel Clipart.*	277
C7-48	Extending boom MEWP. *Source: Inverness Tree Services Ltd.*	278
C7-49	Extending boom MEWP. *Source: CITB.*	278
C7-50	Multi-boom articulated. *Source: RMS.*	278
C7-51	Multi-boom articulated. *Source: CITB.*	278
C7-52	Multi-boom rough terrain. *Source: CITB.*	278
C7-53	Scissor lift. *Source: HSE, HSG150.*	278
C7-54	Scissor lift. *Source: RMS.*	278

Element C8

C8-1	Electrical distribution voltages. *Source: Parliamentary Office of Science and Technology.*	283
C8-2	Impedance. *Source: G Self.*	284
C8-3	Basic electrical circuitry. *Source: RMS.*	284
C8-4	Unearthed and earthed electrical systems. *Source: G Self.*	285
C8-5	Unearthed and earthed electrical systems. *Source: G Self.*	285
C8-6	Electrical equipment near water. *Source: RMS.*	286
C8-7	Contact with high voltage buried cable. *Source: RMS.*	286
C8-8	Effects of alternating current flowing in the human body. *Source: RMS.*	287
C8-9	Used coiled up-risk of overheating. *Source: RMS.*	288
C8-10	Max current capacity exceeded. *Source: RMS.*	288
C8-11	Worn cable - risk of electrical fire. *Source: RMS.*	288
C8-12	Evidence of overheating. *Source: RMS.*	288
C8-13	Creation of static charge. *Source: Simco UK.*	289
C8-14	Construction site generator. *Source: RMS.*	291
C8-15	Construction site power supply. *Source: RMS.*	291
C8-16	110V generator. *Source: RMS.*	291
C8-17	110V extension lead. *Source: RMS.*	291
C8-18	UK standard reduced voltage system. *Source: G Self.*	293

C8-19	Cartridge fuse. *Source: Ambiguous.*	294
C8-20	HBC fuse. *Source: Ambiguous.*	294
C8-21	Circuit breaker. *Source: Ambiguous.*	294
C8-22	Power supply isolation. *Source: RMS.*	295
C8-23	Isolation. *Source: Regulation 12 - Electricity at Work Regulations (EWR) 1989.*	295
C8-24	Plug-foil fuse, no earth. *Source: RMS.*	296
C8-25	Earthing. *Source: RMS.*	296
C8-26	110V centre tapped earth transformer. *Source: RMS.*	297
C8-27	Battery powered drill - 12V. *Source: RMS.*	297
C8-28	110V powered drill. *Source: RMS.*	297
C8-29	110V powered drill. *Source: RMS.*	297
C8-30	Isolation. *Source: Regulation 12 - Electricity at Work Regulations (EWR) 1989.*	297
C8-31	A typical circuit diagram for a RCD. *Source: G Self.*	298
C8-32	Residual current device. *Source: RMS.*	298
C8-33	Plug-in residual current device. *Source: RMS.*	298
C8-34	Double insulation symbol. *Source: HSG 107.*	299
C8-35	General arrangement for an earth free work environment. *Source: G Self.*	299
C8-36	Quotation regarding the frequency of inspection and testing. *Source: HSE, HSG107.*	301
C8-37	Suggested intervals of inspection and test. *Source: HSG107 - Maintaining portable and transportable electrical equipment.*	301
C8-38	PAT labels. *Source: RMS.*	302
C8-39	BS7671 and EWR 1989. *Source: Electricity at Work Regulations (EWR) 1989, Introduction.*	302
C8-40	Maintenance of system. *Source: Regulation 4(2) - Electricity at Work Regulations (EWR) 1989.*	303
C8-41	Work on electrical equipment made dead. *Source: Regulation 13 - Electricity at Work Regulations (EWR) 1989.*	304
C8-42	Lock off. *Source: RMS.*	304
C8-43	Work on or near live conductors. *Source: Regulation 14 - Electricity at Work Regulations (EWR) 1989.*	304
C8-44	Competent person. *Source: Regulation 16 - Electricity at Work Regulations (EWR) 1989.*	305
C8-45	Requirements for a competent person. *Source: Memorandum of guidance on the Electricity at Work Regulations (EWR) 1989 - HSR25.*	305
C8-46	Electric supply line. *Source: Regulation 16 of the Electricity Safety, Quality and Continuity Regulations (ESQCR) 2002.*	305
C8-47	Working near power lines. *Source: HSG144.*	307
C8-48	Overhead power lines. *Source: Lincsafe.*	307
C8-49	Live overhead line training. *Source: Narec.*	310
C8-50	Use and maintenance of system. *Source: Regulation 4(4) - Electricity at Work Regulations (EWR) 1989.*	310
C8-51	Insulating gloves. *Source: BS EN 60903/Clydesdale Ltd.*	310
C8-52	Hazard - fuse wired out. *Source: RMS.*	311
C8-53	Hazard - defective apparatus. *Source: RMS.*	311
C8-54	Hazard - damaged cable. *Source: RMS.*	311
C8-55	Hazard - taped joints. *Source: RMS.*	311

Element C9

C9-1	Assessing the competence of individual CDM co-ordinators. *Source: CDM 2007 ACOP, Regulation 4.*	320
C9-2	Working above ground level. *Source: RMS.*	324
C9-3	Ladder not tied or footed. *Source: RMS.*	325
C9-4	Improper use. *Source: RMS.*	325
C9-5	Poor storage. *Source: Lincsafe.*	325
C9-6	Stepladder. *Source: RMS.*	325
C9-7	Scaffolds. *Source: HSG150.*	327
C9-8	Clip-in vertical ladder for 'Span-Type' tower scaffold. *Source: Ambiguous.*	327
C9-9	Tower scaffolds. *Source: Ambiguous.*	328
C9-10	Falsework. *Source: BMA Construction Engineers Inc.*	329
C9-11	Hazards associated with falling materials. *Source: RMS.*	330
C9-12	Chute for falling materials. *Source: Midland Power Hoists.*	330
C9-13	Use of roof ladders. *Source: HSG150, HSE.*	331
C9-14	Access system for roof work. *Source: HSE, HSG284.*	332
C9-15	Cradle. *Source: www.apollocradles.co.uk.*	332
C9-16	Boatswains chair. *Source: Photo, Pete Verdon.*	333
C9-17	Personal suspension equipment. *Source: RMS.*	333
C9-18	Safety nets. *Source: RMS.*	334
C9-19	Soft fall arrest system. *Source: www.sitesafetysolutions.co.uk.*	334
C9-20	Soft fall arrest system. *Source: www.sitesafetysolutions.co.uk.*	334
C9-21	Hydraulic demolition jaws. *Source: RMS.*	336
C9-22	Hydraulic demolition grapple. *Source: RMS.*	336
C9-23	Fans. *Source: RMS.*	337
C9-24	Brick guards. *Source: HSG150 Safety in Construction.*	337
C9-25	Protection of public. *Source: RMS.*	337
C9-26	Excavation hazards. *Source: RMS.*	340
C9-27	Buried services. *Source: RMS.*	341
C9-28	Excavation hazards. *Source: RMS.*	341
C9-29	Marking of services. *Source: RMS.*	342
C9-30	Methods of supporting excavations. *Source: CDM 2007 Regulation 31.*	342
C9-31	Battering. *Source: RMS.*	343
C9-32	Drag (trench) box. *Source: SRV Construction.*	343
C9-33	Open sheeting. *Source: Trench Control Ltd.*	343
C9-34	Close boarded excavation. *Source: BS6031.*	343
C9-35	Open sheeting. *Source: BS6031.*	343
C9-36	Close sheeting. *Source: RMS.*	344
C9-37	Open sheeting. *Source: RMS.*	344
C9-38	Excavator. *Source: RMS.*	344
C9-39	Permit to dig. *Source: Reproduced by kind permission of Lincsafe.*	346

Element C10

C10-1	Workplace accident statistics 2008/09. *Source: HSE.*	349
C10-2	Vehicle overturned. *Source: Lincsafe.*	349
C10-3	Regulation 37 of CDM 2007. *Source: Construction (Design and Management) Regulations (CDM) 2007.*	350
C10-4	Coupling. *Source: Wikipedia.*	351
C10-5	Synchronised vehicle lifting system. *Source: Rotala.*	351
C10-6	Tilted LGV cab and prop. *Source: HSE.*	352
C10-7	Poor maintenance of vehicle tyres. *Source: RMS.*	352
C10-8	Reduced risk of collision - people/vehicles. *Source: RMS.*	352
C10-9	Means of segregation. *Source: Regulation 17(1) of WHSWR 1992.*	355
C10-10	Crossing point. *Source: HSE, HSG76.*	355
C10-11	Segregating pedestrians and vehicles. *Source: RMS.*	355
C10-12	No segregation - high visibility clothing. *Source: RMS.*	356
C10-13	Control of vehicle movement. *Source: RMS.*	356
C10-14	Barriers and markings. *Source: RMS.*	356
C10-15	Visual warning on a dumper truck. *Source: RMS.*	356
C10-16	Size of the road risk problem. *Source: RoSPA.*	358
C10-17	Road risk. *Source: HSE 1996.*	358

Element C11

C11-1	Water steam characteristics. *Source: Ambiguous.*	367
C11-2	Steam saturation curve. *Source: Spirax-sarco Ltd.*	367
C11-3	Steel pipe blown open at a tee junction by water hammer. *Source: Kirsner Consulting Engineering, Inc.*	368
C11-4	Diagrammatic arrangement of No. 5 Blast furnace. *Source: HSE.*	369
C11-5	Section of dismantled furnace shell. *Source: HSE.*	369
C11-6	Prior to event. *Source: HSE.*	370
C11-7	Furnace movement (5,000 tonnes 0.75 metres vertical) during explosion. *Source: HSE.*	370
C11-8	Properties of liquefied petroleum gas. *Source: Various.*	370
C11-9	High pressure storage spheres. *Source: VTV.*	371
C11-10	Steel pressure vessel with heads on skid mount. *Source: Gizelle; Mbeychok.*	371
C11-11	Mounded LPG storage tanks. *Source: GR.*	372
C11-12	Concrete encased moulded storage tanks. *Source: GR.*	372
C11-13	Typical single-stage vapour compression refrigeration. *Source: Ambiguous.*	373
C11-14	Two-pipe steam heating system. *Source: ITT Corporation.*	373
C11-15	The term vessel explained in ACOP to PSSR 2000. *Source: HSE.*	374
C11-16	Carbon steel vessel. *Source: Calor Gas.*	374
C11-17	Comparison of pressures. *Source: Ambiguous.*	375
C11-18	Frequencies of examination based on earlier prescriptive legislation, as examples only not as a basis of written schemes. *Source: RMS.*	378
C11-19	Pressure systems. *Source: J Stranks; Health and Safety in Practice (Safety Technology); Pitman Publishing; 1996.*	379
C11-20	Description of steam systems devices. *Source: RMS.*	380
C11-21	Description of air systems devices. *Source: RMS.*	380
C11-22	Description of air receiver devices. *Source: RMS.*	380
C11-23	Waterwall header. *Source: NTSB.*	382
C11-24	View of matching fracture halves. *Source: NTSB.*	382
C11-25	Failure point of boiler. *Source: Garry J Bases.*	384
C11-26	Mobile Air compressor. *Source: Speedy Hire plc.*	387

Relevant statutory provisions

RSP-1	Risks from road side work. *Source: RMS.*	414
RSP-2	Risks from street light repair or tree felling. *Source: RMS.*	414
RSP-3	Schedule 1 examples. *Source: Notification of Installations Handling Hazardous Substances Regulations 1982 (as amended).*	423

List of abbreviations

LEGISLATION

ADR	European Agreement concerning the International Carriage of Dangerous Goods by Road 2009
ATG	Automatic Gauging System
BPA	British Pipeline Agency Ltd
BR	Building Regulations 2000
CCA	Civil Contingencies Act 2004
CDGUTPER	Carriage of Dangerous Goods and Use of Transportable Pressure Equipment Regulations 2009
CDM	Construction (Design and Management) Regulation 2007
CHIP	Chemicals (Hazard Information and Packaging for Supply) Regulations 2009
CHPR	Construction (Head Protection) Regulations 1989
COER	Control of Explosives Regulations 1991 (as amended by the Manufacture and Storage of Explosives Regulations 2005)
COMAH	Control of Major Accident Hazards Regulations 1999 (amended 2005)
COSHH	Control of Substances Hazardous to Health Regulations 2002 (and as amended 2004)
CSR	Confined Spaces Regulations 1997
CUR	Road Vehicles (Construction and Use) Regulations 1986
DSEAR	Dangerous Substances and Explosive Atmospheres Regulations 2002
EPS	Equipment and Protective Systems Intended for Use in Potentially Explosive Atmospheres Regulations 1996
ESQCR	Electricity Safety, Quality and Continuity Regulations 2002
EWR	Electricity at Work Regulations 1989
EESR	Electrical Equipment (Safety) Regulations 1994
FAR	Health and Safety (First-Aid) Regulations 1981
FPA	Fire Precautions Act
FPWR	Fire Precautions (Workplace) Regulations
FSA	Fire (Scotland) Act 2005
FSSR	Fire Safety (Scotland) Regulations 2006
HASAWA	Health and Safety at Work etc Act 1974
HSCER	Health and Safety (Consultation with Employees) Regulations 1996
IHLS	Independent High-Level Switch
LOLER	Lifting Operations and Lifting Equipment Regulations 1998
MAR	Health and Safety (Miscellaneous Amendments) Regulations 2002
MHSWR	Management of Health and Safety at Work Regulations 1999
NCTCR	Notification of Conventional Tower Cranes Regulations 2010
NIHHS	Notification of Installations Handling Hazardous Substances Regulations 1982
NOMAS	Dangerous Substances (Notification and Marking of Sites) Regulations 1990
NRSWA	New Roads and Streets Works Act 1991
PER	Pressure Equipment Regulations 1999
PSSR	Pressure Systems Safety Regulations 2000
PUWER	Provision and Use of Work Equipment Regulations 1998
RIDDOR	Reporting of Injuries, Diseases and Dangerous Occurrences Regulations 1995
RRFSO	Regulatory Reform (Fire Safety) Order 2005
RTA	Road Traffic Act 1999
RTRA	Road Traffic Regulation Act 1984
RVLR	Road Vehicles Lighting Regulations 1989
SMSR	Supply of Machinery (Safety) Regulations 2008
SPVSR	Simple Pressure Vessels (Safety) Regulations 1991
SSSR	Health and Safety (Safety Signs and Signals) Regulations 1996
WAH	Work at Height Regulations 2005
WHSWR	Workplace (Health, Safety and Welfare) Regulations 1992

GENERAL

AA	Automobile Association
ABS	Active Braking Systems
AC	Alternating Current
ACOP	Approved Code of Practice
ADR	European Agreement concerning the International Carriage of Goods by Road
AITT	Association of Industrial Truck Trainers
ALARP	As Low As is Reasonably Practicable
AWHE	Access and Work at Height Equipment
AZDN	Azodiisobutyronitrate
BATNEEC	Best Available Technology Not Entailing Excessive Cost
BCEC	British Crane and Excavator Corporation Ltd
BLEVE	Boiling Liquid Exploding Vapour Explosions
CA	Competent Authority
CA	Control Authorities
CBM	Condition Based Maintenance
CCTV	Closed Circuit Television
CE	Conformité Européene
CENELEC	European Committee for Electro-technical Standardisation
CEN	European Committee for Standardisation
CITB	Construction Industry Training Board
CIWH	Condensation Induced Water Hammer
CNC	Computer Numeric Controls
COF	Coefficient of Friction
CVCE	Confined Vapour Cloud Explosion
DC	Direct Current
DfT	Department for Transport

DVLA	Driver and Vehicle Licensing Agency
EC	European Community
EEA	European Economic Area
EEBAD	Earthed Equipotential Bonding and Automatic Disconnection
EHSR	Essential Health and Safety Requirements
EN	European Standards
EPI	Epichlorohydrin
ETSI	European Telecommunications Standards Institute
EU	European Union
FLT	Fork Lift Truck
FMEA	Failure Mode and Effects Analysis
FOPS	Falling-object protective structures
GB	Great Britain
GEEP	Generic Emergency Evacuation Plan
HAZOP	Hazard and Operability Study
HBC	High Breaking Capacity
HOSL	Hertfordshire Oil Storage Ltd.
HRA	Human Reliability Analysis
HSC	Health and Safety Commission
HSE	Health and Safety Executive
HSL	Health and Safety Laboratory
HV	High Voltage
IAD	Insulated Aerial Device
IDLH	Immediately Dangerous To Life or Health
IEC	International Electrotechnical Commission
IEE	Institute of Electrical Engineers
IET	Institution of Engineering and Technology
IIE	Institution of Incorporated Engineers
KATE	Knowledge, Ability, Training and Experience
LEL	Lower Explosive Limit
LEV	Local Exhaust Ventilation
LFL	Lower Flammable Limit
LGV	Large Goods Vehicle
LPG	Liquefied Petroleum Gas
MAG	Metal Active Gas
MAPP	Major Accident Prevention Policy
MEWP	Mobile Elevated Work Platform
MIG	Metal Inert Gas
MIIB	Major Incident Investigation Board
MMA	Manual Metal Arc
MRI	Magnetic Resonance Imaging
MVS	Majority Voting Systems
NDT	Non-destructive Testing
NTSB	National Transportation Safety Board
OBR	Oscillatory Baffled Reactor
OfSEP	Off-site Emergency Plan
PCHE	Printed Circuit Heat Exchanger
PCV	Passenger Carrying Vehicle
PEEPS	Personal Emergency Evacuation Plans
Pmax	Maximum Explosive Pressure
PPE	Personal Protective Equipment
PPM	Planned Preventative Maintenance
PTV	Pendulum Test Value
PTW	Permit to Work
Rccb	Residual Current Circuit Breaker
RCD	Residual Current Device
ROPS	Roll-over protective structures
RPE	Respiratory Protective Equipment
RTITB	Road Transport Industry Training Board
Rz	Roughness Value
SADT	Self Accelerating Decomposition Temperature
SAT	Slip Assessment Tool
SCBA	Self-Contained Breathing Apparatus
SDR	Spinning Disc Reactor
SELV	Separated Extra Low Voltage
SRV	Slip Resistance Value
SWL	Safe Working Load
SWR	Steel Wire Rope
SWWA	South West Water Authority
TIG	Tungsten Inert Gas
UCVCE	Unconfined Vapour Cloud Explosion
UEL	Upper Explosion Limit
UFL	Upper Flammable Limit
UK	United Kingdom
VCA	Vehicle Certification Agency
VICES	Ventilation, Ignition, Containment, Exchange, Separation
WCF	Windsor Castle Fire 1992

© **RMS**

Element C1

General workplace issues

Learning outcomes

The intended learning outcomes are that the student will be able to:

C1.1 Explain the need for, and factors involved in, the provision and maintenance of a safe working environment, with specific reference to access and egress, pedestrians, and slips, trips and falls.

C1.2 Explain how safety signs are used in the workplace.

C1.3 Explain the assessment of risk and safe working practices associated with work in confined spaces.

C1.4 Outline the main issues associated with maintaining structural safety of workplaces.

C1.5 Explain the hazards, risks and controls when working at heights.

C1.6 Explain the hazards, risks and controls for lone working.

Content

C1.1 - Safe working environment 3
    Safe place of work 3
    Safe means of access and egress 3
    The design of surfaces to reduce slipping 4
    Wet Coefficient of Friction (cof), slip resistant testing of footwear and surfaces 4
    Workplace (Health, Safety and Welfare) Regulations (WHSWR) 1992 8
C1.2 - Safety signs 9
    Common safety signs and their categorisation 9
    Use, location and compliance issues 10
    Signals 12
    Health and Safety (Safety Signs and Signals) Regulations 1996, Regulations 2, 3, 4 and 5 14
C1.3 - Confined spaces 14
    Description of conditions that constitute a confined space 14
    Examples of where confined space entry may occur in the workplace 15
    Factors to be considered when assessing risk 15
    Factors to be considered in designing safe working practices 18
    Flammable atmospheres 19
C1.4 - Structural safety of workplaces 20
    Causes of damage to the structure of buildings 20
    Failure modes of workplace structures 22
C1.5 - Working at height 22
    Main hazards and risks for work at height in general workplaces 23
    Main precautions and safe working procedures for work at height 23
    Hierarchy of control measures with reference to the Work at Height Regulations (WAH) 2005 25
C1.6 - Lone working 29
    Main hazards and risks, alternatives, precautions and safe working procedures 29
    Particular problems facing lone workers 30

ELEMENT C1 - GENERAL WORKPLACE ISSUES

Relevant statutory provisions

Confined Spaces Regulations (CSR) 1997
Health and Safety (Safety Signs and Signals) Regulations (SSSR) 1996
Management of Health and Safety at Work Regulations (MHSWR) 1999
Workplace (Health, Safety and Welfare) Regulations (WHSWR) 1992
Work at Height Regulations (WAH) 2005

C1.1 - Safe working environment

Safe place of work

LEGAL REQUIREMENTS FOR A SAFE PLACE OF WORK

Employer's common law duty to provide a safe place of work

The position at common law is that employers must take reasonable care to protect employees from foreseeable injury. If an employer knows of or should have known of a hazard and fails to do anything about it in reasonable time, he may be in breach of his duty of care.

An employer's general duties were identified by the House of Lords in the case of Wilsons and Clyde Coal Co. v English (1938) as follows:

- A safe place of work, including safe access and egress.
- A safe system of work.
- Safe plant and appliances.
- Safe and competent fellow workers.

If the employees' workplace is unsafe because of a third party and the employer does nothing then the employer, as well as the third party, may be liable. This might happen where the employer is a contractor on a building site and his employees are working in unsafe conditions due to an act or omission by the main contractor. The duty of care cannot be delegated and is not removed because the employee is working on someone else's premises.

The common law duty may be confirmed to be fulfilled through regular inspection of the workplace. It does not extend to abnormal hazards that could not have been foreseen. If there is a sudden, unexpected snowfall, the employer is not liable until there has been a reasonable time to deal with it. If the employee is working at a site not owned by the employer, circumstances will determine whether it is inspected. For example, the employer of a painter and decorator would not be expected to inspect every household prior to work being carried out.

Employer's statutory duty to provide a safe place of work

The Health and Safety at Work etc. Act (HASAWA) 1974 sets out a duty to ensure a safe place of work, as far as is reasonably practicable. This is further clarified in the duties set out in the Workplace (Health, Safety and Welfare) Regulations (WHSWR) 1992 (as amended).

PRACTICAL CONSIDERATIONS FOR A SAFE PLACE OF WORK

When determining practical considerations, it is necessary to take regard to where the worker is located. They may be standing in a warehouse determining the quantity of stock, in a sewer or on a scaffold, and each has features that may present a hazard and would require control. For example, the stock storage area may have to be cordoned off to ensure fork lift trucks do not collide with the worker and the scaffold platform must be capable of taking the worker's weight and be wide enough for the work being done.

In addition, it is important to consider the work being done, as this can quickly make a place of work unsafe, for example, a shop worker stacking shelves could quickly make the workplace unsafe by leaving boxes and sealing straps in a disorganised way.

Other practical considerations in the provision and maintenance of a safe place of work include:

- Provision of good ventilation.
- Reasonable temperatures.
- Suitable and sufficient lighting.
- Cleanliness and dealing with waste.
- Adequate space.
- Suitable workstations and seating.
- Condition of floors.
- Establishing traffic routes.

When ensuring a safe place of work it is important to consider how good standards in a workplace could diminish and what actions are necessary to ensure they are maintained. This will include arrangements for cleaning work surfaces, maintaining lighting levels, reapplying markings to identify work/storage areas and dealing with spillages.

Safe means of access and egress

LEGAL REQUIREMENTS FOR SAFE MEANS OF ACCESS AND EGRESS

There is a specific common law duty, emphasised in Wilsons and Clyde Coal Co. v English (1938), to provide reasonably safe access to and egress from a place of work; this is reinforced by the statutory duty set out in the Health and Safety at Work etc. Act (HASAWA) 1974 to ensure, so far as is reasonably practicable, access to and egress from it that are safe and without risk.

PRACTICAL CONSIDERATIONS FOR SAFE MEANS OF ACCESS AND EGRESS

When determining practical considerations for safe means of access and egress, it is important to take regard of such matters as clearly marked gangways, walk routes that are free from obstruction, the maintenance of floors and staircases and the organisation of traffic routes (including pedestrian traffic). A critical consideration when establishing traffic systems is the safety interface between pedestrians and traffic.

ELEMENT C1 - GENERAL WORKPLACE ISSUES

It is important to ensure that every workplace is organised in such a way that pedestrians and vehicles can circulate in a safe manner; this will often mean careful separation of pedestrians from vehicles. The routes that people use should be clearly defined and marked. Consideration should also be made to the safety of doors and gates, as well as escalators and moving walkways.

The workplace may be some distance from the ground, as with construction workers, or several miles underground, as with miners. Therefore, such things as approach roads, portable access equipment (ladders, etc.), and shoring of underground workings must be considered when providing safe means of access and egress. Particular thought should also be given to emergency egress.

When determining access and egress, account should be made of those with a disability and care should be taken to ensure that the workplace, including doors, passageways, stairs and access to showers, washbasins, lavatories and workstations are suitable for disabled persons.

As with the provision of a safe place of work, it is essential to make arrangements to ensure means of access and egress are maintained. This will include arrangements to maintain surfaces that are slip resistant, dealing with obstructions, repairing items that become loose that could cause a trip or fall and ensuring that doors work as they should.

The design of surfaces to reduce slipping

In order to ensure the safe movement of people slip resistant surfaces should be provided:

- At the entrance of buildings, for example a mat that provides both slip resistance and can absorb water brought in on footwear.
- On designated walkways.
- On changes of level, such as stairs, steps, ladders, footholds to vehicles.
- On ramps or slopes.
- Where walkways intersect with internal transport routes and people may need to stop suddenly.
- In work areas where spills of liquids or dry contaminants are likely.
- Where liquids are decanted or containers filled or stored.
- On access areas used for inspection or maintenance.
- Locations where workers need to go that are exposed to the weather and where surfaces may become covered in environmental grime or slippery growth.

When designing and selecting a slip resistant surface consider:

- The consequences of slipping; a slip while holding a knife or at height could have major consequences.
- The type of contamination likely, for example, liquid or dry; water, oil or blood; visible or not.
- Ability to control contamination, for example, drainage.
- Level of use of the surface.
- The range of people using the surface, for example, age, disability.
- What people might be doing on the surface, for example, walking, climbing, carrying, turning, and moving fast.
- Environmental issues, weather, hot or cold.
- Level of control over footwear used.
- The surface option, for example, smooth or rough profile and wear durability.
- The slip resistance rating, (pendulum test value, PTV) and the roughness (Rz) needed.

Figure C1-1: Slip resistance surface on steps.   *Source: RMS.*

Figure C1-2: Anti-slip flooring.   *Source: RMS.*

Wet Coefficient of Friction (cof), slip resistant testing of footwear and surfaces

COEFFICIENT OF FRICTION (COF)

The coefficient of friction is a number that represents the friction between two surfaces.

The symbol usually used to represent the coefficient of friction is µ.

µ = R̲ where µ is the coefficient of friction and R is the normal reaction force and F is the friction force.
    F

The frictional force, F, will act parallel to the surfaces in contact and in a direction to oppose the motion that is taking place or trying to take place. The coefficient of friction is dependent on both the surface of the material and that of the material sliding over it.

There are essentially two components of friction that establish a given coefficient of friction, roughness and molecular adhesion. The first is an interaction between the peaks and troughs inherent in the micro roughness of the two sliding surfaces, which is a form of interlocking of the surfaces that requires a particular level of force to overcome it.

The second component of friction is a molecular adhesion between the two surfaces. Whilst not a major component in very rough surfaces, it becomes the major component when the surfaces are smooth, and in particular when one surface is rubber or plastic. With a very slightly damp, soft rubber in contact with a smooth surface, such as glass, molecular adhesion takes place and the slight dampness appears to enhance the adhesion. Far higher values of µ can be obtained in these situations than with the rough surfaces.

The wet coefficient of friction is, as it suggests, a representation of the friction of two surfaces separated by a liquid. As described above, in some cases this can lead to molecular adhesion, however in other situations it may act to effectively smooth out the peaks and troughs that make up the roughness of a surface, leading to a reduced coefficient of friction. When establishing the slip resistance of surfaces and footwear it is important to consider the effects of likely contaminants on the surface and establish a wet coefficient of friction for the surface, contaminant and likely material in contact with these.

SLIP RESISTANT TESTING OF SURFACES AND FOOTWEAR

The method of testing the slip resistance of surfaces and footwear is based on the use of two instruments, a pendulum coefficient of friction test and a surface micro roughness meter.

The pendulum coefficient of friction test involves the use of a device with a material fitted to the bottom of a pendulum that is set at a known height and swung so that it passes over the surface of the test material in a controlled manner.

The material on the pendulum is a rubber slider which provides an indication of how the surface would behave if footwear was presented to it. This is used to establish a slipperiness value called a pendulum test value (PTV), previously known as a slip resistance value (SRV).

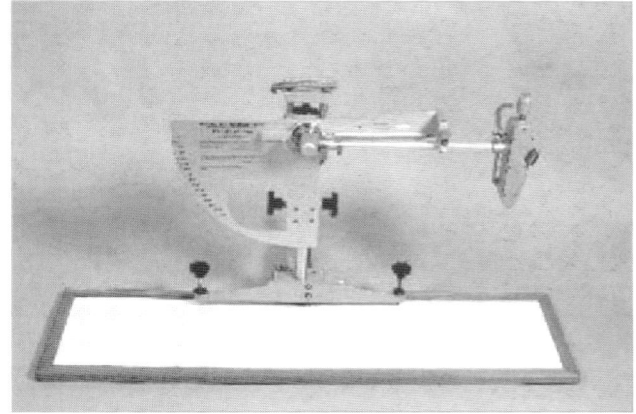

Figure C1-3: Pendulum coefficient of friction tester. *Source: HSE/HSL.*

The pendulum equipment is large and heavy, but provides good representative results. Results are summarised as follows:

Pendulum test value (PTV)	Slip potential classification
0-24	High slip potential
25-35	Moderate slip potential
36+	Low slip potential

Figure C1-4: Slip potential classification PTV.   *Source: HSE/HSL.*

As roughness is such a large component of the coefficient of friction of surfaces, it is possible to obtain an indication of slipperiness by measuring the surface roughness of walking surface materials.

This can also provide a ready indication of the changing characteristics of the surface, such as wear.

Roughness is expressed in a roughness value, Rz; this is used to indicate the level of slip potential of the surface.

In *figure ref C1-6*, the classification relates to a surface in a pedestrian area that may get wet with water.

Figure C1-5: Roughness measuring instrument.
Source: Taylor Hobson.

ELEMENT C1 - GENERAL WORKPLACE ISSUES

Surface roughness (Rz)	Slip potential classification
Below 10 μm	High slip potential
10-20 μm	Moderate slip potential
20+ μm	Low slip potential

Figure C1-6: Slip potential classification, roughness. Source: HSE/HSL.

The HSE has developed a web based slip assessment tool (SAT) to assist with the evaluation of slipperiness of floor surfaces.

This can be used to guide the measurement and analysis of resistance measurements.

The roughness factor can be used to guide the selection of materials for the surface of work and walk surfaces.

It may be particularly important to select a material with a high roughness for situations where contaminants are likely to reduce the coefficient of friction.

The roughness of the surface must be balanced with the need for and ability to clean the surface; whilst a rough surface may reduce slips it may make it difficult to clean.

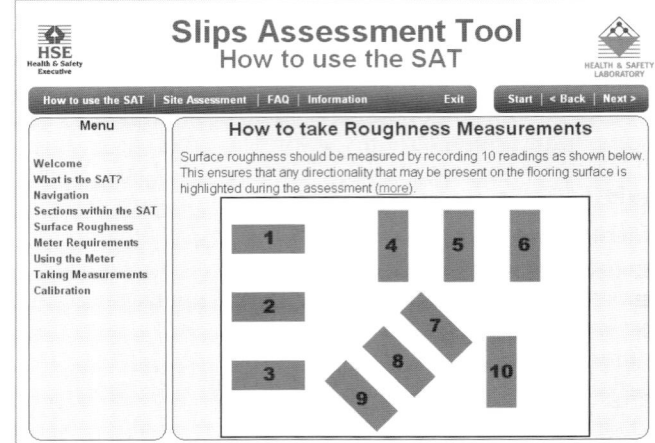

Figure C1-7: Slip assessment tool. Source: HSE.

Minimum roughness (Rz)	Contaminant
20 μm	Clean water, coffee, soft drinks
45 μm	Soap solution, milk
60 μm	Cooking stock
70 μm	Motor oil, olive oil
70 + μm	Gear oil, margarine

Figure C1-8: Roughness suitable for contaminants of different viscosity. Source: HSE/HSL.

DIFFERENT COEFFICIENT OF FRICTION BETWEEN ONE SURFACE AND ANOTHER

The coefficient of friction between one surface and another varies depending on the two materials involved, due to the two characteristic components of friction outlined above. As can be seen by the example set out in *figure ref C1-9* where one surface was rubber, for example, a shoe, and the other was a common walking surface of asphalt, a given coefficient is established.

This can be compared with the coefficient for a shoe and another common walking surface, for example, concrete. This shows that the concrete had a higher frictional resistance and therefore larger coefficient of friction. The higher the coefficient of friction the more resistance to slip there is between the two surfaces.

Material 1	Material 2	μ
Rubber	Asphalt (Dry)	0.5-0.8
Rubber	Asphalt (Wet)	0.25-0.75
Rubber	Concrete (Dry)	0.6-0.85
Rubber	Concrete (Wet)	0.45-0.75

Figure C1-9: Coefficient of friction of different materials. Source: Roy Beardmore.

EFFECTS OF CONTAMINATION ON SURFACES IN TERMS OF COF

The presence of a contaminant on a surface can greatly influence the coefficient of friction. As can be seen in *figure ref C1-9* where the material of the walking surface was wet the coefficient of friction was reduced. Not only does the presence of a contaminant such as water or oil affect the value of the coefficient of friction, but also the manner in which it affects it is very dependent upon factors such as the contact pressure, the size and shape of the contact area, the velocity of movement and the viscosity of the liquid. This makes the measurement of μ in wet conditions much more complex. As described above, one of the most important effects of contamination on surfaces is that liquid contamination can fill in the peaks and troughs of the surface material and flow between these peaks and troughs, acting as a lubricant and reducing the coefficient of friction.

Studies have also found that it is possible for contaminant to form a hydrodynamic squeeze film between the heel of a shoe and a contaminated floor, a feature that could lead to aquaplaning. The level of surface roughness required for solid-to-solid contact increases significantly with the viscosity of the contaminant. Dry contaminants, such as dust and powders, can also affect the coefficient of friction. As with liquids, they can fill in the roughness troughs of the two materials, which changes the nature of the surface. They can also act like tiny spheres between the two surfaces and have a "ball-bearing effect".

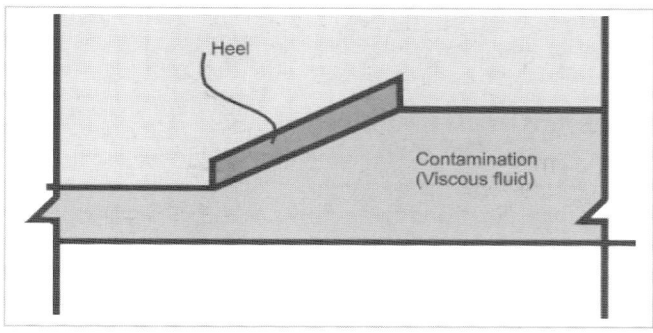

Figure C1-10: Hydrodynamic effect.   Source: CIRIA.

METHODS FOR CLEANING FLOORS AND THE APPROPRIATE FOOTWEAR TO WEAR WHILST CLEANING

Cleaning of floors allows the:

- Removal of surface dirt and contaminant, enabling the surface to be disinfected effectively (if appropriate).
- Original slip resistance of the surface to be restored.
- Removal of microbial soiling, particularly important in the health care, food and catering industries.

Methods for cleaning floors include vacuum dust removal, washing, drying, sealing and polishing. Cleaning arrangements should be in place to deal with the routine removal of low level natural contamination and higher level process derived contamination. Specific cleaning arrangements should also be in place to deal with spillages and other accidental contamination.

The HSE offers the following advice for cleaning in kitchens and other similar areas where contamination and the risk of slipping is high.

Wet cleaning

- The cleaner should wear suitable footwear with good slip resistant qualities that relate to the surface being cleaned.
- Sweep the floor and ensure equipment is clean.
- Prevent people from walking on wet smooth floors until they are totally dry.
- Close area, use barriers, clean in sections, as last resort use cones.
- Warn those affected "wet cleaning in progress"; remove signs as soon as the floor is dry.
- Use the right balance of cleaning solution to water.
- Observe the bucket solution condition and change when dirty.
- After use, rinse cleaning equipment thoroughly.
- Do not dispose of dirty fluid in food and hand sinks.
- Wet the mop well and mop the area.
- Leave solution on the floor for a few minutes to loosen dirt and grease.
- Gently scrub the wet floor (and grout if tiled) with a brush.
- Use a squeegee to push the dirty water residue to the drain, or soak up using a mop.
- Give cleaned area a final mop over.
- Dry off floor with dry mop/squeegee.

Machine cleaning

Steam cleaning

- Steam penetrates deep into flooring; heat and pressure mobilise any grease.
- Some machines recover the dirty water; others have flat head mops which soak it up.
- Leaves floors almost dry.

Mechanical brush (scrubber) methods

- Can clean into the grain of a slip-resistant floor.
- Important that settings and cleaning concentrations are correct and accessories maintained.
- Different brush systems are available, suitable for small, awkward and large floors.
- Some machines leave the floor dry.

Appropriate footwear for cleaning activities

Selecting suitable footwear with good slip resistant qualities is not as straightforward as choosing one from a brochure that says it is slip resistant, as they have to match the surface being cleaned and contaminants from the process or cleaning. Footwear that performs well in the wet may not be suitable for oily surfaces. Manufacturers will often provide data on surfaces and contamination that the footwear has been tested on. The sole tread pattern and sole compound are both important for slip resistance.

Generally a softer sole and close-packed tread pattern work well with fluid contaminants and indoor environments. A more open pattern works better outdoors or with solid contaminants. Confidence in the choice

ELEMENT C1 - GENERAL WORKPLACE ISSUES

of footwear for the environment in question may be improved by conducting field trials. It should be noted that footwear marked as 'oil resistant' does not mean that it is slip resistant to oil, but that the sole will not be damaged by oil.

IMPORTANCE OF GOOD HOUSEKEEPING

Maintenance of a safe workplace may be achieved through the development of a housekeeping procedure. Good housekeeping implies "a place for everything and everything in its place". Laid down procedures are necessary for preventing the spread of contamination, reducing the likelihood of accidents resulting from slips, trips, and falls and reducing the chances of unwanted fire caused by careless storage of flammable waste. Exposure to dust can cause health problems and is an explosion hazard. Dust can be reduced by keeping it damp so it is less likely to become airborne. It can be removed from floors and surfaces by wetting it before 'sweeping' or by using a vacuum cleaner.

Figure C1-11: Housekeeping in office.   *Source: RMS.*

Figure C1-12: Housekeeping in garage.   *Source: RMS.*

Workplace (Health, Safety and Welfare) Regulations (WHSWR) 1992

The main requirements of the Workplace (Health, Safety and Welfare) Regulations (WHSWR) 1992 (as amended) are:

- **Safety** of those using the workplace, including segregation of pedestrians and vehicles, provision of handrails, drainage, fencing or covers for tanks and pits, the operation of doors and gates and escalators or moving walkways.
- **Maintenance** of the workplace and equipment in efficient working order and good repair, cleanliness and arrangements for waste.
- Provision of **welfare** facilities, including rest rooms, changing rooms, accommodation for clothing, toilets, washing facilities and drinking water.
- Provision of a safe **environment,** including lighting, ventilation temperature and the dimensions of rooms and available space).

In addition, the requirements to establish and maintain a safe place of work would include:

- Provision of good ventilation.
- Reasonable temperatures.
- Suitable and sufficient lighting.
- Cleanliness and dealing with waste.
- Adequate space.
- Suitable workstations and seating.
- Condition of floors.
- Establishing traffic routes.

The WHSWR 1992, Regulation 12, specifies that:

"Every floor in a workplace and the surface of every traffic route in a workplace shall be of a construction such that the floor or surface of the traffic route is suitable for the purpose for which it is used.

Without prejudice to the generality of paragraph (1), the requirements in that paragraph shall include requirements that:

a) *The floor, or surface of the traffic route, shall have no hole or slope, or be uneven or slippery so as, in each case, to expose any person to a risk to his health or safety; and*

b) *Every such floor shall have effective means of drainage where necessary".*

The WHSWR 1992 also sets out requirements for maintaining the workplace so that it is safe, Regulation 5 states: *The workplace and the equipment, devices and systems to which this regulation applies shall be maintained (including cleaned as appropriate) in an efficient state, in efficient working order and in good repair.*

When considering specific requirements that relate to safe means of access and egress, the WHSWR 1992, Regulation 17, states that:

"Every workplace shall be organised in such a way that pedestrians and vehicles can circulate in a safe manner".

In addition, the WHSWR 1992 sets out specific requirements for some access/egress issues and considers the safety of doors and gates, as well as escalators and moving walkways.

The WHSWR 1992, Regulation 8, specifies requirements for lighting, *"Every workplace shall have suitable and sufficient lighting".*

This would aid movement in, around and out of the workplace. Lighting provision and levels should take into consideration:

- Changes of level, or direction of pedestrian or vehicle routes.
- Cross over points for pedestrians and vehicles.
- Significant, sudden changes between light levels, for example where there is movement of pedestrians and vehicles between illuminated warehouses and external work areas in the hours of darkness.

The WHSWR 1992 were amended by the Health and Safety (Miscellaneous Amendments) Regulations (MAR) 2002 to take account of disability and to ensure that the workplace, including doors, passageways, stairs, showers, washbasins, lavatories and workstations used or occupied directly by disabled persons is suitable for them.

C1.2 - Safety signs

Common safety signs and their categorisation

Safety signs are defined as those combining shape, colour and a pictorial symbol to provide specific health and safety information and instruction.

The Health and Safety (Safety Signs and Signals) Regulations (SSSR) 1996 require that safety signs comply with the requirements set out in Schedule 1 to the SSSR 1996.

The Regulations cover five main categories of signs:

1)	*Prohibition*	Circular signs. Red and white. For example, - No smoking. - No pedestrian access. - No children. - No unauthorised access.	Prohibition
2)	*Warning*	Triangular signs. Black on yellow. For example, - Toxic substance. - Site traffic. - Electrical hazard. - Deep excavation.	Warning
3)	*Safe condition*	Rectangle/square signs. Green and white. For example, - Fire exit. - First aid. - Emergency assembly point. - Eye wash station.	Safe Condition
4)	*Mandatory*	Circular signs. Blue and white. For example, - Safety helmets must be worn. - Hearing protection must be worn. - Safety boots must be worn. - All visitors must report to site office.	Mandatory

ELEMENT C1 - GENERAL WORKPLACE ISSUES

5)	*Fire-fighting*	Rectangle/square signs. White and red. For example, ■ Fire extinguisher. ■ Fire hose. ■ Emergency fire telephone. ■ Fire alarm call point	

Figure C1-13: Categories of safety signs. *Source: RMS.*

Figure C1-14: Warning, Mandatory and prohibition. *Source: RMS.*   Figure C1-15: Warning and safe condition. *Source: RMS.*

Use, location and compliance issues

USE

Safety signs and signals are not a substitute for other controls. They are for situations where, having conducted a risk assessment and applied all appropriate techniques for collective protection and higher level controls, the employer cannot reduce risks other than by the provision of signs to provide warnings or instruction. The provision of safety signs does not automatically indicate that risks have been adequately reduced; this will only be considered to be the case if, after provision of a sign, there is no longer a significant risk of harm.

LOCATION

Signs should be installed at a suitable height and position appropriate to the line of sight, taking into account obstacles. They will be located either at the access point to an area with a general hazard or in immediate proximity to a specific hazard. The location of signs will depend on the hazards in the workplace and the existence of residual risks; the following indicate specific locations that should be considered:

- Important locations, such as where dangerous substances are stored must be indicated by a suitable warning sign.
- Containers and visible pipes used for dangerous substances must be marked with a suitable warning sign/label. They must be on the visible side of containers and at important locations of the pipe, for example, at joints and valves, and at intervals.
- Places where there is a risk of colliding with obstacles or of falling must be permanently marked with a safety colour and/or with signs.
- Traffic routes must be permanently marked with a safety colour.
- Signs and/or a safety colour must be used to permanently mark the location and identification of fire-fighting equipment.
- Care should be taken to ensure that too many signs are not located together as this can lead to confusion or difficulty in observing the intended information or instruction.
- If illuminated signs are used they should not be placed where other light sources would prevent them being properly visible.

COMPLIANCE ISSUES

Permanent signboards must be used for signs relating to prohibitions, warnings and mandatory requirements and the location and identification of emergency escape routes and first-aid facilities. The pictograms used can differ slightly to those depicted in Schedule 1 of SSSR 1996, but must still convey the same intent. Where there is a risk related to the movement of traffic, including pedestrians, in a workplace the appropriate sign normally used to comply with the Road Traffic Regulation Act (RTRA) 1984 must be used, even if the RTRA 1984 does not apply to the workplace.

GENERAL WORKPLACE ISSUES - ELEMENT C1

Figure C1-16: Prohibition signs.   *Source: RMS.*

Figure C1-17: Warning and mandatory sign.   *Source: RMS.*

The appropriate sign, acoustic or visual signal must be used where the occasion requires; to signal danger, to call people to take a specific course of action, for emergency evacuation and to guide persons carrying out hazardous or dangerous manoeuvres. Safety signs can be supplemented by other signs that provide additional or supplementary information. For example, where a noise hazard is identified by a warning sign - 'hearing protection available on request' may be added as supplementary information.

Supplementary safety signs can be used to mark obstacles, for example, the edge of a raised platform and dangerous locations, or an area where objects may fall or an area where work is going on that the public should not access. These may be yellow and black or red and white - in each case they consist of alternate colour stripes set at 45° angles. These supplementary signs must not be used as a substitute for other warning signs.

Any safety signs provided must be kept up to date, maintained in good condition and removed if they no longer apply. Illuminated signs need to be provided with an alternative power supply that will ensure the sign remains visible when it is needed. It is important to ensure that illuminated signs and signals are checked for correct functioning at intervals.

Figure C1-18: Mandatory sign.   *Source: RMS.*

Figure C1-19: Safe condition sign.   *Source: RMS.*

Figure C1-20: Hazard identification - obstruction.   *Source: RMS.*

Figure C1-21: Hazard identification - restricted width.   *Source: RMS.*

ELEMENT C1 - GENERAL WORKPLACE ISSUES

Signals

The SSSR 1996 establish principles for acoustic, verbal and hand signals. Acoustic signals have to be able to be heard and would usually be set at a level of 10dB above the level of ambient noise and at an appropriate frequency. Where variable and constant frequencies are used the variable frequency should indicate a higher level of danger, or need for action, than a constant signal. The signal for evacuation must be constant.

Verbal signals can be used to direct hazardous operations and may be made by either human, for example, when directing lifting operations or artificial voices such as those used to indicate that a vehicle is reversing. Spoken messages must be clear, concise and understood by the listener. People involved need a good knowledge of the language used. Where English is not the first language of most staff the codes used do not have to be in English.

Code word	Meaning
Start	Start an operation
Stop	Interrupt or end an operation
End	Stop an operation
Raise	Raise a load
Lower	Lower a load
Forwards	Move forward
Backwards	Move backwards
Right	Move to signaller's right
Left	Move to signaller's left
Danger	Emergency stop
Quickly	Speed up a movement

Figure C1-22: Codes for verbal signals.   Source: Health and Safety (Safety Signs and Safety Signals) Regulations (SSSR) 1996.

Hand signals may be used to direct hazardous operations such as cranes or vehicle manoeuvres. A standard set of signalling codes as proposed by Part IX of Schedule 1 of the SSSR 1996 are set as follows.

Hand signals must be precise, simple, expansive, easy to make and to understand, and clearly distinct from other such signals.

Meaning	Description	Illustration
General signals:		
Start Attention Start of Command	Both arms are extended horizontally with the palms facing forwards	
Stop Interruption End of movement	The right arm points upwards with the palm facing forwards	
End of the operation	Both hands are clasped at chest height	
Vertical movements:		
Raise	The right arm points upwards with the palm facing forward and slowly makes a circle	

GENERAL WORKPLACE ISSUES - ELEMENT C1

Lower	The right arm points downwards with the palm facing inwards and slowly makes a circle	
Vertical distance	The hands indicate the relevant distance.	

Horizontal movements:

Move forwards	Both arms are bent with the palms facing upwards, and the forearms make slow movements towards the body	
Move backwards	Both arms are bent with the palms facing downwards, and the forearms make slow movements away from the body	

Meaning	Description	Illustration
Right *to the signalman's*	The right arm is extended more or less horizontally with the palm facing downwards and slowly makes small movements to the right	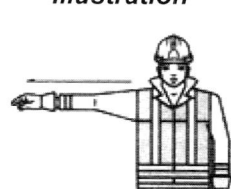
Left *to the signalman's*	The left arm is extended more or less horizontally with the palm facing downwards and slowly makes small movements to the left	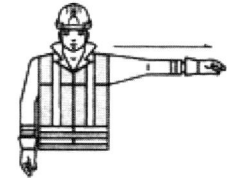
Horizontal distance	The hands indicate the relevant distance.	
Danger **Emergency stop**	Both arms points upwards with the palms facing forwards	
Quick	All movements faster	
Slow	All movements slower	

Figure C1-23: Hand signals. *Source: Health and Safety (Safety Signs and Safety Signals) Regulations (SSSR) 1996.*

ELEMENT C1 - GENERAL WORKPLACE ISSUES

Health and Safety (Safety Signs and Signals) Regulations 1996, Regulations 2, 3, 4 and 5

The objective of the Health and Safety (Safety Signs and Signals) Regulations (SSSR) 1996 is to provide control of the use of safety signs (and signals) and standardisation of the format used, where they are directed at people at work.

The objectives are met by the following:

- Signs are defined by Schedule 1 to the regulations as those combining shape, colour and a pictorial symbol to provide specific health and safety information and instruction.
- Sign categories are specified - prohibition, warning, mandatory, safe conditions (emergency escape or first aid) and fire-fighting signs.
- Supplementary safety signs (strips) can be white with yellow or fluorescent orange/red, but must not substitute for the provision of signs as defined above.
- Signals are specified and have a defined meaning.
- The use of signs and signals is specified.

Regulation 2 of the SSSR 1996 sets out detailed interpretation, for example:

"'Safety sign' means a sign referring to a specific object, activity or situation and providing information or instruction about health or safety at work by means of a signboard, a safety colour, an illuminated sign, an acoustic signal, a verbal communication or a hand signal.

'Hand signal' means a movement or position of the arms or hands or a combination thereof, in coded form, for guiding persons who are carrying out manoeuvres which create a risk to the health or safety of persons at work".

The SSSR 1996 do not apply to situations where other specific arrangements are in place to meet the same objective, including the transport and supply of dangerous substances, for regulating transport (road, rail water and air) or on board a sea-going ship.

The SSSR 1996, Regulation 4, requires employers to provide and maintain specific safety signs whenever there is a significant risk which has not been avoided or controlled by other means, for example, by engineering controls and safe systems of work. Where a safety sign would not help to reduce that risk there is no need to provide a sign.

The regulation also requires that hand signals and verbal communication set out in Schedule 1 of SSSR 1996 are used. The duty extends to the marking of containers and visible pipelines that contain dangerous substances; these should be marked with appropriate warnings and may be supplemented by the name and/or the formula of the substance. The SSSR 1996 does not cover colour coding of pipes in accordance with their content, but BS 1710 "Specification for identification of pipelines and services" does.

Regulation 5 of the SSSR 1996 requires employers to:

- *Provide comprehensive information to employees on the measures to be taken in connection with safety signs.*
- *Provide suitable and sufficient instruction and training in the meaning of the signs and the measures to be taken.*

C1.3 - Confined spaces

Description of conditions that constitute a confined space

The Confined Spaces Regulations (CSR) 1997 defines a confined space as:

"Any place, including any chamber, tank, vat, silo, pit, pipe, sewer, flue, well, or other similar space, in which, by virtue of its enclosed nature, there arises a reasonably foreseeable specified risk".

Figure C1-24: Confined space - definition. Source: CSR 1997.

A 'specified risk' is defined as a risk of:

a) Serious injury from a fire or explosion.
b) Loss of consciousness of any person arising from an increase in body temperature.
c) Loss of consciousness or asphyxiation of any person at work arising from gas, fumes, vapour or lack of oxygen.
d) Drowning of any person at work arising from an increase in the level of a liquid.
e) Asphyxiation of any person at work arising from a free flowing solid or inability to reach a respirable environment due to being trapped by a free flowing solid.

The employer must ensure compliance with the regulations in respect of work carried out by his employees. The employer must also ensure compliance so far as is reasonably practicable with the regulations in respect of work carried out by persons other than employees in so far as they relate to matters which are within the employer's control.

GENERAL WORKPLACE ISSUES - ELEMENT C1

Figure C1-25: Confined space - chamber. *Source: RMS.*

Figure C1-26: Confined space - sewer. *Source: RMS.*

Figure C1-27: Confined space - tank. *Source: RMS.*

Figure C1-28: Confined space - open tank. *Source: RMS.*

Examples of where confined space entry may occur in the workplace

Chamber	Caisson, cofferdam, or interception chamber for water.
Tank	Storage tanks for solid or liquid chemicals.
Vat	Process vessel which may be open, but by its depth confines a person.
Silo	May be an above the ground structure for storing cereal, crops.
Pit	Below ground, such as a chamber for a pump, inspection pit in a garage or vehicle production tracks.
Pipe or duct	Fabricated from concrete, plastic steel etc, used to carry liquids, gases or services, such as trucking ducts and those used for control of a watercourse.
Sewer	Brick or concrete structure for the carrying of liquid waste.
Flue	Exhaust chimney for disposal of waste gases.
Well	Deep source of water.

Factors to be considered when assessing risk

A failure to appreciate the dangers associated with confined spaces has led not only to the deaths of many workers, but also to the demise of some of those who have attempted to rescue them.

A confined space is not only a space that is small and difficult to enter, exit or work in; it can also be a large space, but with limited/restricted access. It can also be a space that is badly ventilated for example, a tank or a large tunnel.

Regulation 4, Work in confined spaces, of the CSR, states that:

"No person at work shall enter a confined space to carry out work for any purpose unless it is not reasonably practicable to achieve that purpose without such entry".

The initial stage of the risk assessment will need to consider if entry is the only way to carry out the task, and if the task cannot be reasonably done by other means, the risks must be determined by analysis of each hazard and preventative control.

Further, Regulation 5, Emergency arrangements, of the CSR, sates that:

"No person at work shall enter or carry out work in a confined space unless there have been prepared in respect of that confined space suitable and sufficient arrangements for the rescue of persons in the event of an emergency, whether or not arising out of a specified risk".

It is important that the risk assessment take account of:

- The need for safe access.
- Provision and maintenance of safe atmospheres.
- The task, materials and equipment.
- The persons at risk.
- Reliability of safeguards.
- Emergency arrangements.

External factors such as weather conditions, temperature, proximity of other tasks, must also be included. Together with clear consideration of the individuals responsible for isolation and making ready, those who need to enter and those who will monitor or might be required for rescue. The whole process of confined space entry should be documented and subject to a written permit to work. The risk assessment should consider the effectiveness of such documentation.

SAFE ACCESS TO AND EGRESS FROM CONFINED SPACES

Openings affording safe access to confined spaces, and through divisions, partitions or obstructions within such spaces, need to be sufficiently large and free from obstruction to allow the passage of persons wearing the necessary protective clothing and equipment. The openings must also be sufficient to allow access and egress for rescue purposes. Practice drills will help to check that the size of openings and entry/exit procedures are satisfactory. For example, as well as provision of openings that allow for safe access, a safety sign warning against unauthorised entry and platforms to enable safe working within the confined space may be provided. Consideration should be made of the access and egress needs in an emergency, special equipment may be needed to hoist a person from a confined space or a second egress point may be required, for example, in a sewer.

Access and egress arrangements should be adequate in size, number, ease of use and secure. It is important that they be maintained to be available when they are needed; this may mean securing them open and/or positioning people to ensure they remain available.

PROVISION AND MAINTENANCE OF SAFE ATMOSPHERES

General factors to consider

There are a number of factors that should be considered when determining risk related to the provision and maintenance of safe atmospheres. Consideration needs to be given to:

- Previous contents, whether they have been removed or part remains as a vapour or gas.
- Residues, for example, deposits or sediments that may release toxic or flammable material when disturbed.
- Oxygen deficiency and oxygen enrichment.
- Physical dimensions; the atmosphere may vary in parts of the confined space, for example, low lying compartments.
- Cleaning chemicals or chemicals introduced as part of the task could affect the atmosphere, for example, vapours from adhesives used to glue a replacement tank lining or the products of combustion from a welding operation.
- The ambient temperature may be too hot or too cold to ensure ease of breathing or control of body core temperature (with external tanks the internal temperature will rise significantly when exposed to sunlight from early morning throughout the day).
- Temperature changes may also cause toxic materials to be released.
- Ingress of substances or dangerous fumes from adjacent work.
- Contamination, for example, methane can leach into groundwater and be released or limestone may give off carbon dioxide in the presence of acid groundwater.
- Failure of forced ventilation.

Testing the atmosphere

Testing of the atmosphere may be needed where knowledge of the confined space indicates that the atmosphere might be contaminated or to any extent abnormal. The appropriate choice of testing equipment will depend on particular circumstances. For example, when testing for toxic atmospheres, chemical detector tubes or portable atmospheric monitoring equipment is appropriate.

However, there may be cases requiring monitoring equipment specifically designed to measure for flammable atmospheres.

Testing should be carried out by persons experienced and competent in the practice and records of the findings should be kept. Personal gas detectors should be worn whenever appropriate to mitigate the hazard of local pockets of contaminates and to confirm a suitable atmosphere is maintained for each individual.

GENERAL WORKPLACE ISSUES - ELEMENT C1

Respiratory protective equipment (RPE)

Where RPE is provided or used in connection with confined space entry (including emergency rescue) it must be suitable for the purpose for which it is intended, i.e. correctly selected and matched to both the job and the wearer. RPE will not normally be suitable unless it is breathing apparatus with an independent air supply that ensures the individual is provided with a safe atmosphere to breath. Suitable breathing apparatus includes a properly fitting helmet or face-piece with necessary connections such that a person using it in toxic, asphyxiating or irritant atmosphere breathes ordinary clean and dry air.

TASK, MATERIAL AND EQUIPMENT

The tasks to be conducted in the confined space, along with the materials and equipment used, could significantly affect the risk. If the task is one where the lining to a confined space is to be replaced the task may involve a sequence of maintenance activities, for example:

- Examination of the condition of the walls of confined space, which could introduce the need for electrical equipment in the form of lighting.
- Cleaning out slurry or other residues, which could release toxic substances.
- Cleaning the inside walls of the confined space, which may involve chemicals or noisy percussion equipment.
- Removal of a lining from the sides and out of a restricted opening, which may involve extreme physical effort that could cause body core temperature to rise and lead to manual handling issues.
- Making the surface of the walls of the confined space ready to receive a new lining, involving grinding and cleaning operations.
- Fitting the new lining, using an adhesive.

As can be seen by this example, the tasks conducted inside a confined space, as well as the materials and equipment involved, can greatly influence the risk. The task must be clearly identified, described and subject to a formal assessment. Whenever possible entry should be avoided by the use of, for example, long reach tools for recovery of objects, pressure hoses for cleaning used from outside the confined space.

Typical safeguards to control the risks related to the task, materials and equipment will include isolation procedures to remove sources of hazard like electricity, fluids and moving parts. These will include:

- Lock off and/or fuse removal.
- Removal of sections of pipe work to and from the vessel with the possible need to use blank off spades.
- Removal and isolation of sources of heat (electrical, gas, steam).
- Isolation of moving equipment such as mixers or turbines.

Ropes, harnesses, lifelines, resuscitating apparatus, first aid equipment, protective clothing and other special equipment will usually need to be provided or used for or in connection with confined space entry or in case of emergency rescue. When a safety harness and line are used it is essential that the free end of the line is secured so that it can be used as part of the rescue procedure. The harness and line will need to be adjusted and worn so that the wearer can be drawn up head first through any access/egress opening. Power operated lifting equipment may be necessary for this purpose.

PERSONS AT RISK

Consideration of the persons at risk includes those that enter the confined space, those involved with supporting them and those that may be involved in rescuing them. It is important to consider the effects on the risk of the individuals involved, and this may involve their:

- Medical condition, for example, physical fitness and need for medication.
- Physical attributes, for example, size, strength and agility.
- Mental attributes, including capacity to work to formal instructions, temperament and capability to work in a confined space (claustrophobia).
- Understanding of the risk and controls.

RELIABILITY OF SAFEGUARDS

The risks related to confined space work can be significant if they are not adequately controlled. The safeguards to be provided generally rely on human intervention to ensure they are used and remain effective; therefore the risk increases if there is less assurance that these safeguards are put in place and remain effective. The absence of a formal procedure that ensured safeguards were taken and remained in place would lead to increased risk.

Risk increases in situations where the safeguards need to be in place for a significant time; because it will rely on repeated monitoring that the safeguards remain effective. This can decline over time and when teams of workers hand over the task to each other; leads to reduced reliability of the safeguards and increased risk.

Reliability of safeguards can be reduced in a number of ways, for example:

- Equipment provided to force air into the confined space could fail.
- Higher than low voltage electrical equipment may be introduced to do difficult or unplanned jobs.
- Isolation may not be secured and get re-instated.
- The people assigned to the work may not be available and other, untrained, workers used.

ELEMENT C1 - GENERAL WORKPLACE ISSUES

- Monitoring of the atmosphere may only be intermittent and conducted in a small number of locations.
- Unplanned substances may be introduced to deal with a problem.

To take account of reliability factors all safeguards should be subject to a permit to work procedure and should be evaluated to ensure their effectiveness before entry is allowed and monitored as the work progresses. Much confined space work involves the use of a range of personal protective equipment (PPE), including breathing apparatus. This places a heavy reliance on an individual, rather than collective, control and presents a lower reliability. Where the use of breathing apparatus is required a standby person should monitor duration of exposure, within a 50% margin for air carried in a cylinder. For air supplied from a compressor a reservoir should be used, such that on failure of the compressor (and standby compressor) there is sufficient capacity for escape.

It is important that good communication is established at all times to enable communication:

- Between those inside the confined space.
- Between those inside the confined space and those outside.
- To summon help in case of emergency.

This will enable the confirmation that safeguards remain in place or that their reliability has failed and action needs to be taken.

Factors to be considered in designing safe working practices

OPERATING PROCEDURES

Written operating procedures should be used for all confined space work that establish a safe system of working. They may need to take account of work above ground (surface or gantry tanks) and work below ground (tanks, sewers etc.). Operating procedures will normally require a formal document control system, such as a permit to work system, to be used to:

- Describe (and restrict) the work to be done.
- A process to determine the hazards.
- Define the controls to reduce the risk to an acceptable level.

The importance and limitation of a permit to work system is captured in the Health and Safety Executive (HSE) guidance to the Confined Spaces Regulations (CSR) 1997.

"A permit to work system is a formal written system and is usually required where there is a reasonably foreseeable risk of serious injury in entering or working in the confined space. The permit to work procedure is an extension of the safe system to work, not a replacement for it. The use of a permit to work system does not, by itself, make the job safe. It supports the safe system, providing a ready means of recording findings and authorisations required to proceed with the entry. It also contains information, for example, time limits on entry, results of the gas testing, and other information that may be required during an emergency and which, when the job is completed, can also provide historical information on original entry conditions".

Example - entry into confined spaces

Possible Lay-Out for a Permit-To-Work Certificate

PLANT DETAILS (Location, identifying number, etc.				ACCEPTANCE OF CERTIFICATE Accepts all conditions of certificate			
WORK TO BE DONE					Signed	Date	Time
WITHDRAWAL FROM SERVICE	Signed	Date	Time	COMPLETION OF WORK All work completed - equipment returned for use	Signed	Date	Time
ISOLATION Dangerous fumes Electrical supply Sources of heat	Signed	Date	Time				
CLEANING AND PURGING Of all dangerous materials	Signed	Date	Time	EXTENSION	Signed	Date	Time
TESTING For contamination	Contaminants tested Signed	Date	Results Time				
I CERTIFY THAT I HAVE PERSONALLY EXAMINED THE PLANT DETAILED ABOVE AND SATISFIED MYSELF THAT THE ABOVE PARTICULARS ARE CORRECT (1) THE PLANT IS SAFE FOR ENTRY WITHOUT BREATHING APPARATUS (2) BREATHING APPARATUS MUST BE WORN Other precautions necessary : Time of expiry of certificate : Delete (1) or (2)	Signed Date		Time	THIS PERMIT TO WORK IS NOW CANCELLED. A NEW PERMIT WILL BE REQUIRED IF WORK IS TO CONTINUE	Signed	Date	Time
				RETURN TO SERVICE	I accept the above plant back into service Signed	Date	Time

Figure C1-29: Example PTW certificate (confined spaces).

Source: HSE Guidance note on permits to work.

The operating procedures will need to consider who is authorised to issue a permit to work, establish controls and require those that enter to work to the controls. The form is signed by all parties to reinforce the gravity of the system of working. A possible permit to work certificate lay-out for confined spaces is shown in *figure ref C1-29*.

A permit to work should be cancelled when the operations to which it applies have finished. This could be the completion of the task, the need to redefine the task or the hand over of the task to others.

EMERGENCY ARRANGEMENTS

The Confined Spaces Regulations (CSR) 1997, Regulation 5 (1), prohibits any person to enter or carry out work in a confined space unless there are suitable and sufficient rescue arrangements in place. In the event of failure of a ventilation system provided to ensure a suitable atmosphere, either a back-up system should automatically take over or a system of work should be in place (for example, alarm and air reservoir) to evacuate the confined space before anyone is put at risk.

Emergency arrangements need to take account of the following in order to be suitable and sufficient:

- Provision and maintenance of resuscitation equipment.
- Provision and maintenance equipment to enable the emergency rescue to be carried out effectively.
- Restrict, so far as is reasonably practicable, the risks to health and safety of any rescuer.
- Be *immediately* put into operation when circumstances arise requiring a rescue.

The arrangements for emergency rescue will depend on the nature of the confined space, the risks identified and consequently the likely nature of an emergency rescue. The arrangements might need to cover:

- Rescue and resuscitation equipment.
- Special arrangements with local hospitals for example, for foreseeable toxic effects).
- Raising the alarm and rescue.
- Safeguarding the rescuers.
- Safeguarding third parties.
- Fire fighting.
- Control of plant.
- First aid.
- Public emergency services.

TRAINING FOR WORK IN CONFINED SPACES

Statutory requirements relate back to HASAWA 1974, section 2(2)c. Employers have a duty to provide such information, instruction, training and supervision to ensure the health and safety at work of employees. Specific training for work in confined spaces will include:

- Awareness of CSR 1997.
- The need to avoid entry unless it is not reasonably practicable to do so.
- Understand the work to be done (hazards and precautions).
- Understand the safe system of work, particularly permit to work.
- How emergencies arise, need to follow emergency procedures.

Specific training may include:

- Atmospheric testing equipment and interpretation of readings.
- Use, maintenance, cleaning of breathing apparatus or escape sets.
- Use of other PPE and limitations.
- Use of communication methods.
- Training in evacuation procedures.

Practical refresher training should be carried out at a suitable frequency. Standby team(s) for rescue would need to be trained additionally in:

- Use of rescue equipment, including lifelines, harness, lifting equipment.
- Dealing with failure of equipment whilst in use.
- Emergency arrangements and response.
- Resuscitation procedures and the use of any other related medical equipment.
- Emergency first aid.
- Use of fire fighting equipment.
- Liaison with local emergency services in the event of an incident.
- Training practice recovery with a full-weight dummy.

Flammable atmospheres

HOW FLAMMABLE ATMOSHPERES ARISE AND WHERE THEY ARE FOUND

The wide variety of flammable substances found in the workplace includes paints, solvents, welding gases and petrol and flammable materials include dusts from wood, flour and sugar. The presence of a substance or material in the atmosphere does not mean it is a flammable atmosphere; it is necessary for a quantity of the substance or material to be present in proportion with the oxygen in the air to make it a flammable atmosphere. The amount necessary and proportion to air varies for different substances and materials. There is a range, percentage of substance or material in air that is necessary for flammability. Too little or too much of a substance or material may prevent flammability.

See also Element C2.1 - Properties of flammable and explosive materials and the mechanisms by which they ignite.

ELEMENT C1 - GENERAL WORKPLACE ISSUES

> *An explosive atmosphere is an accumulation of gas, mist, dust or vapour, mixed with air, which has the potential to catch fire or explode. An explosive atmosphere does not always result in an explosion, but if it caught fire the flames would quickly travel through it and if this happened in a confined space (for example in plant or equipment) the rapid spread of the flames or rise in pressure could also cause an explosion.*

Figure C1-30: Explosive atmosphere.   Source: HSE Guidance INDG370.

Flammable atmospheres may arise for a number of reasons and in various places; some examples are set out below:

- A flammable atmosphere may arise due to a manufacturing process that includes mixing a flammable solvent with a paint to enable it to be applied at point of use properly. Normally this process would be enclosed, but a fault could occur in a pump seal leading to the flammable solvent being released under pressure, causing it to be released in small particles of liquid that are easily vaporised.
- A furniture manufacturing process may involve using glues that contain flammable solvents, if the lids are left off the glue containers the solvent will be free to escape to atmosphere, and this could build up over time.
- When petrol is delivered to a location, if the connecting delivery pipe is not fitted properly the fuel could leak out in small quantities, which could build up over the duration of the delivery.
- Where flour is being produced a conveyor may breakdown, requiring it to be opened for repair. In order to carry out the repair a significant amount of flour dust may be liberated into the atmosphere, particularly if a bad practice like using an airline to blow dust off conveyor components is used.
- Flammable atmospheres may increase over time due to by-products of natural digestion of waste, for example, in sewers, leading to a build up of methane.

CONTROL MEASURES FOR ENTERING FLAMMABLE ATMOSPHERES, INCLUDING PURGING TO KEEP FLAMMABLE ATMOSPHERES BELOW LOWER EXPLOSION LIMITS (LEL)

Work requiring entry in an area that has high potential for the presence of an explosive atmosphere must be strictly controlled and planned to minimise risk. For this reason the work would be subject to a permit to work. Part of the permit to work would be the assessment of the atmosphere to determine the level of flammability and the extent of the affected area. Measurements would be taken with equipment that was suitable for the expected substance or material and the flammable nature of the atmosphere.

Following the first priority of any risk management strategy consideration would be made of the possibility of elimination of the flammable atmosphere, by reducing the quantity of flammable substance or material in the atmosphere to below the lower explosive limit (LEL). In some cases it may be possible for the flammable atmosphere to be allowed to disperse by natural means, particularly if it is in the open air and no sources of ignition are present. In other cases it may be necessary to take positive action to eliminate the flammable atmosphere from the work area by means of forced ventilation, called *purging*, with air or an inert gas, such as nitrogen. The use of inert gases for purging may be useful in situations where it is not proposed to enter the flammable area to carry out hot work. If it was proposed to enter an enclosed area after inert gas purging this could bring a different hazard, as the inert gas would replace oxygen in the air.

In situations where the work area cannot easily be purged or the process has reduced but not eliminated the flammability hazard, it may be necessary to enter the work area. It is important that all sources of ignition are controlled; electrical equipment would need to be suitable for the flammable atmosphere and non-sparking tools used. Anti-static clothing may be required and care taken with controlling hot surfaces of equipment and plant.

See also 'Fire and explosion prevention and protection' in Element 2 - Principles of fire and explosion.

C1.4 - Structural safety of workplaces

Causes of damage to the structure of buildings

The causes of damage to structures includes adverse weather, overloading, corrosion, subsidence and unauthorised modifications to buildings. It is important that controls be established to ensure structural safety. The Workplace (Health, Safety and Welfare) Regulations (WHSWR) 1992 were amended by the Health and Safety (Miscellaneous Amendments) Regulations (MAR) 2002 to require:

"Where a workplace is in a building, the building shall have a stability and solidity appropriate to the nature of the use of the workplace".

Ensuring structural safety and compliance with WHSWR 1992 (as amended) will require control measures to ensure appropriate design and maintenance, as well as control on use and modification of the building. Each of the most common causes of damage to the structure of buildings are covered below, along with an outline of the controls that relate to them.

ADVERSE WEATHER CONDITIONS

Severe weather conditions will often result in loss of roofing materials, collapse of signs and overturning of portable accommodation (portacabins). Strong winds can put additional loading on windows, cladding and sheeting applied to a building fitted with scaffolding.

Partially built buildings may be particularly at risk of collapse in these circumstances. Heavy rain or snow could cause the roof of a structure to collapse where it collects.

OVERLOADING OF STRUCTURES

The overloading of structures may be due to factors like:

- Under specification at the design stage.
- Inadvertent additional loading for storage reasons.
- Introduction of equipment and plant that is beyond the weight capacity of a floor.
- Addition of pipes and other suspended equipment to a roof or below a floor.
- Maintenance work adding loading in order to lift or move equipment.

Structures, racking and flooring may become overloaded and subject to collapse if materials stored are not managed correctly. Where storage racking is provided, each cell should be marked with the safe working load. Each vertical section of storage cells should be similarly plated with the safe working load for that group of cells. Prefabricated offices in work areas or warehouses should not be used to store materials on the roofs; such roofs should be signed to prevent this practice.

Consideration should be given to restricting total weight and identifying distribution of weight on all floors above ground level (where a cellar is below ground level, consider all floors above the cellar). Floors are particularly at risk during refurbishment when building materials might be concentrated within a small area; similarly during demolition, if materials are allowed to accumulate in large quantities.

DAMAGE FROM IMPACT

Damage may occur to walls, door edges, storage racking, overhead pipe work and lights, both within and external to the building, through contact with a variety of vehicles, such as fork lift trucks, heavy goods vehicles and mobile plant. Protective devices that may limit the risk include use of height/width clearance plates, physical barriers to protect overhead services, physical barriers and line marking to protect walls and doorways.

HOT AND CORROSIVE ATMOSPHERES

Work processes that evolve hot or corrosive atmospheres will progressively weaken structures with time. Temperature change will cause expansion and contraction of the building fabric, which may exceed the design specification over time. This could lead to fixings becoming loose or cracking of welded joints. Corrosive atmospheres will erode the surface of the structure and may affect electrical insulation and cause hydrogen embitterment of steel supports, if the levels exceed the design specification. The corrosive atmosphere may accentuate differences in materials used and lead to rapid galvanic corrosion and early failure of load-bearing parts of the structure.

VIBRATION

Vibration from mobile and fixed equipment, if not suitably reduced with vibration buffers, may result in structural damage, or undermining of foundations. The vibration may also be sufficient to cause the loosening of positioning components, for example, bolts, which could lead to a structural part of the building becoming insecure and progressive collapse of the building.

ALTERATION TO STRUCTURAL MEMBERS

The alteration of structural members may take place to:

- Add fittings or fixings for pipes or conveyors.
- Provide clearance for material moving equipment, for example, conveyors or lift trucks.
- Provide new access routes.
- Provide space to locate plant.
- Extend a building, by adding an extension to a structural member.
- Add lifting points.

Before any building is modified or changed, a structural engineer should be involved in the design change phase; reference to the safety file for new builds will also be essential. Local building regulation / planning permission may be necessary; also liaison with the local fire and rescue service and a fire risk assessment is likely to be required.

SUBSIDENCE

Subsidence may occur over time due to natural ground movement. The design should have considered this possibility and footings suitable for the location should have been agreed with the local building regulation department and carried through into the build. Subsidence can also occur as a result of extreme weather that resulted in flooding and subsoil erosion of the ground. Softening of the ground from roof drainage may lead to subsidence and consequential cracking of walls. Erosion of soil due to rainwater runoff can undermine shallow foundations, leading to subsidence and tilting of walls. Damaged drains and inspection chambers may also lead to ground softening. The fracture of a water main in the vicinity of a structure could rapidly inject water into the ground around foundations, changing the state of the soil. The water and soil mixture will not be capable of supporting the same weight of structure as dryer soil, leading to major subsidence. Tunnelling by vermin can also affect the stability of light structures.

ELEMENT C1 - GENERAL WORKPLACE ISSUES

The construction of new structures next to existing structures or other excavation works may also weaken the subsoil and lead to subsidence.

DETERIORATION OF BUILDING MATERIALS

Buildings will deteriorate from general wear and tear, from the effects of the environment, external issues will include sunlight, temperature change and ingress of rain, which will particularly affect cladding of wood and some synthetic materials. Internally, issues to consider will include changes in temperature, humidity and the corrosive effects of waste by products of processes.

The ingress of water from whatever cause can lead to the deterioration of timber and mortar from the effects of wet rot. Dampness may come from driving rain, roof runoff or missing/damaged rainwater gutters. This concentrates water to a particular part of the wall. The results are clearly visible externally as stains and eroded mortar, etc. and any timber built into the wall is liable to be affected. Rusting of steelwork and reinforcement may cause cracking of surrounding masonry leading to further deterioration.

Timber beams and roof trusses naturally deflect under load. The shape and structure of joints and members may vary according to the moisture in the air. An increase in stress may occur due to overloading due to this deflection.

Regular monitoring and maintenance of the building fabric will be required to ensure maximum life.

EXCAVATIONS

Excavations that are dug near to an existing structure or partially built structure could lead to collapse of the building in the area nearest to the excavation. In normal conditions the load of the building is born by the soil around it. The removal of the soil for the excavation means that the outward acting forces created by the weight of a building acting on the soil it is standing on may lead to the collapse of the sides of the excavation. This will lead to an unsupported part of the structure. This may be sufficient to cause part of the foundation to fail and that part of the building supported by the foundation to collapse. In addition, water erosion of the sides of the excavation could cause accelerated collapse.

Excavations will need to be secured from collapse by the use of appropriate shoring; spoil/materials and vehicles should not be allowed to stand near the edge of the excavation as it can lead to collapse of the sides.

UNAUTHORISED MODIFICATIONS TO BUILDINGS

Unauthorised modifications to buildings account for a large number of unprecedented structural collapse. Buildings rely on load bearing systems for stability and strength. Modifications to a building could lead to the removal of load bearing structures or damage to them that reduces their capacity. Modifications can also increase the load on a structure by adding in additional floors and equipment that the building was not capable of supporting. It is essential that all alterations be fully controlled, involving a professional consideration of the proposed modification and its consequences.

Failure modes of workplace structures

The structural safety of workplaces can be threatened by natural disasters such as weather and earthquake or man-made disasters such as fire or explosion or from alterations that affect the integrity of the structure. This includes situations where load bearing roof beams are cut, for example, to make room for the movement, installation or removal of plant and equipment. This action may put the remaining beams under increased loading leading to the collapse of the structure. A similar increased loading can occur when holes are cut through the floor or when beams are used as lifting points.

The holes created concentrate the stress experienced by the floor in the area of the hole and reduce the cross-sectional area of the floor supporting the weight it is carrying.

Removal of part or the whole of internal load bearing walls can cause the structure above the wall, being supported by it, to collapse. This increase in load on lower level floors and the beams supporting them can cause them to fail, leading to a progressive collapse of the structure.

An awareness of these failure modes is important when considering structures that are in use, but they are also important to consider with regard to structures under construction, particularly as full load bearing capacity of the building may not be in place when alterations to the structure or support system take place.

C1.5 - Working at height

The workplace for some employees may be at height. This could be, for example, on a ledge or scaffold platform, on the edge of a pit or excavation, or in the carrier of a lifting machine. Working at height can lead to falls, which account for almost 50% of fatal accidents in the workplace. Falls from height lead to around 70 deaths and 4,000 major injuries in the UK every year. Many falls occur because safe access and egress has not been provided or the workplace itself is not safe, being of fragile structure, lacking edge protection or having a slippery floor surface. *See also details of the Work at Height Regulations (WAH) 2005 which are covered in the Relevant Statutory Provisions section and Element C9.3 - Working at height from fixed or temporary platforms.*

GENERAL WORKPLACE ISSUES - ELEMENT C1

Main hazards and risks for work at height in general workplaces

The main hazards associated with work at height are that a worker or materials could fall from height or that they may come into contact with the structure or services while working. Falls of workers may be from ladders, machinery, open edges, through roof lights or through fragile roofs. The types of task workers may conduct that involves work at height include shelf staking, window cleaning, unloading a vehicle, machine maintenance, electrical maintenance, painting and decorating, cleaning gutters, putting up a display, order picking and roof work.

The risks of falls from height are substantial, however long or short the work. Some activities involve infrequent work at height, for example, stock taking or inspection of equipment. This means that, very often, people with little or no experience find themselves exposed to the dangers of working above ground level.

Risks related to work activities at height are increased by the presence of fragile roofs, roof lights, voids, deteriorating materials and the weather. Almost 20% of those killed in accidents on construction sites were doing roof work. Some involved falling off the edge of flat or sloping roofs, but many were killed by falling through fragile materials, something that could also happen to non-construction workers that access roof areas. Asbestos cement, fibreglass and plastic deteriorate with age and become more fragile. Similarly, steel sheets may rust or may not be supported properly. This presents a serious risk to workers who work on these materials without means to prevent falls.

Adverse weather can have a significant effect on the safety of those working at height. Rain, snow and ice increase the risk of slips and falling from a roof, loading deck, process plant or vehicle. When handling large objects, such as sheet steel, high winds can be a serious problem and may cause the person to be blown off the structure they are on. Extremely cold temperatures can increase the likelihood of brittle failure of materials, such as plastic roof lights.

ALTERNATIVES

In order to reduce or eliminate the risks associated with work at height the alternatives to work at height should be considered first. This will involve arrangements to eliminate the need for the work to be done at height and usually involves as much work as possible being done before materials are moved to height for final fixing, for example, pre-painting panels. Another approach is to ensure materials are brought down to a low level before being worked on, for example, the lowering of a light unit to enable cleaning and bulb changing. In some cases, work can be done on materials located at a height from the ground, for example, cleaning windows, picking fruit or painting.

If the work has to be done at height then it is necessary to consider the alternative types of equipment. Many accidents involving falls could have been prevented if the right equipment had been provided and properly used. There are many work at height systems available, ranging from tower and general scaffold, suspended access equipment, mobile elevating work platforms (MEWPs), boatswain's chairs, rope and harness systems and ladders. The choice of system will depend on the individual circumstances of the work.

In order, these are the priorities when choosing the work at height system to be used:

- Platform with guard rails - if regular access is needed that causes people to work at height, modifications should be made to the existing plant or structure to provide a permanent safe working platform with guardrails.
- Mobile elevating work platform, suspended access equipment - only when it is not practical to provide a work platform with guardrails, should other means of access (for example, boatswain's chairs or rope access) be used.
- Fall limiting equipment - only where no other method is practicable, or when work platforms cannot comply with all the requirements for safe work (for example, a guardrail has to be removed to land materials) should a way of arresting falls (for example, a harness and lines, nets and air bags) be relied upon. A harness or nets may also be needed to protect people when putting guardrails or other protection in place.

Ladders are a means of access, not a working platform. They should only be used as workplaces for a short time, and then only when it is safe to do so. It is generally safer to use a tower scaffold or mobile elevating work platform, even for short-term work.

Main precautions and safe working procedures for work at height

ORGANISATION AND PLANNING OF WORK AT HEIGHT

Regulation 4 of the Work at Height Regulations (WAH) 2005, as amended 2007, states that all work at height must be properly planned, appropriately supervised and carried out in a manner which is, so far as reasonably practicable, safe. Planning must include the selection of suitable equipment, take account of emergencies and give consideration to weather conditions impacting on safety.

WAH 2005 Regulation 5 states that those engaged in any activity in relation to work at height must be competent; and, if under training, be supervised by a competent person.

WAH 2005 Regulation 6 states that work at height must only be carried out when it is not reasonably practicable to carry out the work otherwise.

© RMS

ELEMENT C1 - GENERAL WORKPLACE ISSUES

Employers must also make a risk assessment, as required by Regulation 3 of the Management of Health and Safety at Work Regulations (MHSWR) 1999.

If work must be performed at height, then priority must be given to providing a secure platform that will, where practicable:

- Be securely footed on stable ground.
- Take account of the gradient of the ground, especially where mobile platforms are used.
- Provide a stable access and will not overturn.
- Be secured to an existing structure, where necessary and wherever possible.
- Support the weight of the worker(s) and equipment to be used.
- Provide a sound footing to stand on and for materials needed.
- Provide guard rails to the platform.
- Provide barriers on open edges, holes and openings in the platform floor, the edges of roofs and working areas.

Before accessing a roof, ensure that:

- There is safe access and egress.
- Crawling boards or roof ladders are used to spread the weight of people and materials.
- Roof openings/lights are clearly identified and protected by barriers.
- People do not attempt to walk on the purlins or the roof ridge.

When planning work at height it is important to select the most appropriate equipment for the work to be done. Collective measures must be given priority over personal measures and account needs to be taken of such factors as:

- Working conditions and the risks to the safety of persons at the place where the work equipment is to be used.
- In the case of work equipment for access and egress, the distance to be negotiated.
- Distance and consequences of a potential fall.
- Duration and frequency of use.
- Need for easy and timely evacuation and rescue in an emergency.
- Any additional risk posed by the use, installation or removal of that work equipment or by evacuation and rescue from it.

Unauthorised access to workplaces where a person may fall a distance should be prevented and the danger of falling indicated.

INSPECTION OF EQUIPMENT AND WORKPLACES

Equipment should be inspected at the time it is installed or erected and periodically after that and where 'exceptional circumstances' are likely to have affected it.

Care should be taken to check the condition of the surface, parapet, rail or other fall protection measures of workplaces at height each time the workplace is used.

FRAGILE SURFACES

Care should be taken to avoid work on or access near fragile surfaces where it is reasonably practicable to avoid them. If they cannot be avoided, platforms, coverings, guardrails or similar equipment should be provided.

Where risks of falling still remain measures need to be taken to minimise the distance and consequences of a fall. Warnings of the fragile nature of the structure should be posted or, if not appropriate, people warned of the danger.

CONTACT WITH STRUCTURES OR SERVICES

It is important to allow adequate clearance when equipment is used, particularly near overhead power lines and when using equipment that has adjustable height, such as a mobile elevating work platform (MEWP).

AVOIDING WORKING IN ADVERSE WEATHER CONDITIONS

Adverse weather can include wind, rain, sun, cold, snow and ice. Each of these conditions, particularly in extreme cases, can present a significant hazard to work at height.

In some cases adverse weather must be considered formally and work may have to cease until conditions improve, for example, work on a roof in icy conditions or high winds. Similar approaches may have to be taken for operating a mobile elevating work platform (MEWP) in windy conditions.

FALL OF MATERIALS

WAH 2005 Regulation 10 states:

"That every employer shall take reasonably practicable steps to prevent injury to any person from the fall of any material or object; and where it is not reasonably practicable to do so, to take similar steps to prevent any person being struck by any falling material or object which is liable to cause personal injury".

It is also a requirement that no material is thrown or tipped from height in circumstances where it is liable to cause injury to any person. Materials and objects must be stored in such a way as to prevent risk to any person arising from the collapse, overturning or unintended movement of the materials or objects. WAH 2005 Regulation 11 requires that every employer ensure that where an area presents a risk of falling from height or being struck from an item falling from height, that the area is equipped with devices preventing unauthorised persons from entering these areas and the area is clearly indicated.

Hierarchy of control measures with reference to the Work at Height Regulations (WAH) 2005

The WAH 2005 (as amended 2007) set out a hierarchy for safe work at height. This requires the duty holder to:
- Avoid work at height where they can.
- Use work equipment or other measures to prevent falls where they cannot avoid working at height.
- Where they cannot eliminate the risk of fall, use work equipment or other measures to minimise the distance and consequence of a fall should one occur.

WAH 2005, Regulation 6 - Avoidance of risks from work at height:

1) In identifying the measures required by this regulation, every employer shall take account of a risk assessment under regulation 3 of the Management Regulations.
2) Every employer shall ensure that work is not carried out at height where it is reasonably practicable to carry out the work safely otherwise than at height.
3) Where work is carried out at height, every employer shall take suitable and sufficient measures to prevent, so far as is reasonably practicable, any person falling a distance liable to cause personal injury.
4) The measures required by paragraph (3) shall include:
    a) His ensuring that the work is carried out:
        i) From an existing place of work.
        ii) (In the case of obtaining access or egress) using an existing means; which complies with Schedule 1, where it is reasonably practicable to carry it out safely and under appropriate ergonomic conditions.
    b) Where it is not reasonably practicable for the work to be carried out in accordance with sub-paragraph (a), his providing sufficient work equipment for preventing, so far as is reasonably practicable, a fall occurring.
5) Where the measures taken under paragraph (4) do not eliminate the risk of a fall occurring, every employer shall:
    a) So far as is reasonably practicable, provide sufficient work equipment to minimise:
        i) The distance and consequences.
        ii) Where it is not reasonably practicable to minimise the distance, the consequences, of a fall.
    b) Without prejudice to the generality of paragraph (3), provide such additional training and instruction or take other additional suitable and sufficient measures to prevent, so far as is reasonably practicable, any person falling a distance liable to cause personal injury.

AVOID WORKING AT HEIGHT

Where possible, work at height should be avoided by conducting the work at ground level. This means that organisations should review work done to determine a response to this requirement. This could be achieved by using different equipment or methods of work.

This may affect those that manually fill equipment hoppers located at height, requiring consideration of bulk delivery and automatic feed systems. Where workers have to lubricate or adjust equipment set at height by hand, options to automate or route the lubrication/adjustment mechanisms to ground level should be considered. Pre-assembly of materials such as roof trusses, either before delivery or on the ground on site, instead of assembly at a height should be considered.

If materials are pre-painted or pre-drilled this can greatly reduce the work needed to be done at height, for example, decorative wooden panels for a retail display, boat or building can be pre-treated to avoid weather treatment being brushed on at a height. Long reach handling devices can be used to allow cleaning or other tasks to be conducted from the ground.

Where equipment, such as light units, requires maintenance an option may be to lower it sufficiently to enable bulbs to be changed and cleaning to be conducted from the ground.

USE AN EXISTING SAFE PLACE OF WORK

Do not work at height unless it is absolutely unavoidable. If work must be performed at height, use an existing safe place of work that will meet the requirements of WAH 2005 Schedule 1, where possible:

WAH 2005 Schedule 1 - Requirements for existing places of work and means of access or egress at height.

ELEMENT C1 - GENERAL WORKPLACE ISSUES

Every existing place of work or means of access or egress at height shall:

a) *Be stable and of sufficient strength and rigidity for the purpose for which it is intended to be or is being used.*
b) *Where applicable, rest on a stable, sufficiently strong surface.*
c) *Be of sufficient dimensions to permit the safe passage of persons and the safe use of any plant or materials required to be used and to provide a safe working area having regard to the work to be carried out there.*
d) *Possess suitable and sufficient means for preventing a fall.*
e) *Possess a surface which has no gap:*
   i) *Through which a person could fall.*
   ii) *Through which any material or object could fall and injure a person.*
   iii) *(Giving rise to other risk of injury to any person, unless measures have been taken to protect persons against such risk.*
f) *Be so constructed and used, and maintained in such condition, as to prevent, so far as is reasonably practicable.*
g) *The risk of slipping or tripping.*
h) *Any person being caught between it and any adjacent structure.*
i) *Where it has moving parts, be prevented by appropriate devices from moving inadvertently during work at height.*

By using more permanent workplaces design features that provide collective protection of those at risk can be provided more easily, making it less necessary to rely on personal protective measures. The additional task of erecting a temporary workplace at height has its own added risks, which should be avoided where this is possible.

PROVIDE WORK EQUIPMENT TO PREVENT FALLS (INCLUDING MEWPS)

Careful consideration during the risk assessment and planning phases should establish which equipment is best suited for the working environment and work to be done. There are various types of fall protection that should be evaluated in relationship to the activity and environment. This could be edge protection in the form of scaffolding or barriers (temporary or fixed), or consideration of the building of temporary walls.

When planning work at height it is important to select the most appropriate equipment for the work to be done. Collective measures must be given priority over personal measures and account needs to be taken of such factors as:

- Working conditions and the risks to the safety of persons at the place where the work equipment is to be used.
- In the case of work equipment for access and egress, the distance to be negotiated.
- Distance and consequences of a potential fall.
- Duration and frequency of use.
- Need for easy and timely evacuation and rescue in an emergency.
- Any additional risk posed by the use, installation or removal of that work equipment or by evacuation and rescue from it.

To maintain safe access and egress, temporary staircases should be considered before the use of ladders. Where ladders are used it is more difficult to maintain a 'three-point contact' as workers may have to use their hands to carry or move items to different levels.

Guardrails, fencing and toeboards

Guardrails are designed to prevent people falling whilst toeboards prevent materials falling. Toeboards are usually planks laid on their edge to create a ledge which prevents waste, tools and other materials from being kicked or knocked over the edge of the working platform. **See also - Relevant Statutory Provisions section and Element C9.3 - Working at height from fixed or temporary platforms.**

Material guards, a form of fencing that provides more substantial protection to prevent larger amounts of material from falling over toeboards. They have the added advantage of providing additional protection to prevent people falling, particularly where their work would make them bend down below guard rails. The Work at Height Regulations (WAH) 2005 requires that these means of protection must:

- Be of sufficient dimensions, of sufficient strength and rigidity for the purposes for which they are being used, and otherwise suitable.
- Be so placed, secured and used as to ensure, so far as is reasonably practicable, that they do not become accidentally displaced.
- Be so placed as to prevent, so far as is practicable, the fall of any person, or of any material or object, from any place of work.

Working platforms

The Work at Height Regulations (WAH) 2005 defines a "working platform" as:

- Any platform used as a place of work or as a means of access to or egress from a place of work.
- Any scaffold, suspended scaffold, cradle, mobile platform, trestle, gangway, gantry and stairway which is so used.

Schedule 3 of WAH 2005 sets out requirements that work platforms must fulfil, and this comprises:

- Condition of surfaces on which the work platform rests.
- Stability of supporting structures.
- Safety on working platforms.
- Loading of platforms.
- Stability of working platforms.

The following practical precautions should also be considered, the platform should be:

- Wide enough - at least 600 mm wide - to allow people to pass back and forth safely and to use any equipment or material necessary for their work at that place.
- Free of openings and traps, through which feet could pass and cause workers to trip, fall or be injured in any other way.
- Constructed to prevent materials from falling. As well as toe boards or similar protection at the edge of the platform, the platform itself should be constructed to prevent any object which may be used on the platform from falling through gaps or holes, causing injury to people working below. This relates to fixed working platforms as well as mobile ones. Fixed platforms may provide access to vehicles, plant or storage areas. If a Mobile Elevated Work Platform (MEWP) or cradle is used and it has meshed platform floors, the mesh should be fine enough to prevent materials, especially nails and bolts, from slipping through. For scaffolds, a close-boarded platform would suffice, although for work over public areas, a double-boarded platform sandwiching a polythene sheet may be needed.
- Kept free of tripping and slipping hazards. Where necessary, handholds and footholds should be provided. Platforms should be clean, tidy and mud should not be allowed to build up on them.

Access boards

Access/crawling boards and roof ladders spread across a supporting structure distribute the weight of workers and equipment over a greater area, so that the load can be sustained by a fragile structure, such as a roof. They also provide hand and foot holds and may be equipped with guard rails and toe boards.

Figure C1-31: Ladder hoop. *Source: RMS.*

Figure C1-32: Roof ladder and guard rails. *Source: RMS.*

Ladders

To maintain safe access and egress, temporary staircases should be considered before the use of ladders. Where ladders are used it is more difficult to maintain a 'three-point contact' as workers may have to use their hands to carry or move items to different levels. Schedule 6 of WAH 2005 sets out specific requirements relating to ladders, fixed and movable. Ladders may only be used if a risk assessment confirms no other suitable equipment is justified because of the low risk and the work is of a short duration or existing features on site cannot be altered, for example, to provide a stair. The schedule also sets out a number of practical requirements that have to be complied with as a legal requirement, for example:

- A ladder must be so positioned as to ensure its stability during use.
- A portable ladder must be prevented from slipping during use by:
    a) Securing the stiles at or near their upper or lower ends.
    b) An effective anti-slip or other effective stability device.
    c) Any other arrangement of equivalent effectiveness.

ELEMENT C1 - GENERAL WORKPLACE ISSUES

- A ladder used for access must be long enough to protrude sufficiently above the landing place to ensure a firm handhold.

Ladder hoops are attached to fixed vertical or steeply sloping ladders to create a "tunnel" for safe climbing. Maintenance workers may make use of them to gain access to a roof or similar areas; they are often used where access is required to large process plant that is installed over a number of floors.

There is a risk of fatigue when climbing vertical ladders, because the climber needs to exert energy to pull and step their body up the ladder. The ladder hoops are designed to prevent people falling away from the ladder through fatigue, but do not prevent sliding down the ladder. Hoops need to be used in conjunction with rest platforms, set at intervals of 9 metres, to allow the climber to rest and recover from fatigue.

Mobile elevating work platforms

Mobile Elevating Work Platforms (MEWPs) can provide excellent safe access to high level work.

When using a MEWP make sure:

- Whoever is operating it is fully trained and competent.
- The work platform is fitted with guard rails and toe boards.
- It is used on suitable firm and level ground. The ground may have to be prepared in advance.
- Its tyres are properly inflated.
- The work area is cordoned off to prevent access below the work platform.
- If being used on a public highway in poor lighting that it is well lit.
- Any outriggers are extended and chocked as necessary before raising the platform.
- Everyone knows what to do if the machine fails with the platform in the raised position.

Do Not

- Operate MEWPs close to overhead cables or other dangerous machinery.
- Allow a knuckle, or elbow, of the arm to protrude into a traffic route when working near vehicles.
- Move the equipment with the platform in the raised position unless the equipment is especially designed to allow this to be done safely (check the manufacturer's instructions).

Figure C1-33: Mobile elevated work platform "Cherry Picker". *Source: RMS.*

MITIGATE DISTANCE AND CONSEQUENCES OF A FALL

Fall arresting systems

Fall arrest systems include equipment designed to minimise the distance and consequence of falls, such as nets and air bags. Fall arrest systems are preferred to personal protection systems because they provide collective protection and, unlike a fall arrest harness, does not rely on individual user discipline to guarantee acceptable safety standards.

The WAH 2005 requires that a fall arresting safeguard may only be used if:

- A risk assessment has demonstrated that the work activity can, so far as is reasonably practicable, be performed safely while using it and without affecting its effectiveness.
- Use of other, safer work equipment is not reasonably practicable.
- A sufficient number of available persons have received adequate training specific to the safeguard, including rescue procedures.

A fall arresting safeguard must be suitable and of sufficient strength to arrest safely the fall of any person who is liable to fall.

In addition, it must:

- In the case of a safeguard that is designed to be attached, be securely attached to all the required anchor points.
- The anchors and the means of attachment must be suitable and of sufficient strength and stability for the purpose of supporting the foreseeable loading in arresting the fall and during any subsequent rescue.
- In the case of an airbag, landing mat or similar safeguard, be stable.
- In the case of a safeguard that distorts in arresting a fall, afford sufficient clearance.

Suitable and sufficient steps must be taken to ensure that in the event of a fall the safeguard does not itself cause injury to that person. Fall arresting systems such as safety nets, air/bean bags or crash mats may be used to minimise the impact of falls. They can simplify systems of work and can protect not only workers, but others such as supervisors.

Where safety nets are used, they must be installed as close as possible beneath the surface that people can fall from, securely attached and able to withstand a person falling onto them. These must be installed and maintained by competent personnel. If the work height increases, the nets must be repositioned at each higher level to ensure the minimum fall distance is maintained as the work progresses.

Personal fall protection systems

Personal fall protection systems include work positioning systems, rope access and positioning techniques, fall arrest systems and work restraint systems. Schedule 5, Part 1, WAH 2005 requires that a personal fall protection system may only be used if:

- A risk assessment has demonstrated that:
  - Work can, so far as is reasonably practicable, be performed safely while using that system.
  - Use of other safer work equipment is not reasonably practicable.
- The user and a sufficient number of available persons have received adequate training specific to the operations envisaged, including rescue procedures.

In addition, Schedule 5, Part1, requires that a personal fall protection system must be:

- Be suitable and of sufficient strength for the purposes for which it is being used, having regard to the work being carried out and any foreseeable loading.
- Where necessary, fit the user.
- Be correctly fitted.
- Be designed to minimise injury to the user and, where necessary, be adjusted to prevent the user falling or slipping from it, should a fall occur.
- Be so designed, installed and used as to prevent unplanned or uncontrolled movement of the user.

Each of the different personal fall protection systems (work positioning systems, rope access and positioning techniques, fall arrest systems and work restraint systems) has requirements related to their use set out in Schedule 5 of WAH 2005. Fall arrest systems (harnesses) are useful when other means of fall protection are not reasonably practicable. The harness itself may cause injury when the person comes to a sudden stop, therefore the use of an inertia reel harnesses (the same principle as a car seat belt) may be preferable. When using harnesses in a mobile elevating work platform (MEWP), the harness should always be fixed to the inside of the cradle.

INSTRUCTION AND TRAINING AND/OR OTHER MEANS

Where a risk of a fall remains, after fall protection has been provided, the WAH 2005 requires that additional training and suitable and sufficient other measures must also be taken to prevent injury to any person falling a distance liable to cause injury. This may include training them in techniques that would limit the effect of the fall, controlling what equipment they use that might fall with them, ceasing processes in the area that may cause the worker to be disorientated/overcome leading to a fall, covering items that the person may fall onto and providing means to assist those that have fallen. In addition, Regulation 5 of the WAH 2005 requires:

"Every employer shall ensure that no person engages in any activity, including organisation, planning and supervision, in relation to work at height or work equipment for use in such work unless he is competent to do so or, if being trained, is being supervised by a competent person".

Workers should receive full training and instruction on the use of equipment and systems of working that will minimise the distance and consequences of a fall. Where harnesses are to be used, this should include how to wear the fall arrest harnesses, how to fit it to fixing points, what is a suitable fixing point and fixing at a height that minimises the fall (for example, above the head where possible).

Training should also include the checks that need to be made on fall arrest systems before they are used, this will include checks on the security of nets and the adequacy of airbags. Workers will also need to be trained in how to get off/out of this equipment safely when it has arrested a fall and on emergency arrangements for rescue, where workers cannot assist themselves.

C1.6 - Lone working

Main hazards and risks, alternatives, precautions and safe working procedures

Lone workers are those who work by themselves without close or direct supervision. They are found in a wide range of situations and some examples are given in the following list.

People in fixed establishments where:

- Only one person works on the premises for example, petrol stations, kiosks, shops and also home workers.
- People work separately from others for example, in factories, warehouses, leisure centres or fairgrounds.
- People work outside normal hours for example, cleaners, security, facilities management staff or contractors conducting special tasks better done at this time.

ELEMENT C1 - GENERAL WORKPLACE ISSUES

Mobile workers working away from their fixed base:

- On construction, plant installation, maintenance and cleaning work, electrical repairs, painting and decorating.
- Agricultural and forestry workers.
- Service workers for example, rent collectors, postal staff, home helps, drivers, district nurses.

The hazards that lone workers may experience are essentially the same hazards that people working together may encounter. The major difference is that a lone worker may be more at risk of harm than when working with other workers. For example, a lone worker may be more likely to experience threats or violence whilst working. They may be more likely to do things on their own that would normally need more than one person, for example over exertion while conducting manual handling, operating equipment that needs two people to do safely or carrying out tasks that are outside their limit of competence. In addition, if things go wrong there will not be other workers on hand to provide assistance, for example, provide first aid, help someone trapped under a fallen load, come to the worker's aid when overcome by chemicals or rescue them from falling into a river/water filled tank.

Although there is no general legal prohibition on working alone, the broad duties of the Health and Safety at Work etc Act (HASAWA) 1974 and Management of Health and Safety at Work Regulations (MHSWR) 1999 still apply. These require the identification of hazards of the work, assessing the risks involved, and putting measures in place to avoid or control the risks. Consider the following risk factors:

- Safe access and egress for one person.
- Any special risk associated with the workplace.
- Ease of handling of temporary access equipment, such as portable ladders or trestles.
- All plant, substances, goods livestock and people involved in the work can be safely handled within the capacity of one person.
- Requirements for one person to operate essential controls for the safe running of equipment.
- The risk of violence.
- The presence of any female special risks.
- The presence of any young worker special risks.

Where the risks are higher, consideration should always be made to finding alternative ways of working that avoid lone working. When the risk assessment shows that it is not possible for the work to be done safely by a lone worker, arrangements for providing help or back-up should be put in place. Work may be done faster, safer and more effectively by using two workers.

Where a lone worker is working at another employer's workplace, the host employer should inform the lone worker's employer of any risks and control measures that should be taken. This helps the lone worker's employer to assess the risks, decide the right level of supervision and control measures.

Establishing safe working for lone workers is no different from organising the safety of other employees. Employers need to know the law and standards that apply to their work activities and then assess whether the requirements can be met by people working alone. The control measures for lone working may include instruction, training, supervision, protective equipment, emergency procedures etc.

Particular problems facing lone workers

MEDICAL CONDITIONS

The medical condition of a lone worker may affect their health and safety or that of others that may be affected by their work. The medical condition may be one that is progressive and a previously unaffected worker may develop, over time, a condition that presents significant risk. Consider the following actions:

- Check that lone workers have no medical conditions making them unsuitable for working alone.
- Consider both routine work and foreseeable emergencies which may impose additional physical and mental burdens on the individual.
- Ensure they have access to first-aid facilities and mobile workers should carry a first-aid kit suitable for treating minor injuries.

TRAINING

The lone work may require the worker to conduct a wide range of tasks that would normally be shared by a group of people that together have competence to conduct them. Working alone may mean doing work in a very specific way, whereas other ways of working may allow latitude.

Lone workers have to be capable of a degree of self supervision and may have to be taught ways of checking and assurance that establish confidence the work is done safely. For these reasons lone workers may require more that the usual level of training.

Specific training may also be required under the following circumstances:

- Where there is limited supervision.
- To determine if workers are experienced enough to understand the risks and precautions of lone working fully and to avoid panic reactions in unusual situations.

GENERAL WORKPLACE ISSUES - ELEMENT C1

- To ensure they are competent to deal with circumstances which are new, unusual or beyond the scope of training for example, when to stop work and seek advice from a supervisor and how to handle aggression.
- To ensure they are able to respond correctly to emergencies, and also give information on established emergency procedures and danger areas.
- To ensure they are able to administer self first aid.

SUPERVISION

Though a lone worker is said to be 'not to be under direct or close supervision' this should not be taken to be no supervision. Supervision regimes have to be established as necessary to ensure the worker's health and safety; the following factors should be considered:

- Sufficient to ensure that employees understand the risks associated with their work and that the necessary health and safety precautions are carried out.
- It can provide guidance in situations of uncertainty.
- Supervision can be carried out when checking the progress and quality of the work. It may take the form of periodic site visits, combined with discussions in which health and safety issues are raised.
- It is important when an employee is new to a job, undergoing training, doing a job that presents special risks, or dealing with new situations. This may mean that they may need to be accompanied by a supervisor at first.
- The level of supervision required should be based on the findings of a risk assessment and competency and experience of the worker.

MONITORING AND EMERGENCY PROCEDURES

Procedures for monitoring and emergencies should be built into the safe system of working. Methods should be established that confirm safe conditions exist or identify when an emergency is taking place.

This can be done by utilising a number of means, for example:

- Supervisor's periodically visiting and observing people working alone.
- Regular contact using either a telephone or radio.
- Automatic warning devices, which operate if specific signals are not received periodically from the lone worker, for example, electronic systems for monitoring security staff have entered or left an area.
- Other devices designed to be operated automatically by the absence of activity.
- Checks that the worker has returned to their base or home on completion of a task.
- Manually operated alarms and listening/advice devices.
- Emergency telephones located where the worker is, connected to a permanently controlled call centre.
- Provision of personal emergency first aid resources.
- Provision of other emergency resources related to the work.
- Procedures that ensure the worker and/or others monitoring the worker can obtain assistance from emergency services.

LIFTING OBJECTS THAT ARE TOO HEAVY FOR ONE PERSON

Some tasks may not be suitable for lone working because they involve lifting or movement of objects that are too heavy for one person. This may be an item that needs to be moved to be worked on/installed/removed or equipment used in the work, for example, a heavy generator used to power electrical tools.

Figure C1-34: Two people lifting heavy object.   *Source: RMS.*   Figure C1-35: Heavy electricity generator.   *Source: RMS.*

MORE THAN ONE PERSON NEEDED TO OPERATE ESSENTIAL CONTROLS OR TRANSPORT

There are some high-risk activities where at least one other person may need to be present. Examples include some high-risk confined space working where a supervisor may need to be present, as well as someone dedicated to the rescue role, and electrical work at or near exposed live conductors where at least two people are sometimes required.

Some equipment may require two people to be present in order to operate it safely; this can apply to some forms of large processing plant and transport equipment.

Employers need to be aware of any specific law on lone working applying to their industry; examples include supervision in diving operations, vehicles carrying explosives, fumigation work.

Element C2

Principles of fire and explosion

Learning outcomes

The intended learning outcomes are that the student will be able to:

C2.1 Outline the properties of flammable and explosive materials and the mechanisms by which they ignite.
C2.2 Outline the behaviour of structural materials, buildings and building contents in a fire.
C2.3 Outline the main principles and practices of fire and explosion prevention and protection.
C2.4 Outline the contribution of typical mechanical and systems failures to major accidents.

Content

C2.1 - Properties of flammable and explosive materials and the mechanisms by which they ignite 35
    Properties of solids, liquids and gases 35
    Meanings of terms related to fire and explosion..35
    The fire triangle...38
    Ignition sources..39
    Mechanisms of explosions, mechanisms of fire-spread...40
    Effects of atomisation and oxygen content on the likelihood and severity of a fire/explosion..........................42
    How failure of control measures can bring about an explosion 42
    Oxidisation 43
    Vapour cloud and boiling liquid expanding vapour explosions..43
    Control of vapour phase explosions 49
    Control of amount of material, prevention of release, control of ignition sources and sensing of vapour........49
    Dust explosions...50
    Actual incidents of dust explosions...52
C2.2 - Behaviour of structural materials, building and building contents in a fire 54
    Behaviour of building structures and materials in fire...54
    Behaviour of common building contents in fire 57
    Behaviour of structural materials and contents relating to actual incidents 58
C2.3 - Fire and explosion prevention and protection 59
    Structural protection..59
    Key features of plant design and process control..60
    Segregation and storage of flammable, combustible and incompatible materials 62
    Hazardous area zoning...64
    Exclusion of ignition sources 65
    Inerting..65
    Methods of explosion relief...65
C2.4 - Major accidents 66
    The contribution of typical mechanical and systems failures to major accidents 66

ELEMENT C2 - PRINCIPLES OF FIRE AND EXPLOSION

Relevant statutory provisions

Building Regulations (BR) 2000, Approved Document B
Dangerous Substances and Explosive Atmospheres Regulation (DSEAR) 2002
Electricity at Work Regulations (EWR) 1989

C2.1 - Properties of flammable and explosive materials and the mechanisms by which they ignite

Properties of solids, liquids and gases

When assessing the potential for any fire or explosion, one of the most important factors to consider is the fuel type. The obvious initial consideration is whether a material is combustible or not. However, once we have confirmed combustibility, the physical state of the material and the way in which it is presented within the workplace is of utmost importance. In general, a combustible solid material is considered to be a lower hazard than a flammable liquid, vapour or gas. However, this is not always the case, as the particle size is of vital importance with a solid material. As the particle size of a solid material decreases to a fine dust format, a dust explosion hazard may exist. Any such dust explosion can be far more devastating than many gas explosions.

A flammable liquid has to vaporise before its flammable vapour can burn. The ease with which this happens will be affected by the type of flammable liquid itself, factors such as the speed at which the liquid vaporises (vapour pressure) and if the liquid is under pressure whilst in use. Any flammable gas is an obvious hazard, but the danger it presents will be affected by factors such as the materials 'flammable or explosive range'.

As can be seen from these few examples, it is the fuel, a flammable or explosive material, which influences other factors. In controlling fires and explosions a great deal of effort is made to control the ignition sources within the workplace, but this control has to be applied in a relevant way to the type of fuel and the way in which the fuel is presented.

Meanings of terms related to fire and explosion

FLASH POINT

'Flash Point' is defined as the lowest temperature at which, in a specific test apparatus, sufficient vapour is produced from a liquid sample for momentary or flash ignition to occur. It must not be confused with ignition temperature, which can be considerably lower.

FIRE POINT

The lowest temperature at which the heat produced will enable combustion to continue after a substance is ignited.

AUTO-IGNITION TEMPERATURE

'Auto ignition temperature' is the lowest temperature at which a substance will ignite spontaneously, and will burn without a flame or other ignition source. It is sometimes called 'Spontaneous-ignition temperature'.

VAPOUR DENSITY

This term is sometimes used in the 'fire world' and can cause confusion, as it is often mistaken for the 'density of a vapour' (relative density). Vapour density is the density of a gas or vapour compared to the density of hydrogen, at the same temperature and pressure. This is worked out by using the molecular weights of the atoms concerned. The molecular structure of methane is CH_4 and a molecule of hydrogen is H_2. Therefore the vapour density for methane, as an example, is:

$$\frac{16}{2} = 8$$

The approximate atomic weight of carbon is 12 and hydrogen is 1. Therefore a molecule of methane has a weight of $12 + (4 \times 1) = 16$ and a molecule of hydrogen has a weight of $2 \times 1 = 2$.

This figure of vapour density is, in a way, therefore of little value as it is a theoretical comparison to hydrogen.

RELATIVE DENSITY

Relative density is the ratio of the specific density of a substance to the specific density of a standard substance under specified conditions. For liquids and solids the standard is usually water at 4°C or some other specified temperature. For vapours and gases the standard is often air at the same temperature and pressure as the substance.

For fire safety and fire protection reasons we are particularly concerned with the comparison of a flammable material and its vapours in relation to air. The vapour density of air at standard temperature and pressure is taken as 28.97. We can therefore see that the *relative density* for methane when compared to air is:

$$\frac{16.04}{28.97} = 0.55 \text{ (a relative density less than 1, which makes it lighter than air).}$$

As can be seen, the difference between vapour density and relative density is significant. It is important to ensure that the relative density of a vapour is used when considering its hazards and the necessary safety measures.

Density effects - gases and vapours

Few materials have a molecular weight less than air (molecular weight of approximately 29), so under normal conditions most gases and vapours are heavier than air. Hydrogen (H_2) (molecular weight of approximately 2), methane (CH_4) (molecular weight of approximately 16) and acetylene gas (C_2H_2) (molecular weight of approximately 26) are exceptions. The higher the molecular weight of a gas/vapour the greater its (specific) density at constant temperature.

In order to establish a reference point, air is given a specific density of 1. This enables a relative density to be established for other substances and to predict the effect of them being placed together. Flammable or explosive gas/vapours heavier than air (relative density greater than 1), such as propane (which has a relative density of 1.52 when compared to air), can spread and accumulate at low level, for example, in pits, sumps or drains. Also, vapours less dense than air at ambient temperature may spread at low level when they are cold, because the specific density of the substance when cold could be greater than the surrounding warmer air.

Gas or vapour	Molecular weight	Relative density (air)
Air	28.97	1
Acetylene, C_2H_2	26.04	0.90
Cyclohexane	84.16	2.91
Ethane, C_2H_6	30.07	1.04
Hydrogen, H_2	2.016	0.07
Methane, CH_4	16.04	0.55
Propane, C_3H_8	44.10	1.52

Figure C2-1: Densities of flammable gases/vapours. *Source: RMS/Multiple.*

Accumulations of gas/vapour less dense than air (relative density of less than 1), for example hydrogen and methane, can occur at high points in poorly ventilated buildings. Consideration needs to be given to work activities that represent a source of ignition when they take place where gas accumulation might occur in this way, for example, maintenance work at a height.

The relative density of a flammable vapour or gas with air is important when considering local exhaust ventilation (LEV) requirements provided to prevent a build up of the vapour or gas; it will indicate whether LEV is required at high or low level, or both.

Density effects - liquids

Densities of liquids are determined by comparing the weight (mass) of a given volume of a substance with the weight (mass) of the same volume of water at the same temperature. In order to establish a reference point, water is given a specific density (specific gravity) of 1. This enables a relative density to be established for other substances and to predict the effect of them being placed together.

Some oils and fats have densities greater than 1 and would sink if mixed with water; however materials such as petrol and benzene have densities less than 1 and would float on water. Low density liquids can spread and remain on top of denser (immiscible) liquids, for example, petrol and many organic solvents are less dense than and immiscible with water, therefore petrol would spread and remain on top of water. When spilt or discharged into drainage systems these low density liquids may create a flammable or toxic hazard because they lie on the surface of the water. Selection of fire fighting equipment is important when dealing with fires involving solvents that are insoluble in water.

As indicated above, density also varies with temperature. This is why the layering or stratification of immiscible liquids may occur in process and storage vessels upon heating. Increased temperatures may also cause a reduction of density, which increases the volume of the liquid. If the liquid is in a closed container the increased pressure exerted may cause the container to burst. Storage containers should therefore never be totally filled with liquids - an expansion gap is necessary to allow for changes in ambient temperature. The gap necessary should be calculated for the type of substance to be stored and the maximum temperature likely to occur. The gap is referred to as the ullage space.

See also 'San Carlos 1978' later in this Element.

LIMITS OF FLAMMABILITY

A flammable gas, vapour or dust will only burn in air if the mixture lies between certain limits. They are normally given as a percentage and are called:

- Upper flammable/explosive limit (UFL/UEL) - the highest mixture (concentration) of fuel and air that will just support a flame.
- Lower flammable/explosive limit (LFL/LEL) - the lowest mixture (concentration) of fuel and air that will just support a flame.

At a mixture (concentration) in air below the LEL there is not enough fuel to continue an explosion. Methane gas has a LEL of 5 % by volume at 20°C.

PRINCIPLES OF FIRE AND EXPLOSION - ELEMENT C2

If the atmosphere has less than 5% methane, an explosion cannot occur even if a source of ignition is present. When the methane (CH_4) mixture reaches 5% an explosion can occur if there is an ignition source. LEL concentrations vary greatly between combustible gases, vapours and dusts.

Gas or vapour	LFL/LEL %	UFL/UEL %
Acetylene, C_2H_2	2.5	81
Cyclohexane	1.3	8
Ethane, C_2H_6	3	12.4
Hydrogen, H_2	4	75
Methane, CH_4	5	15
Propane, C_3H_8	2.1	10.1

Figure C2-2: Flammable/explosive limits gases/vapours. *Source: RMS/Multiple.*

It is important to note that it is only vapour that burns; a solid or liquid must be heated to a temperature where the vapour given off by the solid or liquid can ignite before combustion takes place.

CRITICAL TEMPERATURE AND PRESSURE

Critical temperature

Any liquid when heated will eventually boil. If this happens at atmospheric pressure it is known as the 'normal boiling point'. If the pressure is increased, a higher temperature must be reached before the liquid will boil. However, there is a temperature where no matter what pressure is applied, the liquid will boil and vaporise. This is known as the 'critical temperature'.

Some common examples are:

	Critical temperature (°C)
Butane	153
Chlorine	144
Ethylene	10
Hydrogen	-240
Methane	-83
Propane	96

Figure C2-3: Critical temperature examples. *Source: FST.*

When a gas with a fairly high critical temperature, such as propane (a form of LPG), is kept as a liquid under pressure it is important that ullage space is left inside the container. Ullage (air/vapour) space is necessary for sealed containers to allow for liquid expansion if ambient temperature increases. Air is compressible, but liquids are not. The thermal expansion of the liquid alone may be sufficient to rupture the container. Assuming that correct ullage spaces are left, then the only increase in pressure will be due to the vapour pressure inside the ullage space, which storage containers should be designed to withstand.

Critical pressure

The pressure that must be applied to a gas at fractionally below its critical temperature in order to liquefy it is called its critical pressure.

	Critical pressure (atmosphere)
Butane	36
Chlorine	76
Ethylene	51
Hydrogen	13
Methane	46
Propane	43

Figure C2-4: Critical pressure examples. *Source: FST.*

MAXIMUM EXPLOSION PRESSURE

The maximum explosive pressure (Pmax) is one of the explosion indices used, along with maximum rate of explosion pressure rise, to quantify the likely severity of a gas, vapour or dust explosion. Each mixture of flammable material with air will produce a different explosion pressure dependant upon the material itself and the flammable material (fuel)/air mixture. The maximum explosion pressure is reached if the mixture is at its ideal or stoichiometric mixture.

ELEMENT C2 - PRINCIPLES OF FIRE AND EXPLOSION

Fuel	Lower explosive limit (kg/m³)	Maximum explosive pressure
Coal	0.035	780 kPa (7.8 bar)
Aluminium	0.035	650 kPa (6.5 bar)
Starch	0.045	1,100 kPa (11.0 bar)

Figure C2-5: Maximum explosion pressures. *Source: FST.*

RATE OF PRESSURE RISE

When considering the severity of an explosion another consideration would be the rate of pressure rise (K_{st}). The slower the initial pressure rises within an explosion, the greater the chance of detecting the pressure rise and providing a form of intervention that limits the effects of the explosion, for example, inerting to suppress, or providing sufficient blow out relief panels to vent the explosive force.

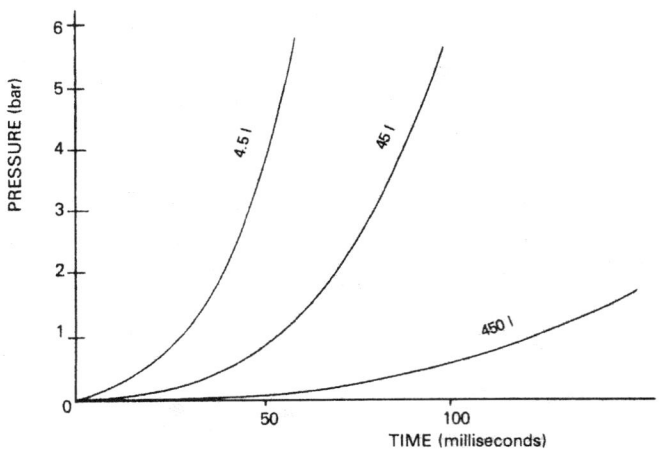

Figure C2-6: Explosion pressure curves for hexane/air mixtures in vessels of different sizes. *Source: Ambiguous.*

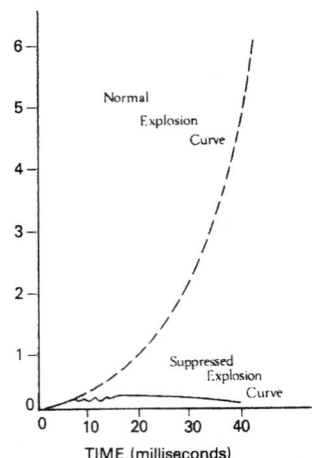

Figure C2-7: Suppressed explosion curve for a hexane/air mixture in a one gallon vessel. *Source: Ambiguous.*

The fire triangle

The fire triangle is a simple approach that depicts fire as having three essential components: fuel, oxygen and heat. The oxygen is contained in the air of most workplaces and anything that burns is a fuel for a fire, for example:

- Flammable liquids.
- Flammable gases.
- Flammable chemicals.
- Wood.
- Paper and card.
- Plastics, rubber and foam.
- Loose packing materials.
- Waste materials.

The heat is derived from various sources of ignition, for example, naked flames or hot surfaces.

When these three components combine in the right proportions, the chemical reaction of combustion takes place.

The three components are portrayed as coming together in a triangle, which shows their dependency on each other for the combustion process.

This approach is useful when considering the components needed to make a fire and how they are extinguished. If one or more of the components of a fire is removed, the fire will be extinguished.

This can be done by:

- **Cooling** the fire to remove the heat.
- **Starving** the fire of fuel.
- **Smothering** the fire by limiting its oxygen supply.

Additionally, the fire may be extinguished by **chemical Interference** with the flame reactions.

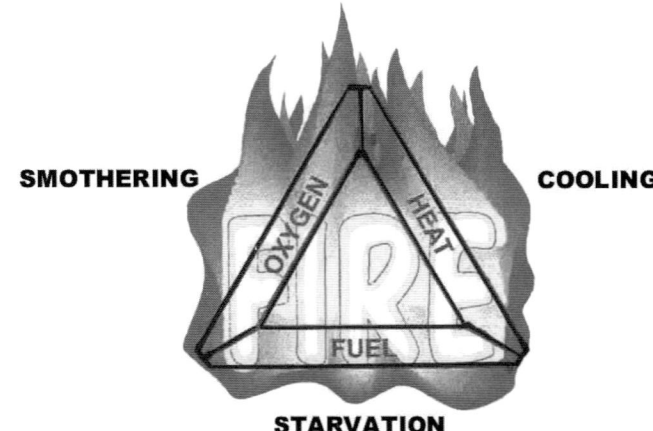

Figure C2-8: The fire triangle. *Source: CorelDraw! 5.0 clipart.*

Ignition sources

HAZARDS

Ignition sources can be found in many forms. Some of the more common forms are *listed below*:

- Smoking, smokers' materials.
- Naked flames and sparks, such as from welding operations.
- Electrical faults or switches causing arcing and sparking.
- Sparks from machinery or electric motors.
- Electrostatic discharge.
- Hot surfaces, such as overheating machinery or lighting.
- Non-intrinsically safe equipment used in a flammable atmosphere.
- Radiated heat from a legitimate source.
- Friction.

Flammable materials may ignite in many ways, some familiar, some less so. Knowledge of the most important ignition scenarios is essential for designers seeking to reduce the likelihood of fire in buildings. The common element is heat transfer. Heat may be transferred by radiation through space, by conduction, upon direct contact with a heat source, or by convection (where air or other heated fluid moves to carry heat from the source to a site of ignition). All ignitions are caused by a version of heat transfer, although other factors may influence them.

Naked flame

The most common ignition source is flame. A match flame transfers heat primarily by convection and may be simply represented in laboratory testing. Larger flames, 0.5 m high or more, transfer heat primarily by radiative (electromagnetic radiation) transfer and may ignite objects without coming into direct contact with them. The larger the flame the more probable radiative ignition becomes.

Hot surfaces

Hot surfaces can also cause fire. A heated metal block can transfer sufficient heat (by conduction) to raise the temperature of some materials above their ignition temperature. An example of ignition by this means is the kitchen fire in which a towel is ignited by contact with an electrically heated cooking element.

Arcing

An electrically caused fire can occur if electrical energy is converted to thermal energy and the heat generated is transferred to a combustible material at a rate that will cause the material to reach its ignition temperature. One mechanism involved in converting electrical energy to thermal energy in an electrical system is arc heating. "Arcing" may be explained as a discharge of electricity from one conductor across an insulating medium (often air) to another conductor. The electrical discharge of an arc can involve temperatures of several thousand degrees Celsius. Arcing may occur when insulation partially breaks down on a conductor and the energy in the conductor is sufficient to jump across the air gap between the exposed part of the conductor and a nearby material capable of conducting the electrical energy away, for example, to earth. These are unintended arcs, which may arise from faulty electrical systems. Unintended arcs are also created when switches break contact. These can be a significant source of ignition for flammable gases, vapours and dusts. In addition, some processes create arcs intentionally, as part of the process, for example, arc welding. These intentional arc processes make use of the high levels of energy involved in an arc to melt metal.

Sparking

Sparks generate very high temperatures in a very small space, but except when flammable gas, vapour and dust mixtures are involved it is rare that a spark will cause ignition, in the absence of other factors. Sparks may be generated by grinding or cutting processes, electrical motors, metal tools and equipment contacting each other or unwanted metal contacting parts of process machinery, for example, in food processing.

Smoking

Smoking and smoking materials have been a significant source of ignition. Since the Health Act 2006, Part 1, prohibited smoking in the workplace the significance has decreased. However, because it is now prohibited it increases the risk of illicit smoking in locations where people are less likely to be discovered smoking. The location chosen to smoke may be a storage or process area where combustible materials are located and the smoker is not likely to be found. Discarded smoking materials may not be fully extinguished or contained, as proper smoking material disposal equipment is not provided.

Where legally acceptable smoking facilities are provide, if they are not located away from combustible materials or where flammable gases or vapours may be present they could be a source of ignition. Smoking materials discarded into general combustible waste may present a significant source of ignition.

Electrostatic discharge

This is the transfer of electrostatic charges between bodies at different electrostatic potentials. The electrostatic charge may be created by direct contact or induced by an electrostatic field.

ELEMENT C2 - PRINCIPLES OF FIRE AND EXPLOSION

Examples of how electrostatic charges are created by direct contact include:

- Walking across a nylon carpet on a dry day, which can generate a electrostatic charge of 35,000 volts.
- Opening a plastic bag, which can generate a charge of 20,000 volts.

Electrostatic discharge can provide a source of high energy to a small location and may be sufficient to ignite flammable gases, vapours and dusts. It represents a significant potential source of ignition in situations where flammable liquids are discharged from a tanker to a storage vessel or flammable dusts are moved through process pipes.

Mechanisms of explosions, mechanisms of fire-spread

HOW AN EXPLOSION/FIRE OCCURS

Combustion

Definition

Combustion is defined as being a chemical reaction during which heat energy and light energy are emitted.

The combustion process

Though the combustion process is defined as a chemical reaction (or series of reactions) where heat and light energy are emitted, this is a very simplistic approach, and it would be better describing the chemical reactions in the combustion process as happening very quickly, at very high temperatures, and in very small volumes. The tiny reactions that take place are exothermic and give out sufficient excess heat to energise the next chemical reaction. Combustion is therefore a chain reaction, or indeed, a series of branching chain reactions. Many experts have studied the chemistry of fire, but it would probably still be true to say that it would be difficult to write down all the chemical reactions that are taking place when combustion occurs. As an example of the complex nature of combustion, the burning of hydrogen can be considered:

This reaction is simply denoted chemically as: **$2 H_2 + O_2 = 2H_2O$**.

This equation suggests that two molecules of hydrogen combine with one molecule of oxygen to form two molecules of water when they collide. Collisions like this must happen, but they are very rare and do not explain the extremely rapid reactions in a hydrogen/oxygen explosion. The flame reactions depend on the activities of 'broken off bits' of molecules. These tiny fragments are very reactive, very unstable, and can only exist for a fraction of a second. However, they are very mobile and capable of rapid reproduction. These fragments are known as 'free radicals'. If we consider the equation again, we can see that the component parts can be broken up into hydrogen atoms (H), oxygen atoms (O), and hydroxyl radicals (OH). Inside a flame all three components are very hot, in high concentrations and completely free to react. If we therefore consider these three component parts separately:

If an oxygen atom collides with a hydrogen molecule, this can happen: *$*O* + H_2 \rightarrow *OH + H*$*.

(*denotes very energetic fragment or free radical).

A hydrogen atom will collide with oxygen to give: *$*H + O_2 \rightarrow *OH + *O*$*.

Finally, the *OH radical reacts with hydrogen to form water vapour plus one free radical: *$*OH + H_2 \rightarrow H_2O + H*$*.

As can be seen the combustion process is a series of chain reactions and branching chain reactions. If the above reactions are put together the complex nature of combustion becomes apparent:

$$\begin{array}{c}
H_2O \qquad\qquad\qquad H_2O \\
\nearrow \qquad\qquad\qquad \nearrow \\
*H + O_2 \rightarrow *OH + H_2 \rightarrow *H + O_2 \rightarrow *OH + H_2 \rightarrow H* \\
\searrow \qquad\qquad\qquad \searrow *O + H_2 \rightarrow *OH \\
\searrow \qquad\qquad\qquad\qquad\qquad \searrow *H \\
\searrow \\
\searrow \qquad\qquad\qquad\qquad H_2O \qquad\qquad H_2O \\
\qquad\qquad\qquad\qquad \nearrow \qquad\qquad \nearrow \\
\searrow *O + H_2 \rightarrow *OH + H_2 \rightarrow *H + O_2 \rightarrow *OH + H_2 \rightarrow *H \\
\searrow *H + O_2 \rightarrow *OH \qquad \searrow *O \\
\searrow *O
\end{array}$$

Points where water vapour is given off are denoted as **H_2O**.

In the above, we have considered the exothermic reactions found in a simple fuel, hydrogen, which is a relatively stable gas. Hydrogen will only react (combust) if there is sufficient heat being produced to decompose the adjacent molecule. We should also note that endothermic reactions are necessary for certain materials/compounds that must absorb heat when they react.

These materials/compounds are infrequently encountered in the workplace as they are unstable, because no heat has to be supplied to decompose them. Good examples of endothermic materials/compounds would be carbon disulphide and acetylene, as both will explode readily.

Explosion

Definition

An explosion may be defined as "rapid flame propagation throughout an area containing flammable gases, vapours or dusts".

The explosion process

Explosions can occur in flammable gases, vapours and certain types of dusts. For the explosion to occur the gas, vapour or dust must be mixed with air in such proportions that the mixture is within the flammability range for that substance. Explosion can occur with such gases as hydrogen, propane, acetylene and examples of dusts that may cause explosion hazards are aluminium, coal, flour and polythene. In a dust explosion, there is an initial smaller **primary explosion**, which is then followed by a devastating **secondary explosion**. See also - Dust explosions - later in this element.

THE STAGES OF COMBUSTION

Fire tends to grow in stages. The graph in **Figure C2-9** shows that fires start with a slow induction period, which is where the conditions for fire are not quite right for ignition.

For example, heat may be present and exposed to a source of fuel, but not sufficiently long enough to raise the temperature of the fuel to a high enough level for ignition to take place.

Once ignition is reached, combustion grows very quickly and is highly dependent on the level of oxygen in the area of the fire.

It then reaches a steady state, where heat available and the fuel/oxygen used are balanced. Once the fuel is consumed, the fire decays.

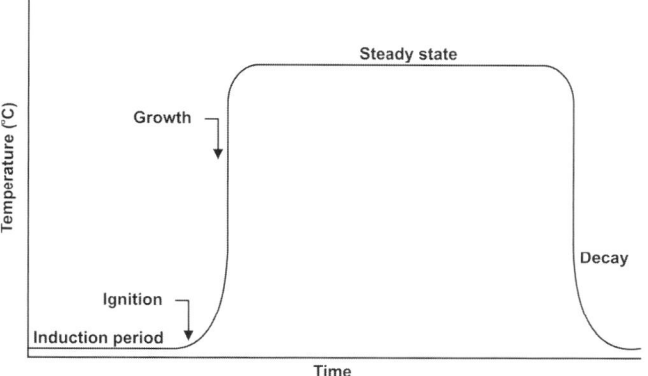

Figure C2-9: Stages of combustion.   Source: RMS.

Induction

This represents the early stages of a fire, when the combustion process is starting. This may often be a slow process such as in a smouldering fire, where the chemical decomposition of a material and the heat build up to an ignition point may take a considerable time.

Ignition

Ignition occurs when a heat source, for example a spark, contains sufficient heat energy to cause combustion of one or more molecules of a flammable material.

Growth

Once true ignition and combustion have taken place, this phase will often grow very quickly and is only limited by the availability of oxygen. The growth rate will then reach a plateau and will remain at that level until the fuel is consumed.

Steady state

The steady state is reached when the fuels that are present within the fire area are burning at their full potential, due to being fed with sufficient oxygen levels to sustain their maximum burn rate. This stage will continue whilst sufficient fuel and oxygen levels are present.

Decay

This is the final stages of a fire. As the fuel runs out the combustion process will quickly slow down, and eventually come to a stop.

MECHANISMS OF UNCONFINED VAPOUR CLOUD EXPLOSIONS, CONFINED VAPOUR CLOUD EXPLOSIONS

There are two known mechanisms for generating unconfined/confined vapour cloud explosions. The first is **deflagration**, where the flame accelerates to high speed, which requires a mechanism for generating the flame acceleration. In the case of an unconfined vapour cloud explosion, this may be due to turbulence in the flow of unburned mixture ahead of the flame, generated as the explosion propagates in free air. This turbulence increases the turbulent burning velocity, which in turn generates more turbulence ahead of the flame. This cycle results in flame acceleration until the maximum burning turbulent velocity and maximum flame speed are attained.

High turbulent burning velocity can create a strong shock wave ahead of the flame, leading to high temperature and pressure. Turbulence may be accentuated as the unconfined vapour cloud encounters natural barriers that cause 'congestion', such as trees, buildings or similar obstacles. In the case of a confined vapour cloud explosion, deflagration can develop from the turbulence as the flame passes through process plant or ducts.

The second mechanism is **detonation**, which may arise from the coming together of a strong shock wave and a fast-moving chemical reacting flame front. The combination can make a transition to propagation of the flame front faster than the speed of sound and produce over-pressures in excess of 1,000 kPa (10 bar). When the combustion flame speed in an ignited vapour cloud increases up to and above the speed of sound a detonation is said to occur. Detonation is not likely to occur in most situations of unconfined vapour cloud explosions. However, this mechanism can develop from a confined vapour cloud deflagration or directly in a very reactive mixture that has strongly focused shock waves, for example, in pipework or highly congested regions of process plant.

Effects of atomisation and oxygen content on the likelihood and severity of a fire/explosion

ATOMISATION/PARTICLE SIZE

The size of the fuel droplets/particle is an important parameter in combustion; the smaller the size of the droplet/particle, the easier the combustion. This is because a mass of solid combustible material reduced to small particle size has more surface area than the larger single mass. The same principle applies to liquids, when a quantity of liquid is 'atomised' (reduced to small droplets) the surface area increases. This larger surface area enables more vapour to be generated and released from the surface of the material by an ignition source and more surface area to be surrounded by oxygen, making the combustion process easier and faster.

A 0.1 mm droplet/particle burns in 0.01 seconds, while a 0.2 mm droplet/particle burns in 0.04 seconds. The combustion time is thus more or less the square of the value of the size of the droplet/particle. As a consequence, a larger droplet/particle may not burn internally when it starts to reach the cooler end of the flame. This incompletely burnt fuel causes the formation of soot and coke.

Mean particle size (microns)	*Kst*	*Pmax*
290	1,100 kPa m/s (11 bar m/s)	390 kPa (3.9 bar)
29	5,900 kPa m/s (59 bar m/s)	820 kPa (8.2 bar)
<20	20,500 kPa m/s (205 bar m/s)	910 kPa (9.1 bar)

Figure C2-10: Effects of particle size of sugar on explosion indices. *Source: Explosion Testing Ltd.*

Atomisation or the small particle size of flammable materials makes the likelihood of a fire or explosion occurring increase. In addition, the high rate of combustion makes the severity of the fire or explosion greater.

OXYGEN CONTENT

Oxygen enrichment of the atmosphere, even by a few percent, considerably increases the risk of fire. A higher oxygen content atmosphere makes the likelihood of a fire or explosion increase. Sparks or other ignition sources that would normally be regarded as harmless can cause fires. In addition, a higher oxygen content atmosphere will make the severity of a fire or explosion greater, as the additional oxygen accelerates the combustion process.

Materials that do not burn in air with the usual level of oxygen content, including fireproofing materials, may burn vigorously or even spontaneously in oxygen enriched air. Oil and grease are particularly hazardous in the presence of oxygen as they can ignite spontaneously and burn with explosive violence. They should never be used to lubricate oxygen or enriched air equipment (special lubricants that are compatible with oxygen can be used under certain conditions).

How failure of control measures can bring about an explosion

The physico-chemical properties relate to both the physical state of a substance, for example, atomisation of a solid substance and the chemical properties of a substance, for example, flammability. Heating may cause violent combustion or explosion, due to the chemical properties of the substance or the substance may spontaneously ignite on contact with air when finely dispersed.

Physico-chemical properties include:

- Flashpoint (liquids) or flammability (solids).
- Flammability (on contact with water).
- Pyrophoric properties (on contact with air).
- Explosive properties.
- Auto-ignition temperature (for liquids) or relative self-ignition temperature (for solids).
- Oxidising properties.

PRINCIPLES OF FIRE AND EXPLOSION - ELEMENT C2

If we consider the above factors and apply them to a combustible dust, any failure of control measures that will bring about the release of the dust (especially if in small particles) into an uncontrolled area, where there are potential ignition sources, can present an immediate explosion hazard. Similarly, a control measure in the form of a level fill alarm on a flammable storage tank may become defective. This could then allow a flammable liquid product to overflow and leak into the atmosphere, which when combined with its ability to vaporise easily, would quickly allow a large area to be covered with a flammable vapour/air mixture, as happened at Buncefield. Control measures in the workplace may include control of the temperature of a flammable material being used or created in a process. If the control measures failed this could lead to the flammable material reaching higher temperatures than intended, with the possibility of it reaching its auto-ignition/self-ignition temperature.

Oxidisation

The chemical process of altering a substance by the addition of oxygen is generally perceived as the oxidisation process. The combustion process itself is a chemical reaction involving oxygen, but this an exothermic reaction where heat energy is released. Oxidisation of a substance often involves some form of heat output. If this heat cannot be dissipated into the atmosphere then the heat build up can take the material through its induction phase and up to its ignition point, where true combustion can take place. This can happen for example in coal stocks, where oxidation of the outer surface of the coal produces heat; if the stacks are not turned over to allow the heat to escape, then ignition can and has occurred.

Oxidising agents are chemical compounds that readily transfer oxygen atoms and therefore allow materials to burn that would otherwise not be capable of sustained combustion, and increase the burning rates of combustible materials. They add to the severity of a fire by increasing the supply of oxygen. Examples of oxidising agents include hydrogen peroxide (H_2O_2), and sodium hypochlorite (including bleach ($NaClO$)).

Vapour cloud and boiling liquid expanding vapour explosions

UNCONFINED VAPOUR CLOUD EXPLOSIONS

The term unconfined vapour cloud explosion (UCVCE) describes an explosion of flammable vapour-air mixture either in the open air or in partially confined circumstances due to the presence of partial obstructions such as buildings, structures and trees. Unconfined vapour cloud explosions usually take the form of a deflagration. A feature of unconfined vapour cloud explosions is low initial turbulence and hence low flame speeds. However, where the explosion is constricted by structures or trees the expansion generated flow (created by combustion) of the unburnt gas passing through the obstacles will generate turbulence. This increases the burning velocity by increasing the flame area and enhancing the molecular process of combustion. This, in turn, increases the expansion generated flow, which leads to further turbulence. This cycle generates higher combustion velocities and increased pressure at the flame front. These pressure waves can increase to a destructive level.

Buncefield, 2005

The unconfined vapour cloud explosion incident at Buncefield was one of the most significant health, safety and environmental incidents of this type to take place in the UK in recent times.

In the early hours of Sunday 11th December 2005, a number of explosions occurred at Buncefield Oil Storage Depot, Hemel Hempstead, Hertfordshire. At least one of the initial explosions was of massive proportions and the incident involved a large fire that engulfed a high proportion of the site. Over 40 people were injured; fortunately there were no fatalities. Significant damage occurred to both commercial and residential properties in the vicinity and a large area around the site was evacuated on the advice of the emergency services. The fire burned for several days, destroying most of the site and emitting large clouds of black smoke into the atmosphere.

Figure C2-11: Buncefield Oil Terminal.

Figure C2-12: Buncefield: Tank 912 indicated by the arrow.

Source: Chiltern Air Support.

ELEMENT C2 - PRINCIPLES OF FIRE AND EXPLOSION

The Major Incident Investigation Board (MIIB) set up to investigate the explosion and fire carried out a joint investigation into the cause of the incident with the Health and Safety Executive and the Environment Agency, as the Competent Authority in England and Wales for the regulation of major accident hazards.

Circumstances

In December 2005 there were three operating sites at the depot; Hertfordshire Oil Storage Ltd (HOSL), British Pipeline Agency Ltd (BPA), BP Oil UK Ltd. All three sites were 'top-tier' sites under the Control of Major Accident Hazards Regulations 1999 (COMAH). In total the depot had hazardous planning consent to store 194,000 tonnes of hydrocarbon fuels.

Fuel was transported to these sites through three pipelines:

- The Finaline between Lindsey Oil Refinery, Humberside and the HOSL West site.
- UKOP North line between Stanlow Oil Refinery, Merseyside and BPA.
- UKOP South line between Coryton Oil Refinery, Essex and BPA.

A parcel of unleaded petrol was being delivered through the UKOP South line into HOSL's Tank 912, a tank that had a capacity of 6 million litres. The tank was fitted with an automatic tank gauging system (ATG), which measured the rising level of fuel and displayed this on a screen in the control room. On Sunday 11 December the ATG display stopped registering the rising level of fuel in the tank, although the tank continued to fill. Consequently the three ATG alarms, the 'user level', the 'high level' and the 'high-high level', could not operate as the **tank reading** was always indicating that the levels were below the levels that would activate these alarms. Due to the practice of working to alarms in the control room, the control room supervisor was not alerted to the fact that the level of petrol in the tank continued to rise and the tank was at risk of overfilling.

The tank had two forms of level control. These were the ATG that enabled the employees in the control room to monitor the filling operation and an independent high-level switch (IHLS), which was meant to close down operations automatically if the tank was overfilled. The IHLS was designed to automatically close valves on any pipelines importing product, as well as sounding an audible alarm, should the petrol in the tank reach an unintended high level. The IHLS failed to register the rising level of petrol, so the 'final alarm' did not sound and the automatic shutdown was not activated. Subsequently, the level within the tank exceeded its ultimate capacity and petrol started to spill out of vents in the tank roof, forming a vapour cloud. The vapour cloud ignited, causing a massive explosion and a fire.

The first ATG gauge had stuck intermittently after the tank had been serviced in August 2005. However, neither site management nor the contractors who maintained the systems responded effectively to its obvious unreliability. The IHLS needed a padlock to retain its check lever in a working position. However, the switch supplier did not communicate this critical point to the installer and maintenance contractor or the site operator. Because of this lack of understanding, the padlock was not fitted.

Figure C2-13: Catastrophic bund wall failure at pipe penetrations.   Figure C2-14: Loss of sealant between penetrating pipe and bund wall.

Source: www.buncefieldinvestigation.gov.uk.

The Explosion Mechanism Advisory Group (Group) of the BMIIB reported that a possible source of the initial explosion was the emergency generator cabin. Deflagration during the unconfined vapour cloud explosion could have occurred due to constrictions as the explosion propagated through process pipework, however this type of pipework constrictions were not present at Buncefield. The Group also studied the damage done by the explosion and concluded that the trees and shrubbery surrounding parts of the site would probably have caused turbulence, leading to flame acceleration as it propagated as a deflagration.

> *This would have caused the flame to accelerate to its maximum flame speed, possibly in the region of 400 m/s, creating a high over-pressure at the flame front and an additional over-pressure due to the semi-confined nature of the explosion. It is estimated that the magnitude of the total maximum over-pressure would be no less than about 1000 mbar. This pressure magnitude in the area of the trees is not inconsistent with some estimations of over-pressures.*

Figure C2-15: Effects of trees and shrubbery on unconfined vapour explosion.   *Source: Explosion Mechanism Advisory Group.*

The Group considered an alternative scenario that may have resulted in direct initiation of a detonation. It was possible that the explosion that vented from the emergency generator cabin underwent a transition to detonation, as a result of the presence of a parked car outside the cabin affecting turbulence and causing flame acceleration.

> There was general agreement within the group that localised detonations might occur; however, a consensus could not be reached on the likelihood of these being sustained over the length of the car parks.

Figure C2-16: Likelihood of detonation arising from the unconfined vapour explosion. Source: Explosion Mechanism Advisory Group.

The Group gave consideration to a scenario where both deflagration and detonation could occur. It considered that a possibility remained that a detonation may have occurred in limited sections of the vapour cloud to the south part of the car parks before deflagration took place amongst the trees and shrubbery, or visa versa. The Health and Safety Laboratory (HSL) did work to estimate the dynamic over-pressures caused by the explosions:

- Estimates from damage to building structures suggested no more than 20 kPa (200 mbar).
- Estimates at the sources of ignition were likely to be significantly greater than 20 kPa (200 mbar).
- Estimates from car damage suggested pressures in excess of 200 kPa (2,000 mbar).
- Estimates from damage to trees, lamp posts and telegraph poles suggested 100 kPa (1,000 mbar).

Figure C2-17 illustrates the over-pressures caused by the explosions, the shaded area in the middle of the site shows where the pressure is estimated to have been higher than 100 kPa (1,000 mbar).

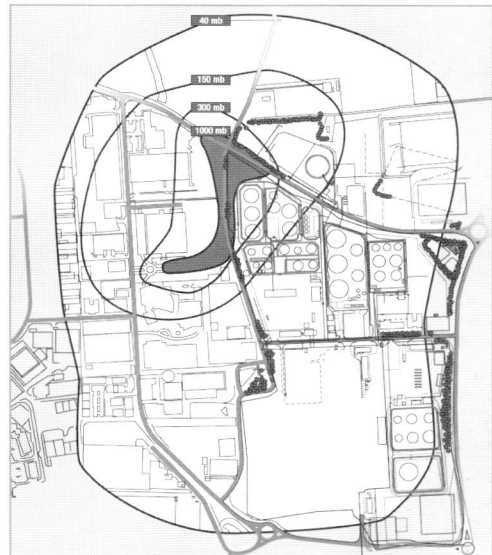

Figure C2-17: Overpressure effects of explosion.
Source: Explosion Mechanism Advisory Group.

Main factors

Failures of design and maintenance in both overfill protection systems and liquid containment systems were the technical causes of the initial explosion and the seepage of pollutants to the environment. However, underlying these immediate failings lay root causes based in broader management failings:

- Management systems in place at HOSL relating to tank filling were both deficient and not properly followed, despite the fact that the systems were independently audited.
- Pressures on staff had been increasing before the incident. The site was fed by three pipelines, two of which control room staff had little control over in terms of flow rates and timing of receipt. This meant that staff did not have sufficient information easily available to them to manage precisely the storage of incoming fuel.
- Throughput had increased at the site. This put more pressure on site management and staff and further degraded their ability to monitor the receipt and storage of fuel. The pressure on staff was made worse by a lack of engineering support from Head Office.
- Cumulatively, these pressures created a culture where keeping the process operating was the primary focus and process safety did not get the attention, resources or priority that it required.

The investigation determined the following improvement points:

- There should be a clear understanding of major accident risks and the safety critical equipment and systems designed to control them.
- There should be systems and a culture in place to detect signals of failure in safety critical equipment and to respond to them quickly and effectively.
- Time and resources for process safety should be made available.
- There should be effective auditing systems in place that test the management systems and ensure that these systems are actually being used on the ground and are effective.
- At the core of managing a major hazard business should be clear and positive process safety leadership with board level involvement and competence to ensure that major hazard risks are being properly managed.

Flixborough, 1974

The classic example of an unconfined vapour cloud explosion was that which occurred in 1974 at the Nypro UK chemical plant at Flixborough. On Saturday 1st June 1974 the Flixborough Works of Nypro (UK) Limited (Nypro) exploded killing 28 people and injuring 36 others on site. The explosion was estimated to be the equivalent of 15-45 tonnes of TNT.

ELEMENT C2 - PRINCIPLES OF FIRE AND EXPLOSION

If the disaster had occurred during the normal working week the death toll would have certainly been greater. Outside the site, 53 casualties were recorded together with extensive property damage over a wide area (1,821 houses and 167 shops/factories).

The explosion occurred following the uncontrolled release of cyclohexane from a temporary pipe line which had been used to bypass a reactor taken out of service for repair. The cyclohexane collected over the plant due to inversion conditions. Normally the air temperature decreases with altitude. In inversion conditions the reverse is true (i.e. temperature increases with altitude). The unusual condition did not allow the vapour cloud to disperse and it collected within explosive limits.

It should be noted that the presence, layout and design of structures within the area of the explosion can help to magnify its effects.

Circumstances

- No 5 reactor (R2525) was discovered to be leaking on the cyclohexane train and was shut down in order to be depressurised and cooled prior to a full inspection. The next morning (28th March 1974) a 2 metre crack was found by the Plant Manager.
- The gap between the flanking reactors (No. 4 and No. 6) was bridged by a 50 cm dog-leg pipe between 2 expansion bellows. The inlet and the outlet of the pipe were at different levels and unsupported.
- The assembly was subjected to temperature and pressure more severe than had been encountered since the dog leg was fitted but still within what should have been normal margins.
- The bridging pipe ruptured, which released large quantities of cyclo-hexane that mixed with air to form an unconfined vapour cloud, which then exploded.

Main factors

- No proper design study had been carried out, nor had the need for support of the bypass pipe been appreciated.
- British Standards were not consulted.
- No safety testing had been carried out.
- The key post of Works Engineer was vacant and none of the senior personnel, who were chemical engineers, were capable of recognising what should have been a simple engineering problem. A junior engineer was present, but his concerns were discounted as was his latter sketch for supports.
- There was an inadequate nitrogen supply upon which the hazardous process system depended.
- There was nitrate stress corrosion on the reactor (R2525) thought to have initiated the sequence of events which led to disaster.
- Many of the stainless steel pipes had suffered from embrittlement due to contact with zinc. The stainless steel pipes had also suffered from creep cavitation fractures which can be produced in a relatively short time under temperature and pressure.
- The events in the control room cannot be determined with certainty as all control room personnel were killed and the instruments destroyed.

BOILING LIQUID EXPANDING VAPOUR EXPLOSIONS (BLEVES)

Gases, such as butane and propane, are stored in cylinders under pressure in their liquid phase. When the valve to the cylinder is opened the resulting drop in pressure restores the substance to the gaseous state. If, however, the closed cylinder is in a fire, the increase in temperature will mean its contents will revert to the gaseous state, with a resulting increase in pressure inside the cylinder.

As the heat turns the liquid into a vapour the liquid level drops. As there is less and less liquid to absorb the heat, the metal container just above the liquid level absorbs the heat and the structure of the metal starts to change and weaken. The metal melts and thins, such that it can no longer contain the pressure of the contents and ruptures. The contents burst out catching fire as they go and sending chunks of the metal container into the surrounding area. This is known as a boiling liquid, expanding vapour explosion (BLEVE).

A BLEVE will consist of:

- A blast wave (usually low pressure).
- High thermal radiation.
- Projectiles being sent long distance.

Severe burn range from the high thermal radiation associated with a BLEVE:

- Aerosol can.   10 metres.
- LPG cylinder.   35 metres.
- LPG rail transport.   250 metres.

Pressure can build up in drums due to the difference between filling temperature and ambient temperature. If the ambient temperature is higher, ejection/splashing of the liquid contents or vapour release may occur on opening the drum.

In June 1993 at Ste. Elizabeth de Warwick, Quebec, Canada, the fire brigade responded to a large cattle barn fire. A 4,900 litre propane tank was close to the fire with its relief vent operating, shooting flames over 5 metres into the air.

The fire fighters applied water to the propane tank in an effort to cool it, but the tank BLEVEd and split into two large pieces. One piece was blasted into an open field while the other one travelled over 47 metres where it struck a fire engine, then travelled a further 232 metres where it struck a passing vehicle, trapping the occupant. Four fire fighters were killed when the metal struck the fire engine, one being thrown 47 metres. The blast also injured three fire fighters and four members of the public.

In April 1998 in Albert City, Iowa, two pipelines carrying liquid propane were struck by a vehicle. The liquid propane rapidly converted to gas and was ignited by a nearby ignition source. The fire impinged on the main propane tank containing 83,000 litres, which was situated between three buildings. The tank vented allowing the gas to escape and was left to vent while water was applied in an attempt to keep the tank cool. However, the gas was not vented fast enough and the weakened metal tank split sending large sections in four directions. The blast extinguished the fire. Two fire fighters were killed and a number of people were badly burned, including the fire chief. The pieces of the tank destroyed buildings and travelled up to 77 metres away.

Mexico City, 1984

The Mexico City explosion represented one of the most significant work-related explosions to have occurred in recent times, it resulted in a large number of deaths and huge devastation. It was an example of the mechanism and effects of large scale boiling liquid expanding vapour explosions (BLEVE).

Circumstances

At approximately 05:35 hours on 19 November 1984 a major fire and a series of catastrophic explosions occurred at the government owned and operated PEMEX liquefied petroleum gas (LPG) Terminal at San Juan Ixhuatepec, Mexico City, Mexico. As a consequence of these events some 500 individuals were killed and the terminal destroyed. Three refineries supplied the facility with LPG on a daily basis. The plant was being filled from a refinery 400 km away, as on the previous day it had become almost empty. Two large spheres and 48 cylindrical vessels were filled to 90% and 4 smaller spheres to 50% full.

A drop in pressure was noticed in the control room and also at a pipeline pumping station. An 8-inch pipe between a sphere and a series of cylinders had ruptured. Unfortunately, the operators could not identify the cause of the pressure drop. The release of LPG continued for about 5-10 minutes when the gas cloud, estimated at 200 m x 150 m x 2 m high, drifted to a flare stack. It ignited, causing violent ground shock. A number of ground fires occurred. Workers on the plant then tried to deal with the escape of gas taking various actions. At a late stage somebody pressed the emergency shut down button.

About fifteen minutes after the initial release the first BLEVE occurred. For the next hour and a half there followed a series of BLEVEs as the LPG vessels violently exploded. LPG was said to by observers to 'rain down' and surfaces covered in the liquid were set alight. The explosions were recorded on a seismograph at the University of Mexico.

Main factors

The total destruction of the terminal occurred because there was a failure of the overall basis of safety, which included the following factors:

- The *layout of the plant* was inadequate and had not taken account the probability of an event of this type. The positioning of the vessels did not provide sufficient separation by distance or barriers.
- The terminal's fire water system was disabled in the initial blast. Also, the water spray systems were inadequate. The survivability of critical active/passive *fire protection systems* had not been ensured.
- The installation of a more effective *gas detection and emergency isolation* system could have averted the incident. The plant had no gas detection system and therefore when the emergency isolation was initiated it was probably too late.
- The emergency response and incident control was ineffective. Traffic chaos, which built up as local residents sought to escape the area, hindered the arrival of the emergency services. The *emergency plan* had not sufficiently accounted for the need of emergency vehicles to gain access at the time of such an emergency.

CONFINED VAPOUR CLOUD EXPLOSIONS

The term confined vapour cloud explosion (CVCE) describes an explosion of flammable vapour-air mixture within a confined volume due to such things as a building, vessel, pipelines or ducts. As the flame propagates through the vapour it produces combustion products. The confinement prevents expansion of the combustion products and results in a pressure increase. The confinement also produces turbulence that increases the burning velocity by causing an increase in the flame area and affecting the molecular process of combustion. This leads to more turbulence, and higher combustion velocities and a further increase in pressure. The pressure acts on the structure confining it, until the structure fails or the vapour-air mixture is consumed. Because of the pressures involved, failure of the structure may be catastrophic.

Hickson and Welch, 1992

The Hickson and Welch explosion at its site in Castleford was a significant example of a confined vapour cloud explosion. It involved the death of employees and substantial damage to the plant.

ELEMENT C2 - PRINCIPLES OF FIRE AND EXPLOSION

The incident could have been prevented if the hazards and the risks associated with this non-routine clean-out operation had been accurately assessed beforehand and suitable precautions taken. However, fundamental errors and incorrect assumptions were made, which led to an incident in which five people lost their lives. The incident also revealed defects in fire precautions affecting the means of escape from parts of the main office block.

In view of the nature of the incident, and public concern, the Health and Safety Commission (HSC) instructed the Health and Safety Executive (HSE) to carry out a formal investigation under Section 14(2) (a) of the Health and Safety at Work etc. Act (HASAWA) 1974 and make a special report. For the sake of brevity this report concentrates on the cause of the incident and the precautions that should have been taken to prevent it but omits reference to many satisfactory arrangements identified during the investigation.

Following the investigation by the HSE, Hickson & Welch Ltd was prosecuted. The company was convicted for an offence under Section 2 of the Health and Safety at Work etc. Act (HASAWA) 1974 at Leeds Crown Court on 30 July 1993 and was fined £250,000 with £150,000 costs awarded against it.

Circumstances

At the time of the incident, approximately 1.20pm on 21 September 1992, a process vessel known as '60 still base', used to distil an organic liquid in batches, was being raked out to remove an accumulation of semi-solid residue or sludge that was rich in dinitrotoluenes and nitrocresols. Before raking, heat was applied to the residues for about three hours through an internal steam coil. This started a self-heating (exothermic) runaway reaction in the residue leading to a confined vapour cloud explosion within the still, involving deflagration and a jet flame

The jet of flame erupted from an access opening on the side of a batch still at the factory. The flame cut through an office/control building nearby killing two employees instantly. Three other employees in these offices sustained severe burns but escaped. Two later died in hospital.

The flame also struck a much larger four-storey office block, shattering windows and setting rooms on fire. There were 63 employees in this building, including a number who were returning from lunch. All managed to escape with the exception of a young employee, who was overcome by smoke in a second floor toilet. Although she was rescued by fire service personnel approximately 40 minutes later, she died on 23 September 1992 from the effects of smoke inhalation.

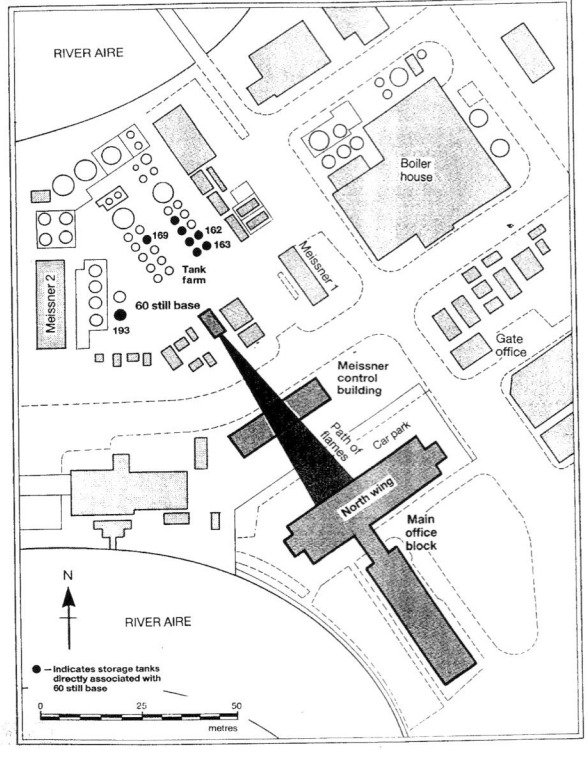

Figure C2-18: Plan of area around 60 still base showing path of the jet flame. *Source: HSE report on the fatal fire at Hickson and Welch Ltd.*

Main factors

The investigation revealed several important lessons:

- Where the batch distillation of highly energetic materials (such as mononitrotoluenes or other organic nitro compounds) is carried out still residues should be analysed, monitored and removed at regular intervals to prevent possible build up of unstable impurities.
- The use of chemical plant for a different process or purpose should be treated as a plant change procedure, requiring rigorous assessment. Consequently before plant is used to carry out non-routine operations authorisation should be obtained from an appropriate level of management, who should ensure that plant hazards have been identified, risks assessed and the precautions determined.
- Safe systems of work covering all aspects of operation and maintenance of all process plant should be established and defined in comprehensive instructions including those operations undertaken at infrequent intervals. These systems should be monitored by management and reviewed at appropriate intervals.
- The nature, operation and limitations of control systems on process plant should be determined, and their implications for health and safety taken into account, before non-routine operations requiring their use are authorised.
- Organisations should assess and monitor the workload and other implications of restructuring levels of management and supervision to ensure that critical personnel have adequate resources, including time and cover, to discharge their responsibilities.
- Persons authorised to issue permits-to-work should be sufficiently knowledgeable about the hazards associated with relevant plant. If 'authorised' personnel are relocated to former workstations refresher training should be given and recorded before re-authorisation.

PRINCIPLES OF FIRE AND EXPLOSION - ELEMENT C2

- The design and location of control and other buildings near chemical plant that processes significant quantities of flammable and/or toxic substances should be based on the assessment of the potential for fire and explosion and/or toxic releases at these plants. Organisations should assess the suitability of existing control buildings and if they are found to be vulnerable, reasonably practicable mitigating action should be taken.
- Organisations should regularly monitor and audit their own compliance with performance standards defined in their fire risk assessment. Particular attention should be paid to the effects of material alterations, for example, installation of pipework and cable ducts and other work in areas concealed by false ceilings, to ensure that the fire-resisting integrity of protected routes is maintained and fire training records should be regularly updated.
- When exercising their on-site emergency plans organisations should ensure that roll call information on missing persons is passed immediately, accurately and directly to the Senior Fire Officer in charge. Roll call procedures should be practised routinely to ensure that they are effective when carried out at all periods of the working day.

Control of vapour phase explosions

Control of explosions is best carried out at the earliest point as possible after initiation, during the vapour phase. This will involve **plant design and structural protection** to withstand smaller explosions in order to protect the main body of plant and equipment. **Process control** should be employed to identify the characteristics that can lead to vapour phase explosions, including levels of vapour in the explosive range. It is important that flammable materials that could contribute to the explosion are **segregated** from possible explosion initiation locations and **stored** in a manner that would protect them if such an explosion occurred.

It is important that **hazardous area zoning** is established to identify areas of higher risk and enable the control of sources of ignition. Hazardous zones are identified by the use of a zone number to illustrate the likelihood of explosive atmospheres being present, zones 0, 1 and 2 for gases, vapours and mists.

Should an explosion occur; mechanisms like **providing inert gas** to the explosion area and **explosion relief** may limit the effects. *See also C2.3 - Fire and explosion prevention and protection - later in this element.*

Control of amount of material, prevention of release, control of ignition sources and sensing of vapour

Given the incidents detailed above and the factors involved, it should be clear that controls on the amount of flammable or explosive material are paramount. Control measures, both in the way of physical mechanical/electrical controls and management controls, must be in place to ensure that the release of any hazardous material is prevented.

When looking at previous incidents that have occurred, it can be seen that the 'human element' often plays a part in failures that result in the release of flammable or explosive materials and/or the creation of a dangerous situation. Systems should be designed to eliminate human error and **prevent release** of flammable materials wherever possible, but any system is only as good as how it is managed/maintained and implemented.

The **amount of material** present should be controlled by process equipment, such as fill alarms and overfill protection devices. Any electro/mechanical system can of course fail and management must ensure that active monitoring is in place so that failure of any component part can be highlighted and corrective actions taken before materials are released and a dangerous situation is created.

In hazardous areas, **ignition sources** are often controlled by using defined hazard areas, zoned to illustrate the likely presence of explosive atmospheres, such as zone 0, 1 and 2 for gases, vapours and mists. By using this information, and for example the ATEX marking scheme for electrical equipment, verification can be made that ignition sources related to electrical equipment are approved for use in the explosive atmospheres that are present. Other, sources of ignition can include friction causing hot surfaces, vehicles, heat sources, hot pipework, welding equipment, and grinding equipment. The zoning also helps to identify where these other ignition sources need to be controlled by engineering methods and permit to work systems.

Flammable gases, vapours or dusts will only ignite/burn or explode when they are present in the atmosphere within the flammable or explosive range for the specific material concerned. Monitoring may be required to **sense the gas, vapour or mist** and determine when the lower flammability limit/lower explosive limit (LFL/LEL) is being approached, as this is the point at which combustion or explosions can occur. This monitoring equipment may need to link to warning devices, to enable the safe evacuation of workers before an explosion occurs, the shut down of equipment, to stop the limit being released, or eliminate ignition sources. The need to warn staff of an imminent explosion risk is a requirement under the Regulatory Reform (Fire Safety) Order 2005 and the Dangerous Substances and Explosive Atmosphere Regulations (DSEAR) 2002.

It may also be important to detect if the air/fuel mixture is above its upper flammability limit (UFL) or upper explosive limit (UEL), because if the air/fuel mixture is too rich it cannot be ignited. Although, this is not a good control to rely on in all circumstances as any dilution of the mixture by ventilation will weaken the mixture to a point below the UFL/UEL so that a fire or explosion can then occur.

Dust explosions

EXAMPLES OF INDUSTRIES/PLANT WITH POTENTIAL DUST EXPLOSION HAZARDS

The type of industries that are typically at risk are those dealing with agricultural products, foodstuffs, pharmaceuticals, chemicals, pigments, polymeric materials, rubbers, coal and wood products. The types of plant, equipment and processes that present a potential dust explosion hazard are diverse. The food industry, where flour, custard powder, instant coffee, sugar, dried milk, potato powder and soup powder and other similar products are being handled, is known to present dust explosion hazards. Common processes that generate explosive dusts include flour milling, sugar grinding, spray drying of milk/instant coffee and the conveyance/storage of whole grains or finely divided materials. Any similar industry that handles combustible dusts can have risks of dust explosion when creating, moving, handling and storing products. The hazard is more likely to be present when processes such as heating or drying of materials are also in place. In a lot of cases, the importance of local exhaust ventilation (LEV) cannot be emphasised enough, as it is vital that all steps should be taken to give sufficient ventilation and dust extraction so that explosion hazard levels are not reached. Consideration should be given to the possibility that the LEV equipment could become the primary source of a dust explosion as all the right conditions may be present in this equipment, i.e., finely divided combustible dust suspended in air.

MECHANISMS OF DUST EXPLOSIONS

Dust explosions can occur in any building used for the manufacture or handling of fine particulate combustible material. This type of explosion can occur if a combustible dust is suspended in air as a dust cloud in such proportions that it will support combustion. In these conditions the surface area exposed to the air is very large in comparison to the mass of the powder.

If ignition does occur the entire material may burn very rapidly. Energy can be released suddenly as heat and this can cause gaseous reaction products to be formed. If the dust cloud is contained, the rapid release of heat and gaseous products that are formed causes an increase in pressure that most industrial plant cannot contain.

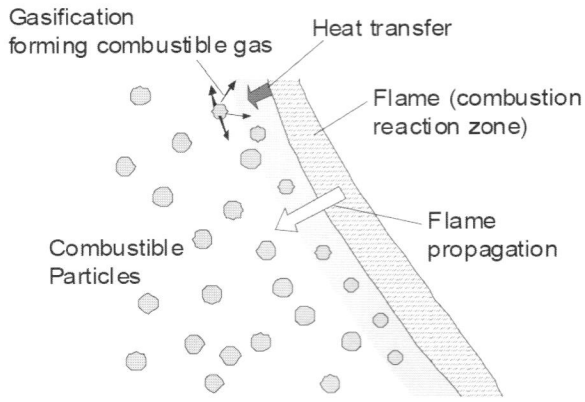

Figure C2-19: Mechanism of a dust explosion. *Source: IOP Publishing.*

The importance of particulate size, dispersal, explosive concentrations, ignition energy, temperature and humidity

Dust explosions can only occur if certain conditions are present:

- The dust must be combustible.
- The dust must be capable of becoming airborne.
- The dust particle size and distribution must be capable of propagating flame.
- The concentration of dust must fall within the explosive range.
- An ignition source of sufficient heat energy must be in contact with the dust.
- The atmosphere must contain sufficient oxygen to sustain combustion.
- The humidity of the air and dust must be low enough not to inhibit ignition.

The severity of the explosion can depend on many factors, including:

Particle size   As a general rule, a dust will not explode if its particle size is greater than 500 microns and will give only weak explosions if over 200 microns. If a material is finely ground it may ignite more readily or at a lower energy.

Dispersal   Ignition of a highly turbulent, well dispersed dust suspension will result in a more severe explosion hazard.

Concentration   Explosions can occur and may propagate within a range of concentrations in air between values known as the lower and upper explosive limits. Although the explosive limits for dusts will vary for differing materials and circumstances, it has been found that for the majority of organic materials the lower explosive limit is 10-50 g/m3. This would resemble a dense fog.

Ignition   Ignition energies vary between flammable dusts and for the same dust depending on particle size and moisture content. The ignition temperature of most dust suspensions is between 200°C and 900°C, the majority falling between 300°C and 600°C.

The ignition source energy is usually above 5 mJ.

Humidity — As the moisture content of the dust increases and reaches 16% by mass, the energy required for ignition increases and the explosion severity decreases.

Overall assessment of dust explosibility

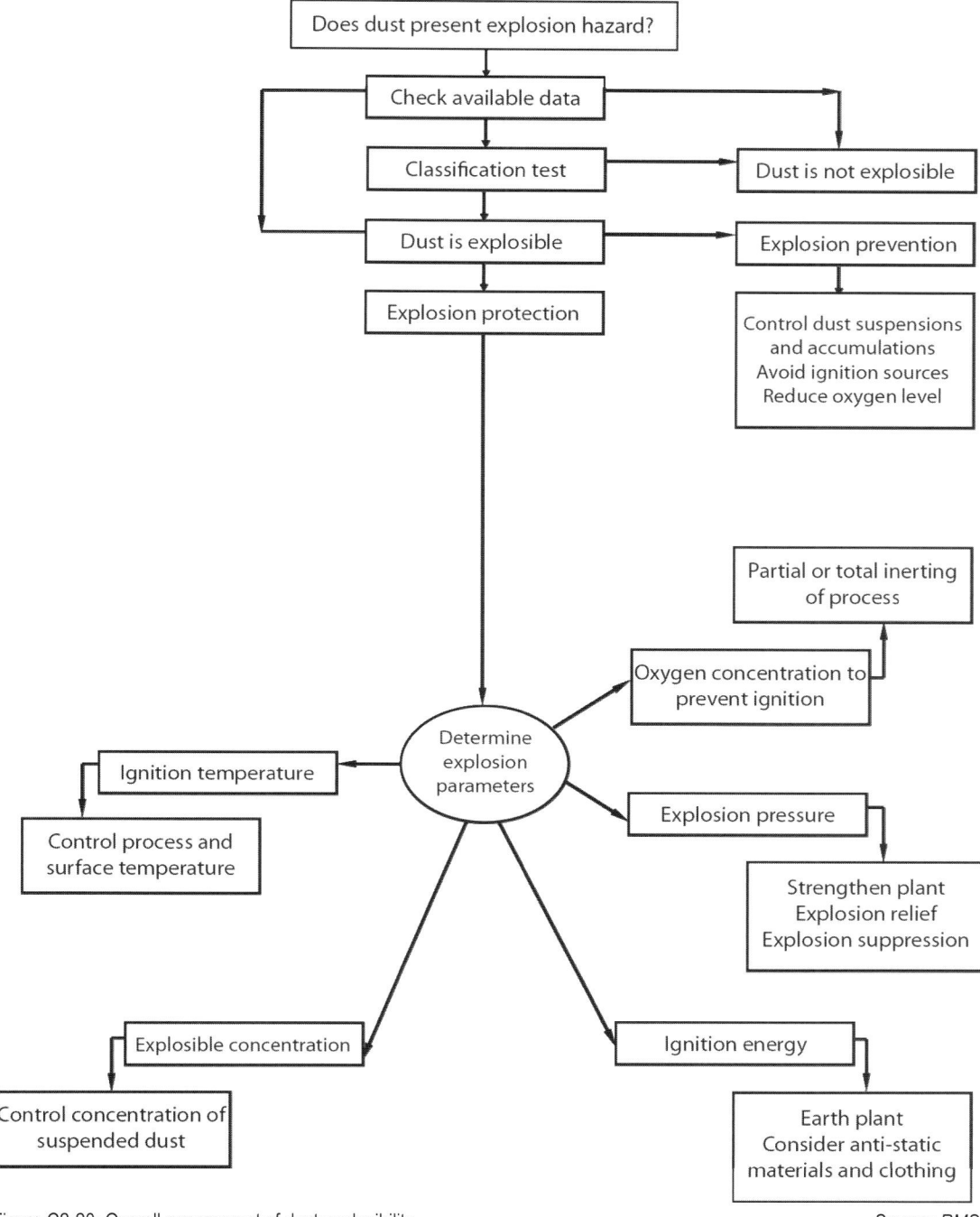

Figure C2-20: Overall assessment of dust explosibility. Source: RMS.

PRIMARY AND SECONDARY EXPLOSION

Dust explosions can be divided into two types. Firstly, a **primary explosion**, which usually occurs in an enclosure or handling plant located within a building. Structural damage of lightweight plant may occur at this stage, as pressures of 800-1,000 kPa (8-10 bars) are produced, but more concerning is the consequent air turbulence created within the workplace. The pressure wave created combined with the air turbulence may dislodge dust off all horizontal surfaces within the workplace, and cause an airborne suspension of combustible dust throughout the entire workplace. This dust can then be ignited by either the initial ignition source, the combustion bi-products of the primary explosion or any other ignition source with sufficient heat energy. Secondly, a **secondary explosion** will then occur throughout the entire workplace with devastating effects. Entire buildings have been destroyed by such effects.

As an example of the problems of secondary explosion and the need for good housekeeping as a prevention method, a layer of flour 0.3 mm thick on the floor in a building would be capable of producing an explosive cloud 3 m high.

ELEMENT C2 - PRINCIPLES OF FIRE AND EXPLOSION

Actual incidents of dust explosions

GENERAL FOODS, BANBURY 1981

Failure of plant in the General Foods Ltd factory at Banbury, Oxfordshire, on Wednesday 18 November 1981, led to an emission and build-up of corn starch powder, which ignited and exploded, injuring nine workers and causing substantial damage.

The emission was caused by a malfunction of a conveying system, which resulted in a feed bin being overfilled. The control system was not capable of detecting that the conveying system was attempting to fill an already full bin.

Circumstances

Corn starch, in fine powder form, particulate size of approximately 15 microns, was the basic ingredient for custard powder production. Twenty people were working in the desert processing area. Two bins needed filling, number 1 and number 2, number 1 was filled first and the filling lever changed to number 2. After a time it was noticed that corn starch powder was coming out of the top of number 1 bin. The lever was checked and found to be in the correct position to fill number 2 bin, but this was not happening, the already full number 1 bin was being filled instead.

By this time large quantities of powder were escaping from number 1 bin, mainly from the top dust filter and an inspection panel on the sides. The overfilling had created large pressures inside the bin, causing the top of the bin to bow and the failure of the filter and inspection panel. This created a dense fog of corn starch powder. An explosion occurred. The electrical supply to the filter unit had been severed and it was concluded that arcing from wires was the most likely source of ignition. The compressed air supply to the filter unit had also ruptured causing the powder to be dispersed over a wide area.

In this incident only a primary explosion was involved and this occurred outside the process plant. It was estimated that approximately 1 tonne of corn starch powder was emitted from the bin, but that most of it was deposited on the floor. It was estimated that the explosion could have occurred with a concentration of powder derived from as little as 30 kg of corn starch powder, the lower explosive limit for corn starch is approximately 60 g/m^3. If the powder had continued to be emitted and the powder had filled more of the first floor of the process area the damage would have been more severe.

Windows and bricks were blown out on all four sides of the building, projecting bricks up to 12 metres and smaller fragments up to 30 metres. There was little pressure damage inside the building. It was estimated that there was a pressure rise of 7-16 kN/m^2. There was flame damage over an area of approximately 60 m^2.

Further serious fire damage was prevented by the operation of the sprinkler system.

Main points

- The results of an investigation into the process plant failure detailed the causes of the equipment failure and concluded with recommendations for preventing a repetition of this explosion at similar plants as follows:
- Those who design such plants or use existing plants should carry out analysis to identify possible modes of failure and to ensure that the necessary precautions to reduce the risk of failures and mitigate their effects.
- Employers using the plant should have an adequate safety policy, with effective organisation and arrangements to carry it out, to ensure that the dangers are fully appreciated and that safe systems of work are established and implemented.
- Staff employed should be properly informed of the process hazards and adequately trained to ensure safe operation of the plant and properly instructed as to the action to be taken in the event of plant failure developing.
- Proper arrangements should be made for plant maintenance to ensure that plant failure cannot initiate conditions in which an explosion might occur.
- There should be provision of suitable buildings, with adequate explosion relief, to put plant of this type in.

IMPERIAL SUGAR, GEORGIA USA, 2008

On February 7, 2008, a series of sugar dust explosions occurred at the Imperial Sugar manufacturing facility in Port Wentworth, Georgia, which resulted in 14 worker fatalities.

The primary explosion occurred in the conveyor system beneath silos 3, 2 and 1 and lofted sugar dust that had accumulated on the floors and elevated horizontal surfaces, propagating more dust explosions through the buildings. Secondary dust explosions occurred throughout the packing buildings, parts of the refinery, and the bulk sugar loading buildings causing severe damage and destruction.

Circumstances

The Imperial Sugar manufacturing facility housed a refinery that converted raw cane sugar into granulated sugar. A system of screw and belt conveyors, and bucket elevators transported granulated sugar from the refinery to three 35 metre tall sugar storage silos. It was then transported through conveyors and bucket elevators to specialty sugar processing areas and granulated sugar packaging machines.

PRINCIPLES OF FIRE AND EXPLOSION - ELEMENT C2

In 2007, Imperial Sugar installed a stainless steel frame, with top and side panels, to fully enclose each belt assembly to protect the granulated sugar from falling debris and reduce the possibility of unintentional contamination.

The enclosures were not equipped with a dust removal system and were not equipped with explosion vents. It was later determined that the panels on the belt conveyor allowed explosive concentrations of sugar dust to accumulate inside the enclosure.

Figure C2-21: West bucket elevator tower; silos 3, 2, and 1; and south packing building destroyed by the sugar dust explosions and fires.

Figure C2-22: Inadequate housekeeping, heavy dust accumulation on conduit and spilled sugar on the floor (Imperial Sugar photo 1990).

Source: U.S. Chemical Safety and Hazard Investigation (CSHI) Report No. 2008-05-I-GA September 2009.

Prior to the enclosure of the conveyor, during more than 80 years of operation, sugar dust released inside the large open volume of the silo tunnel most likely never accumulated to concentrations above the lower explosive limit (LEL).

However, after the steel belt was enclosed, sugar dust was contained and remained suspended inside the unventilated enclosed space. Because the enclosure was one-tenth the volume of the tunnel, sugar dust could easily accumulate to concentrations above the LEL. Imperial Sugar had no written policy or procedure to require the classifying of hazardous areas or require electrical devices to be used that were rated for such areas at the Port Wentworth facility.

Furthermore, multiple potential dust ignition sources were identified inside the enclosure by the investigators:

- Some electrical devices used were rated for use in hazardous areas, but non-rated devices were also installed in the same location, often near the rated devices.
- In addition, many non-hazard classified electrical devices were observed installed in dusty work areas and equipment enclosures.
- Electrical devices in dusty areas were poorly maintained, such as having missing covers or open doors on many breaker panels and other electrical enclosures.

Figure C2-23: Non-dust rated and rated electrical devices in the silo tunnel. *Source: CSHI report.*

Main points

- The investigation determined that the first dust explosion was initiated in the enclosed steel belt conveyor located below the sugar silos.
- Sugar conveying equipment was not designed or maintained to minimise the release of sugar and sugar dust into the work area.
- No explosion relief was incorporated in the conveyor enclosure.
- No consideration had been given to zoning of areas with respect to control of ignition.
- Inadequate housekeeping practices resulted in significant accumulations of combustible sugar and sugar dust on the floors and elevated surfaces throughout the packing buildings.
- Airborne combustible sugar dust accumulated above the lower explosive limit inside the newly enclosed steel belt assembly under silos 1 and 2.
- An overheated bearing in the steel belt conveyor most likely ignited a primary dust explosion.
- The primary dust explosion inside the enclosed steel conveyor belt under silos 1 and 2 led to massive secondary dust explosions and fires throughout the packing buildings.
- Imperial Sugar's emergency evacuation plans were inadequate. Emergency evacuation drills were not conducted and prompt worker notification to evacuate in the event of an emergency was inadequate.

ELEMENT C2 - PRINCIPLES OF FIRE AND EXPLOSION

C2.2 - Behaviour of structural materials, building and building contents in a fire

Behaviour of building structures and materials in fire

GENERAL CONSIDERATIONS

The properties of building materials vary considerably and may affect the ones chosen for a particular hazard situation. However, the choice of materials used may also be affected by other parameters such as economics, availability and aesthetics. The principal consideration should be to ensure that the material and its application comply with the law. All building works, with very few exceptions, are controlled by some form of building legislation. The principal aim of this legislation is that materials are used correctly so that the safety of life is ensured.

When considering the type of material to be used, and its application, the following criteria should be assessed:

- Ignitability.
- Flammability.
- Surface spread of flame.
- Heat release.
- Smoke (or gas) release.
- Fire resistance.
- Flame penetration.
- Smoke (or gas) penetration.

All the above relate to the safety of the occupants of a building, as they may affect the means of escape, whilst others factors are more important from the point of view of damage to the structure and contents.

Other considerations that may affect the choice of building materials include:

- The use or uses of the building.
- The dimensions (compartmentation) of the building.
- The design and layout, including escape routes.
- Whether or not the material will burn.
- The ability of the material to support and spread flame across its surface.
- The behaviour of the material when it is burning.
- The effects of high temperature on non-combustible materials.

The effects of fire on building materials will vary according to its application to the structure. Consideration must be given to the effects of materials being combined in use. The reaction of fire on an isolated material is likely to be entirely different to when that material is used in a different format, applied differently or used in conjunction with other materials.

FIRE PROPERTIES OF COMMON BUILDING MATERIALS AND STRUCTURAL ELEMENTS

Metals

Metals may require surface protection to minimise the danger of fire spreading by conduction. Unprotected metal used structurally may also present a danger of collapse in fire, as all metals soften and melt at high temperature. Structural steel loses 2/3rd of its strength at 600°C, at this temperature it begins to sag and distort.

In addition, metals expand when they get hot. A steel joist 10 m long will expand by 8 cm when heated to 600°C. This expansion factor, especially as the length of the beam increases, can cause walls to be pushed out with a resultant structural collapse.

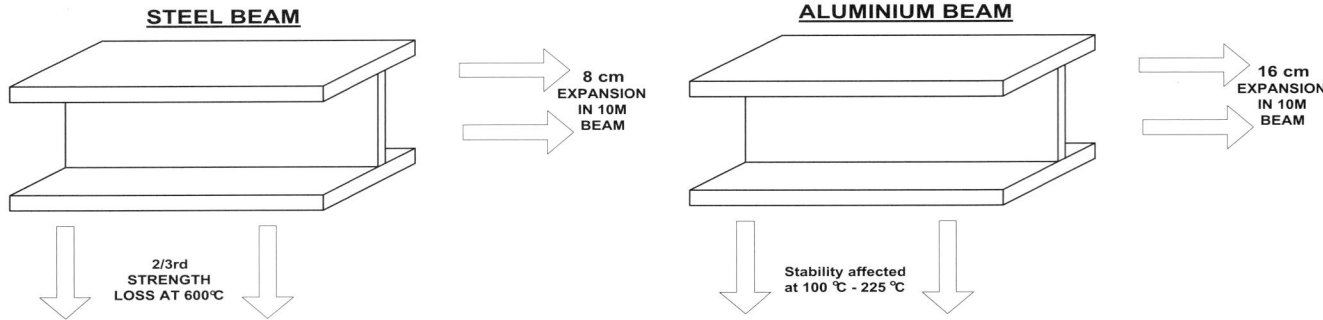

Figure C2-24: Properties of steel and aluminium beams.   Source: FST.

Aluminium alloys are now being used in building construction, because of:

- The reduction in weight (aluminium is 1/3rd the weight of steel).
- Its resistance to corrosion.
- The ease of handling and working.
- Its high strength to weight ratio.

However, these types of alloys have the following disadvantages:

- Very rapid loss of strength in fire (stability affected at 100°C - 225°C).
- High expansion rate (twice that of steel).

- High thermal conductivity (3 times that of steel) giving a greater risk of fire spread.
- Low melting points (pure aluminium 658°C).

Both steel and aluminium alloy structural members must be protected from the effects of fire. This can be done in one of the following ways:

- Solid protection.
- Hollow protection.
- Sprayed or applied mineral coatings.
- Intumescent coatings.
- Hollow section filled with water.
- By filling hollow webs of beams etc. with lightweight blocks of concrete.
- By design features such as suspended ceilings.

Concrete

Concrete is strong in compression, but weak in tension. It is therefore reinforced with steel in parts of the concrete that will be subject to tensile stress, for example, the lower half of a concrete beam. The fire resistance of concrete elements is influenced by the following:

- Size and shape of the element.
- Distribution and properties of reinforcement.
- The load being supported.
- The type of concrete and aggregate.
- Protective concrete cover provided to reinforcements.
- Conditions of end supports.

As already stated, the concrete relies heavily on reinforcement steels for its integrity in tensile conditions. If the steel reinforcement is allowed to heat up then it begins to lose strength. A point is reached at which reinforcing metals lose 50% of their strength - this point is called the 'critical temperature'. The critical temperature for mild steel reinforcements is 550°C and high yield steel reinforcements is 400°C. Reinforced concrete can also be subject to relatively lower temperature cracking and spalling, where parts of the concrete are broken away from the surface. This may be caused by expansion of the reinforcing steel or a build up of pressure caused by the heating of trapped moisture within the concrete. This can occur at temperatures as low as 200°C and can be 'explosive' in nature, tearing off layers of the concrete and exposing the reinforcing steel to higher temperatures. The reduction in cross-sectional area of the concrete may lead to its failure to bear the load on it and subsequent failure of the structure.

Bricks

Brickwork can provide a vital role as a non-combustible and fire resistant element of the structure of a building and can also be used to protect other elements of a structure from the effects of fire, for example, load bearing columns, staircases, shafts and ducts. Load bearing brickwork has inherent fire resistance and requires no further protection. The duration of fire resistance is dependent upon the thickness of the wall:

- A 100 mm brick wall gives approx. 2 hours fire resistance.
- A 200 mm brick wall gives approx. 4 hours fire resistance.

The fire resistance is also affected by the type of construction of the brick itself. If the brick is hollow cast or has holes throughout its width, then it is more susceptible to spalling, with the bottom face falling off. This would obviously reduce the fire resistance of that type of brick.

Wood

The fire resistance of wood as an element of structure depends upon the following:

- The density of the wood.
- Its thickness and cross sectional area.
- The quality of workmanship and/or detailing.

Wood has a very low thermal conductivity and this factor, combined with its production of a protective skin of charcoal in a fire, retards its rate of combustion. Carefully constructed joints that eliminate cracks and air spaces contribute substantially to fire resistance. Due to this slow rate of burning and the fact that timber will distort and sag for a considerable way before collapse occurs, it is a fairly good material to use when considering fire in buildings.

Wood can be treated with fire retardant materials to increase its safety within fires. Fire retardant coatings can be applied to wood that has a class 3 or class 4 rating for surface spread of flame, which can raise the classification to class 1.

Building boards and slabs

Fire resistance and surface spread of flame characteristics are inherent qualities of board materials. Different materials are given a different classification, some examples of which are shown in *figure ref C2-25:*

Plasterboard.	Class '0.
Wood-wool slabs.	Class '0.
Mineral fibre board.	Class '0.
Chipboard.	Class '3'.

ELEMENT C2 - PRINCIPLES OF FIRE AND EXPLOSION

Soft-board.	Class '4'.
Plywood.	Class '3'.

Figure C2-25: Material classifications.　　　　　　　　　　　　　　　　　　　　　*Source: FST.*

If the performance quality of boards is lower than may be desired, this can be increased by the addition of a layer, or impregnation, of a fire resistance substance to the board material. Escape routes and circulation spaces within buildings should have both ceilings and walls comprising materials of class '0' standard.

We should also consider the effects of the wall linings on the speed of development of a fully developed fire, for example, flashover. This is illustrated in *Figure C2-26* which is extracted from test results achieved by the Building Research Establishment.

Wall lining	**Flashover time**
Dense non-combustible material, for example, brick.	23 minutes 30 seconds.
Fibre insulating board with skim of plaster.	12 minutes.
Hardboard with 2 coats of flat oil paint.	8 minutes 15 seconds.
Non-combustible insulating material.	8 minutes.

Figure C2-26: Wall lining test results.　　　　　　　　　　　　　*Source: Building Research Establishment.*

As can be seen, even materials that are classed as being non-combustible can affect the development of a fire due to their insulating properties.

Insulated core panels ('sandwich panels')

In modern buildings one type of construction that is commonly used, but is causing great concern, is 'sandwich panels'. These consist of two outer skins of sheet metal (normally a light alloy) with an infill of heat insulating foam. In some cases, the foam used is polyurethane or styrene foam. This type of construction causes problems in buildings that are on fire, due to a sudden and unannounced building collapse as the panels fall out of their framework.

They can also cause very rapid fire spread, once the internal foam is on fire. These structures present problems to fire brigades, who on arrival at the scene of such a fire may have to consider attacking the fire from outside the building, so as not to endanger the lives of fire-fighters.

Figure C2-27: Insulated core panel (sandwich panel). *Source: HM Government, Fire Safety Guide - 1.*

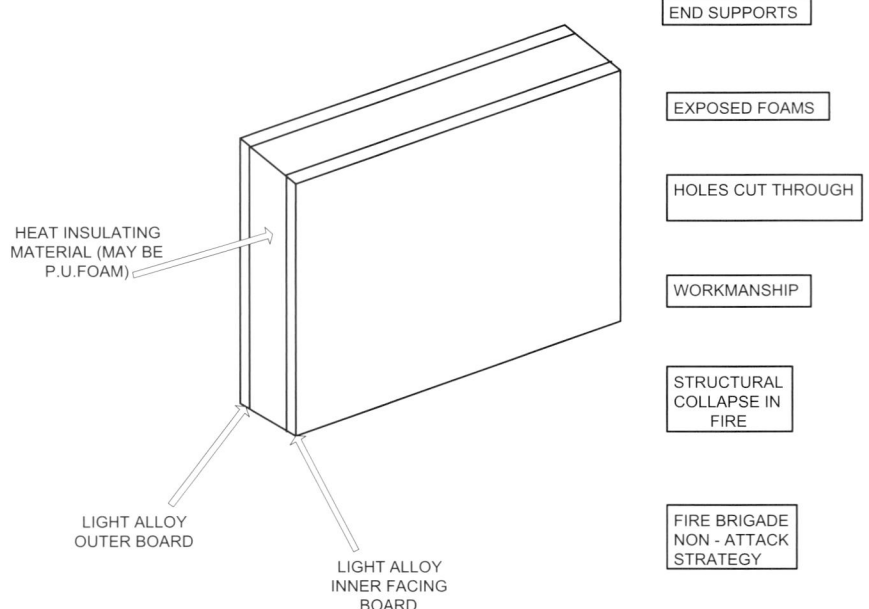

Figure C2-28: Sandwich panel (insulated core panel).　　　　　　*Source: FST.*

Glazing materials

Glass is a non-combustible material and therefore will not contribute to the fire load of a building. However, glass panels in doors or walls do provide a weak point in fires, due to their early collapse or their ability to pass radiated heat, allowing fire to spread. Fire resisting glazing can be used to give up to 1½ hours of fire resistance. The actual fire resistance duration is dependant upon the nature and dimensions of glass, the type of frame and the glazing detail.

Wired glass

This can be used to give up to 1½ hours fire resistance, dependant upon the materials and design of the frame. The glass is usually 6 mm thick and up to 1.6 square metres in area.

Laminated glass (pyran)

This type of glass is now becoming more common in use. It comprises 3 to 5 layers of glass with interlayers of intumescent material, which reacts at 120°C forming an opaque shield. This glass then prevents radiated heat passing through and can therefore be used in many more situations than the traditional wired glass.

Behaviour of common building contents in fire

FIRE SPREAD DUE TO BUILDING CONTENTS

When considering the behaviour of common building contents in fires, it is important to take into account the possibilities and effects of fire spread within a building due to the types of materials that are stored and used within it. Materials may be divided into two categories, **high** or **normal** risk. This may be based on two different tests. The first test specifies materials high or normal risk dependent upon the maximum rate of temperature rise, the second test specifies on the volume of smoke produced. As can be expected, some materials will be classified as high in one test but normal in another. These tests are used because the rate of temperature rise and the amount of smoke produced from a material in a fire will have a major influence on the occupants of the building and their immediate ability to use the means of escape provided. The tests are therefore useful in helping to make an assessment of the risk to life from the use of particular materials.

A few materials tested in this way fall into the high category in both tests, and therefore present a high risk:

- Acrylic fibre.
- Acrylic mixture.
- Acrylic over locks.
- Expanded polystyrene.
- Flexible polyether (PU foam).
- Polypropylene silver.
- Rigid PU foam (low density).

When considering the above factors, it is worth bearing in mind that a large proportion of materials can now be treated or enhanced in some way to make them less susceptible to fire. For example, fire resistant paper is available, which is intumescent based. With any fire resistance treatment it is important to know if the fire resistant properties are inherent and will therefore stay with the product throughout its life or if the fire resistance is added and therefore has a shelf life or can be diminished by actions such as cleaning/washing.

The building contents may also comprise flammable substances used in the process, which can rapidly increase fire spread. *See also - Section C2.3 - 'Segregation and storage' later in this element.*

PAPER-BASED MATERIALS AND FABRICS

Smooth hard surfaces normally will not spread flame as fast as soft or fuzzy surfaces. Thick surfacing materials will usually spread flame more slowly than thin materials, but studies indicate that flame spread is relatively independent of thickness for most materials thicker than 6 mm. The absorption of heat by base materials to which a finish material may be applied will tend to reduce the rate of surface burning, provided there is intimate contact between the two surfaces. This is most significant where thin surfacing materials are concerned. The method of fastening the surfacing material to the base material is very important. The moisture content of a material can also affect the rate of surface spread of flame, particularly with cellulosic materials, as can the proportion of combustible matter it contains.

Fire retardant paper is available and may be used for wall linings. Fabrics, such as those used in furnishings, carpets and blinds, may be treated at time of manufacture with fire retarding substances to limit the effects of fire.

PLASTICS

There are two basic types of plastic:

1) Thermoplastics - which will soften and melt when heated, allowing the plastic to be shaped and re-shaped. It has low fire resistant characteristics and readily melts in a fire. These include nylon, acrylics, polythene, PVC, ABS and polystyrene.
2) Thermosetting - which undergoes a chemical change when heated and sets to a hard infusible form. To a degree they resist heat and fire. These include melamine formaldehyde, phenol formaldehyde, urea and polyester resin.

Thermoplastics melt at relatively low temperatures, temperatures that develop in a fire can cause the plastic to melt and allow burning parts of the plastic item to fall onto other materials, aiding fire spread.

Though thermosetting plastics can have an amount of fire resistance, the temperatures created by fire can cause combustion of the plastics and failure of plastic structures. It is important to remember that most plastics involved in fire emit a large amount of smoke and toxic fumes. Many types of expanded cellular plastics linings can be a very serious hazard if unprotected and may be a cause for concern when they are protected, if the protection provided is insufficient or ineffective. Unprotected expanded cellular plastics linings or those with only thin surface protection should be regarded as likely to present a high risk unless their performance has been checked in tests.

Behaviour of structural materials and contents relating to actual incidents

WINDSOR CASTLE FIRE, 1992

A fire occurred in the Private Chapel at Windsor Castle on the 20th November 1992, whilst the Castle was undergoing restoration work, including improvements to fire prevention and detection.

Circumstances

The fire was caused by the inadvertent use of a spot light, to the rear of curtains in the Chapel at a height of between 3 and 5 metres. The cotton backing of the curtains was exposed to heat from the light, which in turn caused the wool intermediate lining to become overheated, ultimately setting alight to the brocade outer facing fabric of the curtain.

The fire developed rapidly, assisted by the surface spread of flame across untreated (absence of fire resistant coatings) wood panelled walls, some covered with silk, exacerbated in many areas by the hanging of paintings, tapestries and by the large uninterrupted, high level ceiling void running the entire length (60 metres) of the St. Georges hall. Fire spread was rapid, assisted by voids in the structure, including false ceiling, gaps between panelling and flooring that extended for long distances, the absence of fire resistant glass, fire doors or compartmentalisation between rooms.

Main points

Prior to the fire the fire authority had expressed views about the adequacy of the fire protection in the Castle, which being Crown property was outside their authority. The report (E2 WCF 18003, 20th November 1992) by Her Majesty's Chief Inspector of Fire Services made a number of detailed recommendations including:

- An automatic fire detection system should be installed throughout the Castle.
- The Castle should be upgraded to limit fire spread to a standard that would be acceptable to meet current Codes of Practice or Building regulations.
- Training should be provided to Castle staff, including the internal fire brigade.

CHANNEL TUNNEL FIRE, 2008

On 21 August 2006 a fire broke out on a shuttle train travelling from the UK to France. The train was brought to a controlled stop 20.5 km from the UK portal and all 34 people on board were evacuated without injury.

Cirumstances

The immediate cause of the incident was a fire in the load compartment of a goods vehicle on the penultimate wagon of the HGV shuttle. The goods vehicle was transporting packaging material comprising rolls of corrugated paper, brown paper, empty wooden boxes, sheeted cardboard and also a chair.

Before the shuttle entered the tunnel, smoke had begun to emerge in discrete puffs from the top of the load compartment of the goods vehicle. This was recorded by an unmonitored security camera located some 100 metres from the entrance to the tunnel and facing towards the tunnel.

The first detection of smoke was by a fixed tunnel smoke detector station located in the Running Tunnel North, as the shuttle entered the tunnel.

The heat of the fire caused the overhead catenary to become parted and the tunnel concrete lining was damaged to a depth of about 30 mm, exposing steel reinforcement at the crown of the tunnel in the proximity of the fire over a length of 10 m.

Main points

The fire investigators established the likely cause of the fire in the vehicle was a cigarette, discarded whilst the vehicle was being loaded, emphasising the need to prohibit smoking when loading vehicles.

BUNCEFIELD, 2005

See Element C2.1 for Buncefield.

WINDSOR TOWER FIRE (MADRID), 2005

The Windsor Tower, in Madrid, was completely gutted by fire on 12 February 2005, when floor slabs above the 17th floor progressively collapsed due to buckling of unprotected steel perimeter columns. The transfer structure at the 17th floor level resisted further collapse of the building.

PRINCIPLES OF FIRE AND EXPLOSION - ELEMENT C2

Circumstances

The Windsor Tower was a 32-storey concrete building (3 stories below ground) with a reinforced concrete central core. A typical floor of the building comprised two-way spanning slabs supported by the concrete core, internal reinforced concrete columns with additional internal steel beams and steel perimeter columns. The Windsor Tower's original structural design (whilst in compliance with the Spanish building codes in 1970) did not require fire protection to steelwork and the initialisation of water sprinkler systems for fire protection of the building.

Main points

The fire was believed to have been caused by an electrical short-circuit on the 21st floor during, a three year refurbishment programme, including improvements to:

- Fire protection to the perimeter steel columns using a board cladding system.
- Fire protection to the internal steel beams using a spray intumescent protection.
- Installation of a water sprinkler system.
- A fire protected escape stair.
- A new aluminium cladding system.

When the fire occurred, fire protection for all steelwork below the 17th floor had been completed except for a proportion of the 9th and 15th floors (which all buckled in the fire, but did not collapse). When the fire spread below the 17th floor, the protected perimeter columns survived and the remaining structure did not collapse.

The original concrete reinforced steel central column of the structure remained intact, preventing a total collapse of the structure.

New escape stair survived in the fire

Perimeter slabs largely collapsed (5m ~ 10m deep)

South-west view

Figure C2-29: Collapse of upper floors. *Source: www.911myths.com.*

SUMMIT TUNNEL FIRE, 1984

The fire occurred in the Summit Tunnel on 20 December 1984 when a goods train carrying more than 1,000,000 litres of petrol, in thirteen tankers, caught fire in the Yorkshire (north) side of the tunnel.

Circumstances

One-third of the way through the tunnel, a defective axle bearing derailed the fourth tanker, which promptly knocked those behind it off the track. Only the locomotive and the first three tankers remained on the rails. One of the derailed tankers fell on its side and began to leak petrol into the tunnel. Investigators determined that vapour from the leaking petrol was probably ignited by a hot axle box.

Following the fire, the damage caused by the fire to the tunnel was found to be minimal. About 800 metres of track had to be replaced, together with all the electrical services and signalling. The brick lining (six layers thick) had stood up remarkably well, most of the tunnel was scorched, but still serviceable. Although bricks in the area of the blast relief shafts had become vitrified by the intense heat (at least 1400°C.) and had flowed like molten glass.

The tunnel's builder; George Stephenson, stated at the tunnels unauguration: "I stake my reputation and my head that the tunnel will never fail so as to injure any human life".

Main points

- Fire fighters in the tunnel, when it filled with flames, were saved by the fact that blast relief shafts 8 and 9 acted as flame vents (although they were not designed for that purpose).
- The amount of damage to the primary structure of the tunnel was minimal.

C2.3 - Fire and explosion prevention and protection

Structural protection

The spread of fire from the point of origin to other parts of the same building results from the same processes as that which establishes fire growth at the point of origin, i.e. by conduction, convection and radiation. Fires spread, firstly, by radiant heat, hot gases and smoke passing through any existing gaps or openings in the surrounding construction (including doorways).

Secondly, by burning through or opening up gaps within the construction and thirdly by heat conducted through the construction - so igniting combustible materials in direct contact or in close proximity to the other side. The fire and hot gases will then spread along any available routes such as corridors, stair and lift wells, service ducts and cavities.

OPENINGS

In order to prevent fire spread it is important to ensure that the separating elements of construction (walls, floors, supporting elements and doors) have the necessary fire resistance and those gaps and other openings in or between elements are properly fire-stopped. Openings should be protected by the provision of fire barriers, such as shutters, cavity barriers and fire curtains. Attention must also be paid to the design of details involving ducts, pipes and services passing through fire-resisting walls and floors - particularly those elements forming the enclosures to fire compartments and to escape routes.

VOIDS

A particular hazard exists in extensive voids in horizontal or vertical constructions, which, if fire penetrates them, act as 'chimneys' or 'flues' that convey flames and hot gases over considerable distances. This can be greatly aggravated when the voids are lined with combustible materials.

COMPARTMENTATION

When designing to prevent the spread of fire from the point of origin, various parts of a building may be required to be enclosed or separated by fire-resisting construction, the most notable technique being called *compartmentalisation*. A fire compartment can be defined as:

'*a building or part of a building, comprising one or more rooms, spaces or storeys, constructed to prevent the spread of fire to or from another part of the same building, or an adjoining building*'.

Requirements for compartmentalisation are generally based on the occupancy and size of buildings. When considering the size of compartments, consideration can be given to the installation of a sprinkler system. In general the size of a compartment can be doubled if there is a sprinkler system installed.

Key features of plant design and process control

DESIGN OF PLANT

Risk assessments must be made to ascertain if a fire or explosion risk exists. If this is the case, then prevention measures must be taken.

Sources of ignition

Elimination of one of the conditions needed for a fire or explosion to occur - removal of ignition sources - the main ones being:

- Flames.
- Hot surfaces.
- Incandescent materials.
- Spontaneous heating.
- Welding or cutting operations.
- Friction or impact sparks, for example, foreign body in process.
- Electric sparks.
- Electrostatic discharge sparks.

Process plant

- Plant separation should be provided to minimise the total amount of dust available to the explosion, physical separation by distance is preferred. Where plant must be linked for production purposes then 'chokes' (which act as plant separators) such as screw conveyors and rotary valves should be installed.
- Plant should be designed to withstand and contain a fire or explosion whenever possible; also the use of inert gases, such as nitrogen, may be appropriate in enclosed plant or machinery.
- Provision of view panels and sensors to detect if flammable/explosive material feed systems are operating correctly is an important consideration at the design stage.

Vapour dust removal

- Where there is a risk of vapour or dust release it should be captured at the source by a local exhaust ventilation system. Centralised dust collection systems are usually preferred, since all the extracted material is controlled in one area, which can be zoned according to the hazard.
- Alternatively, dedicated extraction systems, drawing vapours or dust from a small number of locations, may be used to reduce the risk of large scale explosive ignition occurring.
- All dust collection systems can create routes that enable burning material to spread when a fire or explosion occurs, this should be controlled by the installation of early detection and close down systems.

Intermediate and final storage

- Contents gauges and level alarms should be provided to all process and storage vessels.
- Where the risk of overfill is high, consideration should be given to an overflow collector vessel to prevent uncontrolled spillage from the primary vessel.

Other considerations

Design plant/workplace to prevent a build up of dust or other flammable residues, including:

- Negate horizontal surfaces, for example, incline light fittings to at least 60°.
- Use of false ceilings to prevent dust settling on roof beams.
- Internal walls should be smooth and washable.
- Floor/wall joints to be curved to prevent build up in corners.

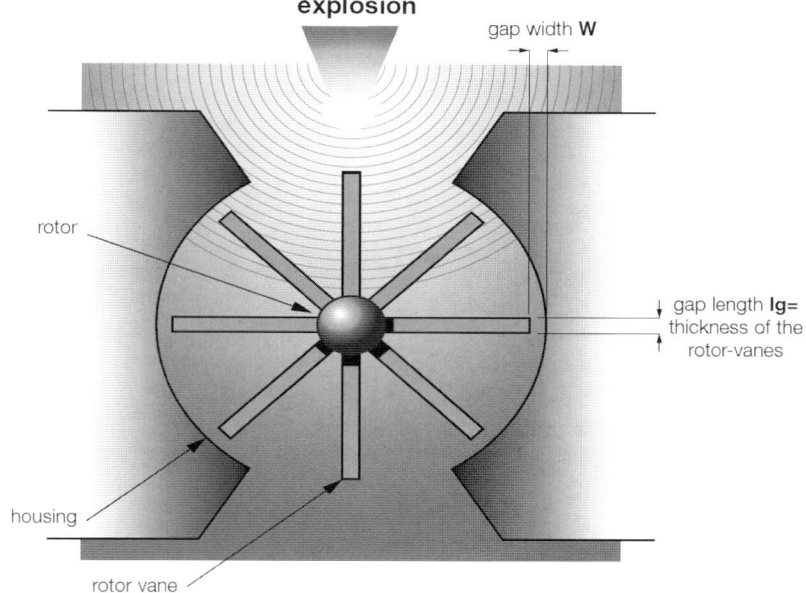

Figure C2-30: Important dimensions of rotary valves used as chokes. *Source: HSG103.*

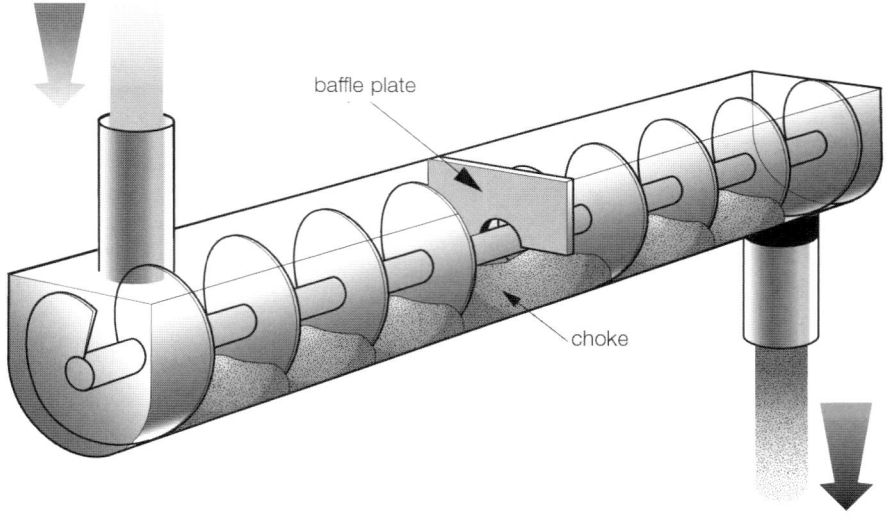

Figure C2-31: The use of a screw conveyor as an explosion choke. *Source: HSG103.*

PROCESS CONTROLS

Various plant controls may be important in controlling the possibility of fires and explosion. Listed *below* are some typical issues that may need to be controlled.

- If powdered products are being dried, the maximum safe temperature that equipment can be operated at must be known, so as to prevent auto-ignition of the powder.
- Plant should be interlocked to ensure ignition sources are removed before tasks are conducted that can release flammable/explosive materials.
- Overloading or blockage of feed systems may cause machinery to overheat. This may need to be detected by a system control, rather than reliance upon operators to see the problem.
- Air pressures may need to be monitored to detect system failures such as faulty relief panels, or collection bag failure, both of which would cause large volumes of dust to escape into the air.
- Local exhaust ventilation should be interlocked so that the process can only run if the ventilation system is operating correctly.
- Automatic monitoring of the atmosphere outside plant to determine leaks that could lead to an explosive atmosphere being created.

ELEMENT C2 - PRINCIPLES OF FIRE AND EXPLOSION

- Detection may need to be installed after a grinding plant, so that any sparks or potential ignition sources can be detected and extinguished before they create an explosion.
- Process controls should be in place so that any deviation from a safe working condition will cause the operation to close down.

MITIGATION MEASURES

The most important mitigation measure is maintaining the plant and process workplace in a clean condition; this includes:

- Regular and efficient housekeeping system to remove waste.
- Regular cleaning of horizontal surfaces so as to remove accumulated dust and the secondary explosion risk.

Segregation and storage of flammable, combustible and incompatible materials

SEGREGATION AND STORAGE

Precautions for the storage of high fire and explosion hazard materials should be risk assessed to comply with the Regulatory Reform (Fire Safety) Order 2005 and the results should be included within the organisation's fire risk assessment records. Where this legislation does not relate to the circumstances the general duties of the Health and Safety at Work Act 1974 should be followed and the material should be stored in a way that ensures safety, so far as is reasonably practicable.

Ideally, a material assessed as being a high fire or explosion hazard should be stored in a separate area to ensure adequate segregation from processes that could initiate a fire, either in a separate building or in a single storey extension to the main building or in a safe place in the open air - with suitable weather protection.

Except as discussed below, where it is not reasonably practicable to avoid locating the storage area in an occupied building the store should be separated from the rest of the premises by partitions of not less than 30 minutes fire resisting construction. High fire or explosion hazard materials should not normally be stored below an occupied floor or in a basement. Where such materials are kept in the same building as domestic or other occupied premises, separation of not less than 1 hour fire resisting construction should be provided between storage and occupied areas. Fire separation can also be established by distance, the distance necessary being influenced by the quantity being stored.

Quantity stored (litres)	Distance from occupied building, boundary, process unit, flammable liquid storage tank or fixed ignition source (metres)
Up to 1,000	2
1,000 - 100,000	4
Above 100,000	7.5
The **maximum stack size** should be 300,000 litres, with at least 4 metres between stacks.	
Containers should not be stored within the bund of a fixed flammable liquid storage tank or within 1 metre of the bund wall.	

Figure C2-32: Minimum separation for flammable liquids. *Source: HSE, HSG51.*

The layout and operation of storage areas outside the work area should be carefully planned. The storage arrangements should ensure segregation of flammable and combustible materials from incompatible materials, for example, oxidising substances should be segregated from flammable substances. The layout should provide for the stable and safe storage of all materials and should allow ready access to all parts of the store for both people and fork lift trucks. The methods of stacking and mechanical handling adopted will be determined by the needs of the organisation, but when the store is designed due regard should be given to the effect that a fire in the store could have on the premises and its occupants. Matters such as stack heights, clearance around and above the aisle widths and total quantities stored should be considered as part of the overall assessment of fire risk.

A store should be used exclusively for storage. Production and ancillary processes, especially any that might introduce sources of ignition, for example, shrink wrapping of the product onto trays and fork lift truck battery charging, should be excluded. Where this standard cannot be achieved and it is necessary to carry out such operations, they should be separated from the materials stored by a safe distance or carried out in a separate bay set aside for the purpose.

Smoking should be prohibited in all storage areas and other ignition sources excluded. For example, direct fired heaters or heaters with high surface temperatures capable of igniting the material should not normally be used.

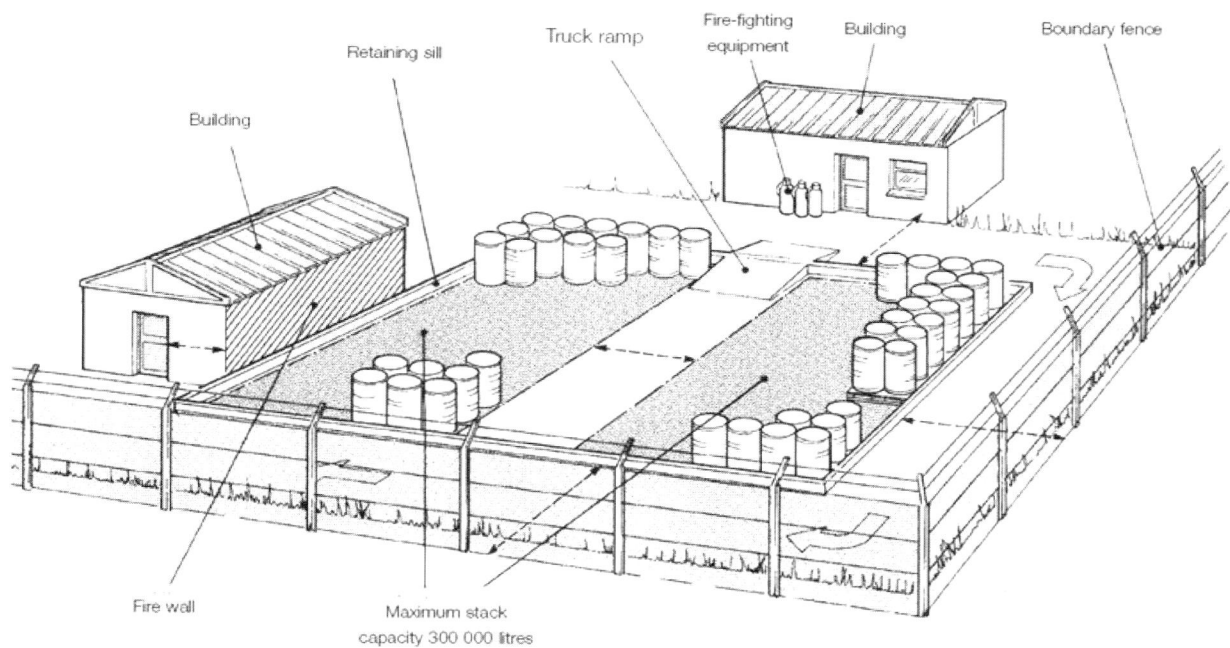

Figure C2-33: General layout of external store for flammable liquids. *Source: HSE, HSG51.*

Where it is necessary to introduce a source of ignition, for example, when conducting maintenance work involving 'hot work' such as welding, cutting or grinding, there should be clear instructions on any additional fire precautions required and close supervision provided, preferably including a permit-to-work system. The work area should be inspected for signs of smouldering fires immediately on completion of the job and once or twice during the following hour.

Access to storage areas should be restricted. The number of people working in the areas should be limited and, where possible, other workers in the premises should not have to pass through the storage area or use it as their only means of escape from the premises.

In some premises, it may not be reasonably practicable to provide a separate store, but safe storage can be achieved by other means. In assessing whether the arrangements provided for storage are adequate in such cases it will be necessary to consider the characteristics and quantity of materials stored, the conditions of storage and use, the nature of the building and the adequacy of emergency procedures and fire precautions.

Examples of situations where separate storage facilities may not be required include:

- Where the quantity stored is insignificant compared with that required for work in progress.
- Where finished or partly finished goods present a reduced fire risk because of their form, outer covering or packaging.
- Where a single storey building has a large volume of free space at ceiling level, so that there is no risk of smoke logging during the early stages of a fire and where the disposition of stored materials has been taken into account in the general fire precautions.
- Where safe storage can be achieved by other means, for example, by spatial separation, the provision of fire or smoke detectors, linked to an alarm system, water-spray protection, automatic smoke vents and smoke curtains (using one or more of these as circumstances dictate).

Where flammable liquids are used, there is likely to be a need to store a limited quantity in the work area. It is important that only the minimum quantity for frequently occurring activities is stored. Typically this should be no more than was required during half a day or one shift, to meet the approved code of practice to the Dangerous Substances and Explosive Atmospheres Regulations (DSEAR) 2002.

When not in use containers should be kept closed and stored in suitable fire resisting cabinets or bins that contain spills (110% of the volume of the largest container stored). Stores should be located away from the process area. The flammable liquids should be stored separately from other dangerous substances that increase the fire risk or might affect the integrity of the container/store, for example, oxidisers and corrosive substances.

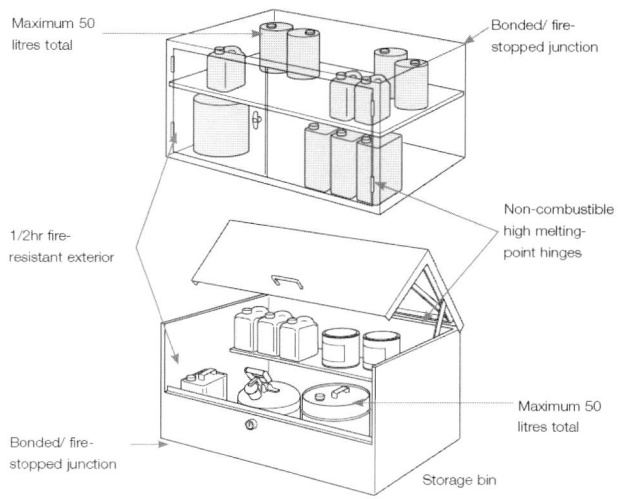

Figure C2-34: Work area storage - flammable liquids. *Source: HSG51.*

ELEMENT C2 - PRINCIPLES OF FIRE AND EXPLOSION

It is recommended that the maximum quantities that may be stored in the work area in this way be no more than 50 litres of extremely, highly flammable and those flammable liquids with a flashpoint below the ambient temperature of the work area. The amount for other flammable liquids with a higher flashpoint of up to 50°C is 250 litres.

The HSE set out in their document HSG51 "The storage of flammable liquids in containers", five general principles for ensuring that the risks of fire and explosion from the storage of flammable liquids in containers are controlled and minimised.

"An aid to remembering these five principles is the acronym 'VICES'. There is no order of priority of the principles implied by the use of the acronym.

V   Ventilation

Is there plenty of fresh air where containers are stored? Good ventilation means vapours given off from a spill, leak, or release, will be rapidly dispersed.

I   Ignition

Have all ignition sources been removed from the storage area? Ignition sources can vary widely. They include sparks from electrical equipment or welding and cutting tools, hot surfaces, smoking, and open flames from heating equipment.

C   Containment

Are your flammable liquids stored in suitable containers? Will a spillage be contained and prevented from spreading to other parts of the storage area or site? A means of controlling spillage would be the use of an impervious sill or low bund. An alternative is to drain the area to a safe place, such as a remote sump or a separator.

E   Exchange

Can you exchange a flammable liquid for a less flammable one? This is a basic question you should always ask. Can you eliminate the storage of flammable liquids from your operation altogether?

S   Separation

Are flammable liquids stored well away from other processes and general storage areas? Can they be separated by a physical barrier, wall or partition?"

FLAMMABLE

Flammable is defined as 'capable of burning with a flame'. Flammable liquids are classed as:

- Extremely flammable - liquids with a flashpoint lower than 0°C and a boiling point lower than or equal to 35°C.
- Highly flammable - liquids with a flashpoint lower than 21°C but which are not extremely flammable.
- Flammable - with a flash point lower than 55°C, but which are not extremely or highly flammable.

COMBUSTIBLE

Combustible is defined as capable of 'burning'. Combustible dusts can be created from many materials, such as coal, wood, grain and sugar. Many solid materials may be combustible and when stored in large quantities represent a significant fire risk, for example, paper, wood and textiles.

INCOMPATIBLE MATERIALS

Incompatible materials are materials that should not be mixed together due to the interaction or reaction between them. Some materials may be incompatible because one may be a fuel and the other an oxidiser; oxidisers promote the combustion process vigorously.

Hazardous area zoning

Areas where explosions may occur are divided into zones. Each zone is classified dependant upon the likelihood and persistence of an explosive atmosphere being created. Classification of hazardous area zoning for *gases, vapours and mists* is:

Zone 0   Explosive atmosphere in air with gas, vapour or mist present continuously, or for long periods of time.

Zone 1   Explosive atmosphere in air with gas, vapour or mist likely to occur in normal operation occasionally.

Zone 2   Explosive atmosphere in air with gas, vapour or mist not likely to occur in normal operation, but if it does it will be for a short period only.

Classification of hazardous area zoning for *dusts* is:

Zone 20   Explosive atmosphere in air with a cloud of combustible dust present continuously or for long periods of time.

Zone 21   Explosive atmosphere in air with a cloud of combustible dust likely to occur in normal operation occasionally.

Zone 22   Explosive atmosphere in air with a cloud of combustible dust is not likely to occur in normal operation, but if it does it will be for a short period only.

Exclusion of ignition sources

In hazardous areas, ignition sources are often controlled by using zoning to illustrate the likely presence of explosive atmospheres. By using this information, and for example the ATEX marking scheme for electrical equipment, verification can be made that ignition sources related to electrical equipment are approved for use in the explosive atmospheres that are present. In this way, ignition sources may be excluded from areas where flammable atmospheres may be present.

Other sources of ignition can include friction causing hot surfaces, vehicles, heat sources, hot pipework, welding equipment, and grinding equipment. The zoning also helps to identify where these other ignition sources need to be controlled by engineering methods and permit to work systems.

Inerting

'Inerting' means the displacement of the atmosphere by a non-reactive gas to such an extent that the resulting atmosphere is non-combustible. The inert gas replaces the oxygen in the air to such an extent that combustion is not viable. Inert gases that may be used include nitrogen, carbon dioxide, argon, or helium.

The process of inerting is similar to the use of a portable carbon dioxide gas fire extinguisher to extinguish a fire. Inerting is most effective when applied to confined atmospheres where the risk of ingress of oxygen to displace the inert gas can be controlled. The inert gas is held in the confined atmosphere at a pressure slightly above atmospheric in order to minimise oxygen ingress. However, leaks of the inert gas to the workplace atmosphere could take place.

Inerting can be used as a preventative measure where inerting enables a process with a significant risk of fire or explosion to take place in a manner that prevents a fire or explosion. It may also be applied as a reactive measure, flooding the space where a fire or explosion is detected with inert gas to stop the combustion process.

Inerting produces an immediately dangerous to life or health (IDLH) oxygen-deficient atmosphere. If the space inerted is large and entry to it is required, this should only be done using self-contained breathing apparatus (SCBA).

Many factors will influence the overall reliability of an inerting system. The Health and Safety Executive (HSE) suggest the following examples in their document HSG103 "Safe handling of combustible dusts":

- Location and number of atmospheric sampling points.
- Type of sensor head.
- Frequency of calibration of the sensor.
- Contaminants in the system that interfere with sensor readings.
- Provision of safe means of control or shutdown, if the oxygen concentration exceeds a predetermined level.
- Adequate supplies of inert gas for all foreseeable needs.
- Number of locations where air may enter the plant.
- Safety margin allowed when setting control levels for oxygen.
- Reliability of any electronic control system.

Methods of explosion relief

VENTING/EXPLOSION PANELS

Venting is the most common system used for explosion relief and involves incorporating deliberate points of weakness in the plant and buildings. The objective is to prevent the explosion pressure from exceeding the design strength of the plant or building. This is normally done by the use of lightweight roofs, lightweight wall panels, louvres and vents.

The venting must be designed to the correct size and installed in the correct place for an explosion to be efficiently vented to outside. The size of vents required will depend upon the explosion properties of the flammable or combustible material involved, the strength of the plant or building and the opening pressure of the vents.

To operate successfully an explosion relief vent must open reliably at a pressure well below that which the plant or building it is protecting can withstand. It must also open instantaneously and fully. They must be sited such that they are not too close to an obstruction or wall as this may limit release of the explosion.

Vent panels may become dangerous missiles in the event of an explosion, so they may need to be fixed to the plant or building with chains, or some similar device. Care needs to be taken to site the vents to prevent the fireball or pressure wave that is produced in an explosion from creating further dangers.

BURSTING DISCS

Certain plant and machinery will have explosion relief built into it in the form of a bursting disc. This is a purpose designed weak spot, which ruptures at a predetermined pressure and immediately vents the over pressure safely; to prevent a more damaging over pressurisation and an explosion occurring.

ELEMENT C2 - PRINCIPLES OF FIRE AND EXPLOSION

CONTAINMENT AND SUPPRESSION

It may not be possible or desirable to provide explosion relief venting, and a method of explosion containment or suppression may need to be installed.

An explosion may develop pressures up to 1,000 kPa (10 bars), which buildings cannot withstand, but small items of plant, such as grinding equipment, may be designed to contain the pressure rise. This method is not usually cost-effective on larger items of plant or machinery.

An explosion suppression system will detect an explosion in its early stages by detecting a pressure increase. The system will then inject an extinguishing agent (often dry powder) into the path of the explosion so that the flame front is extinguished, and the explosion stops.

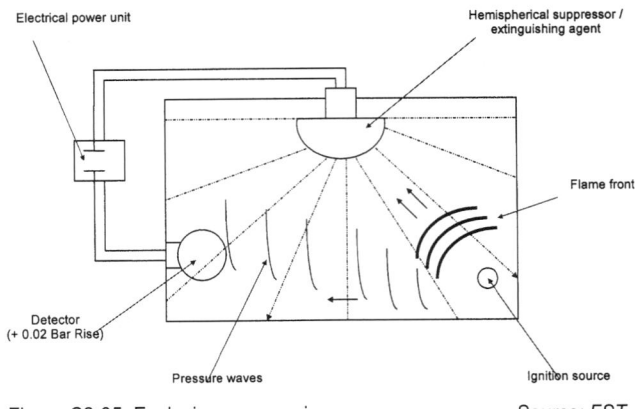

Figure C2-35: Explosion suppression. Source: FST.

C2.4 - Major accidents

The contribution of typical mechanical and systems failures to major accidents

FLIXBOROUGH, HICKSON AND WELCH AND BUNCEFIELD

Please refer to earlier in the element.

PIPER ALPHA, 6 JULY 1988

A series of explosions occurred on the Piper Alpha platform on the 6th July 1988 killing 167 people. The platform owned by Occidental Petroleum, was a key platform in the UK's North Sea oil production. At its peak it accounted for 10% of British North Sea oil production. Standing about 30 metres above the surface of the water, it was designed to accommodate over 200 men.

Circumstances

A pump had been shut down during the day shift, using a permit to work, in order to remove a safety pressure valve for recertification. A blind flange assembly was put in its place. At the end of the working day the suspended permit was returned to the control room, but not displayed.

During the night the working pump failed and the night shift switched to and started the pump that was fitted with the blind flange. Condensate entered the relief line and gas escaped from the flange assembly, which was not airtight.

Main findings

A public enquiry was held headed by Lord Cullen.

The explosion was due, in part, to management failure within a permit to work system, but failing in the design of the rig included:

- The containment wall where the gas was released was fire, but not blast resistant.
- The location of gas pipelines that ended where the oil fire had started and, as consequence, ruptured in the heat and caused an explosion that engulfed the rig in thousands of tonnes of burning gas.
- The accommodation block, whilst flame resistant, did not provide a flame or explosion proof safe exit to the lifeboats.

Permit to work system

- The valve locking off procedure was not included in the permit.
- The permit was not displayed in the work area.
- Work on the suspended pump had not been inspected by the designating authorities (DAs) to ensure it had been correctly isolated.
- DAs were not trained in inspection and permit issue.
- Although the permit system was monitored and frequently audited, failures had not been identified or actions had not been implemented. This included common deviations, such as the inclusion of multiple jobs on one permit and poor or inaccurate description of work to be carried out.

Lord Cullen's report concluded that Occidental had "adopted a superficial attitude" to safety, as they had been made aware of the problems in a report provided to them 12 months prior to the incident.

"The safety policy and procedures were in place: the practice was deficient".

Figure C2-36: Piper Alpha extract. Source: Extract from Lord Cullen's report into the Piper Alpha disaster.

GRANGEMOUTH, 1987

The HSE report describes three separate maintenance related incidents at BP Oil Grangemouth Refinery Limited, which resulted in the deaths of five contractors.

BP incident 1 grangemouth

Circumstances

On the 13th March 1987 gallons of inflammable fuel were released when a valve was removed from a flare system by contractors, the drain line, which was of small diameter, had become blocked with pyrophoric (material with potential for spontaneous ignition in air) scale before the valve was released, preventing the drainage of hydrocarbon. A flammable vapour cloud formed from the rapidly spreading pool of liquid released and was ignited by a nearby air compressor.

Main findings

- Potential ignition sources had not been rigorously excluded, means of escape were inadequate.
- Permit to work procedures had been devised and were being implemented without sufficient awareness or identification of the hazards.

BP incident 2 grangemouth

Circumstances

A major explosion and fire occurred in the hydrocracker plant on 22 March 1987 when the plant was being put back into service after repairs following maintenance by contractors. The sequence of events followed the manual opening, at least three times, of an air operated control valve on the high pressure (HP) separator. This action allowed the remaining liquid in the HP separator to drain away and for high pressure gas to break through into the low pressure (LP) separator. As the pressure relief on the LP separator had been designed for a fire relief incident, not a gas breakthrough, the vessel subsequently exploded.

Main findings

- The control valve did not close automatically because the low level trip on the HP separator had been disconnected several years earlier.
- The operators did not trust the main level control reading and referred to a chart recorder for a back up level reading.
- There was an offset on this chart recorder, which led them to incorrectly assume that the level in the HP separator was normal.

BP incident 3 scotland

Circumstances

A fire within a crude oil storage tank in the BP Dalmeny Oil Storage Terminal on 11 June 1987 killed one man who was removing the thick sludge that had accumulated at the bottom of the tank. Ignition was caused by smoking and there had been persistent deliberate evasion of safety rules by some of the contractor's team.

Main findings

- Safety rules had not been effectively enforced by either the contractor or the refinery operator. Terminal rules required all matches and lighters to be surrendered at the security gate, but this was not enforced.
- Employee, contractor violations of this type are highly susceptible to management influence, as most underlying causes of system violations are created by management, accepted by management or condoned as normal working practice by management neglect.

ALLIED COLLOIDS LTD, 1992

On the 21st July 1992 an intense fire broke out in a storeroom in the raw materials warehouse of Allied Colloids Ltd, in West Yorkshire. Firewater run-off caused significant river pollution and was reported as a major accident to the EC, as required by the SEVESO Directive.

Circumstances

The fire was preceded by the rupture of containers of azodiisobutyronitrile (AZDN), which were kept at high level in a storeroom within the raw materials warehouse and, as far as can be determined, were accidentally heated by an adjacent, leaking steam condensate pipe. AZDN is an unstable, flammable solid when heated, with a self-accelerating decomposition temperature (SADT) of 50°C. AZDN is incompatible (violent exothermic reaction) with oxidising chemicals. The HSE investigation team concluded that AZDN powder released from rupturing drums came into contact with oxidising agents, such as sodium persulphate, in the storeroom, causing the subsequent major fire.

Main findings

- Incompatible substances should be segregated.
- Equal priority should be given to assessing risks in all areas, including non-production departments or warehouses.

ELEMENT C2 - PRINCIPLES OF FIRE AND EXPLOSION

- Safety related engineering maintenance requests should be specifically identified and given the appropriate priority according to risk potential.
- Managers, supervisors and operators of chemical warehouses should receive adequate training in their duties and specifically in respect of the placement and segregation requirements for chemical storage.
- Organisations should ensure that they are able to advise emergency services and other relevant public authorities of the potential toxicity of products of combustion from mixed chemical fires on their premises.
- Sites where fire water run-off could create a major environmental accident should consider, with relevant bodies, how best to contain fire water run-off or to mitigate any effects it might have.
- Organisations should regularly monitor and audit their safety performance in storage facilities.

Element C3

Workplace fire risk assessment

Learning outcomes

The intended learning outcomes are that the student will be able to:

C3.1 Outline the main legal requirements for fire safety in the workplace.
C3.2 Explain the processes involved in the identification of hazards and the assessment of risk from fire.
C3.3 Describe common fire detection and alarm systems and procedures.
C3.4 Outline the factors to be considered when selecting fixed and portable fire-fighting equipment for the various types of fire.
C3.5 Outline the factors to be considered in the provision and maintenance of means of escape.
C3.6 Explain the purpose of, and essential requirements for, emergency evacuation procedures.

Content

C3.1 - Legal requirements...71
    The regulatory powers of a fire authority with respect to fire safety...71
    Dual enforcement 73
    Requirements of the RRFSO 2005...73
    Reference to the Building Regulations 76
C3.2 - Identification of hazards and the assessment of risk from fire 76
    Fire hazards and assessment of risk..76
    Five steps to fire risk assessment..77
C3.3 - Fire detection and alarm systems and procedures 83
    Factors in design and application of fire detection and alarm systems 83
    Principal components of Alarm systems - detection and signalling..87
    Manual and automatic systems 89
C3.4 - Fixed and portable fire-fighting equipment..90
    Classification of fires..90
    Extinguishing media and mode of action...90
    Design and application of fixed fire-fighting systems/equipment..92
    Siting, maintenance and training requirements - fixed fire fighting systems 98
    Portable fire fighting equipment 99
    Siting, maintenance and training requirements - portable fire fighting systems............................ 103
    Environment, including fire water runoff 104
C3.5 - Means of escape 104
    Factors to be considered in the provision and maintenance of a means of escape 104
    General requirements for means of escape 107
C3.6 - Emergency evacuation procedures.. 113
    Purposes of and essential requirements for evacuation arrangements 113
    Provision of fire wardens and their role 118
    Emergency evacuation plans.. 118

ELEMENT C3 - WORKPLACE FIRE RISK ASSESSMENT

Relevant statutory provisions

Regulatory Reform (Fire Safety) Order (RRFSO) 2005
Fire Safety (Scotland) Regulations (FSSR) 2006
Fire (Scotland) Act (FSA) 2005
Health and Safety at Work etc Act (HASAWA) 1974
Management of Health and Safety at Work Regulations (MHSWR) 1999
Building Regulations (BR) 2000, Approved Document B
Health and Safety (Safety Signs and Signals) Regulations (SSSR) 1996

Tutor references

Regulatory Reform (Fire Safety) Order 2005 - A short guide to making your premises safe from fire, June 2006
Fire Safety Risk Assessment - Offices and Shops, June 2006
Fire Safety Risk Assessment - Factories and Warehouses, June 2006
Fire Safety Risk Assessment - Residential Care Premises, June 2006
Fire Safety Risk Assessment - Sleeping Accommodation, June 2006
Fire Safety Risk Assessment - Small and Medium Places of Assembly, June 2006
Fire Safety Risk Assessment - Large Places of Assembly, 5 June 2006
Fire Safety Risk Assessment - Educational Premises, 5 June 2006
Fire Safety Risk Assessment - Theatres, Cinemas and Similar Premises, 8 June 2006
Fire Safety Risk Assessment - Open Air Events and Venues, March 2007
Fire Safety Risk Assessment - Transport Premises and Facilities, February 2007
Fire Safety Risk Assessment - Healthcare Premises, September 2006
Fire Safety Risk Assessment - Animal Premises and Stables, October 2007
PAS 79:2007, Fire Risk Assessment - Guidance and a Recommended Methodology

C3.1 - Legal requirements

The regulatory powers of a fire authority with respect to fire safety

THE POWERS OF INSPECTORS UNDER THE REGULATORY REFORM ORDER 2005

The enforcing authority specified by the Regulatory Reform (Fire Safety) Order (RRFSO) 2005 is the Fire and Rescue Authority in the case of most premises; however the RRFSO 2005 recognises that fire safety in some premises is a complex and technical area so that it has been enforced in earlier legislation by the Health and Safety Executive (HSE). The HSE enforce the RRFSO 2005 in nuclear installations, a ship under construction, conversion or repair and construction sites. The fire service maintained by the Secretary of State for Defence enforces the RRFSO 2005 for premises occupied solely for the purposes of armed forces of the Crown. The relevant local authority enforces the RRFSO 2005 in relation to premises requiring a safety certificate under the Safety of Sports Grounds Act, as amended 2005 by RRFSO or Fire Safety and Safety of Places of Sport Act, as amended by RRFSO 2005. A fire inspector authorised by the Secretary of State will enforce the RRFSO 2005 in Crown premises or the United Kingdom Atomic Energy Authority premises.

Fire inspectors are duly authorised officers of the enforcing authorities. They are provided with powers under the RRFSO 2005 to enable them to regulate compliance with the RRFSO 2005. Inspectors must, if so required, produce to the occupier of the premises evidence of their authority. Powers of inspectors authorised under the RRFSO 2005 are covered in Article 27 of the Order, which sets out a general power to "do anything necessary for the purpose of carrying out this Order and any regulations made under it". In addition, the Order creates the following specific powers:

- To enter any premises to inspect it and anything in it, where this may be done without the use of force.
- To make inquiries:
   (i) To ascertain if the Order applies or has been complied with.
   (ii) To identify the responsible person in relation to the premises.
- To require the production of any records (including plans):
   (i) Which are required to be kept.
   (ii) Which it is necessary to see for the purposes of an examination or inspection.
- To inspect and take copies of records.
- To require facilities and assistance.
- To take samples of any articles or substances for the purpose of ascertaining their fire resistance or flammability.
- To cause articles and substances that may cause danger to be dismantled or subjected to any process or test (but not so as to damage or destroy it unless this is, in the circumstances, necessary).

Where an inspector proposes to dismantle or test any article or substance, it must done in the presence of a person present in and responsible for the premises, where this requested by the person. Before starting to dismantle or test any article or substance inspectors must consult such persons as appear to them appropriate for the purpose of ascertaining what dangers, if any, there may be carrying out the dismantling or testing.

ENFORCEMENT NOTICES

Part 3 of the RRFSO 2005 details the different types of enforcement notices that can be used and the conditions for serving them. The types of notices are alterations notices, enforcement notices and prohibition notices.

Conditions for serving

Alterations notice

- Issued on premises at the discretion of an enforcing authority.
- Issued if premises constitute a serious risk, or may constitute a serious risk if changes were to be made to them or their use.
- If a notice is issued the person receiving must inform the enforcing authority of any proposed changes.
- Appeals can be made within 21 days of the serving of the notice to a Magistrate's Court, which suspends the notice till the hearing.

Enforcement notice

- This notice performs a similar function to an 'improvement notice' served under the Health and Safety at Work etc Act (HASAWA) 1974.
- Issued where there is a failure to comply with any of provisions of the Order.
- Requires that person to take steps to remedy the failure within such period from the date of service of the notice (not being less than 28 days) or as may be specified in the notice.
- The notice will specify the provisions that must be complied with and may include directions as to the measures which the enforcing authority considers are necessary to remedy the failure.

ELEMENT C3 - WORKPLACE FIRE RISK ASSESSMENT

- The enforcing authority may withdraw the notice at any time before the end of the period specified in the notice.
- If an appeal against the notice is not pending, the enforcing authority may extend or further extend the period specified in the notice.
- If the notice would cause the premises to be altered the enforcing authority must consult any other relevant enforcing authority.
- Appeals can be made within 21 days of the serving of the notice to a Magistrate's Court; which suspends the notice till the hearing.

Prohibition notice

- Issued where the risk to 'relevant persons' is so serious that use of premises should be prohibited or restricted.
- The notice will specify the provisions that must be complied with and may include directions as to the measures which the enforcing authority considers are necessary to remedy the failure.
- The notice may direct that the use to which the prohibition notice relates is prohibited or restricted until the specified matters have been remedied.
- It may take effect immediately or at a time specified in the notice, depending on the opinion of the enforcing authority.;
- The enforcing authority may withdraw the notice at any time before the end of the period specified in the notice.
- Appeals can be made within 21 days of the serving of the notice to a Magistrate's Court, the notice remains in force till the hearing.

In addition to the above, Article 37 in Part 5 (Miscellaneous) of the RRFSO 2005 deals with fire-fighters' switches for equipment such as luminous discharge tubes. As part of this Article the fire authority can serve a notice on the responsible person regarding the location, colour and marking of the fire-fighters' switch.

Once the enforcing authority is of the opinion that conditions in or on the premises are such that any of the above notices can be served, they may choose to do so. However, they may need to consult with other enforcing authorities or the relevant local authority before issuing the notice, particularly if it required the premises to be altered. The notice can be served in person, by post, by leaving it at the "responsible persons" proper address, by electronic transmission or if there is no apparent responsible person, by affixing it to some conspicuous part of the premises.

Effects

Once a notice is issued they would normally have immediate effect unless stated otherwise. Being issued with a notice is not an offence; however non compliance with a notice becomes an offence.

Procedures, rights and effects of appeal

If a person has been issued with a notice they may appeal against the notice. Appeal is made by way of 'complaint for an order' at the Magistrate's Court and must be done within 21 days from the date that the notice was served. Once an appeal is commenced the 'alterations' and 'enforcement' notices are suspended. This however is not the case with a 'prohibition notice' which remains in force while the appeal is considered.

The Magistrates Court is the level of court that is utilised to hear appeals against notices served under the RRFSO 2005. However, cases may be referred to Crown Court, for example, if a person appealing against a notice disagrees with the decision made by the Magistrates Court.

Penalties for failure to comply

If a notice is served on the 'responsible person' but they fail to comply with the notice this is seen as a separate offence to the original non-compliance that led to the notice being served. Article 32 sets out the following offences relating to failure to comply with notices:

- Fail to comply with any requirement imposed by an enforcement notice.
- Fail to comply with any prohibition or restriction imposed by a prohibition notice.

In each case, failure to comply with a notice is considered to have serious potential and as such the penalty on summary conviction is the maximum that is allowed, presently £5,000. If the matter is taken on indictment it could lead to an unlimited fine, 2 years imprisonment or both.

PROSECUTION

Summary and indictable offences

Part 4 of the RRFSO 2005 details the offences that may occur related to the Order.

Offence	Summary	Indictment
Failure to comply with regulations made under Article 24 which places 'relevant persons' at risk of death or serious injury.	Statutory maximum (presently £5,000).	Unlimited fine, 2 years imprisonment or both.

Offence	Summary	Indictment
Failure to comply with an alterations notice.	Statutory maximum (presently £5,000).	Unlimited fine, 2 years imprisonment or both.
Failure to comply with an enforcement notice.	Statutory maximum (presently £5,000).	Unlimited fine, 2 years imprisonment or both.
Luminous tube signs.	Level 3 (presently £1,000).	Not applicable.
Failure to comply with requirements imposed by Article 23 (general duties of employees at work) which places 'relevant persons' at risk of death or serious injury.	Statutory maximum (presently £5,000).	Unlimited fine.
False entry in records etc.	Level 5 (presently £5,000).	Not applicable.
Intentional obstruction of an inspector.	Level 5 (presently £5,000).	Not applicable.
Failure to comply with any requirements imposed by an inspector.	Level 3 (presently £1,000).	Not applicable.
Pretend with intent to deceive, to be an inspector.	Level 3 (presently £1,000).	Not applicable.
Failure to comply with prohibition under Article 40 (duty not to charge employees).	Level 5 (presently £5,000).	Not applicable.
Failure to comply with any prohibition or restriction imposed by a prohibition notice.	Statutory maximum (presently £5,000).	Unlimited fine, 2 years imprisonment or both.

Figure C3-1: Summary and indictable offences.   Source: Part 4 of the Regulatory Reform (Fire Safety) Order (RRFSO) 2005.

Part 4 also explains that the legal onus for proving that an offence was not committed is on the accused; this is similar to that found in the HASAWA 1974. A new disputes procedure to deal with situations where a responsible person and an enforcing authority cannot agree on the measures which are necessary to remedy a failure to comply with the Order is also outlined within this part; this is via the Secretary of State's office.

Dual enforcement

In most work situations to which the Regulatory Reform (Fire Safety) Order (RRFSO) 2005 applies there should not be dual enforcement of legislation. However, where some dangerous substances are involved in the workplace two pieces of legislation will apply the RRFSO 2005 and the Dangerous Substances and Explosive Atmosphere Regulations (DSEAR) 2002. The RRFSO 2005 contains similar content to DSEAR 2002 to enable the Fire Service Authority to enforce arrangements for flammable substances and combustible materials in general workplaces. This does give the potential for dual enforcement by the Fire Service Authority, who are the prime enforcer of RRFSO 2005, and the Health and Safety Executive (HSE), who enforce DSEAR 2002.

The government has given guidance on this, in as much as, if the factors being considered are due to process risks then they should be enforced by the HSE under DSEAR 2002. If the factors are to do with 'general fire precautions' they should be enforced by the Fire Service Authority under the RRFSO 2005.

Requirements of the RRFSO 2005

The Regulatory Reform (Fire Safety) Order (RRFSO) 2005 applies to England and Wales. The legislation was introduced in Scotland via 2 separate pieces of legislation, the Fire Safety (Scotland) Regulations (FSSR) 2006 and the Fire (Scotland) Act (FSA) 2005. In principle, the laws in both England and Scotland cover the same matters. Enforcement of the law in Scotland is however separated out and put in place via the Fire (Scotland) Act (FSA) 2005 in Scottish law.

For the purposes of this publication, the subject is covered under the English legal system; for those affected by Scottish law reference would also need to be made to the Fire (Scotland) Act (FSA) 2005.

THE REGULATORY REFORM (FIRE SAFETY) ORDER (RRFSO) 2005

As the name suggests this legislation reforms a number of pieces of legislation relating to fire. The main pieces of legislation replaced with this single order were the Fire Precautions Act (FPA) and the Fire Precautions (Workplace) Regulations (FPWR).

ELEMENT C3 - WORKPLACE FIRE RISK ASSESSMENT

The Licensing Act and Housing Act, along with many other pieces of legislation were amended. The Regulatory Reform (Fire Safety) Order (RRFSO) 2005 became the primary piece of legislation dealing with fire. The legislation applies to most non-domestic premises (other than offshore installations, ships, agricultural or forestry land, mines and boreholes) and includes premises relating to the voluntary sector and self-employed in England and Wales.

For example:

- Factories and warehouses.
- Offices and shops.
- Pubs, clubs and restaurants.
- Hotels and hostels.
- Premises that provide care.
- Community halls.
- Schools.
- Tents and marquees.
- Open air public gatherings (concerts, shows etc).

The RRFSO 2005 represents a move towards greater emphasis on fire prevention through the implementation of measures derived from risk assessments. The RRFSO 2005 abolished Fire Certificates, removing their legal status. However, the fire precautions they imposed should not be discarded without due consideration and good reason. *It replaces fire certification under the Fire Precautions Act 1971 with a general duty to ensure, so far as is reasonably practicable, the safety of employees with regard to fire.* In addition, it places a general duty in relation to non-employees to take such fire precautions as may reasonably be required in the circumstances to ensure that premises are safe, and also a duty to carry out a risk assessment. The main duty-holder is the "*responsible person*" in relation to the premises. The duties on the responsible person are extended to any person who has, to any extent, control of the premises. In summary, the RRFSO 2005 requires the responsible person to:

- Carry out a fire risk assessment, identifying the risks and hazards.
- Consider who may be especially at risk.
- Eliminate or reduce the risk from fire as far as is reasonably practicable and provide general fire precautions to deal with any residual risk.
- Take additional measures to ensure fire safety where flammable or explosive materials are used or stored.
- Create a plan to deal with any emergency and, in most cases, document the findings.
- Review the findings as necessary.

The 'responsible person' has a duty for the safety of 'relevant persons'. Relevant persons would be:

- Any person who is lawfully on the premises.
- Any person in the vicinity of the premises who is at risk from a fire on the premises.

The RRFSO 2005 has become the principal piece of legislation regulating fire at work and comprises 5 parts:

- Part 1   General.
- Part 2   Fire Safety Duties.
- Part 3   Enforcement.
- Part 4   Offences and Appeals.
- Part 5   Miscellaneous.

Each part is then subdivided into the individual points or articles, as they are called in the Order. It makes provision for the creation of regulations and is supported by a series of guidance documents in the form of fire safety guides. *See also - Relevant statutory provisions.*

Part 2 of the RRFSO 2005 sets out the following fire safety duties:

- Duty to take general fire precautions.
- Risk assessment.
- Principles of prevention to be applied.
- Fire safety arrangements.
- Elimination or reduction of risks from dangerous substances.
- Fire-fighting and fire detection.
- Emergency routes and exits.
- Procedures for serious and imminent danger and for danger areas.
- Additional emergency measures re dangerous substances.
- Maintenance.
- Safety assistance.
- Provision of information to employees, employers and self employed.
- Training.
- Co-operation and co-ordination.
- General duties of employees.

In addition, there is a schedule, schedule 1, that covers the risk assessment process, plus details of the various legislation that has been repealed or amended.

The RRFSO 2005 is very comprehensive, encompassing all of the **general requirements** for fire safety in premises in one document. The onus of responsibility to ascertain the control measures that are needed rests on the 'responsible person'. The requirement to conduct fire risk assessments, originally established by the Management of Health and Safety at Work Regulations (MHSWR) 1999, means that existing premises should have risk assessments associated with them that would satisfy the requirements of RRFSO 2005. Risk assessments should also be carried out prior to the design of new premises or alteration of existing premises.

The risk assessment should be reviewed according to the following principles:

- Reasons exist to suspect that it is no longer valid.
- Significant changes in the premises are proposed, for example, technical or organisational measures.
- Change to the building structure, contents, activities or occupancy.
- Young person(s) are employed.
- At regular intervals.

Fire safety regulations

The RRFSO 2005 provides for the Secretary of State to make regulations with regards to premises in relation to risk to relevant persons. For example, regulations may be made "for securing that persons employed to work in the premises receive appropriate instruction or training in what to do in case of fire". Regulations made under RRFSO 2005 provide **specific legal requirements** to define and regulate fire precautions covered by the general requirements of the RRFSO 2005. It should be noted that regulations carry the full force of the law and breaches can lead to significant prosecutions, just as they might for breaching an Act or Articles within an Order.

There are a number of specific regulations that relate to fire safety that were created under the Health and Safety at Work etc Act (HASAWA) 1974. These regulations include the Health and Safety (Safety Signs and Signals) Regulations (SSSR) 1996 and the Dangerous Substances and Explosive Atmosphere Regulations (DSEAR) 2002.

Approved codes of practice and guidance

There is no general government code of practice issued for fire safety. The nearest to this would be the Approved Document B, which applies to the construction of new buildings and building alterations. As an approved document it is intended to provide guidance for some of the more common building situations. There is no obligation to follow the solutions contained within the document and people are free to meet the relevant requirements of the Building Regulations in some other way. However, there is much fire safety guidance both past and present ("Fire Safety an Employers Guide" - HSE Books as an example). There is also an extensive range of British Standards (BS) that relate to fire safety standards in buildings, for example, BS 9999: 2008 that relates to fire safety in the design, management and use of buildings and is now being used extensively as an alternative to (or in conjunction with) the Approved B Document. In addition, the publicly available specification (PAS) PAS 79:2007 "Fire risk assessment. Guidance and a recommended methodology", available from the British Standards Institute (BSI), gives a structured approach and corresponding documentation for conducting and recording significant findings of fire risk assessments.

Government fire safety guidance documents have been published to support the duties expressed in the RRFSO 2005 and suggest ways in which they may be met. They seek to consider the practical application of these duties and as such the fire safety guidance documents for RRFSO 2005 are written to be premises type specific. The premises specific documents all follow a similar format, but provide specific guidance for the type of premise in question for matters such as means of escape and other issues. They are purely for guidance and are aimed at existing premises and therefore should not be used to design fire safety in new buildings, as the building may be subject to Building Regulations. The guidance documents do not set prescriptive standards, but provide recommendations and guidance for assessing the adequacy of fire precautions in premises. There is no obligation to adopt any particular solution that is denoted in the guidance documents. However, they provide useful information that indicates what may be suitable for the particular type of premise. Fire safety arrangements do not have to be the same as those shown in the guidance documents, but the responsible person must demonstrate that they meet an equivalent standard. There are 12 premises specific fire safety guidance documents and one supplementary guide relating to the RRFSO 2005:

- Fire safety in offices and shops.
- Fire safety in factories and warehouses.
- Fire safety in premises providing sleeping accommodation.
- Fire safety in premises providing residential care.
- Fire safety in educational premises.
- Fire safety in small and medium places of assembly.
- Fire safety in large places of assembly.
- Fire safety in theatres and cinemas.
- Fire safety at open air events and venues.

ELEMENT C3 - WORKPLACE FIRE RISK ASSESSMENT

- Fire safety in healthcare premises.
- Fire safety in transport premises and facilities.
- Fire safety in stables and agricultural premises.
- Means of escape for disabled people (supplementary guide).

THE FIRE SAFETY (SCOTLAND) REGULATIONS (FSSR) 2006

The Fire Safety (Scotland) Regulations (FSSR) 2006 are regulations that were made by Scottish Ministers under the powers contained in the Fire (Scotland) Act (FSA) 2005, and further build upon the requirements of that FSA. Reference should be made to the Regulatory Reform (Fire Safety) Order (RRFSO) 2005 for the equivalent legislation for England and Wales.

The FSSR 2006 finished their period of public consultation in November 2005, were laid before the Scottish Parliament on 7th September 2005 and took effect from 1st October 2006, along with part 3 of the Fire (Scotland) Act (FSA) 2005 (all other parts of the Act having already been brought into force on 2nd August 2005).

Some of the main parts of the FSSR 2006 are broken down into the following sections:

- Relevant premises.
- Responsible person(s).
- Third-party fire-safety services and 'safety assistance'.
- Definition of competency.
- Risk assessments.
- Provision and maintenance of fire fighting equipment.
- Employee training, 'fire marshals/wardens'.
- Means of escape and emergency lighting.
- Signage.
- Provision and maintenance of fire alarm systems.
- Information for employees, contractors and the parents of children employees.
- Offences.
- Timescale.
- General.

Reference to the Building Regulations

The powers to make building regulations are contained in the Building Act (BA) 1984. The Act provides that they may be made for the purpose of:

- Securing the health, safety, welfare and convenience of persons in or about buildings.
- For furthering the conservation of fuel and power.
- For preventing waste, misuse or contamination of water.

To this end the current Building Regulations (BR) 2010, as amended 2011, contain a broad range of what are termed functional requirements with which building work must comply. These requirements cover subjects such as structure, fire safety, sound insulation, and ventilation, conservation of fuel and power, and facilities and access for disabled people. They are grouped under thirteen parts (A, B, C, etc) within the Building Regulations.

C3.2 - Identification of hazards and the assessment of risk from fire

Fire hazards and assessment of risk

FIRE HAZARDS

A hazard can be described as something with the potential to cause harm to people, damage to property or impact on the environment. A fire may cause harm to people in a number of ways. Contact with flames from a fire can have a direct effect on people, causing burns that can quickly overwhelm the body and cause death. In addition, there are a number of other effects that a fire can have on people. A study by the Health and Safety Executive (HSE) related to the effects of fire in the offshore gas and oil industry established the following effects of fire.

Toxic gases and smoke

Carbon dioxide is toxic above 5% concentration and causes hyperventilation above 2%, where the subject may inhale large quantities of other toxic components contained in smoke. Hydrogen cyanide will incapacitate a subject within minutes and sulphur dioxide and nitrous oxide have similar effects. Virtually all hydrocarbons will generate smoke. Dense smoke production will obscure escape routes. Smoke inhalation may cause death some hours after exposure.

Hot gases and hot objects

Objects with temperatures above 45°C may cause pain if in contact with skin for more than 10 seconds and those with temperatures above 100°C will cause burns within seconds. Convected hot air or hot gases above

120°C will result in skin pain after 10 minutes. Below this temperature cooling by sweating is possible, giving longer endurance times.

Thermal radiation

Physiological effects of thermal radiation may involve voluntary exposure over relatively long times (for example many minutes) in order to assist with fire fighting or during escape from a fire. The effects typically include high pulse rates, increased and laboured respiration, increased sweating and increased body temperature. The effects may be increased with increasing temperature, up to the point where pain/injury occurs.

At skin temperatures above 44°C, pain is felt and injury continues whilst the temperature remains above this point. The rate of injury increases by a factor of 3 for every degree above 44°C, such that at 50°C, the injury rate is ~100 times that at 44°C. In addition, for heat fluxes greater than 12.5 kW m^{-2}, 33% of the final burn occurs during cooling.

The extent of injury is often related to the thermal dose, which may involve a high heat flux over a short duration. Thermal radiation is a particular hazard in the event of fire balls or where escape routes are blocked by fire.

A severe fire has the potential to cause major loss, including injury or death to people. Millions of pounds of damage are caused by fire every week and the smoke from a fire or the run off of fire fighting water can cause environmental pollution. Because the hazards of flames, toxic gases and smoke only reveal themselves when a fire occurs, in the majority of cases it is sufficient to consider fire hazards as three distinct areas of concern, reflecting the components that are brought together to establish a fire and depicted by the fire triangle:

- Sources of fuel - flammable gases, liquids and vapours; combustible dusts; textiles; paper and packing materials, plastics, rubber and foam and waste materials.
- Sources of heat (or ignition sources) - must be identified and controlled, relevant to the nature and types of fuel within the workplace.
- Sources of oxygen - oxygen may be found in the workplace in the form of cylinders, piped oxygen or chemicals such as oxidising agents. It may also be necessary to consider the effects of air movement within the workplace, for example, air conditioning/air handling systems and the associated trunking. Such systems will provide additional air to any fire area and may spread fire or smoke to other areas within the workplace.

ASSESSMENT OF RISK

Having identified the fire hazards within the workplace and the people who may be harmed by any resultant fire, an assessment of the risk or probability of a fire occurring and its consequences on the people within the workplace must be made. When making this assessment the existing fire safety control measures should be considered. The existing control measures must be evaluated to determine if they are adequate, or if additional measures are required. Some people may prefer to allocate a risk rating to the workplace for example moderate or low risk, but this is not necessary.

The RRFSO 2005 sets out specific requirements regarding the carrying out of fire risk assessment, Article 9 specifies:

"The responsible person must make a suitable and sufficient assessment of the risks to which relevant persons are exposed for the purpose of identifying the general fire precautions he needs to take to comply with the requirements and prohibitions imposed on him by or under this Order".

In addition, the RRFSO 2005, Article 9, requires that a new work activity involving a dangerous substance may not commence unless:

- A risk assessment has been made.
- The measures required to satisfy the RRFSO 2005 have been implemented.

As soon as practicable after the assessment is made or reviewed, the responsible person must record the information where:

- Five or more employees are employed.
- A licence under an enactment is in force in relation to the premises.
- An alterations notice requiring this is in force in relation to the premises.

The prescribed information to record is:

- The significant findings of the assessment, including the measures that have been or will be taken by the responsible person pursuant to the RRFSO 2005.
- Any group of persons identified by the assessment as being especially at risk.

Five steps to fire risk assessment

The purpose of a fire risk assessment is to identify where fire may start in the workplace, the people who would be put at risk, and to reduce the risk where possible. The RRFSO 2005, Article 9, sets out the following duties:

"(1) The responsible person must make a suitable and sufficient assessment of the risks to which relevant persons are exposed for the purpose of identifying the general fire precautions he needs to take to comply with the requirements and prohibitions imposed on him by or under this Order".

ELEMENT C3 - WORKPLACE FIRE RISK ASSESSMENT

When undertaking a fire risk assessments there are five steps that need to be taken:

Step 1 - Identify fire hazards.

Step 2 - Identify people at risk.

Step 3 - Evaluate, remove or remove and protect from risks.

Step 4 - Record, plan, inform, instruct and train.

Step 5 - Review.

STEP 1 - IDENTIFY FIRE HAZARDS

How could a fire start

A fire may start when the three main components of a fire - heat, fuel and oxygen - are brought together. It is important to identify the presence of the separate components, situations where they are in proximity with each other and situations where they may be brought into proximity with each other.

- ***Identify sources of ignition*** - smokers' materials, naked flames, heaters, hot processes, cooking, machinery, boilers, faulty or misused electrical equipment, lighting equipment, hot surfaces, blocked vents, friction, static electricity, sunlight focused through glass objects such as paper weights, metal impact and arson.
- ***Identify sources of fuel*** - flammable liquids, flammable chemicals, wood, paper and card, plastics, foam, flammable gases (consider methane release from groundwater penetrating into cellars) and liquefied petroleum gas (LPG), furniture, textiles, packaging materials, waste materials including shavings, off cuts and dust.
- ***Identify sources of oxygen*** - natural ventilation, doors, windows, forced ventilation systems, air conditioning, oxidising materials, oxygen cylinders or piped oxygen systems.

What could burn

A fire may grow and spread quickly from its original source if there are materials readily available to burn; these materials should be identified. Some materials burn more readily than others and these should be particularly identified.

Common flammable solids

Flammable solids form the majority of fuels within workplaces and are certainly the most common type of fuel to be ignited first when a fire starts. There are very few solid materials that will not burn, the principal factors being the format that the fuel is in and the heat output of the available ignition sources. When assessing fuels within the workplace we need to consider the size of the particles of fuel and how they are presented in the workplace. For example, we could probably extinguish a small naked flame by dropping a cupful of sawdust on top of it from close range if we emptied the cup's contents in one go. However, if the sawdust is fine enough and is suspended in the air in the right proportions a tiny static spark could be sufficient to cause a dust explosion. Common examples of flammable solids would be paper, plastics, soft furnishings, foams and wood.

Common flammable liquids

Flammable liquids are known fire problems due to their capability to ignite easily and spread fire quickly. The prime considerations would be the flashpoint for the liquid concerned, its rate of vaporisation and its flammable or explosive range. The lower the flashpoint, the higher the rate of vaporisation and the wider the flammable range, the more dangerous the product. Common examples of flammable liquids would be petrol, thinners and oils.

Common flammable gases

The most common flammable gases used in work activities would be acetylene, propane, butane and natural gas. Any flammable gas has the potential to fill an area with a gas/air mixture, which can then ignite and cause an explosion throughout the entire area, with devastating effects. As with flammable liquids, one of the main considerations would be the explosive range of the gas as the wider the range, the greater the potential to ignite the gas cloud.

The RRFSO 2005, Article 9 (2), sets out a requirement that where a dangerous substance is or is liable to be present in or on the premises, the risk assessment must include consideration of the matters set out in Part 1 of Schedule 1 of the RRFSO 2005.

"*The matters are:*

(a) The hazardous properties of the substance.

(b) Information on safety provided by the supplier, including information contained in any relevant safety data sheet.

(c) The circumstances of the work including:

   (i) The special, technical and organisational measures and the substances used and their possible interactions.

   (ii) The amount of the substance involved.

(iii) Where the work will involve more than one dangerous substance, the risk presented by such substances in combination.

(iv) The arrangements for the safe handling, storage and transport of dangerous substances and of waste containing dangerous substances.

(d) *Activities, such as maintenance, where there is the potential for a high level of risk.*

(e) *The effect of measures which have been or will be taken pursuant to this Order.*

(f) *The likelihood that an explosive atmosphere will occur and its persistence.*

(g) *The likelihood that ignition sources, including electrostatic discharges, will be present and become active and effective.*

(h) *The scale of the anticipated effects.*

(i) Any places which are, or can be connected via openings to, places in which explosive atmospheres may occur.

(j) Such additional safety information as the responsible person may need in order to complete the assessment".

STEP 2 - IDENTIFY PEOPLE AT RISK

Identify those people at risk:

- Determine who may be at risk and where are they located.
- People in the workplace (staff, visitors, contractors, public).
- People near to the workplace that might be affected (neighbouring workplaces and public).
- The level of discipline and training that they may have had.

Identify those people who may be specifically at risk:

- Identify how could fire, heat, smoke spread and trap people.
- Consider how people will be warned of a fire (audible, visible or buddy arrangements).
- People working near to fire danger.
- People working alone or in isolated locations.
- Children or parents with babies.
- The elderly, infirm or disabled.
- Vulnerable people, the young and those with cognitive difficulties.

The RRFSO 2005 sets out specific requirements relating to risk assessment in respect of young persons, Part 2 of Schedule 1 set out the matters particularly to take into account.

"The matters are:

a) *The inexperience, lack of awareness of risks and immaturity of young persons.*

b) *The fitting-out and layout of the premises.*

c) *The nature, degree and duration of exposure to physical and chemical agents.*

d) *The form, range, and use of work equipment and the way in which it is handled.*

e) *The organisation of processes and activities.*

f) *The extent of the safety training provided or to be provided to young persons.*

g) *Risks from agents, processes and work listed in the Annex to Council Directive 94/33/EC on the protection of young people at work".*

STEP 3 - EVALUATE, REMOVE, REDUCE AND PROTECT FROM RISK

Evaluate the extent to which risks are minimised at source.

- **Sources of ignition -** removal of unnecessary sources of heat or replacement with safer alternatives, ensuring electrical fuses are of the correct rating, ensuring safe and correct use of electrical equipment, enforcing a 'hot work' permit system, safe smoking policy, arson reduction measures.
- **Potential fuel for a fire -** removal or reduction of the amount of flammable materials, replacing materials with safer alternatives, for example, use of higher flash point or non-flammable solvents. Ensure safe handling, storage and use of materials, safe separation distances between flammable materials and ignition sources, use of fire resisting storage, repair or replace damaged or unsuitable furniture, control and removal of flammable waste, care of external storage due to arson, good housekeeping.
- **Sources of oxygen -** closing all doors and windows not required for ventilation particularly out of working hours, shutting down non essential ventilation systems, not storing oxidizing materials near heat sources or flammable materials, controlling the use of oxygen cylinders and ensuring ventilation to areas where they are used.

Evaluate the extent to which risks fire growth and spread are minimised.

- **Unsatisfactory structural features that could lead to fire spread -** unprotected openings in floors/walls and ceilings will allow fire to spread easily. Large voids below or above floors will allow fire/smoke to spread undetected and any unprotected vertical shaft will quickly allow fire/smoke to spread up through the

ELEMENT C3 - WORKPLACE FIRE RISK ASSESSMENT

building, combustible wall, floor or ceiling linings, open voids, open ducts, breeches in fire resistance. The provision of and suitability of fire doors and shutters. Then take remedial actions, such as: removal, covering or treatment of large areas of combustible wall and ceiling linings, improve fire resistance of workplace, install fire breaks into open voids.

- **Work practices** - the management of the workplace, its contents, and the people within it are major factors in the number/type of fire hazards that are created, how fire spreads and the ability to respond to a fire. For example, a workplace where poor housekeeping standards are allowed will easily lead to the obstruction of fire exits and fire equipment. In addition, combustible materials will be allowed to be too near to sources of ignition with the resultant increased probability of fire occurring and spreading.

Consider existing fire safety measures in the workplace and consider possible improvements, such as the following:

Fire detection and warning

- Install rapid detection fire alarms to enable fire to be detected quickly enough to allow people to escape to a place of safety.
- Ensure alarms used are recognised and understood by those who may be affected.
- Explain how to raise the alarm to all staff, or others who may be affected, at site inductions.
- Explain what staff, or others who may be affected, need to do in the event of an alarm at site inductions.
- Ensure fire notices are posted together with any emergency exit signs.

Means of escape

Determine how long it will take for people to escape, to a place of safety, once they are aware of a fire. Consideration should be given to whether the time is reasonable for each category of worker; taking account of their risk exposure and any issues of disability. This will include:

- The adequacy of the number of fire exits provided.
- The location of the fire exits in relation to the risk.
- The travel distance to reach a means of escape.
- Determination of any fire exits that may become unusable in the event of a fire.
- Identification of exits.
- The suitability of the fire exit door and ease of use.
- Inspections to ensure exit routes are free from obstructions and blockages.
- Determining the appropriateness of lighting.
- Regular drills to ensure staff are trained in the use of the escape routes, including alternatives, if their dedicated route is blocked.

Means of fighting fire

Establish the arrangements for fire fighting by considering those who might be at significant risk and whether there is a need to appoint Fire Marshals with specific training. In new premises automatic fire sprinkler extinguishing systems will be in place and the role of all occupants will be to exit rather than tackle a fire. If fire extinguishers or hoses are provided, then the following must be determined:

- Suitability and number of fire extinguishers or hoses.
- Their location.
- Their maintenance frequency and who will be responsible.
- The competency of all staff to use the equipment when necessary.

Maintenance and testing

Ensure:

- All fire doors, escape routes, lighting and signs are regularly checked.
- All fire fighting equipment is regularly checked.
- All fire detectors and alarms are regularly checked.
- All other equipment provided to help means of escape arrangements are regularly checked, for example, evacuation chairs for stairwells.
- Those who carry out maintenance and testing are competent.
- There is relevant information available for those who carry out maintenance and testing.

Fire procedures and training

Ensure there is adequate fire procedures established, this will include:

- Availability of an emergency (fire) plan.
- Establishing a regular review of the emergency (fire) plan to ensure it takes account of all reasonably foreseeable circumstances.
- Consideration of the emergency (fire) plan and its availability to all staff.
- Consideration of others, such as contractors or visitors and their understanding of the emergency (fire) plan and how it might affect them.
- A check that all employees understand the emergency (fire) plan, including those with specific duties, to ensure they are trained and practiced though drills in testing it.

WORKPLACE FIRE RISK ASSESSMENT - ELEMENT C3

- The identification and suitability of procedures to follow throughout workplace.

STEP 4 - RECORD, PLAN, INSTRUCT, INFORM AND TRAIN

Record

The RRFSO 2005, Article 9, requires that as soon as practicable after the risk assessment is made or reviewed, the responsible person must record the finding. This requirement to record is a legal duty in situations where:

"(6) The responsible person must record the information prescribed by paragraph (7) where:

(a) The responsible person employs five or more employees.
(b) A licence under an enactment is in force in relation to the premises; or
(c) An alterations notice requiring this is in force in relation to the premises".

"(7) The prescribed information is:

(a) The significant findings of the assessment, including the measures which have been or will be taken by the responsible person pursuant to this Order.
(b) Any group of persons identified by the assessment as being especially at risk".

In practice, this should be seen as a minimum duty and should not limit those in smaller organisations or those that have a small number of employees and a large numbers of volunteers who work in a premise from making full and proper records. It is necessary to record the significant hazards identified in step 1, any people especially at risk identified in step 2 and what was done about what was found at step 3.

Significant Hazard	People at risk	Evaluate risk of fire occurring	Evaluate risk to people	Remove and reduce hazards	Remove and reduce risks to people	Review date

Figure C3-2: Risk assessment record example.   Source: RMS.

Fire plan

When the records of the risk assessment are complete a fire plan for the building should be produced. The plan will include practical information on fire detection and alarms; actions to be taken when the alarm sound including location of assembly points and those responsible for co-ordinating the evacuation, including identification of escape routes. The plan will detail any fire suppression systems or equipment and who is responsible for their use and maintenance.

Inform, instruct and train

Workers and others affected should be **informed** of the plan and **instructed** in their role or actions in the event of discovering a fire or the fire alarm sounding. **Training** needs should to be identified and carried out. Typically, this will be included at inductions, when workers are moved to a different location and when a new process or materials are introduced. New information, instruction and training should be given to workers when the structure of the building is altered or when some aspect of the plan is changed, for example, if the alarm sounder is changed from a bell to a siren type or if a manual call point alarm system is supplemented by a smoke detection system.

Where necessary, staff with identified roles, such as fire wardens, security, receptionists, will need to undergo additional training to enable them to carry out their role timely and without doubt.

When improvements or changes are made it is essential others affected are kept informed, for example, when in shared occupancy or close proximity with neighbouring properties.

STEP 5 - REVIEW

The RRFSO 2005, Article 9, requires:

"(3) Any such assessment must be reviewed by the responsible person regularly so as to keep it up to date and particularly if:

(a) There is reason to suspect that it is no longer valid.
(b) There has been a significant change in the matters to which it relates including when the premises, special, technical and organisational measures, or organisation of the work undergo significant changes, extensions, or conversions, and where changes to an assessment are required as a result of any such review, the responsible person must make them.

(4) The responsible person must not employ a young person unless he has, in relation to risks to young persons, made or reviewed an assessment".

Reasons for review

The fire risk assessment and fire safety measures (including procedures) must be reviewed on a regular basis, if not reviewed for other reasons.

ELEMENT C3 - WORKPLACE FIRE RISK ASSESSMENT

Reasons that would cause a review to take place are:
- Changes to the people at risk.
- Alteration to the building.
- Changes to work process/activities/procedures.
- Introduction of new equipment.
- Changes to furniture and fittings.
- Storage of dangerous substances.
- Becoming aware of shortcomings in fire safety arrangements.
- Changes in legislation.
- Elapse of time.
- Incidents, such as if a near miss or a fire occurs.

People

Changes to number or type of people (for example young persons, those with disability) present will require a risk assessment to be reviewed. For example, if additional people are added to the workplace in new circumstances, such as the introduction of a night shift or security staff patrols at night.

Alterations to the building

Any alteration to the building may have an effect on the way that fire and smoke could spread through the structure, and it could have an effect on the means of escape from fire for the people in the building. These factors should be reviewed and where necessary risk assessed prior to the alterations being made, to ensure that the alteration can safely go ahead. The impact on fire safety measures within the building whilst the building works are on-going should be reviewed. It is important that the fire safety measures in the building are to an acceptable standard during the alterations; temporary measures may need to be implemented and staff will need to be informed of these.

It is important to note that any alteration that makes the means of escape from fire worse than it was prior to the alteration is a 'notifiable alteration' under Building Regulations, and cannot be undertaken without permission.

Changes to work procedures

Changes to a work process/activity/procedure may have altered the probability of a fire starting and the effects of any fire if started. A review of the procedure/process and an assessment of the risks that this may create should be done, so that any necessary amendments to the fire risk assessment and fire safety measures that exist in the building can be made.

Introduction of new equipment

Changes to workplace equipment or layout may amend the escape routes and could reduce fire standards. This would make review of the risk assessment necessary. New equipment could also introduce additional fire hazards that need to be reviewed and where necessary risk assessed.

Changes to furniture and fittings

Any change to furniture and fittings may have an impact on the escape routes that are available. This can happen not necessarily by changing the furniture, but just by relocating it within the same room. Any change to new or different furniture or fittings could also have an adverse affect on the speed of fire spread if done incorrectly. In both cases a review of the fire risk assessment and fire safety standards in the areas of concern should be made.

Storage of dangerous substances

If new substances are proposed or introduced into the workplace, then a review of the risk assessment will be necessary due to increased risks. If dangerous substances are introduced when there were none present beforehand, then this may have serious implications. The RRFSO 2005 links with the DSEAR 2002 to impose various safety measures to be implemented.

Becoming aware of shortcomings in fire safety arrangements

Each employee has duties under the legislation to make the responsible person aware of any serious and imminent dangers that are created and any shortfall in the fire safety arrangements. The employee has a responsibility as far as is reasonable given their level of training and instruction.

It should be noted that should the responsible person become aware of any shortfalls, they have a duty to act on their findings. The responsible person may also become aware of the shortcomings as part of an inspection, test of equipment or drill. These shortfalls could have a significant effect on the risk assessment and should be considered at time of review.

Legislative changes

If an amendment to legislation or new legislation is made, the fire risk assessment will need to be reviewed to ensure compliance.

Elapse of time

The assessment needs to be reviewed at regular periods. Many organisations carry out annual re-assessment, though legislation such as Control of Substances Hazardous to Health Regulations (COSHH) 2002 cites a maximum period of five years. This may be seen as sufficient in a very stable organisation where little changes.

Incidents

Incidents that occur may confirm or challenge the level of risk and suitability of controls in place and as such have a major bearing on a risk assessment that has been conducted. It would be prudent after any incident (good or bad) to review the risk assessment in the light of findings from the incident and assess if changes to the fire safety measures in place are required. Consider the following:

- Observations made during a fire drill.
- Observations made by routine inspections.
- Changes to number or type of people present.
- If a near miss or fire occurs.

C3.3 - Fire detection and alarm systems and procedures

Factors in design and application of fire detection and alarm systems

CATEGORIES OF FIRE ALARM AND DETECTION SYSTEMS AND THEIR OBJECTIVES

Fire alarm systems are generally designed and installed to BS 5839 Part 1: 2002 + A2: 2008 and Part 6: 2004. There are various parts of this standard but the main two are Part 1, which deals with larger premises such as offices, hotels, industrial buildings etc.; and Part 6, which is designed for and applied to the residential setting for houses and flats. In both cases systems may be installed in buildings to satisfy one, or both, of two principal objectives, namely protection of life and protection of property. Other possible objectives exist, such as protection against business interruption and protection of the environment.

Property risk/protection

In this situation the objective is to summon the Fire and Rescue Service in the early stages of a fire.

- **Category P1:** systems installed throughout all areas of the building. The objective of a Category P1 system is to offer the earliest possible warning of fire so as to minimise the time between ignition and the arrival of fire-fighters.
- **Category P2:** systems installed only in defined parts of the building. The objective of a Category P2 system is to provide early warning of fire in areas of high fire hazard level, or areas in which the risk to property or business continuity from fire is high.

Life risk/protection

In this situation the objective is to protect people from loss of life or injury.

- **Category M:** category M systems are manual systems and, therefore, incorporate no automatic fire detectors (call points and sounders only).
- **Category L:** systems are automatic fire detection systems intended for the protection of life. They are further subdivided into:
- **Category L1:** systems are installed throughout all areas of the building. The objective of a Category L1 system is to offer the **earliest possible warning of fire**, so as to achieve the longest available time for escape.
- **Category L2:** systems are installed only in defined parts of the building. A Category L2 system should include the coverage necessary to satisfy the recommendations of the standard for a Category L3 system; the objective of a Category L2 system is identical to that of a Category L3 system, with the additional objective of affording **early warning of fire in specified areas of high fire hazard level** and/or high fire risk.
- **Category L3:** systems are designed to give a warning of fire at an early enough stage to enable all occupants, other than possibly those in the room of fire origin, to escape safely, **before the escape routes are impassable** owing to the presence of fire, smoke or toxic gases.
- **Category L4:** systems are installed within those parts of the escape routes comprising circulation areas and circulation spaces, such as corridors and stairways. The objective of a Category L4 system is to enhance the safety of occupants by **providing warning of smoke within escape routes**.
- **Category L5:** systems in which the protected area(s) and/or the location of detectors is designed to satisfy a specific fire safety objective (other than that of a Category L1, L2, L3 or L4 system).

COMMON FIRE DETECTION EQUIPMENT

There are opportunities to detect fires at each of the four stages of a fire's development:

1) Invisible products of combustion, including carbon monoxide detectors.
2) Visible smoke.
3) Heat.
4) Flame.

The methods of detection available reflect these stages of the fire. Automatic detection systems should be installed by specialist firms and conform to British Standard 5839 Part 1: 2002 + A2: 2008 and BS 5839 Part 6: 2004.

ELEMENT C3 - WORKPLACE FIRE RISK ASSESSMENT

Smoke detection

There are different types of smoke detectors, the main ones being optical/multi-sensor, ionisation and beam detectors.

Optical smoke detectors operate on the principle of infra red light refracting off smoke particles entering the detection chamber, onto a light sensor which in turn triggers the alarm. This type of detector is good at detecting larger particles of smoke (visible products). This makes this type of detector more sensitive to smouldering fires such as modern fabrics or furnishings. Optical detectors are more prone to false alarms caused by steam, found in some textile processes, or dusty environments such as those arising from building works.

Beam detectors comprise a transmitter and receiver. The transmitter emits an infra red beam from the transmitter (TX) to the receiver (RX), and the beam detects obscuration by smoke.

Ionisation detectors operate on the principle of smoke particles passing between two electrodes (set in the vicinity of a small radioactive source), causing ionisation of surrounding air and a small current flow. The added weight of the smoke particles slows down the transmission rate, which in turn triggers the alarm. This type of detector is more suitable for fast flaming fires as it detects small particles of smoke (invisible products of combustion) such as those involving paper or wood in the incipient stages of fire. Ionisation detectors are more prone to false alarms from burning odours, i.e., those smelt outside a kitchen when food is overcooked and burnt.

Heat detection

There are two main methods of operation for heat detectors - rate of rise and fixed temperature - and the majority of modern heat detectors will in fact respond to either.

1) **Rate of rise heat detectors** will respond to a rapid increase in temperature. Rate of rise detectors are most suitable for areas where a smoke detector is undesirable, for example, a room where flammable liquids are used.

2) **Fixed temperature heat detectors** have a sensing element fixed at a particular temperature. When this is reached, the detector operates. Fixed temperature heat detectors are ideal for kitchens or boiler rooms where a rate of rise heat detector would be unsuitable because heat is part of the process.

Photo thermal detectors analyse both change in temperature as well as density of smoke or smoke-like phenomena. This can considerably reduce the potential for false alarms.

APPLICATION OF FIRE DETECTION EQUIPMENT

The following are the types of fire detection equipment that may be encountered in the workplace. These are described in order that the application and limitations of the various types may be appreciated. The amount of maintenance and the extent of electrical cabling and controls required for spot detectors of the ionisation chamber, photo-electric and thermal type make the installation of these forms of detectors only justifiable in certain locations and applications.

Type	Suitability	Speed/sensitivity	Other factors
Smoke detectors.	Buildings with relatively clean, ambient atmospheres.	Generally give the earliest warning.	False alarms may be given by fumes, dusts, steam, smoke and other particulate matter.
Ionisation. Optical.	Particularly effective for compartments containing electrical/electronic equipment.	Ionisation detectors generally more sensitive to optically dense smoke, for example from burning poly vinyl chloride (PVC).	Fast air flows can cause Ionisation detectors to false alarm.
Heat detectors:	Most buildings.		
(1) Rate of rise.	Not usually suitable for compartments containing electrical/electronic equipment.	Rate of rise detectors quicker than fixed temperature devices if a fire develops heat quickly.	Abnormal temperature increases may cause false alarms.
(2) Fixed temperature.		Fixed temperature includes Quatzoid glass bulbs.	Fixed temperature devices less prone to false alarms.
Flame detectors. Infra red. Ultra violet.	Generally for supplementing heat or smoke detectors in tall compartments where the view is unobstructed.	Quickest warning where flames are immediately present, for example fires involving flammable liquids.	Infra red detectors may be operated by gas flames and other heat sources under some conditions and the ultra violet may be operated by lightening, ultra violet lamps and flame cutting equipment.

Type	Suitability	Speed/sensitivity	Other factors
Laser beam/infra red detector.	Tall compartments. Cable tunnels.		One unit can cover a large volume.
Carbon monoxide detectors.	Risks containing electrical equipment.	Sensitive to decomposition breakdown products released during early stages of combustion process.	May be used as stand alone detection system, or integrated with more traditional detection.

Figure C3-3: Fire detection equipment. *Source: FST.*

The following list shows the types of fire detection strategies that have been used and may be used to detect fire. Fire detection is normally carried out by one of five strategies:

- **Spot detectors** - static detector covering certain size floor area.
- **Line detector** - linear heat detector cable that can be laid around an area to give protection.
- **Beam detector** - beam of light (normally Infra-red) covering a large floor area.
- **Sampling detectors** - range of pipe work connecting different areas back to a detector head. The air from each area can be sampled in turn.
- **Scanning detectors** - moving detector that sweeps a large area.

COMMON ALARM SYSTEMS

The purpose of a fire alarm is to give an early warning of a fire in a building, for two reasons:

1) To increase the safety of occupants by encouraging them to escape to a place of safety.
2) To increase the possibility of early extinction of the fire, thus reducing the loss of or damage to the property.

BS 5839, Part 1: 2002 lays down guidelines which should be followed when installing a fire alarm system. The British Standard is designed to give guidance to the user when involved in design and maintenance of a fire alarm system.

DESIGN FEATURES AND APPLICATION OF ALARM SYSTEMS

Method of raising the alarm

Hand-operated alarm system

For example, a hand bell or whistle. Their limitation is the size of building in which it is possible to hear the device and the need for it to be located conveniently. Some are portable and could, therefore, be prone to loss or theft.

Call points

Call points should be positioned 1.4 m above floor level, on escape routes. The maximum distance a person has to travel to reach a call point should not exceed 30 m (direct distance) or 45 m (actual distance).

Wiring and control panels

Wiring

A wide variety of different cables can be used in various parts of a fire alarm system. Because of their varying abilities to resist both fire and electrical or mechanical damage many of these cables may be restricted in their suitability for specific applications.

The following cables would be acceptable subject to their use:

- Mineral insulated copper clad.
- PVC in conduit.
- Pirelli F P 200.

However, in modern self monitoring systems, lower standards of wiring may be acceptable for certain components of the fire alarm system.

Control panel

This must show the state of the systems: normal - fault - fire. The panel should be sited in an area of low fire risk - preferably at ground level near to an entrance that is likely to be used by the Fire and Rescue Service in the event of a fire and ideally be visible to the Fire and Rescue Service without having to enter the building.

Power supplies

Normal supply for the system is from public mains electrical system. Standby supplies are most commonly a battery with automatic charger (life of at least 4 years). Alternatively, they may be batteries with a standby generator; the standby system should be able to maintain the system for a period of 24 hours.

Radio link systems - advantages

- No wiring needed.
- Easier, cheaper and quicker to install.
- System can be extended beyond a single building.

ELEMENT C3 - WORKPLACE FIRE RISK ASSESSMENT

- No damage to existing surfaces of the building.
- Each detector or call point can be identified.
- Temporary cover for special risks can be arranged.

Radio link systems - disadvantages

- Due to limits of allowed frequency spectrum this can lead to interference between simultaneous signals.
- Each detector call point and sounder has to be supplied with its own power batteries or local mains.
- Radio path may be interrupted by temporary or permanent screening.
- The receiver may be blocked by interfering signals from other sources.

Signals

The alarm system will utilise audible signals, such as bells or sirens. The wiring of sounder circuits should be arranged such that, in the event of a short circuit, at least one alarm sounder will continue to sound.

Sound levels

The sound levels should be 65 dB (A) or 5 dB (A) above any other noise that is likely to persist for longer than 30 seconds. Where sleeping people are to be woken the sound levels should be 75 dB (A) at the bed-head. Noise levels of above 120dB (A) may cause hearing damage in these areas. Special provisions may also be necessary to assist those with hearing and other impairments to know that an alarm has been activated, for example, visual signals or recorded messages.

Single stage alarm

The alarm sounds throughout the whole of the building and calls for total evacuation.

Two-stage alarm

In certain large/high rise buildings, it may be better to evacuate first the areas of high risk, usually those closest to the fire or immediately above it. In this case, an evacuation signal is given in the restricted area, together with an alert signal in other areas. If this type of system is required, early consultation with the Fire and Rescue Authority is essential.

Staff alarms

In some premises, an immediate single stage (total) evacuation may not be desirable, for example night clubs, shops, theatres, cinemas. A controlled evacuation by the staff may be preferred in order to prevent distress and panic to the occupants. If such a system is used the alarm must be restricted to the staff, by the use of coded announcements or direct contact by radio communications, and only used where there are sufficient members of staff present that are trained in the action of what to do in the event of fire.

Zones

When a fire signal is given it is necessary that there should be no confusion as to its point of origin and to achieve this, it is necessary to sub-divide the building into zones.

The size and number of the zones should comply with the following:

- The floor area of a single zone should not exceed 2,000 m^2.
- The search distance should not exceed 30 m.

If the total floor area of the building is 300 m^2 or less, then it may be considered as a single zone. If a total floor area exceeds 300 m^2, then all zones should be restricted to a single storey.

Careful zoning will minimise the search distance. Search distance is defined as 'the distance that has to be travelled by a searcher within a zone in order to visually determine the position of a fire'.

Zone boundaries should, if possible, be boundaries of fire compartments. However, it is permissible to have two complete fire compartments in one zone or two complete zones in one fire compartment. Where the building is in "multiple occupation", the zoning arrangement should take account of this. Each occupation should have its own zoning arrangement independent of the other occupancies. When detectors and/or call points are fitted in stairways or lift shafts, they should be treated as separate zones.

Remote indicator lamps outside doors may be useful, especially if doors are likely to be locked. More sophisticated detector alarm systems have control panels that illustrate more clearly the location of fires.

Testing of the alarm system

Daily check - panel indicates normal operation; if it does not the fault and any action taken must be recorded in the log book for the alarm system.

Weekly check - one detector, call point or end of line switch should be operated to test the control and indicating equipment as well as to test alarm sounders. If there are more than 13 zones, more than one zone may need to be tested to ensure the interval between tests on one circuit does not exceed 13 weeks.

Annual checks and after a fire - to be carried out by a competent person for example installing engineers.

Standby power - Visual check on batteries, check oil, fuel and coolant on generators. Any defect recorded in log book with the action taken.

Principal components of Alarm systems - detection and signalling

The principal components of a fire alarm system for detection and signalling the presence of fire consists of a control panel, usually located close to the main entrance to the building. The control panel is connected electrically, by fire resistant cables, to one or more automatic detectors and one or more manual call points.

When a fire is detected the control panel will then activate audible/visible alarm and indicate on the panel the zone where the fire was detected. The control panel will include a battery back up system to provide standby power in the event of failure of the mains electrical supply to the unit.

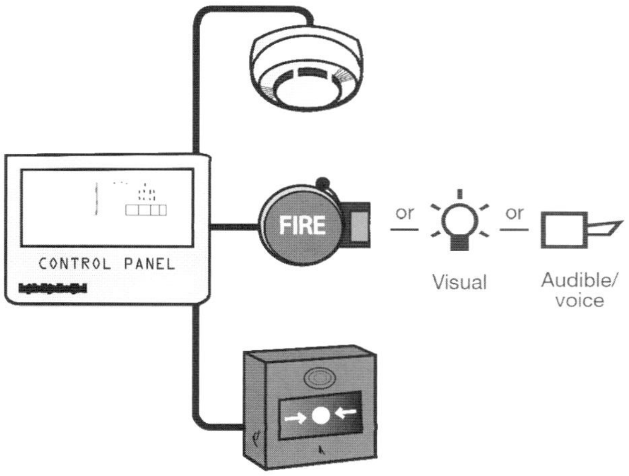

DETECTION

Smoke detection

Ionisation detectors

Figure C3-4: Fire detection and warning system. *Source: Fire Safety Risk Assessment - Guide 1 - Office and Shops/RMS.*

Ionisation type detectors consist of one or two ionisation chambers and the necessary amplification circuits.

The ionisation detector has, as a sensing element, the ionisation chamber which utilises the principle of air being made electrically conductive (ionised) by bombardment of the nitrogen and oxygen molecules in the air with alpha particles emitted by a minute source of radioactive material. A voltage applied across the ionisation chamber causes a very small electrical current to flow as the ions move to the electrode of opposite polarity. When visible or invisible combustion particles enter the chamber they attach themselves to the ions and cause a reduction in mobility and thus a reduction in current flow. The reduced current flow increases the voltage on the electrodes which, at a pre-determined level, results in an alarm.

The device is very sensitive to smoke and to the products of combustion from various materials. This type of detector is unsuitable for use in cable ways in its present state of development since the products of heating PVC at relatively low temperatures contain only small quantities of particulate matter and thus are not easily detectable.

Photo-electric cell smoke detectors

Photo-electric detection of smoke in varying degrees of density has been employed for several years, particularly where the type of fire anticipated is expected to generate a substantial amount of smoke before temperature changes are sufficient to actuate a heat detection system. This type of detector operates on the principle where smoke entering a light beam either obscures the beam path or reflects light on to a photo cell.

Photo electric cell detectors may be used as individual sensing heads or grouped in a cubicle with air sampled from the protected zone.

Laser or beam type

The laser or beam type detector employs a beam carried between elements at extreme ends or sides of the protected area. Smoke between the light source and the receiving photo cell reduces the light reaching the cell, thus causing actuation. Given an unobstructed clear space, light beam detectors of the photo electric type have been installed for distances up to 90m.

Sampling type

This system utilises large bore plastic pipework in the form of a bus line with spurs. Air inlet holes are drilled at suitable sampling points. A sample of the atmosphere within the risk area is drawn into the sampling pipework by the action of the sampling fan. Once a smoke contaminated sample enters the pipework there is rapid detection. Each bus line is separately monitored by a photo electric cell and an alarm is given by measurement of increases in obscuration values.

Flame detectors

A flame detector responds to the appearance of radiant energy visible to the human eye (a wavelength of approximately 4,000 to 7,000 angstroms; 1 angstrom is 1×10^{-10}m) or to radiant energy outside the range of human vision. These detectors are sensitive to glowing embers, coals, or actual flames that radiate energy of sufficient intensity and spectral quality to initiate response of the detector. There are four basic types of flame detectors:

Infra red - this device has a sensing element responsive to radiant energy outside the range of human vision (above 7,700 angstroms).

Ultra violet - this device has a sensing element responsive to radiant energy outside the range of human vision (below approximately 4,000 angstroms).

Photo electric - this device employs a photo cell which either changes its electrical conductivity or produces an electrical potential when exposed to radiant energy.

Flame flicker - this device is a photo electric type which includes means to prevent response to visible light unless the observed light is modulated at a frequency characteristic of the flicker of a flame.

Thermal detectors

Fusible links

Fusible links are devices where a link is formed by solder which fuses under conditions of high temperature, thus allowing mechanical initiation of the fire protective equipment.

Fusible links have the disadvantages of being slow in action, the solder is permanently stressed mechanically and therefore subject to creep, and inaccuracies may develop due to corrosive effects. In more modern designs the solder is not permanently stressed mechanically, but is allowed to melt and flow to break an electrical circuit.

Bi-metallic strips

Bi-metallic strips are two metals joined together to form a composite strip. The individual metals have widely differing coefficients of expansion so that under the application of heat the composite strips will curve and thus can make or break a contact in a electrical circuit. The manufacturing process is complex in respect of the formation of the join between the two metals, and lack of sensitivity and inaccurate working can result from faulty production.

The firetec system

This system is based on the use of differential thermocouples. Each detector contains two thermocouples connected in opposition. One thermocouple is exposed directly to the heat whilst the other is shrouded in high alumina ceramic. The resultant output of the combined detectors is directly proportional to the temperature difference.

The firewire system

This system consists of a number of sensing elements connected in series to form a loop, the ends of which are connected by wiring to a monitoring and control unit which indicates a warning if overheating or a fire occurs. The sensing elements consist of flexible stainless steel capillaries of standard lengths.

Each length of capillary contains a co-axial centre electrode separated from the capillary by a temperature sensitive material. The ends of the capillary are terminated by an end fitting assembly comprising stainless steel coupling mat, locating sleeve and a concentric pin which forces the connection to the central electrode.

Electrical resistance detector

This form of detector is based on the Wheatstone bridge principle and detects a change of voltage due to a change of resistance of a wire when heated. An alarm indication is initiated when the voltage reaches a certain level.

Heat energy detecting cables

Linear heat energy detection in the form of heat energy detecting cables can be used to detect abnormal temperatures in cable installations and other critical areas.

Rate of rise detectors

Fire detectors that operate on the rate-of-rise principle function when the rate of temperature increase at the detector exceeds a stated rate. Detectors of this type invariably combine two functioning elements, one of which initiates an alarm on a rapid rise of temperature. The various types of rate of rise detectors are as follows:

Contra-operating bi-metallic strips giving a rate-of-rise of temperature feature

This detector consists of one bi-metallic strip enclosed in a housing of high thermal capacity and another element open to the environmental conditions. The device remains immune to relatively slow changes of ambient temperature, but will operate to make or break an electrical circuit when a rapid rate-or-rise in temperature occurs.

Pneumatic detectors incorporating a rate-of-rise of temperature facility

In pneumatic detectors the heating effect on an enclosed quantity of air gives an increase in pressure which is exerted on a diaphragm which actuates the protection and alarm features. A compensating vent takes care of normal changes in ambient temperature.

Another type of pneumatic detector comprises a glass element with two spherical bulbs; one of these is exposed to external temperature, the other is contained within the case. These bulbs are joined by two connecting tubes. One of these tubes is blocked with a porous plug, and the other contains two electrical contacts bridged by a slug of mercury. Rapid rises in temperature cause the mercury to either make or break the circuit across the two contacts. The porous plug determines the sensitivity of the detector and acts as a compensator for small rates of rise of temperature above ambient.

Thermocouple detectors incorporating a rate-of-rise of temperature facility

Two dissimilar metals joined together at a point form a temperature sensitive junction that may be used to produce a thermo electric effect, corresponding to change in temperature.

The device is extremely sensitive and has a high speed of response, but its efficiency depends on the condition of the junction which for this reason must be adequately protected against physical damage and atmospheric effects which may reduce the speed of response and sensitivity.

The device also requires the use of compensating leads and it must be protected from any spurious effects such as induced voltage.

Figure C3-5: Smoke detector.   Source: RMS.

Exploding quartzoid glass bulb

The exploding glass bulb is essentially a temperature heat sensitive release valve.

The bulb contains a liquid that has a freezing point below any natural climatic figure and a high co-efficient of expansion. A small amount of vapour is trapped when the bulb is hermetically sealed. When the liquid expands under the influence of heat energy from a fire, pressure in the bulb rises slowly until all the vapour is absorbed. Further rise of temperature causes a rapid rise in pressure sufficient to shatter the bulb. The detector bulbs are designed for various rupture temperatures, and are designated by the colour of the bulb. In water spray installations of the "dry system" type the exploding glass bulb is used to control automatic water spray deluge valves.

In this application the bulb acts as a detector in the compressed air detector line. Groups of detectors are mounted in separate systems of detector pipework which is charged with compressed air and connected to the water spray deluge valve control mechanism. Under normal conditions the air pressure in the detector pipework holds the deluge valve in the closed position.

Rupture of a detector bulb automatically releases air pressure in the small bore detector pipework causing the water valve to open and water to flow to the projectors concerned. In water spray installations of the "wet system" type the quartzoid bulb acts as a detector/activator and is mounted directly on the water spray control valve casing.

Rupture of the detector bulb automatically opens the valve which distributes water to a limited group of spray projectors designed to cover the risk. In automatic water sprinkler installations the quartzoid bulb is used to detect and extinguish or control an outbreak of fire by distributing water automatically over the area commanded by the individual sprinkler head.

Manual and automatic systems

MANUAL SYSTEMS

Regardless of the detection system that is installed, there should always be the opportunity for the building occupants to raise the alarm themselves.

In anything other than very small buildings, where hand operated fire alarms can be considered, there will normally be the traditional manual/electrical call points.

The individual raising the alarm breaks the glass by pressing on it with their finger, and an electrical contact is then made that causes the fire alarm warning devices to operate throughout the workplace.

Figure C3-6: Manual call point. *Source: RMS.*

It may be worth noting that call points may need two actions to operate them if fitted with anti-tamper devices.

These can be found in the form of clear plastic covers that encase the call point. These may have to be lifted upwards, often breaking a seal or setting off a local alarm, to enable the call point to be accessed. Anti-tamper devices are becoming more common in public areas, where they have been installed as an attempt to reduce the number of malicious false alarms being made.

AUTOMATIC SYSTEMS

The majority of serious fires occur at night when people are not present to deal with them. In the day time many large fires start in parts of buildings (for example store rooms) that are infrequently visited. It is dangerous to rely on people to detect fire and manually raise the alarm because they may either not be there at the crucial moment or may well react incorrectly.

ELEMENT C3 - WORKPLACE FIRE RISK ASSESSMENT

The most effective precaution against delay in a fire being discovered and the alarm being raised is to install an automatic detection system that is linked to an alarm monitoring organisation that can provide 24 hour protection.

The purpose of an automatic system is to ensure that in the event of fire, occupants are warned so that they can be evacuated at an early stage, and to ensure that the Fire and Rescue Service arrives at the premises before the fire has got out of control.

Automatic systems should be installed by specialist firms and should conform to British Standard 5839, Part 1, 2002.

C3.4 - Fixed and portable fire-fighting equipment

Classification of fires

A basic understanding of the classification of fires needs to be understood in order to provide and use the correct fire fighting system and equipment for the likely fires that will occur in premises.

In addition, many portable fire-fighting equipment (fire extinguishers) state the classes of fire for which they are suitable.

There are 5 classifications for fires:

CLASS A	 [A symbol]	Fires involving solids (wood, paper, plastics, etc., usually of an organic (carbon) source.
CLASS B	 [B symbol]	Fires involving liquids or liquefiable solids (petrol, oil, paint, fat, wax, etc.).
CLASS C	 [C symbol]	Fires involving gases (liquefied petroleum gas, natural gas, acetylene, etc.).
CLASS D	 [D symbol]	Fires involving metals (zinc, sodium, magnesium, aluminium and many metal powders and swarf, etc.).
ELECTRICAL HAZARDS	 [lightning symbol]	Although not a class of fire, fires in live electrical equipment cause an additional hazard requiring special consideration and the provision of suitable fire fighting equipment. This is a pictogram/statement used with extinguishers to identify their suitability for use on electrical equipment.
CLASS F	 [F symbol]	Fire involving cooking fats/oils.

Figure C3-7: Classification of fires. *Source: Rivington design/FST.*

Extinguishing media and mode of action

WATER

Water extinguishers should only be used on Class A fires - those involving solids like paper and wood. Water works by cooling the burning material to below its ignition temperature, therefore removing the heat part of the fire triangle causing the fire to go out. In addition to the cooling effect, steam is produced in the fire area due to the effects of the heat on the water; this aids in the extinguishing process by tending to smother the fire.

Water is the most common form of extinguishing media and can be used on the majority of fires involving solid materials. However water must not be used on liquid fires or in the vicinity of live electrical equipment.

FOAM

Foam is especially useful for extinguishing Class B fires - those involving burning liquids and solids which melt and turn to liquids as they burn. Foam works in several ways to extinguish the fire, the main way being to smother the burning liquid, i.e. to stop the oxygen reaching the fire zone. Foam can also be used to prevent flammable vapours escaping from spilled volatile liquids. Foam extinguishers are ideally suited for use on Class A fires, and may often be used in preference to water type extinguishers. However foam extinguishers contain water in the vicinity of live electrical equipment unless it has passed an electrical conductivity test and then only with great care from a distance of more than one metre.

POWDER (DRY POWDER)

One of the ways in which powder works to extinguish a fire is the smothering effect; it forms a thin film of powder on the burning liquid thus excluding air. It also chemically interferes with the flame propagation process. The high performance powders now on the market can be used on Class A fires, but the normal powders will only subdue this type of fire for a short while. Powders generally provide extinction faster than foam, but there is a greater risk of re-ignition. If used indoors, a powder extinguisher can cause problems for the operator due to the inhalation of the powder and obscuration of vision. It is therefore imperative that the exit route is clear and available before the extinguisher is operated.

Powder extinguishing media can be used on live electrical equipment, but may cause damage to it.

VAPORISING LIQUIDS

A few years ago vaporising liquid (Halon) extinguishers were commonplace as they were excellent extinguishers for tackling a number of different types of fires. Unfortunately the decomposition products from these extinguishers are harmful to the environment and as a result they have been withdrawn from general use. There are a select number of industries, for example, the aircraft industry, where the advantages of using these products outweigh the disadvantages and these specific industry types can still use this type of extinguisher. The extinguishers work by chemical interference with the reactions that take place in a fire, which is why they are so successful at extinguishing fires.

CARBON DIOXIDE (CO_2)

Carbon dioxide replaces the oxygen in the atmosphere surrounding the fuel and the fire is extinguished. Because it replaces the oxygen, CO_2 is an asphyxiant and should not be used in very small, confined spaces unless the operator can withdraw quickly. Unless the fire is completely extinct, it will take hold again as soon as the CO_2 disperses, dispersal usually occurs within a few seconds.

CO_2 can be used on live electrical equipment; however the operator needs to get very close to the burning equipment as the carbon dioxide needs to be injected through any air vents that are present so that the electrical equipment is filled with CO_2. It can be used for small Class B fires in their early stages, indoors or outdoors, with little air movement.

When working correctly a CO_2 extinguisher is very noisy due to the rapid expansion of gas. This expansion causes severe cooling around the discharge horn and can freeze the skin. Operators should be aware of these occurrences.

As most carbon dioxide extinguishers last only a few seconds they may only be used to tackle small fires.

CLASS C FIRES

It will be seen that only extinguishing media suitable for Class A and B fires have been dealt with above. Except in very small occurrences, a Class C fire should not normally be extinguished, and should only be extinguished if the gas supply can be isolated.

If a leak from a gas cylinder or pipework is burning, the danger area can be identified, i.e. the flames can be seen, and anything which is being affected by the flame can be seen. Where possible the area around the fire should be protected until the leak can be stopped at source by closing the valve, etc. This removes the third side of the fire triangle, the fuel. Any remaining small Class A or B fires can be dealt with using the correct extinguisher. If, however, the fire is extinguished before shutting off the supply, the area of danger cannot then be seen. The possibility of a highly flammable gas cloud spreading throughout the area must be appreciated.

CLASS D FIRES

Class D (metal) fires rarely occur and usually relate to industries that have a known metal fire risk, for example where aluminium swarf is produced. They should have special powder extinguishers on site to deal with such a fire. The powder inside the extinguisher may vary depending upon the metal risks involved.

It may also be possible to deal with metal fires by using a supply of dry sand to smother the fire. Powders such as graphite and talc can be used, but specific extinguishing agents may also be used dependant upon the metal fire risk.

CLASS F (COOKING FATS/OILS) - WET CHEMICAL

Due to the extreme difficulties in extinguishing deep fat fires with hand held extinguishers, a new type of extinguisher was designed a number of years ago. The 'Wet Chemical' extinguisher is specifically designed for use on cooking oils and fats. The extinguishing agent is water salts and it extinguishes the fires by making chemical changes to cooking oils via 'saponification' (fat turned into soluble soaps). By this method the constituency of the oil is chemically changed so that it changes to a 'soap like' solution which is non-combustible. It is worth noting that this type of extinguisher is the only one with a class F rating, so it should be supplied for any kitchen with a deep fat fryer, unless the fryer is a very small table top type where a fire blanket should be sufficient.

Design and application of fixed fire-fighting systems/equipment

When designing new buildings the opportunity to design fixed fire fighting (suppression) systems into the new build is now preferred over the use of portable fire fighting equipment. Fixed systems include local fire detection and suppression using water sprinklers or injection of suppression gases into specific areas to extinguish fires or prevent secondary explosions. Fixed systems now replace the use of internal hose reels systems in many buildings.

HOSEREELS

Hosereels are being used less in buildings today for various reasons. They are of little use to the modern Fire and Rescue Service and the disadvantages of their use by people with limited training can be significant as they create a number of health and safety hazards, including the risk of slip, trip and manual handling injuries. This, coupled with the potential risk from legionella (bacteria in stagnant line water stored at room temperature), is causing various organisations to review their use, and in some cases to withdraw them from use. If this course of action is taken, then the number of portable fire extinguishers in the premises may need to be increased to compensate.

Hosereels - use

Hosereels are designed for use on Class A - Carbonaceous fires. The hosereel acts as a replacement for water fire extinguishers and it is said that one hosereel equates to 4 x 9 litre water extinguishers.

Modern hosereels have an adjustable nozzle and can be adjusted to give a jet of water, water spray or a combination of both. The water jet is normally used for its "striking power" in attacking the seat of a fire. The jet of water should be "played" across the fire surface and into the heart of the fire to extinguish embers, etc. The spray pattern setting has less pressure at point of contact with the burning material and as such is less prone to spreading burning material than a single water jet setting. The water spray can therefore be used if the burning material is easily disturbed with the possibility of spreading the fire. The spray pattern produced allows larger areas to be covered in one go rather than if the water jet is used.

The water spray can also be used for protection purposes by placing a curtain of water droplets between the fire and the person operating the hosereel and therefore providing a barrier which reduces the radiated heat that is absorbed by the operator.

Hosereels - limitations on use

Hosereels should be connected to a permanent water supply so they are not limited by discharge time factors as are extinguishers.

New hosereel, when manufactured, should comply with BS EN 671 Part 3: 2009: "Fixed fire fighting systems", which permits up to a maximum of 30 metres of hosereel in one piece. However, equipment purchased and installed prior to BS EN 671 Part 3: 2009 being applicable would have been manufactured to BS 5306 Part 1: 2006 Fire extinguishing installations and equipment on premises. This allowed up to 45 metres on one drum of hosereel and equipment manufactured to this standard may remain in use until it is replaced. Each of these standards limits the range for use of any one hosereel by virtue of the distance that it is located away from a fire and the length of the hose.

One additional limiting factor to the use of hosereels is the friction drag created by pulling the hosereel along the floor. Considerable physical strength is required to pull 30 metres of hose, and for this reason consideration should be given to shorter lengths of hosereel being located at more frequent intervals.

Another limiting factor is the likely route through which the hosereel will need to pass. If this route includes a lot of corners, turns or doors, then hosereels may not be the most suitable fire-fighting equipment to be provided. A point to remember is that every door between the 'fire room' and the main escape route will be wedged open by the hosereel and may allow smoke and hot gases to make their way to other parts of the building.

Hosereels - advantages/disadvantages

Advantages

- Continuous supply of water - no time constraint.
- Greater quantity of water is delivered than from an extinguisher which has a better effect at extinguishing the fire.

- The person who is attempting to extinguish the fire does not need to get as close as when using extinguishers.
- A spray pattern can be produced to protect the user from radiated heat.

Disadvantages

- Considerable physical effort may be required to pull the hosereel to the fire, especially if the route is twisting and has lots of obstructions.
- Any doors through which the hosereel is pulled will become wedged open by the reel. This will present the possible problem of smoke travel within the building.
- Can only be used on Class 'A' Carbonaceous material fires.
- May create a trip hazard on the escape route.
- People may stay in the fire area for too long, and put themselves at excessive risk.

AUTOMATIC SPRINKLER SYSTEMS

Automatic sprinkler systems are used more than any other fixed fire protection system and over 40 million sprinklers are fitted worldwide each year. The purpose of an automatic sprinkler system is to detect the fire, extinguish or control the fire and to raise the alarm.

Sprinkler systems have been proven in use for well over 100 years. Possibly the oldest in Britain was fitted in 1812 at the Theatre Royal Drury Lane, London, and in updated form is still in use today.

All areas of the building to be protected are covered by a grid of pipes with sprinkler heads fitted into them at regular intervals. Water from a tank via pumps or from the town main (if it can give enough flow) fills the pipes.

Each sprinkler head will open when it reaches a specific temperature and spray water on to a fire. The hot gases from a fire are usually enough to make it operate. Only the sprinklers over the fire open. The others remain closed. This limits any damage to areas where there is no fire and reduces the amount of water needed. The sprinkler heads are spaced, generally on the ceiling, so that if one or more operate there is always sufficient flow of water. The flow is calculated so that there is always enough to control a fire taking into account the size and construction of the building and the goods stored in it or its use.

Sprinkler systems are designed to protect a pre-determined maximum fire loading. Changing the fire load, for example, by changing the goods stored for more combustible materials, or the packaging of low combustible goods, can affect the performance of the system in controlling a fire. This should form part of the fire risk assessment review. Changing the floor layout can also adversely affect the design, by increasing the area protected by some of the sprinkler heads. No sprinkler head should be expected to cover an area greater than that specified for the class of system in the relevant design standard.

Sprinkler heads can be placed in enclosed roof spaces and into floor ducts to protect areas where a fire can start without being noticed. In a large warehouse sprinklers may be placed in the storage racks as well as at the roof.

At the point where the water enters the sprinkler system there is a valve. This can be used to shut off the system for maintenance. For safety reasons it is kept locked open and only authorised persons should be able to close it. If a sprinkler opens and water flows through the valve it lets water into another pipe that causes a bell to ring. In this way the sprinkler system both controls the fire and gives an alarm using water, not electricity.

Classification of sprinkler systems

Installations can be classified under four headings, each designed to protect buildings of certain occupancy risks, for example school (light), foam plastic store (extra high).

1) Light hazard system.
2) Ordinary hazard system.
3) High hazard system.
4) Extra high hazard system.

Each installation consists of a range of pipes, suitably graded in size and generally suspended from a roof or ceiling, connected through controlling valves to one or more water supplies. The pipework is fitted throughout the building; it is designed to protect with sprinkler heads, spaced between approximately 2 and 3 metres apart, according to the risk in the building.

The sprinkler heads cover all parts of the building, including concealed spaces, stairways and passageways. The maximum area that one sprinkler head can cover varies between approximately 2.5 m^2 and 9 m^2 according to the classification of risk, type of system and location of the heads.

Types of sprinkler system

Wet system

In this system the pipework is charged with water under pressure at all times. This system is employed where there is no risk of frost, in climates where freezing is unknown or where the building is continuously heated during the winter months. The wet system sprinklers are usually fitted pendant below the sprinkler pipework.

Dry pipe

In buildings where the water in the sprinkler pipes is likely to freeze, a "dry" pipe system is used. All installation pipes which would normally carry water are charged with air at a moderate pressure and the water is held back out of the reach of frost by a differential air valve which lifts and allows water to enter the pipework system when a sprinkler head opens and releases the air in the pipes.

Alternative wet and dry

This is the system which is adopted for the protection of buildings in which freezing is only likely for part of the year. In this system the pipework is charged with water in the summer and with compressed air in the winter.

In this system the pipework is arranged with a gradual fall towards the installation and the sprinkler heads are fitted above the pipes to facilitate draining.

Pre-action system

This is a combination of a standard dry, or alternative wet/dry sprinkler system, and an independent approved system of heat or smoke detectors installed in the same area. The heat or smoke detectors will operate at a lower temperature than the sprinklers and the pre-action valve will allow water to flow into the pipework before the first sprinkler head operates.

In an extensive building there may be several installations, some of which may be wet and some alternate according to its susceptibility to frost. It should be borne in mind that each installation is self-contained so that one system is unaffected by another, having its own controlling valves, separate connections to the water supplies, and a separate alarm gong for each system. In addition each system is numbered and painted a different colour. Apart from the obvious advantages of the foregoing it also serves as a reliable guide as to the section of the building involved in a fire and in many instances the room in which the fire originated.

Features of a sprinkler system

Main supply pipe

The water supply pipe feeds water to the system and is usually a large pipe of up to 30 cm diameter. The sprinkler system is normally fed by two separate supplies.

Controlling valves (wet system) - sprinkler stop valve

This valve is of the usual wedge type and is provided on the supply side as a means of cutting off the water supply to the installation following the extinguishment of the fire and is normally kept strapped and padlocked in the open position, a strap being used so that in the event of the key not being available to open the lock, the strap can be cut thus enabling the stop valve to be closed. Upon arrival at a fire or where a sprinkler system has actuated, the officer in charge of the first attendance will station a firefighter at the stop valve to ensure that it is *not* closed down until he/she gives orders to that effect.

Pressure gauges

Two pressure gauges are fitted to each set of valves; one is connected to the supply side of the stop valve and the other to the delivery or installation side of the valve. The former indicates the pressure in the mains or other sources of supply, the latter to record the pressure in the installation. Also in the case of the latter, to record the air pressure on the installation when the system is on air, in the case of the alternative system.

Distribution pipes

From the main valve there is a series of distribution pipes which reduce in size as they get nearer to the sprinkler heads.

Sprinkler heads

Two main types of sprinkler heads are in use throughout the country, all conforming to a similar design and principle of operation. These are fusible soldered strut or quartzoid bulb. The main components of a sprinkler head are:

- Main body with screw thread for screwing into pipework.
- Yoke, i.e. 'V' shaped casting.
- Distributor at the base of the yoke.
- Diaphragm (a flexible metal plate with a hole in the centre secured between the yoke casting and the main body).
- Glass valve (a hemispherical glass valve which seats against the diaphragm).
- Glass valve cap (a small brass cap which butts against the underside of the glass valve and is recessed to house one end of a metal strut).

Fusible soldered strut

With a fusible soldered strut sprinkler head, the strut is composed of three pieces of metal joined together with a low melting point solder. When this solder is softened by the heat of the fire, the strut falls apart and the glass valve is thrown clear. The water escapes in a solid half inch jet, impinges upon the distributor plate and is scattered in all directions in the form of a drenching spray. In order to protect against deterioration in the operation, certain corrosive resistant coatings are applied to the sprinkler by the manufacturer.

It is also recommended that petroleum jelly be applied to all heads periodically. The operating temperatures at which sprinkler heads are designed to operate are identified by various colours.

Colour of yoke arms	Soldered strut
Uncoloured	66-74°C
White	93-100°C
Blue	141°C
Yellow	182°C
Red	227°C

Figure C3-8: Fusible soldered strut - operating temperatures for sprinkler heads. *Source: FST.*

Quartzoid bulb type

The main structure of the head is retained but in place of the struts a barrel shaped bulb made of Quartzoid (a transparent material) of unusual strength and toughness is used. This bulb is hermetically sealed after being filled with a highly expandable liquid (coloured). When the head is exposed to a rise in temperature pressure within the bulb rises quickly, and fractures of the bulb results.

These sprinkler heads are made to operate at various temperatures. In temperate climates and for general use, the usual operating temperature for normal situations is 68°C, but for use in special conditions, such as is met in drying stoves, ovens, etc. higher operating temperatures are necessary.

Figure C3-9: Quartzoid bulb sprinkler head. *Source: www.bintouqfire.com.*

The Quartzoid bulb is so strong that it can stand any hydraulic pressure which may be applied to the interior of the sprinkler head. The filling in the whole range of Quartzoid bulbs cannot freeze however severe the frost may be. These sprinklers are equally suitable for the coldest as well as the hottest climate. The bulb is completely resistant to acid or any corrosive action and in any situation will preserve its effectiveness unimpaired for an indefinitely long period. The operating temperatures at which sprinkler heads are designed to operate are identified by various colours.

Sprinkler rating	Colour of bulbs
57°C	Orange
68°C	Red
79°C	Yellow
93°C	Green
141°C	Blue
182°C	Mauve
204 to 260°C	Black

Figure C3-10: Quartzoid bulb type - operating temperatures for sprinkler heads. *Source: FST.*

The diffuser breaks up the water flow into carefully controlled droplets which penetrate the fire plume and cool the burning material to below its ignition point, thus controlling the fire. Only the sprinkler(s) directly over the fire are operated.

Water supplies and systems

The water supplies for a sprinkler system must be reliable under all conditions and adequate for the appropriate class of risk. They are divided into grades according to the number and type of water supplies available.

There are generally at least two separate water systems on a high risk site:

- Hydrant system (internal and/or external).
- Spray water system.

Figure C3-11: Quartzoid bulb operation sequence. *Source: COMPCO Fire Systems.*

ELEMENT C3 - WORKPLACE FIRE RISK ASSESSMENT

Hydrant system

The main hydrant systems form ring mains and are for general use in protecting buildings and other such risks. The system is generally kept primed with clean water but not under pressure, with the pumps being on manual start. The water supply can be from a river or the sea. There are external manifolds into which the Fire and Rescue Service can connect their pumps to supplement the system. Some hydrants are coupled to dry risers which are only pressurised when water is pumped into the low level inlet.

Spray water system

The spray water system is the main fire protection system comprising high velocity waterspray, medium velocity cooling sprays, sprinkler and selected internal/external hydrants.

The spray water system is the main fire protection system comprising high velocity waterspray, medium velocity cooling sprays, sprinkler and selected internal/external hydrants. The system can also supply high velocity water to serve low expansion foam base injection equipment protecting gas turbines and fuel oil tanks.

The water systems form ring mains and are supplied from trunk mains pressurised from a tank charged partly with water from a jockey pump and partly with air from a compressor, with the fire pumps available to cut in when the mains pressure falls when water is being taken from the system. These systems generally use town or raw water supplies.

The pressure tank is a cylindrical steel vessel with convex ends filled with air under pressure and water. The general requirements for a pressure tank are:

- It must be housed in a readily accessible position in a sprinkler protected building or in a separate building of incombustible construction used for no purpose other than for the housing of fire protection water supplies. The tank must be adequately protected against mechanical damage. The temperature of the room should be maintained above 4°C.
- When used as a single water supply, the tank must be provided with an approved arrangement for maintaining automatically the required air pressure and water level in the tank under non-fire conditions. The arrangement should include an approved warning system to indicate failure of the devices to restore the correct pressure and water level. This arrangement is also advocated in cases where the tank provides the duplicate supply.
- The tank must be fitted with air pressure gauges and a gauge glass to show the level of the water. Stop valves and back pressure valves must be provided on both the water and air supply connections to the tank and they must be fixed as close to the tank as possible.

High velocity water sprays

Effective fire protection is afforded by projectors which project a fine spray. The main difference between a water spray projector system and a sprinkler system is that the projectors are not only located overhead but may be sited all around the area of risk. They can be installed to discharge in a horizontal, or even, in certain circumstances, an upward direction. The main application is for the protection and containment of plant using or storing insulating oil (for example, immersion of electrical tansformers in zoned areas), lubricating oil, fuel oils and other flammable liquids. High velocity water sprays project water at high velocity to emulsify oils and liquids at risk. ***They may be used as an extinguishing system as well as for protection from fire.***

The water sprays system is characterised by the type of water projectors selected and these characteristics vary in regard to their density of flow, discharge angle, maximum spacing between projectors and maximum range from the equipment to be protected. The type, characteristics and range of projectors differ with each manufacturer, consequently projector coverage, design and configuration of systems offered will vary. Each water spray nozzle should include a thimble strainer integrated within the nozzle to prevent blockage of the nozzle exit by any debris in solution or inadvertently picked up in the pipework. The point of projectors must not be moved once set; otherwise the area will no longer be fully protected.

Medium velocity water sprays

This system is used for protecting such risks as Bulk Hydrogen, Chlorine and Propane stores and has been used for cooling the external surface areas of bulk gas turbine fuel storage tanks. ***It is not an extinguishing system*** and unlike high pressure water spray systems operates at a lower pressure of 1.4 to 3.5 bar at the sprays. Volatile liquid fire situations cannot be extinguished by the application of medium velocity water sprays but close control of a fire can be obtained at the same time rendering adjacent plant and structures safe by the cooling effect of the water film. This form of protection also gives protection to personnel when fighting fires on this type of risk. Without it, close approach to the seat of the fire might not be possible.

GAS FLOODING AND DRENCHER SYSTEMS

Chemical fire extinguishing systems that are designed and installed in buildings to detect and extinguish fires are commonly called inerting or extinguishment flood systems.

Inerting can be defined as the displacement of the atmosphere in a confined space by a non-combustible gas (such as nitrogen) to such an extent that the resulting atmosphere does not sustain combustion. Traditional flood systems, such as those using carbon dioxide or nitrogen, where the displacement of air within the enclosure is necessary for their successful operation may be considered to be inerting systems.

For systems that use specialist chemicals such as Inergen the manufacturers claim that it is safe for people to be inside the area with the system active and operated. In order for there to be sufficient air to breathe, the system cannot have displaced all of the air from the enclosure and works in a different way to standard inerting chemicals. It may be more useful therefore to think of these systems as extinguishment flood systems.

Carbon dioxide flooding

Fixed carbon dioxide installations in the United Kingdom are usually of the high pressure type in which the gas is stored in liquid form in drawn steel cylinders each containing from 22 to 35 kg (50 to 80 lb) of CO_2 at a pressure of 48-58.5 bar depending on the atmospheric temperature. The cylinders may be used singly or may be connected to a manifold in batteries.

Characteristics of fixed installations

Carbon dioxide is stored in the cylinders as a liquid, and when released it travels in the same form through the pipework to the discharge nozzles. In the case of high-pressure systems, a discharge horn is fitted to the nozzle to prevent the entrainment of air with gas, minimise turbulence, and reduce the high velocity of the discharge. The release of pressure allows the liquid to turn partly to 'snow', solid CO_2 which emerges at a temperature of -79°C, and partly to gas. Carbon dioxide extinguishes a fire principally by reducing the oxygen concentration in the vicinity of the burning material.

Operation of CO_2 systems

A single cylinder is often manually operated by a pull handle, provided either close to the cylinder or at a point outside the space protected. The handle is connected to a cable which, when pulled, withdraws a pin holding a weight in place above the operating level on the cylinder, so that the withdrawal of the pin allows the weight to drop on the lever and so open the cylinder. A battery of cylinders can be similarly operated. Above the lever of each cylinder is a weight and all the weights are held up by a common operating shaft. When the support, which keeps the shaft in place, is released (by pulling the releasing handle) the weights fall on the respective levels and so operate the cylinders.

A fixed CO_2 installation may be operated manually, as we have described above, or automatically by means of air-expansion thermostats or, more usually, by fusible links.

The systems are classified as manual or automatic according to the method of actuation, although the automatic system will also have some means of manual control. Before work or inspections are carried out in any enclosure protected by automatic CO_2, or other chemical extinguishing equipment, the automatic control is rendered inoperative and the equipment left on hand control; a notice to this effect is attached to the equipment, and a permit-to-work system is normally employed.

The automatic control is restored immediately after the persons engaged on the work or inspections have come out of the protected enclosure. Any precautions which are taken to render the automatic control inoperative are noted on any Permit for Work issued for work in the protected enclosure. If it is necessary to enter a space flooded with CO_2 breathing apparatus must be worn because CO_2, although not toxic, is an asphyxiant and excludes oxygen from the room.

Environmentally friendly flood systems

Due to the removal of Halon systems from buildings alternatives are now readily available. There is generally no straight replacement for Halon; however an American company has now launched Fike 25 which utilises existing pipework. All other alternative systems are a complete new refit.

There is a choice of inert gases such as argon, nitrogen, argonite or suppression systems such as Du Pont FE-200®.

Inert gases extinguish fires by diluting the air in the room to such an extent that there is not sufficient oxygen for a fire to continue. The suppression systems works by interfering with the chemical combustion process.

WATER MIST SYSTEMS

Figure C3-12: Cylinders for flood system. *Source: AFE.*

Water mist systems are hailed as one of the most rapid, safe and environmentally friendly ways of suppressing fires. Water mist systems can be used for total flooding, in-cabinet protection and local applications, and these can be combined to suit almost any scenario imaginable.

In its various modes, water mist systems are ideally suited for the protection of art galleries, computer and telecommunications equipment, generating plant, robotic machinery, cable tunnels, kitchens, and many similar applications. Water mist works by a mixture of cooling and smothering.

ELEMENT C3 - WORKPLACE FIRE RISK ASSESSMENT

FIXED FOAM INSTALLATIONS

Fixed foam installations are used against flammable liquids, and generally consist of foam pourers or foam-making branches fed with a supply of foam. The foam is normally the mechanical type foam produced by mixing foam-making compound and water and passing it through a foam-making generator. These generators are designed to mix the correct proportions of foam compound and air with the quantity of water which is flowing, to generate foam and then deliver it through pipework to the point of discharge. The foam so produced normally has an expansion ratio of approximately 8:1. High expansion foam with an expansion ratio of 1,000:1 will be discussed at the end of this sub-section.

It is less easy to arrange for fixed foam installations to operate automatically than is the case with other extinguishing agents. Not only is it vital that the system should operate immediately a fire starts, but it is equally important that it should be shut down as soon as the supply of compound or solution is exhausted; otherwise water alone will reach the foam pourers, with potentially disastrous results.

It is because of this that completely self-contained fixed installations are generally limited to relatively small risks, such as isolated indoor transformers. Small scale fixed foam systems, incorporating a supply of wet chemical extinguishing agent and a pressurizing gas supply, are frequently installed in kitchens over deep fat frying ranges.

For large risks, like oil storage tanks, the fixed installation consists of fixed piping (arranged to suit the risk) terminating in foam pourers or fixed monitors; the piping is run back to an appropriate point and terminates in a coupling, usually protected by a glass panel marked with the words 'foam inlet', together with an indication of the particular risk involved. This arrangement ensures that foam can be applied where it is required; as long as foam compound and water under pressure is available to a foam generator or foam inductor at this point, a continuous supply of foam can be channelled to the required spot.

Use of high expansion foam

It has been shown that high expansion foam, with an expansion ratio of 100:1, may be used as a practical method of fire protection, particularly for special risk areas which are otherwise difficult to protect effectively. High expansion foam can fill an entire building in a matter of minutes; it is a good heat insulator and is effective on ordinary surface fires as well as on flammable liquids.

DRY POWDER INSTALLATIONS

Dry powders, offer the advantage of a quick knock-down of fire and they have negligible toxic effects. Their major disadvantage is that they require a lot of clearing up once an installation has operated. Compacting of the powder is also a problem, due to heat or vibration or moist atmospheres during storage. This could present difficulties in the maintenance of the system especially after discharge when compacting could take place in valves, etc. Recently developed powders (for example 'Monnex') appear, however, to be free of this problem.

A dry powder installation consists of dry powder containers linked by pipework to discharge nozzles covering the areas of risk. When a fire occurs it is necessary to pressurise the powder so that it is forced through the pipework and discharge nozzles. This is usually done with CO_2. A line detector is linked to a lever which then actuated allows the head of a CO_2 cylinder to be pierced. The carbon dioxide thus released pressurises the dry powder and forces it over the protected area. Dry powder installations can usually be operated either automatically or manually.

Fixed fire fighting siting, maintenance and training requirements

HOSEREELS

Siting of hosereels

- One hosereel should be provided for every 800m^2 or part thereof.
- Hosereels should be sited in prominent and accessible positions at each floor level adjacent to exits in corridors on exit routes in such a way that the nozzle can be taken into every room and every part of the room.
- Preferably hosereels should be installed into recesses so as not to obstruct the means of escape.
- Any doors fitted to hosereel cupboard doors should open through 180 degrees.

Maintenance of hosereels

(A) Monthly inspection

A check should be made to ensure that the hosereel system is intact and has no obvious signs of damage. The operating valves should be checked to ensure that they are in the correct position and that they are free moving.

(B) Annual test

- The hosereel should be run out to its full length and checked for damage or defects.
- The hosereel valve and the nozzle should be checked to ensure free movement throughout its operating range.

- The water supply should be switched on and the nozzle operated to check that a suitable water jet is obtained.
- It would be good practice to check that 24 litres min. of water is supplied from the topmost reel - with the 2 topmost reels operating at the same time.
- Whilst the hosereel is pressurised, a check should be made for any leaks from the system.

Training related to hosereels

Though the Regulatory Reform (Fire Safety) Order (RRFSO) 2005 does not specify specific training for fire extinguishers it does require "suitable and sufficient instruction and training on the appropriate precautions and actions to be taken by employee". It further requires that training be carried out periodically where appropriate.

If an employee is expected to make use of hosereels this Article confirms that initial and periodic training must take place. The need for training of employees will increase if hosereels are installed in buildings as people may be tempted to stay in buildings for too long when attempting to fight the fire. Consideration should be given to using teams of two or more to operate hosereels to help assure an individual's safety.

SPRINKLERS

Siting of sprinkler systems

Sprinkler systems will be sited in accordance with the finding of the risk assessment; particular focus will typically be given to areas of high risk, where flammable materials processes are stored or carried out. Low risk workplaces and safe exits will also typically be covered.

Maintenance of sprinkler systems

Daily checks

- The alarm connection to the Fire and Rescue Service or the remote manned centre should be tested daily if it is not automatically monitored.
- Check water levels and air pressures in pressure tanks if not automatically monitored.

Weekly checks

Check and record:

- All water and air pressure gauge readings on installation, trunk mains and pressure tanks.
- All water levels in elevated private reservoirs, rivers, canals, lakes, water storage tanks and pressure tanks.
- Test each water motor alarm for 30 seconds.

Automatic pump starting tests:

- Check oil, fuel levels.
- Simulate a pressure fall to operate automatic start.
- Check pressure at which pump cuts in - is it correct?
- Check the electrolyte level and density of any lead acid batteries.
- If heating systems are fitted to prevent freezing, they should be checked.

Quarterly checks

A complete check is done normally by an engineer, plus a check should be made to ensure that there have been no structural changes or alteration of layout of contents that would impede the effectiveness of the sprinkler system.

In addition, there are checks at 6 month, 1 year, 3 year and 15 year intervals. These are normally completed by a service engineer.

Training relating to sprinkler systems

All staff, and others, in the workplace should be trained in fire extinguishing systems purpose and function. The responsible person should liaise with any maintenance or modification engineers proposing to work on any fixed system. This should occur before any work is carried out to ensure alternative fire protection arrangements are in place if the work is potentially liable to compromise the system in the event of a fire.

Portable fire fighting equipment

Though there is a wide range of portable fire fighting equipment available the most common type of portable fire fighting equipment is the fire extinguisher.

TYPES OF FIRE EXTINGUISHER

From 1st January 1997 all types of new certified fire extinguishers should have a red body. In addition, BS EN 3 allows manufacturers to use up to 5% of the extinguisher casing in another colour in order to differentiate between extinguishers that use a different extinguishing medium.

British Standard BS 7863 Part 1: 1984 and Part 2: 1980 recommends that manufacturers affix different colour coded panels (for example, labels or bands) using the existing colour code scheme noted below when describing the different extinguishers.

ELEMENT C3 - WORKPLACE FIRE RISK ASSESSMENT

Extinguisher medium	Colour code	Extinguisher medium	Colour code
Water	Red	Wet chemical	Yellow
Spray foam	Cream	Carbon dioxide	Black
Dry powder	Blue		

Figure C3-13: Colour coded panels recommended for manufactures to use by BS 7863. *Source: FST.*

Water - red and white

Foam - red and cream

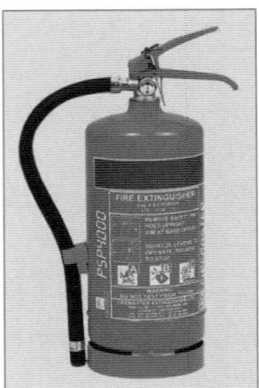
Powder - red and blue

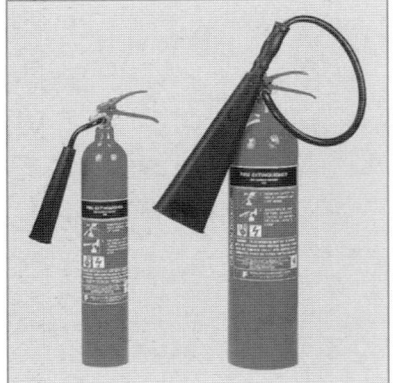
Carbon dioxide - red and black

Wet chemical - red and yellow

Fire blanket - red and white

Figure C3-14: Various fire extinguishing media. *Source: FST.*

APPLICATION OF FIRE EXTINGUISHERS

Summary matrix - fire extinguishing media use on classes of fire

	Method	Class 'A'	Class 'B'	Class 'C'	Class 'D'	Electric	Class 'F'
Water	Cools	Yes	No	No	No	No	No
Spray foam	Smothers	Yes	Yes	No	No	No	No
Wet chemical	Chemical	Some manufacturers	No	No	No	No	Yes
Dry powder	Smothers and Chemical	Limited	Yes	Yes and Isolate	Special Powders	Yes - Low Voltage	No
Vapourising liquids	Chemical and Smothers	Special uses					
Carbon dioxide	Smothers	No	Yes - Small Fires	No	No	Yes	No

Figure C3-15: Summary matrix - fire extinguishers. *Source: RMS.*

Method of operation

There are now only two basic methods by which fire extinguishers are operated - stored pressure type and gas cartridge type. The method of operation will be marked on the extinguisher.

Application of fire extinguisher related to their fire ratings

Some attempt is made at showing the limits of the fire extinguisher by stating its fire rating. However, this is only done for Class A and Class B.

Class A fire ratings are achieved by an extinguisher successfully putting out a designated size of test fire. The test fire is made from Pinus Silvestris (commonly called Scots Pine) and the rating achieved relates directly to the length and number of pieces of timber used to construct the test fire, for example a 13A rated extinguisher, extinguished a fire constructed of 14 layers of sticks, each transverse layer consisting of 13 sticks (500 mm each), the test fire being 1.3 metres long.

Class B fire ratings are similarly achieved but the fires consist of specified containers of flammable liquid (aliphatic hydrocarbon). The test fire rating achieved relates directly to the volume in litres of fuel, for example a 55B rated extinguisher extinguished a fire consisting of 55 litres of fuel with a surface area of 1.73 square metres.

As can be seen from the illustrations given above, the procedure for test fire ratings is quite involved and, if required, further guidance on this matter may be sought from EN 3 1996. Fire extinguishers are installed into buildings in relation to their fire ratings:

Class A fires:	Minimum of 2 extinguishers per floor, unless maximum of 100 m^2 on upper floor area and in single occupancy.
	Floor area m^2 x 0.065 = Class A fire rating required in building/floor area.
Class B fires:	Assess premises in four ways: ■ Each room/enclosure to be considered separately. ■ Fire risks over 20 m apart consider separately. ■ Fire risks less than 20 m apart treat as an undivided or divided group. ■ Risk of a spillage fire.
Spillage:	Rating required = 10 x volume of spillage.
Undivided group:	Containers less than 2 m apart consider as a single container. Therefore total surface area of all containers is used.
Divided group:	Containers more than 2 m apart but less than 20 m apart consider as separate risks. Therefore surface area of largest containers is used.

Figure C3-16: Fire extinguishers in relation to their fire ratings. *Source: FST.*

Extinguisher rating	Max area for 3 foam extinguishers m sq	Max area for 2 extinguishers m sq	Max area for 1 extinguisher m sq
21 B	0.42	0.26	0.14
55 B	1.1	0.69	0.37
144 B	2.88	1.8	0.96

Figure C3-17: Maximum area of a Class B fire. (Demonstration examples only, this is not a comprehensive list). *Source: FST.*

Maximum area of Class B fire (deep liquid) for which extinguishers (foam extinguishers only) are suitable			
Extinguisher Rating	Maximum area for three extinguishers m^{-2}	Maximum area for two extinguishers m^{-2}	Maximum area for one extinguisher m^{-2}
21B	0.42	0.26	0.14
34B	0.68	0.42	0.23
55B	1.10	0.69	0.37
70B	1.40	0.88	0.47
89B	1,78	1.11	0.59
113B	2.26	1.41	0.75
144B	2.88	1.8	0.96
183B	3.66	2.29	1.22
233B	4.66	2.91	1.55

Figure C3-18: Maximum area of Class B fire. *Source: BS 5306, part 8.*

Fire extinguishers - limitations

Fire extinguishers are limited firstly to the class of fire on which they can be successfully used. It would not be good practice and may be dangerous to use extinguishers on types of fires for which they are not approved. In summary the mode of action, advantage and limitations of all fire extinguishers can be summarised ***see Figure C3-19.***

ELEMENT C3 - WORKPLACE FIRE RISK ASSESSMENT

Extinguishing Media	Mode of action (method)	Advantage	Limitation
Water	Principal method is cooling, but smothering does take place in immediate fire area.	Simple to use, good throw of water so person can stay a distance away from the fire.	Small water jet on older portable extinguisher type, so harder to cover large surface areas. Newer type gives a spray design which gives better area cover, but shorter throw. Not to be used in vicinity of electrical equipment or flammable liquids.
Foam	Principal method is smothering but cooling also occurs, plus if used on a flammable liquid the vapours given off are suppressed.	Can be used as a replacement for water, but has advantage of other uses. All modern foam extinguishers are the spray type, so area coverage is good.	Due to spray pattern, distance of throw is reduced so operator has to get closer. If used as a replacement for water is not as effective as a water jet if being used on a small area such as a waste bin due to overspray. Not to be used in vicinity of electrical equipment.
Dry Powder	Principal quoted method is smothering, but it also affects the flame propagation process.	Very quick knock down of flames. Can be used on various types of fire.	Extremely messy in use, loss of vision in area with potential hazard to operator. Powder dust would create a health hazard to anyone with a breathing issue such as asthma. Powder does not penetrate inside a solid fuel area easily and there is no cooling effect. Re-ignition can therefore be an issue.
Vaporising Liquid (Halon)	Chemical interference with combustion process.	Quick knock down of flames and can be used on various types of fire.	Damages environment, and gases given off when used on fires can be harmful to people. Only allowed to be used by a few specific industries.
Wet Chemical	Chemical interference with fuel product by 'saponification'.	Only extinguishing media approved for use on cooking oils and fats and is effective in use.	Has limitations due to surface area of oil involved and it is necessary to verify that size of extinguisher is suitable.
Carbon Dioxide (Gaseous)	Extinguishes by smothering as it replaces and suppresses oxygen levels in the immediate fire area to below 16%.	Excellent for use on electrical equipment as extinguishing media does not conduct electricity. Can also be used on very small flammable liquid fires.	Only effective if access to air vents of equipment can be achieved at close proximity. If this is not possible, the gas will 'bounce' off electrical item and not enter the component part and the fire will not be extinguished. The gas does replace and suppress oxygen levels, so care should be taken if being used in a very small confined area. Once discharged the operator should withdraw from the immediate area. Gas expansion causes area around nozzle to get very cold and causes loud noise.

Figure C3-19: Summary matrix - extinguishing media. *Source: FST.*

Duration of discharge

The effectiveness of a fire extinguisher is limited by the duration of discharge. Some extinguishers only last for very small periods of time and for this reason can only be used on small fires. The minimum duration of discharge for extinguishers is as shown in the following table.

Nominal charge of extinguisher (kg or litres)	*Minimum duration of discharge of extinguisher (seconds)*
Up to and including 3	6
More than 3 but less than or equal to 6	9
More than 6 but less than or equal to 10	12
More than 10	15

Figure C3-20: Minimum duration of discharge - extinguisher. *Source: FST.*

WORKPLACE FIRE RISK ASSESSMENT - ELEMENT C3

Range of discharge

The extinguisher is also limited by the range (or throw) of the discharge. This would affect the maximum distance that a person could be from a fire and still be effective in extinguishing the fire. Since it would not be safe for the operator of an extinguisher to get too close to a fire, if the range of discharge is too short then it will not be possible to extinguish the fire using this equipment.

Portable fire fighting systems siting, maintenance and training requirements

SITING OF EXTINGUISHERS

Portable fire extinguishers should always be sited:

- On the line of escape routes.
- Near, but not too near, to danger points.
- Near to room exits inside or outside according to occupancy and/or risk.
- In multi-storey buildings, at same position on each floor, i.e. top of stair flights or at corners in corridors.
- Where possible in groups forming fire points.
- Where possible in shallow recesses, if sited on a wall.
- So that no person need travel more than 30 metres to reach an extinguisher.
- With the carrying handle about one metre from the floor to facilitate ease of handling, and removal from wall bracket, or on purpose designed floor stands.
- Away from excesses of heat or cold.

Figure C3-21: Extinguisher well sited on escape route.

Figure C3-22: Incorrectly sited plant.   *Sources: FST.*

MAINTENANCE OF EXTINGUISHERS

British Standard Code of Practice BS 5306: Part 3: 2009 - "Fire extinguishing installations and equipment on premises" details the inspection, maintenance and testing of portable fire extinguishers as follows:

(a) Monthly inspection

The British Standard recommends a monthly check of extinguishers. The monthly check should include:

- Located in proper place.
- If discharged.
- Correct pressure.
- Any obvious damage.

(b) Annual inspection and maintenance

A more thorough inspection of extinguishers, spare gas cartridges and replacement charges should be carried out by a competent person on an annual basis. This may include internal and external inspection dependent upon the type of extinguisher.

(c) Test by discharge

Extinguishers should be tested by discharge at intervals as detailed below. The time interval should be taken from the date of manufacture or the last actual discharge.

Extinguisher type	Interval of discharge
Water (stored pressure)	Every 5 years
Foam (all types)	Every 5 years
Water (gas cartridge)	Every 5 years
Powder (gas cartridge)	Every 5 years

Extinguisher type	Interval of discharge
Powder (stored pressure valve operated)	Every 5 years
Carbon Dioxide (all types)	Every 10 years

Figure C3-23: Extinguisher intervals of discharge. *Source: BS 5306, part 3.*

The above information is only a portion of the information on maintenance, inspections and testing. For further details the British Standard should be consulted.

TRAINING REQUIREMENTS FOR EXTINGUISHERS

Though the RRFSO 2005 does not specify specific training for fire extinguishers it does require "suitable and sufficient instruction and training on the appropriate precautions and actions to be taken by employee". It further requires that training be carried out periodically where appropriate. If an employee is expected to make use of extinguishers this Article confirms that initial and periodic training must take place. Any person, who may be called upon to use a fire extinguisher, should be trained in the selection and practical use of the equipment.

Environment, including fire water runoff

The RRFSO 2005 places a duty on the 'Responsible Person' to 'mitigate the effects of the fire'. This incorporates environmental damage that may result as a direct consequence of the fire itself and fire fighting operations. The major pollutant at fires is water run off, which is caused by the water used for fire fighting which does not turn to steam, entering into the water courses. This water contains many pollutants and is very damaging to the marine environment.

The fire risk assessment required under the RRFSO 2005 should therefore consider the drainage system on site, as well as the water table level and any natural water sources such as rivers or streams. Dependant upon the perceived risk, drain covers, sandbags, portable dams and various items of specialist equipment may need to be made available to the fire and rescue service to help in the containment of water run off and the subsequent environmental protection. There are various documents available via the Environmental Protection Agency website which will assist with this issue.

C3.5 - Means of escape

Factors to be considered in the provision and maintenance of a means of escape

LEGAL FACTORS

The RRFSO 2005, Article 14, specifies the following requirements with regard to emergency routes and exits:

"(1) Where necessary in order to safeguard the safety of relevant persons, the responsible person must ensure that routes to emergency exits from premises and the exits themselves are kept clear at all times.

(2) The following requirements must be complied with in respect of premises where necessary (whether due to the features of the premises, the activity carried on there, any hazard present or any other relevant circumstances) in order to safeguard the safety of relevant persons:

  (a) Emergency routes and exits must lead as directly as possible to a place of safety.

  (b) In the event of danger, it must be possible for persons to evacuate the premises as quickly and as safely as possible.

  (c) The number, distribution and dimensions of emergency routes and exits must be adequate having regard to the use, equipment and dimensions of the premises and the maximum number of persons who may be present there at any one time.

  (d) Emergency doors must open in the direction of escape.

  (e) Sliding or revolving doors must not be used for exits specifically intended as emergency exits.

  (f) Emergency doors must not be so locked or fastened that they cannot be easily and immediately opened by any person who may require using them in an emergency.

  (g) Emergency routes and exits must be indicated by signs.

  (h) Emergency routes and exits requiring illumination must be provided with emergency lighting of adequate intensity in the case of failure of their normal lighting".

The RRFSO 2005 places a duty on the Secretary of State to make available guidance to assist those that need to comply with the main articles of the Order.

Eleven guides have been established to provide guidance on compliance in a variety of types of premises, for example, offices, factories, healthcare and educational premises. These guides include guidance on establishing appropriate means of escape for the particular type of premises.

The guides to the RRFSO 2005 indicate the following as common themes to consider when considering means of escape:

- The type and number of people using the premises.
- Escape time.
- The age and construction of the premises.
- The number and complexity of escape routes and exits.
- Whether lifts can or need to be used.
- The use of phased or delayed alarm evacuation.
- Assisted means of escape/personal evacuation plans (PEEPS).

DEFINITION OF MEANS OF ESCAPE

The following is a widely accepted definition of means of escape:

"Route(s) provided to ensure safe egress from the premises or other locations to a place of total safety".

Figure C3-24: Definition of means of escape. *Source: Fire safety risk assessment - a guide for offices.*

A careful study of some of the main words used in the definition is useful in order to consider the overall goals of the provision of means of escape.

Route(s)

Good means of escape must be part of the structure of the building and made immovable. The effect of this is to generally rule out the use of most portable self rescue devices which cannot be relied upon to be in position when required.

Egress

It should be possible for the person escaping to turn their back on the fire and make their away to a safe place. This should be possible from all parts of the building.

Place of total safety

A place of total safety is ideally in the open air from where dispersal can take place. Though it is the goal of the means of escape to lead to a place of total safety when evacuating high buildings it is often necessary to devise a 'halfway' place of safety, and this may be defined as a place of 'comparative safety'.

STRATEGIC FACTORS AFFECTING MEANS OF ESCAPE

- Occupancy.
- Construction.
- Time of evacuation.
- Exits.
- Travel distance.
- Management.

Occupancy

This factor divides into:

1) The people in the building (population).
2) The use to which the building is put.

Population

- Number of occupants.
- Physical condition.
- Expected reactions.
- Asleep or awake.

Space is calculated when the area is empty - before the installation of equipment and storage.

Type of accommodation [2] [3]	Floor space factor m^2/person
Standing spectator areas, bars without seating and similar refreshment areas	0.3
Amusement arcade, assembly hall (including a general purpose place of assembly), bingo hall, club, crush hall, dance floor/hall, venue for pop concert and similar events	0.5
Concourse, queuing area or shopping mall [4]	0.7
Committee room, common room, conference room, dining room, licensed betting office (public area), lounge or bar (other than in 1 above), meeting room, reading room, restaurant, staff room or waiting room [5]	1.0
Exhibition hall or studio (film, radio, television, recording)	1.5
Skating rink	2.0
Shop sales area [6]	2.0
Art gallery, dormitory, factory reproduction area, museum or workshop	5.0
Office	6.0

ELEMENT C3 - WORKPLACE FIRE RISK ASSESSMENT

Type of accommodation [2] [3]	Floor space factor m^2/person
Shop sales area [7]	7.0
Kitchen or library	7.0
Bedroom or study bedroom	8.0
Bed-sitting room, billiards or snooker room or hall	10.0
Storage and warehousing	30.0
Car park	Two persons per car parking space

Figure C3-25: Floor space factors[1]. Source: Approved Document B (2000 Edition incorporating 2000 and 2002 amendments).

Notes:

1) As an alternative to using values in the table, the floor space factor may be determined by reference to actual data taken from similar premises. Where appropriate, the data should reflect the average occupant density at a peak trading time of year.

2) Where accommodation is not directly covered by the descriptions given, a reasonable value based on a similar use may be selected.

3) Where any part of the building is to be used for more than one type of accommodation, the most onerous factor(s) should be applied. Where the building contains different types of accommodation, the occupancy of each different area should be calculated using the relevant space factor.

4) Refer to section 4 of BS 5588-10:1991 *Code of Practice for shopping complexes* for detailed guidance on the calculation of occupancy in common public areas in shopping complexes.

5) Alternatively the occupant capacity may be taken as the number of fixed seats provided, if the occupants will be normally seated.

6) Shops excluding those under item 10, but including - supermarkets and department stores (main sales areas), shops for personal services such as hairdressing and shops for the delivery or collection of goods for cleaning, repair or other treatment or for members of the public themselves carrying out such cleaning, repair or other treatment.

7) Shops (excluding those in covered shopping complexes but including department stores) trading predominantly in furniture, floor coverings, cycles, prams, large domestic appliances of other bulky goods, or trading on a wholesale self-selection basis (cash and carry).

Physical condition

It is important to ascertain the degree of agility that can be expected of the people who need to escape. A means of escape route that involves climbing through a window, for example, may be considered to be acceptable with the occupants in their present state, but will they remain agile?

Expected reactions

In a disciplined occupancy, for example, factory premises, office premises, etc. where regular fire drills may be carried out involving everyone, the reaction of the occupants will no doubt be different to a building occupied largely by members of the public.

Asleep or awake

Whether the people who need to escape are asleep or awake is of vital importance, as any sleeping occupancy must have time to react to the alarm and to then respond quickly.

Use of the building

- Nature of contents.
- Furnishings.
- Goods stored or used.
- Processes carried on.

It must be established what kind of occupancy is anticipated, what effect on the spread of fire the contents may have and whether or not smoke in large volumes is expected. Processes of hazardous nature, for example low flash point liquids, obviously require special consideration. The location of such processes adjacent to escape routes or the access thereto will also have to be carefully considered.

Construction

Primary construction: this refers to the main fabric of the building, i.e. walls, floors, roof and internal dividing walls.

The following classifications are awarded according to this primary construction.

Class A   Complete non-combustible construction.
Class B   Traditional construction, i.e. non-combustible walls, combustible floors and/or roof.
Class C   Combustible construction.

Secondary construction: this refers to internal partitioning, wall and ceiling linings, etc. The anticipated effect that the secondary construction would have upon a fire may well lower the original classification based on the primary construction.

Time of evacuation

Class A   3 minutes.
Class B   2½ minutes.
Class C   2 minutes.

General requirements for means of escape

Management needs to ensure that the means of escape from premises are maintained in an efficient state, in good working order and in good repair. Article 17 of the RRFSO 2005 establishes a requirement for this. In addition, Article 14 of the RRFSO 2005 sets out a requirement: "Where necessary in order to safeguard the safety of relevant persons, the responsible person must ensure that routes to emergency exits from premises and the exits themselves are kept clear at all times".

The best way of achieving this is by implementing a good system of fire safety checks and inspections and by profiling a thorough system of planned maintenance and testing for all aspects of the premises that have an effect on the means of escape.

There should be alternative means of escape from most situations. If it is not possible to have direct access to a place of total safety, for example, a final exit door, it should be possible to reach a place of comparative safety, such as a fire protected stairway, within a reasonable distance. In these cases we have an unprotected portion of the escape route and a protected portion.

- Any unprotected part of an escape route should be limited so that people do not have to travel excessive distances, possibly whilst exposed to the dangers of fire and smoke.
- Horizontal protected escape routes should be limited in distance, as they do not provide protection indefinitely.
- Corridors should be sub-divided by fire doors to prevent smoke travel.
- If people cannot turn their backs on a fire and walk away, then fire protection of the escape route must be considered (dead end conditions).
- Fire protected stairways are considered to be 'fire sterile' areas. Therefore, flames, smoke and gases must be excluded from these areas. Fire risks should not be allowed into these areas, for example storage, photocopier, etc., and must not be allowed if they are the only stairs.
- Once a person has entered a fire protected stairway, then they must be contained within a fire protective structure all the way to the final exit door.
- Exits should not be close enough to each other, so that a fire starting between them will render them both unusable. This is accounted for by the application of the 45° rule, i.e. at the point from where a person is trying to escape, if both exits are within a 45° angle from that point, and then they will only be considered as a single exit route.

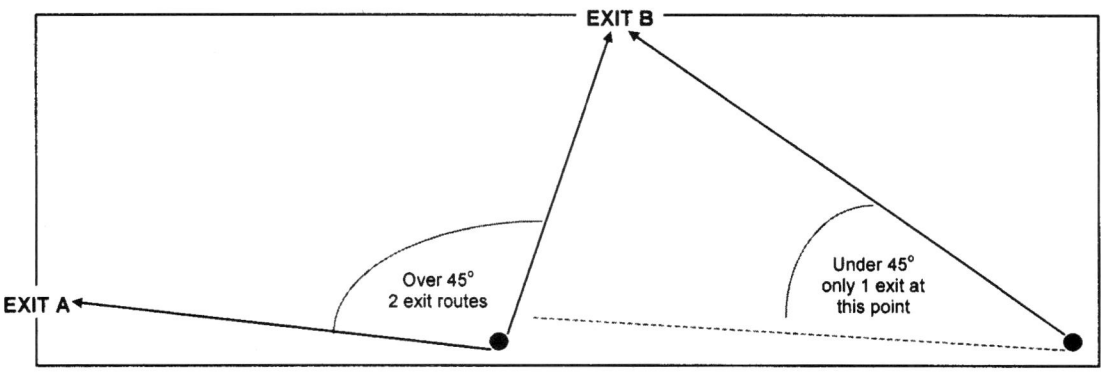

Figure C3-26: Exits - 45° rule.   Source: FST.

- Inner rooms (room within a room) are allowed with certain provisions. However, inner, inner rooms are not allowed.
- Any known fire risks should be located in the building, with consideration to the means of escape, and the effects that they would have on them, if on fire; for example if you have an access room and an inner room, the fire risk should ideally be in the inner room.

ELEMENT C3 - WORKPLACE FIRE RISK ASSESSMENT

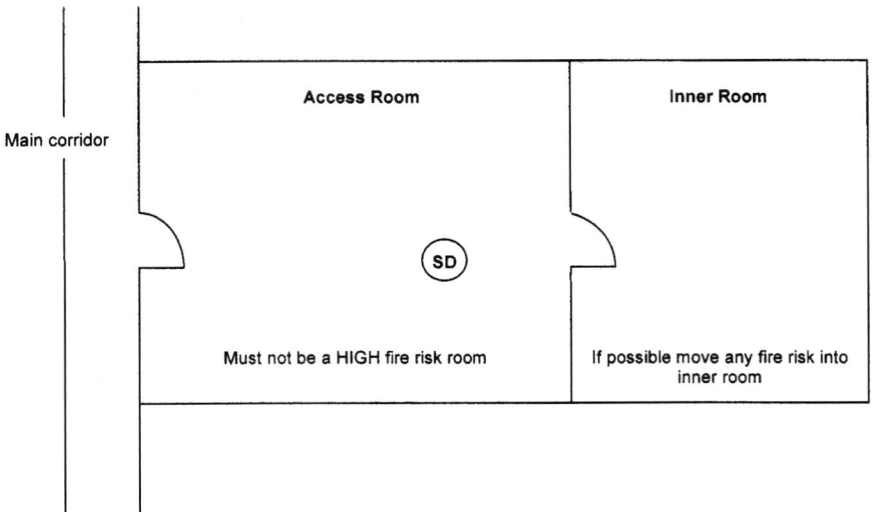

Figure C3-27: Known fire risks. Source: FST.

- When planning for means of escape, if a room or storey has more than one exit, it must be assumed and planned for the eventuality that one of the exits (the largest) will be blocked by fire or smoke.
- In a multi-stairway building, unless the stairway is approached via a protected lobby, i.e. two door protections to stairs, then it must be assumed that a stairway will be rendered unusable due to fire or smoke. An exception to this would be if the stairway is fitted with a smoke control pressurisation system.

TRAVEL DISTANCES

This has been defined as:

> "The actual distance to be travelled by a person from any point within the floor area to the nearest storey exit or final exit, having regard to the layout of walls, partitions and fixings".

Figure C3-28: Definition of travel distances. Source: Fire Safety Risk Assessment - Guide 1 - Office and Shops.

Place of safety in this context can be either ultimate or comparative. If evacuation times are to be maintained, then some limit has to be placed on the travel distance acceptable. It is not possible to set maximum distances which cover a variety of occupancies so it becomes essential to refer to the relative code of practice for guidance. This would include distances to:

- Final exits.
- Doors to a protected lobby.
- Down stairs which are protected routes.
- Doors in a compartment wall.

The guides supporting the RRFSO 2005 for offices, shops and factories suggest where a single escape route is provided in a 'normal' fire risk area the travel distance should not be more than 18 m. If more than one escape route is provided it could be 45 m. If the risk is more or less than normal the guide's advice is that these travel distances could be adjusted.

STAIRS

In the majority of cases stairs are enclosed in a fire resistant shaft. If the structure around the stairs is fire resistant, the doors onto the stairs are fire resistant doors and there is an exit (or two totally separated exit routes) from the base of the stairs, then the stairwell is described as a fire protected stairwell. This type of structure has special significance as it complies with the definition of a storey exit as described in building regulations and fire safety guidance. As such, travel distances are measured to storey exits when deciding upon the compliance of a building design with recognised standards.

In certain buildings a special stairwell (usually called a fire-fighting shaft) is needed. Additional facilities including fire-fighting lifts, fire-fighting stairs and lobbies are included in a fire-fighting shaft. The addition of these measures will allow the Fire and Rescue Service to quickly access the fire floor or to access the floor below a fire from which an operating base can be set up. In general buildings with floor levels over 18 m above, or basements more than 10 m below Fire and Rescue Service vehicle access level, will need to provide fire-fighting shafts.

It may be possible to have an unprotected stairway in a building, but it is not usually counted for means of escape purposes. If an unprotected stairs does form part of the means of escape then the travel distances are measured up to and down the stairs. By taking this approach travel time is reduced before the effects of a fire can prevent people escaping down the stairs. It also usual in such circumstances to install compensating features into the building such as fire detection, sprinklers and/or smoke ventilation.

PASSAGEWAYS

In any area where people work or to which the public are admitted, the contents of that area should be arranged so as to allow free passageway for means of escape.

It may be necessary, for example, in factories or large shops such as DIY shops to mark the gangways with paint. Where the areas used as gangways are subject to change then the marking may be of some other non-permanent but durable material.

DOORS

In simple terminology there are two types of doors when considering fire safety - fire resisting doors and fire exit doors. Of course the fire exit door may also be a fire resisting door. Fire resistant doors along with fire resistant structures serve two purposes:

1) Prevent the spread of fire.
2) Ensure that there is means of escape for persons using the building.

Doors on escape routes should ideally open in the direction of travel, and must do so if more than 60 people may use the door.

It is often difficult to tell visually what a fire door is. However, points to look for are:

- The door will normally be fitted with three hinges.
- The door will normally be fitted with a positive self closing device, for example swing arm device or percomatic closer.
- New fire doors will be fitted with intumescent strips and cold smoke seals.
- New doors should have a colour raw plug inserted into one of its side edges.

Swing arm device

Traditional type of door closer which fits at top of door and joins onto door frame. Once opened it should slowly close and latch the door.

Percomatic closer

A type of door closer which uses spring loaded pistons for its methods of operation. The door closer itself is mounted inside the leaf of the door after a hole has been routed out. The only visible portion is a single or double chain between the door and door frame (hinge side). Again this device is intended to close and latch the door.

Intumescent strips

Intumescent material is material that expands when it get hot. Strips of this material are fitted around both sides and the top of the door. If there is a fire the material intumesces (swells) and fills the gap between the door and door frame, thus preventing fire and smoke from passing through.

Cold smoke seals

Intumescent materials work well if a fire is close to a door or well developed. If the fire is small or distant from the door, by the time the smoke reaches the door it is cold and the intumescent material will not intumesce. Smoke would then pass around the edge of the door. A cold smoke seal is a nylon brush or neoprene strip which again is introduced both sides and at the top of the door. This seal should constantly brush against the door/door frame and therefore prevent the cold smoke from passing through the gap.

FD20/20 and FD30/20 etc

Fire doors are now denoted as FD20/20 and FD30/20, where FD stands for fire door. The first figure stands for stability test rating in minutes, the second figure stands for integrity in minutes.

- Stability - is the time at which collapse occurred.
- Integrity - is the time that cracks or other openings exist through which flame or hot gases can pass and cause flaming of a cotton wool pad.
- The colours on the plug denote the standard of the door, for example white circle with red dot is an FD20/20 door, which requires intumescent materials to be fitted. A white circle with a green dot is an FD30/20 door, which does not require intumescent materials to be added on site.

A number of manufacturers set a plastic plug into the edge of their doors, indicating the potential fire resistance rating when tested in accordance with British Standard 476: Part 20/22: 1987. An explanation of the symbols used is shown below:

Fire resistance rating to BS 476: Parts 8 and 22	Intumescent material to be fitted on site to door manufacturers instructions (Red tree or core)		Intumescent material fitted by door manufacturer during production (Green tree or core)	
	Background.	Core.	Background.	Core.
20 minutes (white background).	White.	Red.	White.	Green.
30 minutes (yellow background).	Yellow.	Red.	Yellow.	Green.
60 minutes (blue background).	Blue.	Red.	Blue.	Green.

Figure C3-29: Fire resistance rating symbols. *Source: www.mawwfire.gov.uk.*

ELEMENT C3 - WORKPLACE FIRE RISK ASSESSMENT

N.B. Red core means intumescent *must* be fitted either in the door or frame on site to manufacturer's instructions. Green core means intumescent is already fitted to the door under the lipping.

Fire exit doors are there to allow people to get out of the building in the event of fire. They need to be wide enough for the number of people who may need to use them. The method of opening doors and any method of securing doors are critical; the functionality of a fire door is quickly undermined if it is left wedged open.

EMERGENCY LIGHTING

Commonly, under the RRFSO 2005 premises require emergency lighting systems. Provision is made in the Order for securing the means of escape, and emergency lighting is one part of this. Under other legislation the provision of emergency lighting may also be required, either directly as in B1 of the Building Regulations (BR) 2000, or as a result of conditions imposed by licences etc.

Two factors that have to be considered with escape routes are the amount of natural light along the route, and the day/night hours worked by staff.

Basically, if an escape route has no natural or borrowed light, or staff work out of normal hours, then escape lighting may be required.

- To indicate clearly the escape routes.
- To provide illumination along such routes to allow safe movement towards and through the exits provided.
- To ensure that fire alarm call points and fire fighting equipment provided along escape routes can be readily located
- The escape lighting should adequately illuminate escape routes in the event of failure of the normal electrical supply to the lighting circuit due to fire.

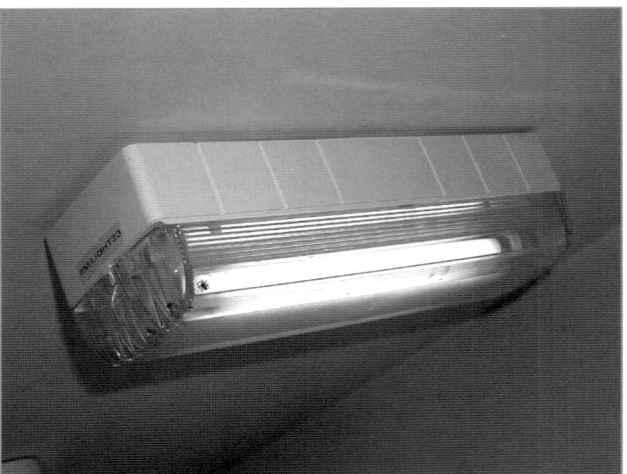

Figure C3-30: Self contained luminaire.　　Source: RMS.

Emergency lighting luminaries should be sited near each exit door and emergency exit door and at points where it is necessary to emphasise the position of safety equipment and hazards, for example:

- Near each intersection of corridors.
- At each exit door.
- Near each change of direction.
- Near other changes in floor level.
- Outside each final exit door.
- Near each fire alarm call point.
- Near fire fighting equipment.
- To illuminate exit and safety signs required by the enforcing authority.

Emergency lighting is usually provided on common access routes in commercial, industrial and multi storey premises.

Types of emergency light	Comments
Maintained	Operates at all times.
Non maintained	Only lights up when power fails.
Sustained	Contains 2 lamps: 1 powered from mains. 1 powered from emergency lighting supply (usually batteries).
Self contained luminaire	Luminaire containing everything: lamp, battery, test facility and controls.
Low level lighting system	Lighting strips (continuous) at floor or skirting board height.

Testing of emergency lighting system

Daily:

- Check no faults - normal power.
- If maintained system, check lamp is lit.
- Any faults to be rectified and action recorded.

Monthly:

- Simulate a power failure to the normal lighting circuit and check that self contained luminaries have energized.

- Simulate a power failure to the normal lighting circuit to check that central battery system energizes (if a central battery system if fitted).
- Simulate a power failure to lighting to check that generator starts up and energizes lights for a minimum of one hour (if generator system fitted).

Annually:

- Longer duration tests should be done, for example 3 hour self contained luminaries should be energized from battery for 1 hour.
- There are also additional tests after 3 years and thereafter annually.
- One other consideration when assessing the need for escape lighting may also be the use of photo-luminescent signs and markings.

EXITS

Entrances, exits and circulation areas are provided in all buildings for normal everyday use and a means of escape should utilise, where possible, existing arrangements. The first approach to this factor should therefore be a question of disposition, number and width of existing exits. The minimum width of an exit should be 750mm or 900mm if it is likely to be used by wheelchair users and 1 metre should be maintained throughout the escape route. This minimum width may need to be increased, dependent upon the number of persons who may need to use the escape route. Consideration should be given to painting tramlines or hatched areas on the floor, or even the use of guardrails to denote the gangways within a workplace. If this is done, then it should make the escape route within the room itself more identifiable.

The escape route should be considered from every point of every room. It should therefore be considered from the individual desks, benches or workstations within a room. There should be a clear path or gangway from each individual's workplace to the exit from the room. Consideration should be given to the spacing between desks, workstations and items of plant or equipment within the building. If there is a main gangway or path through a room or floor, then it should be kept clear at all times.

Once people have escaped from the room itself, the escape route should utilise the normal means of egress from a building, where possible. Only where these routes do not provide adequate means of escape are additional exits and escape routes required.

The route taken should be safe from fire and for this reason will normally be protected from the remainder of the building by fire resistant structures. The protection to the escape route should be such that persons will not be affected by the fire or smoke that is present. One exception to this would be ground floor open plan units where persons can walk away from fire and out of exit doors. Basically if a person can turn their back on a fire from any part and make their way to an exit door then fire resistance may not be required. If there is a possibility that persons could become trapped by fire, then fire resistance may be necessary.

The RRFSO 2005 guides glossary defines the following terms:

Final exits An exit from a building where people can continue to disperse in safety and where they are no longer at danger from fire and/or smoke.

Storey exit A final exit or a doorway giving direct access into a protected stairway, fire-fighting lobby, or external escape route.

DIRECTIONAL SIGNS

Escape routes that form part of the everyday access/egress from a building are not normally identified as escape routes by use of signs etc. The reason for this is that it is recognised that persons working in a building would already know their way in and out of the building.

However, consideration should be given to the access/egress used by different sections of the workforce and their knowledge of other access/egress routes. This approach would not be appropriate if members of the public frequent the building; in this case exit signs etc. would need to be placed along all escape routes. Escape routes which are not in normal use, for example, external fire escape stairways, must be indicated by use of exit signs and directional arrows. In addition, any door fastenings which may need to be opened should have signs to denote operation. Any signs or notices which are used along the escape route should be readily visible and large enough to be read from the furthest point in the room, corridor etc.

Exit signs are normally placed above doorways and openings to which they relate. If it is not possible to site an exit sign above a door, it should be sited immediately next to the doorway, not on the door itself. If the sign is put on the door and the door left open, then the sign will not be seen. Consideration should be given to suspended signs.

The following points should be considered before deciding on the type, size and position of any signs:

- The line of exit route changes direction - therefore a sign bearing a directional arrow is necessary.
- The sign must be capable of being read from both approaches to the exit and so may be required to be double sided.
- The sign must have letters/pictures large enough to be read from the extremities of the room or corridor.
- The sign must not be obscured by light fittings, items of plant, changes in ceiling level etc.

ELEMENT C3 - WORKPLACE FIRE RISK ASSESSMENT

- On landings or at the base of staircases where there is doubt whether the escape route is up or down, a further directional sign is required.
- Signs must be conspicuous and if normal lighting is artificial or work is done in hours of darkness, the sign should be illuminated.

Figure C3-31: Directional arrows. Source: BS 5449.

Supplementary text

It is acceptable to add supplementary text to signs to assist with understanding, for example:

- *Exit* - denotes a doorway or opening that leads to a place of ultimate safety.
- *Fire exit* - denotes a doorway or opening that leads to a place of safety, which has been specifically provided as an alternative exit to be used in the event of the evacuation of the workplace. This does not prevent the door being used for everyday use.

Size of sign

The size of sign is dependent upon the viewing distance from which the sign is seen and the type of sign.

Figure C3-32: Poorly signed fire escape. Source: FST.

For example, whether it is a standard, photo-luminescent, internally illuminated or externally illuminated sign.

All notices should be checked as part of the fire inspection procedure to ensure that they are present and that they are legible. Where safety signs are required then they must incorporate pictograms.

Text only signs do not conform to the Health and Safety (Safety Signs and Signals) Regulations (SSSR) 1996.

C3.6 - Emergency evacuation procedures

Purposes of and essential requirements for evacuation arrangements

EVACUATION PROCEDURES

Purpose of evacuation procedures

The RRFSO 2005, Article 15, requires the Responsible Person to establish *"procedures for serious and imminent danger and for danger areas"*; the duty specifies a requirement to:

- Establish and, where necessary, give effect to appropriate procedures, including safety drills, to be followed in the event of serious and imminent danger to relevant persons.
- Nominate a sufficient number of competent persons to implement those procedures in so far as they relate to the evacuation of relevant persons from the premises.
- Ensure that no relevant person has access to any area to which it is necessary to restrict access on grounds of safety, unless the person concerned has received adequate safety instruction.
- So far as is practicable, require any relevant persons who are exposed to serious and imminent danger to be informed of the nature of the hazard and of the steps taken or to be taken to protect them from it.
- Enable the persons concerned (if necessary by taking appropriate steps in the absence of guidance or instruction and in the light of their knowledge and the technical means at their disposal) to stop work and immediately proceed to a place of safety in the event of their being exposed to serious, imminent and unavoidable danger.
- Save in exceptional cases for reasons duly substantiated (which cases and reasons must be specified in those procedures), require the persons concerned to be prevented from resuming work in any situation where there is still a serious and imminent danger.
- A person is to be regarded as competent where he has sufficient training and experience or knowledge and other qualities to enable him properly to implement the evacuation procedures referred to in that paragraph.

The danger which may threaten people if fire breaks out depends on many different factors. Consequently, it is not possible to construct a model procedure for action in the event of fire in all premises, though some important features are emphasised in the RRFSO 2005, for example, the need for procedures, drills, nominated people to implement procedures, induction, information and training. To avoid delay in evacuating the premises when the fire alarm is sounded, there should be a pre-arranged procedure enabling persons to "stop work and immediately proceed to a place of safety".

It is essential that all staff be familiar with the escape route to be used in the event of fire and also with an alternative route, should the main escape route be impassable. Every employee should therefore be given instruction about their action on hearing the fire alarm as a part of their induction training.

The instruction should identify the alarm, state which route is to be followed, which alternative route is to be used if the first is impassable and where to assemble for a roll call on reaching open air. The responsibility for ensuring that a department is evacuated quickly and safely should rest with the departmental manager or a nominated fire marshal. A search of the department including lavatories and cloakrooms should be made, and on reaching the assembly point the roll should be called to ensure that everyone in the department is accounted for, taking particular care if flexible working hours are allowed.

Approach to evacuation

There are a number of approaches to evacuation procedures which may include the following.

Single stage evacuation (total)

This involves the immediate evacuation of all the occupants of a building on the sounding of the alarm.

Horizontal evacuation

In this type of premises, such as care facilities or hospitals, it is common to initially only evacuate residents from the fire affected area. Residents should be evacuated to a place of safety, normally so that there are two fire door separations between the residents and the fire. The place of safety must then have another direction of escape that is away from the fire affected area.

Figure C3-33: Assembly point. Source: RMS.

It is paramount that the building structure is maintained so that the fire or smoke cannot bypass the fire protection and jeopardise the safety of the people in the place of safety. If the situation gets worse, there must be a method of evacuating residents further away.

This is normally done by moving them horizontally further away from the fire and behind additional fire resistance. In practice there will be a limit to the amount that people can be horizontally evacuated, therefore vertical evacuation or total evacuation may be necessary.

Staff alarm controlled evacuation

In some premises, an immediate total evacuation may not be desirable, for example, night clubs, shops, theatres and cinemas. A controlled evacuation by the staff may be preferred to prevent distress and panic to the occupants. If such a system is used the alarm must be restricted to the staff, by the use of coded announcements or direct contact by radio communications, and only used where there are sufficient members of staff present that are trained in the action of what to do in case of fire.

Two stage evacuation

In certain large/high rise buildings it may be better, in the event of a fire, to first evacuate the areas of high risk, usually those closest to the fire or immediately above it. A two stage evacuation allows a period of time to investigate and respond to the incident before conducting a total evacuation. When using a two stage system a common approach would be that an intermittent signal would alert the people in the building that the first stage had commenced. This enables the investigation to begin, evacuation of the disabled, and the closing down of operations ready for full evacuation. The second stage would usually be a continuous signal to indicate an immediate total evacuation. Following investigation the alarm is then either cancelled or the second stage alarm is activated and the building is totally evacuated. The alarm may be cancelled either because it is a false alarm or the fire has been extinguished.

Phased evacuation

Phased evacuation systems are becoming more common as buildings become taller and house increasing numbers of staff. This form of evacuation is similar to the two stage evacuation. The occupants of the floor on which a fire occurs together with the occupants of the floor directly above it are evacuated immediately a fire is detected by sounding an alarm on those floors affected that signals a requirement to evacuate. The remainder of the occupants receive a different signal to alert them to the incident but remain in the building. If it is necessary for additional floors to be evacuated they will receive the appropriate signal. Further evacuations are usually carried out two floors at a time under the control of fire marshals or the Fire and Rescue Service, this is determined by the way in which the fire develops. A total evacuation could be initiated at any time by sounding the evacuation signal throughout the building.

- Good communications are essential if an orderly evacuation is to be undertaken. If a phased evacuation system is in operation, fire marshals will need to be able to communicate with the senior fire marshal in the control centre by fire telephones, which should be installed on each floor of the building.
- Buildings in which phased evacuation is proposed should incorporate the highest standards of fire protection, and staff should undergo comprehensive training. In particular, each floor should be constructed as a compartment floor, automatic fire detection and alarm system should be installed, smoke control measures are recommended, and if the building is over 30m high an automatic sprinkler installation should be considered.

Allocation of responsibility

Allocation of specific responsibilities will vary according to circumstances. The most important requirements are that there should be no confusion as to who is responsible for each of the various measures that may need to be taken, and that decisions are not delayed unnecessarily because one or more of those responsible are not immediately available.

The ideal is that there should be a designated person in each department, or on each floor, responsible for taking immediate charge at the scene of the outbreak of fire and for taking decisions which may be required pending the arrival of a more senior member of the managerial staff, the fire officer, or the public Fire and Rescue Service. It should be clearly understood that if the designated person is not available then the deputy, or next senior employee, takes charge.

The tasks of the designated people in the departments are to ensure the safety of the occupants, and if the fire is in their department to attempt to contain it, if trained.

Fire action instructions

At conspicuous positions in all parts of the building, and adjacent to all fire alarm actuating points, printed notices should be exhibited stating, in concise terms, the essentials of the action to be taken upon discovering a fire and on hearing the fire alarm.

In the event of a fire, action upon discovery needs to be immediate and a simple fire action plan should be put into effect. A simple fire action notice could include the following points:

- Raise the fire alarm (to warn others).
- Leave the building by the nearest exit.
- Report to the assembly point.

If instructions like "tackle the fire" are included in the action the legal and practical implications must be considered and appropriate training provided.

The roll call system

The roll call system is based on checking that everyone in a building has reached a place of total (ultimate) safety. The names of all the building's occupants are recorded on a list to confirm their arrival at a nominated assembly point. In the event of a fire or practice, following evacuation of the building a designated person checks that everyone on the list answers the roll call. This information is then passed to a central control point.

Advantages of this system include:

- Specific confirmation that staff are out of the building and safe.
- The emphasis lies in getting people out then checking.

Disadvantages of this system include:

- It is dependent on complete and up-to-date lists of their building occupants, which are often difficult if not impossible to maintain at any one time.
- Reactive to evacuation - it doesn't help get people out.
- A lot of time is spent checking lists before the area can be declared clear.
- It assumes all personnel know where to go if the building is evacuated.
- Nominated people, or their substitutes, need to be available to conduct the roll call.

The fire marshal system

This system is based on splitting a building into small manageable areas. In the event of a fire, designated people (Fire Marshals) search their area to ensure that all staff leaves the building. The fire marshals then direct any people who have not evacuated to the appropriate fire exit and onward to their assembly area. They then report that their area is clear, or otherwise, to an allocated person at the assembly point.

Advantages of this system include:

- It has been shown to be the quickest, most efficient way to evacuate a building.
- It allows the Fire and Rescue Service in quickly to rescue people and reduce damage.
- Buildings are split into pre-defined areas for control - no 'grey' areas.
- Pro-active - fire marshals identify dangers and problems arising during - not after evacuation.
- The system uses people to evacuate people and by doing so allows for adverse behaviour.
- It allows for a controlled search of an area, if necessary.

Disadvantages of this system include:

- It may only be in operation during the core working hours for the building.
- The role of fire marshal is normally voluntary - it relies on staff goodwill and their participation.

It is important that all areas of the building are covered by fire marshals, and organisations who choose to adopt this system must ensure that there are sufficient numbers of fire marshals to cover the building at all times; 'extra' fire marshals will be required to cover absences. Absences could include sickness, holiday leave, attendance at meetings or courses or people temporarily absent from their normal place of work.

The actual system of work operated by the fire marshals will be dictated by the building layout, the work practices and number of staff available to conduct an evacuation. In all cases the fire marshals will check areas within the workplace, and instruct staff to evacuate the building by the nearest safe exit. The fire marshals will basically be the last persons to evacuate the area they are checking.

It is always advisable to give fire marshals some visible form of identification such as high visibility jackets as well as some form of communication equipment to enable them to communicate with the person in charge of the fire panel.

Evacuation of disabled people

Alterations may need to be made to enable people with disabilities to access buildings (Equality Act 2010). This may mean that people with disabilities may be found on floors where they were not previously able to gain access. The fire management system should ensure that ***all persons*** who enter buildings can escape in the event of a fire.

There is a misconception in some companies that it is satisfactory to evacuate the person with disability to a safe refuge, for example, fire protected stairwell and to hold them there awaiting the arrival of the Fire and Rescue Service, so that they can carry them down - this is not the case. It remains the responsibility of the 'responsible person(s)' for the premises to ensure all who are present can be evacuated, without assistance from the Fire and Rescue Service, should the need arise.

This issue is not however straightforward as there are many forms of disability that may be encountered. The more common disabilities would be mobility impairment, vision impairment and hearing impairment. All the strategies set out below must be supported by active fire marshals that are made aware of the presence of the people with disability.

Hearing impairment   Evacuation may be assisted by the issue of personal trembler alarms, flashing lights and 'buddy' (work companion assistance) systems or the equivalent for visitors to the building.

Vision impairment   Evacuation may be assisted by use of tactile way-finding and exit signs and 'buddy' systems or the equivalent for visitors to the building.

Mobility impairment   This may vary from someone who is just slower than everyone else in escaping to a person in a wheelchair. Evacuation methods may vary from assisting the person out of the building immediately after the initial rush of occupants to use of evacuation chairs and other escape systems. The worse case scenario should be considered such as the need to evacuate a person in a wheelchair vertically, where the risk factors involved in moving them would need to be known and provided for. An interim step might involve a responsible person remaining with the individual(s) in a designated safe refuge (a place of comparative safety), and the responsible person would then communicate their location at this point so that an informed judgement can be made on the need to evacuate the individual further or not.

The actions required to ensure the safe and effective evacuation of disabled people in an emergency situation need to be given detailed consideration. Management procedures need to be in place that takes account of the various scenarios that may arise.

For example, procedures adopted with regard to disabled people employed in the building may well be different from those for disabled people visiting the building who are therefore unfamiliar with its layout.

BS 5588 'Fire Precautions in the Design, Construction and Use of Buildings' states:

> *"It is neither possible nor desirable ... to recommend which procedure should be adopted in any particular circumstances. Circumstances will vary as to the needs of disabled people and whether their relationship with the building management is a continuing or transient one".*

Figure C3-34: Needs of disabled people.   Source: BS 5588.

Systems of evacuation that may be implemented include:

- Horizontal evacuation.
- Evacuation by lift.
- Evacuation by stairs.
- Use of refuges.

Lifts

An evacuation lift is a lift that has been specifically designed for the evacuation of disabled persons. In essence, these lifts are set within a fire resisting enclosure and have a separate power supply so that their use can be assured during a fire. Evacuation lifts are often utilised in conjunction with 'refuges'.

Refuges

Refuges are relatively safe waiting areas for short periods in the event of a fire in the building. A refuge is an area that is both separated from the fire by a fire-resisting construction with a safe route to a fire exit. It provides a temporary space for people to wait for others who will then help them evacuate.

Disabled people should not be left alone in the refuge, but evacuated as soon as possible by designated staff, and not be reliant upon the Fire Brigade to evacuate the refuge. The use of refuges should always be viewed within the context that buildings should have adequate measures in place to enable the evacuation of all persons.

Evacuation by stairs

At some point it may be desirable or necessary to move people with disabilities down the evacuation stairs. When this involves going down stairs or steps rather than going up, one of the most common systems used is the 'Evac+chair', Evac+chairs can be used by people trained and capable of using the equipment.

It is worth noting however that additional carry handles can be added to Evac+chairs, or other specialist chairs purchased that will allow for evacuation up stairs.

Use of graphic, aural and tactile way-finding and exit sign systems

As part of the control measures put in place for safe evacuation it may be necessary to install additional measures such as graphic, aural and tactile way-finding and exit sign systems. These measures may also be included as part of the access requirements for DDA.

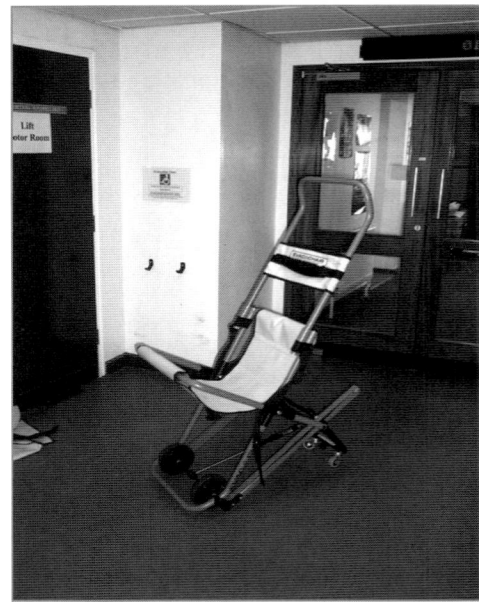

Figure C3-35: 'Evac+chair'.   Source: FST.

Emergency evacuation plan

The needs of the individual should be assessed and if required a personal emergency evacuation plan (PEEP) should be developed.

For more information, see 'Emergency evacuation plans' later in this element.

FIRE DRILLS

To ensure that all employees are familiar with and understand the procedure in the event of fire, repeated practice is desirable. After initial practices to establish the procedure, practice drills should be held at least once a year. Where there is danger of rapid fire spread, more frequent drills are advisable.

An additional method of familiarising employees with escape routes, which will not interrupt normal work, is to instruct them occasionally to leave by their main or alternative escape routes at the end of a working day. This will need to be undertaken with the assistance of the security staff, which may have to guard some vulnerable fire exits while they are insecure, and who will have to check the security of the building at the conclusion of the exercise.

The purpose of fire drills

The responsibility under the RRFSO 2005, Article 15, for carrying out fire drills rests on the responsible person for the premises.

A fire drill is intended to ensure, by means of training and rehearsal, that in the event of fire:

- The people who may be in danger act in a calm and orderly manner.
- Where necessary, those designated carry out their allotted duties to ensure the safety of all concerned.
- The means of escape are used in accordance with a predetermined and practised plan.
- If evacuation of a building becomes necessary, it is speedy and orderly.

Instruction

This should be given frequently at such intervals as will ensure that all employed persons are instructed at least once, in each period of twelve months.

Instruction and training generally should provide for the following:

- The action to be taken upon discovering a fire.
- The action to be taken on hearing the fire alarm.
- Raising the alarm, including the location of alarm call points, internal fire alarm telephones and alarm indicator panels.
- The correct method of calling the fire brigade.
- The location and use of fire fighting equipment.
- Knowledge of escape routes.
- Appreciation of the importance of fire doors and of the need to close all doors at the time of a fire and on hearing the fire alarm.
- Stopping machines and processes and isolating power supplies where appropriate.
- Evacuation of the building.

In addition to the above, certain categories of people should be instructed and trained in any matters specific to their particular responsibilities at the time of a fire.

Examples are:

- Department heads.
- Engineering and maintenance staff.
- Floor managers.
- Security staff (including night security patrols).
- Telephonists.

At least once a year a practice fire drill should be carried out simulating conditions in which one or more of the escape routes from the building are obstructed. During these drills the fire alarm should be operated by a member of staff who is told of the supposed outbreak and, thereafter, the fire routine should be rehearsed as fully as circumstances allow.

Log books

Such details as are necessary to show the training and instruction given should be recorded. The following are examples of matters which may need to be included in such a record:

- Date of the instruction or exercise.
- Duration.
- Name of the person giving the instruction.
- Names of the persons receiving the instruction.
- The nature of the instruction training or drill.

Organisation

In all premises one person should be responsible for organising fire instruction/training and in larger premises to co-ordinate the actions of persons in the event of fire.

Provision of fire wardens and their role

There is no legal requirement for fire wardens/fire marshals. There is however, a legal requirement under the RRFSO 2005 to have procedures in place for serious and imminent danger (fire procedures) and there is a requirement to have 'competent persons' in place to implement these procedures. Regardless therefore of the type of fire evacuation system which is in place, for example, fire marshal/warden floorsweep system or a roll call system, then staff must be available/trained and competent to implement and manage the procedures. It is also worth noting at this stage that there is no specific 'official' differences between the role of a fire marshal and a fire warden. These terms are used differently by various organisations. This is not a problem, providing that the individual understands their role and that the evacuation system is successful.

Emergency evacuation plans

PERSONAL EMERGENCY EVACUATION PLANS (PEEPS)

Where an individual works in a building it is important that their needs are properly identified and adequate written arrangements developed for their safe evacuation. Their needs may match the standard emergency evacuation plan, however if their needs require arrangements different to the standard plan then specific arrangements should be made to take account of their needs.

These arrangements may include the creation of a 'Personal Emergency Evacuation Plan' that identify the needs of a specific individual and details of other people who would assist them in an evacuation. It is vital that all factors are considered, especially when considering mobility issues. As an example, if the individual has a disability such that transferring them from a wheelchair into an evacuation chair would cause them physical harm, for example, brittle bone disease, then evacuation chairs will not suffice. In severe cases fire evacuation lifts and/or evacuation platforms that transfer the individual in their wheelchair down the stairs would need to be considered.

GENERIC EMERGENCY EVACUATION PLAN (GEEP)

In a building where it is probable that people will be present as visitors who will need assistance with evacuation, a similar generic system should be devised and implemented.

Element C4

Storage, handling and processing of dangerous substances

Learning outcomes

The intended learning outcomes are that the student will be able to:

C4.1 Outline the main physical and chemical characteristics of industrial chemical processes.

C4.2 Outline the main principles of the safe storage, handling and transport of dangerous substances.

C4.3 Outline the main principles of the design and use of electrical systems and equipment in adverse or hazardous environments.

C4.4 Explain the need for emergency planning, the typical organisational arrangements needed for emergencies and relevant regulatory requirements.

Content

C4.1 - Industrial chemical processes	121
Factors affecting rate of chemical reaction	121
Heat of reaction	122
Methods of control of temperature and pressure	124
C4.2 - Storage, handling and transport of dangerous substances	126
Hazards presented and assessment of risk	128
Storage methods and quantities	128
Leaking and spillage containment	133
Examples of problems encountered during filling and transfer	135
Handling of dangerous substances	135
Transport of dangerous substances	138
Driver training and Dangerous Goods Safety Advisor	140
C4.3 - Hazardous environments	141
Resistance to mechanical damage and protection against solid bodies, objects, dusts, liquids and gases	141
Wet environments including corrosion and degradation of installation and damage to electrical systems	143
Principles of selection of electrical equipment for use in flammable atmospheres	143
Classification of hazardous areas, zoning	144
Use of permits-to-work	144
Principles of pressurisation and purging	144
Intrinsically safe equipment, flameproof equipment, type 'N' equipment, type 'e' equipment	144
C4.4 - Emergency planning	145
The need for emergency preparedness within an organisation	145
Consequence minimisation via emergency procedures	150
The need for the development of emergency plans to reduce the impact on the organisation	150
The need to develop and prepare an emergency plan	152
Ongoing monitoring and maintenance of emergency plans	152

ELEMENT C4 - STORAGE, HANDLING AND PROCESSING OF DANGEROUS SUBSTANCES

Relevant statutory provisions

Notification of Installations Handling Hazardous Substances Regulations (NIHHS) 1982 (as amended 2002)
Dangerous Substances (Notification and Marking of Sites) Regulations (NOMAS) 1990
Chemicals (Hazard Information and Packaging for Supply) Regulations (CHIP) 2009
Health and Safety (Safety Signs and Signals) Regulations (SSSR) 1996
Dangerous Substances and Explosive Atmospheres Regulations (DSEAR) 2002
Dangerous Goods and Use of Transportable Pressure Equipment Regulations (CDGUTPER) 2009
Regulation for Registration, Evaluation, Authorisation and Restriction of Chemicals (REACH)
Management of Health and Safety at Work Regulations (MHSWR) 1999 - Regulations 8 and 9
Control of Major Accident Hazards Regulations (COMAH) 1999
European Agreement concerning the International Carriage of Dangerous Goods by Road (ADR) 2009

C4.1 - Industrial chemical processes

Unlike other branches of engineering (civil, mechanical, electrical, aerospace), which are concerned with mainly applied physics, chemical engineering is unique in integrating chemistry systematically into industrial chemical production.

Most chemicals produced in industrial processes do not reach consumers, but are used as intermediates in manufacturing processes, such as bleaching agents in the textile and paper industries. Industrial processes fall into two main classes: inorganic and organic. Examples of inorganic include heavy chemicals such as acid or alkalis, which are consumed by industry in vast quantities. Organic includes fine chemicals such as dyes, pharmaceuticals and polymers, which are made from the raw material of hydrocarbons found in crude oil. Most plastics, resins, synthetic fibres, ammonia, methanol, and organic chemicals are manufactured from oil or natural gas. They are called petrochemicals, and there are hundreds of thousands of substances produced worldwide.

Factors affecting rate of chemical reaction

A chemical reaction is a process that leads to the transformation of one set of chemical substances (reactants) to another (products) with different properties to the reactants. Chemical reactions can be either spontaneous, requiring no input of energy, or non-spontaneous, requiring some form of energy such as heat, light or electricity. Chemical reactions involve the movement of electrons in the breaking and forming of new chemical bonds; the rate of reaction can be affected by temperature, pressure and substances called catalysts.

EFFECT OF TEMPERATURE

The rate of reaction of any chemical process will increase with increases in the temperature of the reactants. The rate of reaction is exponential with temperature and increases by a factor of at least two for every 10°C rise. The reaction rate will also increase with increasing concentration of the reactant(s).

For chemical reactions that are exothermic (generate heat energy) caution has to be taken to keep the reaction rate (which is exponential) within control, because the removal of heat, for example, by the use of cooling water, acts at a much slower transfer rate (linear process). Therefore it is essential to maintain the reaction temperature within a narrow band to prevent uncontrollable (run-away) conditions occurring.

Consider a common organic polymerisation manufacturing process, involving the production of urea formaldehyde adhesive resins for the manufacture of chip-board.

The process is relatively simple. Urea is mixed with 36% formaldehyde at a controlled pH and held for approximately 4 hours at 60°C. Polymerisation occurs and the viscosity of the material increases to a pre-determined value, which represents the increased molecular chain length required. If the temperature is not controlled carefully and is allowed to rise above 70°C, the exothermic reaction rate will become uncontrollable, resulting in high temperature, solidification of the reactants and release of volatile toxic materials, i.e. formaldehyde (WEL 2 ppm).

Reaction temperature control is a very important issue when considering scale-up processes from laboratory sized experiments (5 kg), increased through pilot plant (1,000 kg), to final production batch quantities (20,000 kg). The temperature control, particularly cooling, is far easier with small quantities of reactants than with increasing larger quantities, because the ratio of cooling surface decreases with increasing volume of reactants. *See section: "Methods of control of temperature and pressure"*.

EFFECT OF PRESSURE

The most significant use of pressure is the production of compressed gases, the most common being compressed oxygen, liquid nitrogen, and carbon dioxide produced from the fractional distillation of compressed air.

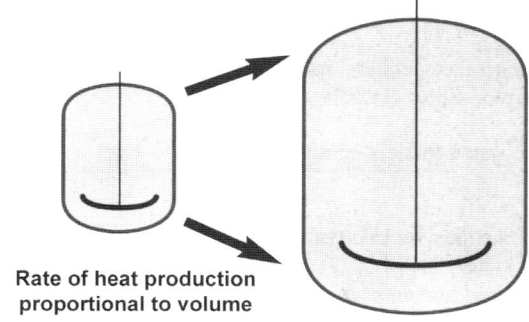

Rate of heat production proportional to volume

Natural cooling capacity proportional to surface area

Figure C4-1: Heat production/volume.   *Source: RMS.*

Other gases are produced either directly or indirectly from chemical processes and for convenience are stored under pressure. Common gases are chlorine, liquefied petroleum gas (propane), sulphur dioxide, hydrogen, ammonia and acetylene.

Some organic processes require reaction at relatively high pressure to prevent degradation of the products. One such reaction is the hydrogenation of castor oil in the manufacture of margarine. The reaction process is designed to be continuous and the reactants are combined at pressures of 200 atmospheres, which allows the products to be produced at much lower temperatures than at atmospheric pressure, below temperatures that would cause degradation.

ELEMENT C4 - STORAGE, HANDLING AND PROCESSING OF DANGEROUS SUBSTANCES

The main concern with pressure processes is over pressurisation leading to catastrophic failure of the plant or storage container.

EFFECT OF CATALYSTS

A catalyst is a substance that alters the rate of a chemical reaction, but is chemically unchanged at the end of the reaction.

Catalysts can be used over and over again, and it is only necessary to have very small quantities present to make a chemical reaction go faster. Certain substances will significantly promote or retard a chemical reaction; common catalysts include:

- Pure elements, for example, palladium, platinum and nickel.
- Pure compounds such as manganese dioxide, silica, vanadium V oxide, iron III oxide.
- Dissolved ions, for example, copper ions, cobalt II ions or a combination of these.

Catalysts that are used to promote reaction rate are often called "positive catalysts" or "promoters". Most catalyst make reactions go faster in order to increase the chance of molecules colliding. There are two main methods by which this is achieved - "adsorption" (where the reactants adhere to the surface of the catalyst) and "formation of intermediate compounds".

Adsorption

An example of the adsorption process is the manufacture of sulphur trioxide (extensively used in its aqueous form as sulphuric acid in lead accumulator batteries) from sulphur dioxide and oxygen, utilising platinum as a catalyst.

In this reaction the molecules of the two gases are adsorbed (adhered) onto the surface of the catalyst and are held in close proximity together, where they react with each other. The sulphur trioxide readily detaches from the catalyst leaving space for more sulphur dioxide and oxygen.

Intermediate compounds

Many catalysts (such as enzymes or lead tetraethyl, formally used in petrol) work by forming intermediate compounds. The chemicals involved in the reaction combine readily with the catalyst, making an intermediate compound. This new compound, however, is very unstable and breaks down to produce the final compound and the catalyst in a reusable form. Usually the reaction occurs at a much lower temperature of reaction than would otherwise be required.

If however we wish to slow down a chemical reaction a "negative catalyst" or "inhibitor" may be used, for example, anti-rust inhibitors used in space heating systems utilising iron radiators.

For the hydrogenation of castor oil in the production of margarine a platinum catalyst, an inhibitor, is used to promote the transition process at the electron transfer level.

The purity of raw materials is important to ensure the desired reaction rate is achieved to prevent the possibility of run away reactions.

Heat of reaction

ENDOTHERMIC REACTIONS - REACTIONS WHICH TAKE IN HEAT ENERGY

Steel

Most commercial endothermic (take in energy) reactions consume large quantities of energy. The most common process is the reduction of iron ore in the manufacture of steel. Iron ore (iron oxide Fe_2O_3,) is reduced with carbon (as coke) in the furnace:

Iron ore + coke + heat energy = iron + carbon dioxide

$2Fe_2O_3 + 3C + $ Heat energy $ = 4Fe + 3 CO_2$.

Other examples of endothermic reactions include photosynthesis and the reaction of ethanoic acid with sodium carbonate.

Photosynthesis

Photosynthesis is the process by which organisms, usually green leafed plants, use the energy from sunlight (photons) to convert carbon dioxide and water into organic materials used in cellular formations and functions such as biosynthesis and respiration. The process consists of:

Carbon dioxide + water + sunlight energy = carbohydrate (sugars) + oxygen

$CO_2 + 6H_2O + $ sunlight energy $ = C_6H_{12}O_6 + 6O_2$

This illustrates the important symbiotic reliance of humans on plants, algae, and many species of bacteria that use photosynthesis in their life cycle.

Ethanoic acid with sodium carbonate

Ethanoic acid is commonly known as acetic acid and in dilute solution it is known as vinegar.

The main use (over a third of the annual production) of ethanoic acid is in the production of vinyl acetate monomer. The monomer is an important component in water-based paints, paper coatings, adhesives and coatings in plastic bottles and petrol tanks. A third of all ethanoic acid produced annually is used to produce acetic anhydride. Acetic anhydride is used to create cellulose acetate, a synthetic textile that is also used as photographic film. Acetic anhydride is also used in the production of certain medicines, such as aspirin and in the production of polyethylene terephthalate, which is mainly used in soft drink bottles.

Sodium carbonate (baking soda) is the combination of a strong base (sodium hydroxide) with a weak acid (carbonic acid). The reaction between ethanoic acid and sodium carbonate is a displacement reaction of the weaker carbonic acid with the stronger ethanoic acid:

Ethanoic Acid + Sodium Carbonate = Sodium ethanoate + water + carbon dioxide

$2 CH_3COOH + Na_2CO_3 = 2 CH_3COONa + H_2O + CO_2$

Carbon dioxide (CO_2) is captured from the reaction and finds application as a pressurised gas, in the soft drink industry, in the process of decaffeination and as a refrigerant.

Uses of sodium ethanoate

Sodium ethanoate is used to neutralise the much stronger acid, sulphuric acid, in the treatment of wastewater streams:

Sodium ethanoate + sulphuric acid = Sodium sulphate + ethanoic acid

$2 CH_3COONa + H2SO4 = Na2SO4 + 2 CH_3COOH$

EXOTHERMIC REACTIONS - REACTIONS WHICH GIVE OUT HEAT ENERGY

Exothermic reactions are reactions that give out heat energy.

Chemical reactions that are exothermic are very common; perhaps the commonest is simple combustion, i.e. fire or explosion. A further example of an exothermic reaction is that involving sodium and chloride to produce salt.

Sodium and chlorine

The chemical reaction between sodium metal and chlorine gas is violently exothermic (give out energy) producing sodium chloride (salt).

Note that virtually all salt used domestically is obtained from sea water trapped in lagoons and evaporated by sunlight or by the mining of underground salt deposits left by former seas.

In chemical processing, if the reaction rate is not accurately monitored or controlled, the energy liberated over a short space of time, can be considerable. If the quantities of material being processed are large; cooling control is critical to avoid runway reactions *(see 'Runaway Reactions' section)*, which will result in loss of control and often ejection of the reactants from processing equipment. For example, when formaldehyde is combined with urea in the production of polymers, an exothermic reaction will occur, which if not controlled carefully, will result in a runaway reaction. Exothermic reactions may follow inadvertent admixture of materials.

EFFECTS OF ENTHALPY CHANGES ON MIXING OF LIQUIDS

Enthalpy is a measure of the total energy of a thermodynamic system. It includes the internal energy, which is the energy required to create a system, and the amount of energy required to make room for it by displacing its environment and establishing its volume and pressure. The unit of measurement for enthalpy in the International System of Units (SI) is the joule (J).

It is not possible to measure the total enthalpy, H, of a system directly. The measurement of change in enthalpy, ΔH, is a more useful quantity than its absolute value. The change ΔH is positive in endothermic reactions, and negative in exothermic processes. ΔH of a system is equal to the sum of non-mechanical work done on it and the heat supplied to it.

When two or more substances of different molecular structure are combined an exothermic (release of heat energy) or endothermic (take up of heat energy) reaction may result. For example, when diluting concentrated sulphuric acid with water, a significant amount of heat energy will be released. If the material is contained in a closed vessel and the rate of temperature rise is not controlled carefully, a rapid expansion, boiling and possible expulsion of the mixture may occur.

Conversely, some mixtures will require large quantities of heat when dissolution occurs, for example, urea in water. Failure to provide heat to a reaction vessel used for this purpose will rapidly lead to temperatures of the vessel and the contents to fall below 0°C, with the potential to freeze any water present in cooling coils which are often associated with such vessels. These internal energy changes (which are not chemical reactions) are known as 'enthalpy changes'.

RUNAWAY REACTIONS

During manufacture chemical changes normally involve the evolution or absorption of heat and are said to be exothermic or endothermic reactions, as outlined above.

ELEMENT C4 - STORAGE, HANDLING AND PROCESSING OF DANGEROUS SUBSTANCES

Of most concern in chemical processing is the exothermic process. If the heat released from such a process cannot be removed efficiently it presents a potential hazard to the operation by remaining in the reaction mass, with the consequence of raising the reaction mass temperature, and hence reaction rate, resulting in a runaway reaction.

If the chemical containment vessel is incorrectly designed or specified, a runaway reaction will result in over pressurisation of the reactor and possible loss of containment and toxic release, due to violent boiling and/or rapid gas generation. In addition, where a runaway reaction occurs, the elevated temperature achieved may well initiate secondary, competing reactions, such as thermal decompositions, which will exacerbate the hazard resulting from a runaway.

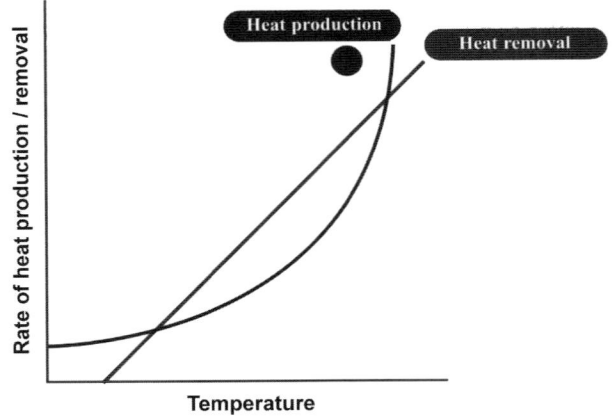

Figure C4-2: Heat production/removal.   Source: HSG 143.

OTHER FACTORS THAT CAN AFFECT THE RATE OF CHEMICAL REACTION

Other factors that can affect the rate of chemical reaction:

- Manufacturing instructions should give specific charging rates for the process. Charging is the addition of quantities of reactant. Appropriate instructions will help prevent the reactant that is being charged (for example, powders or pellets or highly viscous liquids) being charged too quickly and sinking to the bottom of the vessel, resulting in local overheating or sudden cooling or be sufficient to stop the agitator.
- If the reactants are added in the wrong order this may result in an uncontrollable temperature increase (accompanied with volume change) and possible expulsion of the reactor contents.
- Regular cleaning of the inside of the reactors should be carried out to prevent inefficient thermal transfer from the cooling heating coils. Inefficient thermal transfer is often due to build up of scale on the coils from previous residues not cleaned out before starting a new production batch. Cooling water treatment and maintenance will prevent deterioration of thermal transfer on the cooling water side of the coils caused by a build up anaerobic (without oxygen) bacterial growth, which effectively produces an insulating layer on the inside of the coils reducing cooling efficiency.

Methods of control of temperature and pressure

Representative measurement of temperature and pressure is an essential requirement to ensure safe processing of many substances and materials.

TEMPERATURE

Where liquid materials are stored changes in ambient temperature will result in changes in temperature within the stored liquids, due to the movement of heat by convection currents. Many manufacturing processes are carried out at temperatures above ambient and reliance on convection currents alone could result in localised overheating and possibly loss of reaction control (run away reactions).

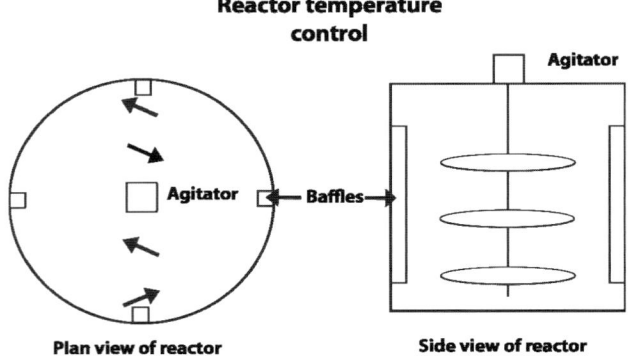

Figure: C4-3: Top and side view of a processing batch reactor agitation components. Source: RMS.

Where large volumes of liquids is to be heated, efficient agitation or circulation is essential to maintain even temperature rise. Reaction rate will typically double or treble with each 10 degree centigrade rise. Control will rely on temperature detection (for example, thermometer, and thermocouple) and display or readout.

For large vessels (or ones containing liquids of high viscosity) detection might need to be measured in more than one part of the liquid to determine efficiency of transfer of heat and to maintain temperature control.

In a similar way, agitators (mixers) are usually fitted with additional paddles along the length of the agitator shaft and baffles are fitted to the inner surface of the reactor to create eddy currents (reverse flow) to improve speed and consistency of mixing.

PRESSURE

Pressure, or overpressure measurement, is particularly important where there is a risk of explosion. Controls will include early detection of pressure rise measured by a detector and displayed in a similar way as with temperature.

Such process vessels will rely on rapid automatic pressure release, frequently using spring loaded pressure relief valves or bursting discs, venting to a safe area.

Where processes involving flammable dusts are concerned control of explosion will be designed into the process and may consist of an over pressure detection device, which causes a suppressant to be released that prevents structural failure of the process vessel due to pressure rise.

Other control devices include weighted lids that lift to reduce the pressure, for example, on grinding mills.

Figure: C4-4: Spring loaded pressure relief valve.
Source: Motherwell Tank Protection UK.

These may be combined with fragile workplace walls and other louvre type vents, which are designed to collapse in such a way that they vent to a safe area to release the over-pressurisation.

The flameless vent system control comprises two parts, an explosion vent and a quenching module. The explosion vent responds to the rapidly building pressure of a deflagration (subsonic combustion where burning material heats the next layer of cold material and ignites it) and opens to relieve this pressure.

As the developing fireball passes through the open explosion vent it is intercepted by the quenching module. A stainless steel precision mesh, retained by a frame of stainless steel, performs as a 3-dimensional flame arrestor to quench the flame.

The quenching module retains the flame and the 3-dimensional mesh arrangement acts as a heat sink that interrupts the explosion in mid-stream as well as absorption of the pressure wave and dust that would normally be ejected by a vented explosion.

Figure: C4-5: Flameless vent IQR System™.
Source: BSandB Pressure Safety Management.

FUTURE DEVELOPMENTS IN THE CONTROL OF TEMPERATURE AND PRESSURE

There are a number of developments in processing reactor design, the aim of which is to reduce process risk (over temperature or pressurisation effects) and production cost.

The current design initiatives are concerned with process intensification (PI), which combines two or more of the conventional process engineering unit operations within one piece of equipment.

New technologies, which the developers claim to be safer (significantly less material in process and very accurate temperature control at the molecular level), cleaner (reduced b-products), smaller and cheaper, include the development of the spinning disc reactor (SDR), the oscillatory baffled reactor (OBR), printed circuit heat exchanger (PCHE), and in-line mixers.

Spinning disc reactor

With the SDR, liquid is fed onto the centre of a rotating disc, which can be heated or cooled by an internally-circulating fluid. Intense interfering waves are formed in the liquid under the influence of the centrifugal force as the liquid moves towards the edge of the disc. This enables very high heat transfer coefficients to be realised between the disc and liquid, as well as very high mass transfer between the liquid and the gas above the liquid.

The waves formed also produce intense local mixing. The liquid flow involves very little back mixing and is therefore almost pure plug flow. The residence time is short, typically seconds.

ELEMENT C4 - STORAGE, HANDLING AND PROCESSING OF DANGEROUS SUBSTANCES

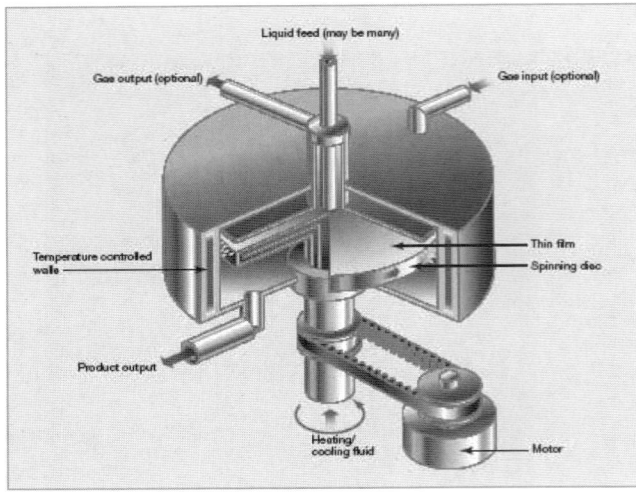

Figure: C4-6: Spinning disc reactor.
Source: www.theengineer.co.uk Clive Whitbourn.

Figure: C4-7: Oscillatory baffled reactor.
Source: www.theengineer.co.uk Clive Whitbourn.

Oscillatory baffled reactor

The OBR offers uniform fluid mixing, excellent particle suspension, and better heat and mass transfer than conventional reactor systems. In a tube with diameter D, orifice-plate internal baffles are placed, spaced 1.5D apart, and with orifices of diameter 0.5D. The oscillating fluid motion interacts with each baffle to form vortices, and the resulting fluid motion gives efficient and uniform mixing in the space between two baffles. This results in significant enhancement of heat and mass transfer, and control of residence time distribution. The mixing is controlled entirely by the oscillations and not by the throughput.

Printed circuit heat exchangers

PCHEs offer genuine savings in space and weight, and hence cost. The super large equipment used in gas treatment plants, for example, a shell-and-tube heat exchanger requiring three shells and weighing 100 tonnes can be replaced by a PCHE weighing only 15 tonnes.

The reactor routes the process stream through a preheating section and into an alternating series of heterogeneous catalyst beds and PCHE cores.

The multiple small reaction stages and heat exchange steps allow the temperature to be controlled precisely and eliminating 'hot spots'. Reactants can be added or products removed at each reactor stage.

Figure: C4-8: Printed circuit heat exchangers.
Source: www.theengineer.co.uk Clive Whitbourn.

Applications range from fuel processing to the production of fine and bulk chemicals. Further information on industrial chemical process safety can be found in the Health and Safety Executive (HSE) publication HSG143 "Designing and operating safe chemical reaction processes".

C4.2 - Storage, handling and transport of dangerous substances

DANGEROUS SUBSTANCES

The Dangerous Substances and Explosive Atmospheres Regulations (DSEAR) 2002 require employers to control the risks to safety from fire and explosions.

DSEAR puts duties on employers and the self-employed to protect people in the workplace (including members of the public) from risks to their safety from fires, explosions and similar events.

Dangerous substances can be found in nearly all workplaces and include such things as solvents, paints, varnishes, flammable gases, such as liquid petroleum gas (LPG), dusts from machining and sanding operations and dusts from foodstuffs.

CHIP refers to the Chemicals (Hazard Information and Packaging for Supply) Regulations 2009, which came into force on 6 April 2009. These regulations are also known as CHIP 4. CHIP is the law that applies to suppliers of dangerous chemicals. Its purpose is to protect people and the environment from the effects of those chemicals by requiring suppliers to provide information about the dangers and to package them safely. At the time of print of this edition the CHIP regulations are gradually being replaced by the European Regulation on Classification, Labelling and Packaging of Substances and Mixtures (EC 1272/2008); known as the CLP Regulation.

DEFINITIONS

The Dangerous Substances and Explosive Atmospheres Regulations (DSEAR) 2002 define a dangerous substance as:

*(a) A substance or preparation which meets the criteria in the approved classification and labelling guide for classification as a substance or preparation which is explosive, oxidising, extremely flammable, highly flammable or flammable, **whether or not that** substance or preparation is classified under the CHIP Regulations.*

(b) A substance or preparation which because of its physico-chemical or chemical properties and the way it is used or is present at the workplace creates a risk, not being a substance or preparation falling within subparagraph (a) above.

(c) Any dust, whether in the form of solid particles or fibrous materials or otherwise, which can form an explosive mixture with air or an explosive atmosphere, not being a substance or preparation falling within subparagraphs (a) or (b) above.

Figure C4-9: Definition - dangerous substances. Source: DSEAR 2002.

The Chemicals (Hazard Information and Packaging for Supply) Regulations 2009 define a dangerous substance as a substance:

(a) Which is listed in Table 3.2 or part 3 of Annex VI of the CLP Regulation.

(b) Which, if it is not so listed, is in one or more of the categories of danger specified in column 1 of Schedule 1.

Figure C4-10: Definition - dangerous substances. Source: CHIP 2009.

That is, a substance that has the following harmful physico-chemical properties (explosive, oxidising, extremely flammable, highly flammable or flammable) or properties that may cause harm to health or environment (very toxic, toxic, harmful, corrosive, irritant, sensitising, sensitising by inhalation, sensitising by skin contact, carcinogenic, mutagenic, toxic for reproduction or dangerous for the environment).

IDENTIFICATION

The Chemicals Hazard Information and Packaging for Supply Regulations (CHIP 4) 2009 requires suppliers to classify substances in accordance with a specified scheme. This classification scheme applies to both the harmful effects on health of substances (for example, toxic, corrosive, irritant etc.) and their physical properties (for example, explosive, oxidising, flammable etc.).

The CHIP 4 Regulations are being progressively replaced by the European Union Regulation on the Classification, Labelling and Packaging of Substances and Mixtures (CLP) Regulation (EC 1272/2008), to be used for the classification of chemicals, data gathering and communication of hazards (for example, the use of Safety Data Sheets in COSHH assessments). The new CLP Regulation creates a Classification and Labelling Inventory. The Inventory will be populated by classifications determined by industry. Much of the information provided on these classifications will be submitted as part of the suppliers' REACH Regulation (EC 1907/2006) registration for those substances that are placed on the market.

The Dangerous and Explosive Atmospheres Regulations (DSEAR) 2002 are also relevant to the storage of dangerous substances. DSEAR 2002 applies to any substance or preparation (mixture of substances) with the potential to create a risk to persons from energetic (energy-releasing) events such as fires, explosions, thermal runaway from exothermic reactions etc. Such substances, which are known in DSEAR 2002 as dangerous substances, include petrol, liquefied petroleum gas (LPG), paints, varnishes and certain types of combustible and explosive dusts produced in, for example, machining and sanding operations.

It should be noted that many of these substances will also create a health risk as well. For example, many solvents are toxic as well as being flammable. DSEAR 2002 does not address these health risks; they are dealt with by the Control of Substances Hazardous to Health Regulations (COSHH) 2002. DSEAR 2002 is concerned with harmful physical effects from thermal radiation (burns); over-pressure effects (blast injuries) and oxygen depletion effects (asphyxiation) arising from fires and explosions.

DSEAR 2002 generally defines a 'highly flammable liquid' as one that has a flash point of less than 32°C.

DSEAR 2002 also defines a 'liquefied flammable gas' as any substance that, at a temperature of 20°C and a pressure of 760 millimetres of mercury, would be a flammable gas, but is in liquid form as a result of the application of pressure, refrigeration or both.

Regulation 7, Schedule 4 of DSEAR 2002 also states that the following **warning sign is to be displayed at the point of entry to any place where explosive atmospheres may occur:**

The distinctive features of this warning sign are:

- Triangular shape.
- Black letters on a yellow background with black edging (the yellow part to take up at least 50% of the area of the sign).

Figure C4-11: Warning sign - explosive atmospheres. Source: DSEAR 2002.

ELEMENT C4 - STORAGE, HANDLING AND PROCESSING OF DANGEROUS SUBSTANCES

Hazards presented and assessment of risk

Risk assessments should consider the implications to health and the environment when assessing the storage, handling, and transport of dangerous materials. For example, consideration should be given to hazards such as whether they are flammable, toxic, corrosive or oxidising and any special health or environmental hazards. Other hazards associated with storage include the possible need for substances to be stored at high or low temperatures with the associated risk (thermal, cryogenic burns) to operators. Some substances will spontaneously ignite when exposed to air, for example, sodium metal and phosphorous. Most organic substances will generate static electricity when transferred to storage with the hazard of electrical discharge at connection and discharge points when off loading or transferring to storage. Some gases are lighter than air, for example hydrogen, others are heavier than air, such as propane and butane; presenting hazards of flammability and explosion if accidentally released.

The assessment of risk should take into account those people that could be harmed by the hazards. Because of the high hazard potential of dangerous substances they could affect workers in the location where they are stored or handled as well as neighbours and the general public. When transport is by road there can be a significant potential to harm large numbers of people in a single incident.

DSEAR 2002, Regulation 5, sets out the considerations to be made when conducting a suitable and sufficient risk assessment of dangerous substances:

(2) The risk assessment shall include consideration of:

   (a) The hazardous properties of the substance.

   (b) Information on safety provided by the supplier, including information contained in any relevant safety data sheet.

   (c) The circumstances of the work including:

      (i) The work processes and substances used and their possible interactions.

      (ii) The amount of the substance involved.

      (iii) Where the work will involve more than one dangerous substance, the risk presented by such substances in combination.

      (iv) The arrangements for the safe handling, storage and transport of dangerous substances and of waste containing dangerous substances.

   (d) Activities, such as maintenance, where there is the potential for a high level of risk.

   (e) The effect of measures which have been or will be taken pursuant to these Regulations.

   (f) The likelihood that an explosive atmosphere will occur and its persistence.

   (g) The likelihood that ignition sources, including electrostatic discharges, will be present and become active and effective.

   (h) The scale of the anticipated effects of a fire or an explosion.

   (i) Any places which are or can be connected via openings to places in which explosive atmospheres may occur.

   (j) Such additional safety information as the employer may need in order to complete the risk assessment.

A similar approach and considerations may be made when assessing the risk of other dangerous substances.

Storage methods and quantities

An assessment of the risks from the storage of dangerous substances will form part of the risk assessment required by the Management of Health and Safety at Work Regulations (MHSWR) 1999.

The overriding concern is to ensure that incidents are prevented and in the event of an incident in the storage area, such as a spillage of toxic or flammable material or a fire, people are able to escape to safety. 'High risk' locations are generally considered to be those where vulnerable populations or large numbers of people may be put at risk. Vulnerable populations include the sick, the old, the disabled and the very young, i.e. hospitals, nursing homes, schools. Large numbers of people may be found in office blocks, residential premises, shopping centres etc.

For some substances that may emit large quantities of heat and toxic fumes, it will be necessary to consider conditions not only on site, but also beyond the site boundary. The quantities and locations of other dangerous substances are also relevant to the assessment, particularly in the context of preventing escalation of an incident.

Dangerous substances should be received by a competent person who understands all the risks that they pose, can decide on where to store them and how to segregate them. They should have regard to their physical and chemical properties, the quantities concerned and the sizes of the packages. Storage will be required at the point of receipt, at the point of use and at the point of disposal/despatch. This will apply to bulk supplies as well as those that are purchased in smaller containers.

Vehicles containing bulk or packaged dangerous substances need to be parked in a safe place during loading or unloading. Palletised dangerous substances should be secured to prevent accidental movement during handling operations.

The site plan should indicate where there is a need to take additional precautions for the storage of dangerous substances. Generally, the areas of significant risk will include the chemical process plant and where hazardous liquids are dispensed. Such areas should be identified and controls established, such as zoning for flammable vapours or dusts. Where an explosive atmosphere may be present all sources of ignition should be controlled. This should be considered as part of the DSEAR 2002 risk assessment.

Locations for storage include:

- External and or internal bulk.
- External or internal bulk storage of solid or liquid raw materials.
- Storage of in-process material, including reactors and intermediate storage.
- External and or internal drums storage facilities.
- Specific locations in the workplace where local storage aids use of dangerous substances.
- Bulk storage of finished products for packaging or dispatch by road or rail.

Incidents such as the unconfined vapour cloud explosion at Flixborough and the fire at Allied Colloids *(see Element C2.4 - Major accidents)* have emphasised certain basic principles of storage, which are:

- Ensure minimum quantities held.
- Segregate storage of incompatible substances.
- Safe distances, i.e. keep the number of workers in the area of risk to a minimum, design control rooms to be remote from processes whenever possible.

BULK

Flammable dangerous substances should be stored in accordance with the requirements of relevant legislation. Typical requirements are:

- Substances are stored in bulk containers and are piped to the place of use.
- There should be adequate identification of bulk containers.
- Bulk containers should be located within bunds (an impervious containment wall and floor that is designed to retain any leakage from containers positioned within the wall).
- Bulk storage should be protected by fire suppression equipment.

The bulk storage should be designed to minimise the need for manual handling, process materials should be pumped whenever possible. Many chemical process facilities are conducted at a height in tall buildings and gravity is utilised to advantage in moving materials around.

INTERMEDIATE

Intermediate storage consists of work in progress. Often this will utilise fixed storage containers that may be used for different substances in accordance with the manufacturing process programme. Intermediate storage will need to be identified, usually in process logs, as distinct from labelling of primary bulk storage of raw materials, which are more permanently marked. Consideration will need to be given to strict maintenance of emptying and refilling records for intermediate storage. Also regimes need to be in place to ensure the cleaning of intermediate storage before refilling, if residues have an adverse chemical reaction with other materials that may be subsequently introduced into the immediate storage container.

DRUM STORAGE

Flammable materials kept in drum storage should be segregated from incompatible materials such as:

- Strong acids and alkalis, oxidising agents and any other unstable or heat sensitive substance.
- Compressed gases and liquids (for example, liquefied petroleum gas and liquid oxygen) that may become over-pressurised in a fire.

Drums may be stored in a variety of sizes of container, typically in drums up to 225 litres capacity, made from a variety of materials, steel and polythene being the most common. Drums should be stored on solid impervious surfaces, distant from occupied buildings and any boundary fence. Where ideal separation distances are difficult to achieve, separation by a physical barrier, such as a non-combustible/impervious brick wall, may be need to be considered.

Drums should be stored on pallets whenever possible. The pallets should be stacked in a safe manner and in a way that minimises the amount of handling and enables easy access. This is best achieved by keeping the drums banded together on the pallets until they are required and not stacking them more than two high. A hazard may be created if other pallets are placed on top of them without additional support to stabilise the stack. Stacking of loose drums is not recommended. It is clearly an advantage if deliveries can be arranged in the form of a set of drums on a pallet, so that drums can be kept strapped together during unloading, stacking and storage. Precautions are necessary to prevent inadvertent mixing with other materials on filling drums or secondary containers and containment of any spillages that might foreseeably occur. Particular care should be taken to keep the floors free of contamination from spillages.

ELEMENT C4 - STORAGE, HANDLING AND PROCESSING OF DANGEROUS SUBSTANCES

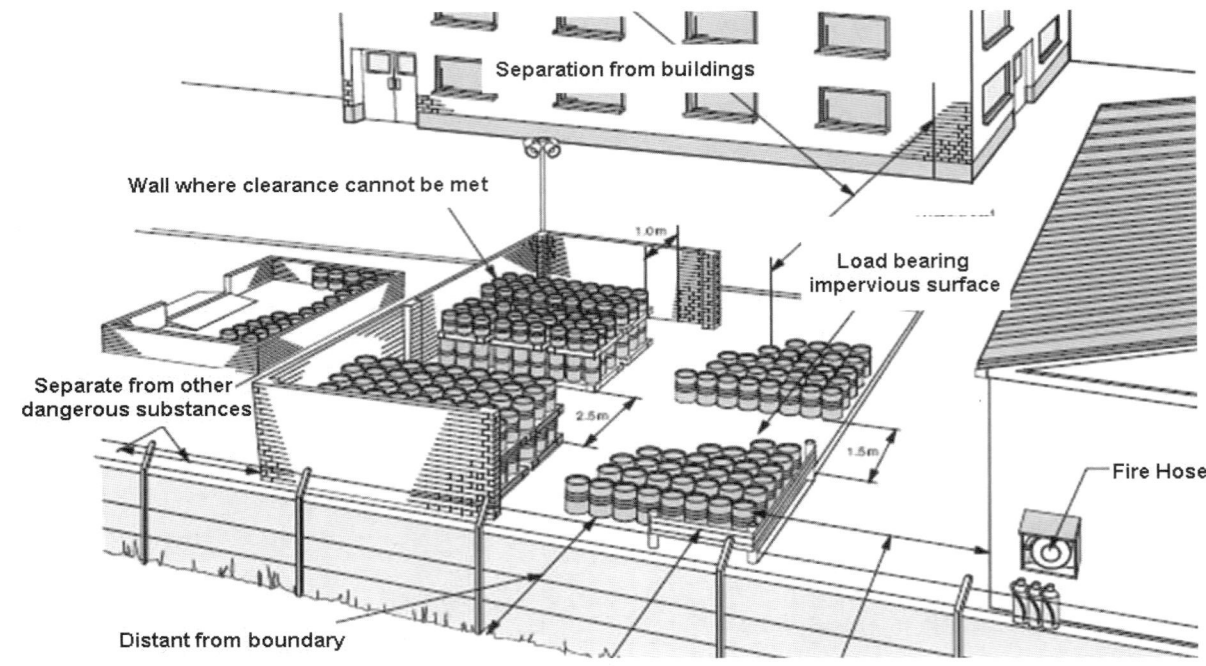

Figure C4-12: Storage of dangerous substances in drums. Source: HSE, HSG 135.

In addition to the need to establish segregation of incompatible dangerous substances, it is important to establish good separation. Separation not only protects people (and property) from the effects of an incident involving dangerous substances in the store itself, but it also protects the store from incidents that may occur elsewhere on site. Consequently, separation is an important means of protection for the storage of dangerous substances, including drum storage.

Separation distances for dangerous substances depend on various factors, including how the dangerous substance is stored and whether the location is considered to be 'high risk' or not. The use of separation as a protective measure for the storage of dangerous substances is essential to reduce the combination of risk in the event of a spillage or fire. Drums may also be damaged if the gangways between stacks are not wide enough for the method of handling used. Access ways of not less than 1.5 metres where single drums are handled manually or 2.5 metres for palletised drums using a fork lift truck are usually adequate.

In addition, it is important to ensure that drums are not unduly confined, such as by stacking them close to building walls or fire walls, it is recommended that at least 1 metre is provided between drums and the wall. Good separation will therefore assist with gaining access to the drums to place them in storage, to inspect them, to retrieve them and to deal with incidents that might occur, such as spills and leaks.

It is also advisable to restrict access to the store by unauthorised people and vehicles. This may prevent accidental damage to drums and the introduction of uncontrolled ignition sources. For outdoor storage, it may be useful to mark the extent of the storage area or erect suitable barriers. The standard of security at the store will depend not only on the nature of the dangerous substances stored, but also the conditions in the area surrounding the store and on the general level of security at the premises.

SPECIFIC LOCATIONS

Dangerous substances will often need to be stored in specific locations in order to make sufficient amounts available for the use of the substances in processes and other work activities. It is usual to control the amount stored to the minimum necessary for immediate use during that day or work shift.

As with storage in other locations, it is important to ensure that incompatible substances are segregated from each other and that access to the dangerous substances is limited to those trained and competent to use them. Many of the good practices needed to control the storage of dangerous substances in the workplace are reflected in the arrangements for storage of flammable dangerous substances.

Flammable dangerous substances for immediate use by workers in the workplace should not exceed 50 litres. Safety storage cabinets should be used for storing flammable liquids in the workplace.

Ideally, these should incorporate the following features:

- Double walls for improved thermal insulation.
- Fitted with low level vents housing flame arrestors in order for the vapours to be safely ducted away.
- Liquid traps to collect any leaks and spills from stored containers within the cabinet.

STORAGE, HANDLING AND PROCESSING OF DANGEROUS SUBSTANCES - ELEMENT C4

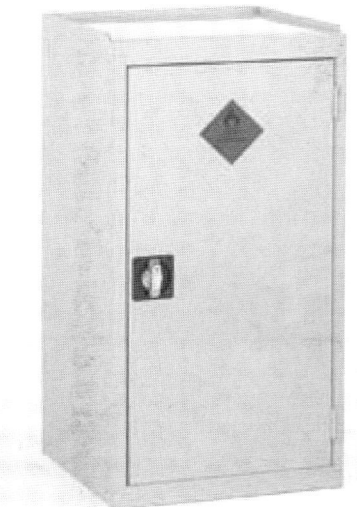

Figure C4-13: Safety cabinet for flammable liquids. *Source: ARCO.*

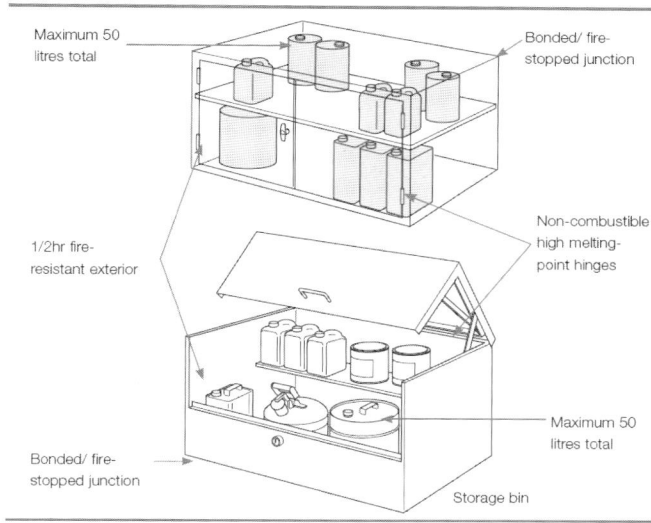

Figure C4-14: Storage of flammable liquids in a workroom. *Source: HSE.*

In addition, provisions should be made to prevent sources of ignition where flammable substances are stored; this will include earth bonding to common ground to reduce the risk of static build up on transfer. Other considerations include the use of the appropriate classification of electrical equipment, the provision of safe vents (flame traps etc.), the possible need to recycle vapours to reduce environmental pollution and the provision of adequate fire suppression equipment.

Containers used to store highly flammable dangerous substances for use in the workplace should be designed to reduce risk by the incorporation of self-closing, spring-loaded caps with a flame arrestor in the neck. The spring loaded cap will snap shut in the event of it being dropped and will act as a safety relief valve, which prevents excess pressure rupturing the container.

Containers that are nominally empty or part empty should be treated as if they are full of the dangerous substance and if they are not needed for immediate use should be returned to the appropriate store.

STORAGE OF INCOMPATIBLE MATERIALS AND THEIR SEGREGATION

In addition to general safe storage practices, segregated storage of incompatible materials is essential. As a minimum, chemicals should be segregated according to similar hazards, such as flammability, corrosion, toxicity and violent reactions when in contact with water or air.

The major hazard categories of dangerous chemicals include:

- Flammables.
- Oxidizers.
- Corrosives.
- Acids.
- Bases.
- Highly reactive.
- Extreme toxics/regulated materials.
- Low hazard.

All chemical manufacturers are required to list all hazards on the labels of outgoing chemical containers and each chemical must be accompanied by a material safety data sheet (MSDS). The chemical label provides a method of determining whether the material is a fire hazard, explosion hazard or reactivity hazard. Most chemicals have multiple hazards and a decision must be made as to which storage area would be most appropriate for each specific chemical.

When establishing a storage scheme, the main consideration should be the flammability characteristics of the material. If the material is flammable, it should be stored in a secure compound or for smaller quantities a flammable cabinet. Certain chemicals will contribute significantly to a fire (i.e., oxidisers), and they should be stored away from flammable materials. Similarly chemicals are corrosive, so that corrosion resistant storage will need to be used. The toxicity of the substance will need to be identified, with particular attention to regulated substances (for example, lead, asbestos, carcinogens, radio active materials, and isotopes).

In some cases, this may mean that certain substances will be isolated within a storage area, for instance, a substance that is an extreme poison, but is also flammable, should be locked away in the flammable storage area to protect it against accidental release.

There will always be some substances that will not fit neatly in one category or another, but with careful consideration of the hazards involved, most of these cases can be handled in a reasonable fashion. Some dangerous substances will spontaneously react when in contact with water (for example, isocyanates explosively decompose) or acids (cyanide compounds will release hydrogen cyanide, ferrous sulphide, hydrogen sulphide).

Where dangerous substances that are violently reactive with water are stored special arrangements will need to be in place with the fire and rescue service, including their location, quantities, identification and the need for the fire service to use alternative fire suppressants when fire fighting in these areas.

Consideration should be given to the segregation of dangerous substances to reduce the risk from mixed spillages or fire. Mixed spillages of oxidants and flammable materials could result in spontaneous ignition and possible explosion. Other substances if not segregated, such as toxic materials, would endanger not only workers but also local emergency or fire fighting personnel called to the scene. The issue of segregation is particularly relevant where both toxic and flammable materials are used together.

Poor segregation substantially increases the risk (of both fire and from toxic fumes) to emergency response organisations and neighbours. Most substances are released as the result of damaged packaging or poor storage conditions, typically too hot or damp. Leakage or spillage of certain materials may act as a source of ignition when they come into contact with each other through an exothermic chemical reaction.

Safe storage includes pallets in good condition and packages shrink wrapped or tied with plastic or metal strapping to prevent falls of materials. Some warehouses are not racked and goods are simply stored in block stacks.

Stack sizes may need to be limited to restrict the severity of any fire. In these cases, standards should be set for the maximum stack size and height. Stacking heights should be limited so that the lowest layer of packages will not be overloaded, resulting in damage from the weight of material above and compromising the stability of the stack.

Where a substance is likely to degrade during storage, the supplier will need to be consulted on the possible hazardous effects of any such degradation.

The information required will include the:

- Recommended storage conditions.
- Indicators that suggest the product is no longer unstable.
- Remedial actions to be taken.
- Maximum storage times.
- Inspection frequencies.

Certain solid substances, such as AZDN, have defined safe storage temperatures above which they will decompose, often with catastrophic results. Where maximum safe storage temperatures are identified, ensure that no heated surfaces above that temperature are present around the stored substance.

The use solely of indirect heating can achieve this, for example, radiators fed remotely by hot water pipes, or indirectly fired gas or oil appliances (i.e. those which take the air for combustion from a safe place and exhaust the products of combustion to the outside air).

Figure C4-15: Storage in racks. *Source: HSG71 Chemical warehousing.*

Figure C4-16: Chemical drum storage.
Source: HSG71 Chemical warehousing.

Figure C4-17: Goods receipt area.
Source: HSG71 Chemical warehousing.

Figure C4-18: Hot air heating system.
Source: HSG71 Chemical warehousing.

Electrically heated radiators that comply with BS EN 60079-14:2003 may be used. In all cases, the heating system should be protected against the build-up of flammable residues on hot surfaces. Stacks should be at least 0.5 m below electric lights. *See also 'Allied Colloids explosion' in Element C2.4 - Major Accidents.*

The following issues may contribute towards a major accident or hazard:

- Failure to understand the properties of substances handled.
- Failure to identify hazards associated with mixing substances.
- Insufficient maintenance of chemical inventories.
- Insufficient labelling of chemical storage containers (raw materials, reactants, intermediates, products, by-products and waste).
- Systems for the location and storage of substances not monitored or reviewed.
- Failure to manage damaged or poorly identified substances.

Leaking and spillage containment

Leaking and spillage can result from a number of sources, for example faulty valves or flanges to pipework; damaged containers such as tins, drums or bags; loss from tanks (typically one tonne) of solids and liquids; filling or emptying bulk or smaller containers. Containers should be stacked in a safe manner that facilitates handling operations and access to deal with leaks. Freestanding (staked upon each other) 225-litre metal drums and similar containers should not be stacked more than four high and preferably on pallets. This will help prevent failure of the drums due to excess weight on them and ensure better stability, which will reduce the likelihood of leaks occurring. The stack design should allow any leaking container to be quickly seen, easily removed and appropriately dealt with. Typical techniques to contain spillage include curbed areas for drum storage and tanker loading of liquids, bunded areas to contain sited tanks, drip trays at decanting points (piped systems and 205 litres drums). In addition, there may be a need to store materials such as absorbent bags, sand or neutralising agents to deal with spillages of flammables or acids and alkalis. Portable tanks are available with two skins (a tank within a tank) to contain any spillage from the internal tank, they are often used where there is a need for portability, such as with construction sites, to minimise the impact of spillage on the environment when storing materials such as fuel oils. Similarly cargo vessels may have double skinned tanks or hulls.

BUNDING

A bund often consists of an area contained by a rectangular wall built upon a concrete slab. The bund floor and walls should be treated to be impervious to any spillage. Storage tanks are located within this containment area. It is necessary to consider the potential escape of tank contents beyond the bund area in the event of the tank developing a hole (known as jetting). The risk of this can be minimised by:

- Keeping the primary container as low as possible.
- Increasing the height of the bund wall.
- Leaving sufficient space between the tank and bund walls.
- Not siting one tank above another.
- Providing screens or curtains.

The bund should be impermeable to the materials stored and water. There should be no direct outlet from the bund:

- Connecting the bund to any drain, sewer or watercourse.
- Discharging onto a yard or unmade ground.

Ideally, pipework should not pass through the bund wall, but over it.

If it is unavoidable for the pipe to pass through the bund wall, the pipe to bund wall seal will require a material that is resistant to dissolution (for example, solvents) or corrosion (for example, acids or alkalis) by the dangerous substance stored, to ensure the bund remains leak-proof. The bund must provide storage of at least 110% of the tank's maximum capacity.

Figure C4-19: Concrete bund. *Source: Safeguard Europe Ltd.* Figure C4-20: Brick bund. *Source: Safeguard Europe Ltd.*

ELEMENT C4 - STORAGE, HANDLING AND PROCESSING OF DANGEROUS SUBSTANCES

If more than one tank is stored in a bund, the system must be capable of storing 110% of the biggest tank's capacity or 25% of the total tank capacity within the bund, whichever is the greater.

FILLING AND TRANSFER

Employers should make sure procedures are established for the safe receipt and transfer of dangerous substances to storage. Workers with responsibility for accepting deliveries must be fully trained and aware of the procedures. They should be informed in advance of what is to be delivered before it arrives on site. Typically, procedures will require that when dangerous substances arrive on site the consignment paperwork is checked against the actual substance expected.

Any substances arriving on site that cannot be identified and matched to the purchase order should not be unloaded into storage tanks. Procedures should be in place for handling such circumstances, including how to contact the supplier for assistance. The delivery vehicle may need to be removed to a remote place while this procedure is undertaken. If a satisfactory response from the supplier is not received then the vehicle and contents should be returned to the supplier.

When the delivery notes are checked ensure that the substance is described clearly and where relevant the concentration of any solution is correct, for example, 15% sulphuric acid is ordered and supplied. Any other relevant purchase specifications or requirements should match the delivery note. Workers should beware of the use of chemical name abbreviations such as ethylenediaminetetraacetic acid, widely abbreviated as EDTA compared with ethylenediaminetetraacetate.

Before offloading the vehicle it is necessary to ensure there is sufficient capacity in the storage tank to receive the delivery with at least a 5% margin of safety (i.e. sufficient ullage in the tank). It should be ensured that the vehicle is correctly positioned, coupled to the correct inlet pipework (check the label) and where appropriate earthed to a common potential with the storage system. Valves should be correctly set to the storage tank that is to receive the transfer. When transfer begins the recipient tank level should be monitored to ensure adequate capacity throughout the filling process.

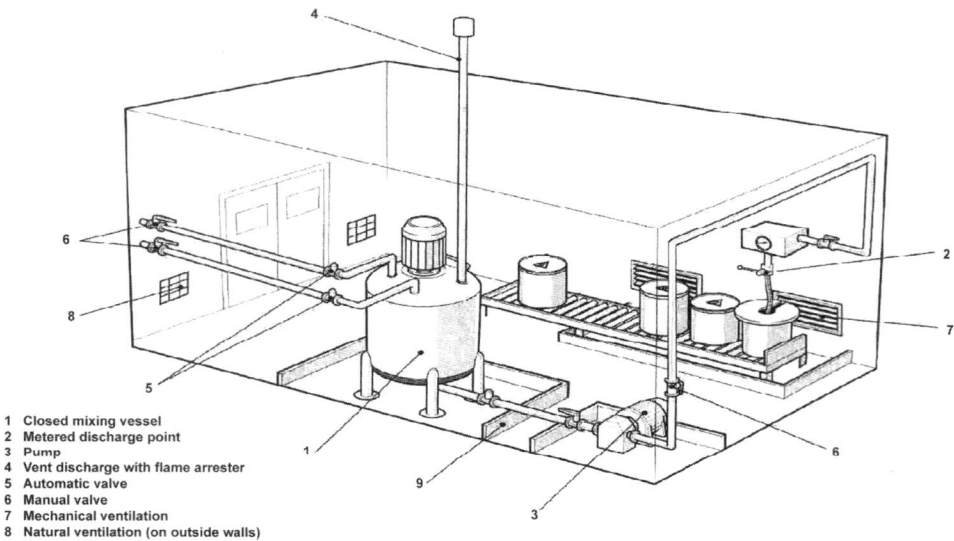

1 Closed mixing vessel
2 Metered discharge point
3 Pump
4 Vent discharge with flame arrester
5 Automatic valve
6 Manual valve
7 Mechanical ventilation
8 Natural ventilation (on outside walls)
9 Leak and spillage retention skills

Figure C4-21: Flammable liquid filling and transfer.   Source: HSG143.

Factors to consider when transferring dangerous substances:

Liquids

- Zoning if flammable solvents or vapours involved.
- Correct positioning of valves.
- Destination container of suitable capacity.
- Provision of overfill devices, including high and extra high level alarms (storage tanks).
- Overfill containment tanks in addition to bunding.
- Spillage containment, such as kerbed areas for tankers.
- High level alarms.
- Starting and stopping of transfer pumps.

Powders

- Containment on conveyors.
- Use of inert gases when blown.
- Zoning if flammable dust is involved.
- Correct positioning of controls.
- Destination container is of suitable capacity.

Examples of problems encountered during filling and transfer

ALBRIGHT AND WILSON, 3 OCTOBER 1996 - INADVERTENT MIXING

An explosion and fire occurred at a factory in Avonmouth, caused by the accidental mixture of two chemicals (epichlorohydrin and sodium chlorite) and resulted in a large plume of smoke that had both on-site and off-site effects. Further chemicals subsequently became involved.

The incident caused some structural damage and several minor casualties (including to fire fighters). Members of the public were advised to shelter indoors with doors and windows closed. Motorways (M48 and M49) were closed, together with both the Severn Crossings, and significant travel disruption was caused.

Circumstances

A mix up occurred in the performance of two contracts and as a result a tanker load of sodium chlorite being supplied by Berk to Albright and Wilson was delivered with the wrong delivery note. The documentation supplied did not relate to the order of sodium chlorite from Berk Ltd., but to a different order by Albright and Wilson for a tanker load of a different chemical, epichlorohydrin (EPI), from a different supplier, Biachem Ltd. Both loads were due for delivery on the same day and at the same factory, the Albright and Wilson's Avonmouth works.

The documentation mix up became possible because, by chance, Berk and Biachem employed the same haulage contractor, A T Stevens Transport, to deliver both tanker loads to Albright and Wilson's Avonmouth works. In turn, Huktra the agent for Berk, employed one subcontractor, Stevens, in respect of both loads.

The agent who was dealing with the matter at Huktra appears to have thought that Biachem did not wish the source of the goods that it was providing to Albright and Wilson to be apparent on the face of the documentation. As a result of that belief, Huktra instructed the driver, who was provided by Stevens, to tender on delivery only the Biachem delivery note. That instruction to the carrier was reinforced by a fax sent by Huktra that said: 'Delivery to Avonmouth 3 October. Please remove all documents and use this delivery note only.'

The delivery note that was referred to and which was attached to that fax was the Biachem delivery note for EPI. However, by mistake, there had been endorsed on it by Huktra the tanker number relevant to the delivery on behalf of Berk of sodium chlorite.

When the driver was carrying out Huktra's instructions, he was driving a tanker full of sodium chlorite, but it had associated with it Biachem's delivery note - the only document that he was under instructions to tender - saying "that the load was EPI".

See Element C2.4 - Major accidents for details on the following examples of transfer related major incidents:

BUNCEFIELD - TANK OVERFILLED RESULTING IN SPILLAGE OF PETROLEUM

A spillage of unleaded petrol occurred from the overfilling of Tank 912 in Bund A in the Hertfordshire Oil Storage Limited West site. The resulting vapour cloud was ignited resulting in an unconfined vapour cloud explosion (UCVCE).

FLIXBOROUGH 1974 - PIPELINE FAILURE

A temporary bridging pipe ruptured and released large quantities of cyclo-hexane, which mixed with air to form an unconfined vapour cloud that subsequently exploded.

MEXICO CITY 1984 - PIPELINE FAILURE

An 8-inch pipe between a sphere and a series of cylinders ruptured releasing liquefied petroleum gas (LPG), which resulted in a series of boiling liquid exploding vapour explosions (BLEVEs).

Handling of dangerous substances

Under the *Notification of Installations Handling Hazardous Substances Regulations (NIHHSR) 1982 (as amended 2002)*, an activity which involves a notifiable quantity of a hazardous substance at a site or in a pipeline under control of a person in control of the site, must be notified to the HSE at least 3 months before the activity commences; or at least 4 weeks before in the case of *ammonium nitrate*. There is a list of notifiable hazardous substances and the notifiable quantities in Schedule 1 of these regulations.

Ammonium nitrate received special attention following an explosion on 21st September 2001, when an earthquake, 3.4 on the Richter scale, triggered an explosion at an artificial fertilizer (ammonium nitrate) factory in Toulouse, France. As a result, 30 people were killed and 3,500 people were injured.

The NIHHSR as amended 2002, require that anyone who handles or stores (or intends to handle or store) 150 tonnes (revised down from 1,000 tonnes) or more of ammonium nitrate (used as a nitrogen fertiliser), or of mixtures containing ammonium nitrate where the nitrogen content exceeds 15.75% of the mixture by weight, should notify the HSE.

FLOW THROUGH PIPELINES

All pipelines should be made of suitable material to withstand the effects of dangerous substances, for example corrosion.

Typical materials include stainless steel, coated mild steel and glass (larger laboratory facilities, used to scale up processes).

All pipework should be identified with the substance and direction of flow arrows. Pipe flanges should be chemically resistant.

Where the risk of static electricity is present from pumping non-conductive substances, earth bonding should be maintained across each flange or valve in the pipe run to ensure a common earth and reduce the risk of static sparks of sufficient energy to be a source of ignition.

Figure C4-22: Labelled pipelines. *Source: HSG 140.*

PRINCIPLES IN FILLING AND EMPTYING CONTAINERS

Factors to be considered when filling and emptying containers include:

- Spillage collection when filling containers, such as drums or tanks.
- Zoning if flammable solvents or vapours are involved.
- Earthing of all metal transfer pipework and storage equipment, from receipt container to supply container, to ensure both are at common electrical grounding and prevent electrostatic discharge.
- Need for ullage provision (compressible air void in sealed containers such as drums or tankers, to allow for contents volume changes with temperature).
- Bunds for storage.
- Capture of any vapours.

PRINCIPLES IN DISPENSING, SPRAYING AND DISPOSAL OF FLAMMABLE LIQUIDS

Dispensing

Dispensing should be carried out in a way that reduces spills and dangerous releases of flammable vapours. The need for dispensing operations should be assessed and, where possible, minimised by the use of enclosed transfer systems. If an enclosed system cannot be used, the containers should be designed to minimise spillage, release of vapour and the effects of fire.

Small safety containers are available that incorporate the following features:

- Metal or heavy-duty plastic construction.
- Pouring and/or filling apertures sealed with self-closing spring loaded caps.
- Pouring and/or filling apertures fitted with flame arresters.
- Use of hoses or other aids when dispensing into small openings.
- Carrying handles for containers with a capacity greater than approximately 2.5 litres.

Containers should be able to resist wear and tear in normal use and any corrosion by the specific liquid being used. They should be strong enough to withstand being dropped. Plastic containers need to be compatible with the fluid that they are intended to contain.

Figure C4-23: Dispensing containers. *Source: HSE, HSG140.*

They should incorporate anti-static features so that any metal components in the transfer system, such as flame arresters or funnels, cannot build up incendive electrostatic charges. The use of containers approved by a recognised testing and approval organisation is recommended.

Spraying

In the spray process, liquid is converted into a fine mist of droplets that is propelled towards a surface where an evenly distributed film is formed. The main spray methods are:

- Compressed air.
- Airless spraying (hydraulic pressure).
- Electrostatic.

Compressed air method

The commonest method of spraying is the compressed air operated spray gun in which liquid is atomised, in either internal-mix or external-mix nozzles by compressed air (30-50 psi). In internal-mix nozzles, liquid and compressed air are combined in a chamber inside the nozzle, whereas in external-mix nozzles liquid and compressed air are ejected through separate orifices to combine outside the nozzle.

Airless method

In airless spraying, liquid is atomised by forcing it through a small orifice (0.1-1.5 mm) at high pressure (typically in the range 50-400 bar). The hydraulic pressure is usually produced by small piston pumps powered by compressed air. The amount of overspray and ricochet may be about 20% as the velocity of the paint droplets falls off rapidly after leaving the nozzle of the gun. The method is limited primarily to applying viscous high-solid heavy-duty coatings to structural steel, because of environmental considerations.

Electrostatic method

In electrostatic spraying, liquid droplets (or solid particles) are given an electrical charge (typically 60-150 kV) causing them to be attracted to an earthed conductive work-piece. The charge is applied either to the liquid stream before its release or to atomised droplets by passing them through an ionising field. Up to 90% of the finish is deposited on the surface.

Spray areas or booths

Ignition sources should be kept out of spraying areas at all times. Even when spraying is not taking place, flammable hazardous area classification is the method used to identify areas where flammable concentrations of gases or vapours are likely to be present. The aim is to reduce to the minimum acceptable level the probability of a flammable atmosphere coinciding with an electrical or other source of ignition. It is normally used to select fixed electrical equipment, but it can also be used in the control of other potential ignition sources such as portable electrical equipment, hot surfaces and vehicles.

For spray booths, the simplest approach is to regard the whole booth interior as zone 1, and to exclude all electrical equipment and other sources of ignition. Adequate lighting of the interior of the booth may be achieved either by using protected lighting, or by allowing light from an overhead fitting to shine through half-hour fire-resistant glass panels sealed into the top of the booth.

Consideration should also be given to the safe disposal of flammable residues, contaminated materials, drying and cleaning operations that may present a fire risk. Other factors to consider include:

- Suitable respiratory protection.
- Hand, forearm protection (to prevent skin inflammation or dermatitis, common with flammable liquid contacts).
- Suitable containment of material overspray (water washed exhaust systems to trap solids and solvents).

Disposal

Waste liquids will generally need to be stored and handled according to the same standards as the flammable liquids from which they were derived. They will also be subject to the same legislation, unless their physical properties have been significantly altered by the processing. If, for example, the storage of the original flammable liquid required a licence from the Petroleum Licensing Authority, the waste material may also be subject to the same licence and conditions.

Waste materials collected from different processes should not be mixed together before disposal, unless the various components are known to be compatible, and only after considering the eventual disposal technique to be used.

Any drums used for waste materials should be sound and not contain any incompatible residues. If a drum is being used as a collecting station for waste liquids, a funnel should be used that fits securely into the drum opening to reduce the possibility of spillage.

Funnels with lids and flame arresters should be used to stop any external ignition from flashing back into the drum and to prevent the drum becoming dangerously pressurised if it is engulfed by fire.

When not in use containers of waste liquids should be securely closed to prevent leakage and returned to storage areas or cabinets.

Figure C4-24: Waste solvent collection. *Source: HSE, HSG140.*

Disposal of flammable liquids should include consideration of the following:

- Segregation.
- Containment and labelling of waste.

ELEMENT C4 - STORAGE, HANDLING AND PROCESSING OF DANGEROUS SUBSTANCES

- Use of a suitable solvent recovery company.
- Safe incineration or alternate disposal.

DANGERS OF ELECTRICITY IN HAZARDOUS AREAS

Electrical hazards in hazardous areas include electrocution and ignition of flammable process materials, such as dusts, gases or vapours, by the use of inappropriate electrical equipment that is not flame proof or intrinsically safe.

Static electricity may be a source of ignition, particularly when non-conductive substances are involved and air is available to support ignition, such as when they are poured into containers or vessels that are not at a common earthed potential, *see figure ref C4-25*. The operator involved in such processes should be wearing electrically conductive boots and be standing on a conductive plate connected to the reactor into which they are charging a flammable chemical.

See also - Dangerous and Explosive Atmospheres Regulations (DSEAR) 2002 - Relevant statutory provisions.

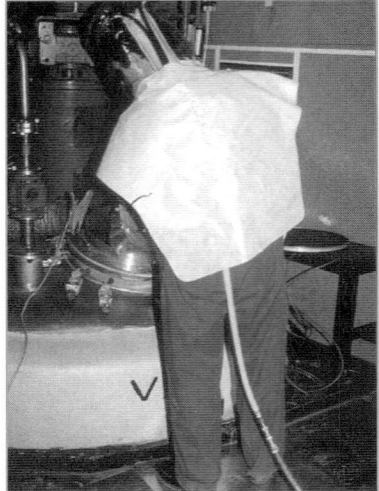

Figure C4-25: Zone 1 - Metal footplate common earth potential when changing flammable chemicals. *Source: HSG140.*

Transport of dangerous substances

KEY SAFETY PRINCIPLES IN LOADING AND UNLOADING OF TANKERS AND TANK CONTAINERS

Drivers of tankers and tank containers must be in possession of sufficient written information to ensure they know the nature of the dangers involved in transporting the dangerous substance and the emergency action to be taken if such dangers arise.

The 'Transport Emergency Card (Road)', known more commonly as a **Tremcard** must be kept in the vehicle cab, so that this 'information in writing' can be easily located by the emergency services in the event of an accident. A **Tremcard** relating to the previous load should be put into a securable compartment or container, which is clearly marked and capable of remaining closed even in the event of a vehicle roll-over.

To meet the requirements of the European Agreement concerning the International Carriage of Goods by Road (ADR) Regulation 5.4.3, instructions in writing must be carried when hazardous goods are transported by road. There is now one set of instructions to cover all dangerous goods.

The driver/haulier is now responsible for providing the instructions in writing on actions to be taken in the event of an accident or emergency that may occur or arise during carriage.

The members of the vehicle crew are required to take the following actions where safe and practicable to do so:

- Apply the braking system, stop the engine and isolate the battery by activating the master switch where available.
- Avoid sources of ignition; in particular, do not smoke or switch on any electrical equipment.
- Inform the appropriate emergency services, giving as much information about the incident or accident and substances involved as possible.
- Put on the warning vest and place the self-standing warning signs as appropriate.
- Keep the transport documents readily available for responders on arrival.
- Do not walk into or touch spilled substances and avoid inhalation of fumes, smoke, dusts and vapours by staying up wind.
- Where appropriate and safe to do so, use the fire extinguishers to put out small/initial fires in tyres, brakes and engine compartments.
- Fires in load compartments shall not be tackled by members of the vehicle crew.
- Where appropriate and safe to do so, use on-board equipment to prevent leakages into the aquatic environment or the sewage system and to contain spillages.
- Move away from the vicinity of the accident or emergency, advise other persons to move away and follow the advice of the emergency services.
- Remove any contaminated clothing and used contaminated protective equipment and dispose of it safely.

Source: United Nations Economic Commission for Europe (UNECE) website.

Additional guidance to members of the vehicle crew must be provided by the haulier on the hazard characteristics of dangerous goods by class, including the explanation of the hazard characteristics represented by danger labels and placards and on actions subject to prevailing circumstances that the driver should take:

Additional guidance to members of the vehicle crew on the hazard characteristics of dangerous goods by class and on actions subject to prevailing circumstances		
Danger labels and placards (1)	Hazard characteristics (2)	Additional guidance (3)
Explosive substances and articles 1 1.5 1.6	May have a range of properties and effects such as mass detonation; projection of fragments; intense fire/heat flux; formation of bright light, loud noise or smoke. Sensitive to shocks and/or impacts and/or heat.	Take cover but stay away from windows.
Explosive substances and articles 1.4	Slight risk of explosion and fire.	Take cover.
Flammable gases 2.1	Risk of fire. Risk of explosion. May be under pressure. Risk of asphyxiation. May cause burns and/or frostbite. Containments may explode when heated.	Take cover. Keep out of low areas.
Non-flammable, non-toxic gases 2.2	Risk of asphyxiation. May be under pressure. May cause frostbite. Containments may explode when heated.	Take cover. Keep out of low areas.

Figure C4-26: Examples of hazard labels and hazard characteristics with guidance for transport crews. *Source: UNECE.*

There is a risk of cross contamination where bulk storage tankers and tank containers that are used for different purposes are delivered to a multi-substance storage area.

The incident at Camelford, Cornwall in July 1988, which involved the inadvertent gross contamination of a service reservoir with aluminium sulphate is an extreme example of what can go wrong.

A relief tanker driver working for the Bristol based distribution firm ISC, arrived at Lowermoor water treatment works on Bodmin Moor and found it unattended. The driver was unfamiliar with the location, had been given a key by another driver and was told simply that "once inside the gate, the aluminium sulphate tank is on the left". However, the key fitted almost every lock used by the South West Water Authority (SWWA). After twenty minutes looking for the correct tank the driver tried the key on a manhole cover and when it unlocked believed he had accessed the correct tank. The driver poured the load of 20 tonnes of aluminium sulphate, used to remove solid particles from cloudy water, into the tank. The tank was a service reservoir and held treated water prior to distribution to the consumers in Camelford. This immediately contaminated the water supply to 20,000 local people and up to 10,000 tourists. The maximum recorded aluminium concentration in the water supply from the contamination was 620,000 micrograms per litre, compared with the maximum concentration admissible at the time by the European Community of 200 micrograms per litre.

In order to avoid this type of error, strict issue and control of access keys is essential. Off loading should be supervised by the site representative and, where appropriate, couplings that are of a unique design and specific to the delivery vehicle for a particular substance should be considered to prevent incorrect connection of pipework at the point of delivery. All receipt couplings should be clearly labelled with the substance name.

Both drivers and those in recipient of dangerous substances are required to observe all the precautions necessary for preventing fire or explosion. Written procedures should be issued, laying down precautions that must be taken during various operations - particularly loading, consigning and unloading. For loading and unloading the precautions include:

- Fire extinguishers should be carried when substances pose a risk of fire or explosion.
- Earth connections must be in use before and during loading and unloading, to prevent the possible build up and subsequent discharge of static electricity.
- No loading or unloading should take place if there is an electrical storm overhead.
- No smoking in the vicinity during loading or unloading.
- For flammable substances (for example petroleum spirit) no matches or lighters are to be carried by the driver.

It should not be forgotten that some manual handling will be involved in loading and unloading, even with bulk materials. For example, this will occur even where solids are transported from silos using conveyors or compressed gas as there may be a need to direct the flow from chutes. Where the loading and unloading of liquids are involved, manual handling will occur at the point of connection/disconnection. Where manual handling is carried out, other risks associated with the close proximity of the person carrying out the manual handling to the substance need to be evaluated, for example exposure to toxic substances and the risk of ignition.

ELEMENT C4 - STORAGE, HANDLING AND PROCESSING OF DANGEROUS SUBSTANCES

Steps should be taken to ensure overfilling of storage and transport vessels receiving dangerous substances are not overfilled. It is essential to ensure that sufficient room for expansion is allowed, the space left for expansion in a storage vessel is known as the ullage. This may require the fitting of alarms to indicate the level of dangerous substance in the storage vessel. This can include high level and extra high level alarms, often supported by automatic filling cut off of filling pumps. Where alarms are not installed, for example on a tanker or tank container for transport levels will need to be monitored visually.

Emergency site arrangements need to be established. Typically this will involve measures to:
- Raise the alarm.
- Initiate evacuation.
- Deal with contamination of individuals (safety drench showers) and the environment.

Wind socks may be necessary to indicate direction routes for airborne contaminants.

LABELLING OF VEHICLES AND PACKAGING OF SUBSTANCES

Tankers and tank containers used to carry dangerous substances must be fitted with the appropriate hazard warning panels. These are often referred to as '*hazchem*' panels. Each panel has five sections which provide information on:

- The emergency action code.
- The substance identification number.
- The symbol indicating the general nature of the substance.
- A source of specialist advice - usually a telephone number.
- The manufacturers or owner's name and logo - this is optional.

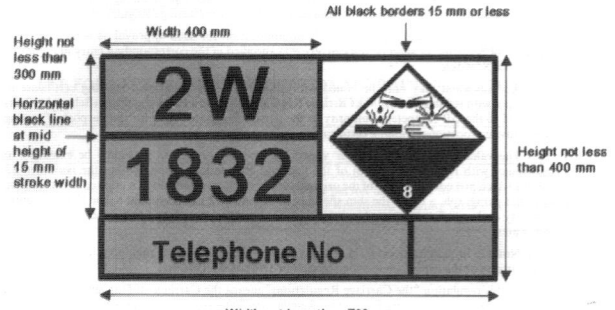

Figure C4-27: HIN - Hazard identification number (kemler code) - does not require a telephone number. *Source: RMS.*

Driver training and Dangerous Goods Safety Advisor

The Carriage of Dangerous Goods and Use of Transportable Pressure Equipment Regulations (CDGUTPER) 2009 effectively implement the requirements of the European agreement concerning the carriage of dangerous goods (ADR; Accord Européen Relatif au Transport International des Marchandises Dangereuses par Route). The Department for Transport (DfT) is the UK "Competent Authority" and the Vehicle Certification Agency (VCA) administers the system for the appointment of bodies for the conformity assessment and periodic inspection of Transportable Pressure Equipment. The CDGUTPER sets out requirements for the safe carriage of dangerous substances, including the training of drivers and the appointment of safety advisors.

DRIVER TRAINING AND SUPERVISION OF VEHICLES

Training of drivers

The Carriage of Dangerous Goods and Use of Transportable Pressure Equipment Regulations 2009 require the training of drivers. Drivers must be given adequate instruction and training so that they are able to understand:
- The nature of the dangers posed by the substance.
- The action to take in an emergency.
- Their duties under the regulations.

Records of instruction and training given to each driver during their employment must be maintained. A copy must also be available to the driver.

Supervision of vehicles

The driver must ensure that when the vehicle is not being driven, it is either:
- Parked in a safe place.
- Supervised at all times by himself or some other competent person over the age of 18.

'Safe place', which can be approved local authority parks or other open air sites where the public have no access, for example, factories or transport depots.

ROLE OF THE DANGEROUS GOODS SAFETY ADVISERS UNDER THE CARRIAGE OF DANGEROUS GOODS AND USE OF TRANSPORTABLE PRESSURE EQUIPMENT REGULATIONS (CDGUTPER) 2009

The Carriage of Dangerous Goods and Use of Transportable Pressure Equipment Regulations (CDGUTPER) 2009 prohibit the transport of dangerous goods by road, railway and inland waterway unless one or more safety adviser(s) are appointed. The number of advisers must be sufficient to ensure that their functions and duties can be carried out effectively. Arrangements must be made to ensure adequate co-operation between the safety advisers appointed. Advisers must be provided with adequate time, means, information and facilities necessary to fulfil their functions and duties.

STORAGE, HANDLING AND PROCESSING OF DANGEROUS SUBSTANCES - ELEMENT C4

No one may be appointed as a safety adviser unless they hold a vocational training certificate appropriate to the modes of transport used and the dangerous goods specified and transported by the employer or one or more. The CDGUTPER 2009 also imposes requirements with regard to the issue, form, validity and renewal of vocational training certificates. Vocational training certificates are mutually recognised throughout the EU.

The role of the safety adviser is to:

- Monitor compliance with the rules governing the transport of dangerous goods.
- Advise the employer on the transport of dangerous goods.
- Ensure that an annual report to the employer is prepared on the activities of the employer concerning the transport of dangerous goods.
- Monitor the following practices and procedures relating to the activities of the employer which concern the transport of dangerous goods:
  - The procedures for compliance with the rules governing the identification of dangerous goods being transported.
  - The practice of the employer in taking into account, when purchasing means of transport, any special requirements in connection with the dangerous goods to be transported.
  - The procedures for checking the equipment used in connection with the transport of dangerous goods.
  - Ensure relevant training of the employer's employees and the maintenance of records of such training.
  - The implementation of appropriate emergency procedures in the event of any accident or incident that may affect safety during the transport of dangerous goods.
  - The investigation of and, where appropriate, preparation of reports on serious accidents, incidents or serious infringements recorded during the transport of dangerous goods.
  - The implementation of appropriate measures to avoid the recurrence of accidents, incidents or serious infringements.
  - Take account of the legal prescriptions and special requirements associated with the transport of dangerous goods in the choice and use of sub-contractors or third parties.
  - Verification that employees involved in the transport of dangerous goods has detailed operational procedures and instructions.
  - The introduction of measures to increase awareness of the risks inherent in the transport of dangerous goods.
  - The implementation of verification procedures to ensure the presence, on board the means of transport, of the documents and safety equipment which must accompany transport and the compliance of such documents and equipment with health and safety regulations.
  - The implementation of verification procedures to ensure compliance with legislation governing loading and unloading of dangerous goods.

The safety adviser must also ensure the preparation of a report on any accident that affects the health or safety of any person or causes damage to the environment or to property and which occurs during the transport of dangerous goods by the employer who has appointed the advisor. A copy of the report must also be provided to the employer. The Secretary of State or any goods vehicle examiner must be provided, on request, with the name of any safety adviser, a copy of any accident and annual reports, and any vocational training certificate.

C4.3 - Hazardous environments

Resistance to mechanical damage and protection against solid bodies, objects, dusts, liquids and gases

In order to protect equipment from damage by solid bodies, objects and dusts or liquids and gases, therefore preventing persons from coming into contact with live or moving parts, the equipment is housed inside enclosures. The degree of protection offered by such an enclosure is the subject of EN 60529:1992; "Specification for degrees of protection provided by enclosures" - commonly called the IP code or Index of Protection. *The table for this is shown in figure ref C4-28*. It can be seen from the table that it specifies categories by a numbering system. The first digit represents the level of mechanical protection and the second digit the level of liquid protection.

First numeral		Second numeral	
(a) Protection of persons against contact with live or moving parts inside enclosure. (b) Protection of equipment against ingress of solid bodies.		Protection of equipment against ingress of water.	
No./symbol	*Degree of protection*	*No./symbol*	*Degree of protection*
0	(a) No protection. (b) No protection.	0	No protection.

ELEMENT C4 - STORAGE, HANDLING AND PROCESSING OF DANGEROUS SUBSTANCES

No./symbol	Degree of protection	No./symbol	Degree of protection
1	(a) Protection against accidental or inadvertent contact by a large surface of the body, for example, hand, but not against deliberate causes. (b) Protection against ingress of large solid objects less than 50 mm in diameter.	1	Protection against drops of water. Drops of water falling on enclosure shall have no harmful effect.
2	(a) Protection against contact by standard finger. (b) Protection against ingress of medium sized bodies less than 12 mm diameter and less than 80 mm in length.	2	Drip Proof: Protection against drops of liquid. Drops of falling liquid shall have no harmful effect when the enclosure is tilted at any angle up to 15° from the vertical.
3	(a) Protection against contact by tools, wires or suchlike more than 2.5 mm thick. (b) Protection against ingress of small solid bodies.	3 	Rain Proof: Water falling as rain at any angle up to 60° from the vertical shall have no harmful effect.
4	(a) As 3 above but against contact by tools, wires or the like, more than 1.00 mm thick. (b) Protection against ingress of small foreign bodies.	4 	Splash Proof: Water splashed from any direction shall have no harmful effect.
5 	(a) Complete protection against contact. (b) **Dustproof** - protection against harmful deposits of dust; dust may enter but not in amount sufficient to interfere with satisfactory operation.	5 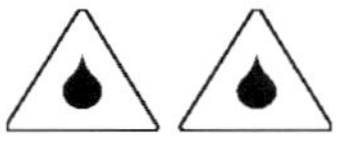	Jet Proof: Water projected from a nozzle from any direction (under stated conditions) shall have no harmful effect.
6 	(a) Complete protection against contact. (b) **Dust tight** - protection against ingress of dust.	6	Watertight Equipment: Protection against conditions on ships, decks, etc. Water from heavy seas or power jets shall not enter the enclosures under prescribed conditions.
IP CODE NOTES: The degree of protection is stated in form IPXX. Protection against contact or ingress of water respectively is specified by replacing first or second X digit number tabled, for example, IP2X defines an enclosure giving protection against finger contact but without any specific protection against ingress of water or liquid.		7 	Protection Against Immersion in Water: It shall not be possible for water to enter the enclosure under stated conditions of pressure and time.
		8	Protection Against Indefinite Immersion in Water Under Specified Pressure: It shall not be possible for water to enter the enclosure.

Figure C4-28: Index of protection ratings. *Source: RMS.*

Note: use of this table is for general guidance only - refer to BS EN 60529 for full information on degrees of protection offered by enclosures.

Example - an enclosure with an IP value of IP56. This means that the 5 = dust proof and the 6 = watertight, so the enclosure is protected from water and dust. The most commonly quoted IP codes are IP2X and IP4X. The X does not mean that no protection is given, but that the level of protection is not specified

Example - an enclosure housing equipment in an AD8 environment (under water) would have an IP code of IPX8.

Wet environments including corrosion and degradation of installation and damage to electrical systems

Many workplaces expose electrical equipment to damage through damp and corrosive environments, for example, laundries, bakeries, chemical plants, breweries, car wash facilities and electroplating processes.

Electroplating involves the use of low voltage high current DC, derived from rectifier units operating at primary voltages of 415 volts AC. Auxiliary equipment typically includes pumps, filters, blowers, centrifuges and heaters (fixed and transportable) as well as hand-held portable tools and instruments. Electroplating uses conductive and corrosive fluids, and the atmosphere in such workplaces is often humid and laden with corrosive mist.

People often have to work close to electrical systems and exposed conductors means that, unless properly controlled, the combination of electricity, water, damp and corrosive conditions can be lethal. Similar hazards, i.e. injury from electric shock, electric burn, electrical explosion or arcing, or from fire or explosion initiated by electrical energy, apply to all workplaces where wet and corrosive environments encountered.

Figure C4-29: Electrical equipment housing held closed with string. Source: HSE.

It is important that the equipment selected is suitable for this harsh environment and is sufficiently protected to prevent harm.

Principles of selection of electrical equipment for use in flammable atmospheres

DSEAR 2002, Schedule 3, *"Criteria for the selection of equipment and protective systems"* sets out the link between zones where explosive atmospheres may be present and the equipment that may be installed in that zone. This applies to new or newly modified installations. The equipment and protective systems for all places in which explosive atmospheres may occur must be selected on the basis of the requirements set out in the Equipment and Protective Systems Intended for Use in Potentially Explosive Atmospheres Regulations (EPS) 1996 unless the risk assessment finds otherwise. The categories of equipment suited to the zones are derived from Annex 1 of the ATEX equipment directive. EPS 1996 sets out two groups of equipment, group I is for use in mines and has category 1 and 2 equipment. Group II equipment is for more general workplaces and has category 1, 2 and 3 equipment. Equipment in category 3 will provide a normal level of performance and reliability that will not present a source of ignition. Category 2 equipment will provide a high level of performance and reliability *"even in the event of frequently occurring disturbances or equipment faults which normally have to be taken into account"*. Category 3 equipment will provide a very high level of performance and reliability *"even in the event of rare incidents relating to equipment and is characterised by means of protection such that: either, in the event of failure of one means of protection, at least an independent second means provides the requisite level of protection, or the requisite level of protection is assured in the event of two faults occurring independently of each other"*. In particular, the following categories of equipment must be used in the zones indicated, provided they are suitable for gases, vapours, mists, dusts or mists and dusts, as appropriate:

- In zone 0 or zone 20, category 1 equipment.
- In zone 1 or zone 21, category 1 or 2 equipment.
- In zone 2 or zone 22, category 1, 2 or 3 equipment.

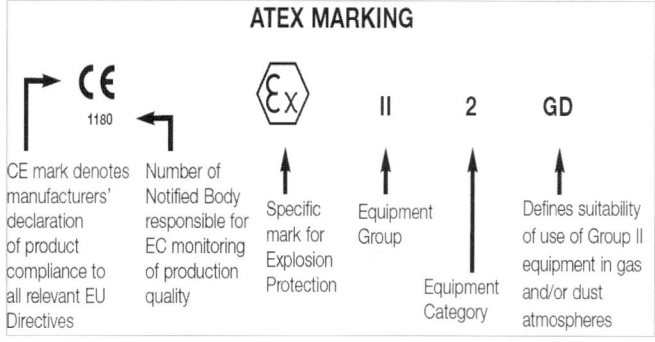
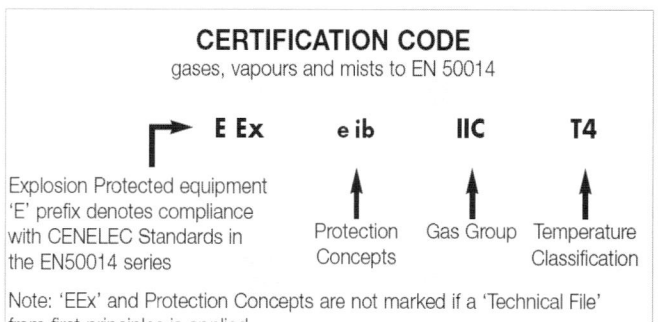

Figure C4-30: Examples of ATEX marking and certification codes for dusts, gases and vapours. Source: Wolf.

Most of the electrical standards have been developed over many years and are now set at international level. Standards set out different protection concepts, with further subdivisions for some types of equipment according to gas group and temperature classification.

Classification of hazardous areas, zoning

It is a requirement of The Dangerous Substances and Explosive Atmospheres Regulations (DSEAR) 2002 to classify areas according to the likelihood of a flammable or explosive substance being within the explosive limits in the area. Combustion is not supported below the lower explosive limit (LEL) as the fuel: air mix is too lean. Above the higher explosive limit the mix is too rich. The classification is set out in schedule 2 of the DSEAR 2002 and essentially reflects the requirements in Annex 1 of the European Directive that established the requirements of DSEAR 2002. The classification is based on the frequency and duration of the occurrence of an explosive atmosphere.

Classification of hazardous area zoning for *gases, vapours and mists* is:

- **Zone 0** - is an area in which a flammable atmosphere is known to be continuously present or present for long periods at a concentration within the upper and lower flammability or explosive limits, such as within a reactor, mixing vessel or storage tank.
- **Zone 1** - is an area in which a flammable atmosphere is likely to occur, at least during normal processing, handling or storage operations.
- **Zone 2** - is an area in which a flammable atmosphere is unlikely to occur except under abnormal conditions and then only for a period of short duration.

Classification of hazardous area zoning for *dusts* is:

- **Zone 20** - Explosive atmosphere in air with a cloud of combustible dust present continuously or for long periods of time.
- **Zone 21** - Explosive atmosphere in air with a cloud of combustible dust likely to occur in normal operation occasionally.
- **Zone 22** - Explosive atmosphere in air with a cloud of combustible dust is not likely to occur in normal operation, but if it does it will be for a short period only.

Use of permits-to-work

Work in hazardous environments, such as flammable atmospheres, must be strictly controlled. This may involve complex planning, organising, control and monitoring arrangements to ensure risks are minimised. This means that work in such environments will often be conducted under the control of a permit to work. This will provide increased assurance that the arrangements necessary are in place and are effective.

Principles of pressurisation and purging

Pressurised gasses and inert gasses are used to create a positive pressure in the equipment, in comparison to the atmospheric pressure outside the equipment, which prevents any flammable atmosphere from entering the protected equipment. These types of systems are safe to use for all zones. Purging is where an atmosphere is purged with an inert gas, such as nitrogen, to replace the oxygen in the atmosphere with the inert gas. This removes the flammable atmospheres and prevents the atmosphere becoming flammable. *See also - Element C2 - Principles of fire and explosion - "fire and explosion prevention and protection" for further details.*

Intrinsically safe equipment, flameproof equipment, type 'N' equipment, type 'e' equipment

Firstly, the possibility of designing out the use of equipment that is likely to produce sparks or heat from the work area should be considered. Only if this is impracticable should flameproof or intrinsically safe equipment be used.

INTRINSICALLY SAFE EQUIPMENT (EX I)

Intrinsically safe equipment is equipment that, by design, cannot produce a spark with sufficient energy to ignite the flammable substance present. The equipment is usually limited to instrumentation and low energy equipment. The limitation of energy also means that components do not become too hot. Powered respirators, test equipment and process instrumentation are common examples of intrinsically safe equipment and are distinguished by their deep blue colour marking. This equipment may be category 1 or 2, category 1 equipment can be suitable for use in zone 0 and category 2 equipment can be used in zone 1 and 2.

FLAMEPROOF EQUIPMENT (EX D)

This apparatus is designed and constructed to withstand an internal explosion, thus preventing the ignition source entering the zone where flammable substances are present, and by having such volume that any inward leakage of flammable substance is unlikely to result in a mixture above the lower flammability limit. Flameproof equipment is easily recognised by its heavy, substantial and costly construction.

The suitability of the apparatus for use in a particular zone is denoted by category and approval markings on the apparatus in accordance with EPS 1996, which establishes the ATEX categorisation for equipment.

STORAGE, HANDLING AND PROCESSING OF DANGEROUS SUBSTANCES - ELEMENT C4

The flameproof quality of an area and its equipment are only as good as the cabling feeding the apparatus, its mechanical protection and the integrity of any plugs and sockets. Designers and installers must ensure that cables, glands and barriers where cables pass through walls are to comparable standards. Flameproof equipment is usually category 2 and therefore suitable for zones 1 and 2.

TYPE 'N' EQUIPMENT

This equipment is usually category 3 and is designed for use in zone 2 conditions and is so constructed that, properly used, it will not ignite flammable atmospheres under normal conditions.

TYPE 'E' EQUIPMENT

This includes equipment such as transformers and squirrel cage motors. They do not produce arcs, sparks or hot surfaces. This equipment is therefore usually category 2 and suitable for zone 1 and 2 conditions.

The basic concepts are detailed in BS EN 60079. It provides information on the selection, installation and maintenance of apparatus for use in potentially explosive atmospheres.

The *apparatus group* is classified in accordance with how easily the burning gas will burn through a narrow gap and the minimum spark ignition energy.

The *temperature class* is based on how hot the equipment gets in fault or worst case normal conditions.

The groups are outlined in *figure ref C4-31*:

Apparatus group	Representative gas	Remarks
I	Methane.	Mining equipment only.
IIA	Propane.	Most flammable gases/vapours are Group IIA.
IIB	Ethylene.	Medium sensitive group.
IIC	Hydrogen.	Most sensitive group; consists of hydrogen, acetylene and carbon disulphide; very small sparks ignite and will burn through very small gaps.

Figure C4-31: Apparatus for use in potentially explosive atmospheres. Source: RMS.

Temperature classification	Temperature limit
T1	Below 450°C.
T2	Below 300°C.
T3	Below 200°C.
T4	Below 135°C.
T5	Below 100°C.
T6	Below 85°C.

Figure C4-32: Temperature classification limits. Source: RMS.

The temperature classification limit must be below the auto-ignition temperature of any flammable gas.

C4.4 - Emergency planning

The need for emergency preparedness within an organisation

GENERAL POINTS

It is important to consider emergency planning, not only as a response to disaster, but also in terms of threat to the commercial survival of the organisation. There have been many attempts to define the word 'disaster'.

'An adverse or unfortunate event; a great and sudden misfortune; a calamity'.

Figure C4-33: "The term disaster". Source: Chambers dictionary.

'Sudden or great misfortune; calamity; ill-luck'.

Figure C4-34: "The term disaster". Source: Oxford dictionary.

In commercial terms the names Piper Alpha, 1998, Buncefield, 2005 and the Windsor Tower fire (Madrid) 2005, immediately convey the meaning of the word 'disaster'. They were all events that happened, that need not have occurred or that could have been contained with the minimum effect on life, environment and plant. Some disasters can be caused by natural events beyond anyone's control - earthquakes, floods, landslides etc. whereas others are due to failures in the protective controls such as - air and rail disasters, civil disturbances and terrorist attacks.

The definition of an emergency is quite flexible. What could be deemed disastrous to a small retailer would perhaps be a minor setback to a large supermarket chain. Whatever the definition or type of emergency, the principles of emergency planning apply to both small and large companies, with the depth of planning increasing in direct proportion to the magnitude of risk.

THE NEED FOR EMERGENCY PREPAREDNESS

The legal requirement for all organisations to plan for emergencies is in the Management of Health and Safety at Work Regulations, regulation 8 "Procedures for serious and imminent danger and for danger areas", and regulation 9 "Contacts with external services".

In regulation 8, the employer has an absolute duty to:

- Have appropriate procedures to be followed in the event of serious and imminent danger to persons at work in his undertaking.
- Have sufficient numbers of nominated competent persons to implement those procedures so far as they relate to the evacuation from the premises.
- Ensure only authorised persons have access to certain areas that may be restricted on the grounds of health and safety.

The employer shall also, so far as is reasonably practicable inform those exposed to serious or imminent danger of the hazard and the steps taken or to be taken to protect them. These people must be enabled to take those appropriate steps even if there is no instruction or guidance at the time of danger, and be prevented from returning to work if the danger is still there.

The competent person referred to in regulation 8 must have sufficient training and experience or knowledge and other qualities to enable him to carry out the evacuation procedures properly.

Regulation 9 places an absolute duty on the employer to ensure that any contacts with external services are arranged, particularly for first aid, emergency medical care and rescue work.

Prompt, effective emergency response reduces accidental losses and the consequences of natural and man-made disasters. There is not enough time during an emergency to decide who is in charge, to survey outside agencies to identify sources of help, or to train people for emergency response. These actions must be taken prior to the emergency.

Disaster can strike at any time. It may seriously damage or even destroy a large proportion of our resources, and a disaster could have fatal repercussions on the financial viability of an organisation. Therefore, emergency planning is, in effect, an orderly assimilation of the arrangements and activities necessary for the control and co-ordination of the event, to minimise loss.

Emergency planning may be considered as a form of risk management and asset protection, as the effectiveness of what we do if an emergency should strike will depend on how well we have prepared the plans and trained the people in their role who will have to implement those plans.

The exercises for testing, not only the plans, but also the people who will have to implement the plans, are essential to prevent confusion during an emergency and ensure the utmost protection and care of lives and property.

It should be emphasised that when planning to minimise the damaging effects of an emergency, the aim is not only to rescue resources, but, first and foremost, to protect life and the environment. A good emergency plan aims to achieve both.

To summarise, the purpose of emergency planning is:

- To envisage the most probable loss factors.
- To consider which areas of the site/business could probably be the scene of a serious incident and what could be the cause.
- To estimate to what extent any foreseeable incident could escalate.
- To assess what the likely impact on the surrounding area and the environment would be.
- To estimate how long disruption can be expected to continue and what can be done to minimise it.
- To establish resources and systems to control the event.
- To define the degree and timescale for the provision of outside help, for example, fire, medical and others.

PERSONAL INJURY

All organisations are required to have some emergency plan for dealing with personal injury. The first person to deal with an injury is usually a first aider. The number of first aiders and approved persons will depend on a number of factors: type of hazard, number of employees, geographical distribution and complexity of the facility and buildings, distance from the public hospital emergency services in relation to the need to administer an antidote in the event of foreseeable poisoning.

EXPLOSIVE DEVICE

Excavation work can sometimes unearth an unexploded bomb that has lain dormant since the 1939-45 war. For organisations that deal with underground services, construction or demolition, this is an emergency that has to be dealt with. Other organisations may have to deal with the threat of a bomb being planted on their premises.

FIRE

All organisations have the threat of fire, some at a higher risk than others, depending on the presence of flammable materials and sources of ignition.

LOSS OF CONTAINMENT

The accidental spillage of chemicals or release of biological agents must be prepared for. The release of chemicals to rivers or the atmosphere or biological agents into the general community will present a major threat to society and adequate arrangements must be in place to deal with all likely scenarios.

CONTROL OF MAJOR ACCIDENT HAZARDS REGULATIONS (COMAH) 1999

Main points of COMAH

For certain organisations, the Control of Major Accident Hazards Regulations (COMAH) 1999 (amended 2005) apply. The main aim of COMAH 1999 is to prevent and mitigate the effects of those major accidents involving dangerous substances, such as liquefied petroleum gas (LPG), chlorine, explosives and toxic chemicals, such as arsenic pentoxide, that can cause serious damage/harm to people and/or the environment. One of the effects of COMAH 1999 is to treat risks to the environment as seriously as those to people.

They require that sites to which they apply must have emergency plans. Regulation 5 requires lower-tier operators to prepare a document setting out their policy for preventing major accidents (a major accident prevention policy or MAPP). Top-tier operators must produce a Safety Report. This is a document prepared by the site operator and provides information to demonstrate to the Competent Authorities (CA) that all measures necessary for the prevention and mitigation of major accidents have been taken.

The purposes and contents of a safety report are set out in Schedule 4 to COMAH 1999. The CA is comprised of HSE and the Environment Agency or in Scotland, HSE and SEPA. This ensures that health and safety and the environment are all considered.

The amendments to the regulations broaden its scope and reflect lessons learned from major accidents in Europe since COMAH 1999 was introduced. They also take account of the results of EC working groups on carcinogens and substances dangerous for the environment. Some new substances have been added, some qualifying quantities have been revised and some changes made to the aggregation rule.

The employer is now meant to consult contractors on his site, as well as his own employees, regarding the on-site emergency plan. The Local Authority must consult members of the public regarding the review of the off-site plan.

Operators of COMAH sites must supply information on safety measures to schools, hospitals and other establishments serving the public, and to make all information supplied available permanently to the public.

COMAH 1999 is enforced by a competent authority (CA) consisting of:

- The Health and Safety Executive (HSE) and the Environment Agency in England and Wales.
- The Health and Safety Executive and the Scottish Environment Protection Agency in Scotland.

The CA operates to a Memorandum of Understanding that sets out the arrangements for joint working. COMAH 1999 places duties on the CA to inspect activities subject to COMAH 1999 and prohibit the operation of an establishment if there is evidence that measures taken for prevention and mitigation of major accidents are seriously deficient.

It also has to examine safety reports and inform operators about the conclusions of its examinations within a reasonable time period. Charging apply to work undertaken by the competent authority on COMAH 1999 compliance. Charges are made on an actual cost basis (i.e. the recovery of the full costs of the time spent by the CA in carrying out COMAH-related activities for a particular establishment).

COMAH 1999 applies mainly to the chemical industry, but also some storage activities, explosives and nuclear sites and other industries, where threshold quantities of dangerous substances identified in the regulations are kept or used. The regulations apply to sites that meet the criteria detailed in Regulation 3 and Schedule 1.

These detail which substances and the quantities involved that COMAH 1999 applies to. There are two thresholds (tiers) for application. Operators of sites that hold large quantities of dangerous substances ('top tier' sites) are subject to more onerous requirements than those of 'lower tier' sites.

Sites that have threshold quantities of dangerous substances on site on the day COMAH 1999 came into force (1st April 1999) are known as 'existing establishments'.

ELEMENT C4 - STORAGE, HANDLING AND PROCESSING OF DANGEROUS SUBSTANCES

Examples - dangerous substances thresholds

Substance	Lower tier sites	Top tier sites
	Tonnes	*Tonnes*
Liquefied extremely flammable gases (including LPG) and natural gas (whether liquefied or not).	50	200
Automotive petrol or other petroleum spirits.	2,500	25,000
Arsenic pentoxide, arsenic (V) and/or salts.	1	2
Chlorine.	10	25
Lead alkyls.	5	50
Oxygen.	200	2,000
Toluene diisocyanate.	10	100
Sulphur trioxide.	15	75

Figure C4-35: Dangerous substances thresholds.   Source: RMS.

Lower-tier sites

The main duties for operators of lower-tier sites are:
- Notify basic details to the CA.
- Take all measures necessary to prevent major accidents and limit their consequences to people and the environment.
- Prepare a major accident prevention policy.

Notify basic details to the CA

Operators who come into scope of the regulations after 1 April 1999 must submit a notification before operation begins (operation begins when the quantity of dangerous substance exceeds one of the thresholds and includes commissioning). The amendment now requires the operator to notify the CA of modifications to the establishment that could have significant repercussions with respect to the prevention of major accidents. Operators must notify certain basic details, which are given in Schedule 3 to the Regulations, to the CA. The amendment to this now allows the notification to be made by e-mail and other means allowed by the recipient. The main points include:

- Name and address of operator.
- Address of establishment.
- Name or position of person in charge.
- Details of dangerous substances on site.
- Site activities.
- Environmental details.

Operators of existing establishments who had previously submitted COMAH safety reports do not need to notify as that report contains all the necessary information.

Take all measures to prevent major accidents and limit their consequences

This is the general duty on all operators that underpins the regulations. It is a high standard that applies to all establishments within scope. By requiring measures both for prevention and mitigation there is recognition that all risks cannot be completely eliminated. This in turn implies that proportionality must remain a key element in the enforcement policy of the HSE and the environment agencies. Thus, the phrase "all measures necessary" will be interpreted to include this principle and a judgement will be made about the measures in place. Where hazards are high then high standards will be required to ensure risks are acceptably low, in line with the HSE's and the environment agencies' policy that enforcement should be proportionate.

Prevention should be based on the principle of reducing risk to a level as low as is reasonably practicable (ALARP) for human risks and using the best available technology not entailing excessive cost (BATNEEC) for environmental risks. The ideal should always be, wherever possible, to avoid a hazard altogether.

Prepare a major accident prevention policy

Regulation 5 requires lower-tier operators to prepare a document setting out their policy for preventing major accidents (a major accident prevention policy or MAPP). The MAPP will usually be a short and simple document setting down what is to be achieved but it should also include a summary and further references to the safety management system that will be used to put the policy into action. The detail will be contained in other documentation relating to the establishment, for example, plant operating procedures, training records, job descriptions, audit reports, to which the MAPP can refer.

The MAPP also has to address issues relating to the safety management system. The details are given in Schedule 2 of the regulations but the key areas are:

- Organisation and personnel.
- Identification and evaluation of major hazards.
- Operational control.
- Planning for emergencies.
- Monitoring, audit and review.

Top-tier operators

Top-tier operators have to comply with the above except that they do not have to prepare a separate major accident prevention policy document - their safety reports have to include the information that lower-tier operators provide in their MAPPs. They also have the following additional duties:

- The preparation of a safety report.
- The updating of the safety report.
- Prepare and test an on-site emergency plan.
- The supply of information to the local authorities.
- The provision of information to the public.

Prepare a safety report

A safety report is a document prepared by the site operator and provides information to demonstrate to the CA that all measures necessary for the prevention and mitigation of major accidents have been taken. The purposes and contents of a safety report are set out in Schedule 4 to the regulations.

The safety report must include:

- A policy on how to prevent and mitigate major accidents.
- A management system for implementing that policy.
- An effective method for identifying any major accidents that might occur.
- Measures (such as safe plant and safe operating procedures) to prevent and mitigate major accidents.
- Information on the safety precautions built into the plant and equipment when it was designed and constructed.
- Details of measures (such as fire-fighting, relief systems and filters) to limit the consequences of any major accident that might occur.
- Information about the emergency plan for the site, which is also used by the local authority in drawing up an off-site emergency plan.

Safety reports are available to the public via the competent authority registers, subject to safeguards for national security, commercial and personal confidentiality. The dates for submission of safety reports are set out in regulation 7. Operators of completely new establishments (so called green field sites) have to provide some information before construction commences and complete the safety report before operation begins.

Update the safety report

The safety report needs to be kept up to date. If there are any modifications to the plant or the way it is operated or if new facts or information become available, the safety report must be reviewed and, if necessary, revised at the time. It must be reviewed after five years even if there have not been any changes.

Prepare and test an on-site emergency plan

Top-tier operators must prepare an emergency plan to deal with the on-site consequences of a major accident. The details are given in Schedule 5 and further HSE guidance is available. For new establishments this must be done before operation begins.

Supply information to local authorities for off-site emergency planning purposes

Local authorities play a key role by preparing, reviewing, revising and testing off-site emergency plans for dealing with the off-site consequences of major accidents at top-tier sites. In order to fulfil this role they need information from operators. Details can be found in Schedule 5 to the regulations. Operators must hold discussions as necessary with their local authorities to determine their exact needs.

The information for the local authority must be supplied no later than the date the on-site emergency plan for the site has to be completed.

Provide information to the public

People who could be affected by an accident at a COMAH 1999 establishment must be given information without having to request it. The details are given in Schedule 6 of the regulations which includes details of the dangerous substances, the possible major accidents and their consequences and what to do in the event of an accident.

As previously mentioned, safety reports are available to the public via public registers. Safety reports are put on the public register shortly after receipt by the CA, unless there is a request for certain information to be withheld (for national security, commercial and personal confidentiality reasons), as provided for in the regulations.

ELEMENT C4 - STORAGE, HANDLING AND PROCESSING OF DANGEROUS SUBSTANCES

The information for people who could be affected by a major accident at the establishment must be supplied 'within a reasonable period of time after the off-site emergency plan has been prepared or revised for the establishment'. Six months would be the normal time.

Consequence minimisation via emergency procedures

The emergency procedure must deal with the minimisation of consequences both in terms of the commercial survival of the organisation and the minimisation of losses. For example, when dealing with a disaster, those involved in the response should work to the following common objectives:

- To save life.
- To prevent escalation of the disaster.
- To relieve suffering.
- To safeguard the environment.
- To protect property.
- To facilitate criminal investigation and judicial, public, technical, or other inquiries.
- To continue to maintain normal services at an appropriate level.
- To inform the public.
- To promote self help and recovery.
- To restore normality as soon as possible.
- To evaluate the response and identify lessons to be learned.

FIRST AID/MEDICAL

The consequences of personal injury can be minimised by fast treatment, which is the role of the first aider. The first aider treats minor injuries that do not require further medical treatment and for serious injuries, sustains and preserves life and prevents deterioration until medical help arrives. Liaison with the emergency services is also essential. This is a requirement of regulation 9 of the MHSWR 1999.

FIRE EVACUATION

If a fire starts, the speed of detection and extinguishment is crucial for consequence minimisation. The objective is to minimise loss to people, the buildings or facility, the product and the environment. Good compartmentalisation will reduce damage from smoke and the installation of interceptor systems will manage the high volume of water used in fire fighting to minimise contaminated runoff water.

Fire marshals have a central role to play in fire evacuation and should be organised by a co-ordinator, a role that should be duplicated in case of absence. This will be in part fulfilment of regulation 7 of the MHSWR 1999, which requires the employer to have assistance in order to fulfil his legal obligations. It also contributes to meeting Article 15 of the Regulatory Reform (Fire Safety) Order (RRFSO) 2005 and Regulation 8 of MHSWR 1999 that both require procedures for serious or imminent danger.

SPILL CONTAINMENT

Stored chemicals should generally be kept in bunded areas to contain spillage. However, the spillage may occur at the point of use or in transit and will require different emergency plans to deal with it. For example, protection of drains, watercourses and porous ground such as soil is essential to prevent environmental damage. There could also be a plan to remove layers of contaminated soil or to neutralise the contaminant in soil or water. Depending on the substance, it may be important to contain the vapour or gas, for example, chlorine, or to release it to atmosphere, for example, propane. The method must be in keeping with the hazard and risk.

The need for the development of emergency plans to reduce the impact on the organisation

A good emergency plan will consider all conceivable emergencies and address any which have a significant probability of occurrence and significant potential for loss. In order to minimise loss, the plan must consider how the business can carry on during, and be restored after, the event.

Prior to drawing up an emergency plan a planning team of key site personnel should be formed. The team's membership should reflect a cross section of the organisation and each member should have total familiarity with their particular operation's procedures and hazards. Although drawing up an emergency/disaster plan may seem a somewhat daunting prospect, the planning team should realise that they will probably have many of the procedures and resources already available to them but that they may need to be reassessed, regrouped or reorganised.

Team effort is important when drawing up a plan. Each area under consideration should be assessed after discussions with front line staff from the area. The 'what if' from the man doing the job will provide relevant expertise and possibly vital information to the planning team. The planning team's emergency plan will ultimately only be as good as the information received from others.

Each company, industry or organisation is unique. Each employs different people and uses different procedures. Each is located in a different area. Nevertheless, the principles of disaster planning apply to all. Although this element highlights areas for consideration and outlines factors to be included, it is only the skeletal framework from which the emergency planning team can begin to work.

When considering the plan, the following potential causes of emergency should be considered:

Natural
- Flooding.
- Gales and other abnormal weather conditions.
- Earthquake.
- Landslide.

Man-made - accidental
- Uncontrolled release of a hazardous substance.
- Building collapse.
- Human error (possibly the hardest to anticipate).
- Fire.
- Explosion.

Man-made - deliberate
- Arson.
- Explosion.
- Bomb threat/attack.
- Terrorist attack.
- Civil disturbance.
- Acts of war.

The plan should be flexible and capable of expansion, with little change, to meet the 'worst case' situation.

POST-INCIDENT RECOVERY

After the incident, it is important for the organisation that things get back to normal as soon as possible. If not, the danger is that the organisation's clients will go elsewhere and never return.

Companies may have a standby system for the computer system that manages the organisation's information. As one goes down, the other one kicks in.

Some companies have standby premises to move into so there is minimum disruption to the undertaking.

Post-incident recovery plans may include letting neighbours know when it is safe to leave their buildings or homes, arranging for clean up of external premises and any environmental issues, and issuing a press statement.

Internal clean up may be done in sections in a logical sequence so work can continue in those sections.

THE ROLE OF EXTERNAL EMERGENCY SERVICES AND LOCAL AUTHORITIES IN EMERGENCY PLANNING AND CONTROL

Regulation 9 of the MHSWR 1999 requires employers to make contact with external services, particularly as regards to first-aid, emergency medical care and rescue work. The emergency services have a duty to provide a response to workplace emergencies in order to provide assistance, particularly where they involve potential harm to the public.

When COMAH 1999 top tier sites are located in a local authority's area they are under a duty to establish an off-site emergency plan (OfSEP) for each site, for the purposes of minimising the consequences of major emergencies to people and the environment. Operators of these sites must provide them with information to enable them to prepare an OfSEP, required by Regulation 10 of COMAH 1999.

Under the Civil Contingencies Act (CCA) 2004 local authorities have a duty to plan for and respond to emergencies. Depending on the type of incident the local authority's role would include:

- Caring for the community by the provision of Rest or Reception Centres.
- Providing emergency feeding.
- Providing plant, materials and labour.
- Providing and operating effective communications.
- Providing emergency transport.
- Co-ordinating the media response with that of other responders.
- Assisting in the establishment of temporary mortuary facilities.
- The co-ordination of counselling support for victims and relatives of those involved.
- Co-ordinating support from the voluntary agencies.
- Provision of environmental health advice.

ELEMENT C4 - STORAGE, HANDLING AND PROCESSING OF DANGEROUS SUBSTANCES

The need to develop and prepare an emergency plan

ON-SITE PLANS

There are many matters to be considered when preparing or reviewing the disaster plant.

Some of these are:

- The areas of the organisation which are hazardous or vulnerable in the event of a potential major accident occurring.
- The areas should be identified the safeguards checked for adequacy.
- The foreseeable consequences of an incident.
- The present resources and arrangements capable of dealing with the initial incident.
- How the incident will affect the neighbouring population, industries or the environment.
- How the alarm will be raised.
- Ensuring all site personnel understand what the alarm means, where to go and how to get there.
- Arrangements for vital services, for example, communication, gas, water, electricity supplies to be provided when your own are out of action.
- Co-ordination with the emergency services.
- Communication of the risks inherent in the operation.
- How to maintain or resume operations during or after an incident.
- Search-and-rescue procedures.
- Number of first aiders.
- Equipment required: emergency protective clothing, first aid and medical supplies, fire fighting, etc.
- Other equipment that may be needed in the event of a disaster, for example, digging or lifting equipment, ladders, transport and other engineering or construction supplies and equipment.
- Where they are located.

OFF-SITE PLANS

As outlined above there is a duty on top tier COMAH sites to contribute to the development of an off-site emergency plan (OfSEP), along with the local authority. This will include incidents that occur on-site but can affect people outside the limits of the site. Plans must also be in place to deal with off-site incidents, such as the involvement of a vehicle carrying dangerous goods in a road accident. This will include most of the above, but may require some additional procedures:

- Good communication so the incident can be co-ordinated from a distance if need be.
- Trained personnel who will be available to deal with off-site incidents.

Ongoing monitoring and maintenance of emergency plans

It is crucial that the emergency plans are closely monitored following an event and after each practice. If something in the plan does not work, then this will have to be reviewed to find a better way. Over time people change jobs and work practices may alter. This can have an impact on the emergency plans that may not be obvious, until an emergency occurs. The plan should be maintained through regular testing and to ensure that nothing gets missed and even subtle changes are dealt with. For example, following a practice evacuation of the building after activating the fire alarms, it may be identified that visitors did not know what to do or where to go. This would require a further procedure to ensure it is known that visitors are on site, they are given information and a member of staff would supervise their leaving the building and take them to the assembly point.

To ensure that monitoring is useful, the plans should be tested by conducting a practice at different times, to ensure all occupants and work scenarios are considered. The maintenance of the emergency plans may be best done following each practice and using direct consultation in order to get the views of the various people involved.

Element C5

Work equipment (general)

Learning outcomes

The intended learning outcomes are that the student will be able to:

C5.1 Outline the criterion for the selection of suitable work equipment for particular tasks and processes to eliminate or reduce risks.
C5.2 Explain how risks to health and safety arising from the use of work equipment are controlled.
C5.3 Explain safe working procedures for the maintenance, inspection and testing of work equipment according to the risks posed.
C5.4 Explain the role of competence, training, information and supervision in the control of risks arising from the installation, operation, maintenance and use of work equipment.

Content

C5.1 - Selection of suitable equipment	155
Suitability of work equipment	155
Control of energy and substances used or produced	158
Ergonomic, anthropometric and human reliability considerations	159
Anthropometric considerations	160
C5.2 - Risk assessment and use	162
The need for conducting risk assessments in the use of work equipment	162
The risks associated with initial integrity, location and purpose of use	163
The risks associated with installation, re-installation, deterioration and exceptional circumstances	163
Risk control hierarchy relating to work equipment	164
C5.3 - Maintenance, inspection and testing	168
The hazards and precautions associated with the maintenance of work equipment	168
The maintenance management strategies	169
Developing a planned maintenance programme for safety-critical components	171
The statutory duties for the maintenance of work equipment	171
Determining inspection regimes for work equipment	172
The need for functional testing of safety-related parts	173
C5.4 - Competence, training, information and supervision	174
The difference between training and competence	174
Circumstances when training is likely to be required	174
Groups of people having specific training needs	174
The relationship between competence, external and self-supervision	175
Specific training needs for certain hazardous types of work equipment	175

ELEMENT C5 - WORK EQUIPMENT (GENERAL)

Relevant statutory provisions

Health and Safety at Work etc. Act (HASAWA) 1974

Provision and Use of Work Equipment Regulations (PUWER) 1998

WORK EQUIPMENT (GENERAL) - ELEMENT C5

C5.1 - Selection of suitable equipment

Suitability of work equipment

GENERAL REQUIREMENTS

The Provision and Use of Work Equipment Regulations (PUWER) 1998 are concerned with most aspects relating to work equipment. PUWER 1998 broadly defines work equipment to include machines of all kinds, appliances, apparatus, tools or installation for use at work. Work equipment includes:

- Air compressor.
- Automatic car wash.
- Automatic storage and retrieval equipment.
- Blast furnace.
- Butcher's knife.
- Car ramp.
- Check-out machine.
- Combine harvester.
- Computer.
- Crane.
- Drill bit.
- Dry cleaning unit.
- Fire engine turntable.
- Hammer.
- Hand saw.
- Laboratory apparatus.
- Ladder.
- Lawn-mower.
- Lift truck.
- Lifting sling.
- LPG filling plant.
- Mobile access platform.
- Overhead projector.
- Portable drill.
- Potato grading line.
- Power press.
- Pressure vessel.
- Quarry crushing plant.
- Resuscitator.
- Road tanker.
- Robot line.
- Scaffolding.
- Scalpel.
- Socket set.
- Soldering iron.
- Solvent degreasing bath.
- Tractor.
- Trench sheets.
- Vehicle hoist.
- X-ray baggage detector.

Not work equipment:

- Livestock.
- Substances.
- Structural items (buildings).
- Private car.

Provision and Use of Work Equipment Regulations [PUWER] 1998

PUWER 1998, Regulation 4 establishes the following requirements for the suitability of work equipment:

1) *Every employer shall ensure that work equipment is so constructed or adapted as to be suitable for the purpose for which it is used or provided.*

2) *In selecting work equipment, every employer shall have regard to the working conditions and to the risks to the health and safety of persons which exist in the premises or undertaking in which that work equipment is to be used and any additional risk posed by the use of that work equipment.*

3) *Every employer shall ensure that work equipment is used only for operations for which, and under conditions for which, it is suitable.*

4) *In this regulation "suitable" means suitable in any respect which it is reasonably foreseeable will affect the health or safety of any person.*

The guidance to PUWER 1998 says that suitability should consider:

- Its initial integrity.
- The place where it will be used.
- The purpose for which it will be used.

Integrity - equipment should be safe through its design, construction or adaptation, for example, sharp edges removed from the pen tray of a flip chart stand, 'home made' tools may not comply as they are often a basic adaptation of scrap material. Equipment adapted to do a specific task should be considered carefully, for example, the addition of a welded bracket may compromise integrity.

Place - equipment should be suitable for the different environments (risks) it is to be used in - wet or explosive. Account must be taken of the possibility that the equipment may cause a problem, for example, a petrol generator used in a confined space, a hydraulic access platform used in a location with a low roof, or the environment may cause a problem to the equipment, for example, lifting equipment used in an acidic atmosphere or a power tool used in a wet place.

Purpose - equipment should be suitable for the specific task it is used for - a hacksaw should not be used to cut metal straps that secure goods to a palette (instead, a purpose designed tool should be used to stop the straps suddenly moving when they are cut); the use of a ladder to do work at a height (instead of a scaffold or other access platform); exceeding the safe working load of a crane or fork lift truck, a swivel chair used as a means of access to a shelf.

ELEMENT C5 - WORK EQUIPMENT (GENERAL)

REQUIREMENTS FOR MAINTENANCE

When selecting work equipment it is important to establish what the requirements for maintenance are. It may be that the equipment has sealed components and must be returned to the manufacturer or periodic maintenance will mean taking the equipment to a specialist dealer/supplier, rendering it out of use for this period. As such, this could put added pressure on the organisation, who may not find it convenient to be without the equipment.

It is essential that this sort of circumstance be considered and arrangements made to deal with it, for example, purchase or hire of extra equipment to be brought into use to allow for maintenance. Maintenance regimes should be carefully considered before selecting equipment. Maintenance staff may not have the specific expertise or skill to work on new equipment, leading to increased risk to themselves and others.

PUWER 1998 - Regulation 22, Maintenance operations, requires:

"Every employer shall take appropriate measures to ensure that work equipment is so constructed or adapted that, so far as is reasonably practicable, maintenance operations which involve a risk to health or safety can be carried out while the work equipment is shut down or, in other cases:

(a) Maintenance operations can be carried out without exposing the person carrying them out to a risk to his health or safety.

(b) Appropriate measures can be taken for the protection of any person carrying out maintenance operations which involve a risk to his health or safety".

Machinery should be designed to enable routine adjustments, lubrication, cleaning and maintenance to be carried out without the removal of guards. In this way effort should be taken to enable lubrication and adjustment to be applied from outside the guard.

AVAILABILITY OF EXPERTISE/SKILLS REQUIRED

The availability of expertise and skill must be considered for all new equipment planned for selection and use, whether this is for long term purchase or short term hire. It may be that the organisation has staff with similar expertise and that they only need a short period of orientation to familiarise themselves, but for many organisations new equipment can mean a radical step forward in technology. It is essential that operation and maintenance of equipment with specific risks be restricted to those that have appropriate skill and expertise.

PUWER 1998 - Regulation 7, Specific risks, requires:

"1) Where the use of work equipment is likely to involve a specific risk to health or safety, every employer shall ensure that:

(a) The use of that work equipment is restricted to those persons given the task of using it.

(b) Repairs, modifications, maintenance or servicing of that work equipment is restricted to those persons who have been specifically designated to perform operations of that description (whether or not also authorised to perform other operations).

2) The employer shall ensure that the persons designated for the purposes of sub-paragraph (b) of paragraph 1) have received adequate training related to any operations in respect of which they have been so designated".

Operators

It is dangerous to assume that because the method of use of new equipment is 'obvious' to those that looked into and sourced it, that it will be so 'obvious' to the operators. It is also necessary to guard against the over enthusiastic operator who feels sure they have the expertise to operate something.

It is essential to take a stepwise approach to the introduction of equipment, for example, driving a fork lift truck is very different to driving a van and the organisation has to anticipate the need to train someone in the use of a fork lift truck before it is put to use in the workplace. Not planning for this at the time of selection may cause the equipment to be used by operators without the appropriate skill or expertise.

Even with what seems to be the same piece of work equipment, for example, when a larger, different model of fork lift truck is hired, it is essential that the operator takes a period of time to formally familiarise with the truck and to practice in a safe place before putting it into use.

Maintenance personnel

As with operators it is essential to consider who is to maintain the equipment before it is selected. If the equipment represents a major leap in technology, aspects of its maintenance may fall outside the skill and expertise of the current maintenance personnel. It may be necessary to train or recruit staff in good time before the maintenance is required.

In addition, new facilities and equipment may be needed in order to conduct the maintenance safely. Accidents often occur because new equipment may appear to be similar to previous equipment. The small differences may be critical and must be emphasised as part of the training of maintenance personnel.

SUITABILITY OF WORK EQUIPMENT FOR THE REQUIRED TASK, PROCESS AND ENVIRONMENT

Regulation 4(3) of PUWER 1998 requires:

"Every employer shall ensure that work equipment is used only for operations for which, and under conditions for which, it is suitable".

This requirement establishes the need to ensure suitability for each specific process that the equipment is used for and the conditions under which it will be used. For example:

- A screwdriver may be used to open a tin of paint, whereas smooth ended opener would be more suitable.
- A forklift truck may be used for access at height, whereas a mobile elevated work platform may be more suitable.
- Wood working equipment, such as a circular saw, may be used to produce a rebate in wood, whereas a more specialised machine, like a spindle moulder, may be more suitable.
- An inflatable boat may be used for work on water, whereas a more stable boat of rigid design may be more suitable.
- Open bladed knives may be used to cut packaging where scissors or a protected blade would be more suitable.

Equipment may not be suitable for specific tasks, for example, a motorised mower may not be suitable for use on a steep sided slope, because of its particular high centre of gravity. A particular chemical process vessel may not be capable of taking the pressures and heat that it may experience in the chemical reaction when processing specific chemicals. A particular lifting sling may not be long enough to lift a wide heavy load at angles that mean the forces will not overload it.

The equipment selection may also need to take account of the environment that it will be used in, for example, in cold wet environments small levers with low level of grip may be hard to operate. Some equipment may have to be capable of operating in very high or very low ambient temperatures. Some equipment may have to be used in rough terrains and need to be specifically suited to this environment.

SUITABILITY OF THE DESIGN, CONSTRUCTION AND ADAPTATION OF WORK EQUIPMENT

Equipment must be suitable, by design, construction or adaptation, for the actual work it is provided to do. This should mean, in practice, that when employers provide equipment they should ensure that it has been produced for the work to be undertaken and that it is used in accordance with the manufacturer's specifications and instructions. If employers choose to adapt equipment then they must ensure that it is still suitable for its intended purpose.

Conformity with relevant standards

Work equipment should be designed and manufactured such that it conforms to all relevant standards. Historically this will have been British Standards. Though many British Standards remain in place today many new standards for work equipment are produced in conjunction with European and international standards organisations. Those that have been agreed at a European level will carry the letters 'EN' in addition to the familiar BS, for example, BS EN 60974-6:2011- *"Arc welding equipment. Limited duty equipment"*. Those that have been agreed at an international level carry the letters 'ISO', for example, BS EN ISO 12100:2010 *"Safety of machinery. General principles for design. Risk assessment and risk reduction"*. Section 6 of The Health and Safety at Work Act (HASAWA) 1974 requires those involved in the design, manufacture, importation and supply of equipment to ensure that it is safe and healthy, so far as is reasonably practicable. This will require them to take account of all relevant standards.

When providing work equipment for use in the workplace care must be taken to ensure it has been manufactured to any product Directive that is relevant to the equipment. This means that, in addition to specifying that work equipment should comply with specific health and safety legislation, such as the Electricity at Work Regulations (EWR) 1989, it is also necessary to specify that it complies with legislation implementing any relevant EC product Directive, for example, the Supply of Machinery (Safety) Regulations (SMSR) 2008, which implements the Machinery Directive 2006/42/EC. In addition PUWER 1998, Regulation 10, requires that new equipment conform to European Community requirements, where they exist, prohibiting the use of equipment that does not comply.

PUWER 1998 - Regulation 10 conformity with Community requirements

PUWER 1998, Regulation 10 requires employers to ensure that an item of work equipment has been designed and constructed in conformity with any essential requirements, relating to its design or construction in any of the instruments listed in Schedule 1 of PUWER 1998 (instruments that give effect to European Community directives concerning the safety of products). This means that work equipment provided for use must conform with legislation made in the UK in response to EC directives relating to work equipment. Only those instruments (regulations) listed in schedule 1 of PUWER 1998 are to be considered. Examples relate to:

- The Supply of Machinery (Safety) Regulations (The Machinery Directive).
- The Personal Protective Equipment Regulations (relating to the supply of personal protective equipment The Personal Protective Equipment Directive).

ELEMENT C5 - WORK EQUIPMENT (GENERAL)

- The Pressure Equipment Regulations (The Pressure Equipment Directive).
- The Simple Pressure Vessels (Safety) Regulations (The Simple Pressure Vessel Directive).

Directives tend to contain details of 'essential health and safety requirements' and a system whereby compliance may be demonstrated. Compliance is usually demonstrated by the attachment of a CE mark and the manufacturer/supplier issuing an EC Declaration of Conformity. When a directive has been translated to UK legislation and it is fully in force only products that conform and bear the 'CE Mark' may be placed on the market or introduced into the UK. However, CE marking is only a *claim* by the manufacturer *that the machinery is safe* and that they have met relevant supply law. Employers carry the duty to ensure equipment is safe when providing equipment under PUWER 1998.

Not all work equipment is covered by a product directive. Directives and legislation derived from them are not retrospective. Second-hand equipment brought into use need not be modified to meet 'essential safety requirements', but will need to comply with regulations 11 to 24 of PUWER 1998. Second-hand equipment imported from outside the EU must comply with 'essential safety requirements' of the relevant product directive. When equipment is in compliance with specific UK legislative, and therefore directive requirements, regulations 11 to 24 of PUWER 1998 do not apply.

CE marking

Article 114A (was article 100A) Directives seek to achieve free movement of goods in the European Community single market by removing different Member States' national controls on the standards of goods and harmonising 'essential health and safety requirements'. Examples of Directives achieving this are shown in the previous section. Suppliers must ensure that their products comply with the legal requirements implementing the Directives, for example, the Supply of Machinery Safety Regulations (SMSR) 2008. It is a common feature of these Directives that compliance is claimed by the manufacturer affixing a 'CE Mark' to the equipment.

SUITABILITY OF WORK EQUIPMENT FOR ITS INTENDED LOCATION OF USE

Regulation 4 of PUWER 1998 states that when selecting work equipment, employers must have regard to the working conditions and to the risks to the health and safety of persons which exist in the premises or undertaking in which that work equipment is to be used. Therefore, the place where the equipment will be used must be given consideration. For example, electrical equipment is not normally suitable for wet or flammable atmospheres unless it is designed for that purpose. For these locations it may be necessary to purchase specialist electrical equipment that is suitable for use in a wet or flammable location. Alternatively, it may be that selection of pneumatic or hydraulically powered equipment is more suitable.

In addition, the physical characteristics of equipment may have to be considered when selecting equipment for a particular location. It may be that the size of the equipment has to fit into a particular space in order to avoid dangers from moving parts and fixed points or the safe movement of workers around the equipment. Equipment size may be limited by headroom or width of aisles, for example, with a fork lift truck. Some equipment may be unsuitable for use in confined locations because they emit noise or dangerous fumes, for example, an internal combustion engine driven generator.

Control of energy and substances used or produced

The European Union Directive 2009,/104/EC "concerning the minimum safety and health requirements for the use of work equipment by workers at work" contains an Annex II, "Provisions concerning the use of work equipment", point 1 of which requires:

"Work equipment must be installed, located and used in such a way as to reduce risks to users of the work equipment and for other workers, for example by ensuring that there is sufficient space between the moving parts of work equipment and fixed or moving parts in its environment and that all forms of energy and substances used or produced can be supplied or removed in a safe manner".

The Approved Code of Practice for Regulation 4 of PUWER 1998 emphasises this as a requirement in the UK.

This will mean selecting equipment that provides appropriate controls for such energy forms as electricity, pneumatics, hydraulics and steam. This will include controls that enable adjustment or limitation of provision, such as valves or switches as well as appropriate vents, drains and earthing. Energy produced may include heat or static electricity arising from the process. In addition, some processes may produce kinetic energy. Care must be taken when selecting equipment that it enables the removal of the kinetic energy in a safe manner, perhaps by the provision of interlocks or brakes.

The Supply of Machinery (Safety) Regulations (SMSR) 2008, Annex 1, sets out the following requirements:

- Isolators must be clearly identified. They must be capable of being locked if reconnection could endanger persons. Isolators must also be capable of being locked where it is not possible, from any of the points to which the operator has access, to check that the energy is still cut off.
- In the case of machinery capable of being plugged into an electricity supply, removal of the plug is sufficient, provided that the operator can check from any of the points to which the operator has access that the plug remains removed.
- After the energy is cut off, it must be possible to dissipate normally any energy remaining or stored in the circuits of the machinery without risk to persons.

- As an exception to the requirement, certain circuits may remain connected to their energy sources in order, for example, to hold parts, to protect information, to light interiors, etc. In this case, special steps must be taken to ensure operator safety.

Ergonomic, anthropometric and human reliability considerations

It is essential to have a balanced strategy in order to achieve safety with machinery. This means not having an over reliance on any one health and safety control measure, but ensuring that they are integrated and complement each other with technical, procedural and behavioural control measures working in harmony. A significant factor in providing work equipment control measures for the use of work equipment are ergonomic, anthropometric and human reliability considerations.

Ergonomists and designers take into account a wide range of human factors and consider biological, physical and psychological characteristics as well as the needs of people - how they see, hear, understand, make decisions and take action. They also consider individual differences including those that occur due to age, fitness/health, or disability and how these may alter the responses and behaviours of people.

The human characteristics and capacities considered in ergonomics include:

Anatomy   Anthropometry - dimensions of the body (static and dynamic).

Biomechanics - application of forces by gravity and muscles.

Physiology   Work physiology - expenditure of energy.

Environmental physiology - effects on humans of the physical environment.

Psychology   Skill psychology - information processing and decision-making.

Occupational psychology - training, motivation, individual differences, stress.

For example, ergonomic design takes account of the size and shape of the human body (anthropometrics) and should ensure that the design is compatible with human dimensions. Operating positions, heights of workstations, reach distances should accommodate the intended operator. Operation of the equipment should not place undue strain on the user. Operators should not be expected to exert undue force or stretch or reach beyond their normal strength or physical reach limitations to carry out tasks.

LAYOUT AND OPERATION OF CONTROLS AND EMERGENCY CONTROLS

Failure of any part of the control system or its power supply of work equipment should lead to a 'fail-safe' condition (more correctly and realistically called 'minimised failure to danger'), and not impede the operation of the 'stop' or 'emergency stop' controls. The measures that should be taken in the design and application of a control system to mitigate against the effects of its failure will need to be balanced against the consequences of any failure. The greater the risk, the more resistant the control system should be to the effects of failure.

At the person-equipment interface the operator may have to manipulate parts of the equipment to pass a message to it; the equipment will act according to the message received and pass a message back to the operator. The operator must be trained to communicate in a way the equipment understands and the equipment must be manufactured to be able to act according to instructions and communicate in an understandable way with the operator. It would be impossible to carry out a task if every time a red button was pressed a different response took place.

It should be possible to identify easily what each control does and what effect it will have on the equipment. Both the equipment controls and their markings should be clearly visible. As well as having legible wording or symbols, factors such as the colour, shape and position of controls are important. Any change in the operating conditions should only be possible by the use of an equipment control, except if the change does not increase risk to health or safety. Examples of operating conditions include speed, pressure, temperature and power.

The equipment controls provided should be designed and positioned to prevent, so far as possible, inadvertent or accidental operation. Buttons and levers should be of appropriate design, for example, including a shrouding or locking facility. It should not be possible for the control to 'operate itself', such as due to the effects of gravity, vibration, or failure of a spring mechanism.

It is important that the action of the equipment stop control should bring the equipment to a safe condition in a safe manner. This acknowledges that it is not always desirable to bring all items of work equipment immediately to a complete or instantaneous stop, for example, to prevent the unsafe build-up of heat or pressure, or to allow a controlled run-down of large rotating parts. Similarly, stopping the mixing mechanism of a reactor during certain chemical reactions could lead to a dangerous exothermic reaction.

Though there are a number of reasons to bring equipment to a controlled rather than immediate stop, PUWER 1998 qualifies this general requirement by 'where necessary for reasons of health and safety', which provides an overriding drive to ensure that it is brought to a complete stop in these circumstances. Therefore accessible dangerous parts must be rendered stationary. However parts of equipment that do not present a risk, such as suitably guarded cooling fans, do not need to be positively stopped and may be allowed to idle.

ELEMENT C5 - WORK EQUIPMENT (GENERAL)

Emergency stops are intended to affect a rapid response to potentially dangerous situations and they should not be used as functional stops during normal operation. Emergency stop controls should be easily reached and actuated. Common types are mushroom-headed buttons, bars, levers, kick-plates, or pressure-sensitive cables.

Warnings given in accordance with PUWER 1998 Regulation 17(3) (c) should be given sufficiently in advance of the equipment starting; circumstances will affect the type of warning chosen. This gives those at risk time to get clear of the equipment. As well as time to get clear of equipment, suitable means of avoiding risks the equipment may present should be provided, for example, adequate provision to enable people at risk to withdraw, for example, sufficient space or exits.

REDUCING NEED FOR ACCESS (AUTOMATION, REMOTE SYSTEMS)

Significant risk reduction through effective design of equipment, particularly machinery, can be achieved by reducing the need for worker intervention in danger zones. As the need for access increases, so do the risk and the need for more sophisticated safeguards.

Automated and remote systems can be considered by the designer to provide the means to keep people away from danger areas. For example, effort should be made to automate such things as lubrication and machinery adjustment for production control. Materials can be fed automatically into machines, reducing the need for the equipment operator's hands to access the danger zone to place the materials in position. Some forms of power press operation have been adapted in this way to prevent the need for the power press operator to put their hand between the press dies to place the material in position.

Where the operator of equipment may need to gain access to the danger zone to see part of the process, vision panels, automatic sensor displays or remote cameras can be provided to reduce the need for access.

Anthropometric considerations

IMPORTANCE OF SIZE OF OPENINGS AND DISTANCE FROM DANGER

Where it is necessary to provide an opening in a guard, it should be at a sufficient distance to prevent any person from reaching the danger point. This may be achieved by positioning the guard at the required distance or by providing a tunnel which extends outwards from it. Access to a guard opening may also be prevented by the use of a false table. The effectiveness of a guard with an opening should be calculated using the distances laid down in BS EN ISO 13857:2008 *"Safety of machinery. Safety distances to prevent hazard zones being reached by upper and lower limbs"*. This should be reinforced by physical tests carried out with the machinery at rest and in a safe condition.

In establishing the safe size of an opening two dimensions are of interest: the size of the opening and the distance to the dangerous part. Anthropometrics, the study of human dimensions, has enabled guided decisions on acceptable opening sizes. **See figure ref C5-1**, which corresponds with BS EN ISO 13857:2008: *"Safety of machinery. Safety distances to prevent hazard zones being reached by upper and lower limbs"*, takes account of anthropometric data and gives the dimensions in millimetres for a regular shaped small opening in respect of the fingertip of a person aged 14 years or over:

Part of body	Illustration	Opening (gap b) mm	Safety distance (sd) mm		
			Slot	Square	Round
Fingertip		$b \leq 4$	≥ 2	≥ 2	≥ 2
		$4 < b \leq 6$	≥ 10	≥ 5	≥ 5

Figure C5-1: Anthropometric data for small openings. *Source: Ambiguous.*

BS EN ISO 13857:2008 *"Safety of machinery. Safety distances to prevent hazard zones being reached by upper and lower limbs"* also contain similar data in respect of people of 3 years of age and above and for most parts of the body including:

- The arm (with various limitations of movement - for example only at shoulder and armpit).
- The finger up to the knuckle joint.
- The hand.
- The leg (both up to the knee and up to the crotch).
- The foot.
- The toe.
- The toe and the toe tip.

See figure ref C5-2, which gives safety distances (sr) for regular opening for persons of 14 years and above for fingertips, fingers, hands and arms.

The dimensions of opening (e) correspond to the side of a square opening, the diameter of a round opening and the narrowest dimension of a slot opening.

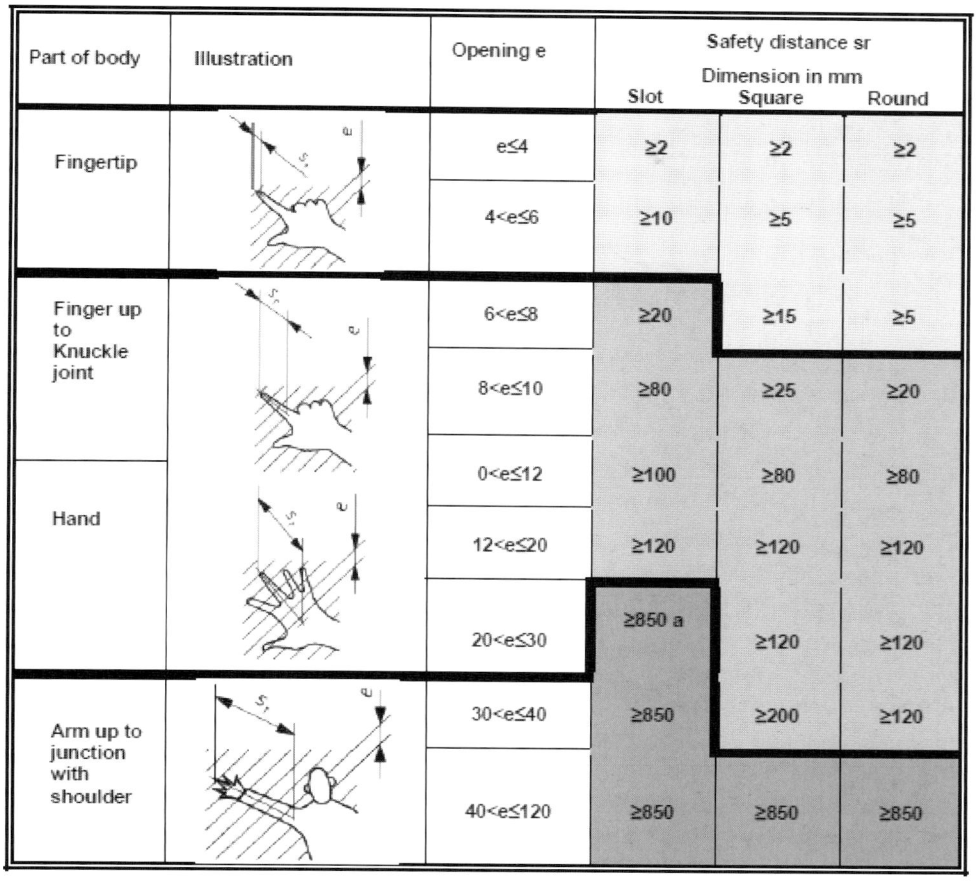

Part of body	Illustration	Opening e	Safety distance sr Dimension in mm Slot	Square	Round
Fingertip		e≤4	≥2	≥2	≥2
		4<e≤6	≥10	≥5	≥5
Finger up to Knuckle joint		6<e≤8	≥20	≥15	≥5
		8<e≤10	≥80	≥25	≥20
Hand		0<e≤12	≥100	≥80	≥80
		12<e≤20	≥120	≥120	≥120
		20<e≤30	≥850 a	≥120	≥120
Arm up to junction with shoulder		30<e≤40	≥850	≥200	≥120
		40<e≤120	≥850	≥850	≥850

The bold lines within the table delineate that part of the body restricted by the opening size.
If the length of the slot opening is ≤ 65 mm, the thumb will act as a stop and the safety distance can be reduced to 200 mm.

Figure C5-2: Reaching through openings.   Source: BS EN ISO 13857:2008.

Where openings are irregular then the smallest regular opening that the irregular opening can be completely inserted into are determined and the corresponding safety distances are calculated.

IMPORTANCE OF HEIGHT OF BARRIERS AND DISTANCE FROM DANGER

If the dangerous parts of a machine cannot be reached then it may be considered safe by position.

Where it is not practicable to use enclosing guards, barriers may be used to prevent people reaching the danger point.

These rely on a combination of height and distance to achieve their purpose. For example, for a danger zone where there is **low risk** from a friction or abrasion hazard extending up to 1.8 m in height it may be protected from reach by the following combinations of height of barrier and distance from the danger zone:

Height of protective structure (barrier) mm	Distance from danger zone mm
1,000	1,100
1,200	1,200
1,400	900
1,600	900
1,800	600
2,000 and above	-

Figure C5-3: Low risk of a friction or abrasion hazard.   Source: BS EN 13857.

ELEMENT C5 - WORK EQUIPMENT (GENERAL)

These distances must be increased if there is a high risk, for example, of entanglement:

Height of protective structure (barrier) mm	Distance from danger zone mm
1,000	1,500
1,200	1,400
1,400	1,100
1,600	900
1,800	800
2,000	600

Figure C5-4: High risk of a friction or abrasion hazard. *Source: BS EN 13857.*

Barriers are not foolproof and they cannot prevent access to a danger zone by a person intent on gaining access. Therefore, as a person's intent on reaching a dangerous part increases, for example, by climbing on chairs, ladders or the barrier itself, the protection provided by a barrier will decrease. When reaching down over the edge of a barrier to a danger zone, the safety distance is dependent on the:

- Distance of the danger zone from floor.
- Height of the edge of barrier.
- Horizontal distance from the edge of the barrier to the danger zone.

Safety distances to prevent danger zones being reached by the upper and lower limbs are contained in the standard: BS EN ISO 13857:2008 "Safety of machinery.

Figure C5-5: Reach distance/barrier. *Source: Proctor Bros Ltd.*

Safety distances to prevent hazard zones being reached by upper and lower limbs".

This builds on the data contained in BS EN ISO 12100:2010 "Safety of machinery. General principles for design. Risk assessment and risk reduction", and must be considered in conjunction with risk assessment. For example, if there is a low risk from a danger zone that is directly overhead, it may be considered out of reach if it is 2.5 m or more above ground. This *'acceptable'* distance is increased to 2.7 m or more if there is a high risk.

C5.2 - Risk assessment and use

The definition of 'use' is wide and includes all activities involving the work equipment, such as stopping or starting the equipment, programming or setting, transporting, repair, modification, maintenance, servicing and cleaning. Most of the above activities would normally be considered as part of 'use' of equipment, however cleaning and transport of the equipment are also included. In this context, 'cleaning' would include removal of waste swarf (metal turnings) from a lathe bed and 'transport' would mean activities like using a lift truck to carry goods around a warehouse.

The need for conducting risk assessments in the use of work equipment

The Management of Health and Safety at Work Regulations (MHSWR) 1999 place a specific requirement that general risk assessments be conducted. These must be suitable and sufficient.

Implicit in this is the need to conduct an initial risk assessment, also, where necessary, a detailed risk assessment and sometimes a technical risk assessment. Therefore, in deriving a suitable and sufficient risk assessment it may be necessary to address the need in three phases:

- *Initial* - to determine broad data on hazards, the consequences arising and the likelihood of the consequence occurring (the risks).
- *Detailed* - a specific assessment of the features that constitute a hazard, how they are encountered and the effects of control measures.
- *Technical* - a comprehensive assessment of the whole or part of the machine and control systems, considering the failure modes and their effects.

In order to have sufficiently risk assessed the use of equipment it may be necessary to conduct very specific and technical risk assessments to confirm the hazards and the suitability of any controls measures. The risk assessment process formalises and documents the way in which designers identify hazards, risks and select the appropriate control measures. The level of risk influences the level and effectiveness of control measures used.

The risks associated with initial integrity, location and purpose of use

Regulation 4 of PUWER 1998 is concerned with the selection of suitable work equipment for particular tasks and processes and if applied correctly makes it possible to eliminate many risks in the workplace. The risk assessment should consider the safety of equipment in respect of:

- Its initial integrity - it should be installed and located in such a way as to reduce any risk to users and others, such as ensuring there is sufficient space between moving parts of machinery. All forms of energy and substances used or produced by equipment should be considered. For example, it may be necessary to provide additional ventilation in the workplace.
- The place (location) where it will be used - some equipment may be unsuitable for the working environment in a particular location because of environmental risks, such as wet or flammable atmospheres and confined spaces.
- The purpose for which it will be used - in practice this means that equipment should be used in accordance with the manufacturer's specifications and instructions. Ergonomic risks, such as working heights and reach distances, should be considered.

The risks associated with installation, re-installation, deterioration and exceptional circumstances

Regulation 6 of PUWER 1998 states that an inspection of work equipment should be carried out where there is a significant risk from:

a) Incorrect installation or re-installation of the equipment.
b) Deterioration of the equipment.
c) Exceptional circumstances which could affect safe operation.

These situations can lead to significant risk of harm to workers and others and need to be considered in the risk assessment process. This will enable control measures and systems to be established that reduce the risk of harm and identify the circumstances that lead to the risk at the earliest point, for example, through inspection.

The extent of the inspection should be proportionate to the risk posed by failure of the equipment. The inspection should always include appropriate testing and checks of safety critical parts, such as limit switches, interlocks and protection devices (guards). Records of such inspections should be retained. If the equipment is moved to another site, records must be transferred. Records should normally include the type and model of equipment, including identity marks, its normal location, the date and name of the inspector, any faults and actions taken, the name of the person to whom faults were reported and the date and details of remedial actions.

Suitable action should be taken to ensure that any defective equipment is not used. In the case of powered equipment, this is likely to involve an isolation procedure. Other examples of suitable measures might include storing the equipment (which should be labelled as defective) in a secure place until repairs are carried out or the item safely disposed of.

INCORRECT INSTALLATION OR RE-INSTALLATION

Re-installation includes assembling the equipment in a new location or site as well as re-assembly after maintenance. Equipment that has been installed or re-installed, for the purposes of PUWER 1998, is normally taken to be equipment that is set into position on a long-term basis and does not normally include repositioning or moving equipment where there is no element of dismantling or re-assembly.

Significant risks may arise from incorrect installation or re-installation. This may relate to such things as racking, scaffolding or a tower crane where incorrect installation/re-installation could lead to collapse when the equipment is put under load during normal use. Poor installation of machines may accentuate vibration and noise or lead to risks of the machine overbalancing. Services connected to equipment that has been installed in an unstable manner could become compromised by the movement of the equipment when it is put into use. Some equipment relies on the separate installation of control measures, such as sensing devices and guards that may not be an integral part of the equipment; these may be installed incorrectly or not at all. Where equipment is re-installed this implies that some dismantling and re-assembly in a new location takes place. In this process critical components that affect the safe functioning of the equipment may become lost or damaged and the equipment may then get re-installed in an unsafe condition.

After installation or assembly at a new site, work equipment must be subject to a suitable inspection by a competent person. The inspection should include any necessary testing and ensure that the equipment is correctly installed and safe to operate. The installer would usually carry this out. It is essential that employers ensure that a commissioning procedure is implemented when buying and installing new machinery.

DETERIORATION OF THE EQUIPMENT

Deterioration of the equipment can occur through use over time; this may lead to critical parts wearing out or them suffering damage due to effects like corrosion. Depending on the part affected the risks arising may lead to catastrophic failure of the equipment. For example, deterioration through wear of the crank of a power press or a wire rope of a crane could lead to reduction in the cross-sectional area of the item and its eventual catastrophic failure. The deterioration of seals on hydraulic components could lead to complete and sudden collapse of the equipment, for example, the boom of a mobile elevated work platform (MEWP); for lift truck mast, person lifting hoist or the bucket of an excavator.

If there is a likelihood that equipment could deteriorate resulting in dangerous situations, inspections should be carried out at suitable intervals set by the competent person, using risk assessment as a guideline. The frequency of inspection should be determined by a risk assessment, to establish the likely periods in which deterioration could present a significant risk. Any manufacturer's guidelines should always be considered. In practice, inspection intervals should be reviewed in the light of experience.

EXCEPTIONAL CIRCUMSTANCES WHICH COULD AFFECT SAFE OPERATION

Exceptional circumstances can affect the safe operation of equipment that was in good condition up until the point of the occurrence. Risk relating to this may be derived from circumstances where the equipment is forced to work outside its normal operating conditions by the work being done. For example, a chemical reaction vessel may be caused to overheat by the effects of the reaction, a centrifuge may be overloaded causing stronger than usual forces on the components or a hospital bed/trolley may be overloaded by an exceptionally heavy patient.

Sometimes the exceptional circumstances relate to environmental issues, such as rain, flood, cold, hot or winds, all of which may affect equipment in different ways, depending on the scale of the circumstances and how well the equipment is designed to deal with them. Equipment left in very cold conditions for a long period may suffer from uneven contraction and then expansion of components when higher temperatures resume. This can lead to the loosening of critical components. High winds can put exceptional forces on equipment exposed to them, for example, a scaffold fitted with weather sheeting.

Exceptional circumstances could relate to accidental circumstances that may have caused serious damage to equipment, for example, a vehicle may hit a barrier or storage vessel while manoeuvring; equipment may get dropped in transportation or a load may get suddenly applied to a crane.

Equipment should be inspected after exceptional circumstances have taken place. For the purposes of PUWER 1998, Regulation 6, relating to inspections, the Health and Safety Executive (HSE) have identified that the following also constitute exceptional circumstances that may give rise to significant risk:

- Major modifications, refurbishment or major repair work.
- Substantial change in the nature of use of the equipment, for example, from an extended period of inactivity.

Risk control hierarchy relating to work equipment

Wherever possible, work equipment risks should always be controlled by the application of the following risk control hierarchy, set out in the ACOP to PUWER 1998:

(a) *"Eliminating the risks, or if that is not possible.*

(b) *Taking 'hardware' (physical) measures to control the risks such as the provision of guards; but if the risks cannot be adequately controlled.*

(c) *Taking appropriate 'software' measures to deal with the residual (remaining) risk, such as following safe systems of work and the provision of information, instruction and training".*

ELIMINATING THE RISKS

Where ever possible risks should be eliminated by establishing intrinsic safety of the work equipment. This is the condition where safety is established by ensuring selection and/or design of components and equipment that ensures no potential to cause harm. In practice, this may actually be the reduction of potential harm to an acceptable level.

For example, the reduction in speed of rotation of a shaft does not eliminate it as a hazard, but may reduce the risk such that it may be considered to be insignificant. By reducing the energy available to the component or equipment, for example, the reduction of force or electrical power required may cause the power or force to be below normal human thresholds of tolerance, thus preventing risk of harm.

Designers should establish health and safety features that reduce risk at the design stage. Consideration should be given to all aspects of use. In addition, design should minimise risks at all phases of the life of the equipment including:

- Construction.
- Transport.
- Installation.
- Commissioning.
- De-commissioning.
- Dismantling.
- Disposal.
- Recycling.

At the design stage arrangements should be made, where practicable, to eliminate the need to expose any dangerous parts during operation, examination, lubrication, adjustment or maintenance.

There are then two principles to bear in mind:

a) As a first principle, as many hazards as possible should be avoided by suitable choice of design features.
b) Secondly, where it is not possible to avoid these hazards, the factors which influence the magnitude of the risk should be examined, i.e. reducing speed or distance of movement, force, torque, inertia, and by use of surfaces that are as smooth as possible.

'HARDWARE' (PHYSICAL) MEASURES

'Hardware' (physical) measures include such things as guards, protection devices, protective appliances, isolation/lock off facilities and equipment controls that ensure operating conditions, including speed, pressure, temperature and power, are regulated to ensure health and safety.

Guards are physical barriers that prevent access to the danger zone of equipment. Protective devices are devices that do not prevent access to the danger zone, but stop the movement of dangerous parts before contact is made with them, for example, a photoelectric trip device.

Protective appliances are used to hold or manipulate material being worked on by equipment in a way that allows equipment operators to control and feed a loose work piece in the danger zone while keeping their body clear of the danger zone, for example, jigs used with a band saw (normally used in conjunction with guards).

In the case of work equipment, 'hardware' (physical) measures may include the brakes on a mobile scaffold, the sheath on a knife, roll over protection and space around equipment.

PUWER 1998 - Regulation 12 Protection against specified hazards

PUWER 1998 - Regulation 12, Protection against specified hazards, sets out the following requirement to use 'hardware' (physical) measures, other then personal protective equipment, when protecting against specific hazards:

"(1) Every employer shall take measures to ensure that the exposure of a person using work equipment to any risk to his health or safety from any hazard specified in paragraph (3) is either prevented, or, where that is not reasonably practicable, adequately controlled.

(2) The measures required by paragraph (1) shall:

(a) Be measures other than the provision of personal protective equipment or of information, instruction, training and supervision, so far as is reasonably practicable.
(b) Include, where appropriate, measures to minimise the effects of the hazard as well as to reduce the likelihood of the hazard occurring.

(3) The hazards referred to in paragraph (1) are:

(a) Any article or substance falling or being ejected from work equipment.
(b) Rupture or disintegration of parts of work equipment.
(c) Work equipment catching fire or overheating.
(d) The unintended or premature discharge of any article or of any gas, dust, liquid, vapour or other substance which, in each case, is produced, used or stored in the work equipment.
(e) The unintended or premature explosion of the work equipment or any article or substance produced, used or stored in it.

(4) For the purposes of this regulation "adequately" means adequately having regard only to the nature of the hazard and the nature and degree of exposure to the risk".

This Regulation covers risks arising from certain listed hazards during the use of equipment. Examples of the hazards that the Regulation addresses are:

- Material falling from equipment, for example molten metal spilling from a casting machine.
- Material held in the equipment being unexpectedly thrown out, for example swarf ejected from a machine tool.
- Parts of the equipment breaking off and being thrown out, for example an abrasive wheel bursting.
- Part of the equipment coming apart, for example a machine tool working loose and flying off a lathe.
- Overheating or fire due for example to friction (bearings running hot), electric motor burning out, cooling system failure.
- Explosion of the equipment due to pressure build-up, for example due to the failure of a pressure-relief device.
- Explosion of substance in the equipment, for example chemical reaction or unplanned ignition.

Where items of equipment have these risks present priority must be made to deal with these by means of 'hardware' (physical) measures. Where this is not practicable, personal protective equipment should be provided.

'SOFTWARE' MEASURES

'Software' measures include things like information, instruction, training and supervision. This will include warnings and instructions fixed to equipment, warnings that equipment is operating (for example signs and signals, such as reversing vehicle sounders), systems of working and maintaining equipment safely, restrictions on use of equipment to those suitable and competent and the use of inspections.

ELEMENT C5 - WORK EQUIPMENT (GENERAL)

Information and instruction

Regulation 8 of PUWER 1998, relating to information and instructions, builds on the general duty in the Health and Safety at Work etc Act (HASAWA) 1974 to provide employees with the information, instruction training and supervision that to the extent that is necessary to ensure, so far as is reasonably practicable, their health and safety. It also links with the general requirement in the Management of Health and Safety at Work Regulations (MHSWR) 1999 to provide information to employees relating to their health and safety. The Health and Safety (Consultation with Employees) Regulations (HSCER) 1996 requires employers to consult their employees on the information required under other regulations, including PUWER 1998, about risks to their health and safety and preventative measures in place.

PUWER 1998 Regulation 8 - Information and instruction

Regulation 8 of PUWER 1998 places a duty on employers to make available all relevant health and safety information and where appropriate, written instructions on the use of work equipment to their workforce. Workers should have easy access to such information and instructions and be able to understand them.

"Every employer shall ensure that all persons who use work equipment have available to them adequate health and safety information and, where appropriate, written instructions pertaining to the use of the work equipment.

Every employer shall ensure that any of his employees who supervises or manages the use of work equipment has available to him adequate health and safety information and, where appropriate, written instructions pertaining to the use of the work equipment".

Information and, where appropriate, written instructions on the following are required:

"(a) The conditions in which and the methods by which the work equipment may be used.
(b) Foreseeable abnormal situations and the action to be taken if such a situation were to occur.
(c) Any conclusions to be drawn from experience in using the work equipment".

Written instructions can include the information provided by manufacturers or suppliers of work equipment, for example, warning labels, signs, instruction placards, instruction sheets and training manuals. It can also include the employer's local instructions and instructions from training courses.

Employers should ensure that any written instructions are available to the workers who use the work equipment. Employers should also ensure that information and instructions are made available to other appropriate people, for example, maintenance instructions need to be provided to those involved in maintaining the work equipment. Supervisors and managers also need access to the information and written instructions. The amount of detailed health and safety information they need to have immediately available for the management of activities involving work equipment will vary, but it is important that they know what information is available and where it can be found.

Information can be made available in writing, or given verbally where it is considered sufficient. It is an employer's responsibility to decide what is appropriate, taking into consideration the individual circumstances. Where the consequences of misunderstanding are high or there are complicated/unusual circumstances the information should be in writing. Other factors also need to be taken into consideration, such as the degree of skill of the workers involved, their experience and training, the degree of supervision and the complexity and length of the activity related to the work equipment.

The information and written instructions should be easy to understand. They should be in clear English and/or other languages if appropriate for the people using them. They should be set out in a logical order, with illustrations where appropriate, and standard symbols should be used. Employers should give special consideration to any employees with language difficulties or with disabilities that could make it difficult for them to receive or understand the information or instructions.

The ACOP to Regulation 8 of PUWER 1998 recommends that any information and written instructions employers provide should cover:

"(a) All health and safety issues relating to the use of the machinery.
(b) Any limitations on these uses.
(c) Any foreseeable difficulties that could arise.
(d) The methods to deal with them.
(e) Any practical tips gained from experience of using the machinery".

Training

In order to ensure the safe use and maintenance of work equipment it is essential that adequate training takes place. The need may be simple and short, but it must take place. Operators of equipment will need different training to those that supervise safe operation or those that maintain the equipment, though there may be some overlap of need. For example, an operator of a fork lift truck will need to have knowledge and skill enough to do this safely, whereas a supervisor/manager does not need the skill to operate the fork lift truck, but must understand the hazards, precautions and rules of safe operation in order to have an expectation and to enforce safe standards. A maintenance person may not have to have all the skill of a fork lift truck operator, but would usually need enough skill to test the equipment after maintenance.

PUWER 1998 - Regulation 9 training

"(1) Every employer shall ensure that all persons who use work equipment have received adequate training for purposes of health and safety, including training in the methods which may be adopted when using the work equipment, any risks which such use may entail and precautions to be taken.

(2) Every employer shall ensure that any of his employees who supervises or manages the use of work equipment has received adequate training for purposes of health and safety, including training in the methods which may be adopted when using the work equipment, any risks which such use may entail and precautions to be taken".

Statutory requirements for certification and authorisation

PUWER 1998 sets out general requirements for training and restriction of those that use equipment. The general statutory duty is not well defined and does not specify processes of certification and authorisation. Training and restriction requirements are developed in the approved code of practice (ACOPs) for wood working machines and power presses, which emphasises the need to restrict use of this equipment to those that have been adequately trained and are designated to the task of using it.

The term designated remains unclear and relates in this context to a system of certification of competence and the giving of authorisation. In addition, the ACOP for the Training of Drivers of Rider Operated Lift Trucks requires a well structured process of training, certification and authorisation of drivers. Instructors carrying out training to this ACOP are required to have been trained to a given standard.

The HSE approves a small number of organisations who accredit and monitor training providers. These are the Construction Industry Training Board (CITB), Road Transport Industry Training Board (RTITB) the Association of Industrial Truck Trainers (AITT) and Lantra - Sector Skills Council for the Environmental and Land-based Sector. Drivers certified under this system are then trained and assessed to a standard expressed in the ACOP. When a driver is trained and certified it then falls to the employer of the driver to determine that they are competent and to authorise them. This authorisation is often represented by the provision of a licence depicting their competence and authorisation. A similar approach may be taken with other forms of work equipment.

Statutory restrictions on use of work equipment

In many workplaces there is a variety of work equipment. Until it is agreed that a person has received sufficient training and has appropriate skill to use the work equipment, they should be prevented from doing so. This may be by specific instruction or, where the risks are particularly high, by physical restraint that prevents the equipment being put into use.

For example, a wood working machine in a general workshop may be locked off and issue of the key controlled and restricted to those that are competent to use it. In the same way, a mobile elevating work platform (MEWP) may be restricted, and a mobile scaffold or ladder restricted by a chain and padlock.

In addition to requirements emphasising the need for training people PUWER 1998 sets out a requirement to restrict use to those 'given the task of using it' where specific risks exist.

PUWER 1998 - Regulation 7 specific risks

"(1) Where the use of work equipment is likely to involve a specific risk to health or safety, every employer shall ensure that:

- *(a) The use of that work equipment is restricted to those persons given the task of using it.*
- *(b) Repairs, modifications, maintenance or servicing of that work equipment is restricted to those persons who have been specifically designated to perform operations of that description (whether or not also authorised to perform other operations).*

(2) The employer shall ensure that the persons designated for the purposes of sub-paragraph (b) of paragraph (1) have received adequate training related to any operations in respect of which they have been so designated".

The term specific risks is not defined, but guidance to PUWER 1998 tends to support restriction where the risks of inappropriate use might lead to serious consequences, though this is not a limiting factor and the principle of restriction to those that are adequately trained should be universally applied.

Older legislation had identified, through the experience provided by accidents, certain equipment (dangerous machines) that required restriction for people under the age of 18 ('young people') **(see the following section),** and though this is no longer mandatory some consideration to the inherent risks of this equipment should be made when deciding restrictions under Regulation 7 of PUWER 1998. The types of machine that were considered to be dangerous were:

- Brick and tile presses.
- Calendars.
- Carding machines used in wool textiles.
- Corner staying machines, as used in upholstery.
- Dough brakes and mixers.
- Garment presses.
- Machines of any type equipped with a circular saw blade or with a saw in a form of a continuous band or strip, planing machines, vertical spindle moulding machines and routing machines being in any case machines used for cutting wood, wood products, fibreboard, plastic or similar material.

ELEMENT C5 - WORK EQUIPMENT (GENERAL)

- Food mixing machines when used with attachments for mincing, slicing or chipping or any other cutting operation or for crumbling.
- Gill Boxes used in wool textiles.
- Hydro extractors.
- Loose knife punching machines.
- Worm pressure extruding machines.
- Wrapping and packing machines.
- Wire stitching machines.
- Washing machines in use in laundries.

- Milling machines used in the metal trades.
- Opening or teasing machines used for upholstery or bedding work.
- Pie and tart making machines.
- Power presses including hydraulic and pneumatic presses.
- Rotary knife bowl chopping machines.
- Semi-automatic wood turning lathes.
- Vegetable slicing machines.

The following machines whether power driven or not:

- Circular knife slicing machines used for cutting bacon and other foods (whether similar to bacon or not).
- Platen printing machines.
- Potato chipping machines.
- Guillotine machines.

Similarly, the Abrasive Wheels Regulations (now revoked) controlled who could fit abrasive wheels - people who did, had to be trained and properly appointed. It might be considered that abrasive wheels represent a specific risk and would require restriction of who can fit abrasive wheels to meet Regulation 7 of PUWER 1998.

C5.3 - Maintenance, inspection and testing

The hazards and precautions associated with the maintenance of work equipment

The principal sources of hazards are associated with maintenance work on:

- Conveyors.
- Lifts and hoists.
- Cranes.
- Concrete pumps.
- Live electrical equipment.
- Storage tanks.
- Hoppers.
- Chemical and degreasing plant.
- Compactors.
- X-ray machinery.

Typical hazards associated with maintenance operations include:

Access	Work at heights, confined spaces.
Chemical	Gases, vapours, mists, fumes, etc.
Electrical	Electrocution, shock, burns.
Mechanical	Entanglements, machinery traps, contact; shearing traps, in-running nips, ejection, unexpected start up.
Physical	Extremes of temperature, noise, vibration, dust.
Pressure	Unexpected pressure releases, explosion.
Structural	Obstructions and floor openings.

Many of the investigated process maintenance incidents were identified as due to lack of, or failure of, permit-to-work systems. These circumstances point to the need for greater attention being paid by management to checking the use of the permit systems.

Maintenance operations require careful consideration if they are to be undertaken without undue risk. More effort is needed by management and workers to control the substantial hazards that are inherent in maintenance operations.

In many of the investigated maintenance incidents the method of work used for the job was itself inherently unsafe and needed to be radically altered before work could be safely carried out. Procedures for handling likely plant failures or breakdown situations must be considered in advance so that the risks are controlled and minimised. Pre-planning of routine maintenance procedures could reduce the number of incidents and accidents.

A safe system of work is required for any maintenance activities that involve the removal of guards. Where the maintenance work involves access into the machine, this system should include a lock-off procedure. A safe system of work is a method of doing a job that eliminates identified hazards, controls others and plans to achieve the controlled completion of the work with minimum risk.

A safe system of work may include a range of precautions from simple lock-off procedures and protective equipment through to a full written permit-to-work. It requires a systematic, imaginative analysis of the job and its hazards. The analysis should be practical and incorporate lessons learned from past experience.

Regulation 22 of PUWER 1998 sets out the following requirements to establish that maintenance work can be conducted safely:

"Every employer shall take appropriate measures to ensure that work equipment is so constructed or adapted that, so far as is reasonably practicable, maintenance operations which involve a risk to health or safety can be carried out while the work equipment is shut down, or in other cases:

(a) *Maintenance operations can be carried out without exposing the person carrying them out to a risk to his health or safety.*

(b) *Appropriate measures can be taken for the protection of any person carrying out maintenance operations which involve a risk to his health or safety".*

The following examples are features of safe working practices that reduce the risk of maintenance work:

- Isolation (for example disconnected or with fuses or keys removed).
- Isolation of equipment and pipelines containing pressurised gas, fluid, steam or hazardous substances. Isolating valves should be locked off and the system depressurised where possible, particularly if access to dangerous parts will be needed.
- Allowing moving equipment to stop.
- Supporting parts of equipment that could fall.
- Allowing components that operate at high temperatures time to cool.
- The switching off of mobile equipment, gear box in neutral, applying brakes and, where necessary, chocking wheels.
- Cleaning of vessels that have contained flammable solids, liquids, gases or dusts and monitoring prior to hot work being carried out.

The maintenance management strategies

When establishing maintenance regimes three basic management strategies are applied, planed preventative, condition based and breakdown maintenance. Each has its role and influence on health and safety.

PLANNED PREVENTATIVE MAINTENANCE

Planned preventative maintenance (PPM) is an important strategy in maintenance and seeks to maximise the life of the component/equipment. This is done by a number of maintenance methods that are both planned and preventative.

The planned method seeks to inspect and replace components on a scheduled basis. Preventative maintenance seeks to take action that tries to keep the condition of the component at its best by carrying out frequent care of the component, for example, lubrication, adjustment, cleaning.

Although all maintenance is preventive in some respect, the primary aim of planned preventive maintenance is to prevent failures occurring while the equipment is in use.

When inadequate maintenance could cause the equipment, guards or other protection devices to fail in a dangerous way, a formal system of planned preventive maintenance may be necessary. A system of planned preventative maintenance could be introduced on a risk basis, highest risk equipment being done first. Over a period of time all equipment could be brought under the scheme. Thus if an item of equipment should fail on an unplanned basis this should be seen as an equipment based incident and may be investigated on the same basis as other incidents/accidents.

CONDITION BASED MAINTENANCE

Condition based maintenance (CBM) is sometimes referred to as "predictive" maintenance. Unlike planned preventive maintenance, which uses information provided by manufacturers to set timescales for changing components, CBM is a technique that involves monitoring the condition of the equipment and predicting equipment failure. Maintenance action is then governed by this monitoring and prediction information. Many CBM systems are controlled by computers.

Condition based maintenance assumes that all equipment will deteriorate and that partial or complete loss of function will occur at some point. CBM monitors the condition or performance of plant equipment through various technologies. The data is collected, analysed, trended, and used to project equipment failures. Once the timing of equipment failure is known, action can be taken to prevent or delay failure. In this way, the reliability of the equipment can remain high.

In order to monitor equipment condition, the technique uses non-destructive testing techniques, visual inspection, and performance data. It replaces arbitrarily timed maintenance tasks (often involving replacement of components whether needed or not) with appropriate maintenance tasks, only when warranted by equipment condition.

As the equipment approaches the end of its life it may fail between condition monitoring periods, this failure could be within the predictive norm and could have direct influence on health and safety. Condition monitoring may have to be increased during this time to prevent an unexpected failure.

BREAKDOWN MAINTENANCE

Breakdown maintenance ensures that when a component comes to the end of its life this has the minimum impact on what surrounds it, for example, safety, productivity.

It is widely accepted that a maintenance strategy based solely on repair at the time of component breakdown is neither efficient nor effective. Its main advantage is the fact that it is fairly transparent that maintenance is required when components are broken. This then ensures no effort is wasted replacing parts that have some life left in them. This approach would also be unacceptable on health and safety grounds if a significant risk would arise from the failure of the component. It does not mean that this type of maintenance is unacceptable in all circumstances. Indeed some effort is being applied to maximise this technique by the study of modes of failure and the classification of the failure on a risk basis. In conjunction with this is the design of equipment that fails to safety, thus allowing the use of breakdown maintenance techniques. The only other issue is the efficient replacement of the component. Once again, considerable effort is going into the design of equipment that makes breakdown maintenance easy to conduct.

> *Breakdown maintenance involves carrying out maintenance only after faults or failures have occurred. It is appropriate only if the failure does not present an immediate risk and can be corrected before risk occurs, for example, through effective fault reporting and maintenance schemes.*
>
> *Planned preventative maintenance involves replacing parts and consumables or making necessary adjustments to preset intervals so that risks do not occur as a result of the deterioration or failure of the equipment.*
>
> *Condition-based maintenance involves monitoring the condition of safety-critical parts and carrying out maintenance whenever necessary to avoid hazards which could otherwise occur.*

Figure C5-6: Different maintenance management techniques.   Source: HSC Approved code of practice for PUWER 1998.

COMBINING THE MAINTENANCE MANAGEMENT STRATEGIES

Maintenance often uses a blend of all methods and strategies in order to gain the best results. Planned maintenance is frequently done by a specialist at intervals in the life of equipment; preventative maintenance is conducted frequently (each day or similar) by a non-specialist (operator); and condition monitored maintenance is particularly useful towards the end of its life and is conducted by specialists.

Maintenance strategies - examples

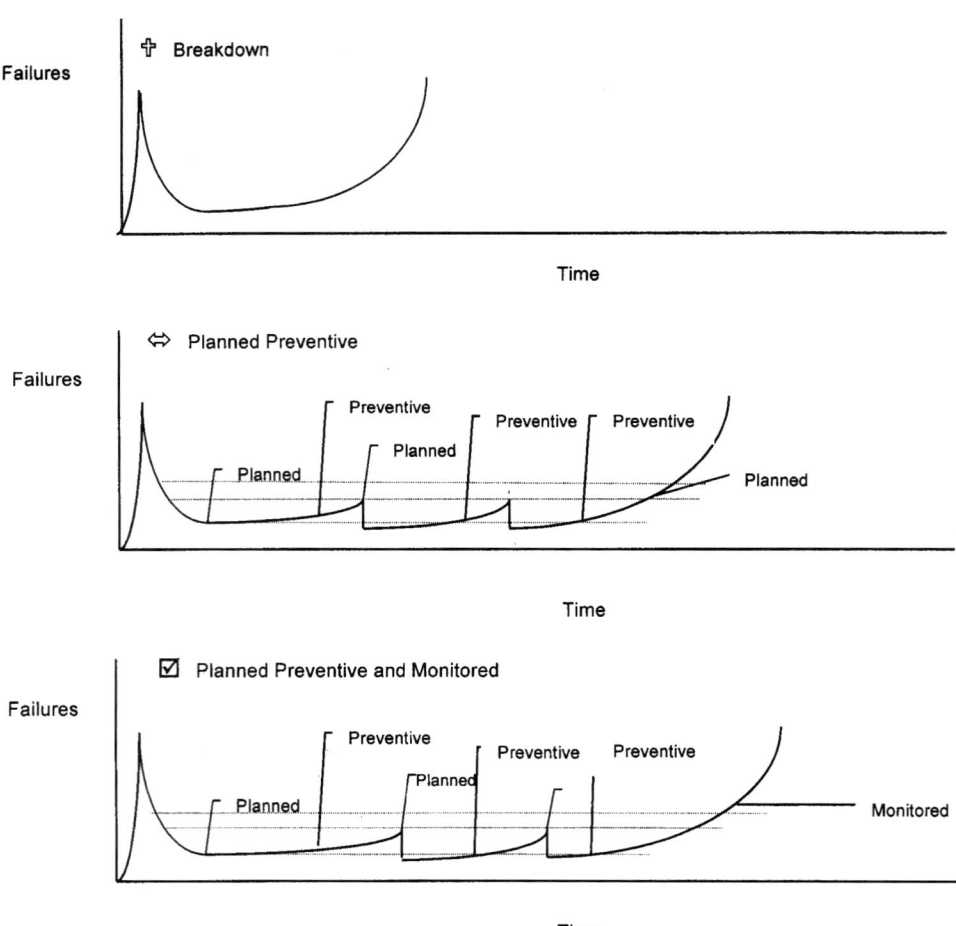

Figure C5-7: Examples of maintenance management strategies.   Source: RMS.

Developing a planned maintenance programme for safety-critical components

BENEFITS OF PLANNED PREVENTIVE MAINTENANCE

The main benefits are:

- Extended life of components.
- Assurance of reliability.
- Confirmation of condition of components.
- Reduced risk/loss producing failure events.
- Ability to carry out work at a suitable time.
- Better utilisation of maintenance staff.
- Less peaks and troughs.
- Less standby facility required.
- Less expensive (last minute) contracted facility required.
- Cost effective actions.

SUPPLIER INFORMATION

Manufacturers and suppliers of work equipment are obliged by section 6 of HASAWA 1974 to provide information on the health and safety of their products. It is reasonable and practicable that they include information on expected maintenance necessary for the equipment when it is in foreseeable use. It is important when developing a planned maintenance programme to consult this data as a source. It should be remembered though, that the specific use the equipment is put to may vary from the standard conditions considered by the manufacturer and could cause the planned maintenance programme to provide more frequent (or less) maintenance than that which is recommended.

RISK

In essence, the risk from failure of equipment is one of the most important factors to consider in a programme of maintenance of work equipment. If the risk of failure is low then the programme may extend the period between maintenance to draw out the most use from the equipment with the least effort and cost. However, not all items of the same type of equipment are identical and some will fail within this averaged maintenance period, but as the risk is low it may be considered of little consequence. Where the risk from failure is high the periods between maintenance may be reduced to develop a higher degree of confidence that the equipment will not fail.

FREQUENCY OF USE

Frequency of use can vary the wear out rate of equipment, in that on average the more the equipment is in use the more maintenance is required. This is not always the case with some components of the equipment; for example, low use may mean more frequent starts and stops in using the equipment and might put additional burden on components like motors or fitting brackets, whose main stress is caused at start of use. Equipment that remains in use after initial start up may not carry the same stresses as that which is taken in and out of use.

COMPETENCY AVAILABILITY

Depending on the equipment and maintenance required the maintenance programme may require specialist competencies. It is important to give this early consideration when developing a maintenance programme as it can take a considerable time to develop skill and expertise. If there is a competency gap it may be necessary to recruit or hire people to supplement the competency of current staff, particularly if a major maintenance programme with enhanced maintenance techniques is to be used.

OTHER FACTORS

- Need for a systematic approach to the identification of safety-critical components.
- Minimum legal requirements.
- Experiences of maintenance staff and users.
- Current best practice expectation for safeguards.
- Resource available.
- Time to introduce.
- Cost and benefit.
- Planning and work done records.
- Training of users/maintenance people.
- Control and confirmation of action through job sheets and procedures.

The statutory duties for the maintenance of work equipment

The Health and Safety at Work etc Act (HASAWA) 1974, Section 2 places a duty on the employer to ensure the maintenance of plant *(equipment)*, so far as is reasonably practicable. In addition, Regulation 5 of PUWER 1998 sets out specific requirements for the maintenance of work equipment, including hired equipment.

ELEMENT C5 - WORK EQUIPMENT (GENERAL)

PUWER 1998 - REGULATION 5 MAINTENANCE

"(1) Every employer shall ensure that work equipment is maintained in an efficient state, in efficient working order and in good repair.

(2) Every employer shall ensure that where any machinery has a maintenance log, the log is kept up to date".

The need for maintenance is considered to be adequately dealt with by the HASAWA 1974. The obligation or outcome of the maintenance is dealt with in PUWER 1998.

'Efficient' refers to its ability to ensure health and safety (not production). As such, a part that clearly protects people and provides health and safety (a safety-critical component), for example, guards, ventilation systems and pressure relief valves, must be maintained such that they perform their function at all times. Efficiency also relates to other parts, whose condition might affect health and safety in a more subtle way, for example, a bearing that through poor lubrication may become a source for a fire or for a high level of noise.

Maintenance must ensure the condition of the equipment is kept above a threshold that would put people at risk. Deterioration to a low level before action should be prevented. Equipment may need to be checked frequently in order to allow maintenance above this threshold. The frequency of checking will depend on the equipment, task and the risks arising from the deterioration of the condition of the equipment. The extent of the maintenance necessary to ensure efficiency will vary greatly dependent on similar factors to the frequency of checking.

In addition to PUWER 1998, other legislation sets out requirements for inspection/examination and maintenance of work equipment, for example, hoists and other lifting equipment, local exhaust ventilation equipment and pressure vessels. It is essential that these are seen as minimum requirements and that in addition to this the equipment must be maintained in an efficient state/working order and good repair, as required by PUWER 1998. In the same way, PUWER 1998 does not require a log of maintenance. The HASAWA 1974 requires the employer to 'ensure maintenance', with the burden of proof on doing so on the accused. Furthermore, some specific legislation will require a record of inspection and confirmation that deficiencies have been remedied, for example, scaffolds, excavations, power presses. Hire equipment will suffer a considerable amount of wear and tear, for example, damage to plugs, insulation, guards, blades etc., which can result in the equipment becoming dangerous to use. All equipment should be inspected for damage prior to hire and on return; written check lists can be used and kept for record purposes.

Determining inspection regimes for work equipment

STATUTORY REQUIREMENTS FOR INSPECTION

Regulation 6 of PUWER 1998 relates to the inspection of most work equipment. Only some power presses and their guards, lifting equipment and winding apparatus, and equipment that are subject to inspection under the Construction (Design and Management) Regulations (CDM) 2007 are not covered. The guidance to PUWER 1998 establishes that inspection of work equipment is only required where its deterioration could present a significant risk, where the foreseeable result would be major injury or worse.

Regulation 6(1) of PUWER 1998 establishes that work equipment must be inspected after installation and prior to first use or after assembly on a new site or location where its safety depends on installation conditions. Inspections must be recorded and carried out prior to removal from premises, sale, hire or loan to another employer.

PUWER 1998 Regulation 6(2&3) - Inspection

"Every employer shall ensure that work equipment exposed to conditions causing deterioration which is liable to result in dangerous situations is inspected:

(a) At suitable intervals.

(b) Each time that exceptional circumstances which are liable to jeopardise the safety of the work equipment have occurred, to ensure that health and safety conditions are maintained and that any deterioration can be detected and remedied in good time.

Every employer shall ensure that the result of an inspection made under this regulation is recorded and kept until the next inspection under this regulation is recorded".

Figure C5-8: Equipment inspection. Source: RMS.

FACTORS THAT DETERMINE INSPECTION REGIMES

The factors to be considered when determining an inspection regime for work equipment includes the type of equipment, where it is used and how it is used.

Type of equipment

The guidance to PUWER 1998 establishes that the types of equipment whose use could result in significant risk as a result of deterioration and which may therefore need to be inspected include:

"(a) Most fairground equipment.
(b) Machines where there is a need to approach the danger zone during normal operation such as horizontal injection moulding machines, paper-cutting guillotines, die-casting machines, shell-moulding machines.
(c) Complex automated equipment.
(d) Integrated production lines".

In addition to this list, it is important to consider the consequence of failure; for example, a small chemical reaction vessel may not be within its scope but could present a large scale problem if the controls on content and process parameters are not inspected for their correct condition and functionality.

Where it is used

The use of equipment in arduous conditions may mean that safety critical parts are at higher risk of damage or being worn out. For example, equipment used in humid conditions could mean that there is a risk of corrosion leading to incorrect functioning or failure of the equipment. Periodic inspection of critical parts may identify their degradation prior to failure in use.

Equipment used in harsh environments, such as that which may be found in coastal environments may also require more frequent inspection. Where the equipment is used may influence the nature of the inspection as well, some safety critical items that deteriorate through use may not need such frequent inspection as those that deteriorate through corrosion.

How it is used

Similarly, if equipment is only used intermittently it may not require frequent inspection, but may need a more complete inspection before it is brought back into use again. Equipment, such as a mobile elevating work platform (MEWP) used to conduct heavier tasks, such as some of those involved in construction, may require a more frequent and searching inspection regime than those in lighter tasks, such as a MEWP used to change bulbs in a warehouse operation.

INSPECTION METHODS

Equipment must also be inspected on a regular basis in order to confirm the condition that it is in. The inspection required is more than a simple daily pre-use check carried out by the operator. The person using equipment, who should be confirmed as competent, should carry out operator checks prior to the use of any equipment. Operator checks should include guards, cables, casing integrity, cutting or machine parts and safety devices such as cut-outs. The inspection required under this regulation should be significant and address a list of identifiable health and safety critical parts.

The inspection procedure may require the completion of an inspection sheet. The purpose of an inspection sheet is to determine deterioration of specific parts, abuse and misuse and to ensure that all items are considered at the time of inspection, by serving as an aide memoire.

The results of the inspection will confirm whether or not a piece of equipment is in a safe enough condition to use. Other regulations, such as the Lifting Operations and Lifting Equipment Regulations (LOLER) 1998, set out specific statutory inspection requirements.

The need for functional testing of safety-related parts

Regulation 19(3) of PUWER 1998 states that:

> "Every employer shall take appropriate measures to ensure that re-connection of any energy source to work equipment does not expose any person using the work equipment to any risk to his health or safety".

Figure C5-9: Regulation 19 of PUWER 1998. *Source: Provision and Use of Work Equipment Regulations (PUWER) 1998.*

Interlocks, protection devices, controls and emergency controls are safety related parts that are placed in work equipment systems to ensure the safety of those using, cleaning and maintaining equipment. Employers should have procedures in place that ensure all safety related parts of systems are periodically checked and their functionality confirmed.

For example, thermal energy may be supplied by circulation of preheated fluid, such as water or steam, in such cases; isolating valves should be fitted into the supply pipework.

Redundancy in the form of more than one isolation valve fitted in series may also be used, but care should be exercised to check the efficacy of each valve function periodically.

The performance of such valves may deteriorate over time, and their effectiveness often cannot be judged visually. Functional testing of safety related parts of equipment should be one of the controls established during risk assessment and should be monitored, reviewed and audited in the normal manner.

C5.4 - Competence, training, information and supervision

The difference between training and competence

Competence can be described as the integration of Knowledge, Ability, Training and Experience (KATE). Training therefore is an essential component to consider when assessing the competence of a person. If a person is lacking one of these components, the gap should be bridged by an increased level of supervision until other action can be taken to establish competence.

Circumstances when training is likely to be required

INDUCTION

Induction training is generally defined as the information, instruction and training given when a person starts a new job, task or process. Its purpose is to orientate the individual to their environment in order to maximise their effectiveness, including health and safety. Thus, a workforce that is aware of the risks is familiar with procedures and systems of work, and knows how to recognise and report unsafe conditions. This ensures that the employee shares a common commitment to health and safety and it contributes strongly to a safer workforce.

Important health and safety topics to be covered

Induction training for new employees should include:

- Review and discussion of the health and safety policy.
- Specific training requirements.
- Fire and emergency procedures.
- Welfare facilities.
- First aid procedures and facilities.
- Personal protective equipment (PPE) provisions - limitations, use and maintenance etc.
- Restriction, for example, areas or equipment.
- Rules, signs and signals.

CHANGES IN WORK ACTIVITIES

When workers are assigned new activities because of a change of their job or temporary transfer to other work, this can present new risks and a need to use different controls. The changes in work activity may be sufficient to make the provision of a complete new induction necessary. In some cases, the changes may be so different as to require detailed remedial training of the worker in the new ways of doing things compared to previous methods. This can be the case; for example, when a person transfers within warehouse operations from the use of a counterbalanced fork lift truck to a reach truck. Though the two types of mechanical handling equipment do similar work their functionality is radically different to each other.

INTRODUCTION OF NEW TECHNOLOGY OR NEW EQUIPMENT AND CHANGES IN SYSTEMS OF WORK

The introduction of new technology will often require the adoption of new work practices and safe systems, for example, improvements in manual handling by using mechanical aids. Such training will include developing skills to interpret equipment control layouts and data display.

Training related to changes in systems of work is required at appropriate intervals to update techniques and ensure awareness of correct methods. Training for change will include information and skills relevant to:

- Introduction of new substances/processes.
- Changes in working procedure.
- Changes in work patterns.
- Review of risk assessments.

REFRESHER TRAINING DUE TO DECLINING SKILLS

As time passes a worker's approach to health and safety can drift away from that intended by the employer. This may simply be because they have forgotten, sometimes because of infrequent use, or because they prefer to have a different understanding or way of working. It is important that regular refresher training be used to reinforce the employer's desired approach. A common refresher period, used for first aiders and lift truck operators is three years. This may be an acceptable interval for some tasks, but the period may need to be shorter for others. Refresher training needs to be provided to managers as well as workers.

Groups of people having specific training needs

SUPERVISORS

Supervisors have specific training needs that relate to their role. They do not need detailed knowledge and skill in the functional operation of the work equipment but they need appropriate training that ensures they know the hazards, controls and correct use of the equipment. In this way, they can have an expectation of practices that ensure correct health and safety, with the confidence that they are able to enforce rules relating to correct use. The training should also enable them to identify work situations that deviate from the normal conditions of use and present different or higher risks. In this way, they can assess the risks from use of work equipment and ensure appropriate controls are in place for different circumstances.

WORK EQUIPMENT (GENERAL) - ELEMENT C5

To ensure responsibilities are known and the organisation's policy is carried out, the main points that should be covered are as follows:

- The health and safety policy.
- Legal framework and the duties of the organisation.
- Health and safety inspection techniques.
- Cause and consequences of accidents.
- Risk assessment.
- Accident prevention techniques.
- Disciplinary procedures.
- The use of reactive and active monitoring techniques.

YOUNG PEOPLE AND VULNERABLE PERSONS

Young people need training most when they start a job or work experience. They need to be trained to do the work without putting themselves and other people at risk. It is important that they have an understanding of, for example:

- The hazards and risks in the workplace and related to work equipment.
- The control measures put in place to protect their health and safety, including restrictions on use.
- A basic introduction to health and safety, for example, first-aid, fire and evacuation procedures.

Young people face unfamiliar risks from the jobs they do and from their work surroundings. They are therefore likely to need more supervision than adults.

Further guidance is contained in HSG165 - "Young people at work: a guide for employers".

Similarly, there are people at work who are especially vulnerable and will need care and supervision in the workplace. A vulnerable adult is someone aged over 18 who may have special needs due to a mental or physical disability, an addiction or a learning difficulty. This covers disabled people, people with mental illness and those with a wide variety of conditions such as autism and Down's syndrome. This vulnerability may mean that the person requires a specific training scheme that is tailored to their vulnerability. In this way, they may learn to use equipment that is within their capability without putting themselves and others at risk.

The relationship between competence, external and self-supervision

Supervision consists of the provision/reinforcement of performance standards of employees to ensure health and safety. It includes monitoring that agreed work practices are followed and the use of motivation techniques such as involvement of the workforce in task design to help ensure compliance with the required actions. The success of information instruction and training activities needs to be measured to enable updating to take place to cater for changes in the workplace. The supervisor has a crucial part to play in this monitoring process.

It is important to balance the amount of supervision against the work being done and the competence of the individual. It is generally appropriate that the level of supervision necessary increases with the level of risk related to the work. It can be said that when considering supervision of individuals it is important to take account of the competence of the person.

In cases where a person has qualifications, but has no experience and is therefore low in competence (for example a young person straight from college) then supervision must increase accordingly.

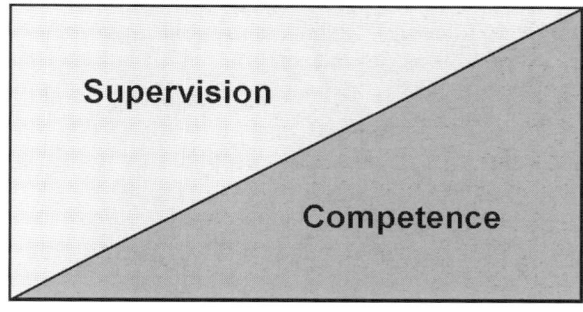

Figure C5-10: Competence v supervision.   Source: RMS.

As the worker develops competence the level of external supervision, provided by a supervisor, can be reduced and the acceptance of the level of self-supervision, provided by the worker, can be increased.

Specific training needs for certain hazardous types of work equipment

Certain hazardous types of work equipment require specific training because they constitute a high risk to the user and those around them. The type of equipment this applies to include chainsaws, woodworking machines, power presses and abrasive wheels.

CHAINSAWS

Chainsaws are used for many projects involving the management of woodland, the removal of trees and the clearance of scrub. In inexperienced hands a chain saw is lethal and training and formal certification is now a requirement of most employers and insurance companies.

WOODWORKING MACHINES

New starters are likely to have the greatest training needs. Refresher training for trained and experienced operators should be provided at least every five years.

The term woodworking machinery covers a wide range of equipment including, bench circular saws, dimension saws, pull over cross cut saws, radial arm saws, band saws, mortisers, spindlers, etc.

ELEMENT C5 - WORK EQUIPMENT (GENERAL)

The training needs for users of this equipment will vary according to their existing levels of knowledge. All training must be specific to the equipment being used and should cover issues such as: appropriate personal protective equipment (PPE), the main causes of accidents, safe working practices, etc.

POWER PRESSES

Regulation 9(1) of PUWER 1998 states:

"Every employer shall ensure that all persons who use work equipment have received adequate training for purposes of health and safety, including training in the methods which may be adopted when using the work equipment, any risks which such use may entail and precautions to be taken".

Regulation 33(1) of PUWER 1998 requires that all guards and protection devices are inspected and tested by a competent person who has been appointed in writing by the employer. If a person is undergoing training for this purpose then they should be under the supervision of a competent person.

The Approved Code of Practice, "Safe Use of Power Presses" that accompanies the regulations states that the competent person should be trained in:

"(a) Power press mechanisms, particularly their safety aspects and including the nature and function of clutch mechanisms, flywheels, brakes and ancillary equipment.
(b) Guards and protection devices - types and functions of each type of guard or protection device, including closed tools where used; method of installation.
(c) The causes and prevention of accidents involving power presses.
(d) The work of the tool setter - safe methods of working, lubrication and co-operation with the press operator.
(e) Tool design - in relation to safe systems of work.
(f) How to carry out an inspection and test of the guard protection device or closed tool, including how to detect defects".

Furthermore, the ACOP also states that:

"Press operators are most likely to need training when they are recruited. However, training needs are also required:
(a) If the risks to which people are exposed change.
(b) If new equipment or technology is introduced.
(c) If the system of work changes".

ABRASIVE WHEELS

The Provision and Use of Work Equipment Regulations (PUWER) 1998 require that persons using work equipment, such as abrasive wheels, and persons who supervise and manage their use should receive adequate training.

Guidance Note HSG 17 "Safety in the use of abrasive wheels" suggests that any training programme should cover at least the following:

a) Hazards and risks arising from the use of abrasive wheels and the precautions to be observed.
b) Methods of marking abrasive wheels with their type, size and maximum operating speed.
c) How to store handle and transport abrasive wheels.
d) How to inspect and test abrasive wheels for damage.
e) The functions of all the components used with abrasive wheels such as flanges, blotters, bushes, nuts etc.
f) How to assemble abrasive wheels correctly to make sure they are properly balanced and fit to use.
g) The proper method of dressing an abrasive wheel (removing dulled abrasive or other material from the cutting surface and/or removing material to correct any uneven wear of the wheel).
h) The correct adjustment of the work rest on pedestal or bench grinding machines.
i) The use of suitable personal protective equipment, for example, eye protection.

Element C6

Work equipment (workplace machinery)

Learning outcomes

The intended learning outcomes are that the student will be able to:

C6.1 Describe the principles of safety integration and the considerations required in a general workplace machinery risk assessment.

C6.2 Describe, with examples, the principal generic mechanical and non-mechanical hazards of general workplace machinery.

C6.3 Describe protective devices found on general workplace machinery.

C6.4 Explain the principles of control associated with the maintenance of general workplace machinery.

C6.5 Describe the requirements for information and warnings on general workplace machinery.

C6.6 Explain the key safety characteristics of general workplace machinery control systems.

C6.7 Explain the analysis, assessment and improvement of system failures and system reliability with the use of calculations.

Content

C6.1 - Safety integration and machinery risk assessment	179
The principles of safety integration from the Supply of Machinery (Safety) Regulations (SMSR) 2008	179
Factors to be considered when assessing risk	182
Purpose of CE marking and the relevance of the CE mark	184
Conformity assessments and the use of harmonised standards	185
C6.2 - Generic hazards	196
Common machinery hazards in a range of general workplaces	196
The types of generic machinery hazards	198
The typical causes of failures	200
Failure modes and prevention in relation to major incidents	207
Failure prevention strategies	213
Non-destructive testing techniques	215
C6.3 - Protective devices	219
The main types of safeguarding devices	219
Characteristics, key features, limitations and typical applications	221
C6.4 - Maintenance	231
The means by which machinery is safely set, cleaned and maintained	231
The means by which machines are isolated from all energy sources	233
C6.5 - Information and warnings	234
The scope of information required for the safe use and operation of machinery	234
Information and instructions regarding the operation and use of machinery	235
C6.6 - Machinery control systems	236
The key safety characteristics of machinery control systems	236
C6.7 - Systems failures and system reliability	239
Meaning of the term 'system'	239
Principles of system failure analysis	240
Use of calculation in the assessment of system reliability	241
Methods for improving system reliability	244

ELEMENT C6 - WORK EQUIPMENT (WORKPLACE MACHINERY)

Relevant statutory provisions

The Supply of Machinery (Safety) Regulations (SMSR) 2008 - Schedule 2
Workplace (Health, Safety and Welfare) Regulations (WHSWR) 1992
Provision and Use of Work Equipment Regulations (PUWER) 1998 (Regulations 10-19)

C6.1 - Safety integration and machinery risk assessment

The principles of safety integration from the Supply of Machinery (Safety) Regulations (SMSR) 2008

The Supply of Machinery (Safety) Regulations (SMSR) 2008 set out requirements to ensure that machinery is designed and constructed taking account of essential health and safety requirements (EHSRs). The term 'machinery' incorporates machinery; interchangeable equipment; safety components; lifting accessories; chains, ropes, and webbing; removable transmission devices and partly completed machinery. The requirement applies to situations where machinery is manufactured for supply to another organisation and when a user manufactures their own machinery. In order to ensure this Regulation 7, "Supply of machinery: general obligations and prohibition", of SMSR 2008 requires the following:

"(1) No responsible person shall place machinery on the market or put it into service unless it is safe.

(2) Before machinery is placed on the market or put into service, the responsible person must:

- a) *Ensure that the applicable essential health and safety requirements are satisfied in respect of it.*
- b) *Ensure that the technical file is compiled and made available in accordance with the requirements of Annex VII (Part 7 of Schedule 2), part A.*
- c) *Provide, in particular, the information necessary to operate it safely, such as instructions.*
- d) *Follow, as appropriate:*
    - (i) *The conformity assessment procedure prescribed by regulation 10.*
    - (ii) *One of the conformity assessment procedures prescribed by regulation 11.*
    - (iii) *One of the conformity assessment procedures prescribed by regulation 12.*
- e) *Draw up the EC declaration of conformity in accordance with the requirements of Annex II (Part 2 of Schedule 2), section A, part 1, and ensure that:*
    - (i) *A copy of it accompanies the machinery.*
    - (ii) *The original is retained in accordance with the requirements of Annex II, part 2, first paragraph.*
- f) *Affix the CE marking to the machinery:*
    - (i) *Visibly, legibly and indelibly.*
    - (ii) *As prescribed in Annex III (Part 3 of Schedule 2)".*

In meeting the essential health and safety requirements, the SMSR 2008, Schedule 2 Part 1, requires the responsible person to conform to Annex 1 "Essential health and safety requirements relating to the design and construction of machinery" of the EU Machinery Directive 2006/42/EC. This establishes a number of **general principles,** including the following.

General principle 1 establishes that the responsible person, the manufacturer or someone working on their behalf, must ensure that a risk assessment is carried out at the design stage in order to determine the health and safety requirements that apply to the machinery. The machinery must then be designed and constructed taking into account the results of the risk assessment. This process of risk assessment and risk reduction requires the responsible person to:

- Determine the limits of the machinery, which includes the intended use and any reasonably foreseeable misuse.
- Identify the hazards that can be generated by the machinery and the associated hazardous situations.
- Estimate the risks, taking into account the severity of the possible injury or damage to health and the probability of its occurrence.
- Evaluate the risks, with a view to determining whether risk reduction is required, in accordance with the objective of the Directive.
- Eliminate the hazards or reduce the risks associated with these hazards by application of protective measures, in the order of priority established in section 1.1.2(b) of Annex 1 of the Directive.

The risk assessment and its outcomes must be documented in the Technical File for machinery, in accordance with Annex VII of the directive.

General principle 2 establishes that the obligations laid down by the essential health and safety requirements only apply when the corresponding hazard exists for the machinery in question when it is used under the conditions foreseen by the responsible person or in foreseeable abnormal situations. In any event, the principles of safety integration referred to in section 1.1.2 of Annex 1 of the directive and the obligations concerning marking of machinery and instructions referred to in sections 1.7.3 and 1.7.4 of the Annex apply.

General principle 3 establishes that:

"The essential health and safety requirements are mandatory. However, taking into account the state of the art, it may not be possible to meet the objectives set by them. In that event, the machinery must, as far as possible, be designed and constructed with the purpose of approaching these objectives".

ELEMENT C6 - WORK EQUIPMENT (WORKPLACE MACHINERY)

General principle 4 establishes that the list of essential health and safety requirements is organised into several sections. The first section has a general scope and is applicable to all kinds of machinery. The other sections refer to certain kinds of more specific hazards. It remains necessary to examine the whole of the list in order to be sure of meeting all the applicable essential requirements. When machinery is being designed, the requirements of the general section and the requirements of one or more of the other sections must be taken into account, depending on the results of the risk assessment.

The following sections set out the five *principles of safety integration* referred to in Annex 1 of the Machinery Directive and referred to in Part 1 of the Supply of Machinery (Safety) Regulations (SMSR) 2008. These principles are sometimes referred to as establishing 'safety by design' and set out a basic methodology for designing and constructing safe machinery and ensures that the essential health and safety requirements are integrated in the design.

MACHINERY MUST BE DESIGNED AND CONSTRUCTED TO BE FIT FOR PURPOSE AND TO ELIMINATE OR REDUCE RISKS THROUGHOUT THE LIFETIME OF THE MACHINERY

Schedule 2, Part 1 of SMSR 2008, first principle of safety integration, requires that machinery be designed and constructed so that it is fitted for its function and can be operated, adjusted and maintained without putting persons at risk when the operations are carried out under foreseen conditions and taking account of reasonably foreseeable misuse. Fitted for its function refers to the safety of the machine rather than the performance of the machine. This will involve consideration of methods to ensure that hazards are removed or protection provided from them while dealing with problems, such as material stuck in the machine during the process and consideration has to be made of foreseeable actions of the operator in the circumstances.

The aim of measures taken in the design and construction must be to eliminate any risk throughout the lifetime of the machinery, including transport, assembly, dismantling, disabling and scrapping. It is important that measures are built into machinery that is intended to be transported between sites where it is used. Design should facilitate assembly and dismantling, particularly where machines will be installed temporarily at work locations; additional measures may be to ensure design prevents errors when fitting and adequate instructions are provided. In consideration of safety measures for disabling and scrapping it may be necessary that components containing hazardous substances are indelibly marked and suitably protected from the action of disassembly. Measures taken need to facilitate the safe removal of the hazardous substances and dissipation of stored energy at the time the machine is disabled, to help ensure health and safety during scrapping.

This is a high standard of duty and will require the duty holders to consider carefully the phases of life of a machine; this is similar to duties under the Construction (Design and Management) Regulations 2007 where the duty related to design encompasses all the phases of the life of a structure.

THE PRINCIPLES MUST BE APPLIED IN ORDER TO ELIMINATE OR REDUCE RISKS AS FAR AS POSSIBLE; TAKE NECESSARY PROTECTIVE MEASURES WHERE RISK CANNOT BE ELIMINATED; AND INFORM USERS OF ANY RESIDUAL RISKS

Schedule 2, Part 1 of SMSR 2008, second principle of safety integration, requires the responsible person to apply specified principles of good practice when selecting the most appropriate methods to prevent risk and satisfy the essential health and safety requirements. It is mandatory that they are applied in the following order:

- Eliminate or reduce risks as far as possible (inherently safe machinery design and construction).
- Take the necessary protective measures in relation to risks that cannot be eliminated.
- Inform users of the residual risks due to any shortcomings of the protective measures adopted, indicate whether any particular training is required and specify any need to provide personal protective equipment.

The responsible person must exhaust all the possible inherently safe design measures before resorting to protective measures. In the same way, the possible protective measures must be exhausted before relying on warnings and instructions to operators. Application of this 3-step method must also take due account of current knowledge and invention, considered by General Principle 3, set out in Part 1 of SMSR 2008 and Annex 1 of the Machinery Directive.

This follows common principles of risk reduction and logically supports the hierarchy set out for employers to meet in the Provision of Work Equipment Regulations (PUWER) 1998, Regulation 11 for protection from dangerous parts of machinery.

Step 1, inherently safe design measures, the EC guide to the Machinery Directive suggests these may include:

- Eliminating the hazard altogether, for example, replacing flammable hydraulic fluid with a non-flammable.
- Designing the control system and control devices in order to ensure safe functioning.
- Ensuring the inherent stability of machinery by its shape and the distribution of masses.
- Ensuring that accessible parts of the machinery do not have sharp edges or rough surfaces.
- Ensuring sufficient distance between moving and fixed parts of the machine to avoid the risk of crushing.
- Avoiding accessible surfaces with extreme temperatures.
- Reducing emissions of noise, vibrations, radiation or hazardous substances at source.
- Reducing, where possible, the speed and the power of moving parts or the travel speed of the machinery itself.

- Locating hazardous parts of machinery in inaccessible places.
- Locating adjustment and maintenance points outside danger zones.

Step 2, protective measures, the EC guide to the Machinery Directive suggests these may include the following technical protective measures:

- Guards: fixed guards, interlocking moveable guards with guard locking where necessary or adjustable guards restricting access.
- Protective devices.
- Insulation of live electrical parts.
- Enclosure of sources of noise.
- Damping of vibrations.
- Containment or evacuation of hazardous substances.
- Devices to compensate the lack of direct visibility.
- Protective structures against the risk of rolling or tipping over or the risk of falling objects.
- Stabilisers.

Step 3, training and personal protective equipment, the EC guide to the Machinery Directive suggests these may include:

- Information or warnings on the machinery in the form of symbols or pictograms.
- Warning acoustic or light signals.
- Indicating of the mass of machinery or parts thereof which must be handled with lifting equipment during the different phases of its foreseeable lifetime.
- Warning against the use of machinery by certain persons such as, for example, young people under a certain age.
- Information relating to the safe assembly and installation of the machinery.
- Specifying the need to provide the necessary information and training to operators.
- Information on the complementary protective measures to be taken in the workplace.
- Specifying the need to provide the appropriate personal protective equipment to operators and ensure that it is used.

Providing warnings and instructions for use is considered as an integral part of the design and construction of the machinery. However the fact that this third step is the last in the order of priority given in section 1.1.2 (b) implies that warnings and instructions must not be a substitute for inherently safe design measures and technical protective measures when these are possible, taking into account the state of the art.

Figure C6-1: Application of training to principles of safety integration.   Source: EC Enterprise and Industry Guide to Machinery Directive.

WHEN DESIGNING AND CONSTRUCTING MACHINERY AND WHEN DRAFTING THE INSTRUCTIONS: USE AND FORESEEABLE MISUSE MUST BE CONSIDERED

Schedule 2, Part 1 of SMSR 2008, third principle of safety integration, establishes a duty to not rely on the specification of intended use for the machine when designing, constructing and drafting instructions. This would be too narrow an approach and allow the duty holder to specify a narrow use, for which protection is provided, in the full knowledge that the machine may foreseeably be used for a different purpose. The duty requires consideration of foreseeable variance from the defined use, misuse. This consideration must include measures to prevent abnormal use, if this would engender a risk. The measures must be chosen in the order of priority set out in the second principle of safety integration.

The EC guide to the Machinery Directive suggests these may include:

- Providing means for restricting the operation of the machinery or of certain control devices to authorised persons.
- Designing machinery to prevent errors of fitting.
- Fitting devices to prevent the travel of mobile machinery when the driver is not at the controls.
- Fitting devices to prevent the operation of machinery unless stabilisers are in position.
- Fitting devices to prevent the overloading of lifting machinery.

Instructions and warnings must draw the user's attention to ways that the machine should not be used that experience has shown might occur.

TAKE ACCOUNT OF OPERATOR CONSTRAINTS DUE TO NECESSARY OR FORESEEABLE USE OF PERSONAL PROTECTIVE EQUIPMENT

Schedule 2, Part 1 of SMSR 2008, fourth principle of safety integration, requires the design and construction of the machinery must take account of constraints to which the operator is subject as a result of foreseeable use of personal protective equipment. In particular, the design, positioning and dimensions of the control devices, for example, on machinery designed to be used in cold conditions the spacing, size and design of foot operated controls should accommodate large boots. In the same way, hand controls for equipment operated in a hot environment need to be operable to someone wearing gloves.

ELEMENT C6 - WORK EQUIPMENT (WORKPLACE MACHINERY)

MACHINERY MUST BE SUPPLIED WITH ALL THE ESSENTIALS TO ENABLE IT TO BE ADJUSTED, MAINTAINED AND USED SAFELY

Schedule 2, Part 1 of SMSR 2008, fifth principle of safety integration, requires that supply must ensure that all essential special equipment or accessories are provided to ensure machinery can be adjusted, maintained and used safely. For example, special fixings may be required to secure an abrasive wheel correctly; if these were not available it may cause the user to over-tighten the fixing, leading to the bursting of the abrasive wheel. Other equipment or accessories that may have to be supplied with the machine may include devices for the removal of parts of the machine for cleaning, devices to feed material in or to remove material jammed in the machinery. It does not establish a requirement to supply standard tools required for adjustment or operation of the machine, for example, screwdrivers or spanners.

Factors to be considered when assessing risk

The factors to be considered when assessing the risk of machinery include:
- Persons at risk.
- Severity of possible injury.
- Probability of injury.
- Need for access.
- Duration of exposure.
- Reliability of safeguards.
- Operating procedures and personnel.

PERSONS AT RISK

The people that are at risk are those that encounter the machinery through its life and include those involved in:
- Manufacture and testing.
- Transport.
- Assembly, installation and commissioning.
- Setting up and use.
- Adjustment, maintenance, clean and repair.
- Dismantling, disabling and scrapping.

When in use, people in the area of the machine must be considered along with those actually using it. People who would not usually be expected to encounter or use it must also be considered, for example, those that supply materials/products for work or remove them after work.

Consideration also needs to be made as to whether the machine is to be used by a young person or someone younger. In considering its foreseeable use consideration has to be made as to whether the equipment will be provided to trained workers or made available to the public, with limited skill and understanding of hazards.

SEVERITY OF POSSIBLE INJURY

This will, in the first instance, depend on the level of energy relating to the hazard encountered. For example, the force exhibited by two moving parts closing together. The second factor influencing the severity of injury is any limitation on the extent to which parts or the whole of the body may encounter the hazard, for example finger in a gap, and head between the parts of a press or the whole body entering an area used by a robot. The third factor is the duration of exposure to the hazard. A brief encounter with the surface of an abrasive wheel may be minor, but if a hand is retained in contact with an abrasive wheel major injury will result.

The severity of possible injury has an important influence on the level of safety precautions necessary to control the risk of harm. Where two machines present the same probability of injury, but in one case the injury is death and in the other a bruised or broken finger, clearly the former carries the higher risk and requires a higher level of safety precautions. Some types of injury, particularly those involving injury to health, are not immediately apparent and may be manifested some time after exposure to a hazard has ceased. Other injuries build up over a long period of exposure to a hazard. These factors contribute to the possible severity of injury arising from machinery and should be taken into account when assessing risk.

PROBABILITY OF INJURY

Probability of injury tends to be summarised as being dependent on three factors:

Technical factors
- Dangerous parts - type of hazard and the ease, with which a hazard may trap, cut or entangle an individual (dependent on speed and surface of the moving part).
- Guards and other devices available.
- Controls and layout of equipment.

Procedural factors
- Planned cleaning and maintenance.
- Systems of working required for dangerous access.
- Lock off procedures.

- Permit to work.

Behavioural factors

- Information and understanding of hazards.
- Instruction.
- Training - skills and procedures.
- Supervision.
- Positive motivational work methods.
- Perception of hazards - accentuated.
- Human error through fatigue and repetition.

NEED FOR ACCESS

- When assessing the risk the need for access should be considered and the significance of this factor to the level of risk considered. Consideration should include:
- Amount of access needed - frequency, proximity and duration of access.
- Circumstances of access - whether the machine is running, switched off, isolated or locked off.
- Reasons for access - whether they are operational requirements, setting, use or maintenance or whether they are informal or an unplanned encounter.

DURATION OF EXPOSURE

Duration of exposure to the hazard increases the probability of contact and then the extent of injury sustained. If duration is taken to be repetitive small exposures that are reliant only on the skill and attention of the individual it can be seen that this could quickly lead to human error and injury. If a long duration of access is required, for example, in order to conduct major adjustments, this long exposure increases the chance that harm may occur.

RELIABILITY OF SAFEGUARDS

The safeguards selected to control risk may involve physical safeguards, protective devices and/or training and personal protective equipment. All safeguards have an amount of reliability. If the safeguard to deal with a risk has a limited reliability then the risk of harm will remain high. Safeguards that rely only on training or personal protective equipment will not normally be as reliable as those that use physical safeguards, such as guards; therefore the risk will remain high. The reliability of safeguards may be diminished by use over time, combined with lack of maintenance, or factors like how easily the user of the equipment can choose not to use the safeguard or defeat it.

The risk assessment should take the reliability of safeguards into account when establishing the safeguards selected to deal with the essential health and safety requirements. The greater the risk, the greater is the need to protect against it. The greater the probability and severity of injury resulting from failure of the safety measures, the greater should be the reliability of the safeguards.

The reliability of a safeguard can be improved by avoiding the motives for its defeat and/or by making defeat more difficult. The design of the safeguarding system should take full account of the human factor, during each phase of the machine's life. Where this aspect of the design is inadequate, motives to defeat the safeguard will commonly arise, often justified by the need to gain access to the danger zone to deal with production problems. Where needs of this kind are identified the design should be modified to eliminate or reduce this need.

Designers should set out to establish likely operating difficulties that may lead to safeguards being compromised and take account of them. Ways to make defeat of safeguards more difficult include:

- The use of interlocking devices or access systems that are coded, for example mechanically, electrically, magnetically or optically.
- Physical obstruction or shielding of the interlocking device while the guard is open.

Where systems rely on special actuators or keys (coded or not) care should be taken over the availability of spare actuators or keys and master keys.

OPERATING PROCEDURES AND PERSONNEL

It is not always possible to eliminate hazards or to design completely adequate safeguards to protect people against every hazard, particularly during such phases of machine life as commissioning, setting, process changeovers, programming, adjustment, cleaning and maintenance, where direct access to the hazardous parts of the machine may be necessary. In situations like this, safe working practices or safe systems of work must be devised and used.

When assessing risk, considerations should include:

Procedures

- Procedures for planned cleaning and maintenance.
- Systems of working required for access to danger zones.
- Lock off procedures.
- Permits to work.
- Positive motivational work methods.

ELEMENT C6 - WORK EQUIPMENT (WORKPLACE MACHINERY)

Personnel

- The competency of personnel that may be required for the proposed tasks involving the machinery.
- Their understanding of hazards and safeguards.
- Their ability to work within parameters of use of the machinery.
- Level of supervision needed.
- Restriction of use and maintenance tasks to those competent and authorised.
- Perception of hazards - accentuated.
- Human error through fatigue and repetition.

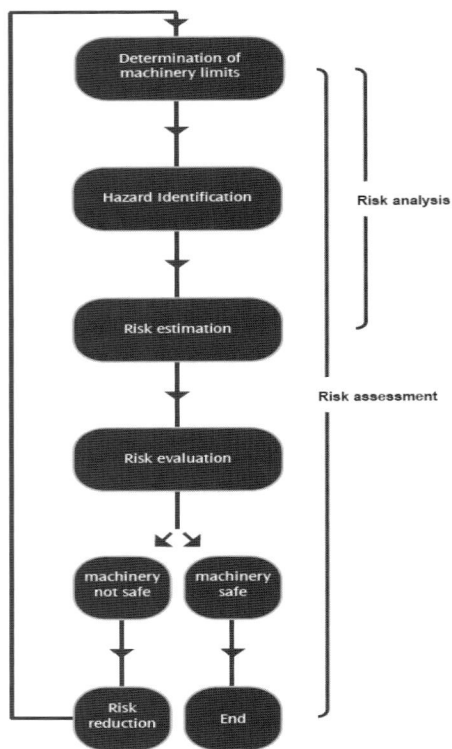

Figure C6-2: Risk assessment. *Source: Rockwell Automation.*

Purpose of CE marking and the relevance of the CE mark

DECLARATION OF CE MARKING

The purpose of CE marking is to provide a visible declaration by the manufacturer, or their authorised representative, that the machinery is in conformity with the applicable requirements set out in European Community harmonisation legislation relating to machinery, being the Machinery Directive 2006/42/EC and in the UK the SMSR 2008. Machinery bearing the CE mark will be taken as meeting the requirements and thereby entitled to free circulation throughout the European Economic Area, provided that it does in fact satisfy those requirements. CE marking can only be applied where conformity with essential health and safety requirements (EHSRs) has been determined. By fixing the CE marking the manufacturer indicates that they are taking responsibility for the conformity of the machine. CE Marking consists of a symbol shown below and the last two figures of the year in which the mark is affixed. The letters "CE" are the abbreviation of the French phrase "Conformité Européene", which literally means "European Conformity". The term initially used was "EC Mark" and it was officially replaced by "CE Marking" in the Directive 93/68/EEC in 1993. "CE Marking" is now used in all EU official documents. "CE Mark" is also in use, but it is NOT the official term.

CE marking must be affixed in a visible, legible and indelible manner in the vicinity of the name of the manufacturer or their authorised representative. It would not usually be smaller than 5mm and the component parts need to be in proportion. It is an offence to affix the CE marking on a machine unless it satisfies the EHSRs and is, in fact, safe. It is also an offence to affix any mark that can be confused with CE marking.

CE marking should not be affixed to a machine for which a Declaration of Incorporation has been issued.

Figure C6-3: CE Mark.
Source: Department of Business Innovation and Skills.

SELECTION AND INTEGRATION OF WORK EQUIPMENT IN THE WORKPLACE

When an employer selects a suitable piece of work equipment, there is often a heavy reliance on information and assurances provided by the manufacturer or supplier. Under the Supply of Machinery (Safety) Regulations (SMSR) 2008 the manufacturer and/or supplier of machinery for use in the workplace is required to ensure that the machinery supplied is safe.

These regulations implement into UK law the EU Machinery Directive 2006 (2006/42/EC) and builds on the requirements of Regulation 6 of the Health and Safety at Work etc Act (HASAWA) 1974. SMSR 2008 states that a manufacturer or distributor may not supply relevant machinery for use within the European Community (Union) unless it is safe and, in particular:

- It satisfies the essential health and safety requirements.
- The technical file has been compiled and made available.
- Information required to operate it safely is provided for example operating instructions.
- The appropriate conformity assessment procedure has been followed.
- An EC Declaration of Conformity has been drawn up.
- The CE marking has been properly affixed to the machinery.
- It is in fact safe.

The requirements are similar, but slightly different, for "partly completed machinery", parts of machines designed to be used with or incorporated into other machinery. Partly completed machinery must have a declaration of incorporation instead of a declaration of conformity.

Selection of work equipment

The Provision and Use of Work Equipment Regulations (PUWER) 1998, Regulation 10 - Conformity with community requirements, places a duty on the employer to ensure that work equipment, including machinery, conforms to UK legislation that gives effect to EU Directives. In the case of machinery, the UK legislation it needs to conform to is the SMSR 2008, which gives effect to the EU Machinery Directive 2006/42/EC.

This will help to ensure the risks associated with the machinery have been taken into account and that it meets the essential health and safety requirements. Assertion of conformity by the manufacturer is identified by declarations and visualised by CE marking. However, this is not an absolute guarantee that it complies as it is only the manufacturer's, or their representative's, assessment. In addition, the particular use the employer is putting the machine to may fall outside the declaration parameters established by the manufacturer in the declaration process.

Integration of work equipment

Work equipment obtained by an employer may be integrated with other work equipment to form an assembly of machines, for example, a packing machine combined with a labelling machine. In a similar way, partly complete machinery may be made up into an assembly of machines. In such cases, there is a duty on the employer to establish that the work equipment making up the assembly of machines, to the extent that it can, conforms to legislative requirements and satisfy the EHSRs.

The safety of the assembly of machines depends not only on the constituent units, but on the interface and interaction between them. The person creating the assembly of machines is considered to be the manufacturer of the assembly of machines; it is therefore incumbent on the employer to ensure that the assembly of machines also complies with requirements of the supply of machinery legislation and essential health and safety requirements. They are then responsible for establishing any declarations and CE marking.

Conformity assessments and the use of harmonised standards

ESSENTIAL HEALTH AND SAFETY REQUIREMENTS FOR MACHINERY

Various product Directives are produced by the European Community to define and control the standards of products manufactured for use within the European Community. They do this by setting out 'Essential Health and Safety Requirements' (EHSR).

These are the features of the product that when it is manufactured will make it safe and healthy for supply into the European Community. The essential health and safety requirements of machinery are set out in Annex 1 of the EU Machinery Directive 2006/42/EC and are listed in Schedule 2 of the SMSR 2008.

The requirements are set out in such a way that they express principles of health and safety and though they are quite specific they do not express how they may be technically fulfilled - this is left to the designer and manufacturer in the first instance.

When applying the essential health and safety requirements it is possible to take account of technical and economic limitations at the time of construction. Conformity with specified published British/European standards (transposed harmonised standards) will be presumed to comply with essential health and safety requirements.

ELEMENT C6 - WORK EQUIPMENT (WORKPLACE MACHINERY)

Section	Element (of essential health and safety requirement)	Relevant
1.1	**General remarks**	
1.1.1	Definitions	
1.1.2	Principles of safety integration	
1.1.3	Materials and products	
1.1.4	Lighting	
1.1.5	Design of machinery to facilitate its handling	
1.1.6	Ergonomics	
1.1.7	Operating positions	
1.1.8	Seating	
1.2	**Control systems**	
1.2.1	Safety and reliability of control systems	
1.2.2	Control devices	
1.2.3	Starting	
1.2.4	Stopping	
1.2.5	Selection of control or operating modes	
1.2.6	Failure of power supply	
1.3.	**Protection against mechanical hazards**	
1.3.1	Risk of loss of stability	
1.3.2	Risk of break-up during operation	
1.3.3	Risks due to falling or ejected objects	
1.3.4	Risks due to surfaces, edges or angles	
1.3.5	Risk related to combined machinery	
1.3.6	Risks related to variations in operating conditions	
1.3.7	Risks related to moving parts	
1.3.8	Choice of protection against risks arising from moving parts	
1.3.9	Risks of uncontrolled movements	
1.4	**Required characteristics of guards and protective devices**	
1.4.1	General requirements	
1.4.2	Special requirements for guards	
1.4.3	Special requirements for protective devices	
1.5	**Risks due to other hazards**	
1.5.1	Electricity supply	
1.5.2	Static electricity	
1.5.3	Energy supply other than electricity	
1.5.4	Errors of fitting	
1.5.5	Extreme temperature	
1.5.6	Fire	
1.5.7	Explosion	

Section	Element (of essential health and safety requirement)	Relevant
1.5.8	Noise	
1.5.9	Vibrations	
1.5.10	Radiation	
1.5.11	External radiation	
1.5.12	Laser equipment	
1.5.13	Emissions of hazardous materials and substances	
1.5.14	Risk of being trapped in a machine	
1.5.15	Risk of slipping, tripping or falling	
1.5.16	Lighting	
1.6	***Maintenance***	
1.6.1	Machinery maintenance	
1.6.2	Access to operating positions and servicing points	
1.6.3	Isolation of energy sources	
1.6.4	Operator intervention	
1.6.5	Cleaning of internal parts	
1.7	***Information***	
1.7.1	Information and warnings on the machinery	
1.7.2	Warning of residual risks	
1.7.3	Marking of machinery	
1.7.4	Instructions	
2	***Supplementary EHSR for certain categories of machine***	
3	***Supplementary EHSR to offset hazards due to mobility of machinery***	
4	***Supplementary EHSR offset hazards due to lifting operations***	
5	***Supplementary EHSR for machine intended for underground work***	
6	***Supplementary EHSR for machinery presenting particular hazards due to the lifting of persons***	

Figure C6-4: Essential health and safety requirements checklist. *Source: SMSR 2008/RMS.*

The responsibility for demonstrating that machinery complies with the SMSR 2008 and the EU Directive rests on the 'responsible person' applying the essential health and safety requirements.

Responsible person under SMSR 2008

This includes:

- The manufacturer of the machinery.
- The manufacturer's appointed representative in the community.
- The person who first supplies the relevant machinery.

The term manufacturer includes any person who assembles machinery or parts thereof.

Machinery under SMSR 2008

The definition of "machinery" is set out in Regulation 4 of the SMSR 2008 and includes:

a) Assemblies that fall within the following descriptions:

"1) An assembly, fitted with or intended to be fitted with a drive system other than directly applied human or animal effort, consisting of linked parts or components, at least one of which moves and which are, joined together for a specific application.

ELEMENT C6 - WORK EQUIPMENT (WORKPLACE MACHINERY)

2) *An assembly as referred to in sub-paragraph 1 paragraph 1 missing only the components to connect it on site or to sources of energy and motion.*
3) *An assembly as referred to in sub-paragraph 1 or 2 ready to be installed and able to function as it stands only if mounted on a means of transport or installed in a building or structure.*
4) *Assemblies of machinery as referred to in sub-paragraphs 1, 2 and 3 or partly completed machinery which in order to achieve the same end are arranged and controlled so that they function as an integral whole.*
5) *An assembly of linked parts or components at least one of which moves and which are joined together, intended for lifting loads and whose only power source is directly applied human effort".*

b) Interchangeable equipment, which are devices assembled with machinery or tractor by operators in order to change its function, but not tools.
c) Components that fulfil a safety function and are placed on the market independently, which are not necessary for the machine to function. For example, protective devices designed to detect the presence of people, power-operated interlocking guards, emergency stop devices, two-hand control devices, extraction systems for machinery emissions, monitoring devices for loading and movement control in lifting machinery, restraint systems to keep people on their seats, roll-over protective structures (ROPS), falling-object protective structures (FOPS).
d) Lifting accessories, for example, lifting slings.
e) Chains, ropes and webbing which is part of lifting equipment or lifting accessories.
f) Removable mechanical transmission devices.

The term machinery also relates to partly completed machinery intended to be incorporated into other machinery.

Particular attention should be paid to those assemblies of machinery as set out in Schedule 2, Part 4 (Annex IV) of SMSR 2008 "Categories of machinery to which one of the procedures referred to in Regulation 11 or 12 must be applied".

These include circular saws (single or multi-blade), band saws and other sawing machinery, spindle moulding machinery, presses (including press-brakes), cartridge operated and other such dangerous machinery that requires special consideration when designing, building and applying the CE mark.

CONFORMITY ASSESSMENTS

There are three methods of conformity assessment under the SMSR 2008, with the choice of method available to the responsible person being dependent, for the most part, on whether the machinery in question falls within Schedule 2, Part 4 of SMSR 2008, which reflects Annex 4 of the EU Machinery Directive 2006/42/EC.

For machinery:

- Not included in Schedule 2, Part 4 of SMSR 2008 (Annex 4), or included in it but manufactured wholly in accordance with published harmonised standards, see procedure 1 - Assessment of conformity with internal checks on manufacture.
- Included in Schedule 2, Part 4 of SMSR 2008 (Annex 4) but either not manufactured wholly in conformity with published harmonised standards or manufactured to be in conformity but not opting to use procedure 1, see procedure 2 - European Community (EC) type-examination.

Included in Schedule 2, Part 4 of SMSR 2008 (Annex 4) and manufactured using a full quality assurance system, see procedure 3 - Full quality assurance.

In the case of each procedure, there is a requirement to draw up a technical file, establish a declaration of conformity and affix a CE marking. Unless the machinery is partly complete, in which case technical information is gathered for adding to a technical file, a declaration of incorporation is established instead and CE marking not applied.

Please **see figure ref C6-6,** which is a diagram that summarises the procedures set out in Articles 12 and 13 of the EU Machinery Directive 2006/42/EC, the annex references are those in the Directive, for the placing on the market of machinery and partly completed machinery.

For the purposes of the UK and conformity with the SMSR 2008, Schedule 2 transposes these requirements into parts containing the same relevant number as the annexes of the Machinery Directive, i.e. Annex VII of the EU Machinery Directive 2006/42/EC corresponds to Part 7 of Schedule 2 of the SMSR 2008.

Machinery type	Conditions	Appropriate conformity assessment procedure
Regulation 10 - Machinery *not* referred to in Schedule 2, Part 4 of SMSR 2008 *(Annex IV)*.	None.	*Conformity assessment procedure with internal checks* on the manufacture of machinery prescribed in Part 8 of Schedule 2 of SMSR 2008 (Annex VIII).
Regulation 11 - Schedule 2, Part 4 of SMSR 2008 *(Annex IV) machinery* manufactured fully in accordance with published harmonised standards and fully covered by such standards.	(i) That the machinery *is* manufactured in accordance with published harmonised standards; *and* (ii) That the published harmonised standards in accordance with which it is manufactured *cover all* the applicable essential health and safety requirements.	(a) *Conformity assessment procedure with internal checks* on the manufacture of machinery prescribed in Part 8 of Schedule 2 of SMSR 2008 (Annex VIII); *or* (b) *EC type-examination procedure* prescribed in Part 9 of Schedule 2 of SMSR 2008 (Annex IX) and the internal checks on the manufacture of machinery prescribed in Part 8 of Schedule 2 of SMSR 2008 (Annex VIII), point 3; *or* (c) *Full quality assurance procedure* prescribed in Part 10 of Schedule 2 of SMSR 2008 (Annex X).
Regulation 12 - Schedule 2, Part 4 of SMSR 2008 *(Annex IV) machinery not* manufactured fully in accordance with published harmonised standards or not fully covered by such standards.	(i) That the machinery is *not* manufactured in accordance with the published harmonised standards which relate to it; *or* (ii) That the machinery is only *partly* manufactured in accordance with the published harmonised standards which relate to it; *or* (iii) That the published harmonised standards in accordance with which the machinery is manufactured do *not cover all* the applicable essential health and safety requirements; *or* (iv) That *no* harmonised standards exist for the machinery.	(a) *EC type-examination procedure* prescribed in Part 9 of Schedule 2 of SMSR 2008 (Annex IX) and the internal checks on the manufacture of machinery prescribed in Part 8 of Schedule 2 of SMSR 2008 (Annex VIII), point 3; *or* (b) *Full quality assurance procedure* prescribed in Part 10 of Schedule 2 of SMSR 2008 (Annex X).

Figure C6-5: Conformity assessments applicable to different types of machinery.

Source: SMSR 2008/RMS.

ELEMENT C6 - WORK EQUIPMENT (WORKPLACE MACHINERY)

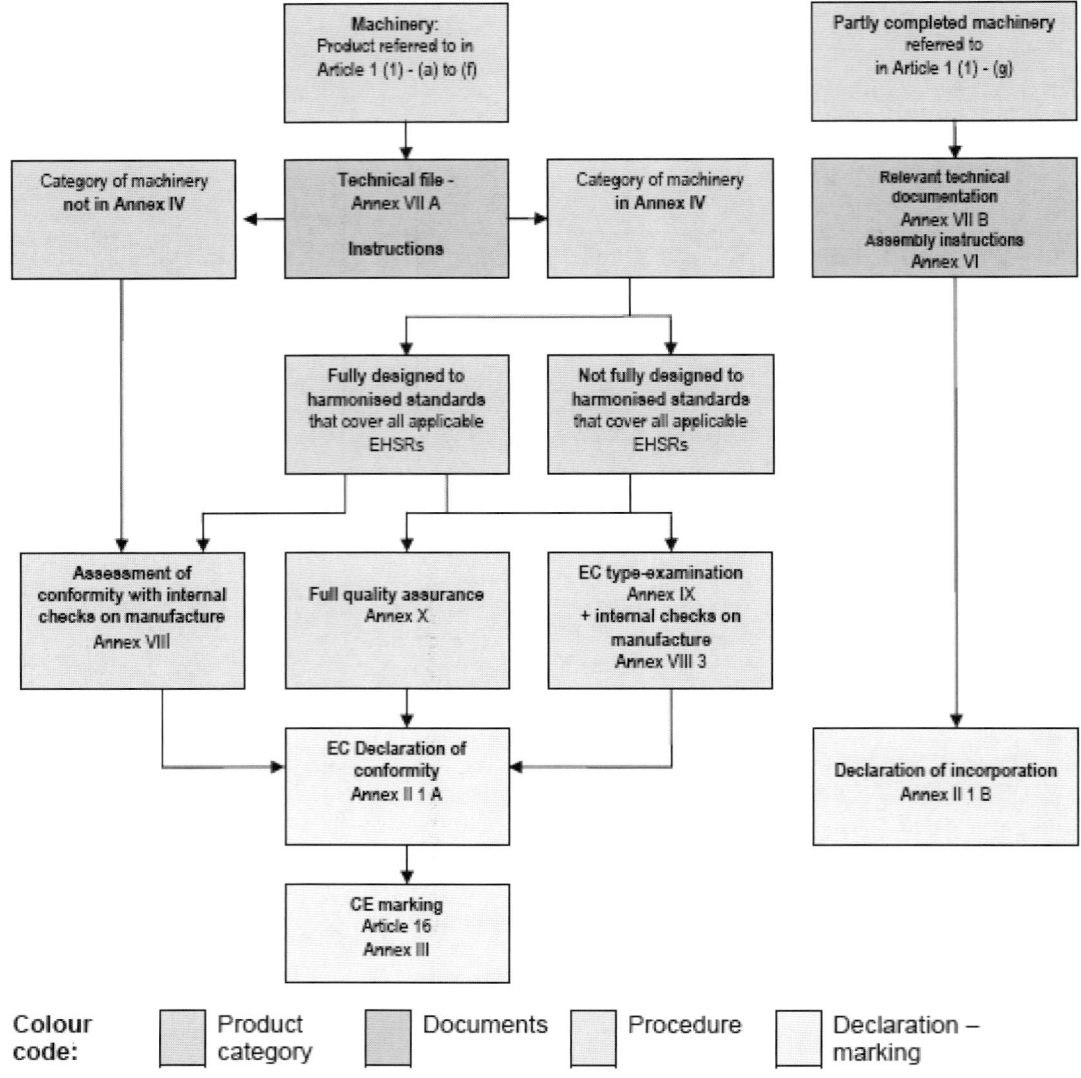

Figure C6-6: Procedures for conformity.   Source: Department of Business Innovation and Skills.

Procedure 1 - Assessment of conformity with internal checks on manufacture (self assessment) - Part 8 of Schedule 2 of SMSR 2008 (Annex VIII)

A responsible person, applying the general principles and having regard to standards, undertakes a risk assessment against the essential health and safety requirements (EHSRs), produces a technical file having applied the necessary internal checks, produces a Declaration of Conformity and affixes the CE marking to the product, thus declaring compliance to the SMSR 2008.

Declaration of incorporation

Where the machinery is incomplete and is intended for incorporation into other machinery or assembly with other machinery to constitute machinery covered by the SMSR 2008, the responsible person must draw up a Declaration of Incorporation for each machine. In this case the partly complete machine must *not* be provided with a CE marking. The declaration should state that the equipment must not be put into service until the machine into which it has been incorporated has been declared to be in conformity. This option is not available for interchangeable equipment modifying the function of the machine or machinery that can function independently.

Procedure 2 - European Community (EC) type-examination (declaration of type approval) - Part 9 of Schedule 2 of SMSR 2008 (Annex IX)

Where a responsible person makes a machine referred to in Part 4 of the SMSR 2008 (Annex 4) that is not manufactured wholly in accordance with published harmonised standards, i.e. those published in the Official Journal of The European Communities, or transposed harmonised standards, those transposed into UK standards, they will be required to have it assessed by a 'notified body'. If compliant, the notified body will issue an EC-type examination certificate. This procedure is also an option open to a manufacturer for machinery that is wholly manufactured to a published harmonised standard. This is the procedure whereby a notified body ascertains and certifies that an example of the machinery satisfies the relevant provisions of the SMSR 2008 and therefore the EU Machinery Directive 2006/42/EC. The procedure requires the following to be included in an application.

- Details of the manufacturer, or representative in the European Community, and place of manufacture.
- A written declaration that the application has not been submitted to another notified body.
- A technical file.
- A representative example of the machine or a statement of where it may be examined.

The notified body will:

- Examine the technical file and verify its appropriateness and relation to the example machine.
- Examine the example machine to determine if it has been manufactured in accord with the technical file, check standards used (if applicable) have been properly applied or examine and test to determine compliance with EHSR where published harmonised standards were not met.

If the example complies, an EC type-examination certificate is issued. The certificate must include the name and address of the manufacturer and the manufacturer's authorised representative, the data necessary for identifying the approved type, the conclusions of the examination and the conditions to which its issue may be subject. Conditions may be applied to the certificate and it will have sufficient information with it such that the approved example machine may be identified. If a certificate is refused, the notified body informs other notified bodies. The responsible person must inform the notified body of modifications; they will consider the modifications and determine if the current certificate remains valid. The manufacturer and the notified body must retain a copy of the certificate, the technical file and all relevant documents for a period of 15 years from the date of issue of the certificate. The manufacturer must request from the notified body the review of the validity of the EC type-examination certificate every five years. If the notified body finds that the certificate remains valid, taking into account the state of the art, it will renew the certificate for a further five years.

Procedure 3 - Full quality assurance - Part 10 of Schedule 2 of SMSR 2008 (Annex X)

For machinery referred to in Part 4 of the SMSR 2008 (Annex 4) a manufacturer that has a full quality assurance system such as BS EN ISO 9001:2008 may produce such machinery under the system and declare conformity. The manufacturer must operate an approved quality system for design, manufacture, final inspection and testing. An application for assessment includes:

- Details of the manufacturer.
- Where the machinery is designed, manufactured, inspected, tested and stored.
- Technical file and sample of the machine.
- Quality system documentation.
- A written declaration that the application has not been submitted to another notified body.

The quality assurance system is approved by a notified body that has been accredited for this type of activity by UKAS and is subject to surveillance and audit by the notified body. The manufacturer is then able to issue relevant declaration documentation and affix CE marking. Where the full quality assurance procedure has been applied, the CE marking must be followed by the identification number of the notified body.

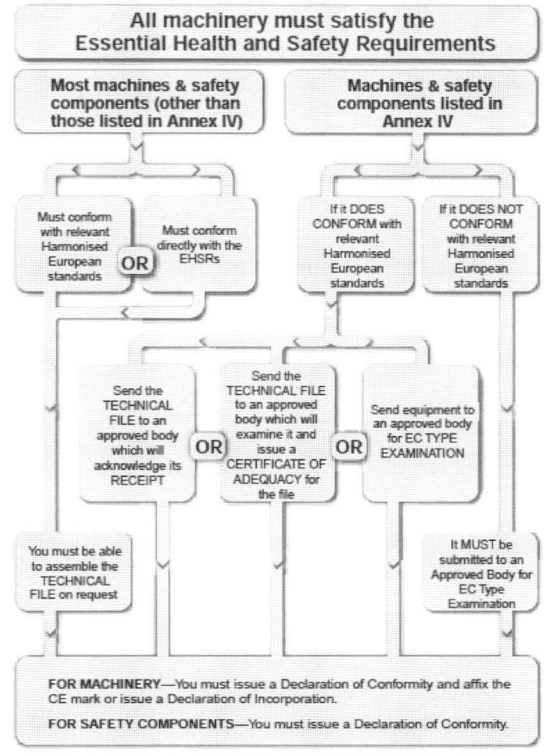

Figure C6-7: Overview procedure for the machinery directive. *Source: Rockwell Automation.*

ELEMENT C6 - WORK EQUIPMENT (WORKPLACE MACHINERY)

USE OF HARMONISED STANDARDS

Harmonised standards

These are non-binding technical specifications adopted by one of the European Standard Organisations (CEN, CENELEC or ETSI) on the basis of a remit issued by the European Commission. These harmonised standards, that cover all the EHSRs, are published in the Official Journal of The European Communities. Where these standards have also been published as identically worded national standards ('transposed harmonised standards') and machinery is made in conformance to them they will be presumed to comply with the EHSRs covered by the European harmonised standards.

The European Committee for Standardisation (CEN) and the European Committee for Electro-technical Standardisation (CENELEC) have been mandated to look at all existing machinery standards to ensure that where necessary they are revised to meet the requirements of the EU Machinery Directive 2006/42/EC. The European Commission periodically publishes in the Official Journal of The European Communities lists of standards that comply with the EU Machinery Directive 2006/42/EC [this list also may carry a note where a Standard has been found not to comply with one or more of the EHSRs].

The standards in support of the EU Machinery Directive 2006/42/EC are of three types. The first, A type, comprises general principles for the design of machinery. The second, B type, covers specific safety devices and ergonomic aspects of machinery. The third, C type, deals with specific classes of machinery by calling up the appropriate standards from the first two types and addressing requirements specific to the class. Only the latter can give a presumption of conformity with the EU Machinery Directive 2006/42/EC, because it defines criteria at a sufficiently detailed level.

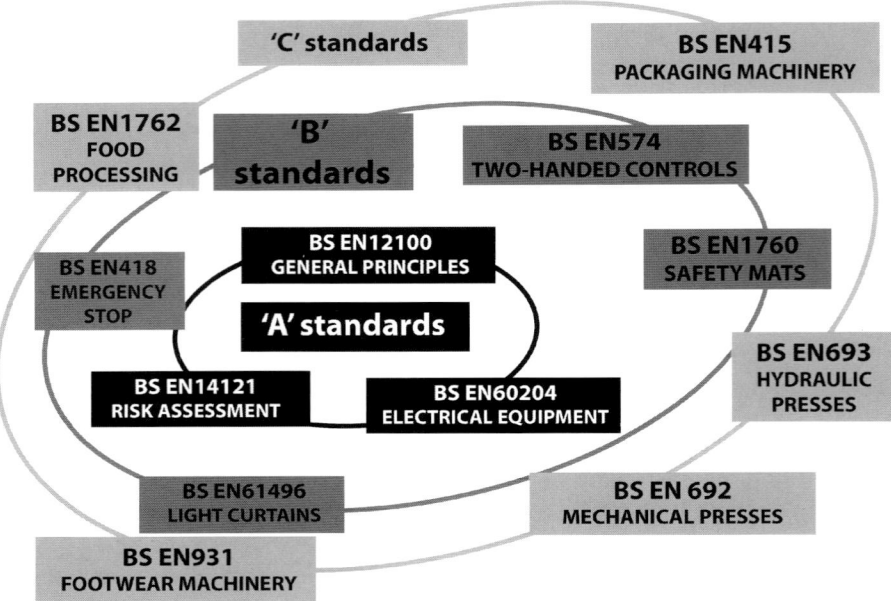

Figure C6-8: Planetary chart - A B and C standards.   Source: RMS.

Conformity assessment for Annex IV machinery

For machinery listed in Schedule 2, Part 4 of the SMSR 2008, drawn from Annex IV of the EU Machinery Directive 2006/42/EC, which expresses a list of machinery posing special hazards, the conformity assessment process can be slightly different. The list of machinery includes circular saws, portable chain saws, presses for the cold working of metal and injection moulding machines. For listed machinery that is *manufactured in conformity with transposed harmonised standards* the responsible person may choose between:

- Procedure 1 - assessment of conformity with internal checks on manufacture.
- Procedure 2 - EC type-examination.
- Procedure 3 - Full quality assured.

For machinery that is *not manufactured in full conformity with transposed harmonised standards* the responsible person must use procedure 2 - EC type-examination or procedure 3 - full quality assurance.

Schedule 2, Part 4 of SMSR 2008 - Annex IV: Categories of machinery to which one of the procedures referred to in regulation 11 or 12 must be applied	
1.	Circular saws (single or multi-blade) for working with wood and material with similar physical characteristics or for working with meat and material with similar physical characteristics, of the following types:
1.1.	Sawing machinery with fixed blade(s) during cutting, having a fixed bed or support with manual feed of the workpiece or with a demountable power feed.

1.2.	Sawing machinery with fixed blade(s) during cutting, having a manually operated reciprocating saw-bench or carriage.
1.3.	Sawing machinery with fixed blade(s) during cutting, having a built-in mechanical feed device for the workpiece, with manual loading and/or unloading.
1.4.	Sawing machinery with movable blade(s) during cutting, having mechanical movement of the blade, with manual loading and/or unloading.
2.	Hand-fed surface planning machinery for woodworking.
3.	Thicknessers for one-side dressing having a built-in mechanical feed device, with manual loading and/or unloading for woodworking.
4.	Band-saws with manual loading and/or unloading for working with wood and material with similar physical characteristics or for working with meat and material with similar physical characteristics, of the following types:
4.1.	Sawing machinery with fixed blade(s) during cutting, having a fixed or reciprocating-movement bed or support for the workpiece.
4.2.	Sawing machinery with blade(s) assembled on a carriage with reciprocating motion.
5.	Combined machinery of the types referred to in points 1 to 4 and point 7 of this Annex, for working with wood and material with similar physical characteristics.
6.	Hand-fed tenoning machinery with several tool holders for woodworking.
7.	Hand-fed vertical spindle moulding machinery for working with wood and material with similar physical characteristics.
8.	Portable chainsaws for woodworking.
9.	Presses, including press-brakes, for the cold working of metals, with manual loading and/or unloading, whose movable working parts may have a travel exceeding 6 mm and a speed exceeding 30 mm/s.
10.	Injection or compression plastics-moulding machinery with manual loading or unloading.
11.	Injection or compression rubber-moulding machinery with manual loading or unloading.
12.	Machinery for underground working of the following types:
12.1.	Locomotives and brake-vans.
12.2.	Hydraulic-powered roof supports.
13.	Manually loaded trucks for the collection of household refuse incorporating a compression mechanism.
14.	Removable mechanical transmission devices including their guards.
15.	Guards for removable mechanical transmission devices.
16.	Vehicle servicing lifts.
17.	Devices for the lifting of persons or of persons and goods involving a hazard of falling from a vertical height of more than three metres.
18.	Portable cartridge-operated fixing and other impact machinery.
19.	Protective devices designed to detect the presence of persons.
20.	Power-operated interlocking movable guards designed to be used as safeguards in machinery referred to in points 9, 10 and 11 of this Annex.
21.	Logic units to ensure safety functions.
22.	Roll-over protective structures (ROPS).
23.	Falling-object protective structures (FOPS).

Figure C6-9: Categories of machine posing special hazards.   *Source: Supply of Machinery (Safety) Regulations (SMSR) 2008.*

TECHNICAL FILE

Before machinery is placed on the market or put into service the responsible person must compile a technical file. The technical file must demonstrate that the machinery complies with the provisions of the EU Machinery Directive 2006/42/EC. It must cover the design, manufacture and operation of the machinery to the extent necessary for the purposes of conformity assessment.

ELEMENT C6 - WORK EQUIPMENT (WORKPLACE MACHINERY)

The requirements for a technical file are set out in Schedule 2, Part 7 "Annex VII: Technical files" of SMSR 2008.

A technical file should include the following:

"(a) A construction file including:

- A general description of the machinery.
- The overall drawing of the machinery and drawings of the control circuits, as well as the pertinent descriptions and explanations necessary for understanding the operation of the machinery.
- Full detailed drawings, accompanied by any calculation notes, test results, certificates, etc., required to check the conformity of the machinery with the essential health and safety requirements.
- The documentation on risk assessment demonstrating the procedure followed, including:
   (i) A list of the essential health and safety requirements which apply to the machinery.
   (ii) The description of the protective measures implemented to eliminate identified hazards or to reduce risks and, when appropriate, the indication of the residual risks associated with the machinery.
- The standards and other technical specifications used, indicating the essential health and safety requirements covered by these standards.
- Any technical report giving the results of the tests carried out either by the manufacturer or by a body chosen by the responsible person.
- A copy of the instructions for the machinery.
- Where appropriate, the declaration of incorporation for included partly completed machinery and the relevant assembly instructions for such machinery.
- Where appropriate, copies of the EC declaration of conformity of machinery or other products incorporated into the machinery.
- A copy of the EC declaration of conformity.

(b) For series manufacture, the internal measures that will be implemented to ensure that the machinery remains in conformity with the provisions of the EU Machinery Directive 2006/42/EC".

The manufacturer must carry out necessary research and tests on components, fittings or the completed machinery to determine whether by its design or construction it is capable of being assembled and put into service safely. The relevant reports and results shall be included in the technical file.

The technical file does not have to include detailed plans or any other specific information as regards the sub-assemblies used for the manufacture of the machinery unless knowledge of them is essential for verification of conformity with the essential health and safety requirements.

The technical file does not have to be permanently available in material form, but must be capable of being assembled and made available within a suitable period of time. The technical file must be made available to the enforcement authorities and the competent authorities of any other European Economic Area (EEA) state for at least 10 years following the date of manufacture of the machinery or, in the case of series manufacture, of the last unit produced.

DECLARATION OF CONFORMITY/INCORPORATION

Declaration of conformity

The requirements for declaration of conformity are set out in Schedule 2, Part 2 "Annex II: Declarations" of SMSR 2008. The declaration of conformity and translations of it must be drawn up under the same conditions as instructions for the machinery and must be type written or hand written in capital letters.

The declaration relates to the condition in which the machine was placed on the market and excludes components and similar items added by the final user. The declaration accompanies each product and declares that it complies with the relevant health and safety requirements or with the example that underwent type-examination.

Schedule 2, Part 2 "Annex II: Declarations" of SMSR 2008 requires that the EC declaration of conformity contain the following particulars:

a) Business name and full address of the manufacturer and, where appropriate, the manufacturer's authorised representative.
b) Name and address of the person authorised to compile the technical file, which must be established in an EEA state.
c) Description and identification of the machinery, including generic denomination, function, model, type, serial number and commercial name.
d) A sentence expressly declaring that the machinery fulfils all the relevant provisions of the Directive and where appropriate, a similar sentence declaring the conformity with other Directives and/or relevant provisions with which the machinery complies. These references must be those of the texts published in the Official Journal of the European Union.
e) Where appropriate, the name, address and identification number of the notified body which carried out the EC type-examination referred to in Annex IX (Part 9 of Schedule 2) and the number of the EC type-examination certificate.

f) Where appropriate, the name, address and identification number of the notified body which notified the full quality assurance system referred to in Annex X (Part 10 of Schedule 2).
g) Where appropriate, a reference to the published harmonised standards used.
h) Where appropriate, the reference to other technical standards and specifications used.
i) The place and date of the declaration.
j) The identity and signature of the person empowered to draw up the declaration on behalf of the responsible person.
k) The manufacturer of machinery or the manufacturer's authorised representative must keep the original EC declaration of conformity for a period of at least 10 years from the last date of manufacture of the machinery.

Declaration of incorporation

Where the machinery is intended for incorporation into other machinery or an assembly with other machines, for example, an electric motor or a conveyor belt section, a declaration of incorporation is required.

A declaration of incorporation is applicable in the case of relevant machinery that is intended for:

- Incorporation into other machinery.
- Assembly with other machinery.
- Is not interchangeable equipment.
- Cannot function independently.

The responsible person draws up a declaration of incorporation for each machine and no "CE" marking is applied to the machinery. The declaration of incorporation states that the machinery must not be put into service until the machinery that it is incorporated into has been declared to be in conformity with the EHSR.

Figure refs C6-10 and C6-11 show sample EC declarations of conformity/incorporation relating to procedure 1 - Assessment of conformity with internal checks on manufacture. Where procedure 2 - European Community (EC) type-examination - is used the name, address and identification number of the notified body that carried out the EC type-examination and the number of the EC type-examination certificate is added.

Where procedure 3 - full quality assurance - is used the name, address and identification number of the notified body that approved the full quality assurance system is added.

Figure C6-10: EC declaration of conformity.   Source: RMS.

Figure C6-11: EC declaration of incorporation.   Source: RMS.

ELEMENT C6 - WORK EQUIPMENT (WORKPLACE MACHINERY)

C6.2 - Generic hazards

Common machinery hazards in a range of general workplaces

The way people work in relation to machinery can be a major contributory factor in machine related accidents. Care is required in the operation, maintenance and cleaning of machinery and, ideally, written safe procedures/permits should cover all three actions listed.

DRILLS (RADIAL ARMS, PEDESTAL) - MAIN HAZARD OF ENTANGLEMENT

Hazards in setting up radial arm and pedestal drill include:

- Failure to securely guard drive pulleys after speed adjustment, leading to risk of entanglement in the rotating parts and potential to be caught in drawing-in zones where the pulley belt meets the pulley wheel.
- Cuts from handling the drills.
- Failure to tighten the drill bit adequately in the drill chuck, leading to the risk of ejection of the drill when the drill is started and the chuck revolves. A similar hazard exists where the chuck key may be ejected if left in the chuck when the drill is started.

Hazards when operating the radial arm drill and pedestal drill include:

- Entanglement of clothing, hair or pendant jewellery in the rotating parts, the drill, chuck and any exposed spindle.
- Puncture of the hand, when the drill is brought down onto the hand instead of the workpiece.
- Ejected waste material (swarf) from the drilling, which could penetrate the eye, cut the hand or arm of the drill operator or gets caught in clothing and increases the risk of entanglement.

CIRCULAR SAWS - MAIN HAZARD OF CUTTING

Hazards in the use of circular saws include:

- Failure to securely guard drive pulleys after speed adjustment, leading to risk of entanglement in the rotating parts and potential to be caught in drawing-in zones where the pulley belt meets the pulley wheel.
- Cuts from handling the saw blades.
- Entanglement of clothing, hair or pendant jewellery in the rotating parts, the blade and any exposed spindle.
- Cuts from contact with the rotating saw blade.
- Ejected waste material from the sawing, which could penetrate the eye.

GUILLOTINES - MAIN HAZARD OF SHEAR

Hazards in the use of guillotines include:

- Cuts from contacting the blade when loading material into the guillotine.
- Cuts from the sheering action of the blade passing fixed points on the guillotine.
- Crush injuries from the clamp devices used to hold down the material being guillotined.
- Cuts from handling the material that has been guillotined or waste material.

PAPER SHREDDERS - MAIN HAZARD CUTTING

The hazards from the use of paper shredders include:

- Drawing-in from the rotating action of the cutters.
- Cuts from the cutting action of the cutters.
- Paper dust evolved from the shredding of the paper.

Some of these hazards are more likely to be encountered by people who carry out unauthorised maintenance work.

PHOTOCOPIERS - MAIN HAZARD DRAWING-IN

The hazards from use of photocopiers include:

- Drawing-in from the rotating action of the paper handling rollers.
- Entanglement in the paper handling rollers.
- Hot surfaces where the toner is fused to the paper.

In addition, there are a number of non-mechanical hazards, for example fumes from the fusing process, toner dust that may not have been fused properly, electricity and glare.

These hazards are more likely to be encountered by people who carry out unauthorised maintenance work.

DISC SANDERS - MAIN HAZARD ABRASION

The hazards from use of disc sanders include:

- Abrasion from contact with the abrasive disc. Electricity where the sanders cables have been abraded by the abrasive disc.
- Entanglement in the rotating parts of the disc and any exposed spindle.

The momentum of the rotating parts means that the abrasive disc does not stop immediately, which can lead to inadvertent abrasion of parts of the user or damage to power cables. Other equipment with similar abrasion hazards are belt sanders and abrasive wheels.

ABRASIVE WHEELS - MULTIPLE HAZARDS

The hazards of the use of abrasive wheels include:

- Friction and abrasion, from contact with the rotating abrasive wheel.
- Entanglement in the rotating abrasive wheel.

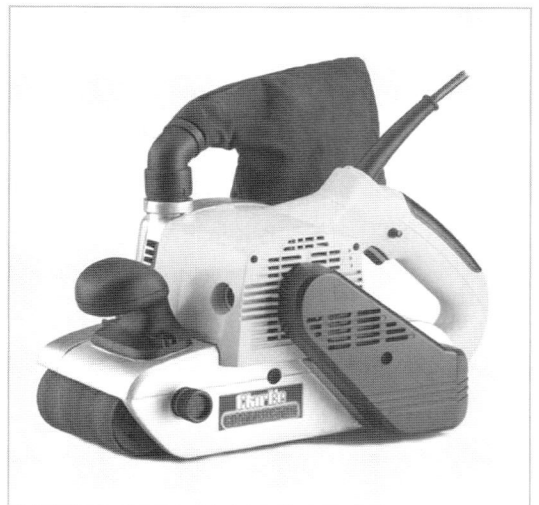

Figure C6-12: Belt sander.   Source: Clarke International.

- Drawing-in of the hands of the user between the rotating abrasive wheel and the fixed work rest.
- Ejection of abraded material or abrasive wheel that could penetrate the eye.
- Ejection of hot particles of abraded material.
- Ejection of the whole piece of material being abraded.
- Rupture and ejection of the abrasive wheel.

LATHES - MAIN HAZARD ENTANGLEMENT

The hazards of the use of lathes include:

- Entanglement in the rotating workpiece or chuck.
- Friction burns or cuts from contact with the rotating workpiece or chuck.
- Drawing-in of the hands of the user between the rotating workpiece and the fixed tool or tool post.
- Ejected waste material (swarf) from the lathe cutting, which could penetrate the eye, cut the hand or arm of the lathe operator or gets caught in clothing and increases the risk of entanglement.
- Ejection of hot pieces of waste material.
- Ejection of the whole workpiece being worked on if it is insecure in the chuck.
- Ejection of the chuck key if it is left in the chuck and the lathe is started.

AUTOMATIC DOORS AND GATES - MAIN HAZARD CRUSH OR IMPACT

The hazards related to doors and gates include:

- Crushing, as the moving part of the system closes towards fixed points, such as the door or gate frame. A similar effect can occur where two doors close together. As a leaf of a door opens it may present a crush hazard as it moves outward towards a fixed point.
- Sheering, as overlapping parts of doors or gates pass over each other or pass over fixed points.
- Impact hazards are created where an automatic door leaf opens out and can then strike someone.
- Drawing-in, where rollers or other similar parts of the door or gate move down guide channels as the door opens or closes. A similar hazard exists with roller doors that create a drawing-in hazard as they wind up to open.
- Entanglement hazards can be created by rotating automatic doors or roller shutter doors as the rotate.

MECHANICAL AND HYDRAULIC PRESSES - MAIN HAZARD CRUSH

The hazards related to mechanical and hydraulic presses include:

- Crushing, as the moving part of the press close towards fixed points, such as where the upper press die is brought together with the lower press die.
- Sheering, as the moving parts of the press, particularly the die, travel over the guides where there may be cutouts in the guides.
- Impact hazards are created where the moving parts of the press can strike someone.
- Entanglement hazards can be created by rotating parts of mechanical presses, such as the crank shaft.
- Ejection of the whole or part of the piece of material being pressed.
- Injection of hydraulic fluid from leaking pressure system.

Similar problems to those highlighted may be relevant when considering the hazards of robotics.

PORTABLE POWER TOOLS

A huge variety of power tools is available, ranging from drills, grinders to more specialist equipment like diamond disc saws or petrol-driven strimmers/brush-cutters.

ELEMENT C6 - WORK EQUIPMENT (WORKPLACE MACHINERY)

Typical injuries are cutting, stabbing, and eye injuries from waste material. Portable tools include equipment powered by battery, petrol and compressed air.

CNC MACHINES

Traditional engineering workshop machinery such as lathes and milling machines may be operated via computer numeric controls (CNC). Rather than relying on the skill of a human operator to control operating parameters and deliver precision products, processes can be partially or completely computerised. Partial control includes microprocessor enhancements that control critical parameters, whilst leaving many control decisions in the hands of the operator, whereas fully programmable CNC machines, which may be used in isolation or as part of an integrated process, with automated feeding and removal of work pieces, fully control the process.

Automation may well increase power ratings, operating speeds etc. leading to potentially greater consequences from the mechanical and non-mechanical hazards present.

Figure C6-13: Example of a CNC machine. *Source: cncmachine-details.info.*

Further hazards may be presented via programming errors or control system faults.

ROBOTICS

The main hazards of robotics are associated with setting up and maintenance. At setting up and maintenance the robotic equipment may make sudden unpredictable movements, leading to risks of impact, crushing, entanglement, shear, cutting, electric shock or burns. At the time of dealing with breakdowns the main hazard is trapped potential energy, which might cause the equipment to cycle, even when isolated from external energy sources, resulting in any of the above injuries.

SUMMARY - MACHINERY HAZARDS

Examples of mechanical hazards	*Examples of machines with this mechanical hazard*	*Examples of non mechanical*
Crushing	Automatic doors and gates or presses	Dust etc
Shear	Guillotine, automatic doors and gates	Radiation
Cutting/severing	Circular saw, paper shredder	Noise
Entanglement	Drills, lathes	Extremes of temperature
Drawing in/trapping	Paper shredder, photocopier, abrasive wheel	Vibration
Impact	Automatic doors and gates or presses	Electricity
Stabbing and puncture	Drilling machine or sewing machine	
Ejection	Grinding wheel - disintegration or sparks, drills	
Injection	Hydraulic or pneumatic presses	
Friction and abrasion	Disc sanders, grinding wheels	

Figure C6-14: Machinery hazards. *Source: RMS.*

The types of generic machinery hazards

MECHANICAL HAZARDS

The main types of mechanical hazards are:
- Crushing.
- Shearing.
- Cutting/severing.
- Entanglement.
- Drawing in/trapping.
- Impact.
- Stabbing/puncture/ejection.
- Friction/abrasion.
- High pressure fluid injection.

Crushing

Caused when part of the body is caught between either two moving parts of machinery or a moving part and a stationary object, for example automatic doors/gates, moving parts of a press or the callipers of a spot welding machine.

Shearing

When two or more machine parts move past one another a shear is created. This can result in a crush injury or even an amputation.

Examples of shearing hazards include guillotines, scissor lifts, and scissor acting mobile elevating work platform and dock levellers.

Figure C6-15: Bench cross-cut circular saw.   *Source: RMS.*

Figure C6-16: Shear.   *Source: RMS.*

Cutting/severing

Saw blades, knives and even rough edges, especially when moving at high speed, can result in serious cuts and even amputation injuries. The dangerous part can appear stationary due to the stroboscopic effect of some light sources.

Examples of cutting action hazards include circular saws, reciprocating saws, slicing machines, abrasive cutting discs, chains (especially chainsaws).

Entanglement

The mere fact that a machine part is revolving can in itself constitute a very real hazard. The risk of entanglement is increased by loose clothing, jewellery, long hair etc.

Examples of rotating action hazards include couplings, drill chucks/ bits, abrasive wheels, flywheels, spindles and shafts (especially those with keys/bolts).

Figure C6-17: Entanglement in chuck of pedestal drill.   *Source: RMS.*

Figure C6-18: Abrasive wheel.   *Source: RMS.*

Drawing in/trapping

Drawings in points are created where parts of machinery rotate towards each other or a fixed point. When a belt runs round a roller a drawing in point is created between the belt and the roller (in the direction of travel). Examples of drawing in/trapping hazards are V-belts, meshing gears, cutters of a paper shredder and conveyors etc.

Impact

Impact hazards are where an object can strike the body, but do not penetrate (unlike stabbing and puncture wounds) or crush it. Automatic moving parts of computer numerically controlled machines or robots may strike someone, similarly the operation of an automatic door may cause an impact with a person.

Stabbing/puncture/ejection

The body may be penetrated by a number of items including:

- Sharp pieces of machinery stabbing or puncturing, such as drilling machines and sewing machines.
- Ejected material, for example waste material (swarf), sparks unsecured material being worked on, broken pieces of machinery, such as a shattered grinding wheel.

Friction/abrasion

Friction burns and abrasion injuries can be caused by coming into contact with rough or relatively smooth surfaces moving at high speed for example a sanding machine, grinding wheel or conveyor belt.

High pressure fluid injection

Injection of fluids through the skin may lead to soft tissue injuries similar to crushing. This is because of the high pressure involved and the fact that this is concentrated over a small area. Air entering the blood stream through the skin may create an embolism, which can be fatal. Examples of equipment that presents hazards of high pressure fluid injection are diesel injectors, spray painting and compressed air jets.

NON-MECHANICAL HAZARDS

BS EN ISO 12100:2010 'Safety of machinery – general principles for design – risk assessment and risk reduction' identifies the main types of non-mechanical hazards as:

- Noise.
- Vibration.
- Electricity.
- Thermal (high/low temperature).
- Radiation.
- Hazardous materials and substances.

Others that may be considered are:

- Falling.
- Collision with equipment.
- Neglecting ergonomic principles.
- Pressure.

Noise

Noise emissions from equipment may be from sources including bearings that are loose or worn, materials falling into or out of equipment as part of the process or from air exhausted from equipment.

Vibration

Vibration may be designed as part of the process or a result of moving parts of the equipment, such as conveyor systems and rotating parts.

Electricity

Electricity hazards may arise from the following sources:

- Power generated electricity at a variety of voltages, often 440v, 230v, 110v. Electricity may be alternating current or direct current. Stored power generated electricity should also be considered; this may be in the form of capacitors.
- Static electricity, for example, from the movement of non-conducting material.
- Chemically derived electricity which is typically used in batteries.

Thermal (high/low temperature)

Many processes rely on the input of high or low temperature as part of the process. In addition, high or low temperature may be evolved by the process, for example, the use of liquefied petroleum gas for fork lift trucks will cause low temperature around the gas cylinder.

Radiation

Radiation may be emitted from processes in a number of forms and may be ionising or non-ionising.

Hazardous materials and substances

Hazardous materials and substances may be part of the process, evolved or introduced along with process materials by mistake, for example, vapours may be released or substances carried on materials from a prior process.

The typical causes of failures

INFLUENCING FACTORS ON MODES OF FAILURE

Stress and strain

The properties of stress and strain relate to the strength and stiffness of a material.

Stress is the load (force) per unit area:

$$S = \frac{F}{A}$$

Where: S = stress
F = force
A = area

The unit of stress is the Newton per square metre (N/m^2) or the Pascal (Pa). This is more usually expressed in meganewtons per square metre (MN/m^2) or Newton's per square millimetre (N/mm^2). Stress is a measure of the **strength** of a material.

Thus a rod that is pulled in tension has a strength which is proportional to its cross sectional area. For example, a rod with a cross sectional area of 4 cm^2 breaks at a pull of 500 MN, so it follows that a rod of the same material of 8 cm^2 cross sectional area will break at a pull of 1,000 MN force.

Strain is a measure of the **stiffness** of a material:

$$\text{Strain} = \frac{\text{change in length}}{\text{original length}}$$

As the units of length are the same they cancel each other out (for example mm/mm), thus strain has no units. The property of the stiffness of a material is the extent to which a material resists being deformed by a force or how springy it is. It is important to note that strength and stiffness is not the same thing. The amount of stress that a piece of solid material (member) is under relates to how **hard** the atoms in the material are being pulled apart, whereas the amount of strain relates to how **far** they are being pulled apart.

Tensile, compressive and shear stresses

Stress can result from a tensile force, a compressive force and from a shear force. Tensile forces are those internal forces that act on a member to pull it apart, whereas compressive forces are those internal forces that push a member together.

Tension

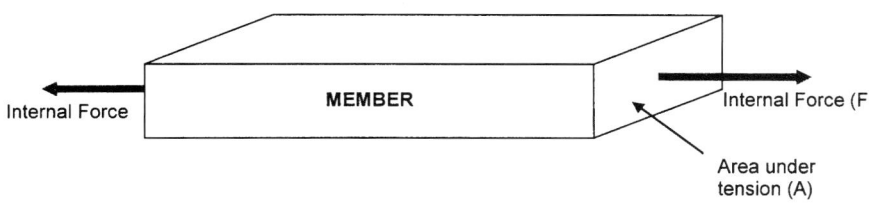

Figure C6-19: Tension.   Source: RMS.

Compression

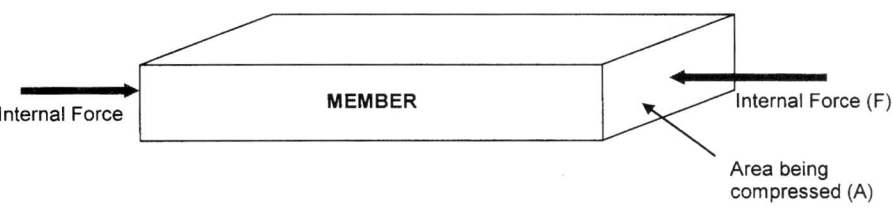

Figure C6-20: Compression.   Source: RMS.

The tensile strength of a material is measured in a tensile testing machine which pulls a test piece apart. Compressive strength is measured by placing a test piece under compressive forces until it fails explosively. In the building industry, designers are usually more concerned with tensile forces than compressive, as most materials are able to withstand compressive forces better.

For example, a brick is able to withstand compressive forces equivalent to a stack of bricks placed on top of it to a height of about 7 km. When compressive forces are applied to a slightly out of true member (for example a scaffold standard), a **bending moment** is created.

A bending moment is a focus of stress at a particular point within the structure **(see section - buckling - later in this element)**. The out of true standard will already have **residual** stresses due to its deformation (i.e. the bend). Residual stresses can be introduced by material defects such as impurities, pitting, corrosion cracks and holes. Residual stresses can also be shape dependant. A rounded corner tends to experience less residual stresses than a square corner. Thus, defects, cracks and sharp changes of shape in materials all represent stress concentrations (residual stresses), which make failure more likely.

ELEMENT C6 - WORK EQUIPMENT (WORKPLACE MACHINERY)

Shear stress

A shear stress is the measure of the tendency for one part of a solid material to slide past the neighbouring part.

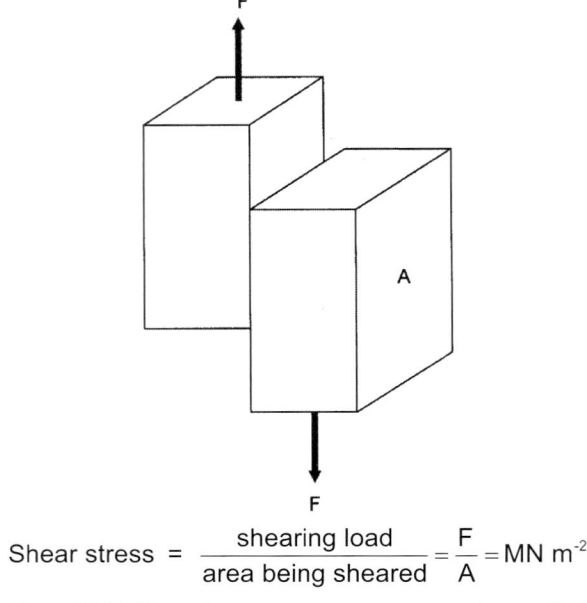

$$\text{Shear stress} = \frac{\text{shearing load}}{\text{area being sheared}} = \frac{F}{A} = MN\ m^{-2}$$

Figure C6-21: Shear stress. Source: RMS.

Stress/strain relationships, yield point, breaking stress, ultimate tensile strength, elasticity and plasticity

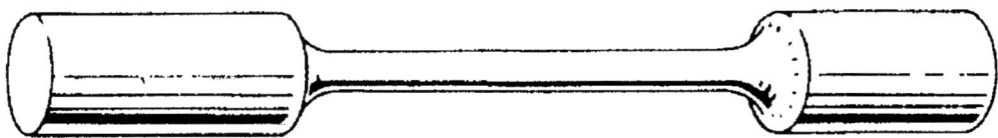

Figure C6-22: A tensile test-piece. Source: Ambiguous.

When a test piece is placed in a tensile testing machine it will produce a load (force) - extension (i.e. change in length) graph. As the initial dimensions of the test piece are known, the data from the tensile test can be translated to a stress strain diagram.

This will reveal a large amount of information about the properties of the material:

- The amount of elastic deformation. This is reversible deformation.
- The degree of permanent plastic deformation. This is not reversible.
- The yield point at which plastic deformation is initiated.
- The stress at which the material breaks, called the breaking stress.
- The maximum tensile stress that the material can support without breaking, called the ultimate tensile strength.

Brittle materials, such as cast iron and glass, display elastic behaviour until they break (i.e. they do not deform plastically). Thus, they will revert back to their original shape once the stress on them is relaxed.

A stress strain graph for most materials will have an initial straight elastic region *(see figure ref C6-23)*. The slope of this elastic region is a measure of the stiffness of the material and is derived from the following formula:

$$E = \frac{\text{stress}}{\text{strain}}$$

Where E is the elastic modulus, or **Young's modulus**, named after Thomas Young (1773-1829). Young's modulus is the ability of a material to withstand elastic deformation (i.e. its stiffness or floppiness).

The stress-strain curve for many materials will also show plastic deformation, in addition to elasticity. This is demonstrated by a curved region on a stress strain graph.

Another term used to describe a material is **ductility**. This is the property, possessed by a typical metal, of being able to be drawn out into a wire.

The tensile stress-strain curve of a hypothetical metal

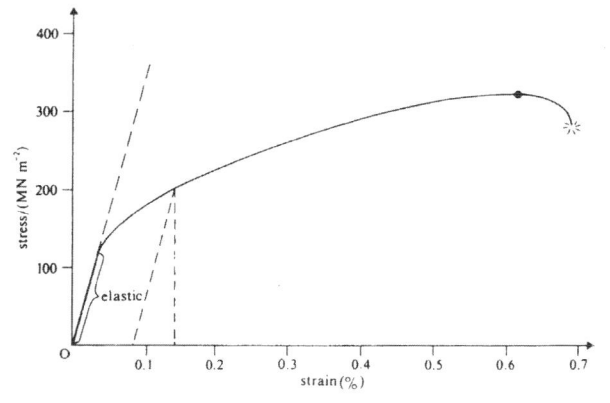

Figure C6-23: Tensile stress-strain curve. *Source: Ambiguous.*

Sketches of the stress-strain curves for cast iron and glass

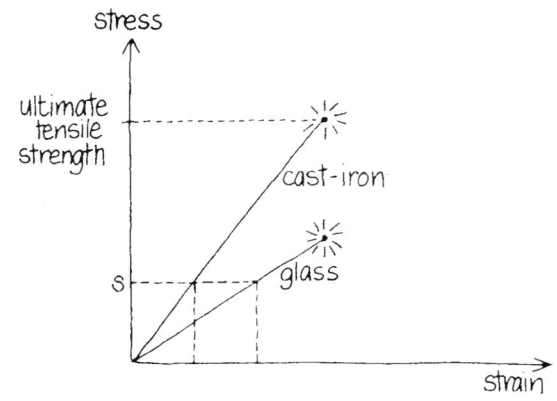

Figure C6-24: Stress-strain curve for iron and glass. *Source: Ambiguous.*

Selected properties of some metallic solids at 20°C (293 K)

Material	Density	Melting Temp	Thermal Conductivity	Electrical Resistivity	Ultimate Tensile Strength	Yield Stress	Ductility (Elongation)	Young's Modulus
	$kg\ m^{-3}$	K	$W\ m^{-1}\ K\ m^{-1}$	$\Omega\ m$	$MN\ m^{-2}$	$MN\ m^{-2}$	%	$GN\ m^{-2}$
Iron, pure	7870	1810	80	9.71	210	120	40	211
Steel, mild	7860	1700	63	12	690	350	20	212
Copper, pure	8960	1356	385	1.67	215	45	60	130
Zinc	7170	693	111	5.92	115	25	25	105

Figure C6-25: Properties of some metallic solids. *Source: Ambiguous.*

Selected properties of some non-metallic solids at 20°C (293 K)

Material	Density	Melting Temp	Thermal Conductivity	Electrical Resistivity	Ultimate Tensile Strength	Ductility (Elongation)	Young's Modulus
	$kg\ m^{-3}$	K	$W\ m^{-1}\ K\ m^{-1}$	$\Omega\ m$	$MN\ m^{-2}$	%	$GN\ m^{-2}$
Carbon, diamond	3300	Λ	20	$\sim 10^{12}$	-	0	1200
Concrete	2400	Λ	0.1	-	~5	0	14
Glass, plate	2500	1400	1.0	$\sim 10^{5}$	~100	0	71
Nylon	1150	470	0.25	$\sim 10^{16}$	70	60-300	1.5
Polythene	920	410	0.2	$\sim 10^{16}$	13	400-800	0.2

Figure C6-26: Properties of some non-metallic solids. *Source: Ambiguous.*

Concrete and diamond breaks down by, for example, charring or burning rather than melting. Dashes indicate data not available. The main modes of failure of structural components are:

- Metal fatigue.
- Ductile failure.
- Brittle failure.
- Buckling.
- Corrosion.
- Wear.
- Creep.

METAL FATIGUE

Notches, holes and irregularities within a material promote the formation of cracks. Providing the crack is below a 'critical length' it will not extend, because making it spread requires too much energy.

ELEMENT C6 - WORK EQUIPMENT (WORKPLACE MACHINERY)

Metal fatigue occurs because the accumulating effects of fluctuating loads promote slow changes in the crystalline structure of the metal. Tiny cracks, which are difficult to detect, then start to extend very slowly through the metal until they reach critical length. The cracks then speed up their extension and run across the material, leading to failure. Prior to rupture, fatigue failure may be practically impossible to spot with the naked eye. The effect of metal fatigue was illustrated in 1953 and 1954 when two Comet aircraft crashed, due to metal fatigue. A modern aircraft is basically a cylindrical pressure vessel, which is pressurised and relaxed each time the aircraft takes off and lands. In the two accidents involving the Comet aircraft cracks started from the same small hole in the fuselage and spread very slowly and undetected until they reached critical length.

The skin of the aircraft's fuselage then tore catastrophically apart and exploded. The aluminium alloy used in the design was particularly susceptible to metal fatigue. As previously stated, fluctuating stresses are the main cause of metal fatigue. Metal fatigue is **promoted** by:

- Static tensile stresses.
- Stress concentration areas such as holes, notches, welds and cracks.
- Corrosive environments.
- Low tensile strength materials such as low tensile steels that have poor fatigue strength, although high tensile steel is sensitive to stress concentrations.

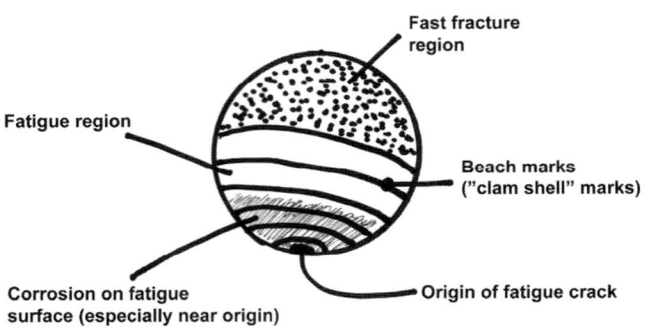

Figure C6-27: Metal fatigue. *Source: RMS.*

Prevention of metal fatigue relies on:

- The reduction of stress concentrations.
- The reduction of fluctuating stresses.

DUCTILE

The property of ductility is the amount of plastic deformation that can take place before fracture. This property allows ductile materials to be shaped (for example a mild steel body panel in a car). The adjacent atoms within the material slide over each other rather than come apart, as they do in brittle failure *(see brittle failure below)*. Ductile failure almost always occurs as the result of a single stress overload to a ductile material. These may be tensile or compressive forces and involve substantial plastic deformation prior to fracture and thus usually shows advance warning. Materials, such as steel, may become more ductile as temperature rises and may then become subject to ductile failure.

BRITTLE FAILURE

Brittle failure is also known as fast fracture as this type of failure occurs without warning or prior evidence of distress.

Figure C6-28: Tensile stress and ductile failure. *Source: Ambiguous.*

Brittle failure is caused by tensile stresses on brittle materials, such as cast iron, glass and pottery. More ductile materials, such as steel become brittle at low temperature and can also be subject to brittle failure.

The main feature of brittle materials is not the lack of tensile strength or lack of stiffness, but rather a lack of toughness. That is the lack of resistance to the propagation of cracks. Once the force which causes fracture is applied, cracks propagate very quickly (usually at several thousand kilometres per hour) in a brittle material - thus to the naked eye the fracture appears instantaneous. The factors that promote brittle failure are:

- High tensile stresses.
- Residual (locked in) stresses.
- Impact loading, which does not give the material time to deform plastically.
- Low and high temperatures.
- The embrittlement of materials through metallurgical changes.
- Work hardening.
- Inappropriate use of brittle materials.
- Welding joints (these may be brittle).
- Thick plated (>100mm) vessels are more prone to brittle failure than thin walled ones. Thick plates are more likely to incorporate defects and thick plate accentuates 'restraint' stress and stress concentrations.

Obviously brittle failure may be avoided by taking the above factors into consideration.

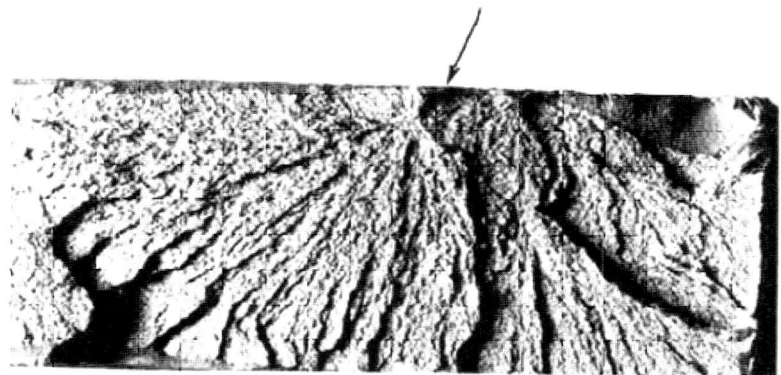

Figure C6-29: Tensile stress and brittle failure. *Source: Ambiguous.*

One example of the embrittlement of materials through metallurgical changes is hydrogen embitterment. This is an effect produced by the adsorption of hydrogen ions during plating or pickling operations. Pickling is the removal of mill scale, lime scale or salt water deposits with a dilute (usually sulphuric) acid containing inhibitors.

BUCKLING

Buckling is caused by excessive compressive forces on a structural member (for example the members that make up the tower of a tower crane). The ability of a material to resist buckling depends on its stiffness and therefore its ability to withstand stresses. A member will be stable only as long as the highest stresses do not exceed the yield stress (elastic stability). Where this does occur, plastic deformation takes place.

Figure C6-30: Tensile stress and brittle failure. *Source: Ambiguous.*

Buckling can be prevented by ensuring the appropriate material choice (i.e. stiffness) of the structural member and by ensuring that forces are not magnified by the member being 'out of true'. For example, a scaffold standard that is not true in a vertical plane will have the vertical forces placed upon it magnified by being 'out of true', thus a bending moment occurs and buckle failure results.

Scaffold standard

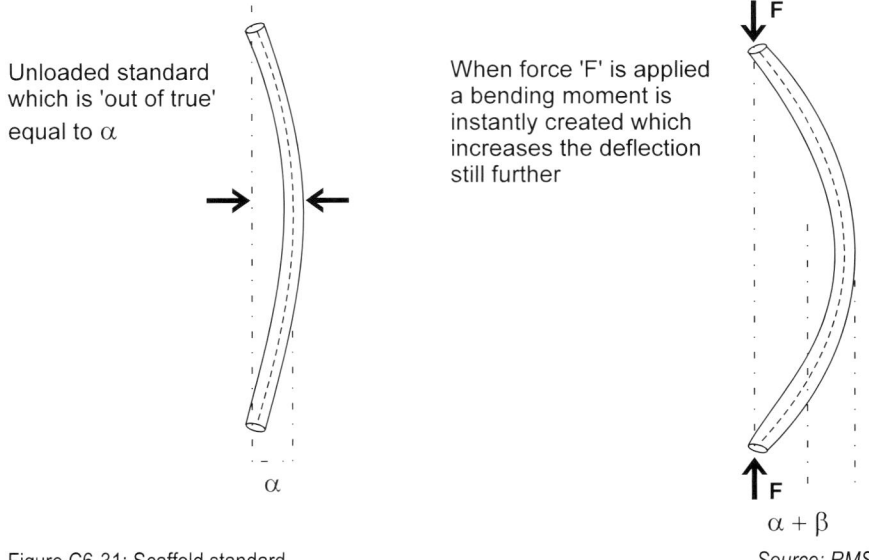

Figure C6-31: Scaffold standard. *Source: RMS.*

CORROSION

Corrosion is the deterioration of a metal through chemical or electro-chemical interaction with its environment. This follows when a material, such as mild steel, is attacked by agents such as polluted air and sea water, which then leads to the formation of rust (oxides). Corrosion is promoted via specific environmental factors, including moisture (made worse by water-soluble pollutants or solid impurities) and high temperatures.

Most corrosion involves an electro-chemical process. Here, a combination of moisture above a critical humidity level, oxygen and an electrolyte combine to promote the liberation, transfer and consumption of electrons. A small potential difference allows electrons to flows from one location (the anode) to another (the cathode).

Where two dissimilar metals are in electrical contact (this includes if it is through an electrolyte) galvanic corrosion can take place. Depending on the relationship of the two metals to each other in the galvanic table one establishes itself as the anode and the other the cathode. For example, if steel and zinc were placed together the steel would become the cathode and zinc the anode. In the process of galvanic corrosion the anode is corroded in preference to the cathode, therefore where steel and zinc are placed together the zinc anode would corrode. Sometimes, in anticipation of this form of corrosion, it is arranged that zinc is placed in contact with steel structures. This would lead to the zinc material being corroded (sacrificed) in preference to the steel, for example, in the case of a ship's hull or pipelines laid in the ground.

Damage to the material from corrosion may take a combination of forms:

1. General thinning of the material, through oxidisation, for example the effects of rust.
2. Passive film formation (tarnishing), which forms a barrier to further corrosion.
3. High temperature oxidation, which, for example, leads to blockages and overheating in pipe-work.
4. Pitting, where the material is selectively attacked.
5. Cracking, where selective attack forms deep cracks.

Precautions against corrosion include:

- Choice of materials.
- Protective coatings.
- Low pH and de-aeration of water.
- Cathodic protection where a sacrificial anode is incorporated into the design (for example a manganese strip is buried alongside a steel pipe and wired to the pipe to protect it from corrosion).
- Designing details to avoid crevices to avoid collection of water, together with good drainage in places where water may collect.

```
Base    Magnesium                              Anodic
        Zinc
        Aluminium (commercial)
        Cadmium
        Duralumin (Al with 4½ % Cu)
        Mild steel
        Cast iron
        Stainless steel
          (Type 430; 18% Cr)
        ACTIVE
        Stainless steel
          (Type 304; 18% Cr 10% Ni)  ACTIVE
        Lead-tin solders
        Lead
        Tin
        Nickel
        Brasses
        Copper
        Bronze
        Monel
        Silver solders  (70% Ag 30% Cu)
        Nickel                        PASSIVE
        Stainless steel  (Type 430)   PASSIVE
        Stainless steel  (Type 304)   PASSIVE
        Silver
        Titanium
        Graphite    (Carbon) (non-metal)
        Gold                                  Cathodic
Noble   Platinum
```

Figure C6-32: Galvanic series in sea water. *Source: 14 Bimetallic Corrosion, Dept. of Industry in association with the Institution of Corrosion, Science and Technology. Courtesy of International Nickel Limited.*

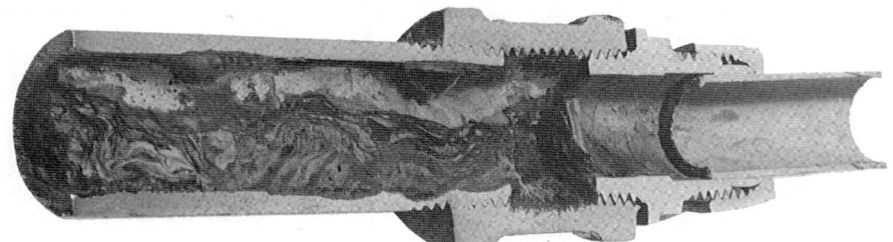

Figure C6-33: Corrosion of galvanised iron pipe. *Source: 14 Bimetallic Corrosion, Dept. of Industry in association with the Institution of Corrosion, Science and Technology.*

The figure above shows the corrosion of a galvanised iron pipe near to a junction with a brass fitting and copper tube, showing the build-up of corrosion products resulting from exposure to hot, moderately soft water. At temperatures above 60°C iron is anodic to zinc. In addition, corrosion is enhanced by copper dissolved from the pipework depositing onto the zinc coating, setting up local bimetallic cells and causing galvanic action that exposes iron.

WEAR

Wear is the loss of material due to the sliding contact between two materials, for example metal to metal. Wear is promoted by a lack of lubrication and the presence of abrasive foreign matter, such as grit.

Lubrication prevents surface contact by separating the two materials with a thick protective oil film under pressure (thick film lubrication) or by a thin layer of grease, only a few molecules thick, (boundary lubrication). Wear can be prevented by maintaining lubrication and/or by choosing materials with compatible surface energies, thereby reducing adhesion.

Abrasive wear can be reduced by the cleaning of surfaces, the keeping out or filtering of contaminant abrasives and the use of hard materials.

CREEP

Essentially, creep is plastic deformation that evolves with time. When creep occurs, the grains of the material slide over each other as time passes, leading to excessive deformation or rupture. Creep is most commonly found in plant and components that have been subjected to high temperatures, such as gas turbines.

Creep can be promoted with only minor variations in temperature. This can lead to drastically reduced component working life. A component with an 11 year life at 500°C can be ruptured within an hour at 700°C.

Measures to prevent creep include:

- Temperature and stresses control in plant, including the minimisation of thermal stresses (for example re-routing hot pipes).
- Use of creep resistant materials (for example 1% chrome, ½ % molybdenum steel).
- Regular inspection for cracks and signs of deformation, such as bulges.
- Maintenance and replacement of creep prone components.

Failure modes and prevention in relation to major incidents

See also - Vapour phase explosions, Flixborough - Element C2

BRENT CROSS, 20 JUNE 1964

Facts

The jib on a 15.2 tonne (15 ton) mobile crane failed and fell onto a passing coach killing seven passengers and injuring a further thirty two. At the time of the accident the crane was erecting a larger scotch derrick crane.

Background

The crane was manufactured by Sheds Engineering Products Ltd, which was later to become the British Crane and Excavator Corporation Ltd (BCEC). The crane was a 15.2 tonne (15 ton) mobile crane with a maximum safe working load (SWL) of 12.7 tonne (12.5 tons) working with a jib radius of 3 metre (10 ft). This was reduced to 7.6 tonne (7.5 tons) SWL with a 24 metre (80 ft) jib and 4.5 metre (15 ft) radius. The load factor/margin of safety was 1.6. The jib was designed to withstand stresses induced by:

- Acceleration/deceleration of slewing motion.
- Wind pressure on the side of the jib.

The Road Traffic Act (RTA) 1999 had been amended to allow a maximum allowable overhang of any crane being moved by road of 2 metres (6 ft). In order to comply the crane was fitted with a gate section (like a giant hinge) enabling the head and heel sections of the jib to fold back one against the other, and bringing the overhang to within the maximum 2 metres (6 ft) allowed.

ELEMENT C6 - WORK EQUIPMENT (WORKPLACE MACHINERY)

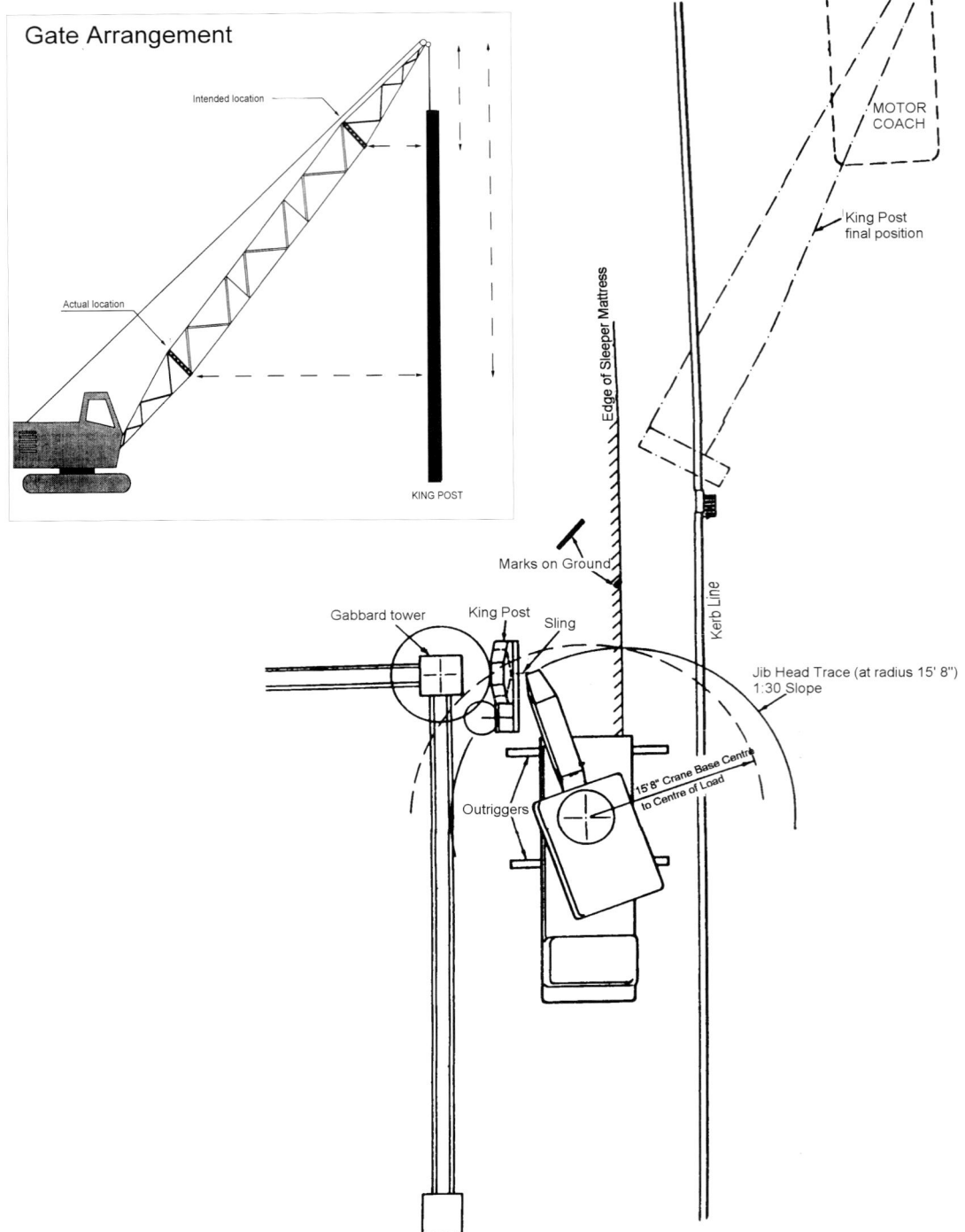

Figure C6-34: Crane failure at Brent Cross. Source: HSE Report on Brent Cross Crane Failure.

The gate was designed by BCEC. The design calculations were destroyed; however, the designer considered that two limitations should be incorporated into the use of the gate:

1) It should always be inserted next to the head section.
2) It should not be used with a jib longer than 12 metres (40 ft) plus the gate.

However, no note of these considerations exists and the instructions were not communicated. The gate was made by Steels Process Plants Ltd, a subsidiary of BCEC.

The gate was designed to be fitted with 12 lugs:

- 4 rectangular 44 mm (1 ¾ inch) thick (no. 236667).
- 8 triangular 25 mm (1 inch) thick (no. 236668).

During fabrication all 12 lugs were fabricated to the 25 mm (1 inch) triangular design (no. 236668). The thickness error was detected for the missing 4 x 44 mm (1 ¾ inch) lugs, however the shape was not. Thus, 4 thicker 44 mm (1 ¾ inch) lugs were locally manufactured by Steels Process Plants Ltd to a triangular shape - rather than the rectangular shape that the design called for. The designer's specification of rectangular lugs was necessary to deal with the compressive forces within the jib.

WORK EQUIPMENT (WORKPLACE MACHINERY) - ELEMENT C6

By using triangular lugs, the scissor-action created when the jib extended was over done on one side, making the jib slightly out of skew.

BCEC did not fit the gate themselves. A service engineer fitted the gate next to the heel section and adjusted the radius indicator, but did not otherwise recalibrate the crane nor was it subjected to a test.

The head and heel sections were 4.5 metres (15 ft) each, which, together with the main section, brought the overall length of the jib to 25 metres (82 ft 9 inches). The crane was lifting a king post, which was estimated to weigh 6.6 tonne (6 ½ tons), but actually weighed 8 tonne (7 tons 17 cwt). The safe working load of the crane with a jib of 25 metres (82 ft 9 inches) length and at the assumed working radius 4.7 metres (15 ft 8 inches) was 7.6 tonne (7.5 tons). The actual working radius was 5.8 metres (19 ft).

The terrain did not permit the crane to face the load (king post) - it was sited alongside the load and had to work over-side. The crane was sited on a 1:30 slope. The mis-manufacture of the gate resulted in lateral bending stresses in the jib. Had the gate been fitted next to the head section, then the bending forces would have been less than a quarter of those on the lower position. The jib failed and fell onto a passing coach killing seven passengers and injuring a further thirty-two.

Main factors

- Incorrect manufacture of the gate (wrong lugs, wrong shape of lugs).
- Incorrect positioning of the gate.
- Failure to inspect.
- Failure to notify designer's limitations on use to the user.
- Crane was operating on a 1:30 slope.
- Estimated weight of load was wrong.
- SWL was exceeded.
- The safe load indicator was defective.
- Failure to test.

LITTLEBROOK D POWER STATION, 09 JANUARY 1978

Facts

Several contractors were involved in the construction of the Littlebrook 'D' power station in Dartford Kent, on behalf of the Central Electricity Generating Board. One sub-contractor Edmund Nuttall Ltd (Nuttalls) was given the job of constructing the shafts and tunnels as part of the cooling system. Access to the two tunnels involved was via a hoist fitted in each of the two access shafts. On 9 January 1978 a single suspension rope of one of the hoist cages, in which nine men were travelling, broke. The safety gear failed to operate and the cage plunged more than 30 metres to the bottom of a 60 metres shaft. Four men were killed and five were seriously injured.

Main factors

- The hoist's suspension rope broke at a part weakened by corrosion and lacking lubrication. Later examination showed that a length of about 35 metres of the rope was completely devoid of lubricant and very corroded, both internally and externally, with many of its wires broken. Tests indicated that at the fracture all the wires had lost 50% of their tensile strength and the outer wires had lost 80%. It was also estimated that at the fracture position there was a loss in breaking strength of approximately 80% before the final fracture occurred.
- The deterioration took place over a relatively short period of time and was not detected.
- Analysis of the water in the shaft showed that it contained salt and the corrosion was consistent with the rope having been impregnated with salt water.
- Both clamping units of the cage safety mechanism were found to be corroded and coated with hard, cement like, material that prevented them from working.

Contributory factors

- The statutory six monthly examination of the hoist was overdue.
- The weekly site inspection had failed to record any defects.
- The maximum load for the hoist was eight passengers.
- The maintenance of the cage safety mechanism had been inadequate to maintain it in good working order in the environment to which it had been exposed.

The subsequent Health and Safety Executive (HSE) investigation could not establish the exact pattern of routine maintenance on the hoist or if the hoist had been maintained in accordance with the manufacturer's (ACE Machinery Ltd) instructions, since the operator (Nuttalls) kept no records. Many defects in Nuttalls' safety management system were noted (including policy, inspection, maintenance, training, resources and monitoring).

As a result of the investigation it was shown that similar hoists were defective. All known users were advised of the need to perform a free-fall (drop) test. One of the key recommendations of the investigation was that all rope suspended passenger hoists should be suspended by at least two ropes. In addition, it was concluded that drop testing of prototypes of safety gear be conducted to establish a maximum number of drop tests before they would require replacement. *See figure ref C6-35.*

ELEMENT C6 - WORK EQUIPMENT (WORKPLACE MACHINERY)

General layout of shaft hoist and tunnel

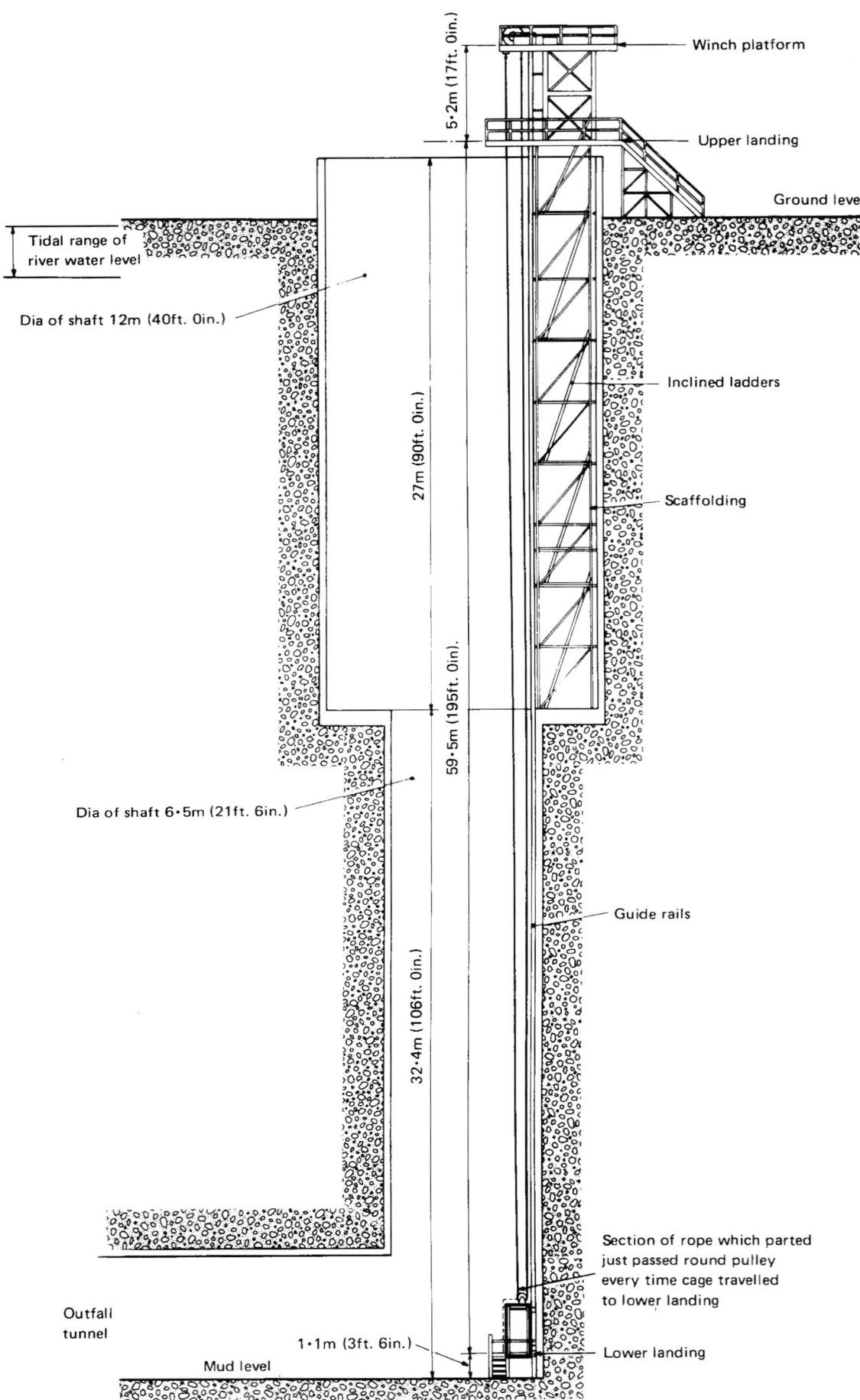

Figure C6-35: General layout of shaft hoist and tunnel. *Source: The hoist accident at Littlebrook 'D' Power Station, HSE Books.*

MARKHAM COLLIERY, 30 JULY 1973

Facts

The day shift was being lowered at No. 3 upcast shaft at Markham Colliery, Derbyshire on 30 July 1973. A double deck cage containing 29 men crashed to the wooden baulks at the pit bottom killing 18 men and seriously injuring another 11.

The accident occurred due to an overwind. The ascending cage rose until it struck the roof girders of the airlock structure fracturing the surrounding concrete and brickwork. As there were no safety catches in the headframe, the cage then dropped back until it was hanging by its suspension chains from the detaching hook. The engineman applied the brake lever and 'saw some sparks under the brake cylinder' and heard a bang. The brake lever seemed to have little effect, so he pressed the emergency stop button expecting to see the drum brought to a sudden stop, but nothing happened.

The descending cage carrying the 29 men struck pit bottom with such force that it fractured 9 of the 17 of the wooden baulks (the speed of impact was estimated to be 27 miles per hour). Although power had been cut off before the crash, the momentum of the winding system unwound the spare coils of overlap rope and then the metal loop, with part of the drum side and brake path was torn away. The rope and loop were pulled over the headgear pulley and then fell down the shaft on top of and alongside the cage containing the men. The drum continued to rotate and the flailing loop of the underlap rope seriously damaged the winding engine house and an adjoining workshop. The subsequent investigation found that:

1) There was a complete failure of the winding engine brake - the centre rod in the spring nest had broken.
2) The centre rod appeared to have failed due to fatigue.

The investigators fitted four strain gauges at 90° to each other to a replacement centre rod, as near as possible to the position where the fracture occurred in the original rod. These tests showed that, in addition to tensile stresses at the gauge positions, there were substantial stresses due to bending when the brake was operated. The gauges at right angles to the winding drum indicated that the magnitude of stresses varied to such an extent that on the one furthest from the drum there was a change from tension to compression as the brake was released.

Later metallurgical examination of the spring nest showed that it had failed because of fatigue. There was evidence that three small cracks had existed for some time and had propagated to a depth of 28 mm (1.1 inches) before the rod broke. Numerous additional small cracks existed both above and below the fracture. These were found in the laboratory by magnetic particle inspection. Experiments showed that these small cracks would not have been revealed by an ultrasonic probe; however, this method would have detected the much larger cracks (of ~ 10 mm (3/8 ") depth).

The centre rod was made from good quality carbon steel. The ultimate tensile strength of the material was 5,340 kg/cm^2 (38 tonf/in^2) and the mean tensile stress induced by the spring nest at the minimum cross section was 870 kg/cm^2 (6.2 tonf/ in^2). Consequently, the static factor of safety was 6.1. The investigation, however, revealed that the bending and alternating stresses, with an amplitude of ± 930 kg/cm^2 (6.6 tonf/ in^2), were superimposed on the tensile stress. These stresses meant that the failure of the rod was inevitable. The centre rod, which was (2.74m) (8 ft 11 7/8 in) long and 51 mm (2") in diameter had been in service for 21 years.

The investigation also showed that winding engine operators were trained 'on the job' and used different operating techniques, which were inconsistent methods of controlling the gear.

Main factors

1) No provision had been made for non-destructive testing (NDT) of the centre rod in the spring nest.
2) The centre rod was a 'single line' component and the safety of the cage was completely dependent upon it.
3) A similar rod had broken in Ollerton Colliery in January 1961, which was attributed to induced stresses. The subsequent instruction to examine centre rods did not give any guidance as to the nature and frequency of examinations or the use of NDT.
4) Ultrasonic tests, which can be carried out in situ, would have revealed large cracks (~ 10 mm (3/8 ") depth) but would not have detected the small cracks in the rod. The probability of detecting the crack that led to failure using ultrasonic methods would therefore have depended on the crack's rate of propagation and the interval between tests.

Recommendations

The investigation recommended that:

1) All winding engines be examined and modified.
2) Winding engines should not rely on 'single line' components or, if this was not possible, they be modified, operated and maintained so as to prevent danger.
3) Appropriate NDT testing is carried out on all safety critical components.
4) A design analysis, including an assessment of the working life of components, is carried out.
5) Control systems are reviewed to ensure that electrical braking was available after the initiation of an emergency or automatic trip device.
6) All solid landings in shafts are replaced by suitable arresting devices.

ELEMENT C6 - WORK EQUIPMENT (WORKPLACE MACHINERY)

7) The training and examination of winding engine operators be reviewed and an operation manual prepared.
8) Every winding engine that can attain a speed in excess of 2 metres/sec (7 ft/sec) is provided with a rope speed indicator.

PORT RAMSGATE, SEPTEMBER 1994

Facts

At 0045 on 14 September 1994 a passenger walkway at Port Ramsgate collapsed killing six passengers and seriously injuring seven more.

In the collapse, one end of the walkway fell 10 metres, embedding itself in the deck of the pontoon that had provided the floating seaward support for the structure.

The Health and Safety Executive's (HSE) investigation established that the immediate cause of the collapse was the failure of a weld in a safety-critical support element of the structure. Further investigation revealed gross deficiencies in the design, which would have ensured failure of safety-critical elements within a fairly short part of the structure's lifespan. The HSE established that the collapsed walkway was of unique design and that similar risks of collapse did not exist at other British ferry ports.

The technical deficiencies arose from the failure of various parties involved, procurement, design and installation, to manage the project effectively and in particular to carry out any reasonable risk assessment of the project.

The problem was that there was no allowance made for roll in the design, and the bearings were assumed to be able to accommodate torsion. This led to the bearings being under-designed. The independent, external design checkers did not notice this problem. Other factors, such as the leaving out of some of the greasomatics and problems during construction, accentuated the problem and speeded up the disaster. The constant swaying motion that the sea put on the bearings and welds of the walkway gradually caused a fatigue failure.

Background

The following is taken from "The Collapse of the Ramsgate Walkway" by J C Chapman.

The life of ship to shore structures is related more closely to the life of a ship, about 20 years, than to the notional 120 years of a highway bridge. Yet the operating conditions of ship-to-shore structures are exceptionally onerous. The support system must accommodate the tidal range, wave effects, and occasional ship impact. Large horizontal movements must also be accommodated.

A single-tier vehicle linkspan, supported at the seaward end on a pontoon had been operating at Ramsgate for several years. Transverse inclination (roll), caused by waves, wind, or eccentric loading was assumed (in accordance with common practice) to be accommodated by the torsional compliance of the linkspan.

When Belgian ferries were relocated to Ramsgate, a second linkspan was required above the existing one. The seaward end was supported on a portal frame erected on the pontoon, which had been designed for that possibility. A covered walkway was also required so that foot passengers could board without interrupting the flow of vehicles. The seaward end of the walkway span was supported on a cantilever platform on the outside of the portal frame. The shore end was supported within an aperture in the passenger access building.

The existing pontoon and vehicle linkspan were designed, fabricated and constructed by an experienced and respected firm of naval architects and engineers. The contract was for a design-and-build. They were certified by Lloyds Register. Similar arrangements were adopted for the new walkway and linkspan.

The walkway consisted of box section trusses with 6 mm steel plate roof, lower sides and floor cladding welded to the trusses and cross members. This made the walkway very stiff, flexurally and torsionally. The shore bearings were steel plates with low friction pads attached. The bearings could slide on steel plates fixed to the web of channel sections, between the upstanding flanges. The slide clearance enabled the walkway to rotate about a vertical axis. The bearing was attached by vertical brackets to tubes within which stub axles, projecting transversely from the end of the walkway structure could rotate. The axles were welded within the central bore of vertical discs, which were site welded to the walkway structure. The seaward bearings were of similar design, but the right hand bearing had a vertical pin projecting downwards through the horizontal plate of the cantilever platform. Vertical movement was limited by a welded collar. This all meant that the articulation system allowed for the three translatory freedoms of the pontoon and two of the rotational freedoms, but there was no allowance for roll, which could be accommodated only by a bearing lifting from its seating, as was observed in service.

Main facts

At 0045, while passengers were boarding a ferry, the seaward end of the main walkway span dropped without warning, about 10 metres to the pontoon deck. The violent deceleration on impact caused the death of six passengers and serious injuries to seven others. The walkway had been in service for only 4 months. There were no unusual external circumstances.

The right hand seaward bearing, including the axle remained on the platform being retained by the pin. The welds connecting the axle to the disc had fractured. The left hand seaward bearing struck the deck and was propelled into the dock. The walkway structure itself was intact.

As part of the certification procedure, the walkway had been tested under the design loading, without apparent damage. One month before the accident the walkway had been inspected by the insurers' inspector, who had been trained to inspect ship-to-shore structures; he had found nothing wrong.

The HSE took the bearings and part of the support platform for examination. Calculations made by the designer/installation contractors and by Lloyds Register were also examined.

The HSE found that the welded connection of the axle of the right hand seaward bearing to the disc had failed in fatigue, thereby detaching the walkway from the bearing. The connection of the left hand seaward axle had failed largely in fatigue and final fracture had occurred when the bearing hit the pontoon deck. Both shore axles had extensive fatigue cracking, but were still connected. This confirmed that an incident during construction involving the right hand seaward bearing was not the cause of failure, because when the incident occurred the shore bearings were not loaded. The lubrication of the axles was deficient, partly through poor design and partly because some automatic lubricating devices had not been fitted.

The prime cause became apparent from the calculations of the designers and checkers. Both had independently made the same conceptual mistake.

Instead of calculating the axle moment at the weld connecting the axle to the disc, they assumed the moment to be zero. They had designed on the basis of shear alone. A smaller, but still major error was the assumption that all four reactions were equal, notwithstanding the rotational movement of the pontoon and the large torsional stiffness of the structure.

The bearings were not fabricated in the same factory as the structure and the drawings were separate. There were no assembly drawings, and this could have increased the risk of incorrect design assumptions.

HSE brought legal proceedings against Port Ramsgate, the operating company, Fartygsentreprenader AB (FEAB) Fartygskonstructioner AB (FKAB), the designers/installation contractors, and Lloyds Register of Shipping, the independent approval organisation. Lloyds Register pleaded guilty, the Port of Ramsgate pleaded not guilty and the Swedish contractors did not plead and did not attend. All parties were charged under the Health and Safety at Work etc Act (HASAWA) 1974 and Port Ramsgate were also charged under the Docks Regulations. (CDM was not in force at the time). All parties were found guilty. The fines, a total of £1.25m, a record at the time, were in proportion of 5:2:1 to FEAB FKAB, Lloyds Register and Port Ramsgate. Costs to the HSE of £713,000 were divided approximately equally. It was not been possible to recover the fines and costs from the Swedish contractors as they went bankrupt.

Consideration was given by the Crown Prosecution Service to manslaughter proceedings, but responsibility for the failings that caused the incident was divided between so many individuals and organisations that no clear case could be established against any of them.

Failure prevention strategies

The prevention of failures in materials depends on the:

- Assessment of the foreseeable modes of failure under normal operating conditions.
- The selection of appropriate materials and structural components.
- The carrying out of appropriate design calculations and the incorporation of an appropriate factor of safety.
- Manufacture using quality assurance techniques.
- Installation that prevents damage and unplanned pre-stressing.
- Determining an appropriate inspection, test and maintenance regime (including non-destructive testing and the use of fracture mechanics).
- Avoiding alterations and ill conceived repairs.
- Use within known and accepted limits.

METHODS OF IDENTIFYING POTENTIAL FAILURE MODES

Identifying potential failure modes

It is important that the designer understands and appreciates the conditions and use in the actual environment in which the item being designed is used. For example, the fan blade fitted to the British Midland B737- 400 that crashed at Kegworth experienced flutter at altitude, a fact that had not been appreciated at the design and test stage. This led to catastrophic failure of the left engine when the blade snapped and went into the engine.

Use of fracture mechanics

Fracture mechanics is used to test the residual strength of materials that contain cracks or flaws. As stated previously, there is a 'critical crack length' beyond which failure will result. For example, if a crack is observed during visual inspection of a pressure vessel, fracture mechanics can be used to predict the future development of the crack, thus avoiding the need to scrap an expensive vessel. By knowing the crack's depth/length, the tensile strength of the material and the fluctuating pressures to which the vessel is subjected the working life of the vessel can be predicted. Monitoring of the development of the crack serves to refine the model used and confirm its accuracy.

There are two techniques which can be used as a predictive tool:

1) Linear elastic fracture mechanics (LEFM).
2) General yielding fracture mechanics.

ELEMENT C6 - WORK EQUIPMENT (WORKPLACE MACHINERY)

These techniques allow the working life of a component or system to be extended and minimise the risk of catastrophic failure. It is important to note that fracture mechanics do not deal with ductile failure, because this type of failure is not affected by cracks (unless the cracks are huge).

RELATED ENVIRONMENTAL FACTORS

The performance of a component or material is greatly influenced by the environment it is placed in. As can be seen by previous explanations of mode of failure, unsuitable materials placed in an offensive environment may be encouraged to fail. Examples include simple forms of steel, whose performance and ductility may be fine in a moderate temperature ambient at 20°C, but may fail in a brittle mode when put into service in the cold temperatures of the North Sea. Similarly, a steel sling used to lift hot forged items may be subject to long exposure to high temperature and the state of the material may become changed, leading to failure at a level below its rated safe working load. It is for this reason that materials suited to this environment need to be selected and in practice the sling may be assigned a *'working load limit'* below the usual safe working load when used in ambient temperatures of 20°C.

Selection of materials

The selection of materials is therefore very important. For example, iron was commonly used for lifting chains. This has been replaced by high tensile steel because of the problem of work hardening and the expense of the annealing process that iron required in order to reduce the probability of brittle failure. As an added benefit, the factor of safety required to offset the fact that as the iron chains became work hardened they became brittle has been reduced through the use of high tensile steel chains.

Purpose of 'safety factors'

If a structure is designed to support three times its normally expected load then its **factor of safety** is 3. The purpose of safety factors is to allow for:

- Sub-standard materials.
- Higher than expected loads.
- Poor quality workmanship.
- Unusual/abnormal conditions.

This factor of safety is often used to calculate the load that a structure must be designed to withstand, for example:

Design load = normal maximum load x factor of safety.

It should be noted that the factor of safety does not represent a margin of spare capacity.

QUALITY ASSURANCE DURING MANUFACTURE AND INSTALLATION

BS EN ISO 9001:2008 requires that:

- Suppliers establish and maintain documented procedures to ensure that purchased product conforms to specified requirements.
- Suppliers establish and maintain documented procedures for inspection and testing activities in order to verify that the specified requirements for the product are met.
- The required inspection and testing and the records to be established be detailed in the quality plan and documented procedures.
- Suppliers ensure that incoming product is not used or processed (except in specific circumstances) until it has been inspected or tested or otherwise verified as conforming to specified requirements and requires that verification be in accordance with the quality plan or documented procedures.
- When determining the amount and nature of receiving inspection, consideration should be given to the control exercised at the subcontractor's* premises and recorded evidence of conformance required.
- Where incoming product is released for urgent production purposes, prior to verification, it shall be positively identified and recorded in order to permit immediate recall and replacement in the event of non-conformance to specified requirements.
- The supplier to inspect, test and identify product as required by the quality plan or documented procedures.
- The supplier is to hold product until the required inspection and tests have been received and verified except when product is released under positive recall procedures.
- The supplier is to arrange for the protection of the quality of the product after final inspection and test and, where contractually specified, this protection shall extend to include delivery to destination.

*It should be noted that the term subcontractor is defined under ISO 9000-2 as an organisation that provides products (including services) to the supplier.

In addition, where servicing is a specified requirement (for example vehicles, washing machines or a photocopier), then the supplier must establish and maintain documented procedures for performing these services.

TESTING DURING MANUFACTURE AND INSTALLATION

Final inspection and testing can have three main forms:

1) An inspection carried out on completion of the product.

2) A last inspection carried out prior to dispatch.

3) A last inspection the supplier carries out prior to transfer of ownership to the customer.

Final inspection should include ensuring that previous inspections and tests have been carried out and that the as-built configuration is the same as the issue status of all parts, sub assemblies etc. specified by the design standard. The inspection record must clearly show whether the product has passed or failed inspections and/or tests according to the defined acceptance criteria. Non-conforming products must be controlled to ensure that they are not used. Therefore, they must be clearly identified and segregated to ensure this.

Inspection, measuring and test equipment used for inspection and test purposes must be controlled, calibrated and maintained. Similarly gauges, tools, jigs etc. must be verified to ensure accuracy. The aim of inspection and testing is to ensure that the product complies with specified requirements. The principle behind this is that inspection and test does not control quality, but merely measures achieved quality in order to give the producer information for remedial action.

The trend in systems where materials failure is critical is towards a regime of written systems of inspection (examination) and test. Examples include pressure systems *(see also - Element C11 - Pressure system hazards and controls)* and lifting equipment. Here a system is broken down into its component parts and subjected to a routine of inspections and tests depending on its failure modes.

Previous incidents and failures, such as the hoist accident at Littlebrook 'D' Power Station and the crane accident at Brent Cross, should be taken into account when determining the nature and frequency of inspections and tests - as should the lessons learnt during the system's life. Perhaps the best example of this philosophy is in the aircraft industry where the identification of a failed component in one airframe can lead to the grounding of all of that type of aircraft worldwide.

FORENSIC EXAMINATION OF FAILED COMPONENTS

Failed components can be forensically examined in order to determine the modes and causes of failure. The first consideration must be to ensure that evidence is not contaminated during any examination or removal process and to ensure that the examination takes place quickly enough so that significant further corrosion etc. does not take place. Careful visual examination, possibly with the aid of a magnifying glass or low power microscope, can reveal much about the mode of failure. The following table considers the indicators that point towards failure modes.

Mode	*Possible indicators*
Tensile fracture	Local 'necking' or extension and decrease in sectional area in direction of load.
Shear fracture	Friction marks with a new-moon shaped gap on the unloaded side of a bolt etc.
Brittle failure	Clean break with no signs of necking. Surface has coarse, angular appearance with 'chevron' markings pointing back to the starting point.
Wear	Shiny new appearance, pitting and fretting of components.
Corrosion	Pitting, colour changes (for example rust and tarnishing).
Fatigue crack	'Beach' or conchoidal marks.

Figure C6-36: Failure modes. *Source: RMS.*

Non-destructive testing techniques

The principle of non-destructive testing (NDT) is to test the integrity of materials without causing damage in the process. Many of the techniques used rely on considerable skill and experience by the person carrying out the tests and rely on tests being carried out at appropriate intervals. Personnel carrying out NDT must be properly trained and qualified.

Most NDT methods will only detect surface flaws (patent defects). However, radiography, used to carry out an internal inspection, is very effective in identifying sub-surface flaws (latent defects). NDT is used by manufacturers to:

- Ensure product integrity and reliability.
- Prevent failure and accidents, and save lives.
- Make profit for users.
- Ensure customer satisfaction.
- Aide better product design.
- Control manufacturing processes.
- Lower manufacturing costs.
- Maintain uniform quality level.
- Ensure operational readiness.

The selection of the most appropriate NDT method for a particular component depends on a number of factors such as:

- Material of construction.
- Thickness of section.
- Type of defect to be detected.
- Cost.
- Inspection equipment available.
- Operator skill.

ELEMENT C6 - WORK EQUIPMENT (WORKPLACE MACHINERY)

NDT TECHNIQUES SUITABLE FOR SURFACE DEFECTS

- Visual inspection.
- Liquid penetrant inspection.
- Magnetic particle inspection.
- Eddy current testing.

Visual inspection

Visual inspection involves direct or indirect inspecting for **surface** condition, defects, roughness and/or dimensional changes.

Despite many other more sophisticated NDT techniques, visual inspection plays an important role in the detection of surface flaws and damage. This can be done unaided or with the use of a microscope. Some signs of damage may be obvious (for example pitting and large surface cracks), but some are not (for example an increase of 1 mm in a 125 mm diameter tube may indicate imminent creep rupture).

Advantages

- A fast, cheap and relatively simple means of surface inspection.

Disadvantages

- Dependent upon the eyesight of the inspector; therefore regular eyesight tests for both visual acuity and colour differentiation are essential.
- Time for continuous viewing must be restricted with frequent rests to reduce fatigue.

Typical applications

Weld inspection:

- Verification of correct weld preparation.
- Inspection for surface defects for example undercuts and cracks.
- Verification of completed weld profile (cap, root).

Condition monitoring in service:

- Detection of corrosion.
- Detection of defects and cracks.

Metrology:

- Measurement of component geometry.
- Measurement of surface roughness.

Etch inspection:

- Detection of grinding defects.
- Detection of incorrect heat treatment (case depth).
- Metallographic examination (weld profile, inclusions, grain size, microstructure).

Visual inspection has many techniques to aid the operator and extend its capability.

- Etching for metallographic examination and to reveal cracks, inclusions and localised variations in composition and hardness.
- Lighting must be at an appropriate level and of the correct type.
- Magnifiers, from low power, x2 to x5, hand held lenses to high power microscopes.
- Borescopes are devices that permit inspection of internal surfaces in piping, engines, air frames etc. They contain systems of lenses, mirrors; prisms and lighting that illuminate the test area and transmit images to the inspector. They may be either rigid or flexible. The flexible type uses optical fibres, the smallest have outside diameters of just a few millimetres and can be steered into position around tight bends.
- Television cameras combined with borescopes, video recorders and image processing equipment permit the remote collection and storage of visual images. This permits inspection in difficult and hazardous sites, for example nuclear installations and underwater pipelines. Image enhancement by computer is also possible.
- Surface replication using strippable films also permits the remote inspection of surfaces.

Liquid dye penetrant inspection

Liquid dye penetrant inspection enhances visual inspection for **surface** flaws by the use of liquid dyes on any non-absorbent material's surface. A brightly coloured or fluorescent liquid dye is applied to a component surface and allowed to penetrate any surface-breaking cracks or cavities. After soaking (approximately 20 minutes), the excess liquid dye penetrant is wiped away from the surface and a developer applied. The developer draws penetrant out of any cracks by reverse capillary action to produce indications on the surface. These (coloured) indications are broader than the actual flaw and are therefore more easily visible. The types of defect that can be detected using this method include: cracks, porosity, seams and laps (defects highlighted in the surface) and leak detection (because the dye seeps out of cracks etc.). Penetrant dyes include:

- Low viscosity oil and chalk.
- Brilliant dye penetrants.
- Water washable fluorescent penetrants.

The surface of the test piece must be clean and undisturbed. Liquid dye penetrant tests can be used on both ferrous and non-ferrous metals.

Advantages

- It can be used on a wide range of materials, i.e. metallic and non-metallic, magnetic and non-magnetic, conductive and non-conductive.
- It has high sensitivity to small surface defects.
- Large areas and large quantities of items can be tested quickly and at low cost.

- Complex geometric shapes can be tested.
- The dye shows the location and shape of the defect directly on the surface.
- The method does not rely on large amounts of complex equipment and dye penetrant may be applied using portable aerosol sprays.
- Penetrant liquids and any associated equipment are relatively inexpensive.

Disadvantages

- Only materials with a relative non-porous surface can be inspected.
- Only surface breaking defects can be detected.
- Surface finish and roughness can affect inspection sensitivity.
- Pre-cleaning is critical as contaminants can mask defects.
- Liquid dye penetrant is applied directly to the surface; the method relies on direct access and the ability to conduct visual examination.
- The method relies on sufficient time to allow dye to penetrate.
- Some skill is required to ensure excess penetrant is not removed from defects as well as from the surface of the item being tested.
- Some cleaning of the tested item may be required after test.
- Chemical handling controls and proper disposal is required.

Typical applications

Liquid dye penetrant testing is used in a number of industries. The aerospace industry use automated fluorescent penetrant testing to look for fatigue cracking in turbine blades; the construction industry uses dye penetrant testing as a quick and simple method for checking that welds and other susceptible areas are free from surface-breaking defects.

Magnetic particle testing

Magnetic particle testing is an electromagnetic test method that provides for the detection of **surface and near surface** discontinuities in ferro-magnetic materials.

A magnetic field is induced in the item under test and a suitable medium (for example iron filings mixed with paraffin) is sprinkled on the surface. Defects are indicated by anomalies in the distribution of these particles. In order to aid detection the particles are often florescent when placed under ultraviolet light. The types of defect that can be detected using this method include cracks, laps, seams, voids, pits and near surface holes.

Advantages

- It has high sensitivity to small surface and near surface defects.
- Large areas and large quantities of items can be tested quickly and at low cost.
- Complex geometric shapes can be tested.
- The magnetic particles show the location and shape of the defect directly on the surface.
- It is quick and simple.
- Thin layers of contaminant or coating do not usually inhibit performance.

Disadvantages

- Material being tested needs to be capable of being magnetised, for example ferrous.
- It will not detect deep internal defects.
- High currents applied to components being tested may cause damage.
- The magnetic particles are applied directly to the surface; the method relies on direct access and the ability to conduct visual examination.
- Handling the component during visual examination may mask the location of defects or cause magnetic particles to be dislodged.
- High power equipment is required to enable the magnetisation of the components.
- Demagnetisation is often necessary after inspection.

Typical application

Magnetic particle testing may be used to test small steel forgings for use in safety-critical applications, which need to be inspected for surface and near surface flaws that might propagate in service. Magnetic particle testing is widely used for this type of application since, in addition to offering adequate sensitivity to defects, the technique can be mechanised for volume production.

Eddy current testing

The most widely used and best-known of the electromagnetic methods is eddy current testing. A current is passed through a coil of electrically conducting material that surrounds the item under test. This produces an electromagnetic field around the item, which produces an eddy current within it. Test instruments detect the nature and profile of the eddy current created and compares this to data derived from a known specimen, which acts as a reference. Impedance changes in the coil could indicate the presence of a defect. Where the data obtained from the item under test differs from that of the known specimen it is deduced that this is because of a defect and the item under test is rejected. This method can be used on electrically conductive materials for detecting and characterising defects, such as **surface and near surface** cracks, gouges and voids.

It can also be used to verify an electrically conducting material's heat treat condition. In addition, wall thickness of thin wall tubing and thickness of conductive and non-conductive coatings on materials can also be determined using this method.

Advantages
- Defects at or near the surface can be reliably detected.
- High-sensitivity to small defects.
- Can test complex shapes.
- Accurate measuring of conductivity.
- Accurate coating thickness measurements.
- Tests provide an electrical read out that can be translated to quick decisions of conformity or non-conformity.
- Lends itself to high speed testing and automation.
- Can be used to test continuous items like wire or pipe.
- No physical contact is required, the electromagnetic field surrounds the item being tested.
- Low cost and portable.

Disadvantages
- Material must be electrically conductive.
- Limited penetration into item being tested.
- Several variables simultaneously affect output indication and therefore though it may be determined substandard, the exact defect may not easily be identified.
- Requires skill to interpret details of result when many variables are involved.
- False indications can result from edge effects and the geometry of the item being tested.
- High power equipment is required to enable the generation of strong electromagnetic fields.
- Exposure to electromagnetic currents may lead to health problems.

Typical applications
Eddy current testing is used for the testing of metal wires for surface and near surface defects at high speeds and high temperatures. During the manufacture of steel wire, at speeds of up to 100 m/s, it is necessary to feed back information on wire quality to the control station as quickly as possible so that actions can be taken before several thousand metres have been processed. An eddy current test, using a small coil probe, is able to detect significant flaws during the high speed process, even at wire surface temperatures of 1200°C. Eddy current testing can also be used for the automated rapid testing of electrically conducting metal components, such as those used in automotive manufacture.

NDT TECHNIQUES SUITABLE FOR SUB-SURFACE DEFECTS
- Radiography.
- Ultrasonic testing.

Radiography

Internal defects are highlighted by transmitting **X-rays or gamma rays** through a material to a film on the opposite side of the item being tested. These rays are highly penetrating and are used to expose the film, which records the intensity of the radiation it has received. As cracks and other flaws are hollow, these show as dark patches on the radiograph.

Radiography may be used on both ferrous and non-ferrous materials. The types of defect that can be detected using this method include porosity, slag inclusions in welds, tungsten inclusions, lack of fusion or penetration, forging laps and cracks (although this method is not particularly suitable for the latter).

Neutron radiography is another technique for producing an image of the interior structure of solid objects. Whereas X-rays cannot discriminate between materials of similar density, neutrons can interact quite differently with materials of similar density and thus give a complementary view to that obtained by X-rays.

Advantages
- Can be used with most materials.
- Can be used to determine sub-surface defects.
- Discloses fabrication errors.
- Reveals structural discontinuities.
- Provides a permanent visual image.

Disadvantages
- Exposure to radiation may lead to health problems.
- The item being tested needs to be accessed on at least two sides.
- Technical understanding required to establish correct exposure.
- High power electrical equipment is required to generate x-rays.

Typical applications
Radiography is important for ensuring that any welds are free from defects.

X-ray radiography is used extensively in the testing of aircraft structures and components, welded assemblies, pressure vessels and piping, electronic circuitry, bridge girders, and similar materials.

Gamma ray radiography is used in testing pipelines, bridge and building fabrications, pressure vessels, large forgings and castings, and armoured vehicle components.

Neutron radiography is used in the testing of nuclear reactor fuel, detecting of hydrogenous materials, detecting of flaws in gas turbine blades and corrosion of aircraft components, quality control of ceramics, detecting of explosive charges, and detecting of the presence of lubrication films inside gear boxes or bearings.

Ultrasonic testing

Ultrasound is defined as (sound) waves at frequencies beyond the upper limit that the human ear can detect (i.e. above 20 kHz). An ultrasonic probe is used to detect cracks in an item under test. This sends ultrasonic waves into the item and picks up reflections from the internal boundaries within the item.

These reflected waves are normally observed on a screen. Simple systems will represent any defects as 'blips', whereas more complex systems may represent the item being tested as an image and defects may show up as differences in image intensity. Angled probes are used to more accurately locate cracks. The types of defect that can be detected using this method include cracks, misalignment, porosity, inclusions, surface conditions and pitting.

Advantages
- High sensitivity, which permits detection of minute defects.
- High penetrating power (6-7 metres in steel).
- High accuracy of defect positioning and sizing.
- Equipment is portable.

Disadvantages
- Complex geometry of the test specimen causes problems during inspection.
- Defect orientation affects detection ability.
- Requires good direct contact (through a contact medium) with the surface of item being tested.
- Contact medium may need to be removed after test.
- Requires expert interpretation.

Typical application

Ultrasonic testing is used in the aerospace and nuclear industries. Large airframe and rocket fuselage sections made up from fibre reinforced composites and honeycomb structures are examined using sequenced multi-probe equipment under computer control and operating to dimensional accuracies and repeatability in the order of one micron.

OTHER NDT TECHNIQUES

- *Acoustic methods* including: acoustic emission, tap testing, acoustic-ultrasonic testing and acoustic microscopy.
- *Electromagnetic methods* including: magnetic flux leakage, magnetography, nuclear magnetic resonance, electric current testing, corona-discharge testing, potential drop testing, dielectric testing, and microwave-radiation testing.
- *Leak-test methods* including: tracer-gas leak detection, pressure-change testing, vacuum-system tests, bubble-leak detection and acoustic leak-testing.
- Hydrostatic and pneumatic testing.
- Cryogenic testing.
- Tensile tests.
- Hardness, impact and manipulating tests.
- Corrosion tests.
- Brittle (coating) lacquer testing.
- Strain-gauge testing.
- Electrical resistivity.
- Thermography.
- Holography.

C6.3 - Protective devices

The main types of safeguarding devices

FACTORS AFFECTING CHOICE OF SAFEGUARDING METHOD

In selecting an appropriate safeguard for a particular type of machinery or danger area, it should be borne in mind that a fixed guard is simple, and should be used where access to the danger area is not required during operation of the machinery or for cleaning, setting or other activities.

As the need for access arises and increases in frequency, the importance of safety procedures for removal of a fixed guard increases until the frequency is such that interlocking should be used.

Where access to the danger area is not required during normal operation of the machinery, safeguards may be selected from the following.

- Fixed enclosing guard.
- Fixed distance guard.
- Interlocking guard.
- Trip device.

Where access to the danger area is required for normal operation, safeguards may be selected from the following:

- Interlocking guard.
- Automatic guard.
- Trip device.
- Adjustable guard.
- Self-adjusting guard.
- Two-hand control device.
- Hold-to-run control.

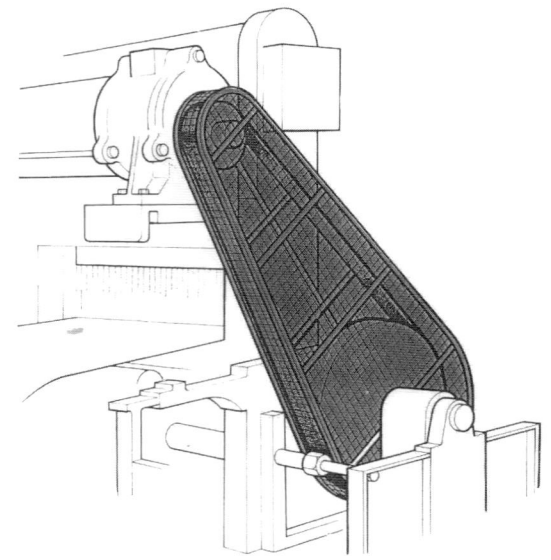

Figure C6-37: Fixed enclosing guard constructed of wire mesh and angle section preventing access to transmission machinery.
Source: BS PD 5304.

Hierarchy of safeguarding methods (PUWER 1998 - Regulation 11 dangerous parts of machinery) as amended by the Health and Safety (Miscellaneous Amendment) Regulations (MAR) 2002

"(1) Every employer shall ensure that measures are taken in accordance with paragraph (2) which are effective:

(a) To prevent access to any dangerous part of machinery or to any rotating stock-bar.

(b) To stop the movement of any dangerous part of machinery or rotating stock-bar before any part of a person enters a danger zone.

(2) The measures required by paragraph (1) shall consist of:

(a) The provision of fixed guards enclosing every dangerous part or rotating stock-bar where and to the extent that it is practicable to do so, but where or to the extent that it is not, then.

(b) The provision of other guards or protection devices where and to the extent that it is practicable to do so, but where or to the extent that it is not, then.

(c) The provision of jigs, holders, push-sticks or similar protection appliances used in conjunction with the machinery where and to the extent that it is practicable to do so, and the provision of such information, instruction, training and supervision as is necessary.

(3) All guards and protection devices provided under sub-paragraphs (a) or (b) of paragraph (2) shall:

(a) Be suitable for the purpose for which they are provided.

(b) Be of good construction, sound material and adequate strength.

(c) Be maintained in an efficient state, in efficient working order and in good repair.

(d) Not give rise to any increased risk to health or safety.

(e) Not be easily bypassed or disabled.

(f) Be situated at sufficient distance from the danger zone.

(g) Not unduly restrict the view of the operating cycle of the machinery, where such a view is necessary.

(h) Be so constructed or adapted that they allow operations necessary to fit or replace parts and for maintenance work, restricting access so that it is allowed only to the area where the work is to be carried out and, if possible, without having to dismantle the guard or protection device.

(4) All protection appliances provided under sub-paragraph (c) of paragraph (2) shall comply with sub-paragraphs (a) to (d) and (g) of paragraph (3).

(5) In this regulation:

"Danger zone" means any zone in or around machinery in which a person is exposed to a risk to health or safety from contact with a dangerous part of machinery or a rotating stock-bar; "stock-bar" means any part of a stock-bar which projects beyond the head-stock of a lathe".

Guard construction

Any guard selected should not itself present a hazard such as trapping or shear points, rough or sharp edges or other hazards likely to cause injury. Guard mounting should be compatible with the strength and duty of the guard. Power operated guards should be designed and constructed so that a hazard is not created by their operation. In selecting the material to be used for the construction of a guard, consideration should be given to the following:

- Its ability to withstand the force of ejection of part of the machinery or material being processed, where this is a foreseeable danger. Its ability to provide protection against hazards identified. In many cases, the guard may fulfil a combination of functions such as prevention of access and containment of hazards. This may apply where the hazards include ejected particles, liquids, dust, fumes, radiation, noise, etc. and one or more of these considerations may govern the selection of guard materials.
- Its weight and size in relation to the need to remove and replace it for routine maintenance.
- Its compatibility with the material being processed. This is particularly important in the food processing industry where the guard material should not constitute a source of contamination of the product.
- Its ability to maintain its physical and mechanical properties after coming into contact with potential contaminants such as cutting fluids used in machining operations or cleaning and sterilising agents used in food processing machinery.

Characteristics, key features, limitations and typical applications

FIXED ENCLOSED GUARDS

A fixed guard is a guard that has no moving parts.

If the guard can be opened or removed, this should only be possible with the aid of a tool. Preferably the fastenings should be of the captive type. Ideally the removal of a single fixing with the appropriate tool should give the access required.

A fixed enclosing guard is a fixed guard that, when in position, prevents access to a danger zone or point by enclosure.

When it is necessary for work to be fed through the guard, openings should be sufficient only to allow the passage of material, but should not create a trap between the material and the guard. If access to the dangerous parts cannot be prevented by the use of a fixed enclosing guard with a plain opening, then a tunnel of sufficient length should be provided.

FIXED DISTANCE GUARDS

A fixed guard that does not completely cover the danger zone or point, but places it out of normal reach. The larger the opening (to feed in material) the greater must be the distance from the opening to the danger zone or point.

A distance guard that completely surrounds machinery is commonly called a perimeter-fence type guard.

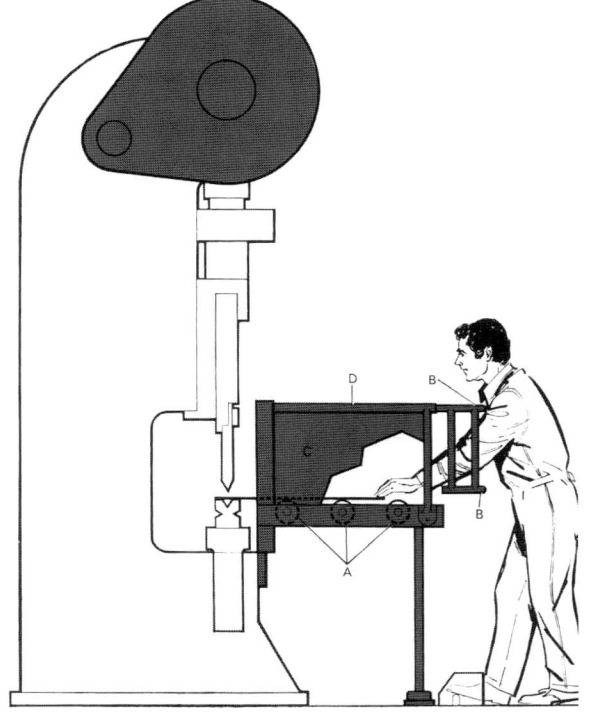

Figure C6-38: Fixed distance guard fitted to a press brake.
Source: BS PD 5304.

Anthropometric considerations

General

Guards should be designed and constructed with the object of preventing any part of the body from reaching a danger zone or point. They should take account of the physical characteristics of the people involved, and in particular their abilities to reach through the openings, and over or around barriers or guards.

Openings in a guard

Where it is necessary to provide an opening in a guard, it should be at a sufficient distance to prevent any person from reaching the danger zone or point. This may be achieved by positioning the guard at the required distance or by providing a tunnel that extends outwards from the danger zone or point.

The relationship between the size of the guard opening and the distance of the opening from the danger zone or point may be described by the formula:

$$Y = \frac{X + 6}{12}$$ where Y = the opening in mm and X = distance from hazard in mm

ELEMENT C6 - WORK EQUIPMENT (WORKPLACE MACHINERY)

Barriers

Where it is not practicable to use enclosing guards, barriers may be used to prevent people reaching the danger zone or point. These rely on a combination of height and distance to achieve their purpose. A guide figure of 1.8 metres height is suggested for perimeter fencing. With the body upright and standing at full height, the safety distance when reaching upward is determined to be 2,500 mm.

Barriers are not foolproof and they cannot prevent access to person's intent on gaining access. Therefore, as a person's intent on reaching a dangerous part increases, for example by climbing on chairs, ladders or the barrier itself, the protection provided by a barrier will decrease.

When reaching down over an edge, the safety distance is dependent on:

- Distance of danger point from floor.
- Height of edge of barrier.
- Horizontal distance from the edge of the barrier to the danger point.

INTERLOCKED GUARDS

An interlocking guard is a guard, similar to a fixed guard, but which has a movable (usually hinged) part so connected to the machine controls that if the movable part is in the open position, the dangerous moving parts at the work point cannot operate. This can be arranged so that the act of closing the guard activates the working part (to speed up work) for example the front panel of a photocopier.

Functions of an interlock

An interlock provides the connection between a guard and the control or power system of the machinery to which the guard is fitted.

The interlock and the guard with which it operates should be designed, installed and adjusted so that:

- Until the guard is closed the interlock prevents the machinery from operating by interrupting the power medium.
- Either the guard remains locked closed until the risk of injury from the hazard has passed, or opening the guard causes the hazard to be eliminated before access is possible.

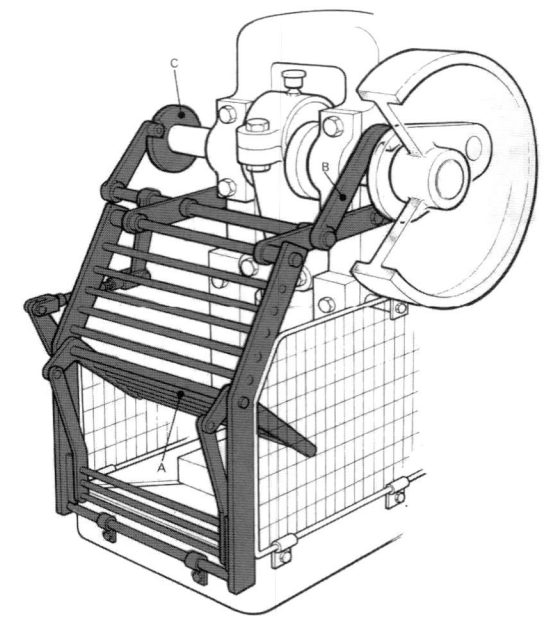

Figure C6-39: Interlocking guard for positive clutch power press.
Source: BS PD 5304.

Interlocking media

The four media most commonly encountered in interlocking are electrical, mechanical, hydraulic and pneumatic. Electrical interlocking, particularly in control systems, is the most common and electrical components are often incorporated in hydraulic and pneumatic circuitry, for example solenoid operated valves.

The principles of interlocking apply equally to all media. Each has advantages and disadvantages, and the choice of interlocking medium will depend on the type of machinery and the method of actuation of its dangerous parts.

Some interlocking systems have more than one control channel, for example dual control systems. It is often advantageous to design these systems so that the similar failures in both channels from the same cause (common cause failures) are minimised. One way of achieving this is by using a different control medium for each channel, for example one hydraulic and one electrical.

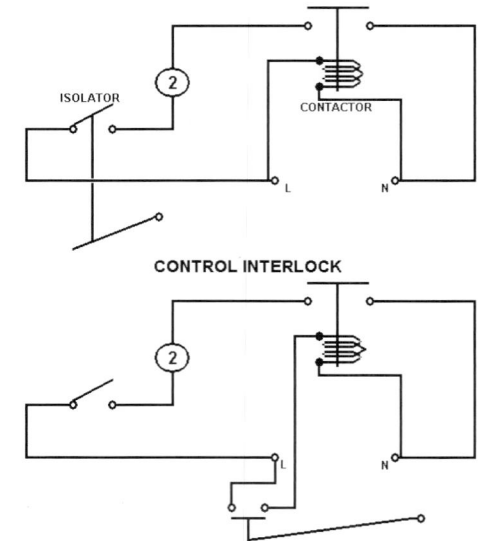

Figure C6-40: Schematic representation of power and control interlocking.
Source: Ambiguous.

Interlocking methods

Methods of interlocking that ensure the power medium is interrupted when a guard is open fall into two groups:
1) Power interlocking.
2) Control interlocking - illustrated by the following schematic diagrams (note: not actual circuit diagrams).

Power interlocking systems eliminate intermediate components used in control interlocking systems, thereby reducing the probability of failure.

Interlocking incorporating braking and/or guard locking

A hazard may exist after interruption of the power medium, for example, due to the continuing release of stored energy. Under these circumstances, systems should incorporate a device (or in dual systems, devices) to either:

1) Cause the hazard to be eliminated as the guard is opened (braking).
2) Prevent the guard from being opened until the risk of injury from the hazard has passed (guard locking).

Guard locking systems

Motion or position *sensing* devices:

a) Rotation sensing device which may be operated on various principles such a centrifugal force, friction, voltage generation.
b) Photoelectric beam.
c) Proximity device.
d) Position switch or valve.

Timing devices:

a) Mechanical, electric or electronic clocks.
b) Delay relay.
c) Sequence valve.
d) Threaded bolt.
e) Dashpot.

Guard *locking* devices:

a) Captive-key unit.
b) Trapped-key unit.

Types of failure of interlocking systems

The most common failures from which an interlocking system may suffer are as follows:

a) Failure, interruption or variation of externally supplied power medium, for example electrical supply, pneumatic or hydraulic ring main.
b) Malfunction due to power medium contamination.
c) Earth faults, i.e. accidental connection of a conductor to earth.
d) Open circuits in electrical systems.
e) Cross connection faults causing, for example, unintended starting or failure to stop.
f) Malfunction due to the electrical environment, i.e. mains borne or radiated interference. (This is normally less of a problem with electromagnetic and electromechanical devices than electronic devices).
g) Disconnection or rupture of hoses or piping.
h) Mechanical failure, for example breakage or seizure.
i) Malfunction due to vibration.
j) Brake failure.

Failure monitoring of interlocking systems

Measures can be taken to minimise the consequences of single failures in interlocking systems. These may include the use of additional control or monitoring channels:

- Dual-control system interlocking without cross-monitoring.
- Dual-control system interlocking with cross monitoring, which may or may not be self-checked.

Probable effect of a failure to danger

Type of system	Probable effect of a failure to danger in a single channel	Action
Single-control system interlocking without indication of failure.	Machinery will continue to operate normally.	Guarding system is ineffective.
Dual-control system interlocking without cross-monitoring, but provided with indication of failure.	Machinery will continue to operate normally. Guarding system remains effective only on one channel.	Note indication failure. Take necessary remedial action.
Dual-control system interlocking with cross-monitoring. Monitoring function self-checked.	Guarding system remains effective.	None.

Figure C6-41: Probable effect of a failure to danger. Source: RMS.

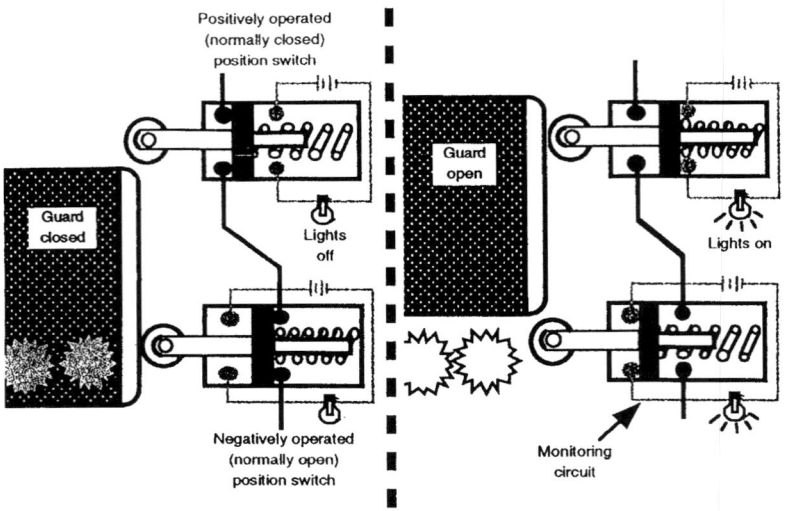

Figure C6-42: Interlocking system. *Source: Paper D (S Tech); Q5; June 1996 Previous NEBOSH Diploma.*

Choice of interlocking system

Selection of the preferred system of interlocking for a particular application should take account of:

a) Frequency with which the approach to the danger zone or point is required.
b) Probability and severity of injury should the interlocking system fail.
c) Resources required for reducing the risk of injury.

Interlocking switch types

a) Cam-operated position switches.
b) Tongue-operated switches.
c) Captive-key switches.
d) Trapped-key control of electrical switches.
e) Inductive proximity switches.
f) Magnetic switches.
g) Diode links.
h) Manually operated delay bolts.
i) Solenoid operated shotbolts.

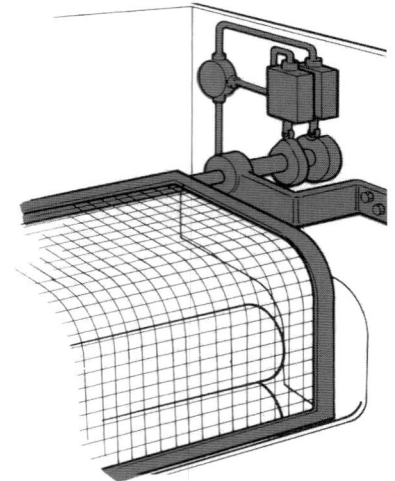

Figure C6-43: Two position switches operating in opposite modes, mounted side by side, each actuated by its own cam mounted on the guard hinge. *Source: BS PD 5304.*

Mechanical interlocks

Can take a number of forms, but usually involve discs, bars and levers arranged so that operation of the machine can only be carried out in a safe order. One such arrangement is used on positive clutch power presses. This utilises an arrangement where a cup type cam prevents the guard from opening until the press stops at the end of its cycle. This is used in conjunction with a lever connected to the guard, which stops the clutch being operated while it is open.

Cam-activated position switches and modes of operation

Cam-operated limit switch interlocks are versatile, effective and difficult to defeat. They can be rotary or linear and in each case the critical feature is that in the safe operating position the switch is relaxed, i.e. the switch plunger is not depressed. Any movement of the guard from the safe position causes the switch plunger to be depressed, tripping the controls and stopping the machine.

A switch can be actuated in either of two modes, positive or negative. In the case of a cam operated electrical switch, positive means the contacts have been opened by a positive mechanical action of the cam (or similar). Negative means the contacts are opened by spring pressure when the cam is rotated. When used singularly positive mode is preferred; negative mode operating interlock switches are not acceptable on their own. For certain high risk machinery, a combination of positive and negative mode is recommended and this arrangement can incorporate a switch failure monitoring circuit.

Magnetic switches

Magnetic switches that have the actuating magnet attached to the guard have the disadvantage that they can be defeated easily by placing a piece of magnetic material near the switch. However, types of magnetic switch that use a shaped magnet has been accepted and in use for many years.

Normal reed switches are not acceptable unless they incorporate special fail safe and current limiting features. Reed switches are often encapsulated and have application in flammable atmospheres. A similar type of switch relies on inductive circuits.

Captive and trapped key systems

Captive key systems

Captive key interlocking systems involve a combination of an electrical switch and a mechanical lock in a single assembly. Usually the captive key part is attached to the movable guard. In order to engage the key in the lock, the guard has to be fully closed. When the guard is closed, the key locates on the switch spindle. First movement of the key mechanically locks the guard shut and further movement actuates the electrical switch to complete the safety circuit.

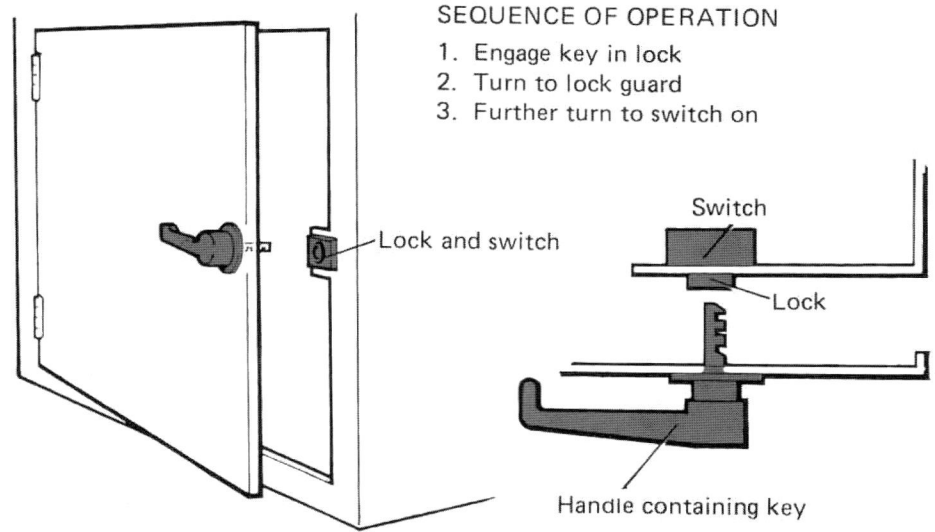

Figure C6-44: Captive key switch.   Source: BS PD 5304.

This type of interlock is suitable for a hinged guard, or for a guard that can be removed bodily from the machine. Where the guard is removed from the machine alignment of the key and switch can be aided by providing a location pin or pins that engage in bushes prior to the key entering the switch.

Time delay captive key switch

The time delay commences when the machine is switched off. When the time delay is completed, the electromechanical bolt is released by energising the solenoid and the guard can be opened for access.

Trapped key system

In a trapped-key system the guard lock and switch, which also incorporates a lock, are separate as opposed to being combined into a single unit as in the captive-key switch. The essential feature of the system is that the removable key is trapped either in the guard lock, or in the switch lock. When the lock on the guard has been closed and locked, this allows transfer of the key from the guard to the switch lock. Closing the switch traps the key, so that it cannot be removed while the switch is in the 'on' position.

If there is more than one source of power, and therefore more than one control to be isolated, then a key exchange box should be used, to which all control isolation keys should be transferred and locked in before the access key, which is of a different configuration, can be released for transfer to the guard lock. Where there is more than one guard, the exchange box will accommodate an equivalent number of access keys.

1 Key, 3 keys trapped.   Insert and turn free key, then turn and release   1 key is trapped, 3 keys released.
                                                          trapped keys in sequence.

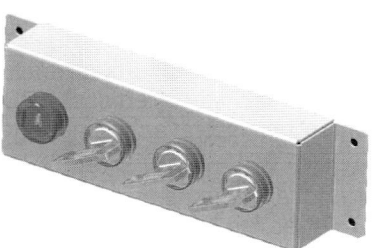 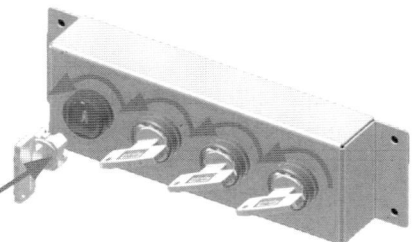 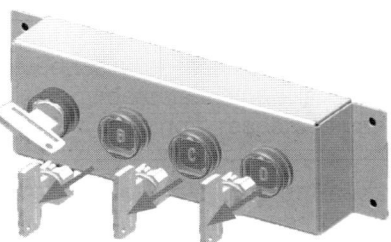

Figure C6-45: Key Exchange Box system.   Source: Castell Safety.

ELEMENT C6 - WORK EQUIPMENT (WORKPLACE MACHINERY)

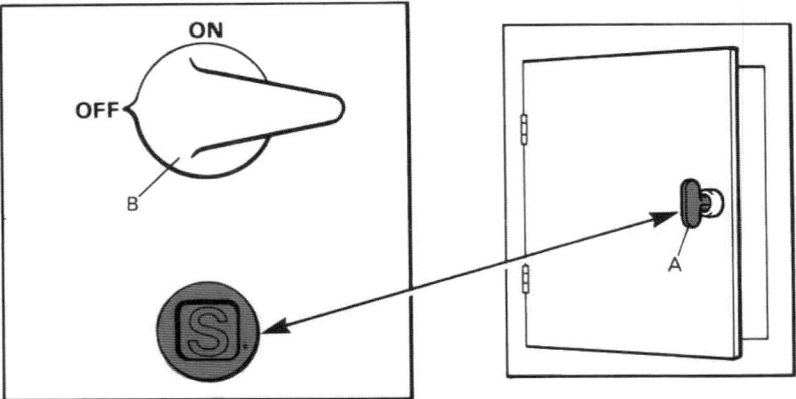

Figure C6-46: Practical application of the trapped-key control system. *Source: BS PD 5304.*

Where, for the purpose of the process or for safety, a number of operations has to be carried out in a definite sequence, the transferable key is locked in and exchanged for a different one at each stage. The exchange box can be integral with the lock. It should be recognised that there is a danger with any interlocking system employing separate identical keys that the keys may be used without authorisation. The operation of such systems should therefore be restricted to responsible persons.

AUTOMATIC GUARDS

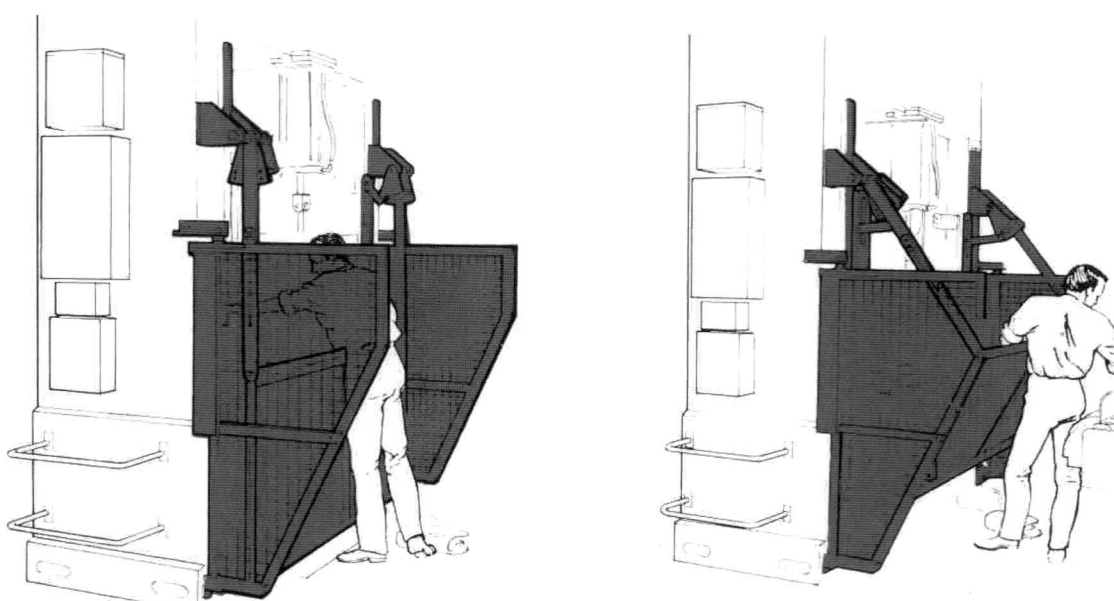

Figure C6-47: Automatic guard for a power press. *Source: BS PD 5304.*

An automatic guard is a guard that is moved into position automatically by the machine, thereby removing any part of a person from the danger area. In some applications this type of guard is known as a 'sweep away guard' for example on a guillotine. An automatic guard operates by physically removing from the danger area any part of a person exposed to danger. The movable part of the guard should be positively actuated by the movement of the dangerous part of the machinery. The mechanism should be so designed that it will withstand long use with minimum maintenance. It can be used only where there is adequate time for such removal to take place and the movement of the person or part of the person can take place without introducing any further danger.

TRIP DEVICES

A trip device is a device that causes working machinery to stop or assume an otherwise safe condition, to prevent injury when a person approaches a danger zone or point, beyond a safe limit. The device will also be required to keep the machine in this condition while the person remains within the danger area unless other means of fulfilling this function are provided.

A trip device should be designed to ensure that an approach to a dangerous part beyond a safe limit causes the device to operate and the dangerous part(s) to stop before injury can be inflicted. The sensitive trip bar fitted in radial drilling machines does not exactly fit this description, but when operated so that minimal deflection trips it and it is properly located, it prevents serious injury. The effective performance of a trip device depends on the stopping characteristics of the machinery, which should be controlled within fine limits. A brake may be necessary.

A trip device should be designed so that after it has been operated it must be re-set; it should not be possible for it to reset automatically or manually by means of the normal start button. An electrical or electronic trip device should be so designed that its effective operation will not be impaired by any function of the machinery or by extraneous influences, for example, an infrared operated trip device may be affected by stray sources of infrared.

There are two main types of trip device:

1) Mechanically actuated (for example trip wires, telescopic probes).
2) Non-mechanically actuated (for example photo-electric and ultra sonic devices).

Mechanical actuated devices

The essential element of a mechanical trip device is a barrier or part of the barrier, for example trip edge, which is moved by part of the body as it approaches a danger zone. This movement operates the device, which can be electrical, mechanical, hydraulic or pneumatic. Trips can also be fitted to drills. It is important to understand that a trip is intended to prevent or minimise injury and that it does not prevent entanglement with the rotating spindle or tool. Operators should, therefore, be trained to take all necessary precautions to avoid the risk of entanglement and to use trip devices correctly.

A trip device consists of three principal components:

1) The actuating switch - usually operated from an adjustable trip probe or horizontal trip wire. Trip wires should actuate the switch in both the pulled and slack wire conditions.
2) A control unit, which provides the electrical interface between the trip switch and motor. It should incorporate a reset button to ensure that after the device has been operated it must be reset before restarting the machine at the normal start control.
3) A brake, which may be either mechanical or electro-dynamic (for example DC injection).

Pressure sensitive mat system

A pressure sensitive mat contains sensors that operate when a person or object applies pressure to the mat.

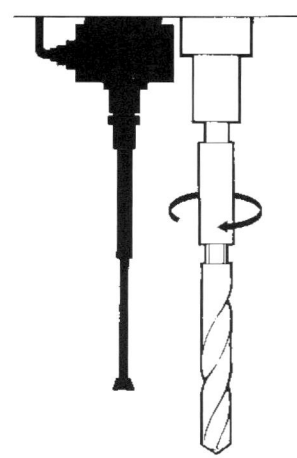

Figure C6-48: Trip device for drilling machines.
Source: BS PD 5304.

By their nature, pressure sensitive mats are exposed to potential damage, which can result in failure.

The dimensions of the mat should take account of a person's speed of approach, length of stride, and the overall response time of the safety system. Care should be taken to ensure that access cannot be gained without actuating the mat. Pressure sensitive mats should be sensitive over the whole sensing area. Where a number of mats are used together, this should include the function between adjoining mats.

A pressure sensitive mat system may be appropriate in circumstances where the use of a fixed guard or an interlocking guard is impracticable, and is particularly suitable for use as an emergency stopping device, as a means of protecting a person who may be inside machinery or in conjunction with other forms of safeguard.

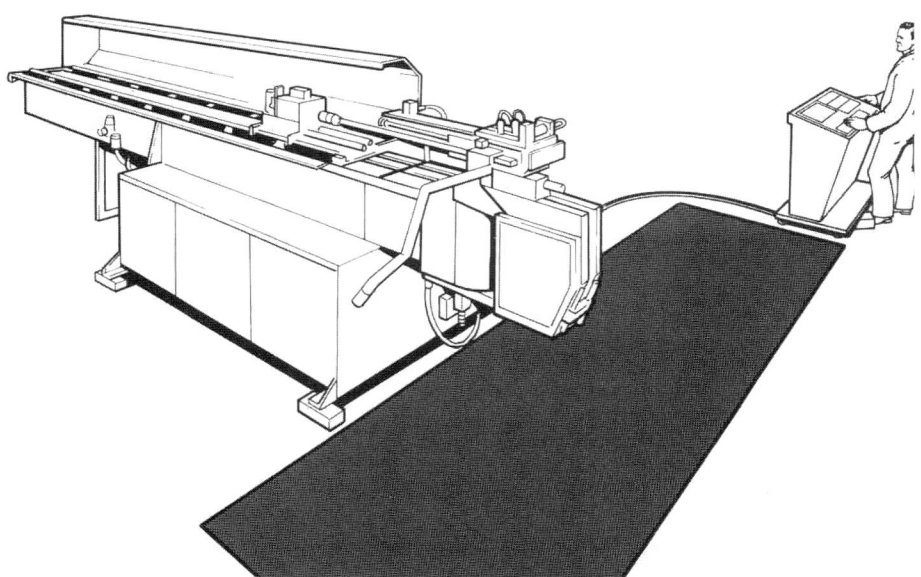

Figure C6-49: Pressure sensitive mat safeguarding the clamping and bending jaws of an automatic horizontal tube bender. *Source: BS PD 5304.*

ELEMENT C6 - WORK EQUIPMENT (WORKPLACE MACHINERY)

The size and positioning if pressure sensitive mats should be calculated using the formula from the standard BS EN 999:1998+A1:2008 "Safety of Machinery. The positioning of protective equipment in respect of approach speeds of parts of the human body". The standard relating to the mats themselves is contained in BS EN 1760-1 "Safety of machinery. Pressure sensitive protective devices.

General principles for the design and testing of pressure sensitive mats and pressure sensitive floors". This requires that the top mat surface should be of a material capable of standing up to high duty wear and be slip resistant. Where heavy loads, such as fork lift trucks, are likely then this should be made clear when specifying the mat to the manufacturer.

The standard also contains the following important points:

- The size, force and positioning of test pieces for testing the mat sensitivity. Where an effective sensing area is built up from more than one sensor it shall have no dead zone.
- A single sensor shall still perform its function after one million actuations by a mass of 75 kg.
- When the actuating force is applied the output signal switching device shall change from an on state to an off state for at least as long as the acting force is applied.
- After the actuating force has been removed the output of the output signal switching devices shall only change to on state after the application of a reset signal (applies to devices with reset).
- For a pressure sensitive mat without reset, the output from the output signal switching device(s) shall change to an on state at power on and after the actuating force has been removed.

Non-mechanically actuated devices

Photoelectric safety systems

Photoelectric safety systems operate on the principal of the detection of an obstruction in the path taken by a beam or beams of light.

The sensing 'barrier' provided by this type of device may consist of a single beam, a number of beams of light, a curtain of light or any combination of these as necessary to provide the required safeguard. The curtain of light may be created by a scanning beam or beams, or a number of fixed beams.

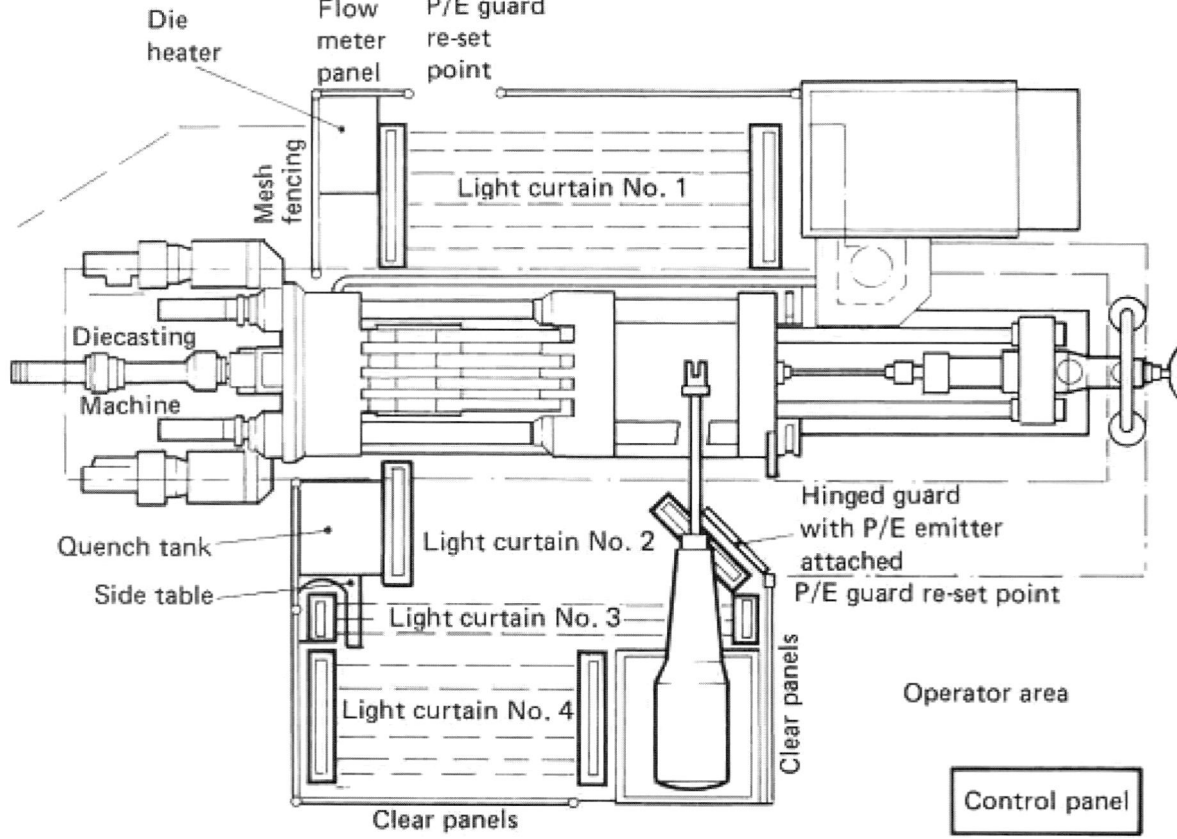

Figure C6-50: Photoelectric safety system used as a presence sensing device inside distance guards fitted around a robot served pressure die casting machine. *Source: HSG 129 Health and Safety in Engineering Workshops.*

The light may be visible or invisible, for example infra-red, and may be continuous or modulated, for example a scanning system.

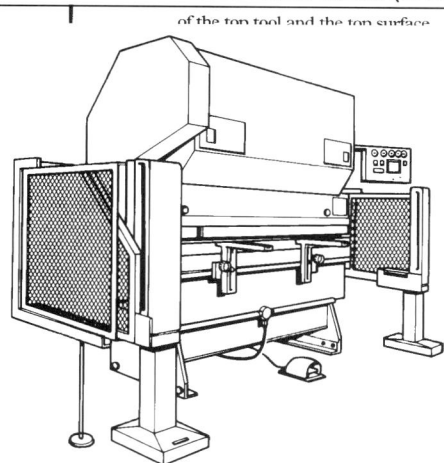

Figure C6-51: Hydraulic press brake using photoelectric safety system. *Source: HSG 129 Health and Safety in Engineering Workshops.*

There are some factors that make photo-electric safety systems unsuitable either as trip devices or for presence detection. Factors that preclude their use as trip devices include:

- Inconsistent or inadequate machine response time/stopping performance due, for example, to:
  - The reaction characteristics of the machinery control circuitry, whether electrical, hydraulic or pneumatic.
  - Poor brake design.
  - Variable speed, load or inertia.
- The inability of the machine to stop part-way through a cycle due to:
  - Nature of the process, for example a multi-station process where stopping between stations would create a production problem.
  - The method of drive, for example positive key clutches or similar mechanisms for engaging the drive so arranged that once started, the machinery can only be stopped when the cycle is complete.
  - Stored energy, for example in the form of stored pressure in pneumatic reservoirs or hydraulic accumulators.
- Tendency for the machinery to eject materials or component parts.

Factors that preclude the use of photo-electric safety systems as trip or presence sensing devices include:

- Risk of injury from thermal or other radiation.
- Unacceptable noise levels.
- An environment likely to affect adversely the efficiency of the photo-electric safety system, for example through extraneous radiation, vibration, dust, excess water, or extremes of temperature.

However, photo-electric safety systems may be acceptable if additional steps are taken to control the risks associated with the above hazards (for example local fixed guards to contain ejection). Further information is available in the Health and Safety Executive guidance HSG 180 "Application of electro-sensitive protective equipment using light curtains and light beam devices to machinery".

ADJUSTABLE/SELF-ADJUSTING GUARDS

Adjustable

An adjustable guard is a fixed guard that incorporates an adjustable element (which remains fixed for the duration of a particular operation) for example on a pillar drill or circular saw. An adjustable guard provides an opening to the machinery through which material can be fed.

The whole guard or part of it being capable of adjustment in order that the opening can be varied in height and width to suit the dimension of the work being done. It is essential in such cases that the adjustment is carefully carried out by a suitably trained person.

Regular maintenance of the fixing arrangements is necessary to ensure that the adjustable element of the guard remains firmly in place when once positioned.

The guard should be designed that the adjustable parts cannot easily become detached and mislaid.

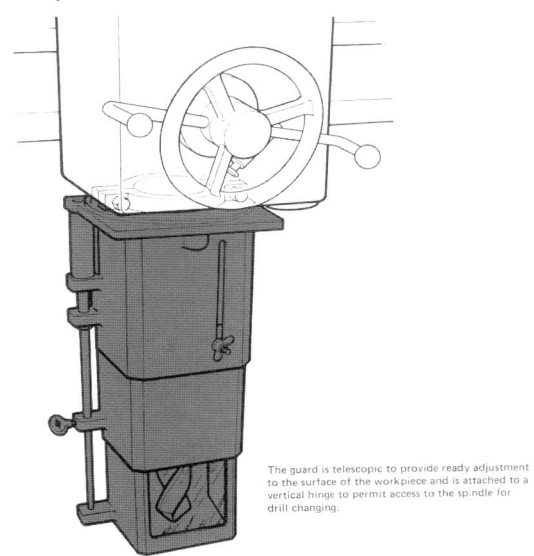

Figure C6-52: Adjustable guard for a radial or pedestal drilling machine. *Source: BS PD 5304.*

Self adjusting

A self adjusting guard is a guard that prevents accidental access by the operator, but allows entry of the material to the machine in such a way that the material actually forms part of the guarding arrangement itself, for example hand held circular saw.

This type of protection is designed to prevent access to the dangerous part(s) until actuated by the movement of the workpiece, i.e. it is opened by the passage of the workpiece at the beginning of the operation and returns to the safe position on completion of the operation.

TWO-HAND CONTROLS

A two-hand control device (2HC) is a device that requires both hands to operate.

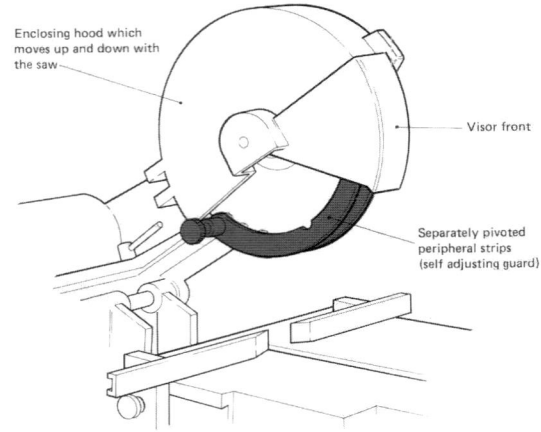

Figure C6-53: Self-adjusting guard arrangement for snipper cross-cutting sawing machine. *Source: BS PD 5304.*

Note that '2HC' devices protect only the operator and then, only provided the assistance of a colleague is not solicited to activate one control.

Where guarding is impracticable two-hand controls offer a means of protecting the hands of the machine operator. It may also be used as a hold-to-run control.

It should be designed in accordance with the following:

- The hand controls should be so placed, separated and protected as to prevent spanning with one hand only, being operated with one hand and another part of the body, or being readily bridged.
- It should not be possible to set the dangerous parts in motion unless the two controls are operated within approximately 0.5s of each other. Having set the dangerous parts in motion, it should not be possible to do so again until both controls have been returned to their off position.
- This effectively discourages two people operating the machine together by co-ordinating their actions and prevents the operator from locking one control in the start position, which would allow them to operate the machinery by means of the other control and leaving one hand free.

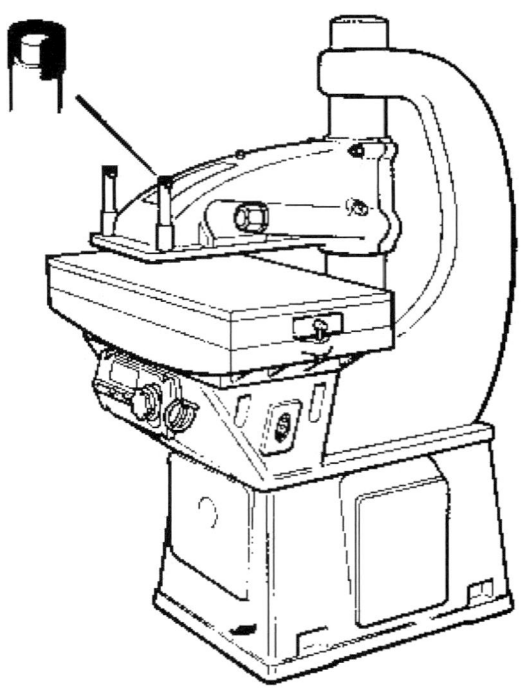

Figure C6-54: Two-hand control device. *Source: BS PD 5304.*

- Movement of the dangerous parts should be arrested immediately or, where appropriate, arrested and reversed if one or both controls are released while there is still danger from the movement of these parts.
- The hand controls should be situated at such a distance from the danger zone or danger point that, on releasing the controls, it is not possible for the operator to reach the danger zone or danger point before the motion of the dangerous parts has been arrested or, where appropriate, arrested and reversed.

MECHANICAL RESTRAINTS

Mechanical restraints are devices that apply mechanical restraint to the dangerous part, which prevents it from moving:

- When the controls fail.
- When the machine is inadvertently activated.

Mechanical restraints are used to physically prevent a dangerous part of machinery from either moving into an undesired area or to stop the part moving at all during procedures such as cleaning or in transit (for example wedges, scotch, strut, and spindle).

Reliance is placed on the strength of the restraint to prevent hazardous movement such as a lift ram falling due to failure of the normal retaining system.

For example, in the plastics industry, many serious accidents have occurred during blade changing and the clearing of blockages, often due to unpowered movement of the blades in granulators. Chocks or in-built mechanical restraints should be used to stop the rotor moving during such procedures.

JIGS

Jigs are protection appliances that are used to hold or manipulate the workpiece in a way that allows people to keep their body away from the danger zone or danger point. They normally need to be used in addition to guards. Even when the best possible guarding is used, the operation of certain types of machines (for example woodworking machines, such as a band saws) often involves considerable risk, and wherever possible appliances such as jigs and holders should be provided and used.

PUSH STICKS

Push sticks are used to feed timber through bench mounted circular saws or food into a food processing machine. The stick used with a circular saw is a short 12 to 24 cm length of wood used to move the last part of the timber to be cut past the blade, the stick keeps the blade at a safe distance from the hands and the fingers. Push sticks and jigs are defined as appliances within the scope of hierarchy of Provision and Use of Work Equipment Regulations (PUWER) 1998 for safeguarding machinery.

C6.4 - Maintenance

The means by which machinery is safely set, cleaned and maintained

SAFE SYSTEMS OF WORK

It is essential to have a balanced strategy for the integration of technical, procedural and behavioural controls in order to achieve safety with machinery. This means not having an over reliance on any one control, but ensuring that they are integrated and complement each other. The principle of taking a risk based approach is essential. This will mean using more of the control options the higher the risk.

PERMITS

A permit-to-work system is a formal written system used to control certain types of work that are potentially hazardous. A permit-to-work is a document that specifies the work to be done and the precautions to be taken. Permits-to-work form an essential part of safe systems of work for many maintenance activities. They allow work to start only after safe procedures have been defined and they provide a clear record that all foreseeable hazards have been considered.

A permit-to-work system should be used whenever the method by which a job is to be done is likely to be critical to the safety of those involved, other nearby workers, the public or the plant itself. A permit to work will be particularly applicable to complex machinery, for example, where it operates over more than one floor, is long in length or may require workers to enter within it in order to conduct maintenance.

Format

A permit-to-work is a document that:

- Specifies the work to be done and the precautions to be taken.
- Predetermines a safe procedure.
- Provides a clear record that foreseeable hazards have been considered in advance.

It defines the appropriate precautions and the sequence in which they are to be carried out. Before maintenance work is begun, consideration should be given as to whether a permit-to-work is required. A permit-to-work system should be only as complicated as the work requires.

Major features of permit-to-work systems

Identifying need

Failure to identify that a permit-to-work system was needed is a frequent cause of incidents. Often it is not a failure to appreciate the risk, but failure to realise that a formal structured system is required to prevent the incident.

Identifying hazards

A common fault with permit-to-work systems is failure to adequately consider all the possible hazards, creating a false sense of security on the part of the workers. Risks from adjacent plant are often ignored, as are the introduction or creation of further hazards after a permit-to-work had been raised.

Implementation

Issuing a permit-to-work does not of itself make the job safe. It merely provides the opportunity for management to check what is necessary for the operation, to ensure that it has been done and to inform those who are to do the work how to proceed.

Completing a permit-to-work without ensuring that its conditions are satisfied can be more dangerous than having no permit-to-work at all. A number of instances have been noted where work was being carried out under a permit-to-work system, but the checks had not been made to ensure compliance.

ELEMENT C6 - WORK EQUIPMENT (WORKPLACE MACHINERY)

Key points of a permit-to-work
- Define the job to be done.
- Specifies the risks.
- Determine the hazards.
- Establish the controls.
- Identify responsibilities.
- Check isolation procedures are adequate.
- Define who should issue (authoriser) the permit.
- Hand over the permit to the operator (acceptor).
- Establish a time limit.
- Hand over formally if the work involves a shift change.
- Regularly monitor work standards throughout the permit duration.

ISOLATION

Regulation 19 of PUWER 1998 deals with isolation from sources of energy.

"(1) Every employer shall ensure that where appropriate work equipment is provided with suitable means to isolate it from all its sources of energy.

(2) Without prejudice to the generality of paragraph (1), the means mentioned in that paragraph shall not be suitable unless they are clearly identifiable and readily accessible.

(3) Every employer shall take appropriate measures to ensure that re-connection of any energy source to work equipment does not expose any person using the work equipment to any risk to his health or safety".

The main aim of this regulation is to allow equipment to be made safe under particular circumstances, such as when maintenance is to be carried out, when an unsafe condition develops (failure of a component, overheating, or pressure build-up), or where a temporarily adverse environment would render the equipment unsafe, for example, electrical equipment in wet conditions or in a flammable or explosive atmosphere.

Isolation means more than simply switching off the equipment using the stop button. Though this is an essential first step isolation includes removing energy sources, for example, switching off the electrical isolator for the equipment. In new workplaces, individual equipment isolators should be provided; i.e. each piece of equipment has its own isolator(s) near to it. One isolator should not control several items of equipment as it is then impossible to isolate a single piece of equipment on its own. This can lead maintenance staff to rely on switching equipment off using the off button before conducting maintenance work. Isolation should also take account of stored energy, which may need to be dissipated before the equipment is worked on.

Isolation should be adequate and secure. Operating an isolation device alone does not afford adequate protection, because there is nothing to prevent the isolator being switched back on. Similarly, removed fuses can be replaced inadvertently, while the person who isolated the equipment is still working on the equipment.

To ensure that this does not happen, the isolator needs to be physically locked in the off position (typically using a padlock and the key being retained by the person in danger). Multiple lock out devices is often used where multiple trades are carrying out work on the same equipment. They are designed to carry a number of isolation padlocks for the different people working on the equipment; the equipment cannot be energised until all the padlocks are removed, thereby protecting the last worker involved in the task.

PROCEDURES FOR WORKING AT UNGUARDED MACHINERY

Greater reliance on information, instruction, training and supervision may be required in respect of the personnel working at unguarded machinery or involved with setting, cleaning or maintenance. The inexperience, lack of awareness of risks and immaturity of young persons should also be taken into account. While it is recognised that young people may need to carry out these operations as part of their training, such work is only permitted provided it is carried out under the adequate supervision of a person who has the necessary knowledge and experience.

Approach to unguarded machinery should be reduced to a minimum. Lubrication should be by remote or mechanical means. Jigs, push sticks or holders should be used where more sophisticated arrangements are not possible. Where other access is absolutely necessary, it must be strictly controlled by a safe system of work. Where it is necessary for removal of waste material, swarf etc., to be cleared then a tool such as a 'swarf rake' should be provided.

Setting

Setting is the process by which cutting tools etc. are replaced or adjusted on a machine to suit the work to be done. Setting will usually require clear access to the tools of the machine to enable adjustment or replacement. For example, the dies of a power press may need to be changed and set into position to enable a new component to be produced. This type of work will usually cause the person doing the setting to open or remove the guard. The setter may be tempted to run the machine without the guard in place to test their setting arrangements. This would be a dangerous practice that must not be allowed. It is important that the guards be replaced before operational checks are made.

Cleaning

Cleaning is the process by which the cutting tools etc. are cleaned of waste materials, such as swarf, and are periodically removed. When machines are in use and producing waste materials they may build up on the cutting tools, operators may be tempted to clean the cutting tool to remove the build up and improve the process.

The machine must either be stationary to enable cleaning or the cleaning be done by the use of an appliance that keeps the operator in a safe position and free from the cutting or entanglement risk that may be associated with the cutting tools.

Maintenance

Any maintenance work, including setting and cleaning, should only be done when the machine is isolated from all sources of power such as electrical, steam, compressed air and flywheels. If the potential for stored energy exists, this should be released and if necessary moving parts, for example, fans, drive shafts, mixers, etc should be physically secured to prevent movement.

The means by which machines are isolated from all energy sources

Isolation means establishing a break in the energy supply in a secure manner, i.e. by ensuring that inadvertent reconnection is not possible. It is important to identify the possibilities and risks of reconnection as part of the risk assessment process, which should then establish how secure isolation can be achieved. For some equipment, this can be done by simply removing the plug from the electrical supply socket. For other equipment, an isolating switch or valve may have to be locked in the off or closed position to avoid unsafe reconnection. The closed position is not always the safe position, for example, drain or vent outlets may need to be secured in the open position.

If work on isolated equipment is being done by more than one worker, it may be necessary to provide a locking device with multiple locks and keys. Each worker will have their own lock or key and fit it to the isolator locking point, in this way all locks must be taken off before the isolating device can be removed. Keys should not be passed to anyone other than the nominated worker and should not be interchanged between nominated workers.

Figure C6-55: Physical isolation of valve.   Source: RMS.

Figure C6-56: Multiple (padlock) lock off device.   Source: RMS.

For safety reasons, in some circumstances, sources of energy may need to be maintained when the equipment is stopped, for example, when the power supply is helping to keep the equipment or parts of it safe. In such cases, isolation could lead to consequent danger, so it will be necessary to take appropriate measures to eliminate any risk before attempting to isolate the equipment.

It is appropriate to provide means of isolation where the work equipment is dependent upon external energy sources such as electricity, pressure (hydraulic or pneumatic) or heat. Where possible, means of dissipating stored energy should be provided. Other sources of energy such as its potential energy, chemical or radiological energy, cannot be isolated from the equipment. Nevertheless, there should be a means of preventing such energy from adversely affecting workers, by shielding, barriers or restraint.

Isolation of electrical equipment is dealt with by regulation 12 of the Electricity at Work Regulations (EWR) 1989. Guidance to these Regulations expands on the means of isolating electrical equipment. Note that these Regulations are only concerned with electrical danger (electric shock or burn, arcing and fire or explosion caused by electricity), and do not deal with other risks (such as mechanical) that may arise from failure to isolate electrical equipment.

Thermal energy may be supplied by circulation of pre-heated fluid such as water or steam. In such cases, isolating valves should be fitted to the supply pipework.

Similar provision should be made for energy supplies in the form of liquids or gases under pressure. A planned preventive maintenance programme should therefore be instigated that assures effective means of isolation. It may be necessary to isolate pipework by physically disconnecting it or fitting spades in the line to provide the necessary level of protection. Redundancy in the form of more than one isolation valve fitted in series may also be used, but care should be exercised to check the efficacy of each valve function periodically. The performance of such valves may deteriorate over time, and their effectiveness often cannot be judged visually.

The energy source of some equipment is held in the substances contained within it, for example the use of gases or liquids as fuel, electrical accumulators (batteries) and radionuclides.

In such cases, isolation may mean removing the energy-containing material, although this may not always be necessary. Also, it is clearly not appropriate to isolate the terminals of a battery from the chemical cells within it, since that could not be done without destroying the whole unit.

Some equipment makes use of natural sources of energy such as light or flowing water. In such cases, suitable means of isolation include screening from light, and the means of diverting water flow, respectively. Another natural energy source, wind power, is less easily diverted, so sail mechanisms should be designed and constructed so as to permit minimal energy transfer when necessary. Effective restraint should be provided to prevent unplanned movement when taken out of use for repair or maintenance.

Regulation 19(3) of PUWER 1998 also requires precautions to ensure that people are not put at risk following reconnection of the energy source. So, reconnection of the energy source should not put people at risk by itself initiating movement or other hazard. Measures are also required to ensure that guards and other protection devices are functioning correctly before operation begins.

C6.5 - Information and warnings

The scope of information required for the safe use and operation of machinery

As part of the requirements set out in Part 1 (Annex I) subparagraph 1.7 of Schedule 2 of the Supply of Machinery (Safety) Regulations (SMSR) 2008, concerning how essential health and safety requirements are dealt with, manufacturers must provide comprehensive information regarding the safe operation and use of machinery.

Instruction manuals provided with machinery by manufacturers or suppliers must be in one or more official European Community languages. The words "Original Instructions" must appear on the language versions and this must be verified by the "Responsible Person".

Each instruction manual must contain, where applicable, at least the following information:

"(a) *The business name and full address of the manufacturer and of the manufacturer's authorised representative.*

(b) *The designation of the machinery as marked on the machinery itself, except for the serial number.*

(c) *The EC declaration of conformity, or a document setting out the contents of the EC declaration of conformity, showing the particulars of the machinery, not necessarily including the serial number and the signature.*

(d) *A general description of the machinery.*

(e) *The drawings, diagrams, descriptions and explanations necessary for the use, maintenance and repair of the machinery and for checking its correct functioning.*

(f) *A description of the workstation(s) likely to be occupied by operators.*

(g) *A description of the intended use of the machinery.*

(h) *Warnings concerning ways in which the machinery must not be used that experience has shown might occur.*

(i) *Assembly, installation and connection instructions, including drawings, diagrams and the means of attachment and the designation of the chassis or installation on which the machinery is to be mounted.*

(j) *Instructions relating to installation and assembly for reducing noise or vibration.*

(k) *Instructions for the putting into service and use of the machinery and, if necessary, instructions for the training of operators.*

(l) *Information about the residual risks that remain despite the inherent safe design measures, safeguarding and complementary protective measures adopted.*

(m) *Instructions on the protective measures to be taken by the user, including, where appropriate, the personal protective equipment to be provided.*

(n) *The essential characteristics of tools which may be fitted to the machinery.*

(o) *The conditions in which the machinery meets the requirement of stability during use, transportation, assembly, dismantling when out of service, testing or foreseeable breakdowns.*

(p) *Instructions with a view to ensuring that transport, handling and storage operations can be made safely, giving the mass of the machinery and of its various parts where these are regularly to be transported separately.*

(q) *The operating method to be followed in the event of accident or breakdown; if a blockage is likely to occur, the operating method to be followed so as to enable the equipment to be safely unblocked.*

(r) *The description of the adjustment and maintenance operations that should be carried out by the user and the preventive maintenance measures that should be observed.*

(s) *Instructions designed to enable adjustment and maintenance to be carried out safely, including the protective measures that should be taken during these operations.*

(t) *The specifications of the spare parts to be used, when these affect the health and safety of operators.*

(u) *The following information on airborne noise emissions:*

  i) *The A-weighted emission sound pressure level at workstations, where this exceeds 70 dB(A); where this level does not exceed 70 dB(A), this fact must be indicated.*

  ii) *The peak C-weighted instantaneous sound pressure value at workstations, where this exceeds 63 Pa (130 dB in relation to 20 Pa).*

  iii) *The A-weighted sound power level emitted by the machinery, where the A weighted emission sound pressure level at workstations exceeds 80 dB(A).*

  iv) *These values must be either those actually measured for the machinery in question or those established on the basis of measurements taken for technically comparable machinery which is representative of the machinery to be produced.*

  v) *Where machinery is likely to emit non-ionising radiation which may cause harm to persons, in particular persons with active or non-active implantable medical devices, information concerning the radiation emitted for the operator and exposed persons".*

In addition, the Provision and Use of Work Equipment Regulations (PUWER) 1998 specifies that:

"(1) Every employer shall ensure that all persons who use work equipment have available to them adequate health and safety information and, where appropriate, written instructions pertaining to the use of the work equipment.

(2) Every employer shall ensure that any of his employees who supervises or manages the use of work equipment has available to him adequate health and safety information and, where appropriate, written instructions pertaining to the use of the work equipment".

The regulation specifies that this includes information and, where appropriate, written instructions on:

- The conditions under which the machinery may be used.
- Foreseeable abnormal situations and the action to be taken.
- Any conclusions drawn from experience in using the work equipment.

The guidance to PUWER 1998 suggests that any information and written instructions provide should cover:

(a) *All health and safety aspects arising from the use of the work equipment.*

(b) *Any limitations on these uses.*

(c) *Any foreseeable difficulties that could arise.*

(d) *The methods to deal with them.*

(e) *Any conclusions drawn from experience of using the work equipment should be either recorded or steps taken to ensure that all appropriate members of the workforce are aware of them.*

Information and instructions regarding the operation and use of machinery

COMPREHENSIBLE INFORMATION AND INSTRUCTIONS

The EU Machinery Directive 2006/42/EC and SMSR 2008 require that information and instructions provided by the responsible person, for example the manufacturer, regarding the operation and use of machinery must be comprehensible to those concerned. In addition, PUWER 1998, Regulation 8, requires that:

"(4) Information and instructions required by this regulation shall be readily comprehensible to those concerned".

This will involve consideration of the language of the user and may mean providing the information in more languages than English. The ability of the worker to understand technical data should also be considered. Technical information may be appropriate for engineers involved with the installation and maintenance of machinery, but consideration has to be made of the capabilities of users. This means that it may be preferable to provided information and instructions in the form of readily understandable symbols or pictograms. Whatever the format, the information and instructions should be set out in a logical order.

In addition, in order to ensure the information and instructions are comprehensible it is important to consider those workers with language difficulties or with cognitive disabilities that could make it difficult for them to receive or understand information or instructions.

MARKINGS AND WARNINGS

In addition to requirements under the SMSR 2008, PUWER 1998 sets out duties on the employer regarding markings and warnings.

PUWER Regulation 23 - Markings

PUWER 2008, Regulation 23 requires that employers ensure that work equipment is marked in a clearly visible manner with any marking appropriate for reasons of health and safety.

There are similarities between regulation 23 and 24 covering markings and warnings. Certain markings may also serve as a warning, for example the maximum working speed, maximum working load or the contents being of a hazardous nature (for example explosive dusts or high temperatures). Markings may also include the numbering of machines in order to aid identification, this may be very important to help ensure correct isolation prior to maintenance.

In order to ensure consistency, markings should follow the approach taken for the Health and Safety (Safety Signs and Signals) Regulations 1996 and similar meanings to colours and shape of markings should apply.

PUWER Regulation 24 - Warnings

PUWER 2008, Regulation 24 requires that employers ensure that work equipment incorporates any warnings or warning devices that are appropriate for reasons of health and safety.

Warnings and warning devices are introduced following the implementation of markings and other physical measures, where appropriate risks to health and safety remain. Warnings are usually in the form of a notice, sign or similar.

Examples of warnings include positive instructions (hard hats must be worn); prohibitions (no naked flames) and restrictions (do not heat above 60°C). In order to ensure consistency, warnings should follow the approach taken for the Health and Safety (Safety Signs and Signals) Regulations 1996 and similar meanings should be given to the colours and shape of warnings.

Warning devices are active units that often provide an audible or visual signal, usually connected to the equipment in order that it operates only when a hazard exists. Warnings given by warning devices on work equipment will not be appropriate unless they are unambiguous, easily perceived and easily understood. Warning devices are also used where the equipment is mobile, such things as a flashing light can warn of the presence of a fork-lift truck and an audible device may warn of a vehicle reversing or a conveyor about to start. Warning devices may also provide an indication of imminent danger, for example, of a blockage to a conveyor that removes material from a machine.

C6.6 - Machinery control systems

The key safety characteristics of machinery control systems

GENERAL REQUIREMENTS

PUWER 1998, Regulation 18 - "Control systems", sets out the following requirement:

"(1) Every employer shall:

  a) *Ensure, so far as is reasonably practicable, that all control systems of work equipment are safe.*

  b) *Are chosen making due allowance for the failures, faults and constraints to be expected in the planned circumstances of use.*

(2) Without prejudice to the generality of paragraph (1), a control system shall not be safe unless:

  a) *Its operation does not create any increased risk to health or safety.*

  b) *It ensures, so far as is reasonably practicable, that any fault in or damage to any part of the control system or the loss of supply of any source of energy used by the work equipment cannot result in additional or increased risk to health or safety.*

  c) *It does not impede the operation of any control required by regulation 15 or 16".*

Failure of any part of the control system or its power supply should lead to a 'fail-safe' condition (more correctly and realistically called 'minimised failure to danger'), and not impede the operation of the 'stop' or 'emergency stop' controls. The measures that should be taken in the design and application of a control system to mitigate against the effects of its failure will need to be balanced against the consequences of any failure. The greater the risk, the more resistant the control system should be to the effects of failure.

Summary of required characteristics, the machinery control system should:

- Make allowance for the failures, faults and constraints to be expected in the planned circumstances of use.
- Not create any increased risk to health or safety.
- Faults or damage to the control system or the loss of energy supply must not result in additional risk to health or safety.
- Not impede the operation of any stop/energy stop controls.

CONTROLS FOR STARTING OR MAKING A SIGNIFICANT CHANGE IN OPERATING CONDITIONS

PUWER 1998, Regulation 14 - "Controls for starting or making a significant change in operating conditions", requires:

"(1) Every employer shall ensure that, where appropriate, work equipment is provided with one or more controls for the purposes of:

  a) *Starting the work equipment (including re-starting after a stoppage for any reason).*

b) Controlling any change in the speed, pressure or other operating conditions of the work equipment where such conditions after the change result in risk to health and safety which is greater than or of a different nature from such risks before the change.

(2) Subject to paragraph (3), every employer shall ensure that where a control is required by paragraph (1), it shall not be possible to perform any operation mentioned in sub-paragraph (a) or (b) of that paragraph except by a deliberate action on such control. Paragraph (1) shall not apply to re-starting or changing operating conditions as a result of the normal operating cycle of an automatic device".

Any change in the operating conditions should only be possible by the use of a control, except if the change does not increase risk to health or safety. Examples of operating conditions include speed, pressure, temperature and power.

The controls provided should be designed and positioned so as to prevent, so far as possible, inadvertent or accidental operation. Buttons and levers should be of appropriate design, for example, including a shroud or locking facility. It should not be possible for the control to 'operate itself', for example due to the effects of gravity, vibration, or failure of a spring mechanism.

STOP CONTROLS READILY ACCESSIBLE AND LEADS TO A SAFE CONDITION

PUWER 1998 Regulation 15 - "Stop controls" requires:

"(1) Every employer shall ensure that, where appropriate, work equipment is provided with one or more readily accessible controls the operation of which will bring the work equipment to a safe condition in a safe manner.

(2) Any control required by paragraph (1) shall bring the work equipment to a complete stop where necessary for reasons of health and safety.

(3) Any control required by paragraph (1) shall, if necessary for reasons of health and safety, switch off all sources of energy after stopping the functioning of the work equipment.

(4) Any control required by paragraph (1) shall operate in priority to any control which starts or changes the operating conditions of the work equipment".

Stop controls must be placed so that they are readily accessible to the user, therefore it is important to consider the activities the user may be involved in and ensure the controls are available to them while they are doing this work. This may include providing supplementary stop controls at points where material is fed in or taken out of machinery as well as the primary operating position. The nature of the work may mean that a different type of control needs to be provided, such as a foot operated stop control, because the person's hands may be occupied while the machine is operating.

The other main requirement of this Regulation is that the action of the control should bring the equipment to a safe condition in a safe manner. This acknowledges that it is not always desirable to bring all items of work equipment immediately to a complete or instantaneous stop.

For example, to prevent the unsafe build-up of heat or pressure, or to allow a controlled run-down of large rotating parts. Similarly, stopping the mixing mechanism of a reactor during certain chemical reactions could lead to a dangerous exothermic reaction.

The Regulation is qualified by 'where necessary for reasons of health and safety'. Therefore, accessible dangerous parts must be rendered stationary. However, parts of equipment that do not present a risk, such as suitably guarded cooling fans, do not need to be positively stopped and may be allowed to idle.

EMERGENCY STOP CONTROLS PROVIDED AND TO BE READILY ACCESSIBLE

The function of an emergency stop control device is to provide a means to bring a machine to a rapid halt. It is provided in such circumstances where it would be of benefit and should be readily available to the operator and/or others. It should be easy to operate and clearly discernible from other controls.

PUWER 1998, Regulation 16 - "Emergency stop controls" sets out the requirement:

"(1) Every employer shall ensure that, where appropriate, work equipment is provided with one or more readily accessible emergency stop controls unless it is not necessary by reason of the nature of the hazards and the time taken for the work equipment to come to a complete stop as a result of the action of any control provided by virtue of regulation 15(1).

(2) Any control required by paragraph (1) shall operate in priority to any control required by regulation 15(1)".

Emergency stop controls are intended to affect a rapid response to potentially dangerous situations and they should not be used as functional stops during normal operation.

They should be easily reached and actuated. This may mean positioning one or more of the devices to ensure that they are available to workers using the machine from different positions, for example while loading materials into the machine.

Emergency stop controls may have to be positioned to take account of whether the worker will be seated or standing and whether their hands will be available to operate it. In some cases, supplementary foot operated emergency controls may be required. Common types are mushroom-headed buttons, bars, levers, kick-plates, or pressure-sensitive cables.

POSITION AND MARKING OF CONTROLS TO BE VISIBLE AND IDENTIFIABLE

PUWER 1998, Regulation 17 - "Controls", sets out the following requirements:

"(1) Every employer shall ensure that all controls for work equipment shall be clearly visible and identifiable, including by appropriate marking where necessary.

(2) Except where necessary, the employer shall ensure that no control for work equipment is in a position where any person operating the control is exposed to a risk to his health or safety.

(3) Every employer shall ensure where appropriate:

a) That, so far as is reasonably practicable, the operator of any control is able to ensure from the position of that control that no person is in a place where he would be exposed to any risk to his health or safety as a result of the operation of that control, but where or to the extent that it is not reasonably practicable.

b) That, so far as is reasonably practicable, systems of work are effective to ensure that, when work equipment is about to start, no person is in a place where he would be exposed to a risk to his health or safety as a result of the work equipment starting, but where neither of these is reasonably practicable.

c) That an audible, visible or other suitable warning is given by virtue of regulation 24 whenever work equipment is about to start.

(4) Every employer shall take appropriate measures to ensure that any person who is in a place where he would be exposed to a risk to his health or safety as a result of the starting or stopping of work equipment has sufficient time and suitable means to avoid that risk".

It should be possible to identify easily what each control does and on which equipment it takes effect. Both the controls and their markings should be clearly visible. As well as having legible wording or symbols, factors such as the colour, shape and position of controls are important.

Warnings given in accordance with PUWER 1998, Regulation 17(3)(c), should be given sufficiently in advance of the machine starting to give those at risk time to get clear. As well as time, suitable means of avoiding the risk should be provided.

This may take the form of a device by means of which the person at risk can prevent start-up or warn the operator of their presence. Otherwise, there must be adequate provision to enable people at risk to withdraw, for example sufficient space or exits. Circumstances will affect the type of warning chosen.

CONSIDERATION OF ERGONOMIC PRINCIPLES

Ergonomic principles

Ergonomic considerations involve the study of the person-equipment interface. The aim of ergonomic principles is to ensure controls suit a variety of individual sizes of worker and work positions in order to provide machinery control systems that are suitable and can be operated effectively.

In considering the ergonomic principles of a machinery control system it is essential to include the machine user's individual attributes and how the attributes may affect their ability to use the controls. This will include hand span, reach and strength capabilities.

Ergonomic principles for machine control systems might include consideration of the position and posture of workers when seated or standing, the height of the controls, layout of controls on a panel and their function. Consideration may have to be given to the colour and other differentiation of controls to avoid their operation in error. Where workers move between machines with similar functions the controls should be standardised for position, function and operation.

Controls with similar function should be grouped together, unless this would lead to confusion. Sufficient space should be provided between the controls to prevent unintentional operation and lighting levels should be sufficient to avoid incorrect operation due to mistakes in selection of the control.

The direction of movement of the control should be consistent with the expected outcome, for example moving a control lever forward moves the machine forward. The forces required to operate controls should be within the worker's capability, but not too light that it may be inadvertently operated or its movement is difficult to control. Inadvertent use of start controls should be prevented by shrouding or recessing the control. Stop and emergency stop controls should be positioned for ease of use/priority and be more pronounced.

The size of the control should take account of clothing or footwear in use while operating the machine, for example gloves in a cold workplace.

It is essential that ergonomic considerations form an active part at the planning stage of the design of machinery, to ensure the suitable location and operation of controls.

WORK EQUIPMENT (WORKPLACE MACHINERY) - ELEMENT C6

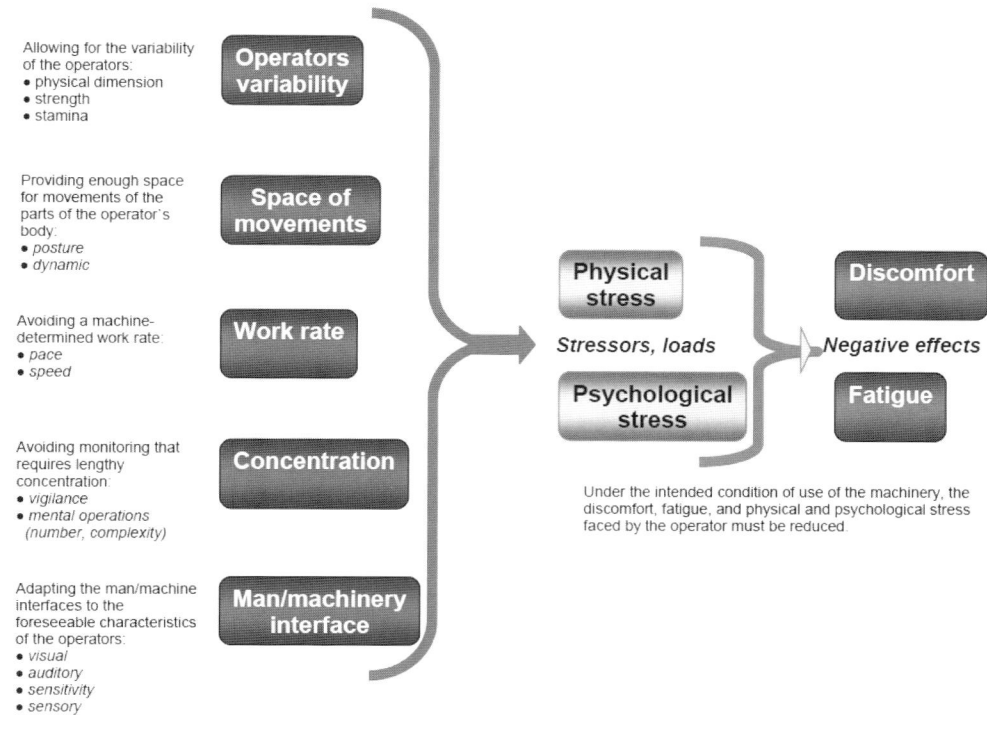

Ergonomic factors   Possible negative consequences

Figure C6-57: Practical application of ergonomic principles to machine design. *Source: Guide to the Machinery Directive.*

Stability

PUWER 1998 - Regulation 20 - "Stability" requires:

"Every employer shall ensure that work equipment or any part of work equipment is stabilised by clamping or otherwise where necessary for purposes of health or safety".

Most machines used in a fixed position should be bolted or otherwise fastened down so that they do not move or rock during use. It has long been recognised that woodworking and other machines (except those specifically designed for portable use) should be bolted to the floor or similarly secured to prevent unexpected movement.

Lighting

PUWER 1998 - Regulation 21 - "Lighting" requires:

"Every employer shall ensure that suitable and sufficient lighting, which takes account of the operations to be carried out, is provided at any place where a person uses work equipment".

Local lighting may be needed to give sufficient view of a dangerous process or to reduce visual fatigue.

C6.7 - Systems failures and system reliability

Meaning of the term 'system'

A system is a set of inter-related elements that starts with an input that undergoes some process and results in an output, which has a monitoring (feedback) loop that evaluates the input, process and output in order to make adjustments that ensure the intended resultant output is provided.

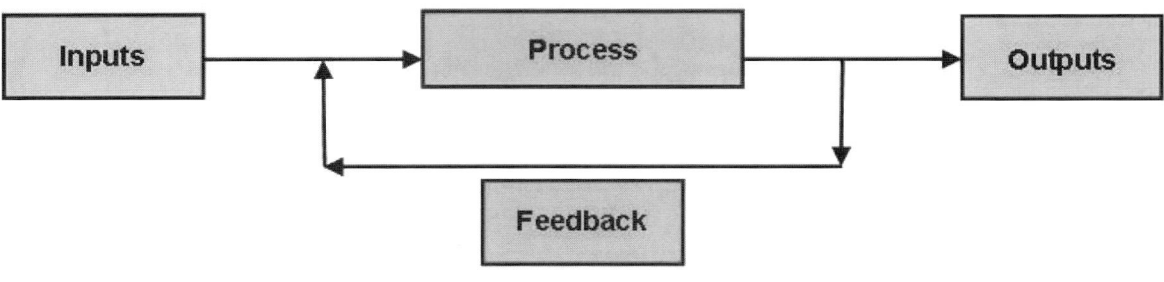

Figure C6-58: System.   *Source: RMS.*

ELEMENT C6 - WORK EQUIPMENT (WORKPLACE MACHINERY)

Principles of system failure analysis

HOLISTIC AND REDUCTIONIST APPROACHES

The *holistic* approach examines the system as a whole. The rationale behind this is the argument that the behaviour of a system cannot be satisfactorily explained merely by the study of its component parts. Thus, the philosophy behind this approach is that the system is synergistic - that is, the whole is more than the sum of its parts. An example of the holistic approach is a hazard and operability (HAZOP) study, which most effectively examines the impact of failure on the whole system, although it can be used at the sub-system level. Thus, the impact of maloperation or malfunction of components is considered in terms of the effect on the system as a whole.

The advantage of holistic analysis is that it draws attention to the relationship between components and the qualitative aspects of the system that may not be appreciated by the reductionist approach.

The *reductionist* approach to analysis of any system involves dividing the system into its individual component parts. An individual component is then isolated and the factors that influence it are examined. Thus, the reductionist approach to failure analysis begins at the component level, by identifying basic modes of failure for each component within the system. Each component failure is then evaluated for its effects on the system. An example of this technique is failure mode and effects analysis (FMEA).

DIFFERENCES BETWEEN SYSTEMIC AND SYSTEMATIC ANALYSIS

Systemic: of the body as a whole.

Systematic: methodical; according to plan, not casually or at random.

This is similar to the differences between the holistic and reductionist approach to complex failure analysis considered above.

A **systemic** analysis considers the whole system whereas a **systematic** analysis considers the component parts of the system in a logical, methodical way that considers each stage of the system in turn. Systemic analysis allows for an intuitive approach that may perceive relationships in an apparently unconnected array of activities.

APPLICATION TO ACTUAL EXAMPLES

Systems may be "hard" or "soft". A "hard" system is, for example, a piece of equipment, a vehicle, a plant that processes a chemical, a smoke or heat detector, an automatic fire alarm system, etc. A "soft" system is a management strategy, for example, to manage contractors, recruit new staff, deal with emergencies, etc. Systems are made up of sub-systems; parts that work together to make the system work.

A forklift truck (FLT) may be considered a system that operates within an environment. It can be analysed as to its failure within that environment by consideration of the task it performs and its movements: hitting overhead pipes, overturning, a wheel going down a pothole, etc.

The FLT (the system) can be broken up into a number of sub-systems. The lifting mechanism and the braking mechanism are two of the sub-systems, i.e. parts of the greater whole. Analysis of the lifting mechanism, for example, using FMEA, will show which parts may fail and how. The failure of component parts in the lifting mechanism, the chain for example, may cause the lifting mechanism to fail while carrying a load or not be able to operate at all. The effect on the system, the FLT, may just be that it cannot perform its duties as a lifting machine and there may be some product damage. Analysis of the braking mechanism could show that failure of the component parts, the brake pads for example, may make the brakes inoperable. The effect on the system (the FLT) could be catastrophic and cause loss by way of personal injury, plant and building damage, loss of product and the inoperability of the FLT.

An analysis of the system and sub-system would have shown the probability of a failure of a weak temporary link (solvent pipeline) between vessels at *Flixborough*, where a major flammable chemical explosion occurred. A HAZOP and/or an FMEA would have shown how the temporary change introduced could have adversely affected the system.

A system to manage contractors will be made up of sub-systems for example, choosing the contractor, site induction, issuing work orders, safe procedures and permits-to-work, supervising them, etc. On analysis, each of these sub-systems can be further broken down so, for example, issuing permits to work becomes a system that can be broken down into sub-systems such as support documentation, permit authorisers and so on until a further breakdown is no longer possible. Controls can be considered at each stage.

The *Piper Alpha* explosion was due, in part, to management failure within a permit-to-work system. The permit-to-work sub-system had not been analysed to find out what effect its failure in operation could be on the whole system.

If a car and passenger ferry such as the *Herald of Free Enterprise* leaving port is considered as a system, then for the numerous problems that developed, for example, management attitude 'to turn the ship around quickly', failure to follow standard procedures in the sub-systems inevitably led to disaster.

Use of calculation in the assessment of system reliability

GENERAL POINTS

Reliability is not confined to single components only; the evaluation of systems, simple or complex, is needed. Evaluation techniques are used for designing reliable systems or for gaining reasonable assurance in advance that a design will meet certain safety and reliability requirements.

System reliability calculations are based on two important operations:

- As precise as possible a measurement of the reliability of the components used in the system environment.
- A calculation of the reliability of some complex combinations of these components.

The calculation of the reliability of components will take account of the probability of failure, for example where a component had a probability of failure of 3 in every 100 this could be represented by a probability of failure of 0.03. This can then be translated to derive a reliability for the component of 0.97.

SERIES SYSTEMS

Generally, the reliability of the series system is computed by multiplying the probability of each component part that it will survive its operating life. Multiplying the probability of survival of A and B in the diagram will give the probability of the system surviving.

Figure C6-59: Series system. Source: RMS.

If there are number of components in the series, the system reliability is given by:

Rs = R1 X R2 X R3 X......X Rn

For example, if A had a reliability of 0.98 and B had a reliability of 0.97 the reliability of the whole system, a series system would be:

Rs = 0.98 x 0.97 = 0.95

A series system has drawbacks, in that one failed component causes failure to the whole system. The accident at Markham Colliery is an example of this, where the one failed component (central pin in the winding mechanism to the lift cage) caused the whole system to fail and hence led to the disaster.

PARALLEL SYSTEMS

If very high system reliabilities are required, for example, on lifts or aircraft, the designer must duplicate components and sometimes whole circuits to fulfil such requirements. Use must be made of parallel reliabilities, called parallel redundancy. In series systems, all components must function for the system to operate. In parallel systems, it is necessary for only one component to operate for the system to operate. The systems can be evaluated in a similar, but more complex, way to the series equation in order to work out the probability of success or failure.

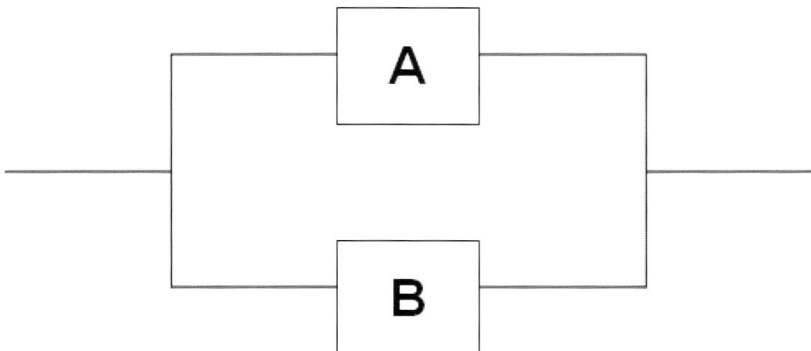

Figure C6-60: Parallel system. Source: RMS.

If there are number of components in parallel, the system reliability is given by:

Rs =   1 - (1 - R1) x (1 - R2) x (1 - R3) ..... x (1 - Rn)

For example, if A had a reliability of 0.95 and B, being an identical component, had a reliability of 0.95 the reliability of the whole system, a parallel system would be:

Rs =   1 - (1 - 0.95) x (1 - 0.95)

Rs =   1 - (0.05) x (0.05)

Rs =   1 - 0.0025

Rs = 0.99 (2 decimal places)

Three components in parallel are represented by:

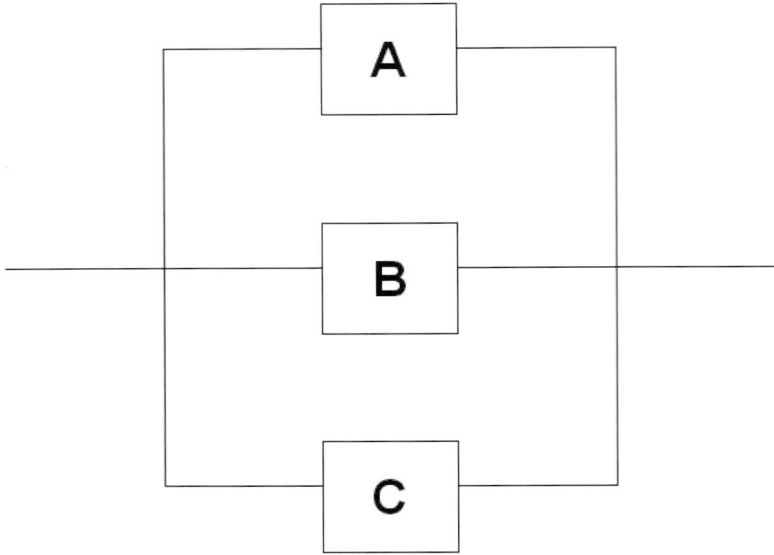

Figure C6-61: Three components in parallel. Source: RMS.

MIXED SYSTEMS

The reliability of a mixed system involving series and parallel components can be calculated as follows:

Figure C6-62: The reliability of a mixed system (series and parallel). Source: RMS.

Where there are systems with components in parallel, with a switch component in and a switch component out, the reliability of the whole system can be calculated as follows:

Reliability of each of the parts of the parallel system, comprising of two components in series, is 0.98 x 0.97 = 0.95

Reliability of the two systems in parallel is:

= 1 - (1 - 0.95) x (1 - 0.95)
= 1 - (0.05) x (0.05)
= 1 - 0.0025
= 0.99 (2 decimal places)

Reliability of the whole system, including the two switches, is then calculated as a series system, with the parallel part of the system represented by a reliability of 0.99:

= 0.99 x 0.99 x 0.99
= 0.97

Reliability of the whole system = 0.97, which is less reliable with the inclusion of the two switches, but is more reliable than the single series system (which would have been 0.99 x 0.98 x 0.97 x 0.99 = 0.93).

Probability of failure of whole system = 1 - 0.97 = 0.03

There are some cases when not all reliability models can be reduced to the series, parallel and stand-by. There are combinations of components that are neither series, parallel, nor stand-by. Again, there are formulae available to evaluate the reliability of these systems.

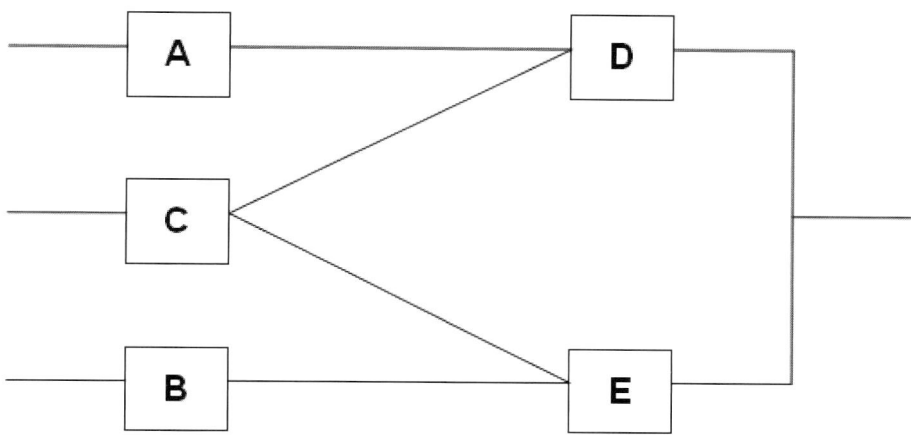

Figure C6-63: Mixed system.   Source: RMS.

In the above system, the two equal paths, A-D and B-E, operate in parallel so that if at least one of them is good, the output is assured. But, because units A and B are not reliable enough, a third equal unit, C, is inserted into the system so that units D and E are supplied with the necessary input. Therefore, the following operations are possible:

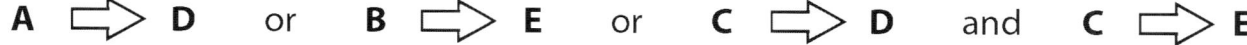

COMMON MODE FAILURES

Failure can occur when an external factor affects the systems. For example, in 1980 a leg sheared off an oil platform (rig), the platform tilted and the generator was knocked off. The generator supplied all the electrical power. The rig was plunged into darkness, the resulting fire could not be dealt with and there was no means of escape. The systems for dealing with the various emergency situations should have been so completely apart from each other that the risk of them all being affected by the same external factor could have been avoided.

PRINCIPLES OF HUMAN RELIABILITY ANALYSIS

Human reliability analysis (HRA) was developed as a means of quantifying the interaction between human and engineering systems. It aims to improve the understanding of the contribution made by all people to engineering systems. This is significantly greater than the previous man-machine interface analysis. HRA is a systematic evaluation of the factors that influence the performance of humans in the workplace and is used to identify potential human errors, their causes and their subsequent effects.

Human behaviour

Human behaviour is controlled by the requirements of the task, the working environment in which the task is performed and the skills, experience, abilities and training of the human performing the task. Human knowledge can be assigned to one of three categories:

1) Skill based knowledge and action.
2) Rule based knowledge and action.
3) Formal reason based knowledge and action.

The skills required from and exercised by an operator of equipment include sensing, perceiving, prediction, familiarity with controls, and decision making. The table below summarises some of the errors made by people contributing to the failure of engineering systems over their lifetime.

Examples of errors

Designer	*Procurer*	*Manufacturer*	*Distributor*	*End user*
Failure to select most appropriate control-display component.	Incorrect specification of system type.	Incorrect production of design.	Incorrect handling and storage.	Use of incorrect operating and maintenance.
Human is assigned a task that they cannot do or that is best done by machine.	Incorrect specification of parameters.	Use of wrong machining and fabrication techniques.	Incorrect monitoring of environment during transit.	Use of incorrect parts in maintenance.

Figure C6-64: Examples of errors.   Source: RMS.

ELEMENT C6 - WORK EQUIPMENT (WORKPLACE MACHINERY)

Applications of human reliability analysis

For example, in the computer industry, the requirement for reliability safety critical software has led to wide studies for reducing errors by software developers. Based on the findings of HRA, computers are used to check the design decisions of humans and hence improve reliability of software. In the transport industry, analysis of incidents involving the transport of dangerous substances showed that over 40% of these incidents were directly caused by human error, rather than by mechanical failure.

Implementation of human reliability analysis

The following steps are taken when implementing HRA.

1) List the system functions to be performed.
2) For each function, list all the actions that must be performed by operators to implement that function.
3) Determine whether any operator tasks have already been specified by a customer procurement document.
4) Determine sub-tasks that must be performed to implement higher order tasks.
5) Describe each task and sub-task in terms of a verb that indicates the nature of the action being performed by the task, for example, monitor, check, read, etc.
6) For each task and sub-task identify error-likely situations.
7) Rank the errors in the order of severity.
8) Document the results.

Type and nature of results

The results of HRA are both qualitative and quantitative. They are qualitative in the respect that they give a listing of the errors and the contributing factors that are likely to be encountered during normal and emergency operation. They also identify systems interfaces that are affected by specific errors. Human reliability analysis gives quantitative results in the respect that it provides relative ranking of errors based on probability of occurrence and severity of consequences.

Methods for improving system reliability

GENERAL POINTS

Regular testing is important to identify fail to danger situations before a demand is placed on the system, but there may be a danger in testing systems too frequently.

Three risk factors need to be considered if the testing of systems is carried out more frequently:

1) Continuance of plant operation whilst protective devices are removed for testing.
2) The likelihood of error/damage in removal/replacement of equipment by test engineers.
3) Potential exists to replace a good component with a component that is defective.

1984 Bhopal, India

A major disaster occurred to the local population following the uncontrolled release of highly toxic vapour when a storage tank containing methyl isocyanate was contaminated with water (major respiratory injury results at exposure to levels at parts per billion). 2,500 people were killed and it is estimated that approaching 500,000 people were injured from the release. The most significant aspect that contributed to the loss was that the plant was operating whilst the protective trip systems and devices were disconnected for testing and maintenance work. It is essential to include testing/maintenance considerations at the design stage, when conducting HAZOPs.

Typically the trip system/devices should be tested to a frequency that gives at least the same reliability as the protective device.

The human element is a very important consideration when calculating the frequency of the test of protective systems and devices, and as a minimum, task analysis should be carried out. For high potential risk considerations other techniques such as psychological profiling will often be required. Formulae are available to calculate these probabilities, but these are outside the scope of this book.

USE OF RELIABLE COMPONENTS

By considering the data available, the most reliable components can be chosen. The most expensive may not always be the most suitable. For example, the reliability of a system may be lessened because a valve has a probability of failure of 0.05. Using the same level of quality valve, a second valve can be placed in parallel so that if one fails the other will come into use. This means, for a dangerous situation to arise, both valves will have to fail together, the probability of which is 0.05 X 0.05 = 0.0025. The probability has gone from 1 in 20 to 1 in 400.

Another method of improving reliability is derating. This means having a safety margin. For example, a resistor rated for a current of 2 amps is run at 1.4 amps. The derating is 1.4 / 2 = 0.7. This is a typical figure for electronic parts.

QUALITY ASSURANCE

Components that are made to a specification within a quality assurance system, where rigorous testing is carried out are more likely to be reliable. It is important that reliability is built in from the design stage, through manufacture, through the building of the system, its use, making changes, and maintaining the system and its component parts.

PARALLEL REDUNDANCY

System reliability can be improved by duplication of critical components in parallel, so that when one component fails (becomes redundant) the other operates to maintain control for example dual braking fitted to a road vehicle. When designing parallel systems consideration should also be given to diversity, which is where alternative mechanisms provide the desired action, for example a pneumatic system may be provided in parallel to support an electronic system.

STANDBY SYSTEMS

A stand-by system is where a component or unit is operating and one or more units are standing by to take over the operation, should the primary one fail. The supporting components or units are normally idle and begin to operate only when the primary unit fails. An example of this is a second water supply pump at a water treatment plant provided to be available by valve switching when required following a failure or maintenance of the primary pump.

These systems therefore require failure sensing and switchover devices to put the stand-by component or unit into operation. The reliability of the sensing/switching device must be taken into consideration, as well as the failure rates of the stand-by units. Standby is therefore only appropriate when the system has the capacity to deal with the time for switchover, which may be either manual or automatic.

MINIMISING FAILURES TO DANGER

Minimising failure to danger is a design consideration at the HAZOP stage. This requires consideration of the operation of safety critical equipment and devices at the time of failure of the device, detector communication link or responder.

Consider a remotely operated steam control valve to a reactor. Such valves are usually controlled using compressed air operating the valve against a spring. A typical arrangement would be that the valve closes at zero supply pressure and opens when compressed air at a known pressure is applied.

At the design stage it would need to be determined which is the more critical to the process, failure to open or failure to close. The reliability of the equipment and air supply would be assessed and the design would ensure the correct sequence of events to ensure a failure to a safe condition results.

Certain high risk facilities, for example, the nuclear industry, may need complex duplication of protective devices to meet the societal level of assurance. Such systems are designed to include 'majority voting systems' (MVS). Majority voting systems use voting logic. For example, consider the temperature of a reactor; it may be decided that this needs to be controlled critically. Any message from the thermocouple that shows overheating will set a sequence in play to shut down the reactor. However, some of the messages from the sensor are spurious. The solution is to install three thermocouples to monitor a single process variable. A voting logic analyser will receive readings from each of the sensors, but any response action (for example reactor shut down) is only initiated by any two of the three sensors. The logic behind this is that there is a probability that one sensor could send a spurious message, but the probability that two will send spurious messages at the same time is remote. Conversely, there is a probability that one sensor might not pick up a change in temperature, but the probability that two will not at the same time is remote.

DIVERSITY

Diversity is concerned with the identification of common mode failure. Common mode failure may cause a parallel system failure, for example if the parallel system requires compressed air and both components are supplied from the same air supply, then failure of the air supply will result in the failure of both components in the parallel system. A single failure of electrical supply may affect many different supply voltages to a plant, including low voltage instrumentation, if not provided with separate back up. Care needs to be taken when considering the need for either redundancy or diversity. The best design systems strive to reduce the need for protective devices as the more protective devices that are included the more likely you are to have spurious trips.

For example, a power press utilises three protective devices to safeguard the operator: electrical, mechanical and pneumatic. If an electrical failure occurred the electric interlock would fail, but in such a diverse system, the mechanical interlock would protect the operator from injury. If both the electrical and mechanical protective devices failed, then the pneumatic interlock would become the protective device. A common fault in the system would be unlikely to affect all three types of safeguarding system. The machine would be guarded by at least one of the systems and the probability of all failing would be very low.

ELEMENT C6 - WORK EQUIPMENT (WORKPLACE MACHINERY)

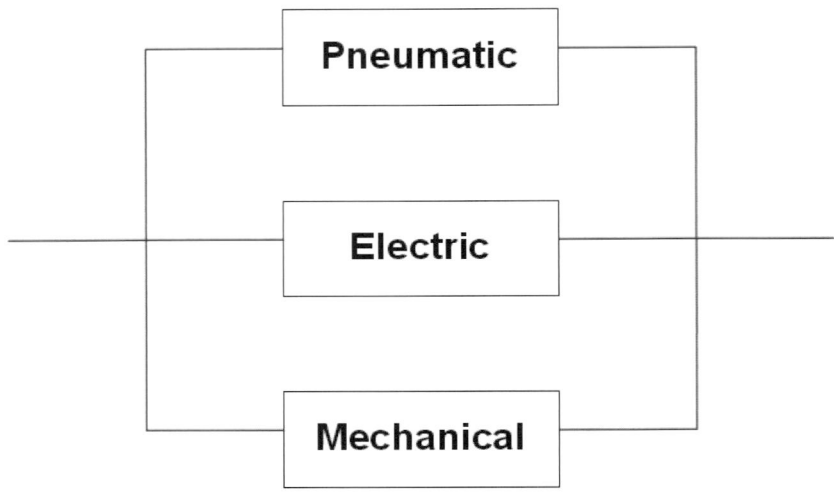

Figure C6-65: Diverse system.   Source: RMS.

PLANNED PREVENTIVE MAINTENANCE

Plant maintenance systems

The risk management approach to maintenance is to minimise costs (of all types, including accidents) and to maximise productivity and equipment life. There are various strategies that can be adopted including emergency maintenance, breakdown maintenance, shutdown maintenance and planned preventive maintenance, including routine condition monitoring.

Although there may be some short-term gains in adopting a total breakdown maintenance strategy (no disruption of production, or use of spare parts, no or low maintenance staff costs) this will become increasingly less cost-efficient as time passes. Breakdown maintenance would be appropriate for non-safety or production critical items where the cost of maintenance outweighs the need for increased reliability.

No matter what maintenance strategy is adopted, some equipment failures will occur. Although the precise timing or location of the failure cannot always be accurately forecast, the fact that a breakdown will occur at some time is mostly predictable - either by examination of historical records or via the risk assessment process. It is important therefore to have a suitable system for emergency maintenance in place. This may be achieved through the use of:

- Contingency plans.
- Model (or generic) risk assessments.
- Safe systems of work (for example permit to work system).
- The provision of appropriate skills and training.

Shutdown maintenance, where the renewal work is carried out when the process is stopped, is still common to the chemical and engineering sectors of industry. Traditionally in the engineering sector this occurred during the Easter break. Chemical plants usually have a cycle whereby they shutdown, for example, every two years. The frequency and duration of the maintenance period is dependent on the nature of the plant and processes being operated. This has the advantage of allowing maintenance to take place without the pressures of production. Many organisations combine the shutdown period with a general process employee holiday. Unless adequate management arrangements are in place, this can lead to a lowering of normal safety standards, particularly when third party maintenance staff is involved.

Planned preventative maintenance seeks to take action which tries to keep the condition of the component at its best by carrying out frequent care of the component for example lubrication, adjustment, cleaning. Monitored maintenance seeks to monitor the conditions of components, for example, noise or frequency levels from a gearbox to estimate bearing wear to determining the point just before failure, at which point it would be replaced. The main benefits of planned preventative maintenance are:

- Extended useable life of components.
- Assurance of reliability.
- Confirmation of condition of components.
- Reduced risk/loss producing failure events.
- Ability to carry out work at a suitable time.
- Better utilisation of maintenance staff.
- Less peaks and troughs in maintenance activity.
- Less standby facilities required.
- Less expensive (last minute) contracted facility required, for example temporary hire of equipment such as fork lift truck.

Routine condition monitoring is the comparison of the state parameters of the plant. Traditionally in engineering systems important parameters have been temperature, coolant and vibration. For example, when a local exhaust ventilation system (LEV) is installed the state parameters (for example capture velocity and static pressures) will be measured during the commissioning process. These are then used as a benchmark against which the efficiency of the system and thus the need for maintenance is measured. This has the advantages of ensuring that the plant is working efficiently, allows early detection of any deterioration and the carrying out of maintenance tasks at the optimum time. In turn, condition monitoring may be extended to the components that comprise the system. This is particularly relevant to the monitoring of critical components such as the motor/fan within an LEV system. Here the motor and its associated bearings can be monitored to identify any deterioration in performance that might threaten the efficiency of the system as a whole.

The role of statutory examinations of plant and equipment

The role of statutory examinations is to provide a means to identify the condition of critical equipment that, if not maintained to an acceptable standard, would create serious risk. The examinations take the form of a physical examination of the equipment by a competent person to identify patent defects, such as surface corrosion or physical damage, in the condition of equipment and its safety devices.

Statutory examinations have been prescribed for a considerable period. Traditionally the period of 14 months (for example LEV under COSHH 2002) was considered an appropriate period. This had the twin advantages of allowing for the movement of Easter, the traditional maintenance period, and gives a variation in the time of year that the examination is carried out. However, having fixed intervals between examinations with universal application takes no account of the actual conditions of use. The trend, however, appears to be moving away from prescriptive statutory examinations towards risk based assessment by a competent person (for example written systems of examination for pressure systems and lifting equipment). The latter example illustrates the prescribed versus risk bases approach. The Lifting Operations and Lifting Equipment Regulations (LOLER) 1998 provide that operational lifting equipment is to be thoroughly examined:

- At least every 6 months for lifting equipment for lifting persons or lifting accessories.
- At least every 12 months for other lifting equipment.
- In either case, in accordance with an examination scheme.
- On each occurrence of exceptional circumstances liable to jeopardise the safety of the lifting equipment.

Note that the law setting out the requirements for statutory examinations does not precisely define a 'competent person' nor does it stipulate that they should be independent of the employer. Although statutory examinations can be delegated to an outside organisation, this does not absolve the employer from the responsibility to ensure that they are carried out.

MINIMISING HUMAN ERROR

Human reliability analysis (HRA) can be used to develop training schemes for skill based behaviour and associated physiological factors, the design of controls, workplace, buildings, environmental conditions, transportation, and communications. A good example is the design of aircraft cockpit control layouts in which human performance at the operator level reaches the highest levels of criticality.

The concept of HRA could be used by management to devise management controls. The collapse of Baring's Bank and the huge losses suffered by a Japanese investment bank of the New York bonds market and Black Monday were attributed to human errors in monitoring and controlling the operations of the traders. HRA is increasingly used in the development of expert and machine intelligent systems to improve the performance of humans and equipment. At the design stage, HRA can be used to identify the features of hardware and job design that are likely to produce a high rate of human error.

Application of HRA requires skilled analysts who understand the plant operation and the tasks performed by operators. The lack of reliable data on operator's behaviour in error-likely situations is a major drawback for the application of the technique.

Analysts must consider that any analysis of operator behaviour is likely to bring about a modification of the behaviour. Operators will modify their behaviour and this can have significant effects on the HRA. One technique to reduce effect on behaviour is to train someone close to the operators in the technique, such as their line manager. The presence of someone known and often in the workplace has less effect on behavioural change, than for example an 'outsider' such as a consultant. Many of the same problems exist in other types of analysis, for example job safety analysis, and can be alleviated where the operators have confidence in the approach being taken and the analysts involved.

Failures of components and hardware can be expressed as probabilities. These may be derived from various studies such as in-service or test failures. Predicting the probability of human failure is far more complex. However, if risk assessments are to be done then human reliability needs to be considered and quantified.

When attempting to quantify human behaviour, it is necessary to be clear about what task or step is to be performed, when this task/step is to be performed and how much time there is available to perform it. The next stage is the consideration of how the person can deviate from the step/task. The most common deviations are when the step/task is not carried out correctly, when a step/task is forgotten in a sequence or is performed out of sequence, or when the step/task is not completed in the time required.

ELEMENT C6 - WORK EQUIPMENT (WORKPLACE MACHINERY)

Error rates can be affected by a variety of conditions. As previously mentioned, observations of task performance can alter error rates, as can environmental conditions, training and skill levels, and various other stressors. Error rates are likely to be high when the person is under very little stress (bored), or under great stress (emergency situations). Human beings also have the ability to recover from errors, often demonstrating what appears to be an innate ability to control errors of great consequence compared to those of small consequence.

Error rates for a control room situation may typically be as follows:

Error rate	Situation
1 in 1	Impending disaster, rapid action needed, panic
1 in 10	No impending disaster apparent, busy, signals, alarms
1 in 100	Quiet but busy, relaxed
1 in 1000	Familiar, routine tasks

Figure C6-66: Error rates for a control room. *Source: RMS.*

For example, we could imagine a situation where studies have been carried out, which may be a number of task analyses, and found out that under no stress conditions there is an error in reading a gauge of 1 in 100 operations (1% of readings). Under pressure, this increases to 1 in 10 operations (10% of readings). If there are 400 readings taken per year, then the probability of an error under no stress and stress conditions within the next 1,000 hours is as follows:

Error rate under **no stress** conditions - based on 400 readings per year and 1 error in 100 readings (1%).

Error rate per year = number of readings per year x 1 error / 100 readings

= 400 x 1/100 per year = 4 errors per year

= 4 errors in 24 (hours) x 365 (days) = 4 errors per 8760 hrs

Error rate per 1000 hrs = 4 x 1000 / 8760 errors per 1000hrs

Therefore error rate per 1000 hrs = 0.46 errors per 1000 hrs

Probability of error under **no stress** P_{f1000} = $1 - e^{-0.46}$

= 0.37

Error rate under **stress** conditions - based on 400 readings and 1 error in 10 readings (10%)

Therefore error rate 1000 hrs = 4.6 errors per 1000 hrs

Probability of error under **stress** P_{f1000} = $1 - e^{-4.6}$

= 0.99

This data can be used in risk assessments to quantify risk once the effect of the error is known. It can help reduce the amount of subjectivity that is usually present when dealing with human error. Once the probability of an accident happening is known, then it is relatively easy to balance the cost of the accident against the cost of controls.

Element C7

Work equipment (mobile, lifting and access)

Learning outcomes

The intended learning outcomes are that the student will be able to:

C7.1 Describe the main hazards and control measures associated with commonly encountered mobile work equipment.

C7.2 Describe the main hazards and control measures associated with commonly encountered lifting equipment.

C7.3 Describe the main hazards and control measures associated with commonly encountered access equipment and equipment for working at height.

Content

C7.1 - Mobile work equipment: hazards and control measures.. 251
    The applications of different types of mobile work equipment.. 251
    The hazards associated with mobile work equipment.. 254
    The hazards associated with the energising (electrical, LPG, diesel) of mobile work equipment........ 256
    The control measures to be used in the use of mobile work equipment 257
    Attachments used on lift trucks.. 259
    Roll-over protection, falling objects protection, speed control and restraining systems................ 260
    The requirements for the training of lift truck operators (basic, specific job training and familiarisation)...... 262
C7.2 - Lifting equipment: hazards and control measures 263
    The applications and different types of lifting equipment including cranes and hoists................ 263
    Main hazards and controls associated with cranes and lifting operations 265
    Main hazards and controls associated with hoists and lifts 266
    General control measures for lifting equipment.. 269
    Control measures for cranes and lifting operations 271
C7.3 - Access and work at height equipment: hazards and control measures.. 277
    The applications and different types of mobile access and work at height equipment 277
    The hazards of access and work at height equipment 279
    The appropriate control measures for use of access and work at height equipment.................. 279

ELEMENT C7 - WORK EQUIPMENT (MOBILE, LIFTING AND ACCESS)

Relevant statutory provisions

Work at Height Regulations (WAH) 2005
Workplace (Health, Safety and Welfare) Regulations (WHSWR) 1992
Provision and Use of Work Equipment Regulations (PUWER) 1998
Lifting Operations and Lifting Equipment Regulations (LOLER) 1998
The Supply of Machinery (Safety) Regulations (SMSR) 2008 Schedule 2

C7.1 - Mobile work equipment - hazards and control measures

The mobile work equipment discussed in this element includes vehicles that are not in general use on the public highways and are used within the confines of a site, such as a warehouse depot or a site involving construction/demolition work. Vehicles that transfer materials to and from such locations on the public highways, together with the hazards and controls when loading and unloading, are discussed in Element 10 "Workplace transport and driving at work".

The term mobile work equipment includes work equipment that is self-propelled, towed, attached, pedestrian-controlled, and remotely-controlled. Examples of mobile work equipment include: various forms of lift truck, such as the counterbalance; reach; rough terrain telescopic materials handler; side loading and pedestrian controlled types. Other examples of mobile work equipment include agricultural tractors and other works vehicles.

The applications of different types of mobile work equipment

LIFT TRUCKS

Counterbalance

Typically counterbalanced lift trucks are used for materials handling in warehouses; delivery and removal of manufacturing materials in the workplace and loading/unloading goods vehicles.

Loads placed on the forks of this type of lift truck are counterbalanced by the weight of the vehicle. The mass of the truck acts as a counterweight, so that the truck can lift and move a load without tipping forwards.

The *rated capacity* of a counterbalance lift truck is the maximum weight in kilos/pounds it can lift at a maximum load centre stated in metres/inches, for example, 907 kg at 0.45 m load centre. The load centre is measured from the heel of the forks to the centre of gravity of the load. If the rated capacity is exceeded it will cause the lift truck to become unstable, causing it to overbalance and tip forwards.

Figure C7-1: Counterbalance lift truck.
Source: HSE, HSG6 - Safety in working with lift trucks.

Reach

Reach lift trucks are used exclusively in warehouses for placing and removing components; typically for order picking work where space is at a premium and their design enables them to work in narrow isles.

With the forks "out" a reach truck behaves in a similar manner to a counterbalance truck. With the fork "in" and the load retracted within the wheelbase the truck is less likely to overbalance and tip forwards. The facility to retract the load within the wheelbase of the reach truck minimises its overall working length, compared with a counterbalance truck, and allows the isle width that they work in to be reduced due to its greater manoeuvrability.

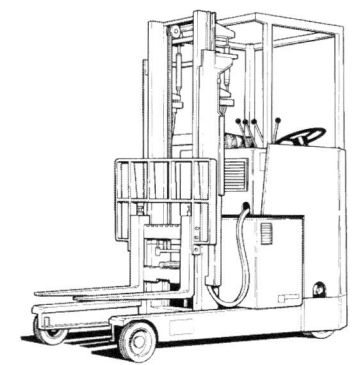
Figure C7-2: Reach lift truck.
Source: HSE, HSG6 - Safety in working with lift trucks.

Rough terrain

Rough terrain lift trucks, as the name suggests, are used to move a variety of materials on soft undulating ground, such as agricultural or construction sites.

Rough terrain lift trucks operate in a similar manner to traditional counterbalanced lift truck equipment found within industry, but with the main difference being the surface they operate on which is typically unmade and not hard standing. For example, the design employed on construction sites is usually of a heavier duty design.

Typical design differences also include:

- Diesel fuelled engines to provide the greater power required.
- Increased load/lifting capacity.
- Enclosed operator cab for protection against the elements.
- Higher chassis position for uneven terrain.
- Large diameter wheels with deep tread, pneumatic traction tyres for muddy, rough terrain.
- Increased security to enable the vehicle to be left unattended.

ELEMENT C7 - WORK EQUIPMENT (MOBILE, LIFTING AND ACCESS)

Figure C7-3: Rough-terrain lift trucks. Source: RMS.

Figure C7-4: Rough-terrain lift trucks. Source: RMS.

Telescopic materials handlers

These lift trucks are often referred to as multi-tool carriers. This versatility makes them particularly useful for agricultural, maintenance and construction work where lift trucks would be unsuitable.

When fitted with forks they can be used as a front-end materials loader and when fitted with a jib they can be used for crane duties. Instead of a vertical mast to raise or lower loads, this type of lift truck is fitted with a telescopic boom. This allows both vertical and forward movement of the forks, enabling the effects of uneven ground to be compensated for and the placement of loads in difficult positions that other lift trucks could not reach.

Figure C7-5: Telescopic handler. Source: Ambiguous.

Figure C7-6: Side loading trucks. Source: Ambiguous.

Side loading trucks

This type of lift truck is used for stacking and moving long loads, such as timber or pipes.

The operator of a side loading truck is positioned at the front and to one side of the lift truck. Side loading lift trucks have a mast and load carriage that moves sideways from the operator's position to pick up or deposit a load.

This enables the centre of gravity of the load to be within the wheelbase of the truck during travelling. During travelling, the load is usually resting on the truck structure.

Pedestrian controlled trucks

Pedestrian controlled trucks usually have a more restricted lifting height compared with other trucks, some may only have just enough to lift a pallet from the floor and enable it to be moved a relatively short distance, they are used extensively in chemical process operations.

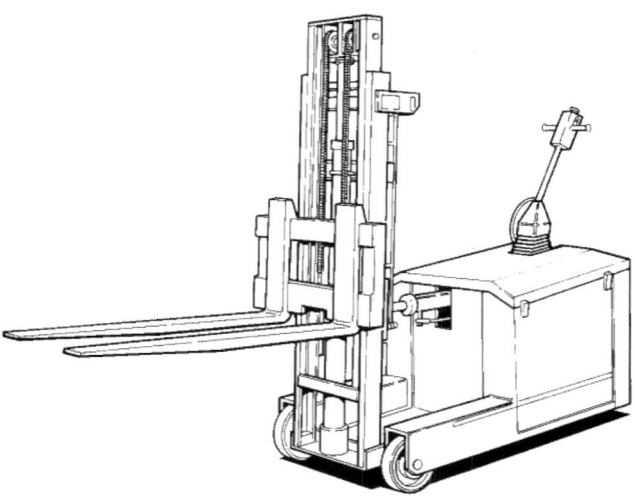

Figure C7-7: Pedestrian controlled trucks.
Source: HSE, HSG6 - Safety in working with lift trucks.

Pedestrian controlled trucks are operated by walking with the truck and controlling it by means of a control handle. They may be equipped with a battery powered lift facility or the lift may be powered by using a hydraulic hand pump.

Some hybrid pedestrian controlled trucks have a facility for the operator to ride on in a standing position at the back of the truck whilst travelling long distances.

AGRICULTURAL TRACTORS

Agricultural tractors are a versatile form of mobile equipment used in farming, forestry and municipal work. Agricultural tractors operate similarly to rough terrain equipment found within industry.

The design employed for agricultural tractors is usually of a heavier duty than general industrial equipment. This is because they typically operate on unmade ground and not hard standing vehicles are often fitted with larger tyres, with deep treads to enable the vehicle to navigate the soft undulating terrain. They may be fitted with two or four wheel drive. When fitted with forks or a bucket they may be used for load handling. They are well suited to towing equipment, such as a trailer or specialist farm equipment.

Figure C7-8: Agricultural tractor. *Source: Massey Ferguson.*

They are usually fitted with a power take-off shaft, which allows power to be transmitted from the rear of the vehicle to other equipment, for example, farm equipment used for planting or muck spreading.

REMOTELY CONTROLLED MOBILE EQUIPMENT

Remote controlled programmable robots are increasingly being used in the movement of goods in warehouses. There are many robotic systems available for use in order picking, ranging from telescopic arms capable of picking up individual small items through to robust pallet or small mobile storage unit moving robots.

Mobile storage unit moving robots

Mobile storage unit moving robots will travel long distances delivering and collecting specific storage units. The system eliminates the need for workers walking long distances to collate orders or collect parts. One such system is the 'KIVA bots', which are short squat orange lifters that glide under storage units, lifting and moving them where they need to go.

The robots are guided by a very simple grid of stickers attached to the floor, which keeps the robots from colliding, and proximity sensors fitted to each unit, to prevent collision with workers.

Figure C7-9: Mobile storage system moving robots.

Source: Kiva Systems.

Remotely controlled narrow isle storage and retrieval systems

Where warehouse floor space is limited remotely controlled narrow isle storage and retrieval systems may be used, which can store at heights in excess of 40 metres.

Some systems are designed to handle standard pallets and have good load carrying capabilities, for example, a 1,250 kilogram load with a horizontal travelling speed of approximately 240 metres per minute and a hoisting speed of 90 metres per minute.

These systems are designed to operate with no workers present in the area to avoid collision or crushing injuries to warehouse staff. This requires adequate fencing with interlock gates and a formal entry system.

ELEMENT C7 - WORK EQUIPMENT (MOBILE, LIFTING AND ACCESS)

Figure C7-10: Remotely controlled narrow isle storage and retrieval systems.　　　　　Source: SSI Schafer.

The hazards associated with mobile work equipment

ROLLOVER

Dumper trucks are particularly at risk from roll over (turning a full 360° or more), particularly when driven at speed or across an incline or a slope created by a steep spoil of earth removed from an excavation.

OVERTURNING

The various circumstances that may cause mobile work equipment to overturn include insecure and unstable loads, manoeuvring with the load elevated, colliding with kerbs and other obstructions, cornering at speed, braking harshly, driving on uneven or soft ground, and mechanical failure.

The stability of mobile work equipment, in particular lift trucks, is particularly affected by the forces generated when turning, especially at speed, or if the equipment is tilted sideways, for example, by travelling across an incline or by the wheels running into a pothole or over an obstruction. The danger of a lift truck being turned on its side is greater with the load in the raised position *(see figure ref C7-11a)*, than in the lowered position *(see figure ref C7-11b)*. This risk is increased if the load is high and the wheelbase of the truck is short and on a slope - *(see figure ref C7-11c)*.

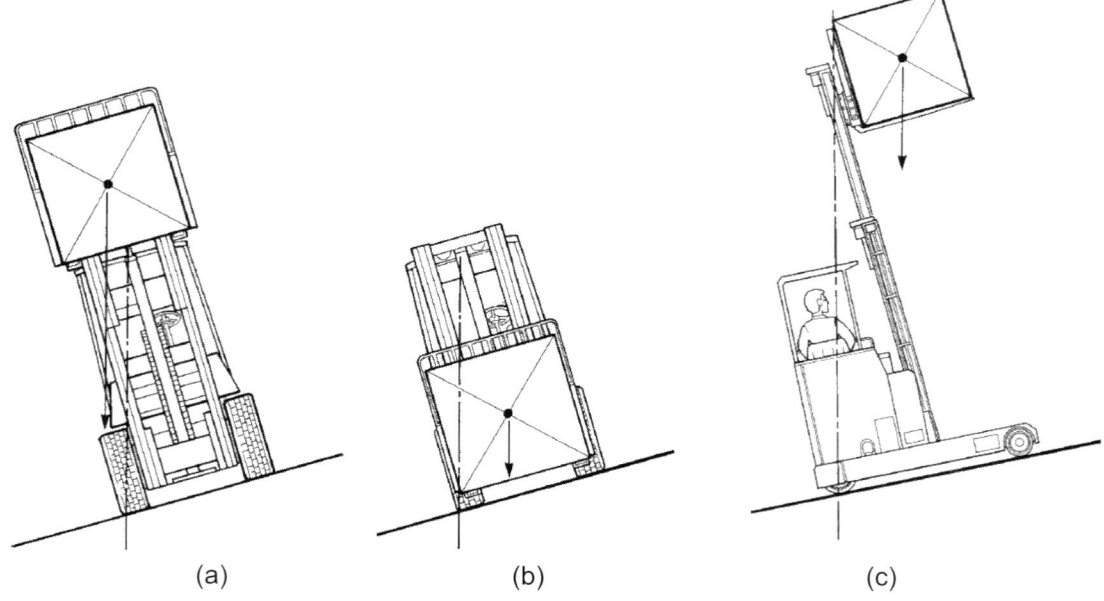

Figure C7-11: Overturning of lift truck.　　　Source: HSE, HSG6 - Safety in working with lift trucks.

Possible causes of a fork lift truck overturning

- Driving too fast.
- Sudden braking.
- Driving on slopes.
- Driving over debris.
- Under-inflated tyres.
- Driving over holes in the floor, such as drains.
- Driving with the load elevated.
- Driving with the load incorrectly positioned on the forks.
- Overloading - exceeding maximum rated capacity.
- Collisions with buildings or other vehicles.

Possible causes of a dumper truck overturning

- Overloading or uneven loading of the bucket.
- Cornering at excessive speed.
- Hitting obstructions.
- Driving too close to the edges of embankments or excavations.
- Mechanical defects that occur because of lack of maintenance.
- Inappropriate or unequal tyre pressures.
- Driving across slopes.

OVERBALANCING

The mass of a counterbalance lift truck acts as a counterweight so that the load can be lifted and moved without the lift truck overbalancing and tipping forwards *(see figure ref C7-12a)*. However, the lift truck can be tipped forward if the load is too heavy *(see figure ref C7-12b)*, if the load is incorrectly placed on the forks *(see figure ref C7-12c)*, or if the lift truck accelerates or brakes harshly while carrying a heavy load.

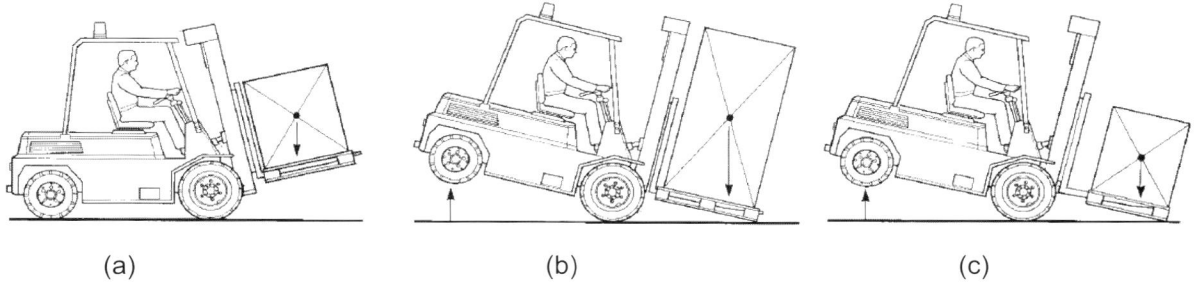

Figure C7-12: Overbalancing of lift truck. Source: HSE, HSG6 - Safety in working with lift trucks.

Other mobile equipment can be affected in a similar way, for example, a tractor towing an overloaded trailer could overbalance and tip backwards. In the case of both lift trucks and tractors this may not cause the equipment to overturn, but the overbalancing can injure the operator and lead to loss of control of steering. The lift trucks are usually provided with rear wheel steering and the tractors front wheel steering. The overbalancing lifts the equipment from the ground preventing the steering wheels from contacting the ground properly.

COLLISIONS WITH OTHER VEHICLES, PEDESTRIANS OR FIXED OBJECTS

People may unexpectedly appear from a part of a building structure or workers intent on the work they are doing may step away from where they are working to collect materials or tools. Often the space in workplaces such as warehouses is restricted. Racking is then increased in height to maximise the floor space. This in turn leads to restricted visibility especially at busy junctions where vehicles come together. This may lead to collisions with other vehicles and pedestrians or, in the avoidance of these, fixed objects such as roof and racking supports.

SUITABILITY FOR CARRYING PASSENGERS

Many types of mobile work equipment are not designed to carry passengers and when incorrectly used for this purpose there is a risk that the passenger will fall off the mobile work equipment or suffer collision injuries to parts of their body from impact with fixed structures, for example, when the equipment passes through narrow doorways.

UNAUTHORISED START-UP

Unauthorised use of mobile work equipment by drivers that are not trained in its use can lead to loss of load or overturning of the equipment; with the potential for serious injury to the unauthorised driver. People may be working on, in or around the mobile work equipment, loading/unloading or making adjustments. An unauthorised start up and movement of the equipment could cause injury to those on, in or around it, leading to entanglement, crush injuries or falls.

ELEMENT C7 - WORK EQUIPMENT (MOBILE, LIFTING AND ACCESS)

SAFE OPERATING STATION/PLATFORM

The failure to provide a safe operating station for the operator can result in poor access to controls or limited visibility, leading to the risk of collision of the mobile work equipment with other equipment, stationary objects or people. In addition, the operator could be at risk of falling from the mobile work equipment while it is moving. In addition to fall injuries there is a risk of the operator being run over by the moving work equipment. The risk of falls from the operating position/platform will increase if the operator reaches significantly outside of the platform area, for example, when painting pipework from a mobile elevating work platform (MEWP). The operating station/platform may also place the operator in close proximity to other hazards, for example, the moving lifting parts of a fork lift truck, moving wheels/tracks or falling objects.

OVERRUN OF SPEED

Overrun of speed is generally taken to be where mobile work equipment is moving at higher than desired speeds, often downhill, with the motion control (for example, accelerator) not applied. This can occur where the momentum of the equipment provides additional speed to that required or expected, this is particularly evident on a steep gradient. For example, a dumper truck may overrun if driven down a steep slope. The effect of overrun of speed may limit the ability of the mobile equipment to control the speed of movement through braking. Mobile work equipment that is normally designed to be used on flat surfaces may not have adequate parking or operator brakes for work on a slope and a moderate slope may counteract braking applied, leading to an overrun of speed. This can lead to loss of control of the equipment, collision with other vehicles or pedestrians, loss of load or overturning.

CONTACT WITH WHEELS AND TRACKS

Pedestrians, passengers and operators of mobile work equipment are at risk of crush, cut or abrasion injuries from contact with the moving wheels or tracks of the equipment. In addition, injury may result from the ejection of soil or stones when the equipment travels on un-made up ground or gravel.

FALLS OF OBJECTS

Drivers and pedestrians are at risk from the hazards of falling materials when mobile equipment is used to carry or lift items that are not adequately secured. This could include loose items that fall from a load being stacked by a fork lift truck or a load falling from the trailer of an agricultural tractor.

MOVING PARTS/DRIVE SHAFTS/POWER TAKE-OFFS

Many mobile vehicles will have partially exposed moving parts, such as the drive shafts/power take off points for fitting various attachments to an agricultural tractor or the lifting parts of a fork lift truck. These exposed parts of the equipment will create hazards to the operator of drawing in or entanglement.

OVER-HEATING

The hazards of overheating are fires or explosions, which are often the result of friction (bearings running hot), electric motor burn out, thermostat failure or cooling system failure. The risk of explosion may result from pressure build-up, perhaps due to the failure of a pressure-relief valve or the unexpected blockage or sealing off of pipework.

FUEL COMBUSTION GASES

LPG and diesel powered vehicles will use an internal combustion engine where the fuel is mixed with air and 'burnt' to power the equipment. In normal use the exhaust will produce carbon dioxide and some un-burnt fuel so the equipment should only be used in a well ventilated workplace. If the work place is enclosed and not ventilated, there is the risk that the fuel will only be partially combusted, producing carbon monoxide (a chemical asphyxiant) gas. This can lead to the risk of acute poisoning to the operator and anyone else in the confined space. In addition, diesel exhaust emissions contain other harmful particles that can have longer term effects, including carbon (soot), nitrogen dioxide, sulphur dioxide and polycyclic aromatic hydrocarbons.

The hazards associated with the energising (electrical, LPG, diesel) of mobile work equipment

Energising of mobile work equipment is concerned with making power available to start, run and operate the equipment. All mobile work equipment carries stored energy necessary for its operation and movement. The energy store will need to be replaced or replenished from time to time and this will expose the person doing it to a number of hazards.

ELECTRICALLY (BATTERY) POWERED EQUIPMENT

The main hazards associated with energising mobile work equipment with electricity include:

- Exposure to corrosive acid (28% sulphuric acid): contained in lead-acid batteries can lead to corrosive burns of the skin and eyes.
- Inhalation of acidic mists can result from the heat generated during charging lead-acid batteries causing the liberation of small particles of acid.

- Re-charging lead-acid batteries causes a breakdown of the acid and the liberation of explosive concentrations of hydrogen. Arcing between the live charging supply and the battery connector could create a source of ignition of the hydrogen.
- When batteries are connected/disconnected to the mobile work equipment a short circuit may occur, resulting in very high temperatures of the conductors and the potential for severe burns to the hands. There is also a possibility that this could cause explosive failure of the battery casing, projecting materials and acids outwards.
- The charging supply presents the hazard of electricity if it is energised and handled before connection to the batteries.
- Batteries are very heavy and if they cannot be charged without removal from the mobile work equipment there is the risk of a manual handling injury to workers involved in the charging process.

LPG POWERED EQUIPMENT

The main hazards associated with energising mobile work equipment with liquefied petroleum gas (LPG) include:

- Loss of LPG, usually propane, when the used cylinder is disconnected or when a full cylinder is reconnected presents the risk of ignition of the escaped gas.
- As the LPG is discharged from the cylinder during use it takes in heat from its surroundings making parts of the exterior of the cylinder cold. Heavy discharge prior to replacement of the cylinder could cause it to be very cold and ice to form on parts of it. This can present the risk of cold burns and difficulty in manual handling the cylinder.
- LPG cylinders are heavy and there is the risk of a manual handling injury when removing and replacing them.
- The LPG cylinder may be set at a height on the equipment, which presents a risk of it falling and injuring the person connecting or disconnecting it.

DIESEL POWERED EQUIPMENT

The main hazards associated with energising mobile work equipment with diesel include:

- Prolonged or repeated exposure of skin to diesel fuel may give rise to dermatitis. Under conditions of poor personal hygiene, excessive exposure may lead to irritation, oil acne, and folliculitis and development of warty growths that may subsequently become malignant. There is limited evidence of diesel fuel having a carcinogenic effect.
- Though diesel fuel is not classified as flammable, it is combustible and may ignite on surfaces at temperatures above its auto-ignition temperature, for example, hot parts of the equipment.
- Diesel fuel vapour in the headspace of fuel tanks and fuel containers may ignite and explode at temperatures exceeding its auto-ignition temperature where vapour concentrations are within the flammability range.
- Diesel fuel represents a significant environmental risk if it is spilt and gets into watercourses, it may cause long-term adverse effects in the aquatic environment.

The control measures to be used in the use of mobile work equipment

The employer, through its managers, needs to carry out an assessment of risk with regard to the safe use of mobile equipment as part of the overall health and safety policy. Consideration should be given to the following control measures for the use of mobile work equipment. In addition, control measures for workplace transport operations are included in Element 10 "Workplace transport and driving at work".

SAFE OPERATION

The organisation should appoint a senior manager to be responsible for the use of mobile work equipment. Users of mobile work equipment should be properly trained and a system should be in place to ensure unauthorised people are not permitted to use mobile work equipment. This may include control of keys or electronic access codes to ensure authority is controlled. Safe operation of mobile work equipment should be supervised and rules enforced.

Operational rules - basic fork lift truck

The following list should only be used as a guide to good practice in the safe operation of fork lift trucks; it also has some applicability to all mobile work equipment:

- Speeds must be consistent with workplace conditions, special care should be taken on greasy or wet roads.
- Operators should always face direction of travel.
- Forks should be between 10 cm and 15 cm from the ground and parallel to the ground unless travelling with a load, when the forks should be tilted back enough to prevent it sliding off the forks.
- The load must be seated as close to the heel of the forks as possible.
- When travelling up or down a slope the forks must always point up the slope.
- Trucks must not be driven over obstacles or holes in the road. These defects must be reported immediately.
- Care should be taken not to drive trucks across a slope.

ELEMENT C7 - WORK EQUIPMENT (MOBILE, LIFTING AND ACCESS)

- Travel slowly and with due care when approaching a road junction, door opening or where pedestrians could be present. Sound the horn as a warning of the presence of the fork lift truck.
- No passengers, unless the fork lift truck is specifically designed to accommodate them.
- All parts of the operator's body must be kept within the limits of the fork lift truck and no part of the body placed between the uprights of the mast.
- The fork lift truck must be stationary with the handbrake applied when the forks are raised or lowered, whether with a load or not.
- Fork lift trucks must not be used to pull or push loads.

PRE-OPERATIONAL CHECKS

It is essential that the person responsible for the use of mobile work equipment, for example, the driver, carries out pre-operational checks to ensure that the mobile equipment is safe for work. These should be carried out when the mobile work equipment has been left standing for any length of time and especially at the beginning of each shift.

The following is a typical approach for pre-operational checks of a fork lift truck (FLT).

Forks	-	Check for alignment and security.
Tyres	-	Check for security, adequate tread, no excessive cuts, and correct pressure if pneumatic.
Hydraulic oil tank	-	Check level of fluid.
Unions, pipes, jacks	-	Check there are no leaks of hydraulic fluid.
Seat	-	Check adjustment to personal requirements and effectiveness of restraints.
Protection	-	Check roll over and falling material protection.
Lift and tilt controls	-	Check effectiveness.
Brakes	-	Foot - check effectiveness on level in forward and reverse.
	-	Handbrake - check effectiveness on slope.
Warning device(s)	-	Check effectiveness.

The above simple list should be adapted after consideration of the information provided by the manufacturer; this may need to be modified to meet the equipment's individual usage and the workplace. Any adverse conditions identified may require more frequent checks or maintenance than the manufacturer has stated.

A system should be in place for the driver to report any significant faults or defects immediately to the supervisor and the equipment should be taken out of use until it is certified safe to use. Each item of mobile work equipment should have an individual log where such tests, as well as other checks and remedial measures, are recorded.

No operator or other person should make any repair or adjustment unless specifically trained and authorised to do so. A system of regular maintenance by competent persons must be in existence and records kept in the log.

SAFE LAYOUT OF AREAS WHERE MOBILE EQUIPMENT IS USED

The layout of the areas where mobile work equipment is used should take account of the size and numbers of mobile work equipment, tasks to be done and manoeuvrability of the equipment. The layout may need to provide specific areas for mobile work equipment to turn around in order to limit the need to operate in reverse.

Consideration of the layout should encompass the weight of the equipment and its ability to negotiate slopes or uneven/soft ground. Any gradient in a mobile work equipment operating area should be kept as gentle as possible unless the equipment is specifically designed for these conditions.

Obstructions and similar hazards that would inhibit safe movement of the mobile work equipment should be identified and where possible removed. Adjustments may be required to limit the effect of blind corners by requiring mobile work equipment to manoeuvre at a position wide of the corner or, where the effect is caused by material stacked in the workplace that the stacks are kept at a reduced height on corners. Traffic routes should be clearly marked and signed. Signs should incorporate speed limits, one way systems and movement priorities or restrictions.

Consideration should be given to adequate lighting of operating areas, in particular entrances/exits, crossing points or where pedestrians may be encountered. Where possible pedestrians should be segregated from areas where mobile work equipment operates. The layout of areas where mobile work equipment operates should take account of the need to park the equipment safely.

PROTECTION OF PEDESTRIANS

It is important to anticipate that drivers of mobile work equipment might misjudge a manoeuvre and collide with pedestrians or structures whilst operating. Where possible pedestrians and mobile work equipment should be segregated from each other. For this reason, barriers that continuously surround the mobile work equipment operating area and provide physical segregation should be used. If this is not practicable, barriers should be located at critical positions where pedestrians might encounter mobile work equipment.

Protection of pedestrians will require clear defined and marked routes that identify pedestrian areas. Separate routes should be provided for access and egress points to all parts of the workplace affected. Safe crossing places should be provided where pedestrians have to cross areas where mobile work equipment operates. This may mean marking crossing points on the ground or the provision of raised walkways and bridges. Any area or route that is used by both pedestrians and mobile work equipment should be wide enough to enable them to pass each other safely.

In addition, signs warning of mobile work equipment operating or the presence of pedestrians should be provided. Signs should be supplemented by visual and audible warning systems that confirm the presence of mobile work equipment operating. These may be operated by the driver, such as a horn on a fork lift truck or automatically, such as an audible reversing signal on a large road vehicle.

In order to protect pedestrians it may be necessary to provide the mobile work equipment with a banksman to control its operation when pedestrians are in the vicinity. Pedestrians present in an area where mobile work equipment is operating should be made more visible by their use of high visibility clothing.

Attachments used on lift trucks

THE USE OF LIFT TRUCKS TO MOVE PEOPLE

Primarily, fork lift trucks are intended for lifting materials and not people. However, they can be used with working platform attachments to allow people to work at height.

The Work at Height Regulations (WAH) 2005, regulation 7(2)(b) places a duty on employers to select the most suitable work equipment for the task to be carried out regardless of the duration of the task.

Often people will use unsafe methods of access to height for short duration and occasional tasks, for example, standing on pallets placed on the forks of a fork lift truck. To encourage safer working practices, in these circumstances, occasional use of working platforms with fork lift trucks is allowed in the UK, the Health and Safety Executive (HSE) have produced guidance on this in the form of a guidance note, PM28 "Working platforms (non-integrated) on forklift trucks".

The working platform must be compatible with the truck on which it is to be used.

It is important to ensure that:

- The truck and working platform combination has adequate stability under all circumstances in which it is intended to be used.
- The platform can be securely attached to the truck.
- Preferably, the raising and lowering of the platform is controlled from within the platform.
- Guards are fitted to prevent contact with hazardous moving parts or controls on the truck.
- The weight of the platform together with its load of people, tools, materials etc. must not be more than half of the actual capacity of the truck (i.e. actual capacity for materials handling).
- To prevent falls and head injuries people should wear harnesses secured to suitable anchorage points on the platform and hard hats.

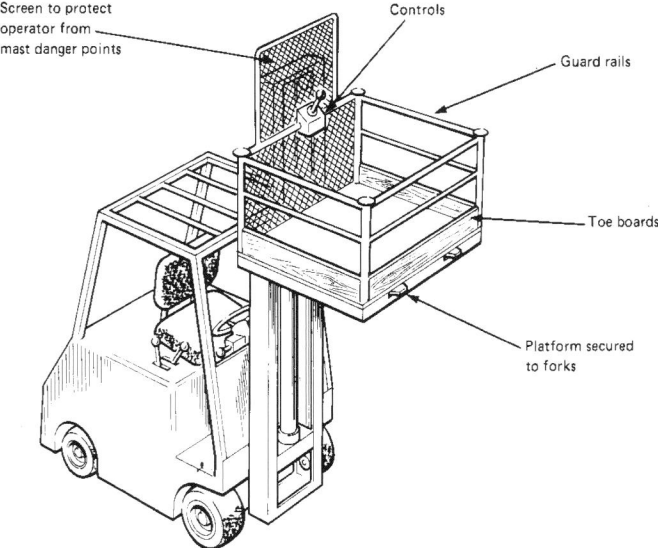

Figure C7-13: Use of working platform on fork lift truck.   Source: HSE.

OTHER ATTACHMENTS USED ON LIFT TRUCKS

It is always important to use the correct tool for the job and to this end there are many specialist attachments that have been made available to enable difficult shaped load to be transferred safely using a lift truck. Their correct selection will reduce significantly the risk of loss of load when moving items.

ELEMENT C7 - WORK EQUIPMENT (MOBILE, LIFTING AND ACCESS)

Examples of some attachments in common use are shown in *figure ref C7-14*.

A fork lift truck drum handling attachment.

A range of under-slung attachments designed for handling typical construction materials, for use under a fork lift truck or telescopic handler.

A bucket fork lift truck attachment for loose or granular material.

A fork lift truck jib attachment for the handling of un-palletised loads.

Figure C7-14: Other attachments used on fork lift trucks.

Source: Contact Attachments Ltd.

Roll-over protection, falling objects protection, speed control and restraining systems

ROLL-OVER PROTECTION

In many mobile work equipment accidents the driver is injured because the equipment does not offer protection when it rolls over or it does not restrain the driver to prevent them falling out of the vehicle and being injured by the fall or the vehicle falling on them.

Vehicles such as dumper trucks, road rollers and fork lift trucks are examples of equipment that may present this risk.

PUWER 1998 Part 3 recognises the importance of this and sets out requirements for equipment to be adapted, where practicable, to provide roll-over protection, for example, the use of roll bar, and restraining systems, for example, lap straps or seat belts.

PUWER 1998 requires that new equipment of this type provided by the employer, including hire equipment, must be fitted with protection and restraint systems, where relevant.

FALLING OBJECT PROTECTION

Falling object protection must be provided to a suitable standard to deflect and protect the driver from objects that might foreseeably fall on them while operating the mobile work equipment, for example, loose items when stacking materials at a height with a lift truck.

Protection is usually afforded by the use a high tensile strength mesh or a cover over the driver and part way down the side of the cab. Mesh protection provides visibility, but will not prevent contact with dust or liquids from damaged containers when they fall.

Other mobile work equipment provides protection in the form of a frame and glass/perspex windows, this provides a complete enclosure.

Figure C7-15: Roll bar and seat restraint.   Source: RMS.

Figure C7-16: Risk of Falling materials.   Source: RMS.

SPEED CONTROL SYSTEMS

Speed control systems or governors may be fitted to mobile work equipment to restrict drivers from driving too fast. Speed controls limit the amount of combustion in internal combustion engines, such as those powered by diesel or LPG.

Battery powered mobile work equipment is limited by gearing or electronic circuitry. These are important to limit the speed of mobile work equipment to a safe level appropriate for the area that the equipment is working in. This is particularly important where pedestrians are present in the same area where mobile work equipment is operated. In this case limiters may limit the equipment to a walking speed.

In addition, it is important that mobile work equipment is fitted with the means for the operator to bring its movement to a timely stop when operating normally; this may involve the use of a 'hold to run' device that brings the equipment to a stop when it is released. It is also important to provide an emergency braking facility that ensures that when a positive action is applied a form of brake operates and the mobile work equipment is brought to an emergency stop.

GUARDS, BARRIERS AND RESTRAINING SYSTEMS

Guards and barriers are important to provide a physical segregation of pedestrians from mobile work equipment. Whilst clear routes may be designated with painted lines it is preferable to provide physical barriers. Where complete enclosure segregation is not possible, barriers and guards may be provided at critical locations to maintain segregation and channel pedestrians and mobile work equipment away from each other, for example, at entrances and exits to buildings.

It is important to fit guards, barriers and restraining systems to some mobile work equipment to prevent people on the equipment falling from it or contacting dangerous parts of the equipment

MEANS OF FIRE FIGHTING

Because mobile work equipment does not operate at a fixed point it does not readily benefit from fixed fire fighting equipment or portable fire extinguishers set in a designated location. The mobile work equipment often carries its own supply of flammable fuel to enable its operation and may be subject to overheating or fire. In order to promptly deal with a fire that might occur with mobile work equipment it is important that it is readily available to the user of the equipment. This will often mean that the fire fighting equipment is positioned on the mobile work equipment, ensuring it is available wherever it is.

VISION AIDS

Mirrors

A range of mirrors are available to improve the vision of mobile work equipment operators and pedestrians, for example, plane, angled and curved mirrors. The choice of mirror will depend on the circumstances of use, for example, angled mirrors may be installed to provide a view round obstructions or corners and curved mirrors can be installed to provide a wider field of view of an area.

Mirrors fitted to mobile work equipment should not be used for reversing. Drivers should, where practicable, look in the direction of travel, since their field of vision is much greater when directly viewed by the eye compared to that through the use of a mirror.

Where the vision of the driver or any pedestrian is restricted (at 'blind spots'), such as at gates or doorways, mirrors should be provided for safe entry of those using them and poor visibility should be dealt with by the careful positioning of mirrors on walls, plant or storage equipment.

Fresnel lenses

The Fresnel lens *(see figure ref C7-17 - diagram 1)* reduces the amount of material required, compared to a conventional spherical lens *(see figure ref C7-17 - diagram 2)*, by dividing the lens into a set of concentric annular sections known as "Fresnel zones".

In each of these zones, the overall thickness of the lens is decreased, effectively dividing the continuous surface of a standard lens into a set of surfaces of the same curvature, with stepwise discontinuities between them.

The Fresnel lens is much thinner, larger, and flatter, and captures more oblique light from a light source, thus allowing low intensity sources of light to be visible over much greater distances.

Fresnel lenses are widely used in vehicle tail lights and in the manufacture of yellow coloured warning lights often fitted to the top of mobile work equipment.

Radar

Simple radar devices may be fitted to mobile work equipment to give audible warnings of obstructions when reversing. Often the warning will consist of a series of bleeps.

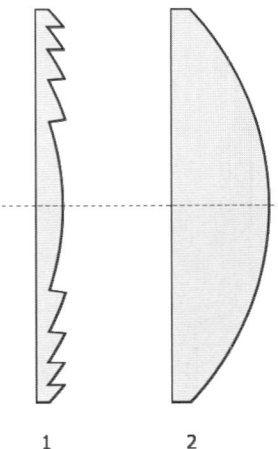

Figure C7-17: Comparison between Fresnel lens (1) and normal lens (2). *Source: Pko.*

The time interval between bleeps shortens as the mobile work equipment approaches an obstruction, until a continuous sound is generated when it is in close proximity to the obstruction. More advanced systems, in addition to an audible signal, will display the information schematically on a screen that is available for the operator of the equipment to view.

CCTV

CCTV (closed circuit television) is readily available to display images not easily observed by the operator of mobile work equipment, such as to the rear of a vehicle. They may be used as a reversing aid, particularly in large vehicles where people would be difficult to see if they located behind the vehicle.

The requirements for the training of lift truck operators

No persons should be permitted to drive a lift trucks unless they have been selected, trained and authorised to do so, or are undergoing properly organised formal training.

The Provision and Use of Work Equipment Regulations (PUWER) 1998, Regulation 9, requires the users of mobile work equipment, including lift truck operators, to be trained, it states:

"Every employer shall ensure that all persons who use work equipment have received adequate training for purposes of health and safety, including training in the methods which may be adopted when using the work equipment, any risks which such use may entail and precautions to be taken."

The legal requirement for training that is set out in PUWER 1998 is supported by a specific Approved Code of Practice (ACOP) for the training of many lift truck operators - "Rider-operated lift trucks: Operator training". The training for lift trucks that are not rider operated, pedestrian controlled lift trucks, should follow a similar approach to that expressed in the ACOP.

SELECTION OF OPERATORS FOR TRAINING

The safe use of lift trucks requires a reasonable degree of both physical and mental fitness. The selection procedure should be devised to identify people who have been shown to be reliable and mature enough to perform their work responsibly and carefully. Lift truck operators should be over the minimum school-leaving age or in some cases, such as dock work, over 18 years. The immaturity of young people and their lack of awareness of risks should be considered before selecting them for training. To avoid wasteful training for workers who lack co-ordination and ability to learn, selection tests should be used.

Consideration must be given to any legal age restrictions that apply to vehicles that operate on the public road. A similar approach may be adopted for similar vehicles used on site though the law is not specific on age limitations in such cases.

Potential operators should be medically examined prior to employment/training in order to assess the individual's physical ability to cope with this type of work. They should also be examined every five years in middle age and after sickness or accident.

Points to be considered are:

General - normal agility, having full movement of trunk, neck and limbs.

Vision - good eyesight is important as operators are required to have good judgement of space and distance. Normally distance vision should not be less than 6/12 with both eyes or corrected by spectacles or contact lenses as appropriate. Operators should have good colour vision.

Hearing - the ability to hear instruction and warning signals with each ear is important.

TRAINING OPERATORS

Safety must constitute an integral part of the lift truck operator skill training programme and not be treated as a separate subject. The operator should be trained to a level consistent with efficient operation and care for the safety of himself and other persons. The training should consist of three stages, the last being the one in which the operator is introduced to their future work environment.

Stage one - should contain the *basic* skills and knowledge required to operate the lift truck safely (including the hazards and controls relating to use and associated tasks like battery charging), to understand the basic mechanics and balance of the machine and to carry out routine daily checks. Basic training should be conducted under strict training conditions with the learning area closed to other personnel.

Stage two - this stage is to provide *specific* job training, this will enable the operator to be made familiar with the type of lift truck they will be operating, site layout, company health and safety rules relating to the job they will be doing and specific features of the work. This training should be tailored to the employer's needs and include:

a) Knowledge of the operating principles of the lift truck the operator is to use, covering any controls that are different from the lift truck used to train the operator, use of any special attachments and the manufacturer's data and instructions for safe and efficient operation.
b) Training and practice in the use of the lift truck in conditions likely to be encountered, for example, gangways, slopes, cold stores, confined spaces and bad weather conditions.
c) Instruction on site rules, such as speed limits and one-way systems.
d) Training and practice in the work to be undertaken, for example, loading and unloading vehicles, stacking and de-stacking, familiarisation with the loads/materials they will be handling, including weight assessment.
e) Safe systems of work, including arrangements to access the lift truck with keys or other means, arrangements to prevent use of the lift truck by others when left unattended and prohibitions on unauthorised operators using the lift truck.

Specific job training should also be conducted under strict training conditions with the learning area closed to other personnel.

Stage three - after successfully completing the first two stages, the operator should be given further *familiarisation training* in the workplace under close supervision of a person with appropriate knowledge. Under strict supervision the operator should apply the training learnt in earlier stages and cover the features of the work that were not feasible to include in stage 2 of the training, such as local emergency procedures.

Basic and specific job training should be carried out by a competent instructor either at the premises of a training organisation or the employer's premises. An operator with basic training on one type of lift truck cannot operate others safely without additional conversion training.

On completion of training the operator should be examined and tested to ensure that they have achieved the required standard. It is recommended that formal check tests be introduced at set intervals, when there is an indication of the operator not working to the required standard or following an accident.

On completion of all stages of training the operator should be issued with the organisation's authority to drive and a record of all basic training, refresher training and tests maintained in the individual's personal documents file.

C7.2 - Lifting equipment: hazards and control measures

The Lifting Operations and Lifting Equipment Regulations (LOLER) 1998, Regulation 2(1), defines 'lifting equipment' as *"work equipment for lifting or lowering loads and includes its attachments used for anchoring, fixing or supporting it"*.

It includes any lifting accessories that attach the load to the lifting machine, in addition to the equipment that carries out the actual lifting function. The scope of these Regulations is therefore very wide and includes a range of equipment from an eyebolt to a tower crane.

Applications and different types of lifting equipment including cranes and hoists

APPLICATIONS OF DIFFERENT TYPES OF CRANE

Mobile cranes

Mobile cranes are used for combined road and off-road lifting applications. Mobile cranes are the ultimate in mobility as they can travel up to 80 km/h and are extremely versatile due to their compact dimensions.

A wide range of sizes of mobile crane are available that have a wide range of load lifting capability. They are often designed to enable the load to be lifted and slewed (rotation of the lifting part of the crane) to a new position, perhaps onto a vehicle for transportation. They are widely used in industry, maintenance and construction work.

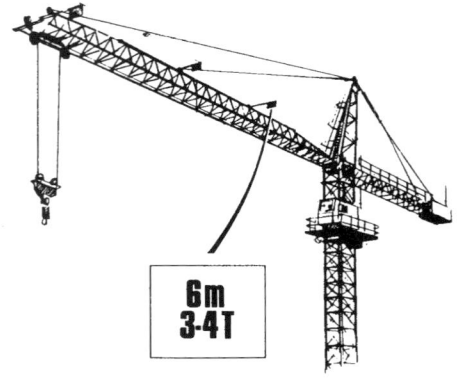

Figure C7-18: Mobile crane. *Source: Liebherr.* Figure C7-19: Tower crane. *Source: Construction Industry Publications Ltd for the Building Employers Confederation.*

Tower cranes

Tower cranes are suitable for the handling of relatively light loads to extremes of height/reach and are particularly suitable when there is limited space for a crane or to enable the frequent placement of loads over a large area. They are widely used in construction operations.

Overhead cranes

Overhead cranes are able to provide lifting operations over a large linear area, for example, a long manufacturing workshop. Because they are set into place above the workshop equipment they are unaffected by the obstructions that they create at floor level.

They can be operated by a driver in a cab fitted to the travelling gantry, above the workplace, or from a pendent suspended from the gantry at floor level. They have a wide range of load carrying capacity and may be designed to lift significant loads.

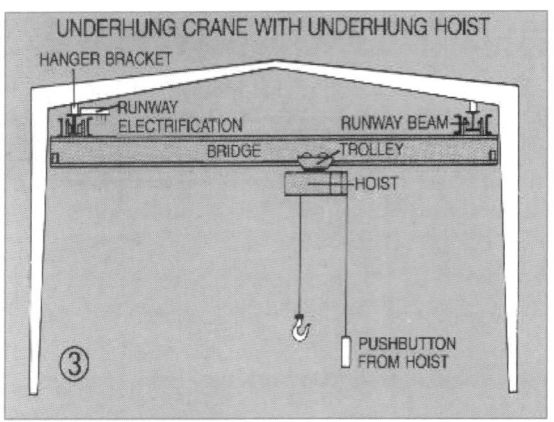

Figure C7-20: Overhead cranes.   *Source: Columbus McKinnon Corp.*

APPLICATION OF DIFFERENT TYPES OF LIFTS AND HOISTS

Lifts and hoists cover any equipment used for transporting people and goods from one position to another or from one place to another.

Examples are:

- Passenger lifts in buildings.
- Patient hoists. For example, a hoist used to lift someone from a seated position and transfer them to another location, such as a bed, a seat or a bathtub.
- Stair lifts.
- Window cleaning suspended cradle for access on high buildings.
- Hoists for moving materials up structures on construction sites, for example, cantilever type hoist.

There are various types of people handling hoists, some designs require the operator to manually raise the person using the hoist, others use electrically driven hoists to lift the person.

These forms of hoist are widely used in hospitals and other care facilities.

WORK EQUIPMENT (MOBILE, LIFTING AND ACCESS) - ELEMENT C7

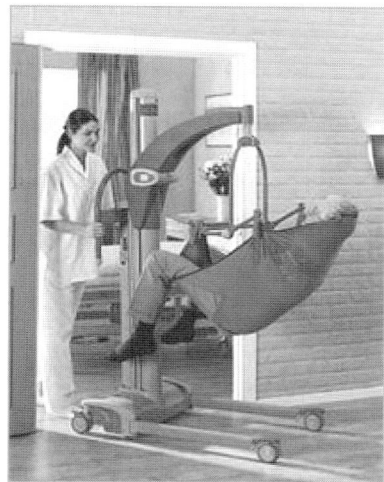

Figure C7-21: Mobile person hoist. *Source: Arjo.*

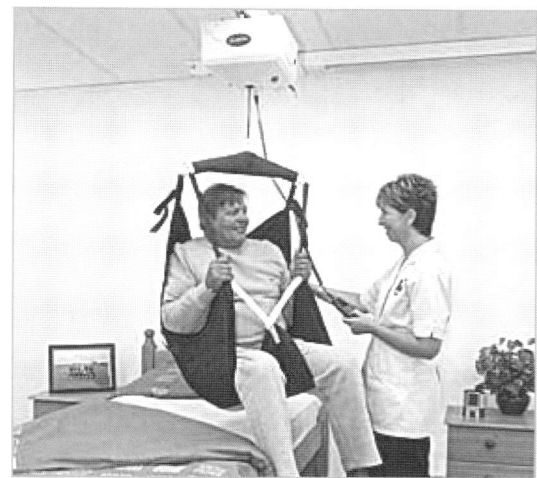

Figure C7-22: Ceiling person hoist. *Source: Dolphin Midlands.*

Hoists for use on construction sites tend to fall into two categories, mobile and fixed. Mobile hoists are widely used to move materials to upper levels of construction operations; they are easily transported and erected. They can have a wide range of attachments fitted to suit the materials being lifted, including buckets, platforms and cages. They can typically be adjusted to lift material from 8 metres to 30 metres and have load carrying capacity up to 500 kg.

Fixed construction tower platform hoists are erected and secured to the structure under construction; they usually involve an enclosing structure and moving platform with a cage around it. They are very robust, generally have a large load carrying capacity and can reach great heights. They may also be designed to carrying people as well as materials.

Figure C7-23: Construction tower platform hoist. *Source: RMS.*

Main hazards and controls associated with cranes and lifting operations

CRANES AND LIFTING OPERATIONS

Hazards

The principal main *hazards* associated with any crane and lifting operation are:

Overturning which can be caused by weak support, operating outside the capabilities of the machine and by striking obstructions.
Overloading by exceeding the operating capacity or operating radii, or by failure of safety devices.
Collision with other cranes, overhead cables or structures.
Failure of load bearing part - placing over cellars and drains, outriggers not extended, made-up or not solid ground, or of structural components of the crane itself.
Loss of load from failure of lifting tackle or slinging procedure.

Controls

The principal main **controls** associated with any crane and lifting operation is to ensure:

- The ground the crane stands on is it capable of bearing the load; check for underground services and cellars.
- The ground is level, if not select a crane, with hydraulic level adjustment stabilisers.
- The load bearing capacity of the crane is sufficient of for the task.
- The correct procedure is followed when erecting or dismantling any crane.
- The crane is positioned so that there is enough room for the lift and to avoid collision hazards.
- Non-essential people are kept clear of the work area.
- The crane is not operated in adverse weather conditions.
- The structural integrity of the crane is maintained, check for any signs of corrosion.
- The correct procedure is followed when erecting or dismantling any crane.

See also "Control measures for cranes and lifting operations" later in this section for more information.

ELEMENT C7 - WORK EQUIPMENT (MOBILE, LIFTING AND ACCESS)

Main hazards and controls associated with hoists and lifts

Hoists are generally lifting equipment that raises the item to be moved from above, often using some form of rope (for example, man made, artificial fibre or wire rope). These include gin wheels and construction site platform hoists. Lifts are generally lifting equipment that raises the item to be moved from below, often using some form of mechanical or hydraulic mechanism. These include passenger and goods lifts, scissor lifts, vehicle inspection lifts and mobile elevating work platforms (MEWPS). The term lift is often used in common language to describe lifting equipment used to move people in a building, even though the lifting equipment often uses a hoist mechanism.

GIN WHEEL HOIST

Gin wheel hoists provide a very convenient way of raising loads. They comprise of a pulley wheel and rope suspended from a fixed point, for example, a scaffold. The material to be moved is attached to one end of the rope and is raised by pulling the other end. Though they are simple pieces of equipment, care is required when assembling and using them.

Gin wheels are in wide use on small construction sites, but are being replaced by small electric hoists that use a single wire rope to raise materials.

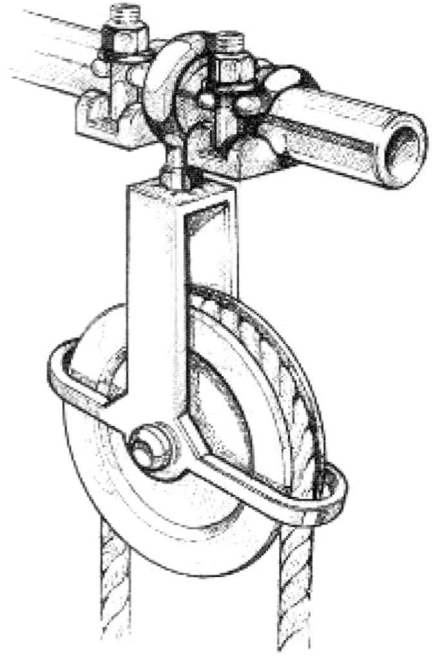

Hazards

The main hazards are:

- The loss of the gin wheel and or any load from its fixing point.
- The loss of load from the hook.

Controls

Ensure that the:

- The gin wheel is securely fixed to the anchorage.
- A proper hook is being used with a safety catch to secure the load.
- A safe working platform exists from which the hook can be loaded or unloaded.

Figure C7-24: Gin wheel. *Source: Ambiguous.*

HOIST/LIFT FOR PASSENGER AND GOODS (INCLUDING CONSTRUCTION SITE PLATFORM)

Hazards

In general, the hazards associated with hoists and lifts are the same as with any other lifting equipment:

- The lift/hoist may overturn or collapse.
- The lift/hoist can strike persons who may be near or under the platform or cage during normal operations.
- The supporting ropes or lifting mechanism may fail and the platform/cage may fall to the ground.
- The load or part of the load may fall.
- The lift/hoist may fail in a high position.
- Persons being raised or lowered may become stranded if the lift/hoist fails.

Controls

The hoist/lift should be protected by a substantial enclosure to prevent anyone from being struck by any moving part of the hoist or material falling down the hoist way. Gates must be provided at all access landings, including at ground level. The gates must be kept shut, except when the platform is at the landing. The controls should be arranged so that the hoist/lift can be operated from one position only, which may be from within the hoist/lift. If an operator is provided they must be trained and competent. The safe working load of the hoist/lift must be clearly marked. If the hoist/lift is for materials only there should be a prominent warning notice on the platform or cage to stop people riding on it. The hoist/lift should be inspected weekly and thoroughly examined every 12 months (six months where it is used to move people) by a competent person and the results of inspection/examination recorded.

Lifts and hoists for movement of goods require:

- Adequate design.
- Sound construction.
- Correct selection and installation.
- Competent operation.
- Regular inspection.
- Adequate maintenance.
- Statutory safety devices.

- Holdback equipment (for rope or lifting mechanism failure).
- Overrun tip systems.
- Guards on hoist/lift machinery.
- Landing gates (securely closed down during operation).

In addition, passenger hoists/lifts require more sophisticated controls:

- Operating controls inside the cage.
- Electromagnetic interlocks on the cage doors.
- The enclosing shaft must be of fire-proof construction, if within a building.

SCISSOR LIFTS

Scissor lifts can provide excellent movement of goods to the desired level. They are therefore particularly useful for loading or unloading good from vehicles and to storage levels in warehouses.

Hazards

- Crush injuries may occur as the platform is raised to or past a fixed part of a structure.
- People, equipment or materials falling from the platform.
- Overload.
- The scissor lift may overturn or collapse.
- The sheer effect of the scissor mechanism as it closes.

Controls

Before using the scissor lift ensure:
- Whoever is operating it is fully trained and competent.
- The scissor lift is fitted with a guard covering the scissor mechanism to a height that is reasonably practicable.
- Anyone in the area is kept clear of the work area.
- That it is not possible to insert a foot or similar part of the body underneath the lifting platform when it is being lowered.
- That there is a safe system of work for the retrieval of items dropped down near the scissor mechanism and for maintenance underneath it.

VEHICLE INSPECTION LIFTS

Vehicle lifts come in a variety of configurations and use different forms of lifting mechanism. Common mechanisms involve screws that rotate and raise/lower the platform and hydraulic systems. They are capable of lifting small vehicles, goods vehicles and large passenger vehicles.

Hazards

- There is a risk of vehicles falling or rolling off the lift due to incorrectly positioned lift mechanisms or uneven lifting, this can cause fatal crushing injuries.
- Crush injury, particularly to the feet, when the lift is lowered to the ground.
- The vehicle lift may overturn, particularly if it utilises portable lifting mechanisms.
- The vehicle lift may collapse, for example, if it is overloaded.

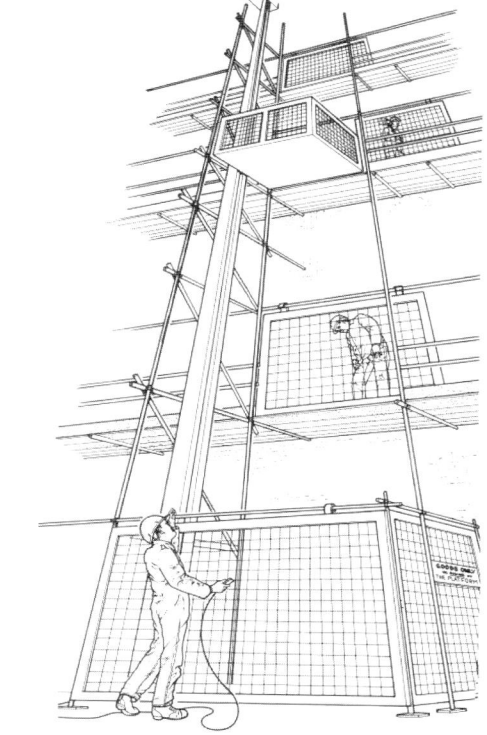

Figure C7-25: Construction platform hoist. *Source: HSE, HSG150.*

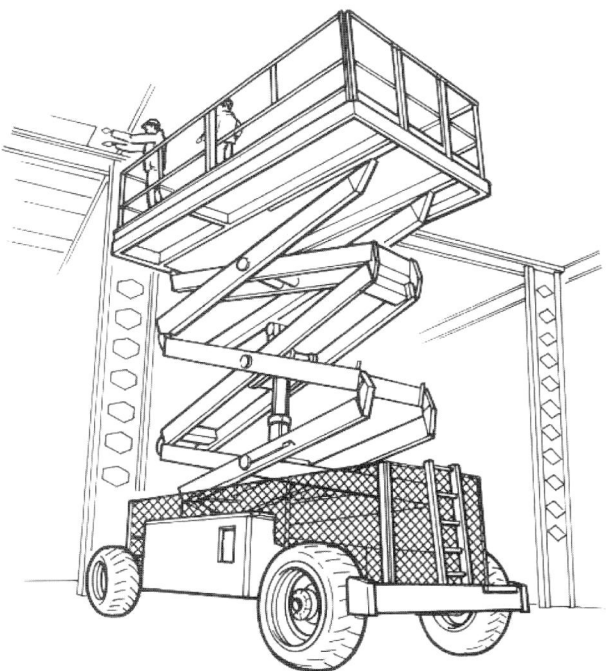

Figure C7-26: Scissor lift. *Source: HSG150, HSE.*

ELEMENT C7 - WORK EQUIPMENT (MOBILE, LIFTING AND ACCESS)

Figure C7-27: Vehicle lift.   *Source: RMS.*

Figure C7-28: Vehicle lift.   *Source: RMS.*

Controls

Always ensure that:

- Vehicle lift mechanisms must be sited on flat, even ground.
- Vehicle should be positioned on the lift centrally or mechanisms fitted to vehicle evenly.
- The need to secure vehicle wheels from movement is considered before raising the hoist.
- Lift is operated steadily and each lifting mechanism raised evenly.
- The stability of the vehicle is checked at a low level before continuing to raise it.
- Stand well clear of the lifting mechanisms and platform when raising or lowering the vehicle.

MOBILE ELEVATING WORK PLATFORMS

Figure C7-29: Mobile elevated work platform (MEWP).   *Source: RMS.*

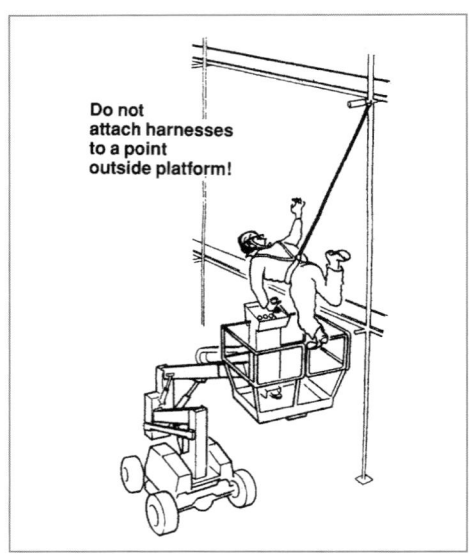

Figure C7-30: Use of harness with a MEWP.   *Source: HSG150.*

A mobile elevating work platform (MEWP) is an efficient means of providing a work platform at a height. The equipment is designed to be movable, under its own power or by being towed, so that it can easily be set up in a location where it is needed.

Various mechanical and hydraulic means are used to elevate the work platform to the desired height, including telescopic arms and scissor lifts. The versatility of this equipment, enabling the easy placement of a platform at a height, makes it a popular piece of access equipment. Often, to do similar work by other means would take a lot of time or be very difficult.

Hazards

They are now widely available and there is a tendency for people to oversimplify their use and allow people to operate them without prior training and experience. This places users and others at high risk of serious injury.

Hazards include:

- Operating too close to overhead cables or dangerous machinery.
- Injuries to the head from pipework or roof beams when the platform is raised.
- Injuries to protruding knuckle, or elbow, of the arm when working near vehicles.
- Falls, if workers overreach guard rails.
- Collision with other vehicles if used on roads.

Controls

Before using a MEWP ensure:

- The operator is fully trained and competent.
- The work platform is fitted with guard rails and toe boards.
- A harness with a lanyard attached to the platform provides extra protection against falls especially when the platform is being raised or lowered.
- It is used on suitable firm and level ground. The ground may have to be prepared in advance.
- Tyres are properly inflated.
- The work area is cordoned off to prevent access below the work platform.
- That it is well lit if being used on a public highway in poor lighting.
- Outriggers are extended before raising the platform.
- Only operate within the defined stable working area for that particular MEWP.
- All involved know what to do if the MEWP fails with the platform in the raised position.

General control measures for lifting equipment

There are a number of general control measures that apply to all lifting equipment, including cranes, hoists and lifts, these include:

- Integrity of lifting equipment.
- Competence of personnel.
- Maintenance.
- Inspection.
- Statutory examination of lifting equipment.

INTEGRITY OF LIFTING EQUIPMENT

It is important that the integrity of lifting equipment is appropriate for its intended use. This will relate to its original design, materials used, initial manufacture, and adaptation and maintenance of condition. Where lifting equipment is designed and manufactured by an employer it is necessary for its integrity to be verified. The lifting equipment should not be unduly susceptible to foreseeable failure modes likely to arise in service, for example, fracture, wear or fatigue. The lifting equipment used should provide an appropriate factor of safety against failure under foreseeable failure modes.

Strength

Regulation 4 of the Lifting Operations and Lifting Equipment Regulations (LOLER) 1998 requires every employer to ensure that:

- *Lifting equipment is of adequate strength and stability for each load, having regard in particular to the stress induced at its mounting or fixing point.*
- *Every part of a load and anything attached to it and used in lifting it is of adequate strength.*

The combined weight of the load and lifting accessories should be taken into consideration when assessing whether the lifting equipment has adequate strength for the proposed use. It is important to consider the load, task and environment in order to match the strength of the lifting equipment to the circumstances of use. For example, if the environment is hot or cold this can affect the lifting capacity of the lifting equipment. In order to counteract this effect equipment with a higher rated safe working load may be needed.

If the load to be lifted is a person, equipment with a generous capacity above the person's weight should be selected in order to provide an increased factor for safety. If the load is likely to move unexpectedly, because of the movement of an animal or liquids in a container, this sudden movement can put additional forces on the equipment and may necessitate equipment with higher strength to be selected. When lifting a load that is submerged in water, the initial lifting weight will be misleading because the load will be supported by the water. When the load emerges from the water the support will no longer be available and this sudden increase in weight can put additional stress on the crane and its lifting accessories.

When conducting the lifting task the lifting accessories may be used in such a way that may reduce its lifting capacity below its stated safe working load; sharp corners on a load and 'back hooking' can have this effect. In these circumstances accessories with a higher rated safe working load may be required.

It is essential to remember when considering the integrity of lifting equipment that it only has an overall lifting capacity equivalent to the item with the lowest strength. For example, in a situation where a crane with a lifting capacity of 50 tonnes is used with a hook of 10 tonnes capacity and a wire rope sling of 5 tonnes capacity, it would give an overall maximum lifting strength/capacity of 5 tonnes.

SWL marked

The safe working load (SWL) must be visibly and clearly marked on all lifting equipment in order to ensure safe use, including lifting machinery and accessories. Where the SWL depends on the configuration of the machinery, it must be marked for each configuration used and kept with the machinery.

Accessories must be marked with supplementary information that indicates the characteristics for its safe use, for example, safe angles of lift.

Equipment designed for lifting people must be clearly marked as such and equipment that is not designed for lifting persons, but which might be used as such, must have appropriate markings to the effect that it is not to be used for lifting people.

COMPETENCE OF PERSONNEL

The Health and Safety at Work etc Act (HASAWA) 1974 places a duty on employers to their employees for the provision of information, instruction, training and supervision as is necessary to ensure, so far as is reasonably practicable, the health and safety at work of the employees.

In addition to this general duty, a further duty exists under The Provision and Use of Work Equipment Regulations (PUWER) 1998. Employers must ensure that any person who uses a piece of work equipment has received adequate training for purposes of health and safety, including training in the methods which may be adopted when using work equipment, any risks which such use may entail and precautions to be taken.

Users of lifting equipment and others involved in lifting operations (for example, those that direct the movement of the load), must be adequately trained, experienced and aged 18 years or over. The only exception is when they are under the direct supervision of a competent person for training requirements.

There are various appointments with specified responsibilities in order to ensure the safety of lifting operations on site.

These are as follows:

- Competent person   -   Appointed to plan the operation.
- Load handler   -   Attaches and detaches the load.
- Authorised person   -   Ensures the load safely attached.
- Operator   -   Appointed to operate the equipment.
- Responsible person -   Appointed to communicate the position of the load (banksman).
- Assistants   -   Appointed to relay communications.

MAINTENANCE AND INSPECTION

It is important that maintenance and inspections be conducted to minimise the likelihood of failure in service through failure modes like corrosion and wear.

Regulation 5 of PUWER 1998 requires work equipment to be maintained in an efficient state, in efficient working order and good repair. Where appropriate to ensure health and safety, maintenance should be carried out in accordance with the manufacturer's instructions, and the maintenance frequency should take into consideration any extended period of activity or inactivity, and also the environment (heat, cold, corrosive).

Inspections must also be carried out at suitable intervals between thorough examinations. Inspections must ensure that the good condition of equipment is maintained and that any deterioration can be detected and remedied in good time.

STATUTORY EXAMINATION OF LIFTING EQUIPMENT

The requirements for statutory requirements are set out in Regulation 9 of the LOLER 1998.

Lifting equipment must be thoroughly examined before being put into service for the first time by a new user. This does not apply to new lifting equipment (unless its safety depends on installation conditions) or equipment that conforms to European Community requirements and has been certified as being examined within the previous 12 months.

Suppliers of used lifting equipment are obliged to certify that a thorough examination has been carried out. Where the safety of lifting equipment depends on the installation conditions it must be thoroughly examined prior to first use, after assembly and on change of location in order to ensure that it has been installed correctly and is safe to operate.

Lifting equipment exposed to conditions causing deterioration that is liable to result in dangerous situations is to be thoroughly examined by a competent person:

- At least every 6 months - lifting equipment for lifting persons and lifting accessories.
- At least every 12 months - other lifting equipment.
- In either case, in accordance with an examination scheme.
- On each occurrence of exceptional circumstances liable to jeopardise the safety of the lifting equipment.

Regulation 10 of LOLER 1998 requires those persons carrying out the thorough examinations specified under regulation 9 to, as soon as is practicable; make a written report of the results of the examination. This is to be signed by the competent person carrying out this task.

Regulation 11 of LOLER 1998 concerns the keeping of information in relation to examinations and specifies that any report written by a competent person, following an examination, must be kept available for inspection for the period of validity of the report.

Figure C7-31: Marking of accessories.   Source: RMS.

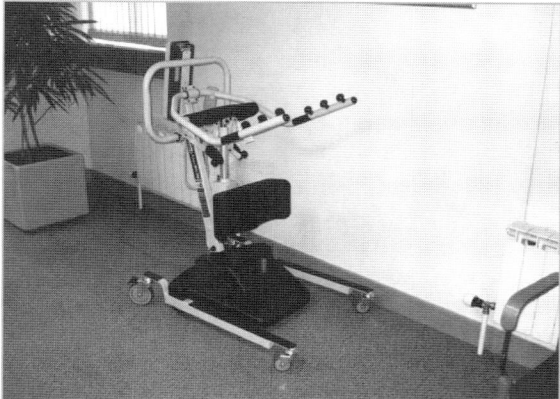
Figure C7-32: Mobile hoist for lifting people.   Source: RMS.

Control measures for cranes and lifting operations

SELECTION

Lifting equipment, and any accessories used for lifting, is pieces of work equipment under the Provision and Use of Work Equipment Regulations (PUWER) 1998.

Regulation 4 of PUWER 1998 states:

1) *Every employer shall ensure that work equipment is so constructed or adapted as to be suitable for the purpose for which it is used or provided.*

2) *In selecting work equipment, every employer shall have regard to the working conditions and to the risks to the health and safety of persons which exist in the premises or undertaking in which that work equipment is to be used and any additional risk posed by the use of that work equipment.*

3) *Every employer shall ensure that work equipment is used only for operations for which, and under conditions for which, it is suitable.*

4) *In this regulation "suitable" means suitable in any respect which is reasonably foreseeable will affect the health or safety of any person.*

In order for lifting equipment to be suitable it must be of the correct type for the task, have a safe working load limit in excess of the load being lifted, and have the correct type and combination of lifting accessories attached.

Lifting equipment used within industry varies and includes mobile cranes, static tower cranes and overhead travelling cranes. The type of lifting equipment selected will depend on a number of factors including the weight of the load to be lifted, the radius of operation, the height of the lift, the time available, and the frequency of the lifting activities. This equipment is often very heavy, which means its weight can cause the ground underneath the equipment to sink or collapse.

Other factors like height and size may have to be considered as there may be limitations in site roads that are located between structures or where overhead restrictions exist. Careful consideration of these factors must be made when selecting the correct crane.

Selecting lifting equipment to carry out a lifting activity should be done at the planning stage, where the most suitable equipment can be identified that is able to meet all of the lifting requirements and the limitations of the location.

Figure C7-33: Lifting operations.   Source: RMS.

Figure C7-34: Lifting operations.   Source: RMS.

SITING - POSITIONED AND INSTALLED CORRECTLY

Lifting equipment must be positioned or installed so that the risk of the equipment striking a person is as low as is reasonably practicable. Similarly, the risk of a load drifting, falling freely or being unintentionally released must also be considered and equipment positioned to take account of this.

All nearby hazards, including overhead cables and uninsulated power supply conductors, should be identified and removed or the risk from them covered by safe working procedures, such as locking-off and permit systems. The possibility of striking other lifting equipment or structures should also be examined.

Detailed consideration must be given to the location of any heavy piece of lifting equipment due to the fact that additional weight is distributed to the ground through the loading of the equipment when performing a lift.

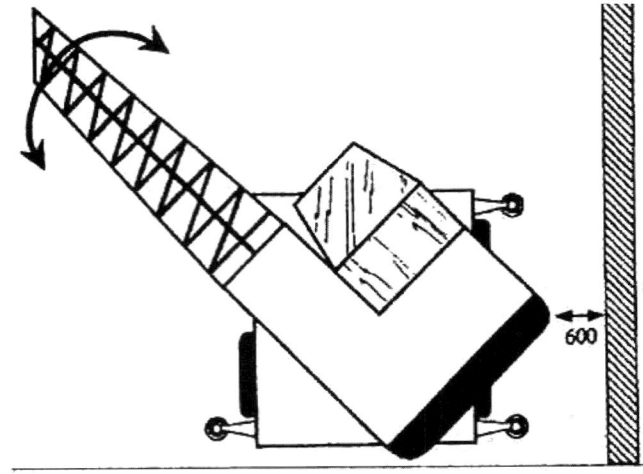

Figure C7-35: Danger zone - crane and fixed item.   Source: RMS.

Surveys must be carried out to determine the nature of the ground, whether soft or firm, and what underground hazards are present such as buried services or hollow voids. If the ground proves to be soft, then this can be covered using timber, digger mats or hard core to prevent the equipment or its outriggers sinking when under load.

The surrounding environment must also be taken into consideration and factors may include highways, railways, electricity cables, areas of public interest. The area around where lifting equipment is sited should be securely fenced, including the extremes of the lift radius, with an additional factor of safety to allow for emergency arrangements such as emergency vehicle access or safety in the event of a collapse or fall.

Where practicable, lifting equipment should be positioned and installed such that loads are not carried or suspended over areas occupied by people. Where this is necessary, appropriate systems of work should be used to ensure it is done safely.

If the operator cannot observe the full path of the load, an appointed person (and assistants as appropriate) should be used to communicate the position of the load and provide directions to avoid striking anything or anyone.

STABILITY

A number of factors can affect the stability of lifting equipment, for example, wind conditions, slopes/cambers, stability of ground conditions and how the load is to be lifted.

Lifting equipment must be positioned and installed so that it does not tip over when in use. Anchoring can be achieved by securing with guy ropes, bolting the structure to a foundation, using ballast as counterweights or using outriggers to extend the stability base of the lifting equipment.

Mobile lifting equipment should be sited on firm ground. Where the ground is not firm; the weight acting on the wheels or outriggers should be distributed over a large surface area by the addition of support material set underneath them.

Figure C7-36: Siting and stability.   Source: RMS.

Care should be taken that the equipment is not positioned over cellars, drains or underground cavities, or positioned near excavations. Sloping ground should be avoided as this can shift the load radius out or in, away from the safe working position.

In the uphill position, the greatest danger occurs when the load is set down. This can cause the mobile lifting equipment to tip over.

In the downhill position, the load moves out of the radius and may cause the equipment to tip forwards.

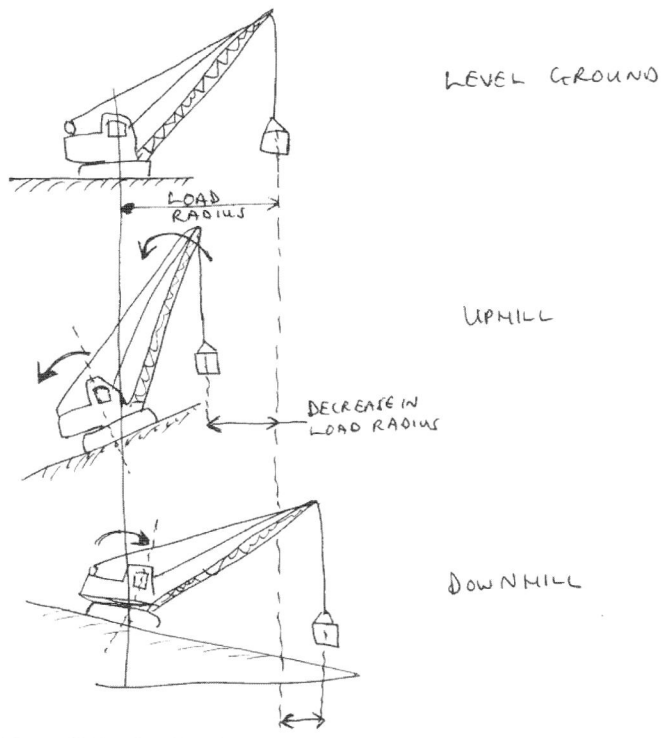

Figure C7-37: Stability of cranes (Hand-drawn). Source: RMS.

PLANNED, SUPERVISED AND CARRIED OUT IN SAFE MANNER

Regulation 8 of LOLER 1998 requires that every employer shall ensure that every lifting operation involving lifting equipment is:

- Properly planned by a competent person.
- Appropriately supervised.
- Carried out in a safe manner.

The type of lifting equipment that is to be used and the complexity of the lifting operations will dictate the degree of planning required for the lifting operation.

Planning combines two parts:

- Initial planning to ensure that lifting equipment is provided which is suitable for the range of tasks that it will have to carry out.
- Planning of individual lifting operations so that they can be carried out safely with the lifting equipment provided.

Factors that should be considered when formulating a plan include:

- The load that is being lifted - weight, shape, centres of gravity, surface condition, lifting points.
- The equipment and accessories being used for the operation and suitability - certification validity.
- The proposed route that the load will take including the destination and checks for obstructions.
- The team required to carry out the lift - competencies and numbers required.
- Production of a safe system of work, risk assessments, permits to work.
- The environment in which the lift will take place - ground conditions, weather, local population.
- Securing areas below the lift - information, restrictions, demarcation and barriers.
- A suitable trial to determine the reaction of the lifting equipment prior to full lift.

Completion of the operation and any dismantling required. It is important that someone takes supervisory control of lifting operations at the time they are being conducted. Though the operator may be skilled in lifting techniques this may not be enough to ensure safety as other factors may influence whether the overall operation is conducted safely, for example, people may stray into the area. The supervisor of the lifting operation must remain in control and stop the operation if it is not carried out satisfactorily.

Figure C7-38: Siting and stability. Source: RMS.

ELEMENT C7 - WORK EQUIPMENT (MOBILE, LIFTING AND ACCESS)

Lifting operations should not be carried on where adverse weather conditions occur, such as fog, poor lightning, strong wind or where heavy rainfall makes ground conditions unstable. It is important that measures be used to prevent lifting equipment overturning and that there is sufficient room for it to operate without contacting other objects.

Lifting equipment should not be used to drag loads and should not be overloaded. Special arrangements need to be in place when lifting equipment not normally used for lifting people is used for that purpose, for example, de-rating the working load limit, ensuring communication is in place between the people being lifted and the operator, and ensuring the operation controls are manned at all times.

Lifting equipment and accessories used in lifting operations should be subject to a pre-use check in order to determine their condition and suitability. In addition, care should be taken to ensure the lifting accessories used are compatible with the task and that the load is protected or supported such that it does not disintegrate when lifted.

SAFE USE OF LIFTING ACCESSORIES

Lifting equipment and any accessories used for lifting are pieces of work equipment under the Provision and Use of Work Equipment Regulations (PUWER) 1998. Regulation 4 states that:

> *'Every employer shall ensure that work equipment is used only for operations for which, and under conditions for which, it is suitable in order to avoid any reasonably foreseeable risk to the health and safety of any person'.*

Figure C7-39: Regulation 4 of PUWER 1998.   Source: Provision and Use of Work Equipment Regulations (PUWER) 1998.

Lifting equipment (accessories) includes slings, hooks, chains eyes and cradles. In order for lifting equipment to be suitable it must be of the correct type for the task, have a safe working load limit in excess of the load being lifted, and have the correct type and combination of lifting accessories attached.

Slings

Slings are available in single, two, three or four-leg or endless form. In practice, it will be found that chain, wire rope and fibre rope slings are available in any of these configurations, but that flat woven webbing is limited to single-leg and endless. Round slings are only supplied in endless forms. The maximum load that a sling may lift will be governed by the slinging arrangements and may vary from the marked safe working load (SWL).

Slings are normally one of the following three types:

- Steel wire rope (SWR).
- Chain.
- Fibre rope (natural or artificial).

Steel wire rope

A strong general-purpose sling available in a wide range of SWL, with very little stretch when subjected to a maximum permitted SWL. They can be supplied as single or multi-leg assemblies employing a wide range of terminal tackle.

Figure C7-40: Single-leg sling.   Source: Ambiguous.

They are constructed in a series of individual wires wound into strands, with a number of strands (usually six) laid in a left or right hand lay over a central strand or core. The main core helps to hold the rope together and prevent it from collapsing when bent. The core can be either fibre or steel depending on the strength and uses of the rope.

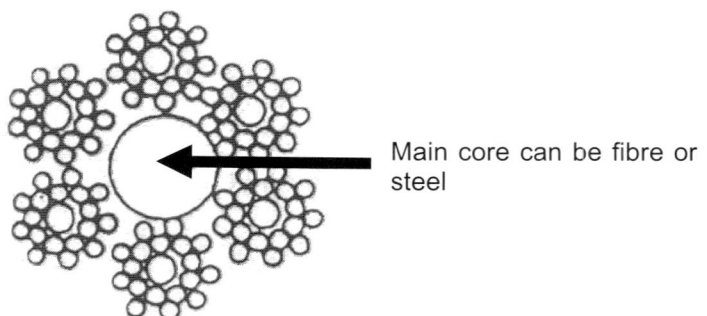

Figure C7-41: Typical wire rope construction 6 x 19 (6 strands with 19 wires in each strand). *Source: Ambiguous.*

Chain slings

Chain slings can be used as an alternative to steel wire rope (SWR). Each has its own advantages and limitations and the latter must be fully appreciated by the slinger if accidents are to be avoided.

Chain slings are able to withstand rougher handling, are less liable to tangle, twist or knot and they are more flexible when not under load tension than SWR. They are capable of gripping a load firmly and are not damaged as easily as SWR or fibre slings by sharp corners or edges of a load (though adequate packing should still be used where necessary).

Chains are available in single, multi-leg or endless configurations and may be fitted with various types of terminal accessories such as hooks, pipe grabs, drum and case clamps etc. They are resistant to abrasion and corrosion and will give warning of excessive loading by the elongation and narrowing of links until eventually they bind together.

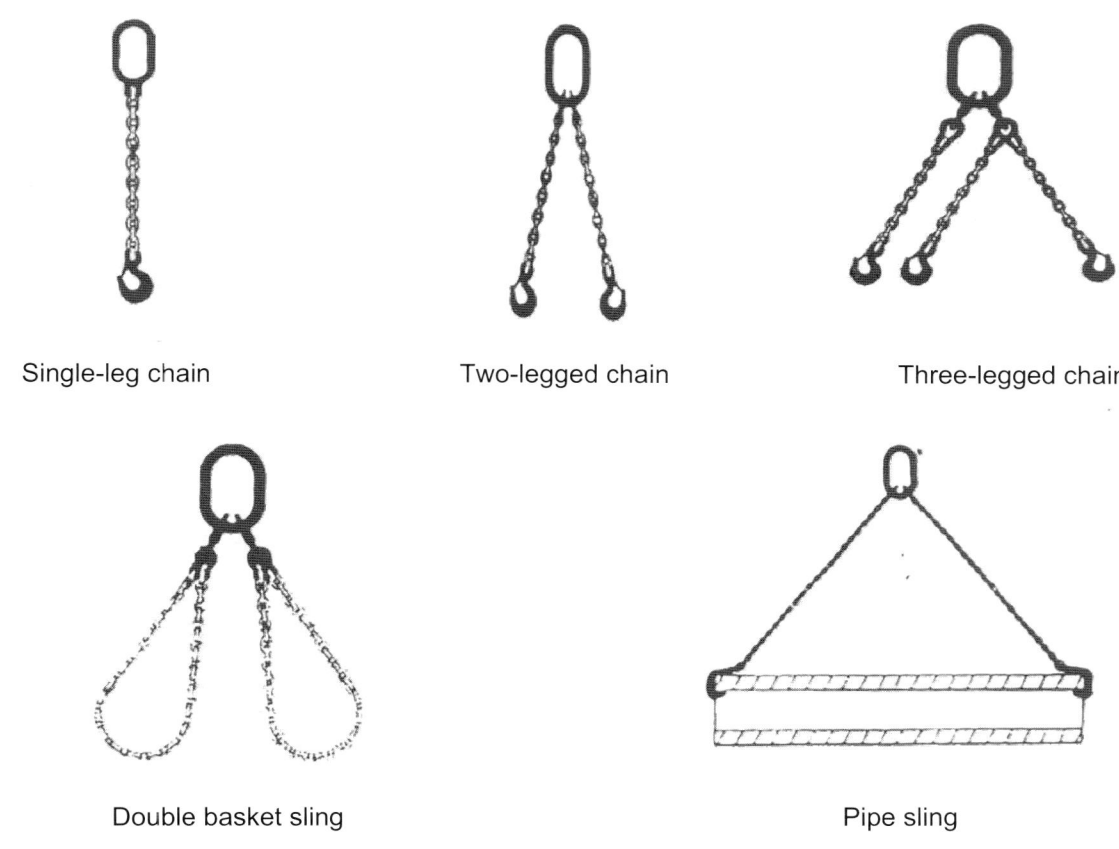

Figure C7-42: Types of chain sling.   Source: Ambiguous.

Fibre rope slings

Fibre rope slings are usually constructed from one of the following materials:

Natural fibre:	Synthetic fibre:
Manila, sisal, hemp.	Terylene polyester, nylon, polypropylene.

Synthetic fibre is used extensively for the manufacture of slings, due to its strength and durability (less liable to damage from rot, mildew). In addition, certain fibres are resistant to various chemical solutions. However, fibre rope slings are more suspect to damage from abrasion and cuts than steel wire rope or chain slings.

This fact should always be taken into account by the slingers when selecting or inspecting these types of slings. All fibre rope slings are liable to wear and mechanical damage, and may also be weakened to some degree by exposure to dampness, chemicals, heat and sunlight.

Man-made fibres are resistant to the following chemicals:

Terylene polyester	High resistance to acid solutions, but is attacked by alkali solutions.
Nylon	High resistance to alkali solutions, but is attacked by acid solutions.
Polypropylene	Resistant to both acids and alkalis.

Where synthetic fibre slings are used in any chemical solution, they should be thoroughly washed and dried naturally before returning to storage. Natural fibre ropes should not be used in chemical solutions. All fibre ropes should be stored in a cool, dry, well-ventilated storage area away from bright sunlight. Particular care should be taken to protect slings from damage caused by sharp edges on the load, by using packing or sleeves. Knots and bends tied in fibre slings will considerably reduce the safe working load of the sling and should be avoided where possible. Fibre rope slings of different materials should not be used when lifting loads due to the different stretching properties of different fibres.

ELEMENT C7 - WORK EQUIPMENT (MOBILE, LIFTING AND ACCESS)

Figure C7-43: Fibre rope sling. *Source: Lincsafe.*

Figure C7-44: Fibre rope sling. *Source: RMS.*

Eyebolts

Eyebolts are normally used for fitting to various items of equipment for the purpose of lifting anchor points when slinging. There are three common types of eyebolts:

Dynamo	To be used for straight lifts only (vertical).
Collar	For both angles (multi-leg) and straight lifts.
Collar and ring	For angle (multi-leg) lifts.

Note: on no account should dynamo eyebolts be used for angled lifts.

Care should be taken to ensure that the load does not rotate when lifting with a dynamo eyebolt since the eyebolt may unscrew.

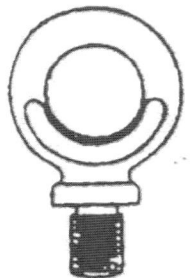
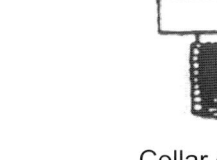
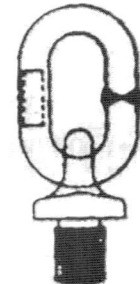

Dynamo eyebolt   Collar eyebolt   Collar eyebolt with ring

Figure C7-45: Eyebolts. *Source: Ambiguous.*

Lifting spreader beam

Designed for the purpose of handling long loads. Can also be used in conjunction with two dynamo eyebolts since a vertical lift would be applied to the eyebolts. Must be a tested piece of lifting equipment marked with a Safe Working Load.

Plate clamp

Used for lifting sheets of metal. These must be free from oil and grease because they rely on the clamping force of the clamp mechanism to prevent the load slipping. Plate clamps are not suitable for heavy loads. Must be a tested piece of lifting equipment marked with a safe working load.

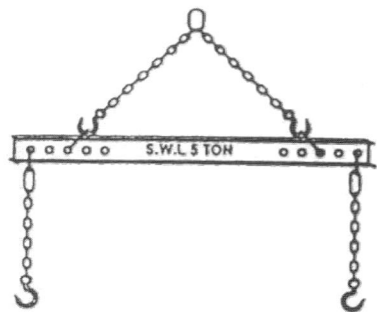

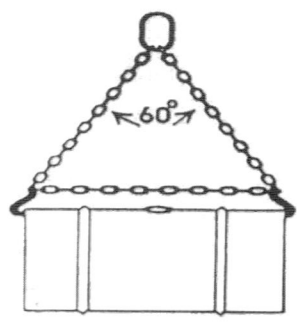

Lifting spreader beam   Plate clamp   Case or drum sling

Figure C7-46: Case or drum sling. *Source: Ambiguous.*

Case or drum sling

They are only suitable for loads of less than 1 tonne. Included angle of lift should always be kept as close as possible to 60 degrees. Drum rims should always be in a sound condition when using this type of sling.

Shackles

Shackles are used as terminal tackle for securing the sling to the load or eyebolt, or to attach a number of slings to the hook of a lifting appliance. Their use is also recommended where it may be necessary to join two slings together so as to increase the sling length. All shackles should be marked with their safe working load and identification mark.

Lifting hooks

There are several types of lifting hooks that may be fitted to the lifting appliance or used as terminal tackle, particularly on chain slings.

The type of hook will normally depend upon the type of lifting or slinging application. The slinger needs to be aware of all safe practices associated with the use of each type of hook. All hooks used for lifting must be fitted with a safety catch, or should be moused, or so shaped to prevent the sling eye or load coming off the hook.

Figure C7-47: Hook with safety latch. *Source: Corel Clipart.*

Lifting equipment is designed with the aim of assisting in lifting items without the need for manual force. Because these accessories are in a constantly changing environment and are in and out of use they need to be protected from damage; a failure of any one item could have fatal effects. For example, lifting eyes needed to be correctly fitted, slings have to be used with the correct technique and all equipment must be stored properly. Accessories must be attached correctly and safely to the load by a competent person, and then the lifting equipment takes over the task of providing the necessary required power to perform the lift.

C7.3 - Access and work at height equipment: hazards and control measures

The applications and different types of mobile access and work at height equipment

MOBILE ELEVATING WORK PLATFORM (MEWP)

Mobile elevating work platforms (MEWPs) can provide a safe way of working at height. They allow the worker to reach the task quickly and easily. They have guard rails and toe boards which prevent a person or materials from falling and can be used in-doors or out. MEWPs are designed to be movable, under their own power or by being towed, so that it can easily be set up in a location where they are needed.

Various mechanical and hydraulic means are used to elevate the work platform to the desired height, including telescopic arms. The versatility of this equipment enables the easy placement of a work platform at a height and makes it a popular piece of access equipment. Often, to do similar work by other means would take a lot of time or be very difficult. They are now widely available and there is a tendency for people to oversimplify their use and allow people to operate them without prior training and experience.

MEWPs include:

- Hydraulic extending boom type 'cherry pickers'.
- Scissor lifts.
- Vehicle-mounted articulating multi-booms.

All of these may be towable units; vehicle-mounted; self-propelled or pedestrian controlled. They are nearly always equipped with outriggers to improve stability in use. Rough terrain MEWPs have been specifically designed and equipped to be used on rough terrain, so that they are safe to use on uneven or undulating ground.

Hydraulic extending boom type

The hydraulic extending boom type, 'cherry pickers', provides vertical height, horizontal reach and extended reach. They are not as versatile as the multi-boom articulated MEWP, but are commonly used in providing ready access for many applications. Extending boom type MEWPs are generally known as 'cherry pickers'.

ELEMENT C7 - WORK EQUIPMENT (MOBILE, LIFTING AND ACCESS)

Figure C7-48: Extending boom MEWP. *Source: Inverness Tree Services Ltd.*

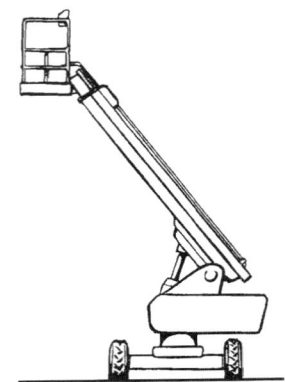

Figure C7-49: Extending boom MEWP. *Source: CITB.*

Articulating and telescopic or multi-boom articulated

These types of equipment give a wide range of reach and height, with good platform mobility. The equipment enables access to be made in more than one plane, i.e. vertical and horizontal, providing greater flexibility for access, although with reduced load capability when compared to a scissor lift. The multi-boom design has enabled their use for specialist work, for instance, machines that enable access to the underside of bridge arches from the roadway above. Some forms of this equipment are vehicle mounted.

Figure C7-50: *Multi-boom articulated. Source: RMS.*

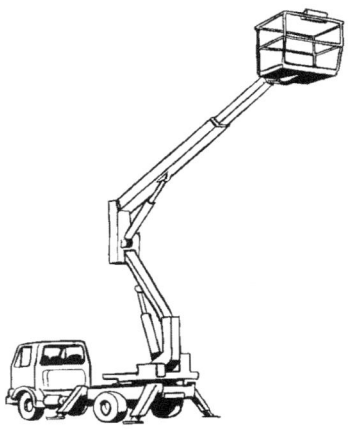

Figure C7-51: *Multi-boom articulated. Source: CITB.*

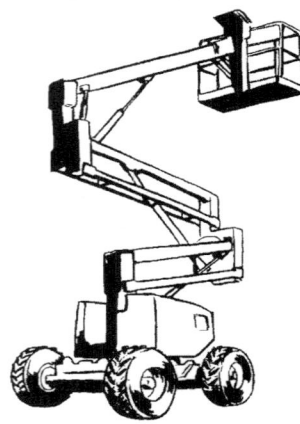

Figure: C7-52: *Multi-boom rough terrain. Source: CITB.*

Figure C7-53: Scissor lift. *Source: HSE, HSG150.*

Figure C7-54: Scissor lift. *Source: RMS.*

Scissor

A scissor lift provides an excellent means of access in a vertical plane; it provides a large work platform from which to work. They may be provided with a form of outrigger in order to improve stability and to enable the lift to be set on the level and ensuring a vertical lift.

Their mobile nature enables workers to gain access to locations at height for inspection, maintenance or construction work. Its size enables it to lift both materials and workers, which makes it suitable for use with roof work tasks where sheets and insulation have to be moved.

The hazards of access and work at height equipment

MECHANICAL STRENGTH

Access and similar equipment of this type is designed to have a certain load bearing capacity. As the equipment is used, the moving parts may become worn out, for example, hydraulic seals may start to leak, and this will reduce the ability of the equipment to carry its full capacity. In the same way, non-moving parts, such as booms and struts, can be damaged by impact and a weak point caused in the item that will reduce its load bearing capacity. The weak point may become obvious when the equipment is working at its fully extended position, as this will increase the forces acting on the equipment. This can lead to sudden catastrophic failure of the equipment. These hazards are more likely if the equipment is mistreated, for example, overloaded, or not maintained.

LOADING CONTROL AND CONTROL DEVICES

The absence of sufficient control devices available to those using the access equipment to work at height could mean that it is operated from the ground. This creates a risk of contact with buildings and structures due to poor communication and co-ordination between the person operating the equipment and those in it.

The absence of load control, including load sensing devices (overload devices) can lead to the overload of the equipment causing failure or possible overturning. In addition, the load capacity of more complicated MEWPS with multiple lift sections can be a complex calculation depending on how far the equipment extends and the weight of the equipment counterbalancing it. This means that it may be easy to overload or overturn such a device if electronic and other indicators do not limit the user to stay within the safe lifting envelope of the equipment.

HAZARDS TO PERSONS ON OR IN THE CARRIER

The principal hazards to persons on or in the carrier of access equipment of this type relate to:

Movement of the carrier. Where the movement might bring the people in contact with fixed or moving parts of equipment or structures. This may lead to contact with these structures, such as to the head with pipes or steelwork or limbs trapped/injured as the carrier moves past fixed points.

Persons falling from the carrier. The work being done by the people in the carrier or poor positioning may cause them to overreach and fall from it. Sudden movement of the carrier could cause them to overbalance and fall over the sides of the carrier.

Objects falling on the carrier. The nature of use of the access equipment may relate to construction, maintenance or demolition. In each case the equipment may be used to assist in the location or removal of materials. This leads those in the carrier to be at risk of injury from materials that could fall during this operation. This may be small fixing bolts dropped by co-workers or larger pieces of steelwork that unexpectedly fall during the process.

EXCEEDING THE SAFE WORKING LOADS/PERSONS PERMITTED

Because it can take time to lower, load and raise the equipment those using it may be tempted to overload it in order to save time. It is also not uncommon for users of the equipment to fail to take account of tools and equipment being lifted as well as the people, leading to too many people in the carrier. This can significantly overload the equipment and change the effective safe working envelope.

The appropriate control measures for use of access and work at height equipment

In establishing appropriate control measures for access and work at height equipment (AWHE) it is necessary to determine whether risks can be eliminated, for example, adjusting the phasing of the work so that it is not carried out at height.

Appropriate control measures for access and work at height equipment include:

- Ground conditions will need to be considered, particularly following any periods of rain causing soft ground. Identify any buried services or cellars that may cause the ground to collapse under the weight of the equipment.
- Ensure parts of the equipment cannot protrude into roads or other transport routes. If there is passing traffic it is important to consider how collisions will be prevented, consider barriers to protect the outriggers, warning signs and possibly someone to control the traffic flow. Equipment used in poor lighting conditions on or near roads and walkways must use standard vehicle lighting to warn road traffic of its presence.
- Identify any overhead obstruction hazards, for example, steelwork, tree branches or power lines to prevent collision damage to the equipment or crush injuries or electric shock to the operator.
- Consideration will need to be given to the selection of the equipment to ensure it meets the requirements for the task. This will include the maximum reach, both vertical and horizontal, that is required for the task, to prevent overreaching of the operators. In addition, the space provided by the equipment and strength of the equipment should be adequate for the maximum number of people and maximum working load.

ELEMENT C7 - WORK EQUIPMENT (MOBILE, LIFTING AND ACCESS)

- Fitted with a suspension or supporting system, i.e. capable of carrying the maximum load, stable without undue movement. Where possible the carrier has an enhanced safety coefficient suspension rope or chain, which is inspected by a competent person every working day.
- Controlled by person in the carrier, i.e. controls for vertical or horizontal movement of the equipment. This will enable more accurate positioning of the equipment and remove the need to communicate to another person the movements required. This can help prevent collisions, crush injuries and the movement will tend to be conducted more smoothly reducing the risk of falling from the equipment.
- Fitted with emergency stop devices, i.e. to stop and isolate movement of the equipment. It is important that the means to stop the equipment in an emergency is available to the operator and, if the operator is someone in a carrier, someone on the ground.
- Fitted with hold to run controls, i.e. when released run controls automatically stop and movement ceases. This will ensure that if the operator is unable to confirm movement it will stop, for example, if they slip over in the carrier or strike their head on an obstruction.
- Prevention of tilting if there is a risk of occupants falling, i.e. locking system to prevent tilt when the platform is raised. The equipment would benefit from a device that could detect that it was tilting outside acceptable limits and would cause the equipment to stop.
- Trapdoors opening in a direction that eliminates any risk of falling, i.e. upwards.
- Protective roof if risk of falling objects endanger persons, i.e. robust mesh cover.
- Marked with maximum number of persons and maximum load, i.e. permanently fixed prominent plate.
- The operator is fully trained and competent.
- The work platform is fitted with guard rails and toe boards.
- Tyres are properly inflated.
- Outriggers are extended as necessary before raising the platform.
- All involved know what to do if the machine fails with the platform in the raised position.
- Ensure the equipment has a thorough examination by a competent person at least once every six months. Inspections may be more frequent depending on the use and operating conditions. Inspection intervals should be stated in the examination scheme.
- Ensure competent personnel undertake planned maintenance in accordance with the manufacturer's instructions.

Element C8

Electrical safety and Electricity at Work Regulations 1989

Learning outcomes

The intended learning outcomes are that the student will be able to:

C8.1 Outline the basic principles of electricity.
C8.2 Outline the dangers of electricity.
C8.3 Outline the issues relevant to the installation, use, inspection and maintenance of electrical systems.
C8.4 Outline the main principles for safe working in the vicinity of high voltage systems.
C8.5 Outline the main hazards, risks and controls associated with the use of portable electrical equipment.

Content

C8.1 - Basic principles of electricity 283
    Differences between low and high voltage 283
    Potential difference, current, resistance, impedance, Ohm's law.. 283
    Basic electrical circuitry 284
    Earthing principles 285
    Significance of direct and alternating currents and electromagnetic radiation 285
C8.2 - Dangers of electricity... 286
    Effect of electric shock on the body... 286
    Factors influencing the severity of the effects of electric shock on the body 286
    Common causes of fire 288
    Electric arcs 289
    Circumstances giving rise to the generation of static electricity 289
    Hazards and controls for static electricity 290
C8.3 - Installation, use and inspection of electrical systems 290
    Meaning of 'duty holders' and 'construction'.. 290
    Control measures 296
    Relationship between BS 7671:2008, IET Wiring Regs 17th Edn and the Electricity at Work Regs 1989 302
    Importance of schemes of maintenance, schedules, plans and records 303
    Safe systems of work on installations made dead.. 304
    Safe systems of work and criteria of acceptability for live working... 304
    Use of permits to work 305
    Meaning of 'competent' person.. 305
C8.4 - Safe working in the vicinity of high voltage systems 305
    Common high voltage systems and prevention of danger 305
    Competent and authorised persons role related to system modifications.. 306
    Safe systems of work and permit-to-work procedures 307
    Safe working near overhead power lines 307
    Underground cables 308
    Substations 309
    High voltage glove working and live line overhead working 309
C8.5 - Portable electrical equipment.. 310
    Conditions and practices likely to lead to accidents 310
    Electrical risks from important portable appliances 311
    Control measures, including portable appliance inspection and testing... 312
    Aspects of supply, e.g. height of cables 312

ELEMENT C8 - ELECTRICAL SAFETY AND EWR 1989

Relevant statutory provisions

Electricity at Work Regulations (EWR) 1989

Dangerous Substances and Explosive Atmospheres Regulations (DSEAR) 2002

IET Wiring Regulations 17th Edition: (BS 7671: 2008)

ELECTRICAL SAFETY AND EWR 1989 - **ELEMENT C8**

C8.1 - Basic principles of electricity

Differences between low and high voltage

Electricity is generated at high voltages and distributed through primary parts of the national distribution system at 400kV; it then passes to secondary, lower voltage parts of the system reducing voltage as it is distributed to points of use.

Large users of electricity will receive electricity at voltages of 33kV or 11kV and transform it to voltages that they can use for their processes.

In other cases, it is distributed at 440v and separated into 230V for general use. In use, this may be further transformed to lower voltages for process reasons or for personal safety.

For example, a 'low voltage transformer' may reduce the voltage to 110V for use with power tools on a construction site. Portable electrical equipment in some chemical process sites may be operated at voltages below 110V, for example 50V, which may be adequate and safer for such things as hand held lighting.

Extra low voltage that below 50V, is safer where there is a risk of wet conditions, perhaps because of the processes being carried out.

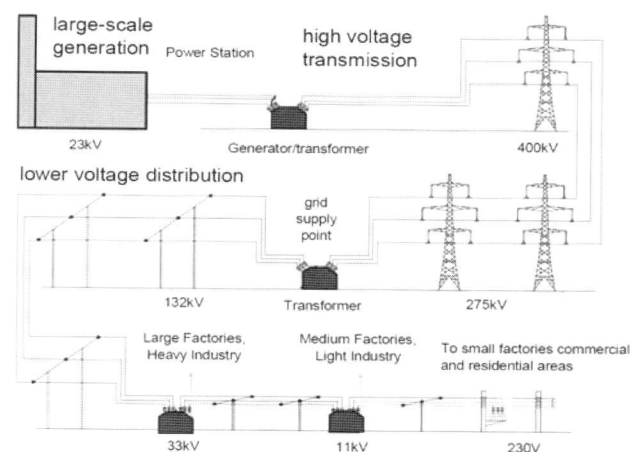

Figure C8-1: Electrical distribution voltages. *Source: Parliamentary Office of Science and Technology.*

The terms high and low voltage are often used differently by the generation/distribution/transmission industry and in general discussion by users. The generation/distribution/transmission industry uses the term low voltage in relation to apparatus running (or generating) electricity in the range 50-1,000 volts AC and 120 and 1500 volts DC; as per the IET (formally IEE) 17th Edn Wiring Regulations.

Equipment manufactured to work in this range must also conform to the Electrical Equipment (Safety) Regulations (EESR) 1994. High voltage is any voltage exceeding low voltage.

Potential difference, current, resistance, impedance, Ohm's law

POTENTIAL DIFFERENCE

The flow of electrons through a conductor is known as current. Just as water flows through a pipe because of the pressure behind it, the electric current flows due to differences in electrical "pressure" or potential difference as it is often known. To further explain, current flows in a circuit as a result of a difference in potential between two points in the circuit. The potential difference between two points in a conductor is the work per unit charge done by the charge in moving from a point of higher potential to a point of lower potential.

The unit of potential difference is called the volt, **V**. One volt of potential difference exists between two points if one joule of work is done by each coulomb of charge in moving between them. Potential difference is measured by an instrument called a voltmeter. Voltmeters are connected in parallel to the component across which one wishes to measure the potential difference. They have a resistance which is several orders of magnitude higher than the resistance of the component. The current which flows through a voltmeter is negligible.

CURRENT

Current is the flow of charge. The unit of current is the ampere, denoted by the letter **I**.

Current is measured using an instrument called an ammeter. Ammeters are connected in series with the part of the circuit through which one wishes to measure the current, **I**, and they have negligible resistance.

RESISTANCE

For any conductor, the ratio of the potential difference across the conductor and the current flowing through it is constant. This constant is called the resistance of the conductor, **R**:

$$\text{Resistance}(R) = \frac{V}{I}$$

The unit of resistance is the Ohm, Ω.

Resistance is a property of a particular conductor and depends on:

- The material of which the conductor is made.
- The length, l, of the conductor ($R \propto l$). (Resistance is directly proportional to length).
- The cross-sectional area of the conductor. (Resistance is inversely proportional to cross-sectional area).
- The temperature of the conductor. (Resistance increases non-linearly with temperature).

ELEMENT C8 - ELECTRICAL SAFETY AND EWR 1989

IMPEDANCE

As an alternating current passes round a circuit under the action of an applied voltage it is impeded in its flow. This may be due to the presence in the circuit of resistance, inductance or capacitance, the combined effect of which is called impedance and is measured in ohms.

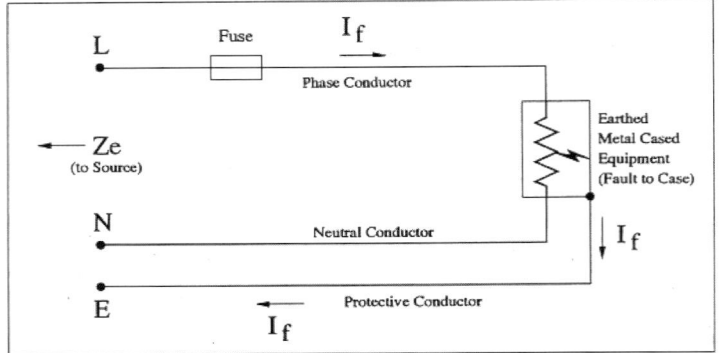

TOTAL EFLI (Z) = EXTERNAL EFLI (Ze) + CIRCUIT EFLI (Zc)

Zc = Impedance of phase conductor plus impedance of protective conductor (fault assumed to have negligible impedance)

Figure C8-2: Impedance. *Source: G Self.*

OHM'S LAW

"For any particular conductor at a constant temperature, the current that flows through it is directly proportional to the potential difference applied across it".

$$I = \frac{1}{R}V \quad \text{or} \quad IR = V \quad \text{or} \quad I = \frac{V}{R}$$

There is a simple relationship between electrical pressure (volts), current and resistance represented by Ohm's Law: voltage (**V**) = current (**I**) multiplied by the circuit resistance (**R**).

$$V = I \times R \text{ or } I = \frac{V}{R}$$

Hence, given any two values, the third can be calculated. Also, if one value changes the other two values will change accordingly.

This basic electrical equation can be used to calculate the current that flows in a circuit of a given resistance or power connected to a particular voltage supply. This will need to be done to determine, for example, the fuse or cable rating needed for a particular circuit. Similarly, the current that will flow through a person who touches a live conductor can be calculated.

Basic electrical circuitry

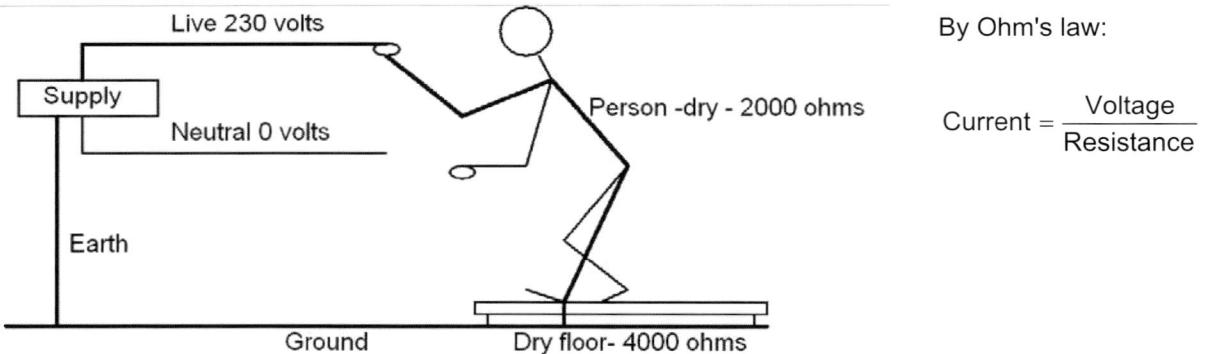

By Ohm's law:

$$\text{Current} = \frac{\text{Voltage}}{\text{Resistance}}$$

Figure C8-3: Basic electrical circuitry. *Source: RMS.*

Resistance in a circuit is dependent on many factors. Most metals, particularly precious metals, allow current to pass very easily. These have a low resistance and are used as conductors. Other materials such as plastics, rubber and textiles have a high resistance and are used as insulators.

If the person is on, say, a dry concrete floor, resistance in the body will only be about 2,000 ohms and the resistance in the floor about 4,000 ohms, therefore:

$$I = \frac{V}{R} = \frac{230 \text{ Volts}}{\approx 2000 + 4000 \text{ Ohms}} = 0.04 \text{ Amps}$$

The current flowing through the operator will be about 40 milliamps that could result in a fatal shock. *(See figure ref C8-3).*

Earthing principles

The conductive mass of the Earth, whose electric potential at any point is conventionally taken as zero helps as a protective measure.

A conductor called an earth wire is connected to the system. It is connected at one end to a plate buried into the ground and the other end connected to the metal casing of the equipment. If for any reason a conducting wire touches the casing so that the equipment casing becomes '*live*' the current will flow to the point of lowest potential.

By fitting the earth wire the path to this point is made easier as the wire has very little resistance and therefore an easier path.

UNEARTHED ELECTRICAL SYSTEM

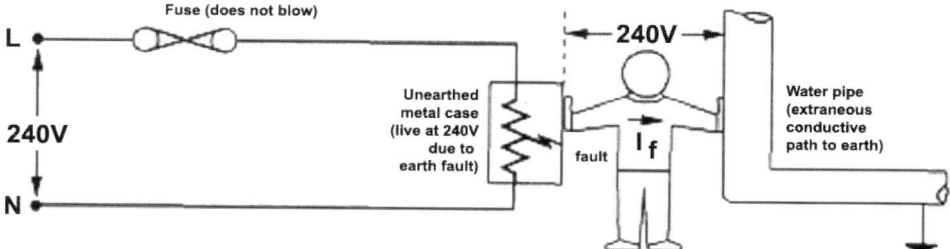

EARTHED ELECTRICAL SYSTEM

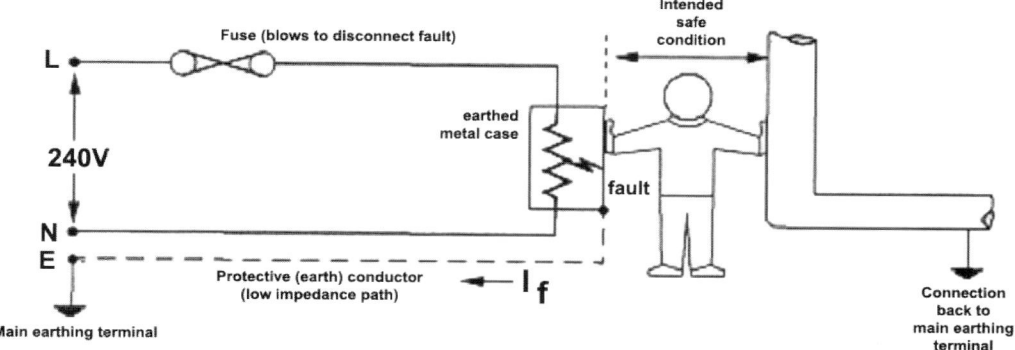

Figures C8-4 and C8-5: Unearthed and earthed electrical systems. Source: G Self.

Significance of direct and alternating currents and electromagnetic radiation

DIRECT AND ALTERNATING CURRENT

In some systems the current flows continually in the same direction. This is known as direct current (DC). However, the current may also constantly reverse its direction of flow. This is known as alternating current (AC). Most public electricity supplies are alternating current. The UK system reverses its direction 50 times per second - it has a frequency of 50 cycles per second or 50 Hertz (50 Hz). Direct current is little used in standard electrical power distribution systems, but is sometimes used in industry for specialist applications. Although there are slight differences in the effects under fault and shock conditions between alternating current and direct current, it is a safe rule to apply the same controls. *See also "Factors influencing the severity of the effects of electric shock on the body – later in the element".*

ELECTROMAGNETIC RADIATION

Electromagnetic radiation may be generated from a number of sources, including radio transmitters. The most severe sources for industrial environments are typically from arc furnaces, induction heaters, and radio frequency (RF) welders and from variable speed motor drives. In medical work, magnetic resonance imaging (MRI) equipment represents an important source.

The significance of electromagnetic radiation in the workplace is related to the harm to a person's health and the effects it can have on electronic devices that have a health and safety effect, for example, proximity devices used for guarding applications. The effects on health are principally that they can cause a heating effect on a person's body, but they may also induce a current in metal parts of a person's clothing or medical equipment placed in the body, causing them to get hot. Electromagnetic radiation can cause the malfunction or failure of electronic devices. If they have a safety critical role this may lead to failure of protective devices or process problems that may lead to catastrophic failure of plant.

ELEMENT C8 - ELECTRICAL SAFETY AND EWR 1989

C8.2 - Dangers of electricity

Effect of electric shock on the body

When an electric current passes through a material, the resistance to the flow of electrons dissipates energy, usually in the form of heat. If the material is human tissue and the amount of heat generated is sufficient, the tissue may be burnt. The effect is similar to damage caused by an open flame or other high-temperature source of heat, except that electricity has the ability to *burn* tissue well beneath the skin, including internal organs.

Nerve cells communicate by creating electrical signals (very small voltages and currents) in response to the input of certain chemical compounds called neurotransmitters. If the electric shock current is of sufficient magnitude it will override the electrical impulses normally generated by the neurons preventing both reflex and volitional (controlled by conscious choice or decision) signals from being able to actuate muscles. These effects may be felt as *pain*.

Muscles triggered by a shock current will involuntarily *contract*. The forearm muscles responsible for bending fingers tend to be better developed than those muscles responsible for extending fingers, if both sets of muscles attempt to contract the "bending" muscles will be stronger and clench the fingers into a fist. If the conductor delivering a shock current touches the palm of the hand, the clenching action will force the hand to grasp the conductor firmly, securing contact with the wire and it will not be possible for the victim to release their grasp. Even when the current is stopped, the victim may not regain voluntary control over their muscles for a while, as the neurotransmitter chemistry will be in disarray. Involuntary muscle contraction is called tetanus. Shock-induced tetanus can only be interrupted by stopping the current passing through the body.

Electric current is able to affect more than just skeletal muscles, such as the lungs and heart, particularly if the path is across the chest. The diaphragm muscle controlling the lungs and the heart muscle can also be caused to be in a state of tetanus by a shock current, leading to *respiratory failure* of the lungs and *fibrillation* of the heart or *cardiac arrest*.

Fibrillation is a condition where all the heart muscles start moving independently in a disorganised manner, rather than in a co-ordinated way. It affects the ability of the heart to pump blood, resulting in brain damage and eventual cardiac arrest.

Factors influencing the severity of the effects of electric shock on the body

The factors influencing the severity of the effects of electric shock on the body include the following:

- Voltage.
- Frequency.
- Duration.
- Impedance/resistance.
- Current and current path.
- Direct/indirect shock.

The amount of current that flows through the body for a given voltage will depend on the frequency of the supply voltage, on the level of the voltage that is applied and on the state of the point of contact with the body, particularly the moisture condition. The effect of electricity on the body and severity of electric shock results from a combination of the current level and the time duration of the passage of that current. The voltage level is relevant mainly in that it causes the passage of the current.

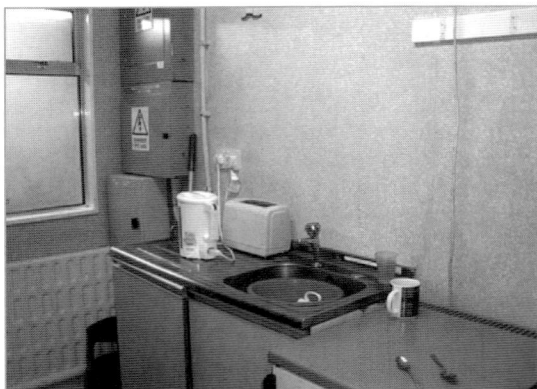

Figure C8-6: Electrical equipment near water. *Source: RMS.*

Figure C8-7: Contact with high voltage buried cable. *Source: RMS.*

VOLTAGE

Voltage is the driving force behind the flow of electricity, like pressure in a water pipe influences the amount of water that flows. The correct name for this term is potential difference, as a voltage is the measure of the difference in electrical energy between two points. Any electrical charge that is free to move will move from the higher energy point to the lower one, taking a quantity of that energy difference with it.

FREQUENCY

Alternating current (AC) is preferred over direct current (DC) for power generation/transmission systems and is used domestically, in industry and commerce, but AC is 3 to 5 times more dangerous than DC at the same voltage and amperage. AC at frequencies of 50 to 60 Hz produces a series of muscle contractions (tetany), which will, if the point of contact is the palm of the hand, cause the hand to grasp the source and prolonging the exposure. DC is most likely to cause a single convulsive contraction. AC has a greater tendency to cause fibrillation of the heart muscles, whereas DC tends to make the heart muscles stand still. Once the shock current is halted, a still heart has a better chance of regaining a normal beat pattern than one that is in fibrillation. Defibrillating equipment, used by paramedics, utilises a DC shock current to halt fibrillation to enable the heart to recover its normal beat. Though both AC and DC shocks may be fatal, more DC is required to have the same effect as AC, for example the 'no let go' threshold for DC is reported to be 4-5 times that of AC.

DURATION

For an electric shock to have an effect a person needs to be in contact with the current for sufficient time. At low current levels the body tolerates the current so the time is not material, however at higher current levels, for example, 50 mA; the person has to remain in contact for sufficient time for the heart to be affected, in the order of milliseconds. In general, the longer a person is in contact with the current the more harm may be caused.

RESISTANCE

The amount of resistance in a circuit influences the amount of current that is allowed to flow, as explained by Ohm's law. It is possible for a person to be in contact with a circuit and to present sufficiently high resistance that very little current is allowed to flow through their body. The example shown in *figure ref C8-3* illustrates this. It should be noted that the level of current flow is also dependent on the voltage; at high voltages an enormous amount of resistance is needed to ensure current flow will remain at a safe level. In an electric shock situation the human body contributes part of the resistance of the circuit, the amount it contributes depends on the current path taken and other factors such as personal chemical make-up (a large portion of the body is water), moisture on and thickness of skin, and any clothing that is being worn, such as shoes and gloves.

CURRENT AND CURRENT PATH

The effect of an electric shock on the body is particularly dependent on the current path through the body. Current has to flow through from one point to another as part of a circuit. If the flow was between two points on a finger the effect on the body would be concentrated between the two points. If the current path is between one hand and another, across the chest, this means the flow will pass through major parts of the body, such as the heart, and may cause fibrillation or cardiac arrest.

In a similar way, a contact between hand and foot (feet), across the chest, can have serious effects on a great many parts of the body, including the heart. These latter current paths tend to be the ones leading to fatal injuries. However, a current path from hand to foot down the one side of the body may not affect the heart and therefore may not be fatal. Although many people may experience shock from 230 volts this may not be fatal if they were, for example, standing on or wearing some insulating material. This may be a matter of fortune and, as a rule; protection should not be relied on.

The amount of current flow through the body has a significant influence on the effect of the electric shock. At low levels of current flow no effect may be experienced; however at progressively higher levels of current flow the larger muscles of the body may be affected. The heart, being made of large muscles, requires a significant current to affect it. At high currents levels burns may occur at the point of current entry and exit from the body, as well as points along the route the current takes through the body.

Current (mA)	Length of time	Likely effects
0-1	Not critical	Threshold of feeling. Undetected by person.
2-15	Not critical	Threshold of cramp. Independent loosening of the hands no longer possible, 'no let go' condition exists.
16-30	Minutes	Cramp like pulling together of the arms, breathing difficult. Limit of tolerance.
31-50	Seconds to minutes	Strong cramp like effects, loss of consciousness due to restricted breathing. Longer time may lead to fibrillation.
51-500	Less than one heart period (750 ms)	No fibrillation. Strong shock effects.
	Greater than one heart period	Fibrillation. Loss of consciousness. Burn marks.
Over 500	Less than one heart period	Fibrillation. Loss of consciousness. Burn marks.

Figure C8-8: Effects of alternating current flowing in the human body.

Source: RMS.

ELEMENT C8 - ELECTRICAL SAFETY AND EWR 1989

DIRECT/INDIRECT SHOCK

Direct shock

Direct shock relates to when a person makes contact with a charged or energised conductor that is intended to be charged or energised. In these circumstances the electrical system is operating in its normal or proper condition. This may occur when someone is working on equipment where conductors are exposed and in the live condition.

Indirect shock

Indirect shock relates to when a person makes contact with electrical conducting material that is normally at a safe potential, but has become dangerously live through a fault condition. Conductive parts of equipment that may become live in a fault condition include the conducting casing of equipment and trunking around electrical cables.

These are normally safe to touch, but under fault conditions could become dangerously live. For example, where the casing of equipment has a poor connection to earth, and when a fault occurs on the equipment, the casing may become live.

Common causes of fire

The principal causes of electrical fires are:

- Overheating.
- Ignition of flammable vapour.
- Ignition of combustible material.
- Breakdown of insulation.

Figure C8-9: Used coiled up-risk of overheating. *Source: RMS.*

Figure C8-10: Max current capacity exceeded. *Source: RMS.*

Figure C8-11: Worn cable - risk of electrical fire. *Source: RMS.*

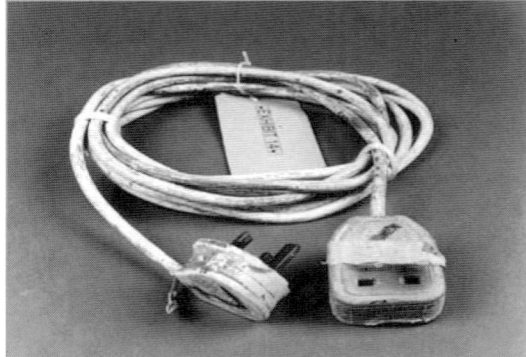

Figure C8-12: Evidence of overheating. *Source: RMS.*

OVERHEATING

Overheating of cables or other electrical equipment may occur through overloading the electrical system with currents above their design capacity. This may occur by placing too many portable appliances on one electrical socket, often by the use of plug in multi-outlet additions or the use of an extension lead with multiple outlets. Overheating will particularly occur where more than one piece of high power consumption equipment is supplied from one socket. Current flow through a conductor creates an amount of heat; if this is not able to be dissipated, for example, where an extension lead is coiled up, this could cause overheating and a lead to a fire.

If fuses with the incorrect rating are used in electrical equipment this will allow the electrical circuit to run at higher currents than its design criteria and may lead to the equipment and conductors overheating. In addition, if poor connections exist in a circuit, perhaps due to lack of maintenance or unskilled personnel, this can lead to localised heating that may be sufficient to cause insulation to ignite.

IGNITION OF FLAMMABLE VAPOUR OR COMBUSTIBLE MATERIAL

Electrical equipment may also act as a source of ignition of flammable vapours, gases, liquids, dust or other combustible material, through the creation of electric sparks, arcs or high surface temperatures of equipment.

This may be due to the normal operation of the equipment or be created by poorly maintained equipment, such as defective motors, heaters and lighting. Combustible material placed close to electrical equipment may ignite due to the heat given off by its operation, due to current flow.

BREAKDOWN OF INSULATION

Insulation around conductors can be broken down by chemical attack when electrical equipment is located in aggressive environments. Mechanical breakdown of the insulation surrounding conductors can occur through normal use, particularly where the conductors are flexible and experience a lot of bending. Mechanical breakdown can also occur through situations where insulation is damaged by the use of the equipment, such as an extension lead abraded by an abrasive wheel or melted by heat from a lamp.

Mechanical damage to conductors in an electrical circuit can occur in situations where the conductors are concealed in a ceiling or floor and work is done that involves driving nails or similar items through the surface and causing accidental damage to the insulation. In addition, the insulation on conductors may age, become brittle and break up. This breakdown of the insulation of conductors can lead to small amounts of extraneous current flow that creates localised heating and may lead to fires.

Electric arcs

MOLTEN METAL SPLASH AND RADIATION

An electric arc is a high temperature electrical discharge between two conductors in close proximity. The energy released is in the form of heat and light. This extremely high temperature can result in the conductor melting. If this phenomenon is controlled it has great benefits for industry, for example, electric arc welding. However, uncontrolled it can lead to molten metal being violently discharged or the light (UV radiation) produced can cause burns and a condition called photokeratitis ('arc eye').

Circumstances giving rise to the generation of static electricity

HOW STATIC IS CREATED

Static electricity is different to mains power electricity as it can be generated naturally. It is familiar in everyday life as the crackling sound when we remove a woollen sweater and the tiny blue sparks seen in the dark. The clinging together of clothing, paper or sheets of material or the sharp shock when we rub and separate from a dissimilar surface, such as when getting out of a car and then touching the body work.

All materials have electrical charge in the atoms that comprise the material. When two materials are in contact some of the electrical charge redistributes by moving from one material to another. This leaves an excess positive charge on one material and an equal negative charge on the other. Therefore, the term static electricity relates to this charge held by the material and consists of an excess or deficiency of electrons on the surface of materials. Its presence is normally only recognised by the occurrence of the discharging spark, unless appropriate instruments are used. If two charged materials remain close together, the charges oppose each other and to external appearances the combination is neutral.

When the surfaces of the two materials are moved apart the two opposite charges separate and the two materials become separately and oppositely charged, one positive and the other negative. If the materials can conduct electricity away, the charges will dissipate on separation and the effects of static electricity will not usually be noticeable. However, if the materials are separated faster than the material can dissipate the charge, particularly where the materials are not very conductive, the amount of static electricity builds up, eventually to a high voltage, possibly thousands of volts.

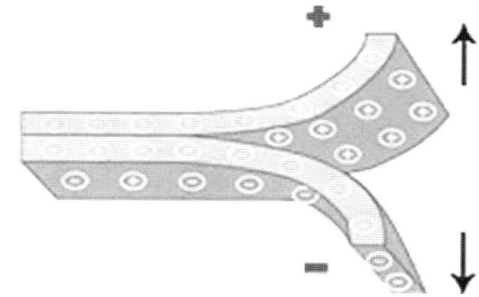

Figure C8-13: Creation of static charge. *Source: Simco UK.*

The materials can remain in that state of charge if the surroundings are sufficiently resistive to withstand the often thousands of volts between them. Dry air would usually provide sufficient resistance for this if they are far enough apart. If the potential difference (voltage) is very large a spark may jump across the gap between the charged material and a conductor.

There are two types of discharge of static electricity:

- **Spark discharge** occurs where a charged conductor is discharged, usually to earth, through another conductor, for example, from an insulated charged container to an earthed vessel, or from a charged insulated vessel through a person and then to earth. When an energetic discharge of this type occurs, the virtually instantaneous action produces a spark that may have sufficient energy to ignite gas, vapour, and

dust or vapour/dust mixtures. A spark discharge through humans to earth may be sufficient to cause a sudden short pain, but they are not usually dangerous. However, the shock may be a nuisance or cause the person to jump back from the source of the static discharge and may cause a person to fall.
- *Brush discharge* occurs where a non-conducting body becomes charged and part discharges to earth. Because only the energy from around the proximity of the discharge is dispersed immediately, this type of discharge is slower, less energetic and less visible. It will ignite gas, vapour and vapour/dust mixtures, but is not usually of sufficient energy to ignite dust.

OCCURRENCE OF STATIC

Static electricity may be generated during the following situations:
- The flow of liquids and powders through pipes, filters, tanks and other non-miscible liquids.
- The pouring of powders from insulating plastic bags.
- Spraying.
- The settling of solids through liquids or bubbles rising through liquids.
- The mixing and stirring of liquids and powders.
- The sieving or grinding of powders and dusts.
- The unwinding of rolled insulating foils.
- Human movement with insulated shoes over nylon or plastic carpets or floors; similarly between layers of clothing.
- The movement of dust or liquids through air.
- The pouring of liquids, granules or powders from insulated containers.
- Manufacture of plastic sheet or bags.
- Production of textiles.
- Printing processes.
- Discharge of chemical liquids or powders through pipes, from a road tanker to fixed storage vessels.

Static electricity build up is particularly a problem where materials that are not very conductive are in contact with each other, for example, plastics and paper, and where two surfaces are rapidly separated.

Electrostatic properties are also used in processes like photocopiers/printers, applying paint to vehicles, removal of airborne pollutants from chimney stacks or air conditioning systems. The particles that are to be applied can be given a negative charge and the surface that they are to be attracted to given a positive charge. This charge will cause the particles to be attracted to the target surface ensuring it provides an even coating.

Hazards and controls for static electricity

HAZARDS

Danger occurs, in particular, when a static spark is created in a flammable or explosive atmosphere. Given the right mix of flammable material and oxygen, a static spark with sufficient energy can start a fire or explosion.

CONTROLS

Spark discharge can be controlled through the bonding and earthing to a common potential of all conducting surfaces.

Brush discharges cannot be earthed out and can only be prevented by the avoidance of non-conductors or the exclusion of oxygen.

Reducing static build up

- Earthing of all exposed non-current carrying metalwork.
- Maintaining an atmosphere with a high relative humidity.
- Ionising the air by controlled voltage discharge.
- Wearing special conducting footwear and clothing that does not allow static build up.
- Placing earthed metal combs or similar devices near to the source of the static.
- For some flammable liquids, a special chemical additive can be obtained to allow static to conduct through the liquid and dissipate.
- The flooding of the free space above liquids and powders with an inert gas to reduce the possibility of ignition.

C8.3 - Installation, use and inspection of electrical systems

Meaning of 'duty holders' and 'construction'

MEANING OF 'DUTY HOLDERS'

The Electricity at Work Regulations (EWR) 1989 place duties upon the following groups of people, who are classed as duty holders:
- Employers and self employed persons.
- Managers of quarries.
- Employees.

Employers and self employed persons

The duty imposed is to comply with the EWR 1989 as far as they are within his/her control.

Managers of quarries

The duty here again is to comply with the EWR 1989 as far as matters are within the Manager's control. They are defined further by saying that it is only so far as the regulations apply to the quarry or part of the quarry of which they are the Manager.

Employees

The duty imposed is a duplication of Section 7(b) of the Health and Safety at Work etc. Act (HASAWA) 1974 - duty to co-operate with the employer to fulfil the employer's duties. The EWR 1989 also place a duty for the employee to comply with the EWR 1989 as far as they are within their control at all levels. These duties are designed to make everyone in an organisation take ownership for safety at all levels and for each person to comply with all aspects of the EWR 1989.

MEANING OF 'CONSTRUCTION'

EWR 1989, Regulation 4 - "Systems, work activities and protective equipment", requires:

(1) All systems shall at all times be of such construction as to prevent, so far as is reasonably practicable, danger.

The term construction in this context has a wide interpretation. It covers the physical condition and arrangement of the components of a system during its life. It includes the following stages:

- Design.
- Planning.
- Installation.
- Manufacture.
- Testing.
- Commissioning.
- Operation.
- Inspecting.
- Maintaining.
- Decommissioning.

Figure C8-14: Construction site generator.　　Source: RMS.

Figure C8-15: Construction site power supply.　　Source: RMS.

Figure C8-16: 110V generator.　　Source: RMS.

Figure C8-17: 110V extension lead.　　Source: RMS.

The Memorandum of Guidance to the EWR 1989 specifies that when assessing the suitability of the construction of electrical systems care should be taken to consider the actual application or use of the electrical equipment in the system.

In particular, the following should be considered:

- The manufacturer's assigned or other certified rating of the equipment.
- The likely load and fault conditions.
- The need for suitable electrical protective devices.
- The fault level at the point of supply and the ability of the equipment and the protective devices to handle likely fault conditions.
- Any contribution to the fault level from the connected loads such as from motors.
- The environmental conditions which will have a bearing on the mechanical strength and protection required of the equipment.
- The user's requirements of the installation.
- The manner in which commissioning, testing and subsequent maintenance or other work may need to be carried out.

STRENGTH AND CAPABILITY OF ELECTRICAL EQUIPMENT

EWR 1989, Regulation 5 - "Strength and capability of electrical equipment" requires:

"No electrical equipment shall be put into use where its strength and capability may be exceeded in such a way as may give rise to danger".

This duty requires an assessment to be made prior to connecting equipment to a system. This involves looking at the design specification and the operating limitations of the piece of equipment and considering the system it is to be used in conjunction with. In particular, attention should be paid not only to the normal operating limits of the system and equipment but also the potential consequences during fault conditions.

The 'strength and capability' refers to the ability to withstand the thermal, electro-magnetic, electro-chemical or other effects of an electrical current that the equipment will be exposed to when connected to a system.

INSULATION, PROTECTION AND PLACING OF CONDUCTORS

Insulation and protection

All solids contain free electrons. Substances that contain many free electrons are good conductors of electricity. Those solids that do not have many free electrons are bad conductors and are called insulators. Examples of insulators are rubber, plastic, glass. The EWR 1989 specify in Regulation 7:

"All conductors in a system which may give rise to danger shall be suitably covered with insulating material and as necessary protected to prevent, so far as is reasonably practicable, danger".

Insulation specifications can be found for systems up to 1,000V AC in the IET Wiring Regulations (17th Edition).

The level of insulation required will depend upon the conditions of use, environmental factors and also the voltage present. This could either be between the conductor and any other conductor near by or between the conductor and earth.

Regulation 7 also places a duty to assess whether or not, once insulation has been applied to a conductor, any mechanical protection is also required to prevent danger. An example of this is an armoured cable sheath.

Placing of conductors

Due to the danger presented by a live conductor the process of planning where they should be positioned is an important part of the design and planning stages of a system. Wherever possible conductors should be placed out of reach.

Consideration should be given to the work that people do when placing conductors and not just normal operating procedures, but also emergency or non-routine operations. An example of this would be putting electrical power supplies to a factory overhead, but failing to consider a window cleaner moving a ladder, the movement of large vehicles and the possibility of fork lift trucks operating in the area.

REDUCING THE RISK OF SHOCK

Those designing, installing, maintaining or using electrical systems have the following means available to prevent persons or animals from contacting dangerous parts of electrical systems:

- Protection from direct contact.
- Protection from indirect contact.
- Protection from external influences.
- Reduced voltage and SELV.

Protection from direct contact

Note - direct contact is contact with a charged or energised conductor that is intended to be so charged or energised.

- Insulation, barriers, enclosures, obstacles, out-of-reach.
- Residual/differential current relay - residual current circuit breaker (Rccb) or residual current device (Rcd).
- Separated extra low voltage, SELV.

Protection from indirect contact

Note - indirect contact is contact with a conducting part that is normally at a safe potential, but has become dangerously live through a fault condition.

- Class I, earthed equipment.
- Earthed equipotential bonding and automatic disconnection (EEBAD) of the supply.
- Class II, double insulated equipment.
- Non conducting location.
- Earth free local equipotential bonding.
- Electrical separation.

Protection from external influences

- Adverse conditions.
- Index of Protection (IP codes) - finger and tool proof, dust proof, rain proof, watertight etc.
- Flora and fauna, vibration, impact, seismic, wind etc.
- Flameproof, intrinsically safe etc.

Reduced voltage and SELV

Pneumatic tools and reduced voltage tools, for example 110 volt centre-tapped, are readily available and should be considered.

Where there is a high risk of electric shock, as with hand lamps, soldering irons, and portable tools in adverse conditions, the use of separated extra low voltage (maximum 50 volts AC/125 volts DC ripple free) is recommended.

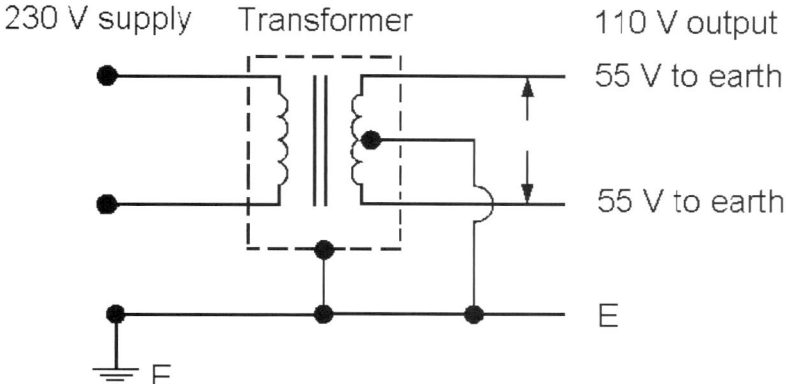

Figure C8-18: UK standard reduced voltage system.   Source: G Self.

EXCESS CURRENT PROTECTION

Excess current is also called over current. There are two types of over current. These are overload and fault current.

Overload occurs in a normally healthy electrical system when equipment has been mechanically overloaded beyond its safe operating load or an excessive number of electrical appliances have been added to the system creating excessive demands. Two things normally happen. Due to the extra current demanded the temperature of the conductors rapidly rises. If left undetected, this will lead to a breakdown in insulation resistance and eventually a fire.

Fault current occurs when an excess of current flows between conductors or from one or more conductors to earth due to a fault condition. The consequences may generate sufficient heat to cause fire and in this case the overload protection will normally take effect.

Under certain conditions only a small fault current will be generated, but this may be sufficient to apply a live potential to the exposed casing or metalwork.

Excess current protection devices rely on the detection of the excess current and disconnection within designed boundaries. The current level for disconnection will always be greater than the normal operating current.

Fuses

These work on the thermal effect produced by the current flow and are designed to melt at predetermined temperatures that are proportional to a level of current flow. There are two types of fuse commonly used - cartridge fuses and high breaking capacity fuses (HBC).

Cartridge fuse

The body of the fuse can be either ceramic or glass with metal end caps, to which the fuse element is connected. The fuse sometimes is filled with silica sand.

Advantage
- Small physical size.
- No mechanical moving parts.
- Accurate current rating.
- Little deterioration over time.

Disadvantage
- More expensive to replace over time.
- Can be replaced with the wrong rated fuse.
- Not suitable for high fault current.
- Can be shorted out.

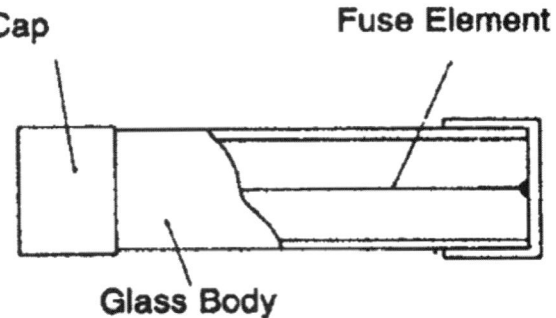

Figure C8-19: Cartridge fuse.   Source: Ambiguous.   Figure C8-20: HBC fuse.   Source: Ambiguous.

HBC fuse

The barrel of the fuse is made from high grade ceramic in order to withstand the mechanical forces of heavy current interruption. The plated end caps give good levels of electrical contact. The fuse element is machined from silver and gives precise characteristics. Some HBC fuses are fitted with indicator bands that show when they have blown.

Advantage
- Discriminates between overload currents of short time duration and high fault currents.
- Simple to observe when blown.
- Consistent in operation.
- Reliable.

Disadvantage
- Very expensive.

Circuit breakers

Circuit breakers work on either a thermal or magnetic field principle and have a wide range of applications and designs. They can be set at manufacture to detect a specific level of current flow that causes them to trip. They can be used in the electrical system to substitute for fuses.

Advantage
- Tripping characteristic is set during manufacture and cannot be altered.
- Will trip for a sustained overload, but not for transient overloads.
- Faulty circuit is easy identified.
- Supply quickly restored.
- Tamper proof.
- Multiple units available.

Disadvantage
- Have mechanically moving parts.
- Expensive.
- Need for regular testing to ensure satisfactory operation.
- Characteristics affected by ambient temperature.

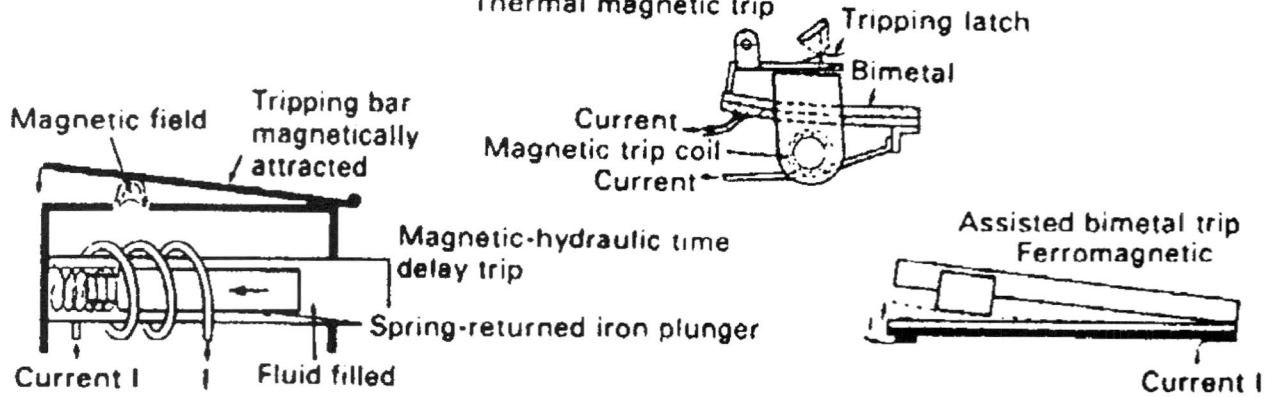

Figure C8-21: Circuit breaker.   Source: Ambiguous.

CUTTING OFF SUPPLY AND ISOLATION

Regulation 12 of the EWR 1989 places a duty to ensure that to prevent danger, where necessary, there must be a suitable means for cutting off the supply of electrical energy to a piece of equipment.

This is to enable the equipment to be switched off and may be done by direct operation of a switch or remote operation via circuit breakers.

A switch is a mechanism that is able to mechanically disconnect the electrical supply from a part of an installation or an appliance. There are two types of switch.

Functional switch - this is the device that the operator of a piece of equipment uses to turn the equipment on or off, for example a light switch.

Emergency switch - this is used on some equipment where a hazardous condition may occur, for example an emergency stop on a lathe.

Note: a piece of equipment can be switched off but still be *live*.

Figure C8-22: Power supply isolation.   Source: RMS.

Regulation 12 also deals with the term 'isolation'.

Isolation means 'the disconnection and separation of the electrical equipment from every source of energy in such a way that this disconnection and separation is secure'.

Figure C8-23: Isolation.   Source: Regulation 12 - Electricity at Work Regulations (EWR) 1989.

The requirement for isolation is to ensure that the supply of electrical energy remains switched off and that inadvertent reconnection is prevented. Isolation is different to switching off and this must be remembered, although there are circumstances when both will occur by the same action.

WORKING SPACE, ACCESS AND LIGHTING

Regulation 15 of the EWR 1989 states:

"For the purposes of enabling injury to be prevented, adequate working space, adequate means of access, and adequate lighting shall be provided at all electrical equipment on which or near which work is being done in circumstances which may give rise to danger".

This duty does not only apply when live conductors are exposed, but also when any work is conducted that may give rise to danger.

Space and access

The need for adequate working space and access is to:

- Allow people to move away from the conductors without hazard.
- Allow people to pass one another with ease and without hazard.

The Regulations do not specifically mention dimensions, but earlier legislation in the form of the Electricity (Factories Act) Special Regulations 1908 and 1944, which were revoked by the Electricity at Work Regulations1989, did and these dimensions are still used as a guideline for voltages up to 3 kV.

The dimensions are detailed in Appendix 3 of the Memorandum of Guidance on the Electricity at Work Regulations (EWR) 1989.

"(a) Those constructed for low pressure and medium pressure switchboards (collection of switches) shall have a clear height of not less than 7 ft and a clear width measured from bare conductor of not less than 3 ft.

(b) Those constructed for high pressure (650 - 3000volts) and extra high pressure switchboards (>3000volts), other than operating desks or panels working solely at low pressure (not exceeding 250volts), shall have a clear height of not less than 8 ft and a clear width measured from bare conductor of not less than 3 ft 6 in.

(c) Bare conductors shall not be exposed on both sides of the switchboard passageway unless either (i) the clear width of the passage is in the case of low pressure and medium pressure (260 - 650 volts) not less than 4 ft 6 in and in the case of high pressure and extra high pressure not less than 8 ft in each case measured between bare conductors, or (ii) the conductors on one side are so guarded that they cannot be accidentally touched".

Lighting

It may be necessary to provide artificial lighting to enable work to be conducted with or on electrical systems without danger. Where possible, this should be properly designed and permanent. Where this is not possible, sufficient temporary lighting to prevent danger should be provided. This may mean provision of lighting from a generator or from a hand held lamp.

ELEMENT C8 - ELECTRICAL SAFETY AND EWR 1989

Control measures

SELECTION AND SUITABILITY OF EQUIPMENT

The British Standard BS 7671:2008, "Requirements for Electrical Installations"/Institution of Engineering and Technology IET 17th edition requirements specifies the need for good workmanship and that proper materials shall be used. Construction, installation, inspection, testing and maintenance shall be such as to prevent danger. Equipment must be suitable for the power demanded and the conditions in which it is installed. Additions and alterations to installations should comply with these regulations.

The Electrical Equipment (Safety) Regulations (EESR) 1994, that relate to the supply of equipment, refer to equipment using between 50 and 1000 volts AC and 75 and 1500 volts DC and require it to be safe. Construction, including flexible cables and cords, must be to EU accepted good engineering practice standards. The EWR 1989 are deemed satisfied if the equipment bears a recognised standard mark, certificate or other acceptable authorisation. Supply of unsafe equipment or components is prohibited.

PROTECTIVE SYSTEMS

Fuses

This is a device designed to automatically cut off the power supply to a circuit, within a given time, when the current flow in that circuit exceeds a given value. In effect, it is a weak link in the circuit that melts when heat is created by too high a current passing through the thin wire in the fuse case. When this happens the circuit is broken and no more current flows. They tend to have a rating in the order of amperes rather than milliamperes, which means they have *limited usefulness in protecting people from electric shock*. They may also act slowly if the current is just above the fuse rating. Using the wrong fuse causes many electrical problems.

The following formula should be used to calculate the correct rating for a fuse:

$$\text{Current (Amperes)} = \frac{\text{Power (Watts)}}{\text{Voltage (Volts)}}$$

For example, the correct fuse current rating for a 2-kilowatt kettle on a 230-volt supply would be:

$$\text{Fuse Current Rating (Amperes)} = \frac{2,000}{230} = 8.7 \text{ A}$$

Fuses are available for appliances as 2, 5, 7, 10 and 13 Ampere ratings. The nearest fuse just above this current level is 10 A.

Typical examples of power ratings are:

- Computer processor   350 Watts.
- Electric kettle   1850 - 2200 Watts.
- Dishwasher   1380 Watts.
- Refrigerator   90 Watts.

In summary a fuse is:

- A weak link in the circuit that melts slowly when heat is created by a fault condition. However, usually too slowly to protect people.
- Easy to replace with wrong rating.
- Sometimes needs tools to replace.
- Easy to override.

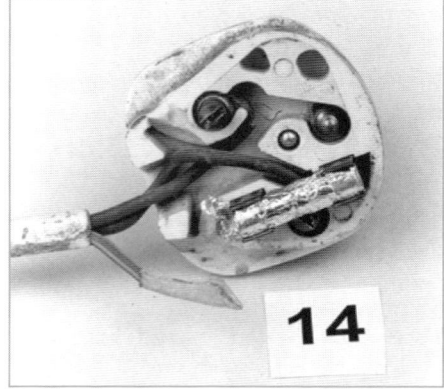

Figure C8-24: Plug-foil fuse, no earth. *Source: RMS.*

Figure C8-25: Earthing. *Source: RMS.*

Reduced voltage systems

One of the best ways to reduce the risk from electricity is to reduce the voltage. This is achieved by the use of a transformer (step down), which will reduce the voltage. A common reduction of voltage from 230V is to 110V.

ELECTRICAL SAFETY AND EWR 1989 - ELEMENT C8

Normally, transformers that are used to reduce voltage are described as "centre tap to earth". In practice, this means that any voltage involved in an electrical shock will be 55V.

Using the earlier example of Ohms Law, if the voltage is 230V then:

$$I = \frac{V}{R} = \frac{230 \text{ Volts}}{\approx 2000 + 4000 \text{ Ohms}} = 0.04 \text{ Amperes or } 40 \text{ mA}$$

However, if a centre tap to earth transformer is used, then:

$$I = \frac{V}{R} = \frac{55 \text{ Volts}}{\approx 2000 + 4000 \text{ Ohms}} = 0.009 \text{ Amperes or } 9 \text{ mA}$$

The examples above show how reducing the voltage **reduces the possible effects of electric shock** on the body by reducing the current that flows through it.

An alternative to reduction in voltage by means of a transformer is to provide battery powered equipment that will commonly run on 12V-24V. The common method is to use a rechargeable battery to power the equipment, which eliminates the need for a cable to feed power to the equipment and gives a greater flexibility of use for the user, for example, drills.

Figure C8-26: 110V centre tapped earth transformer. *Source: RMS.*

Figure C8-27: Battery powered drill - 12V. *Source: RMS.*

Figure C8-28: 110V powered drill. *Source: RMS.*

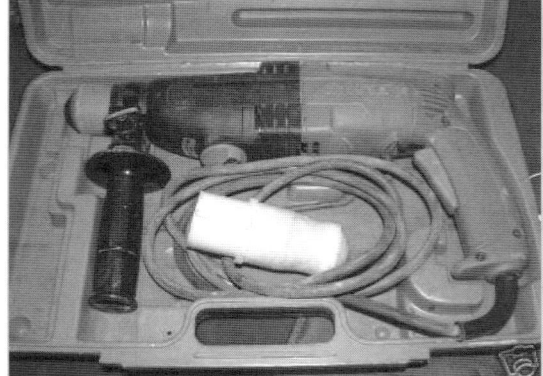

Figure C8-29: 110V powered drill. *Source: RMS.*

Isolation

Regulation 12 of the EWR 1989 places a duty to ensure that to prevent danger, where necessary, there must be a suitable means for switching off the electrical supply to a piece of equipment. Regulation 12 also deals with the term 'isolation'. This is defined as:

> *"The disconnection and separation of the electrical equipment from every source of energy in such a way that this disconnection and separation is secure".*

Figure C8-30: Isolation. *Source: Regulation 12 - Electricity at Work Regulations (EWR) 1989.*

Isolation device

An isolation device is a device that will disconnect all supplies of electrical energy to an installation or piece of equipment. The internal design of the isolator must be such that contact separation from the electrical supply conductors is ensured.

Security in the isolated position is necessary and this can be in the form of a lock off method or supervision by the user. The location of the isolator should be easily accessible and the time and effort required to use the isolator should be reasonable, taking into account the circumstances in which the isolator may be used.

© RMS

ELEMENT C8 - ELECTRICAL SAFETY AND EWR 1989

When carrying out isolation the competent person should be *sure* that the:

- Isolator being used is suitable for the purpose of isolation, rather than switching off.
- Isolator being used to turn off the power is working correctly and reliably.
- Isolator being used is the only way that the circuit can be fed with electrical energy.
- Isolator being used is locked in the off position and cannot easily be turned on again.
- Equipment and method being used to check for voltage works and is reliable.
- Isolation has been successful by confirming the circuit is no longer 'live'.

Some electrical systems and equipment must be earthed before it is safe to work near them.

Residual current devices (RCDs)

RCDs are an electro-mechanical switching device used to automatically isolate the supply when there is a difference between the current flowing into a device and the current flowing from the device. Such a difference might result from a fault causing current leakage, i.e. the current in the neutral (return) conductor is less than that in the phase conductor. Current leakage has possible fire risks or the risk of electric shock when a person touches a system as they may provide a path to earth for the current.

A typical circuit diagram for a RCD is shown in *figure ref C8-31*.

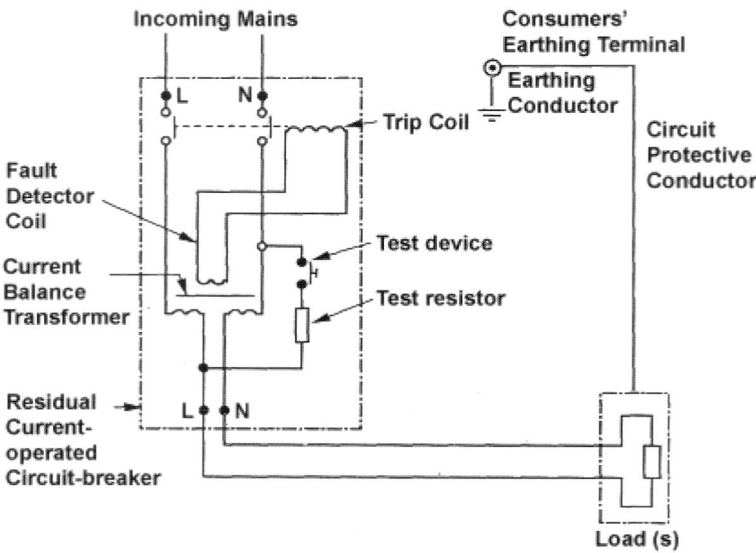

Figure C8-31: A typical circuit diagram for a RCD.   Source: G Self.

RCDs can be designed to operate at low currents and with fast response times. A typical operating current being 30 mA, with tripping occurring within about 15-40 ms, depending upon the magnitude of the current flow. Whilst an RCD will not prevent electric shock, because of its quick acting nature, any current flow through the body should be of sufficiently short duration to *reduce the effect of electric shock and prevent that shock from being fatal*.

A residual current device is:

- Rapid and sensitive.
- Difficult to defeat.
- Easy and safe to test and reset.

Figure C8-32: Residual current device.   Source: RMS.

Figure C8-33: Plug-in residual current device.   Source: RMS.

Double insulation

Double insulated equipment has two layers of insulating material between the live parts of the electrical equipment and the user. Since the casing material of this type of electrical equipment is an insulator and does not conduct electricity, it does not normally have an earth wire. Each layer of insulation must be sufficient in its own right to give adequate protection against shock.

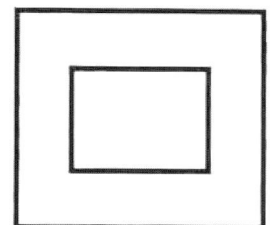

Figure C8-34: Double insulation symbol. *Source: HSG 107.*

If a fault occurs with the live parts and a conductor touches the insulating material surrounding it no current can pass to the user, therefore **no shock occurs**.

Earth free zones

This is a protective measure that is used in areas where research and live testing is carried out. It may only be used in an area with competent persons, effective supervision and where it has been designed by suitably qualified engineers. If the area (zone) is insulated from earth (earth free), then even if live metal is touched there is no path for the electricity to flow to earth.

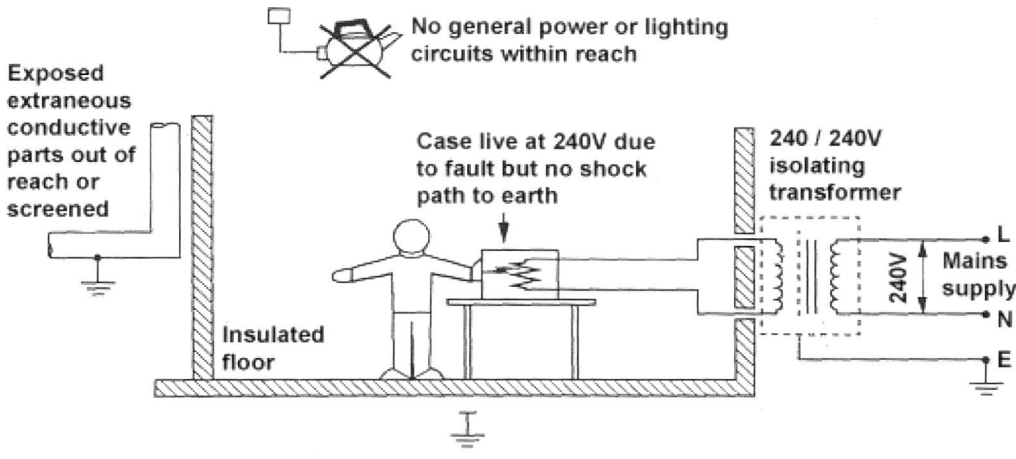

Figure C8-35: General arrangement for an earth free work environment. *Source: G Self.*

INSPECTION AND MAINTENANCE STRATEGY

The legal duty for inspection and maintenance

The requirements relating to the use and maintenance of electrical equipment are contained in EWR 1989. These Regulations apply to all work activities involving electrical equipment. They place duties on employers, the self-employed and employees (the duty-holders), that are intended to control risks arising from the use of electricity. The Regulations are goal-setting, describing safety objectives to be achieved, without prescribing the measures to be taken. This allows the duty-holder to select precautions appropriate to the risk rather than having precautions imposed that may not be relevant to a particular work activity.

The EWR 1989, Regulation 4(2) requires that:

"All systems be maintained, so far as is reasonably practicable, to prevent danger".

This requirement covers all items of electrical equipment including fixed, portable and transportable equipment. The Memorandum of Guidance on the EWR 1989 defines a system. In simple terms, it will include any equipment that is, or may be, connected to a common source of electrical energy and includes the source and the equipment. Thus, the distribution system in a workplace and the equipment connected to it are covered. It must be recognised that there is little benefit in having perfect portable electrical equipment if it is plugged into a defective socket that may be without proper insulation, with a switch that does not work properly, with the polarity reversed or with a high resistance earth connection.

Danger is defined as the risk of injury from electric shock, electric burn, and fire of electrical origin, electric arcing or explosion initiated or caused by electricity. In addition to the EWR 1989, the *general duties covering the use and maintenance of work equipment* are contained in:

- **Section 2, HASAWA 1974:** *"... the provision and maintenance of plant ... so far as is reasonably practicable ... safe and without risks to health".*
- **MHSWR 1999**, which requires an employer to make: *"... a suitable and sufficient assessment of the risks to health and safety of employees ... for the purposes of identifying the measures he needs to take to comply with the requirements ... imposed upon him ... under other relevant law".* Such a risk assessment should include risks arising from the use of electrical equipment.

- **PUWER 1998**, which requires the employer (person in control) to select suitable work equipment (Regulation 5) and to: *"... ensure that work equipment is maintained in an efficient state, in efficient working order and in good repair".*

Guidance from the Health and Safety Executive (HSE) indicates that maintenance is a general term that in practice can include visual inspection, repair, testing and replacement. Maintenance will determine whether equipment is fully serviceable or needing repair. It further suggests that cost effective maintenance can be achieved by a combination of:

- Checks by the user.
- Visual inspections by a person appointed to do this.
- Combined inspection and tests by a competent person or by a contractor.

User checks

The user of electrical equipment should be encouraged, after basic training, to look critically at the equipment and the source of power. If any defects are found, the equipment should be marked and not used again until it is examined by a competent person. There must be a procedure to enable the user to bring faults to the attention of a supervisor and/or a competent person who might rectify the fault. Checks by the user are the first line of defence, but should never be the only line taken. Such checks should be aimed at identifying the following:

- ✓ Damaged cable sheaths.
- ✓ Damaged plugs. Cracked casing or bent pins.
- ✓ Taped or other inadequate cable joints.
- ✓ Outer cable insulation not secured into plugs or equipment.
- ✓ Faulty or ineffective switches.
- ✓ Burn marks or discolouration.
- ✓ Damaged casing.
- ✓ Loose parts or screws.
- ✓ Wet or contaminated equipment.
- ✓ Loose or damaged sockets or switches.

Formal visual inspections

The maintenance strategy should always include formal visual inspection of all portable electrical equipment. User checks and a programme of formal visual inspections are found to pick up some 95% of faults. The frequency depends on the type of equipment and where it is used. The inspection can be done by a sensible member of staff, who has been shown what to look for and has basic electrical knowledge and common sense. They should know enough to avoid danger to themselves or others.

Visual inspections are likely to need to look for the same types of defects as user checks, but should also include the following:

Opening plugs of portable equipment to check for:

- ✓ Use of correctly rated fuse.
- ✓ Effective cord grip.
- ✓ Secure and correct cable terminations.

Inspection of fixed installations for:

- ✓ Damaged or loose conduit, trunking or cabling.
- ✓ Missing broken or inadequately secured covers.
- ✓ Loose or faulty joints.
- ✓ Loose earth connections.
- ✓ Moisture, corrosion or contamination.
- ✓ Burn marks or discolouration.
- ✓ Open or inadequately secured panel doors.
- ✓ Ease of access to switches and isolators.
- ✓ Presence of temporary wiring.

Combined inspection and tests

Periodic testing. Faults such as loss of earth or broken wires inside an installation or cable cannot be found by visual inspection, so some equipment needs to have a combined inspection and test. This is particularly important for all earthed equipment and leads/plugs connected to hand held or hand operated equipment.

Testing procedures. The installation should be tested regularly in accordance with BS 7671/IET requirements. The word 'regularly' is not specified in terms of time intervals other than in certain special cases and a management judgment must again be made to specify an appropriate timetable.

Getting a maintenance programme started

In order to identify what systems will need maintenance, they should be listed. This same listing can be used as a checklist, recording that the appropriate checks have been done. It may also include details of the type of equipment, as well as the checks and tests to be carried out.

There is a growing trend, especially in offices, for employees to bring to work their own electrically powered equipment including calculators, radios, kettles and coffee makers. The number of electrical accidents has grown accordingly and fires from calculator chargers left on overnight are growing in number. All such equipment should be recorded and inspected by a competent person before use and at regular intervals, as if it were company property.

Records of maintenance and tests

Although there is no requirement under the EWR 1989 to keep maintenance logs for portable and transportable electrical equipment, the 'Memorandum of Guidance on the EWR 1989', does refer to the benefits of recording maintenance, including test results. A suitable log is useful as a management tool for monitoring and reviewing the effectiveness of the maintenance scheme and also to demonstrate that a scheme exists. It can also be used as an inventory of equipment and a check on the use of unauthorised equipment (for example, domestic kettles or electric heaters brought to work by employees).

Frequency of inspection and testing

| Question: | "I have been told that I have to have my desk lamp tested every six months. Is this correct?" |
| Answer: | "No. The law requires it to be maintained. It does not require any elaborate or rigorous system of frequent electrical testing". |

Figure C8-36: Quotation regarding the frequency of inspection and testing. *Source: HSE, HSG107.*

Deciding on the frequency of inspection and testing is a matter of judgement by the duty-holder, and should be based on an assessment of risk. This can be undertaken as part of the assessment of risks under the Management of Health and Safety Regulations (MHSWR) 1999.

Factors to be considered when assessing the risk include:

- ✓ Type of equipment.
- ✓ If it is hand held.
- ✓ Manufacturer's recommendations.
- ✓ Its initial integrity and soundness.
- ✓ Age.
- ✓ Working environment.
- ✓ Likelihood of mechanical damage.
- ✓ Frequency of use.
- ✓ Duration of use.
- ✓ Foreseeable use.
- ✓ The type of user.
- ✓ Modifications or repairs.
- ✓ Past experience.

The guidance sets out a table that shows the suggested frequency of formal visual inspections and electrical tests for portable and transportable electrical equipment. The duty-holder, with appropriate advice where necessary, should assess the conditions affecting the equipment that may lead to potential damage and/or deterioration and should determine an appropriate maintenance regime.

Type of business	User checks	Formal visual inspection	Combined inspection and test
Construction	110 V - Weekly 230 V mains - Daily/every shift	110 V - Monthly 230 V mains - Weekly	110 V - Before first use on site then 3-monthly 230 V mains - Before first use on site then monthly
Light industrial	Yes	Before initial use then 6 monthly	6 - 12 months
Heavy industrial/high risk of equipment damage	Daily	Weekly	6 - 12 months
Office information technology, for example desktop computers, photocopiers, fax machines	No	1 - 2 years	None if double-insulated, otherwise up to 5 years
Double-insulated equipment not hand-held, for example fans, table lamps	No	2 - 3 years	No

Figure C8-37: Suggested intervals of inspection and test. *Source: HSG107 - Maintaining portable and transportable electrical equipment.*

Competent persons

EWR 1989, Part II General, Regulation 16 - *"Persons to be competent to prevent danger and injury"* sets out a duty that establishes what a competent person must be:

"No person shall be engaged in any work activity where technical knowledge or experience is necessary to prevent danger or, where appropriate, injury, unless he possesses such knowledge or experience, or is under such degree of supervision as may be appropriate having regard to the nature of the work".

ELEMENT C8 - ELECTRICAL SAFETY AND EWR 1989

Maintaining portable and transportable electrical equipment (HSG107)

A quarter of all reportable electrical accidents at work involve portable equipment and the vast majority cause electrical shock. The Health and Safety Executive guidance HSG107 "Maintaining portable and transportable electrical equipment" provides guidance on inspection and maintenance. In addition to general advice covering equipment that may be connected to a fixed mains or locally generated supply, the guidance also advises on what the legal requirements for maintenance can mean in practice.

HSG107 "Maintaining portable and transportable electrical equipment" covers a whole spectrum of everyday equipment including drills, extension leads, hand lamps, portable grinders, pressure water cleaners, floor cleaners, kettles and similar equipment. The guide advocates 3 types of inspection and test:

- User check - carried out by the user prior to use.
- Formal visual check - carried out by a competent person.
- Combined inspection and testing - carried out by a competent person.

Routine inspection and appropriate testing, where necessary, are normally part of any overall strategy for ensuring that work equipment is maintained in a safe condition.

Figure C8-38: PAT labels. Source: RMS.

Relationship between BS 7671:2008, IET Wiring Regs 17th Edn and the Electricity at Work Regs 1989

THE SIGNIFICANCE OF THE INSTITUTION OF ENGINEERING AND TECHNOLOGY (IET)

The Institution of Engineering and Technology (IET) has more than 150,000 members worldwide in 127 countries and was formed in March 2006 by a merger of the Institution of Electrical Engineers (IEE) and the Institution of Incorporated Engineers (IIE). It is a world leading professional organisation sharing and advancing knowledge to promote science, engineering and technology across the world.

The IET represents engineers, including electrical engineers, in matters that affect them. The IET prepares regulations to direct the conformity of work done by its electrical engineer members relating to the safety of electrical installations for buildings, called the IET Wiring Regulations.

RELATIONSHIP OF IET REGULATIONS TO THE BRITISH STANDARDS INSTITUTE

The IET has co-operated with the British Standards Institute to establish a code of working that both satisfies the IET's need for regulation of members and the national need to establish formal standards. This collaboration has resulted in the codification of the IET Wiring Regulations in to the UK standard BS 7671:2008 Requirements for Electrical Installations.

RELATIONSHIP OF IET REGULATIONS AND BS7671:2008 TO THE ELECTRICITY AT WORK REGULATIONS 1989

Compliance with IET Wiring Regulations and BS 7671 is not a statutory requirement, but the following quotation emphasises how they may be treated in situations of enforcement of the Electricity at Work Regulations (EWR) 1989.

BS 7671 is a code of practice which is widely recognised and accepted in the UK and compliance with it is likely to achieve compliance with relevant aspects of the 1989 Regulations.

> There are however many types of system, equipment and hazard to which BS 7671 is not applicable; for example, certain installations at mines and quarries, equipment on vehicles, systems for public electricity supply and explosion protection. Furthermore, BS 7671 applies only to installations operating at up to 1,000 volts ac or 1500 volts dc.

Figure C8-39: BS7671 and EWR 1989. Source: Electricity at Work Regulations (EWR) 1989, Introduction.

BS 7671:2008, 'REQUIREMENTS FOR ELECTRICAL INSTALLATIONS'

BS 7671:2008 Requirements for Electrical Installations, IET Wiring Regulations 17th Edition, was issued on 1 January 2008 and came into effect on 1 July 2008. Applicable installations designed after the 30th June 2008 should comply with BS 7671:2008.

The revised standard applies to the design, erection and verification of electrical installations, also additions and alternations to existing installations. BS 7671: 2008 includes changes necessary to maintain technical alignment with CENELEC, the European Committee for Electrotechnical Standardisation and The International Electrotechnical Commission (IEC) harmonisation documents.

The main changes from the 16th edition are:
- RCDs must be installed on socket outlets and tested annually.
- Consideration must be given to emergency escape and warning systems.
- Facilities provided to ensure life support systems must have back-up power.
- Equipment installed must not emit dangerous levels of magnetic fields.
- The installation's documentation must be up to date and inspection.
- Testing must be carried out periodically by a competent person.

In summary, these changes mean:
- 30 milliamp RCD protection is required on circuits as follows:
  - All sockets outlets for general use by ordinary persons in offices, workshops, warehouses, labs etc. and all outdoor socket outlets.
  - Cables concealed in walls or partitions at a depth less than 50 mm or where partition is of metallic construction.
  - All circuits, including lighting in a bathroom. Socket outlets can be installed 3 m horizontally from zone 1 in a bathroom.
- Circuit breakers and fuse maximum earth loop impedance values reduced by 4%.
- Periodic inspection and testing of every electrical installation is positively recommended and must be carried out by a competent person with emphasis on disconnection times and distribution board schedules.
- Safety of services (emergency lighting, fire alarms) and continuity of service (life support service) are a specific requirement of installations.
- Installation work must be carried out or supervised by competent person.
- New requirements for protection from voltage disturbances and electromagnetic emissions from equipment now required.
- Disconnection times for construction and demolition sites and agricultural and horticultural sites reduced to 0.2 seconds and the 25V touch voltage requirement has been removed.
- Minimum insulation resistance increased to 1 Megaohm for systems up to 500V.
- Direct contact and indirect contact terminologies are now termed as Basic Protection and Fault Protection respectively.

Content of BS 7671:2008 - the IET Wiring Regulations 17th Edition:

Part 1   Scope, objective and fundamental principles.

Part 2   Definitions.

Part 3   Assessment and general characteristics.

Part 4   Protection for safety.

Part 5   Selection and erection of equipment.

Part 6   Inspection and testing.

Part 7   Special installations.

Importance of schemes of maintenance, schedules, plans and records

Electrical systems must be used, maintained and repaired in a way that prevents danger, both to the user and to those carrying out repairs and maintenance.

> As may be necessary to prevent **danger**, **all systems** shall be maintained so as to prevent, so far as is reasonably practicable, such **danger**.

Figure C8-40: Maintenance of system.   Source: Regulation 4(2) - Electricity at Work Regulations (EWR) 1989.

The obligation to maintain arises only if danger would result from failing to maintain the system. The frequency and depth of maintenance should be sufficient to prevent danger. When ensuring safe maintenance it is important to establish schemes and schedules that relate to the particular system.

It is important that they relate to the specific system, because the use of the system, its location and age may influence the schemes or schedules of maintenance required. The schemes and schedules must be established in such a way that they ensure the condition required is maintained. This may include regimes of planned preventative and condition monitoring maintenance.

It is important that plans of the system are maintained up to date and that changes are noted to ensure danger does not arise from lack of knowledge of the system or from amendments that lead to parts of the system remaining live when they are thought to be dead.

Records of maintenance and repair, including test results, must be kept up to date to enable the competent persons conducting maintenance to determine factors that can validate the established schemes and schedules, or challenge them if there are more faults than would be expected. Records should be kept throughout the working life of the system.

ELEMENT C8 - ELECTRICAL SAFETY AND EWR 1989

Safe systems of work on installations made dead

PRECAUTIONS FOR WORK ON EQUIPMENT MADE DEAD

Regulation 13 of EWR 1989 - "Precautions for work on equipment made dead", deals with working with the conductors dead. The main principle is that once the system is dead, then it must be proven to be dead at the point of work, and steps must be taken to prevent the system in question becoming live or charged until it is safe to do so.

> *Adequate precautions shall be taken to prevent electrical equipment, which has been made dead in order to prevent danger while work is carried out on or near that equipment, from becoming electrically charged during that work if danger may thereby arise.*

Figure C8-41: Work on electrical equipment made dead.   Source: Regulation 13 - Electricity at Work Regulations (EWR) 1989.

Once the isolator has been isolated there is a system called 'lock off' that can be employed to prevent it being made live again.

This involves the padlocking of the isolator in the 'off' position by the worker at risk.

The padlock has a unique key that the worker keeps at all times that they are at risk. This prevents any unauthorised person inadvertently turning the electrical supplies back on.

The worker will also post warning signs to show other workers that the electrical system is being worked on, that the isolations have been carried out and danger could be present if they are turned back on.

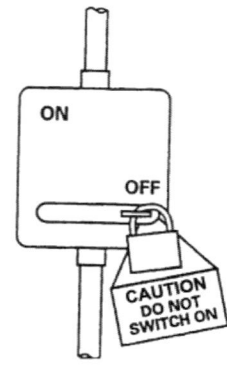

Figure C8-42: Lock off. *Source: RMS.*

Safe systems of work and criteria of acceptability for live working

The duty to establish a safe system of work for live working and the criteria that should be taken into account when considering live working is set out in Regulation 14, of EWR 1989, relating to work on or near live conductors.

CRITERIA OF ACCEPTABILITY FOR LIVE WORKING

> *No person shall be engaged in any work activity on or so near any live conductor (other than one suitably covered with insulating material so as to prevent danger) that danger may arise unless:*
>
> a) *It is unreasonable in all the circumstances for it to be dead.*
>
> b) *It is reasonable in all the circumstances for him to be at work on or near it while it is live.*
>
> c) *Suitable precautions (including where necessary the provision of suitable protective equipment) are taken to prevent injury.*

Figure C8-43: Work on or near live conductors.   Source: Regulation 14 - Electricity at Work Regulations (EWR) 1989.

This duty means that if danger could be present, wherever possible the work should be carried out with the electrical system dead. However it also appreciates that there are times when there is work that must be done with the conductors live, for example, taking voltage readings.

The guidance to the regulations recommends that equipment should be designed with the intent of manufacturing it so that work with the conductors live will not be necessary.

Factors that should be considered in deciding whether to work with the conductors live include:

- When it is not practicable to carry out work with the conductors dead.
- The creation of other hazards, by making the conductors dead such as to other users of the system, or for continuously operating process plants etc.
- The need to comply with other statutory requirements.
- The level of risk involved in working work with the conductors live and the effectiveness of the precautions available set against economic need to perform that work.

SAFE SYSTEMS OF WORK

Safe systems of work should be employed when carrying out work with the conductors live. The safe system of work should take into account all eventualities, and should be documented to ensure adequate management of the task involved.

Suitable precautions that are required to be taken include:

- Only allowing authorised competent personnel to work on or near live conductors.
- Provision of adequate information on the task to be performed.
- The selection and use of suitable test equipment and tools to be used.

ELECTRICAL SAFETY AND EWR 1989 - ELEMENT C8

- Competent supervision of the work either direct or indirect.
- Maintenance of effective controls in any area where there is danger from live conductors.
- Segregation of the workers carrying out the work with the conductors live and any other persons, vehicles or plant.
- Ensuring adequate lighting and access is given.
- Suitably qualified first aid trained personnel available during the work.

Use of permits to work

These are an essential form of documentation and form part of the safe system of work employed to manage the risk of working with the conductors dead.

The permit is really a form of declaration, by an authorised person in charge of the work, for the purpose of making known to other persons exactly what work is being carried out, where and when, and what safety precautions have been taken. It is the duty of the authorised person issuing the permit-to-work to ensure that the safety precautions have been taken, that they are adequate to prevent danger, and that the recipient is fully conversant with the task and the precautions to be taken.

Meaning of 'competent' person

"No person shall be engaged in any work activity where technical knowledge or experience is necessary to prevent danger or, where appropriate, injury, unless he possesses such knowledge or experience, or is under such degree of supervision as may be appropriate having regard to the nature of the work".

Figure C8-44: Competent person.   Source: Regulation 16 - Electricity at Work Regulations (EWR) 1989.

The guidance to the Regulations informs us that the object of this regulation is to:

"Ensure that persons are not placed at risk due to a lack of skills on the part of themselves or others in dealing with electrical equipment".

In order to meet the requirements of this regulation a competent person may need:

- *Adequate knowledge of electricity.*
- *Adequate experience of electrical work.*
- *Adequate understanding of the system to be worked on and practical experience of that class of system.*
- *Understanding of the hazards which may arise during the work and the precautions which need to be taken.*
- *Ability to recognise at all times whether it is safe for work to continue.*

Figure C8-45: Requirements for a competent person. Source: Memorandum of guidance on the Electricity at Work Regulations (EWR) 1989 - HSR25.

Advice and queries regarding qualifications and training can be directed to the IET - Institution of Engineering and Technology.

EMERGENCY RESUSCITATION AND FIRST AID

The Memorandum of Guidance to the EWR 1989, Regulation 14, states that placards giving details of emergency resuscitation procedures in the event of electric shock should be posted at locations where people may be at greater risk of electric shock than most. Such places might include electrical test areas. To comply with the Health and Safety (First Aid) Regulations and be effective, employers should make adequate first aid provision of suitably trained first aiders and appropriate equipment to deal with emergencies relating to work with electricity.

C8.4 - Safe working in the vicinity of high voltage systems

Common high voltage systems and prevention of danger

COMMON HIGH VOLTAGE SYSTEMS

High voltage systems refer to those which exceed 1000 volts AC and 1500 volts DC. The majority of industrial facilities will have a supply from the Electricity Authority coming into their facility and will have a transformer that reduces the voltage down to a useable voltage.

The normal method by which electricity is supplied to a facility is that the electricity is taken by the suppliers from the National Grid. This occurs at 400 kV to 275 kV. The supply voltage is then distributed at 132 kV and transformed down.

This reduction pattern is normally 132 kV down to 33 kV, 33 kV to 11 kV and then it will either be supplied to the facility directly at this voltage, where a substation will be positioned on site to reduce it to 415V AC, or it will be supplied at 415V AC. This is a three phase supply and a 230V AC tap will be taken to supply those pieces of equipment that run at this voltage level.

"No electric line shall be used for the purpose of supply at a voltage greater than 400,000 volts".

Figure C8-46 Electric supply line.   Source: Regulation 16 of the Electricity Safety, Quality and Continuity Regulations (ESQCR) 2002.

Exposure to high voltages normally occurs in three forms:

1) Overhead lines.   2) Underground lines.   3) Substations.

PREVENTION OF DANGER

The Approved Code of Practice that supports the Management of Health and Safety at Work Regulations (MHSWR) 1999 sets out a hierarchy of precautions to take in order to control risks. For work in the vicinity of high voltage systems, application of this hierarchy suggests the following actions:

a) Avoided the work altogether.
b) Divert all power in the high voltage system clear of where the work is take place.
c) Make the system dead while the work is in progress.
d) Work around the high voltage system using appropriate precautions that prevent danger.

In some cases it may be necessary to use suitable combinations of these measures, particularly where high voltage systems pass over or through permanent work areas.

Competent and authorised persons role related to system modifications

Although the EWR 1989 do not distinguish between various voltage limits, the degree of competence that a person would need to prevent danger and injury, as required by Regulation 16, would be considerably more than that needed for work at lower voltages.

EWR 1989 Regulation 16 - "Requirement to prevent danger or, where appropriate, injury".

The Memorandum of Guidance to the regulation uses both of the terms, 'injury' and 'danger'. The regulation therefore applies to the whole range of work associated with electrical equipment where danger may arise and whether or not danger (or the risk of injury) is actually present during the work.

DANGER

The prevention of danger, for the duration of the work will need to be under the control of someone who must therefore possess sufficient technical knowledge or experience, or be so supervised, to be capable of ensuring the danger is prevented. For example, where someone is to isolate some electrical equipment before work on the equipment is undertaken they will require sufficient technical knowledge or experience to prevent danger during the isolation.

INJURY

Regulation 16 also covers those circumstances where danger is present, i.e. where there is a risk of injury, as for example where work is being done on live or charged equipment using special techniques and under the terms of Regulation 14 relating to work on or near live conductors. In these circumstances, people must possess sufficient technical knowledge or experience or be so supervised etc, to be capable of ensuring that injury is prevented.

TECHNICAL KNOWLEDGE OR EXPERIENCE

The scope of 'technical knowledge or experience' may include:

- Adequate knowledge of electricity.
- Adequate experience of electrical work.
- Adequate understanding of the system to be worked on and practical experience of that class of system.
- Understanding of the hazards which may arise during the work and the precautions which need to be taken.
- Ability to recognise at all times whether it is safe for work to continue.

It is important to ensure that any personnel working on high voltage systems must be competent. In assessing competence, the person's knowledge, training and experience in the particular class of work and type of system involved should be considered. The more complex the system, the higher the competence level required.

In the case of high voltage systems, most electricity supply companies organise special high voltage courses that provide legal, technical and practical guidance on distribution systems.

COMPETENT AND AUTHORISED PERSONS

The Authorised Person is responsible for the work on a high voltage system and ensures that those conducting the work, Competent Persons, do so in a safe manner. The Authorised Person will ensure precautions are taken by the Competent Person, for example, ensuring equipment for isolation is issued and that isolation and testing has taken place, usually through the application of a permit-to-work.

The Authorised Person should be:

- Sufficiently senior so as to be able to enforce safe working, usually through a permit-to-work system.
- Aware of the hazards and potential risks involved in the activity to be carried out.
- Understand the control measures necessary for safe working with the high voltage system.

This Competent Person should either be the person in charge of the activity to be carried out or should be the person who is actually going to do the work. Any permit-to-work applied must be issued to a named person and not to a position or group.

Safe systems of work and permit-to-work procedures

SAFE SYSTEMS OF WORK

The risk of death or injury is significant in many high voltage, and particularly high energy systems. Safe systems of work should be employed when carrying out working with or near high voltage systems. The system should take into account all eventualities.

The following general guidelines are suggested:

- Turn off the power before touching any part of a high voltage system, or even getting close to it. Secure isolation by use of a key switch or lockout device.
- High voltage capacitors may hold a charge long after power is turned off. Always discharge capacitors and keep them shorted in storage or when working on them. Even after being shorted, a capacitor can regain significant voltage when open circuited. Ideally, the system should be designed so that the capacitor shorting is failsafe.
- Make sure the metal cases of transformers, motors, control panels and other items are properly grounded (earthed).
- Keep a safe distance from energised or potentially energised components. Don't move conductive objects too close to energised components.
- Use adequate fusing of the power and/or circuit breakers to limit the maximum current.
- Spend some time laying out your circuits. Hot glue, electrical tape and exposed wiring are quick and easy, but could be lethal.

PERMIT TO WORK PROCEDURES

A permit-to-work type system should be used to ensure adequate management of the task involved. This should form part of the safe system of work employed to manage the risk of working on or near high voltage systems. The permit states what work is being carried out, where and when, and what safety precautions have been taken. It is the duty of the Authorised Person issuing the permit-to-work to ensure that the safety precautions have been taken, that they are adequate to prevent danger, and that the recipient Competent Person is fully conversant with the task and the precautions to be taken.

Safe working near overhead power lines

HAZARDS

Every year people are seriously hurt by coming into contact with overhead power lines. A high proportion, about one third - prove to be fatal. These fatalities occur at voltages ranging from 400 kV to 230V. Any lines found on a site should always be treated as live until they are proved to be otherwise.

Overhead power lines usually consist of bare (uninsulated) conductors. These are often referred to as cables. They are supported overhead in a number of ways, the most common being wooden posts or metal towers. A common problem with the type supported by wooden posts is that they are mistaken for telephone cables.

One of the main risks is that of arcing or, as it is sometimes called, a flashover. This occurs when an object, or person, approaches the conductor, the electricity bridges the air gap between and current flows through the object or person. The risk of flashover increases significantly as the voltage applied to the conductor increases. If vehicles are brought closer than the following distance there is a significant risk of flashover:

- 15 m of overhead lines supported by steel towers.
- 9 m of overhead lines supported by wooden poles.

PRECAUTIONS

Regulation 19 of Electricity Safety, Quality and Continuity Regulations (ESQCR) 2002 places a duty for electricity suppliers to prevent access to overhead lines and to provide warning signs that are suitably positioned to 'give due warning of danger in all circumstances'.

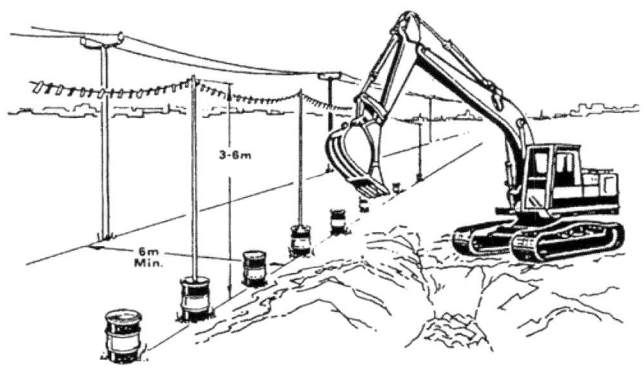 

Figure C8-47: Working near power lines.   Source: HSG144.   Figure C8-48: Overhead power lines.   Source: Lincsafe.

ELEMENT C8 - ELECTRICAL SAFETY AND EWR 1989

Using the principles of prevention stated in the Management of Health and Safety at Work Regulations (MHSWR) 1999, the following approach should be taken when working near overhead power lines:

Avoid where possible:

- If this cannot be achieved then divert the lines clear of the work area.
- If this cannot be done then have the lines made dead temporarily.
- If this cannot be achieved then take suitable precautions to prevent danger.

Suitable precautions depend upon the nature of the work. There are three main categories:

1) Work carried out near to lines.
2) Work where items or vehicles will pass beneath the lines.
3) Work carried out beneath the lines.

Work carried out near to lines

If work is carried out near the lines then barriers are to be used along with warning signs. The recommended minimum distance for the position of the barriers is 6 m (horizontally) from the nearest line. It should always be remembered that some vehicles have a jib that extends long distances, therefore the measurement should be taken with the reach of the jib (maximum outreach) measured (horizontally) from the position of the ground barriers. For very high voltages these distances may be increased further.

Where cranes or vehicles with jibs are working, it may be necessary to place bunting to show drivers of these vehicles the position of the lines. The bunting should be placed at a height of 3-6 m. Where it is used at a height of 6 m the distance (horizontally) from the lines should be increased to a distance of 9 m (horizontally) from the nearest line. The erection of bunting should be pre-planned so as to avoid coming into contact with the lines, and only competent personnel should carry out the work.

Ground barriers should be sturdy enough so that they are not moved easily and should be colour coded with red and white stripes. Types of barrier commonly used include:

- 200 litre drums - filled with rubble or concrete.
- Railway sleepers.
- Earth bank raised to 1 m height and marked by posts to prevent vehicle entry.
- A tension wire fence with flags attached. This type of protection needs to be earthed in consultation with the electricity supplier.

Equipment and materials should never be allowed to be stored between the overhead power lines and the ground barriers.

Work where items or vehicles will pass beneath the lines

Work areas where plant will pass beneath the lines are required to have similar protection devices. The number of passing points should always be kept to a minimum. Each passing place should have a set of goal posts erected at both ends to serve as gateways between the barriers. Appropriate warning signs should be placed around these goal posts and the approaches to them, including the clearance height and notice to drivers to lower jibs.

The goal posts should be constructed of an insulating material and should be marked with red and white stripes to define them and make them visible. If work is to be carried out at night then suitable lighting levels should be achieved by site lighting to ensure good visibility.

Work carried out beneath the lines

The working height and overhead power line height should be defined and where possible ensuring materials used cannot come into contact with the line. Any mobile plant used that has a telescopic facility or raised parts should be physically limited so that it cannot strike the line.

Underground cables

HAZARDS

Because underground cables are concealed below the surface and their exact location is not usually known there is a risk that work near to them could cause contact with the cable. Depending on how contact is made this could lead to penetration of the armour cabling surrounding the conductor, for example by pneumatic drill, excavator or a pick. This may cause a sudden release of energy that rapidly melts part of the conductor and ejects the molten metal in the surrounding area, which can lead to major burns to nearby workers.

In addition, the release of energy can include a high energy flash involving ultraviolet light, which can cause photokeritits to those exposed. The energy from otherwise insulated cable may pass through the item that penetrated the armour and try to find earth, if this is through a person holding the drill or pick major burns and eclectic shock may be caused. The metal work of an excavator may be made live, but the energy not pass to earth immediately. The driver may then provide a ready path to earth for the energy as they step from the excavator to the ground.

PRECAUTIONS

Part IV (Regulations 12 to 15) of Electricity Safety, Quality and Continuity Regulations (ESQCR) 2002 specifies that any conductor that is placed below ground and is not earthed must be insulated from earth and so positioned that no damage can occur inadvertently from an excavation, tool or similar. It also stated that 'a conductor placed below ground used in a suppliers high voltage system but not connected with earth shall be laid in such manner as to ensure, so far as is reasonably practicable, that any person excavating the ground will receive a warning of its presence'.

Suppliers of electricity must keep accurate drawings and plans of the position of where their cables are. This information is to be given to developers and construction personnel as necessary in order for them to ascertain the proximity of buried cables in relation to any excavating they may carry out.

When planning excavation work a survey needs to be carried out, not just for ground conditions and contamination levels, but also for the position of buried services. Technological advances over the last few years has made this job a lot easier than previously and various forms are available including ground radar and portable cable detection devices.

Once identified, the locations of cables need to be marked out to warn workers of the hazard buried below ground. Colour identification can be used to distinguish between the wide range of buried services. Barriers can be used either side of where a buried cable lies to prevent digging or exploratory work being carried out.

Any services, regardless of identification or condition, should be treated as a live cable until proven otherwise. Hand methods of digging, spades and shovels rather than picks or forks, should be used to explore for the position of cables and within 0.5 m of a known buried service.

Substations

HAZARDS

Substations are premises where the transformation of electrical energy occurs. Some industrial complexes may have a substation on site, but employees may not have access to it; whereas other sites will have access as the ownership of the substation is theirs.

The electrical apparatus inside a substation usually includes the input and output cables, the transformer and housing, instrumentation and switchgear. This type of equipment can be at high voltages and present high risk if operated incorrectly. This can mean that those working in substations may be at a significant risk of electric shock, flash or burns.

PRECAUTIONS

The substation should have suitable security measures to ensure only authorised personnel are allowed to gain entry to the premises and safe systems of work employed to control the access and the work carried out within.

Live conductors should be screened or insulated to prevent danger and an adequate working area should be employed when designing the substation with regard to the nature of the work to be carried out there.

Part III (Regulation 11) of ESQCR 2002 deals with substations and places a duty on suppliers to prevent the ingress of water or gasses into any 'suppliers' works' including substations.

Substations are required to have a fence no less than 2.4 m high to prevent access. Safety signs and a sign identifying the supplier, a telephone number and a contact address are to be prominently displayed. Additionally, all reasonable steps are to be taken to prevent fire.

High voltage glove working and live line overhead working

HIGH VOLTAGE GLOVE WORK

Before conducting high voltage glove working it must be confirmed that this work needs to be conducted live and that it is unreasonable that it be made dead.

When this has been confirmed the following precautions should be taken, where they are appropriate to the work:

- The use of people who are properly trained and competent to work on live equipment safely (see regulation 16 of EWR 1989 and earlier in this element).
- The provision of adequate information to the person carrying out the work about the live conductors involved, the associated electrical system and the foreseeable risks.
- Accompaniment by another person or people if the presence of such person or people could contribute significantly to ensuring that injury is prevented.
- The use of suitable equipment, including insulated tools and protective clothing, including insulating gloves.
- The use of suitable insulated barriers or screens.
- The use of suitable instruments and test probes.
- Effective control of any area where there is danger from live conductors.

ELEMENT C8 - ELECTRICAL SAFETY AND EWR 1989

LIVE LINE OVERHEAD WORKING

Live line working makes use of the following safe practices.

Separation of the linesmen, working in close proximity to live high voltage (HV) conductors, and earth, which is provided by means of the insulated aerial device (IAD).

All of the component parts of the IAD, including booms, buckets and bucket liners must be manufactured from materials of high insulation value. The overall working rating of the IAD should be a minimum of 46kV.

Insulation between the linesmen and HV apparatus is achieved by the application of approved insulation material to all live conductors and earthed metalwork within the working area.

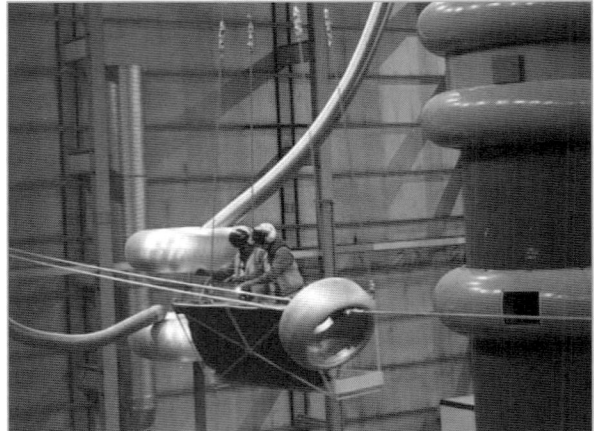

Figure C8-49: Live overhead line training.   Source: Narec.

This includes the use of line hose, blankets and insulator hoods that should be rated to a minimum of 17 kV for work on 11 kV overhead lines, and a minimum of 36kV for work on 33kV overhead lines. Further personal protection of the linesmen is given by the wearing of insulating gloves and sleeves that are rated at 17 kV class 2, 26.5 kV class 3 and 36 kV class 4. Live line working should only be carried out by workers who are properly trained and competent to work on live overhead lines safely.

Before work can begin, a condition assessment of the equipment, including conductors, insulators, and other pole top and line fittings must be carried out in order to minimise the possibility of failure during the work process. Tools and equipment must be kept in a clean and dry condition. Before use they must be inspected to ensure they are in a suitable condition for use and if a defect is found or suspected, then they must not be used.

Any equipment provided under these Regulations for the purpose of protecting persons at work on or near electrical equipment shall be suitable for the use for which it is provided, be maintained in a condition suitable for that use, and be properly used.

Figure C8-50: Use and maintenance of system.   Source: Regulation 4(4) - Electricity at Work Regulations (EWR) 1989.

BS EN 60903 stipulates the following electrical test requirements for insulating gloves according to their voltage class:

Class	Max Working Voltage	Proof Test Voltage (AC)	Max Leakage Current mA Glove Length 11"	14"	16"	18"	Proof Test Voltage (DC)
0	1kV	5kV	12	14	16	n/a	10kV
1	7.5kV	10kV	n/a	16	18	n/a	20kV
2	17kV	20kV	n/a	18	20	n/a	30kV
3	26.5kV	30kV	n/a	n/a	22	24	40kV
4	36kV	40kV	n/a	n/a	24	26	60kV

Figure C8-51: Insulating gloves.   Source: BS EN 60903/Clydesdale Ltd.

C8.5 - Portable electrical equipment

Conditions and practices likely to lead to accidents

UNSUITABLE EQUIPMENT

Portable electrical equipment may lead to accidents through:

- Unsuitable apparatus for the duty or the conditions.
- Misuse.
- Failure to follow operating instructions.
- Wrong connection of system - supply phase, neutral or earth reversed.
- Wrong voltage or rating of equipment.

ELECTRICAL SAFETY AND EWR 1989 - **ELEMENT C8**

Figure C8-52: Hazard - fuse wired out. Source: RMS.

Figure C8-53: Hazard - defective apparatus. Source: RMS.

INADEQUATE MAINTENANCE

Portable electrical equipment may lead to accidents through:

- Inadequate maintenance of the installation and the equipment.
- Wrong or broken connection to portable apparatus.
- Inadequate earthing.
- Poor maintenance and testing.
- No defect reporting system.

USE OF DEFECTIVE APPARATUS

Portable electrical equipment may lead to accidents through:

- Faulty cables, notably extension leads.
- Plugs and sockets.
- Damaged plug or socket.
- Protection devices, such as fuses or circuit breaker, incorrect rating, damaged or missing.
- Overloaded leading to damage or over-heating.
- Short circuit leading to damage, overheating or movement.
- Isolation procedures or systems of work wrong.
- Bad circuit connections.

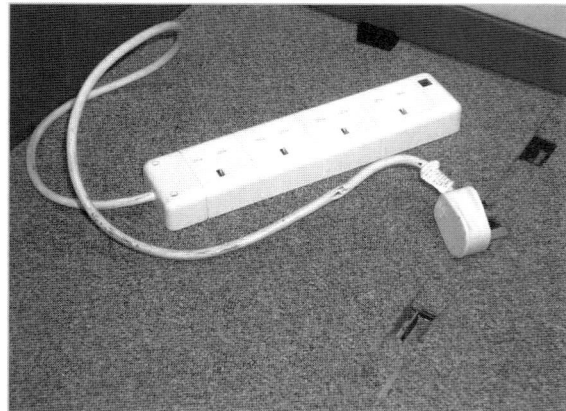

Figure C8-54: Hazard - damaged cable. Source: RMS.

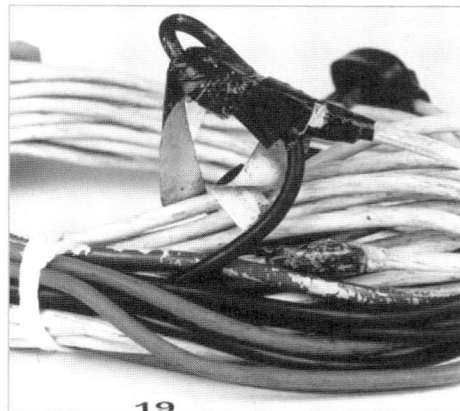

Figure C8-55: Hazard - taped joints. Source: RMS.

General

Portable electrical equipment may lead to accidents through:

- Lack of competence.
- Poor access, lighting and emergency procedures.
- No work planning including permit-to-work.

Electrical risks from important portable appliances

The principal risks related to this type of equipment arise from circumstances where no adequate earth has been established and/or the person becomes part of the system. These types of portable appliances may need to be provided with their own independent earth to establish a path for any fault current and to allow any devices that detect fault to operate correctly.

© RMS

GENERATORS

A portable generator will often be used to provide electricity to portable power tools. If the power tools are double insulated the systems 'floating earth' does not present a problem and additional safety devices are not usually required.

However if the generator is to provide power to replace a standard mains supply and equipment is to be attached that relies on the presence of an earth to operate safely the generator must be provided with an earth connection. With portable generators, reliance should not be made on the contact of the generator skids with the ground. A better earth may be provided by using a low-impedance spike, which is inserted into the ground.

WELDING

There are a number of electric welding systems available, including manual metal arc (MMA), metal inert gas (MIG), metal active gas (MAG) and tungsten inert gas (TIG) systems.

Welding equipment usually operate with an open circuit voltage at about 80V and AC welding equipment set to 80V will have a peak voltage near 120V, so the risk and potential danger of a shock is higher. When changing welding rods it is important to ensure the welding equipment is not live. It is common for welders to tuck the welding rod holder under their arm while they are changing the rod and, even though the welding equipment operates at a relatively low voltage, a path through the body created by contact with the damp area under the arm may prove fatal. Devices are available that reduce the open circuit voltage when welding is not being carried out; they should meet BS EN 60974-1 requirements.

Electric welding operations make use of a live welding rod and a welding return, which is connected to the material being welded, to provide an electrical circuit. In circumstances where there is a fault in the welding return that increases its impedance, there is a risk that the conductive items in contact with the material being welded may provide an alternative route for the welding current. The welding current returns to the welding transformer by other means that the welding return lead.

This may be through wire ropes, metal fittings and pipe work or the earth wires of other electrical equipment. The current can cause considerable damage as it passes through. There is also the potential that the welder may be part of the current return. Welding return leads should be checked for their impedance at intervals, located as near to the welding arc as possible and a good connection secured on 'bright' metal.

Where welding equipment is of a type where there is a high level of insulation between the primary and secondary parts of the welding transformer (double or reinforced insulation to BS EN 60974-1) additional earthing of the material being welded is not recommended. Equipment that does not conform to BS EN 60974-1, this tends to be older welding equipment, should be used with an additional earth lead connected to the material being welded.

Control measures, including portable appliance inspection and testing

Portable appliance inspection and testing should be carried out in accordance with a defined schedule of planned maintenance. Factors affecting the time scales between tests include:

- Number of work hours used.
- Environmental conditions.
- Reported defects or problems during use.
- Voltage dependant upon environment equipment used.

There are 3 types of test in common use and suggested in the HSE guidance document HSG107 "Maintaining portable and transportable electrical equipment":

1) User check - carried out by the user prior to use.
2) Formal visual check - carried out by a competent person.
3) Combined inspection and testing - carried out by a competent person.

Aspects of supply

Supply cables for portable electrical equipment may be providing power at 230 V and can be very vulnerable to damage if not protected, for example, forklift trucks may pass over them as the cables cross a sharp door threshold or a door may close on them causing damage. They can also present a tripping hazard that could cause the cable at one end to become insecure in its connections.

For these reasons, it may be better to route cables at height, rather than across the ground or protect them with cable covers. Supply cables should also be kept as short as possible to reduce the amount of cable exposed to the risk of harm and to enable the cable to remain under the supervision of the user as much as possible.

Construction hazards and controls

Element C9

Learning outcomes

The intended learning outcomes are that the student will be able to:

C9.1 Describe the scope and nature of construction activities.
C9.2 Explain the scope and application of the Construction (Design and Management) Regulations 2007.
C9.3 Explain the hazards associated with working at heights from fixed work or temporary platforms and the necessary precautions and safe working practices.
C9.4 Explain the hazards, precautions and safe working practices associated with demolition work.
C9.5 Explain the hazards associated with excavation work and the necessary precautions and safe working practices.

Content

C9.1 - Scope and nature of construction activities 315
    Types of work 315
    Range of activities 316
    Particular construction issues 317
C9.2 - Scope and application of the Construction (Design and Management) Regulations (CDM) 2007 318
    The duties of clients, designers, CDM co-ordinators, principal contractors and contractors 318
C9.3 - Working at height from fixed or temporary platforms 324
    Working at height 324
    Safe use of temporary (immobile) access equipment 324
    The requirements for the erection, use and dismantling of scaffolds and falsework 328
    Inspection of working platforms above 2 metres 329
    Hazards associated with falling materials and appropriate precautionary measures 330
    Safe methods of roof work 331
    Means of temporary access types and safety features 332
    The use, application, selection and precautions in use of personal and collective fall arrest devices 334
C9.4 - Demolition work 335
    Main techniques in demolition of buildings and the associated hazards and safe working practices 335
C9.5 - Excavations 339
    Hazards and controls associated with excavation work 339
    The requirements for statutory inspections and examinations of excavations 344

ELEMENT C9 - CONSTRUCTION HAZARDS AND CONTROLS

Relevant statutory provisions

Construction (Head Protection) Regulations (CHPR) 1989
Construction (Design and Management) Regulations (CDM) 2007
Work at Height Regulations (WAH) 2005
Lifting Operations and Lifting Equipment Regulations (LOLER) 1998
New Roads and Street Works Act (NRSWA) 1991
Notification of Conventional Tower Cranes Regulations (NCTCR) 2010

C9.1 - Scope and nature of construction activities

In construction activities in the UK there were 42 fatal injuries, with a rate of 2.2 deaths per 100, 000 workers, in 2009/10. This compares to an average rate of 3.2 deaths per 100,000 workers for the previous five years. Thus, the rate for 2009/10 is 32% below the average for the previous five years.

Types of work

BUILDING WORKS

Building works involve most trades within the construction industry such as ground workers, steel erectors, brick layers, carpenters, plasterers, etc all working closely together with the common goal of creating a new finished building or structure.

RENOVATION, ALTERATION AND MAINTENANCE OF EXISTING PREMISES

Renovation

Renovation work involves restoring an existing building or structure to a condition that is representative of its original condition or improved by repair and modernisation using more up-to-date materials and practices. As with new building works, this also involves most of the common trades normally used within the construction industry.

Alteration

Alteration works are required when the layout of an existing building, structure or premises no longer suits the use for which it was originally intended. This can include elements of both new building works and renovation works. Alterations can comprise:

- An extension to an existing structure or demolition and removal of sections of the internal structure to make premises more spacious.
- Alternatively, an alteration may involve dividing the existing structure into smaller, separate sections by the introduction of partition walls of various materials (block-work, brick-work or studding and plasterboard).

Maintenance of existing premises

Maintenance work is an essential element to ensure that the condition of an existing building, premises or structure does not deteriorate and that it remains in as good a condition as is possible. Work is normally carried out on a regular scheduled basis to deal with issues of wear and tear, but can also be required when a problem suddenly occurs that requires urgent attention for example, loss of roofing materials following a storm. Maintenance can be carried out on all components of existing premises, including the building, services, and any final building finish and furnishing.

Occupied premises

Careful planning of maintenance work should occur if the building or premises are occupied. Hazards from paint, dust, falling masonry and excavations should be considered, suitable and sufficient risk assessments should be made and controls implemented.

Unoccupied premises

Unoccupied premises/buildings can pose other hazards, with unstable groundwork, footings, walls, beams supporting floors and roofing. In addition unoccupied buildings are likely to be infested with vermin or suffer intrusion by pigeons in the rafters where roof integrity may have failed, increasing the risks of biological hazards. Again these hazards should be highlighted, suitable risk assessments should be made and controls implemented.

CIVIL ENGINEERING AND WORKS OF ENGINEERING CONSTRUCTION

Civil engineering and engineering works normally relate to heavy construction activities requiring large items of plant and equipment such as cranes and excavators. This work will require specialist knowledge and experience in order to undertake activities such as highway construction, bridge construction, piling works, large foundations, large concrete structures, excavations and utility projects.

Construction work

The term "construction work" as specified in Regulation 2 of CDM 2007 means the carrying out of any building, civil engineering or engineering construction work and includes:

- The construction, alteration, conversion, fitting out, commissioning, renovation, repair, upkeep, redecoration or other maintenance (including cleaning which involves the use of water or an abrasive at high pressure or the use of corrosive or toxic substances), de-commissioning, demolition or dismantling of a structure.
- The preparation for an intended structure, including site clearance, exploration, investigation (but not site survey) and excavation, and the clearance or preparation of the site or structure for use or occupation at its conclusion.
- The assembly on site of prefabricated elements to form a structure or the disassembly on site of prefabricated elements which, immediately before such disassembly, formed a structure.

ELEMENT C9 - CONSTRUCTION HAZARDS AND CONTROLS

- The removal of a structure or of any product or waste resulting from demolition or dismantling of a structure or from disassembly of prefabricated elements which immediately before such disassembly formed such a structure.
- The installation, commissioning, maintenance, repair or removal of mechanical, electrical, gas, compressed air, hydraulic, telecommunications, computer or similar services which are normally fixed within or to a structure.

DEMOLITION

The term demolition refers to 'breaking down' or 'removing'. This includes the dismantling of a buildings or structures that are no longer required or are possibly derelict. Demolition may involve the partial dismantling of a structure in order to conduct construction work to alter or extend it. The term is not limited to the complete removal of a building or structure.

Any project that involves any element of demolition (full or part demolition) falls under the control of the Construction (Design and Management) Regulations (CDM) 2007.

Range of activities

SITE CLEARANCE

Site clearance consists of preparing the site prior to the works being undertaken. This may involve removal of hazardous waste, obstructive trees, unwanted scrub and landscaping. Demolition activities may also be required as part of site clearance prior to construction works beginning. Where there are high levels of contaminants it may also be necessary for ground remediation.

Following completion of construction works, site clearance will involve removal of all waste associated with the construction activities (for example, brick and timber off-cuts, packaging, spoil) to a licensed waste disposal site. It will also include the removal of all plant and equipment used on the construction site with the aim of leaving the site in a clean and tidy state ready for its intended use.

DISMANTLING AND DEMOLITION

Demolition/deconstruction/dismantling activities will generally include a survey of the structure to be demolished in order to identify any potential contamination or hazards that are concealed, for example asbestos dust, lead, chemicals, live utility services. Various techniques will be employed to carry out demolition, including dismantling, which normally is piece by piece in reverse order to construction; demolition may also be carried out in large sections at a time, by machines or demolition by hand - where items are broken into their individual parts to be reclaimed or reused.

Where material recovery is not important long reach cranes with a demolition ball, long reach mechanical pincer jaws and explosive charges may be possible to be used. Protection should be ensured for all workers involved, through controlled access to the area. The danger area should be defined and suitably fenced with controlled access only to authorised personnel. Demolition must be carried out in a structured sequence to prevent any premature collapse of the structure. Falling debris must not be allowed to fall onto any surrounding area or buildings.

EXCAVATION

The interpretation, according to the Construction (Design and Management) Regulations (CDM) 2007, of the term "excavation" includes any earthwork, trench, well, shaft, tunnel or underground working.

Excavation consists of digging below ground level to various depths in order to create a cavity that can be used for exposure of buried utility services, trenching for installation of utility services, casting building foundations or ground investigations. Methods of digging used for excavation work include the use of hand tools (pick, fork, shovel), and by using a mechanical excavator. Major excavations for basements, sub-structures etc, remain as a permanent part in the construction operation.

LOADING, UNLOADING AND STORAGE OF MATERIALS

Construction sites use a host of different materials in the construction process that will require loading or unloading by mechanical or manual means. These can be broken down into materials that are used or removed immediately at site (i.e. excavation spoil, concrete mix, mortar mix) and materials that are stored at site and used or removed at regular intervals as required (bricks, cement, sand, timber, sundries, waste disposal skips). Loading and unloading should be undertaken using the correct procedures that comply with site safe systems of work and wherever possible avoiding the need for manual handling. Storage requirements should be identified and planned for the whole project. This will need to consider security, safe position and suitable ground condition; protection from adverse weather and potential for falls from a height or into an excavation.

SITE MOVEMENTS

Construction sites contain various types of heavy mobile plant and equipment and large numbers of site workers. Construction site projects should be well planned to take into account vehicles moving around the site. In particular, consideration to safe access and egress would include issues of adequacy of space for manoeuvring and ensuring operator visibility. Routes for both vehicles and pedestrians should be provided and be suitably surfaced, clearly defined and separated.

FABRICATION

Fabrication at site can include steel erecting, welding and form-working. Quite often it can involve working at height (where specialist work platforms and fall arrest equipment should be used) and adequate control is essential to prevent the falling of materials and tools. A variety of specialist equipment may be required, for example, a welding machine, bolt gun, or nail gun. This specialist equipment should only be used by competent persons.

DECORATION

Decoration consists of applying various coatings, for example, paints, wallpaper, and artex, necessary to create the final finished appearance to a building or structure. The tools involved with decoration are often handheld and not powered. Various access systems, including mobile elevating work platforms, are required for this type of work.

CLEANING

Cleaning involves applying water, steam or various abrasive or chemical agents to the surfaces to be treated, for example, walls, windows, floors, fabric. The method of application can require the use of various types of equipment ranging from vacuum cleaners, floor polisher through to high pressure jets. Consideration should be given to the correct disposal of waste materials.

INSTALLATION, REMOVAL AND MAINTENANCE OF SERVICES

Various utility services (for example, electricity gas, water and telecommunications) are required on both existing and new construction sites, and are usually buried underground. In new installations this involves a great deal of liaison with the planning authority, utility companies and designer concerning the route the services will take and will involve excavation with heavy plant, loading and unloading of materials. New services are often connected to their source at a location that is situated outside the construction site boundary. Where this occurs, the additional hazard to the general public presents itself and suitable means of traffic control (for example, signing and lighting), guarding and protection of the public (barriers and warning signs) will need to be employed. Removing or maintaining utilities can present other hazards, and these should be isolated correctly prior to any work commencing. This may require involving the utility companies, so proactive planning is essential.

LANDSCAPING

Landscaping usually takes place during the final stages of the construction phase, when there is little or no construction plant travelling around the site. Landscaping may include altering site levels and the introduction of trees, shrubs, grass turf/seed etc. The works generally consist of loading and unloading of materials, manual handling, and cleaning work (footways and roads). Note that care should be taken to avoid planting trees close to underground services or near to building footings.

Particular construction issues

TRANSITORY NATURE OF WORKERS

The building and construction industry is characterised by its intermittent, temporary, transitory nature. Generally, building and construction contractors hire a work force on a project basis. Thus, workers in the building and construction industry are accustomed to travelling from areas where work is not plentiful to fill short-term labour shortages created by expansion and contraction of local construction activity.

TEMPORARY NATURE OF CONSTRUCTION ACTIVITIES AND THE CONSTANTLY CHANGING WORKPLACE

Construction sites constantly change through the build phase, as the trades that are associated with the construction vary greatly at each stage. Consideration needs to be given to site induction for new workers as appropriate. The safe systems of work, risk assessments, site safety procedures and site inductions will need to be updated regularly to suit the most current situation. A construction site will always be an unfamiliar workplace with new hazards and dangers posed as each phase moves to the next.

TIME PRESSURES FROM CLIENTS

Clients have one of the biggest influences on the health and safety of those working on a construction project. Their decisions have substantial influence on the time, money and other resources available for the project. Because of this, the Construction (Design and Management) Regulations (CDM) 2007 make them accountable for the impact their decisions have on health and safety.

WEATHER CONDITIONS

For those working outdoors, adverse weather can create numerous problems. Short-term exposure to the sun can cause excessive sweating, dehydration and fatigue. There are fears that prolonged exposure can cause skin cancer. Strong wind increases risk when working at height and can cause unexpected movement of loads suspended on cranes. Heavy rain may cause soft ground conditions which can increase problems with site traffic and undermine the stability of scaffolds and excavations. Extreme cold leads to snow and ice which increases the likelihood of slips and falls. It may also increase the risk of brittle failure of equipment.

POOR LEVELS OF NUMERACY AND LITERACY OF WORKERS

Poor levels of literacy and numeracy can significantly impede the progress of workers at a workplace. The level of understanding and critical information retention required, for example, when attending a health and safety induction, can be significantly reduced. Where the written word is used instead of a pictographic approach, written critical safety instructions or directions may not be understood and could be unintentionally ignored. Weights and measures, dates and times critical to processes could also be misconstrued or overlooked if workers are innumerate.

NON-ENGLISH SPEAKING WORKERS

Employers need to consider the following with reference to their non-English speaking employees:

- Employers should check that prospective workers have sufficient command of English for their role.
- Worker understanding of instructions and health and safety related notices and warnings should also be checked. Employers have a legal duty to ensure the employee understands notices, symbols etc. related to health and safety. If the employee does not understand or cannot read English, these have to be translated into the employee's language.
- If other members of staff are available who can speak the employee's native language, then they may be able to help the employee understand the working culture and environment in the UK.

The employee's previous experience should be determined; this shows whether they have relevant experience to carry out the work required.

C9.2 - Scope and application of the Construction (Design and Management) Regulations (CDM) 2007

The duties of clients, designers, CDM co-ordinators, principal contractors and contractors

The Construction (Design and Management) Regulations (CDM) 2007 require systematic management of construction projects from concept to completion. Hazards must be identified and, where possible, eliminated, and the remaining risks reduced and controlled. This is achieved by the appointment of people as competent duty holders, with sufficient resources.

The Regulations are split into five parts.

Part 1 - Introduction.

Part 2 - General management duties applying to all construction projects.

Part 3 - Additional duties where a project is notifiable.

Part 4 - Duties relating to health and safety on construction sites.

Part 5 - General.

The duties placed on the duty holders are summarised below.

DUTIES

Clients

For *all* projects, ensure that:

- Work can be carried out safely.
- Adequate welfare facilities are provided.
- Any workplace complies with CDM 2007 Part 4.
- Make relevant pre-construction health and safety information available.

Where a project is notifiable, the client shall:

- As soon as practicable appoint a competent CDM co-ordinator.
- Then appoint a competent principal contractor.
- Promptly provide the CDM co-ordinator and principal contractor with pre-construction information.
- Not allow work to start until the construction phase plan and adequate welfare facilities are in place.
- Provide the CDM co-ordinator with information for inclusion in the health and safety file.
- Keep health and safety file available for inspection and revised as necessary.

Designers

For *all* projects, ensure that:

- The client is aware of his duties.
- Take account of other design considerations.

- Design to avoid foreseeable risk during construction, use and maintenance of the building.
- Give priority to collective measures over individual measures.
- Ensure where it is not possible to avoid risks that they are minimised.
- Provide adequate information about materials used in the design that could affect the health and safety of persons carrying out construction work.

Where a project is notifiable:

- Shall not commence until a CDM co-ordinator has been appointed.
- Provide the CDM co-ordinator with information for inclusion in the health and safety file.

CDM co-ordinators

- Be in a position to give advice to clients.
- Ensure co-operation between persons involved in the project.
- Ensure that designers include among the design considerations the principles of prevention.
- Liaise with principal contractor regarding information for the health and safety plan and health and safety file.
- Identify and collect pre-construction information.
- Ensure that designers comply with their duties.
- Ensure co-operation between designers and principal contractor in relation to any design change.
- Prepare a health and safety file.
- Ensure that a health and safety file is delivered to the client.
- Notify the Health and Safety Executive (HSE).

Principal contractors

- Plan, manage and monitor the construction phase to ensure that it is carried out without risk.
- Liaise with the CDM co-ordinator.
- Ensure adequate welfare facilities are provided.
- Draw up site rules.

Ensure that every contractor is:

- Informed of the minimum amount of time allocated for planning and preparation.
- If necessary consulted about the health and safety plan.
- Given access to the health and safety plan.
- Given any relevant information.
- Informed about the information that may be required for inclusion in the health and safety file.
- Display the notification details.
- Prevent unauthorised access to the site.

Ensure that every worker is provided with:

- Site induction.
- Information that has to be provided by a contractor (see below).
- Any further information that might be necessary.

Contractors

For *all* projects, ensure that:

- They do not start work unless they are aware of their duties.
- Plan, manage and monitor work to ensue that it is carried out without risk.
- Every (sub) contractor that the contractor appoints is provided with relevant information.

Every worker under his control is given information and training which should include:

- Site induction (if not provided by the principal contractor).
- Results of risk assessments and control measures.
- Site rules.
- Emergency procedures and the persons involved in implementing the procedures.
- They do not commence work until unauthorised access to the site has been prevented.
- Ensure that adequate welfare facilities are provided.

Where a project is notifiable the contractor shall:

- Not start work unless he knows the names of the CDM co-ordinator and principal contractor, has been given access to the health and safety plan and the project has been notified to the HSE.
- Provide relevant information to the principal contractor on the health and safety risks created by their works and how they will be controlled.
- Identify any contractors he has appointed to the principal contractor.
- Comply with directions given by the principal contractor and any rules in the health and safety plan.
- Provide the principal contractor with any Reporting of Injuries, Diseases and Dangerous Occurrences Regulations (RIDDOR) 1995 reports.

ELEMENT C9 - CONSTRUCTION HAZARDS AND CONTROLS

APPOINTMENT AND COMPETENCE REQUIRED OF RELEVANT PARTIES

Where a project is notifiable, the client must appoint a CDM Co-ordinator and a principal contractor as soon as is practicable after initial design work or other preparation for construction work has begun.

No person, who is a duty holder under CDM 2007, is allowed to:

- Appoint or engage a CDM co-ordinator, designer, principal contractor or contractor unless the person to be engaged is competent.
- Accept such an appointment unless the CDM Co-ordinator is competent.
- Instruct a worker to carry out or manage design or construction work unless the worker is:
    - Competent.
    - Under the supervision of a competent person.

To be competent an organisation or individual must have knowledge of specific tasks and the risks that may arise.

> "An appropriate health and safety qualification such as the NEBOSH construction certificate will demonstrate that the person has adequate knowledge of health and safety, but this will need to be coupled with a Stage 2 assessment to demonstrate that they have experience in applying this knowledge in the construction environment".

Figure C9-1: Assessing the competence of individual CDM co-ordinators.   Source: CDM 2007 ACOP, Regulation 4.

NOTIFICATION OF PROJECTS

CDM 2007 applies to all construction projects. However, construction projects with a construction phase longer than 30 days or involving more than 500 person days of construction work are notifiable to the Health and Safety Executive (HSE).

Notification by the CDM co-ordinator must be in writing and can be made using the form F10 (rev). A copy of the notification should be posted at the place where the work is to be carried out.

PREPARATION OF PRE-CONSTRUCTION INFORMATION

The purpose of pre-construction information is to provide information to those bidding for or planning work and for the development of the construction phase plan. Pre-construction information is essentially a collection of information about the significant health and safety risks of the construction project that the principal contractor will have to manage during the construction phase.

The pre-construction information will mainly come from:

- **The client** - who has to provide information relevant to health and safety to the CDM co-ordinator. This could include existing drawings, surveys of the site or premises, information on the location of services, etc.
- **Designers** - who have to provide information about the risks which cannot be avoided and will have to be controlled by the principal contractor and other contractors. Typically this information may be provided on drawings, in written specifications or in outline method statements.

The pre-construction information serves three main purposes:

- During its development the plan can provide a focus at which the health and safety considerations of design are brought together under the control of the CDM co-ordinator.
- Secondly, the plan plays a vital role in the tender documentation. It enables prospective principal contractors to be fully aware of the project's health, safety and welfare requirements. This will allow prospective principal contractors to have a level playing field as far as health and safety is concerned on which to provide tender submissions.
- Thirdly, the plan provides a template against which different tender submissions can be measured. This helps the CDM co-ordinator to advise the client on the provision of resources for health and safety and to assess the competence of prospective principal contractors.

The CDM co-ordinator is responsible for ensuring that the pre-construction information is prepared. This does not mean that the CDM co-ordinator must produce the information directly, but the CDM co-ordinator must ensure that it is prepared.

Content of the pre-construction information pack

The contents of the pre-construction information will depend on the nature of the project itself. However, the following areas should be considered:

Description of project

- Project description and programme details, including critical dates.
- Details of client, designers, CDM co-ordinator and other consultants.
- Whether or not the structure will be used as a workplace; therefore the need to comply with the Workplace (Health, Safety and Welfare) Regulations (WHSWR) 1992.
- Extent and location of existing records and plans.

Client's considerations and management requirements

- Arrangements for planning and managing the construction work.

- Structure and organisation.
- Health and safety goals for the project and arrangements for monitoring and review.
- Communication between duty holders.
- Site security and welfare.
- Requirements for health and safety of client's employees and customers, including vehicles, permits to work, restrictions and emergency procedures.
- Activities on or adjacent to the site during the works.
- Site delineation and security arrangements.

Environmental restrictions and existing on-site risks

a) Safety hazards, including:
- Boundaries and access, including temporary access.
- Restrictions on delivery, storage or removal of materials.
- Adjacent land uses.
- Existing storage of hazardous materials.
- Location of existing services - water, electricity, gas, etc.
- Ground conditions.
- Existing structures - stability, or fragile materials.
- Difficulties and damage to structure, for example, height restrictions or fire damage.

b) Health hazards, including:
- Asbestos, including results of any surveys.
- Existing storage of hazardous materials.
- Contaminated land, including results of surveys.
- Existing structures, hazardous materials.
- Health risks arising from client's activities.

Significant design and construction hazards
- Design assumptions and control measures.
- Arrangements for co-ordination of on-going design work and handling design changes.
- Information on significant risks identified during design (health and safety risks).
- Materials requiring particular precautions.

The health and safety file
- Description of its format.
- Conditions relating to its content.

Format of the pre-construction information pack

If the pre-construction information is to be effective in helping to select a principal contractor, the CDM co-ordinator and any other professional advisers who put together the tender documentation will need to determine what the most suitable format for the plan is. Clearly the way the pre-construction information is included in the tender documentation and is structured is essential if responses on health and safety are to be made by prospective principal contractors.

The pre-construction information does not have to be a separate document. If the project is a large and complex one, a separate document that ensures that important information is highlighted, is appropriate. However, on small projects, some of the information outlined will already be in existing tender documentation. In this case, the key information can be highlighted in a covering letter or by use of an index pointing to which information should be considered.

THE CONSTRUCTION PHASE PLAN

The purpose of the construction phase plan is to set out how health and safety is to be managed during the construction phase. The plan is developed by the principal contractor and is the foundation on which the health and safety management of the construction work is based. The contents of the construction phase health and safety plan will depend on the nature of the project itself and be proportionate to the risks involved in the project. Many of the items in the construction phase plan reflect the information considered at the pre-construction phase, but with further consideration for the construction phase. Typically, the construction phase plan will therefore include:

Description of the project
- A description of the project and programme, this will include details of important dates.
- Details of the parties involved in the project and the extent and location of existing records and plans.

Management of the work
- The management structure and responsibilities of the various parties involved in the project, including the client, CDM co-ordinator and other members of the project team, whether based at site or elsewhere.

ELEMENT C9 - CONSTRUCTION HAZARDS AND CONTROLS

- The health and safety standards to which the project will be carried out, including health and safety goals. These may be set in terms of statutory requirements or higher standards that the client may require in particular circumstances.
- Means for informing contractors about risks to their health and safety arising from the environment in which the project is to be carried out and the construction work itself.
- Means to ensure that all contractors, the self employed and designers to be appointed by the principal contractor are properly selected (i.e. they are competent and will make adequate provision for health and safety).
- Means for communicating and passing information between the project team (including the client and any client's representatives), the designers, the CDM co-ordinator, the principal contractor, other contractors, workers on site and others whose health and safety may be affected.
- Arrangements for reporting and investigation of accidents, including passing information to the principal contractor about accidents, ill health and dangerous occurrences that require to be notified to the health and safety executive (HSE) under RIDDOR 1995.
- Arrangements for the provision and maintenance of welfare facilities.
- Arrangements for health and safety induction and training.
- Arrangements that have been made for consulting and co-ordinating the views of workers or their representatives.
- Arrangements for site rules and for bringing them to the attention of those affected.
- Arrangements for risk assessments and written systems of work.
- Emergency arrangements for dealing with and minimising the effects of injuries, fire and other dangerous occurrences.
- Arrangements should be set out for the monitoring systems to achieve compliance with legal requirements; and the health and safety rules developed by the principal contractor.

Arrangements for controlling significant site risks

- Arrangements of controls safety risks', including preventing falls, control of vehicles and safety when working with services.
- Arrangements for control of health risks, including removal of asbestos, manual handling, noise and vibration.

The health and safety file

- Layout and format.
- Arrangements for collecting information.
- Storage of information.

PROVISION OF APPROPRIATE AND RELEVANT INFORMATION TO ALL PARTIES

Relevant information must be provided to appropriate parties to ensure the health and safety of persons affected by the project, and, to assist the persons to whom information is provided to meet their duties under CDM 2007. In order to perform their duties under CDM 2007, every client must ensure that:

- Every person designing the structure that may be bidding for the work (or who intend to be engaged), is conversant with the project-specific health and safety information needed to identify hazards and risks associated with the design and construction work.
- Every contractor who has been or may be appointed by the client is promptly provided with pre-construction information in accordance with the CDM 2007.

The pre-construction information shall consist of all the information in the client's possession (or which is reasonably obtainable), including:

- Any information about or affecting the site or the construction work.
- Any information concerning the proposed use of the structure as a workplace.
- The minimum amount of time before the construction phase which will be allowed to the contractors appointed by the client for planning and preparation for construction work.
- Any information in any existing health and safety file.

PREPARATION OF THE HEALTH AND SAFETY FILE

The purpose of the health and safety file is to provide a source of information needed to allow future construction work, alterations, refurbishment and demolition, including cleaning and maintenance, to be carried out in a safe and healthy manner.

Clients, designers, principal contractors, other contractors and CDM co-ordinators all have legal duties in respect of the health and safety file:

- CDM co-ordinators must prepare, review, amend or add to the file as the project progresses, and give it to the client at the end of project.
- Clients, designers, principal contractors and other contractors must supply the information necessary for compiling or updating the file.
- Clients must keep the file to assist with future construction work.
- Everyone providing information should make sure that it is accurate, and provided promptly.

Preparing the health and safety file

The CDM co-ordinator is responsible for ensuring the health and safety file is prepared. Putting together the health and safety file is a task which should ideally be a continual process throughout the project and not left until the construction work is completed. Early on in the construction project the CDM co-ordinator may find it useful to discuss the health and safety file with the client. This will help determine what information the client requires and how the client wishes the information to be stored and recorded. When the client's requirements are known, procedures may need to be drawn up by the CDM co-ordinator so that all those who will be contributing to the health and safety file (for example, designers and contractors) are aware of:

- What information is to be collected?
- How the information is to be collected, presented and stored.

The CDM co-ordinator may find it useful to detail in the pre-construction information requirements on how and when the information for the health and safety file is to be prepared and passed on. The principal contractor may also find it useful to include similar procedures in the health and safety plan for the construction phase.

Throughout the project those who carry out design work (including contractors) will need to ensure so far as is reasonably practicable that information about any feature of the structure which will involve significant risks to health and safety during the structure's lifetime are passed to either the CDM co-ordinator or to the principal contractor.

Providing this information on drawings will allow for amendments if any variations arise during construction. It will also allow health and safety information to be stored on one document, therefore reducing the paperwork. The principal contractor may need to obtain details of services, plant and equipment which are part of the structure from specialist suppliers and installers, for example, mechanical and electrical contractors and pass this information on.

Contractors have a specific duty in CDM 2007 to pass information for the health and safety file to the principal contractor, who in turn has to pass it to the CDM co-ordinator. This information could include 'as built' and 'as installed' drawings as well as operation and maintenance manuals.

At the end of the project the CDM co-ordinator has to hand over the health and safety file to the client. In some cases it might not be possible for a fully developed file to be handed over on completion of the project. This may happen because the construction work was finished rapidly to meet a tight deadline and completion of the health and safety file was impossible. Clearly a common sense approach is needed so that the health and safety file is handed over as soon as practicable after a completion certificate or similar document has been issued.

Contents of the health and safety file

The contents of the health and safety file will vary depending on the type of structure and the future health and safety risks that will have to be managed. Typical information which may be put in the health and safety file includes:

- A brief description of the work carried out.
- Any residual hazards that remain and how they have been dealt with (for example buried services).
- Key structural principles (for example bracing or sources of stored energy).
- Hazardous materials such as lead paint or pesticides.
- Information regarding the removal or dismantling of installed plant and equipment.
- Health and safety information about equipment provided for cleaning or maintaining the structure.
- The nature, location and markings of any significant services such as underground services; fire fighting services, etc.
- Information and as-built drawings of the structure, its plant and equipment.

Future use of the health and safety file

When the project is finished and the health and safety file has been handed over by the CDM co-ordinator, the client should keep it available for those who need to use it. Usually this will include maintenance contractors, the CDM co-ordinator and contractors preparing or carrying out future construction work.

Ideally, the health and safety file should be kept available for inspection on the premises to which it relates. It may be useful to store the health and safety file so that it is in two parts. One part will be more relevant for day to day use, for example, operational and maintenance manuals.

The other part will be for longer term use, for example, drawings that will only be required when major alteration work is carried out. The health and safety file could be stored electronically, whatever form it is stored, it should be easily accessible.

For ease of reference it may be useful for the CDM co-ordinator to produce a document that summarises the main elements of the health and safety file and acts as a quick reference to where the relevant information is stored. On a project that involves work on part of a structure, for which there is no health and safety file, a file only has to be created in relation to the construction work carried out in the project, not for the whole of the structure. If the client sells all or part of the structure, the health and safety file, or the relevant parts of the health and safety file, should be passed to the new owner.

C9.3 - Working at height from fixed or temporary platforms

Working at height

See also Element C1.5 - 'Working at height' for work at height arrangements in general workplaces.

HAZARDS ASSOCIATED WITH WORKING AT HEIGHTS

Work at height is classified as anything above floor level. HSE statistics show that falls from height account for one in every four fatalities and 60% of all major injuries resulted from falls from a height of less than 2m. The nature and range of the hazards will depend on the location and work activity involved with the work at height.

There are four main types of hazard associated with work at height:

- Falls of persons.
- Falling objects.
- Contact with or crushed against structures.
- Access to normally inaccessible hazards, for example, overhead power cables.

Whether a fall is liable to cause injury may depend on:

- The height of the fall.
- Dangers associated with falling onto or into material below.
- Dangers associated with passing traffic.
- Whether there is rough or uneven ground.
- The type of structure and its security.

Risks related to work activities at height are increased by the presence of fragile roofs, roof lights, voids, deteriorating materials and the weather. Typically 20% of those killed in accidents on construction sites are involved in roof work. Some fall off the edge of flat or sloping roofs but many are killed by falling through fragile materials.

Asbestos cement, fibreglass and plastic deteriorate with age and become more fragile. Similarly, steel sheets may rust or may not be supported properly. This presents a serious risk to workers who work on these materials without means to prevent falls. Adverse weather can have a significant effect on the safety of those working at a height. Rain, snow and ice increase the risk of slips and falling from a roof. When handling large objects, such as roof panels, high wind can be a serious problem and may cause the person to be blown off the roof.

Extremely cold temperatures can increase the likelihood of brittle failure of materials and therefore increase the likelihood of failure of roof supports, scaffold components and plastic roof lights.

Figure C9-2: Working above ground level. *Source: RMS.*

Safe use of temporary (immobile) access equipment

There are many forms of access equipment, some of which are mobile in that they move under their own means or can be towed, notably mobile elevating work platforms (MEWPS). Other access equipment, although it can be moved from place to place, does not have its own means to move and is therefore immobile, for example, ladders, trestles and scaffolds.

LADDERS

Ladders are primarily a means of vertical access to a workplace. However, they are often used to carry out work and this frequently results in accidents. Many accidents involving ladders happen during work lasting 30 minutes or less. Ladders are often used for short jobs when it would be safer to use other equipment, for example, mobile scaffold towers or MEWPs. Generally, ladders should be considered as access equipment and use of a ladder as a work platform should be discouraged.

There are situations when working from a ladder would be inappropriate, for example:

- When two hands are needed or the work area is large.
- Where the equipment or materials used are large or awkward.
- Excessive height.
- Work of long duration.
- Where the ladder cannot be secured or made stable.
- Where the ladder cannot be protected from vehicles etc.
- Adverse weather conditions.

CONSTRUCTION HAZARDS AND CONTROLS - ELEMENT C9

Figure C9-3: Ladder not tied or footed. *Source: RMS.*

Figure C9-4: Improper use. *Source: RMS.*

Before using a ladder to work from, consider whether it is the right equipment for the job and give consideration to the following:

- Pre-use inspection. Make sure the ladder is in good condition. Check the rungs and stiles for warping, cracking or splintering, the condition of the feet, and for any other defects. Do not use defective or painted ladders.
- Position the ladder properly for safe access and out of the way of vehicles.
- Ladders must stand on a firm, level base, be positioned approximately at an angle of 75° (1 unit horizontally to 4 units vertically) and extend about 1 metre above the landing place. Do not rest ladders against fragile surfaces.
- Ladders must be properly tied near the top, even if only in use for a short time. If not tied, ladders must be secured near the bottom, footed or weighted. Footing is not considered effective on ladders longer than five metres. While being tied, a ladder must be footed.
- Keep both hands free to grip the ladder when climbing or descending, with only one person on the ladder at any time. Beware of wet, greasy or icy rungs and make sure soles of footwear are clean.

Figure C9-5: Poor storage. *Source: Lincsafe.*

Figure C9-6: Stepladder. *Source: RMS.*

Stepladders require careful use. They are subject to the same general health and safety rules as ladders. However, in addition, they will not withstand any degree of side loading and overturn very easily. Over-reaching is to be avoided at all costs.

The top step of a stepladder should not be used as a working platform unless it has been specifically designed for that purpose. Ladder stays must be 'locked out' properly before use.

TRESTLES

Trestles are pre-fabricated steel, aluminium or wood supports, of approximately 500 mm - 1 metre width, that may be of fixed height or may be height adjustable by means of sliding struts with varying fixing points (pin

ELEMENT C9 - CONSTRUCTION HAZARDS AND CONTROLS

method) or various cross bars to suit the height required. They are used with scaffold boards or similar platform material to span from one trestle to the other in order to make a work platform.

These can only be used where work cannot be carried out from the ground but where a scaffold would be impracticable.

A good example of where a trestle may be used would be where a plasterer who is installing and plastering a new ceiling. Typical working heights when using a trestle system range from 300 mm to 1 metre, but can be up to above 4 metres.

Edge protection should be fitted wherever practical. As with any work carried out above ground level, a risk assessment, as required by the Management of Health and Safety at Work Regulations (MHSWR) 1999, should be carried out and consideration given to the application of the Work at Height Regulations (WAH) 2005 and/or the Construction (Design and Management) Regulations (CDM) 2007 and/or the Workplace (Health, Safety and Welfare) Regulations (WHSWR) 1992.

There are many configurations of locking and adjustable trestles. Platforms based on trestles should be fully boarded, adequately supported and provided with edge protection where appropriate. Safe means of access should be provided to trestle platforms, usually by stepladders.

Always
- Set up the equipment on a firm, level, non-slip surface.
- On soft ground, stand the equipment on boards to stop it sinking in.
- Place each trestle at 1.5m intervals which allows the scaffold boards to be adequately supported.
- Then open each up to the height required, ensure the locking pins are properly located.

Never
- Do anything that involves applying a lot of side force. The trestle could topple over.
- The maximum safe working load of a scaffold board is 150 Kg evenly spaced.
- The total weight of the user and tools must not exceed this.
- When moving to a new site, carry the equipment with care.
- Never use steps, boxes etc. to gain extra height.

SCAFFOLDS

Independent

The independent tied scaffold is classified into three main types:

- ***Light duty*** - only one platform is used at any one time. The distributed load and height are restricted to $73kg/m^2$ and 61 metres respectively. This scaffold is used for stone cleaning or painting.
- ***General purpose*** - up to four platforms can be used. The distributed load to be carried by the scaffold depends on how far apart the standards are, i.e. the wider apart the less the load which can be supported. At 2.1 metres apart the maximum load should be $180kg/m^2$ and at 2.5 metres apart is reduced to $145kg/m^2$, with the maximum recommended height being 46 metres. This scaffold is for general work with loaded materials.
- ***Heavy duty*** - there are two heavy duty working platforms, maximum distributed load $290kg/m^2$. The maximum recommended height is 46 metres. This is used for heavy masonry work or when large building blocks are used.

As the independent tied scaffold depends on the integrity of the ground to carry the scaffold's full weight, including the materials it might support, it is vital that the weight is spread with the use of base plates and sole boards. This helps to prevent the narrow ended standards being forced into the ground by the weight placed on them.

The independent tied scaffold has a double row of standards. The inner row should be set far enough out from the building to allow working clearance and to lay one width of scaffold board along its length. The outer standards should be set at a distance suitable for the number of boards used on the working platform.

Platform widths can vary from three to seven boards:

- 3 boards - for footing, i.e. for persons to work without materials deposited or as a gangway.
- 4 boards - for footing and storing materials.
- 5 boards - for general work.
- 6 boards - for masons and their materials.
- 7 boards - for masons using trestles.
- All boards must be secured so they do not lift in high winds.

The working platform must be fitted with toe-boards and guardrails. The toe-boards are to help prevent materials falling off and injuring someone. They also help to prevent persons rolling off the platform or their feet slipping off the edge.

Guardrails must be fitted around the working platform, inside the standards, at a height of between 0.9 metres and 1.14 metres.

CONSTRUCTION HAZARDS AND CONTROLS - ELEMENT C9

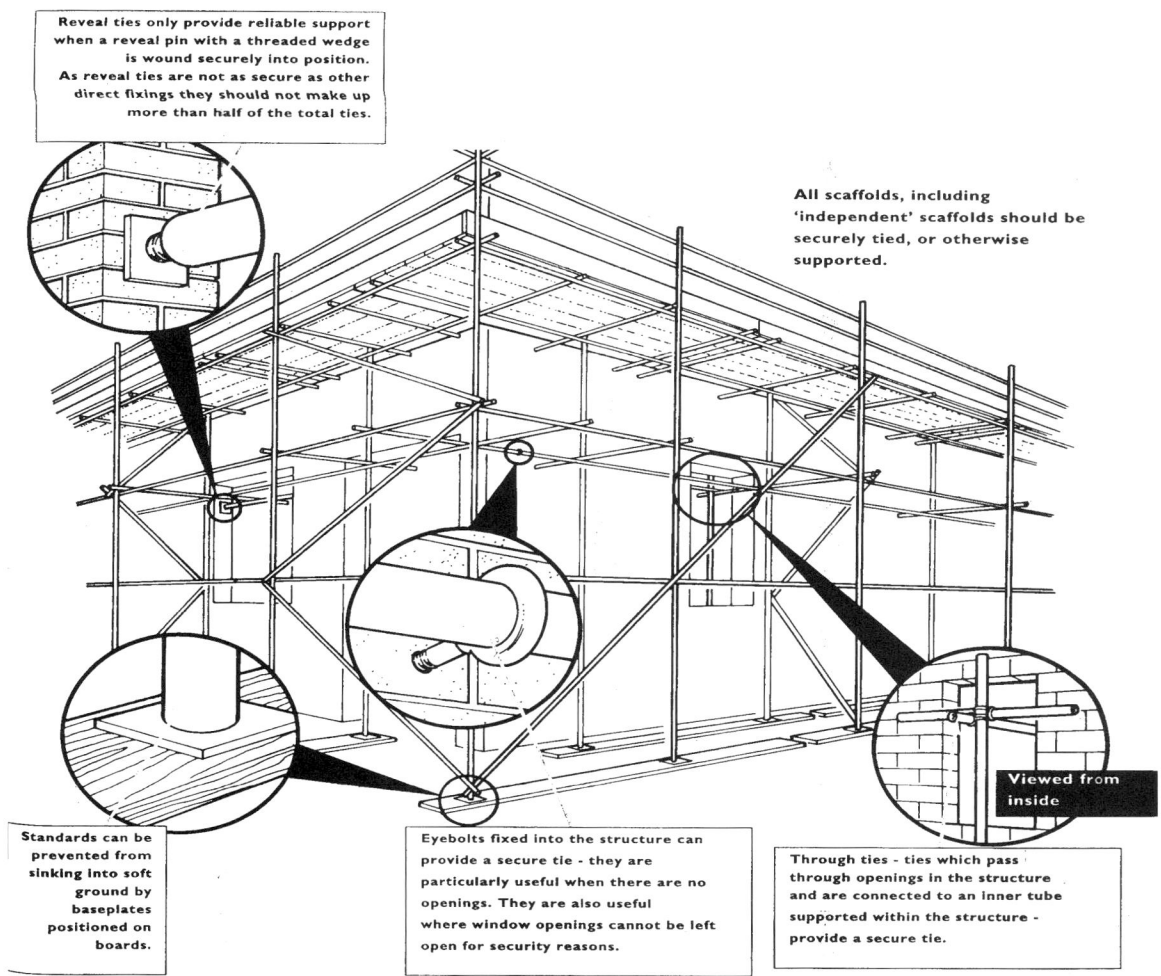

Figure C9-7: Scaffolds.
Source: HSG150.

The standards are set in the vertical position with the ledgers at right angles, running horizontally across the face of the scaffold. The transoms run horizontally from the front to the wall of the building. They are used for supports for the working platforms and to keep the rows of standards evenly spaced. Bracing is used to give stiffness to the structure and may be diagonal/transverse or longitudinal. The stabilising link to the structure is the ties. There are three methods that can be used: through ties, reveal ties and permanent ties. A ***through tie*** is a tube bearing on the inside face of the wall that is used for tying in. At least 50% of the fixings should be through ties as these are the safest.

Reveal ties are where a tube is wedged between two opposite surfaces and a reveal pin is used to make jacking adjustments. As reveal ties are not considered safe, special bolts may be used. They can have their shanks expanded into the face of the building and the scaffold can be secured to them. Permanent ties are also used. These are set into the building during construction to allow future scaffolds to be set up.

Tower scaffolds

A tower scaffold can become unstable very easily so certain factors are considered essential when it is in use:

- It must be set up for use on level ground.
- Access must be by the ladder fitted to the inside of the scaffold and not by climbing up the outside structure.
- The wheels must be turned outwards, which increases the base area, and locked into position.
- When the scaffold is to be moved, it must only be done by pushing or pulling at the base.
- The scaffold should never be moved when either workers or materials are on the platform.

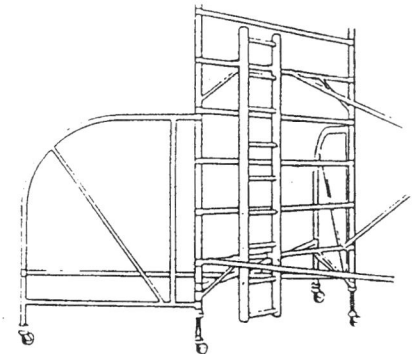

Figure C9-8: Clip-in vertical ladder for 'Span-Type' tower scaffold.
Source: Ambiguous.

The tall, relatively narrow structure of a tower scaffold makes it inherently unstable unless the rules and guidelines are followed. Used correctly, they allow safe access to large areas.

© RMS 327

ELEMENT C9 - CONSTRUCTION HAZARDS AND CONTROLS

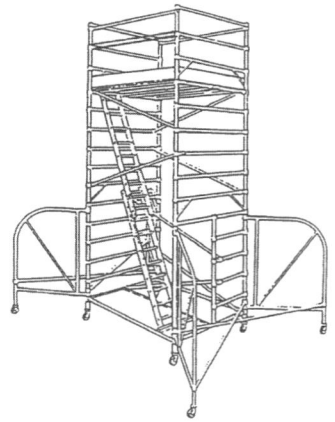
A proprietary tower scaffold with outriggers.

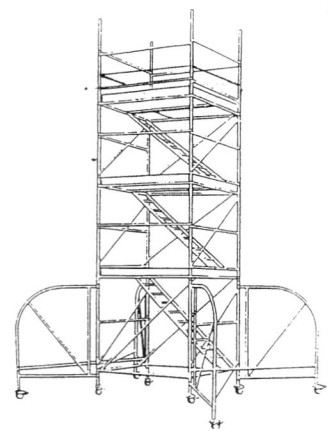
Internal stairway.

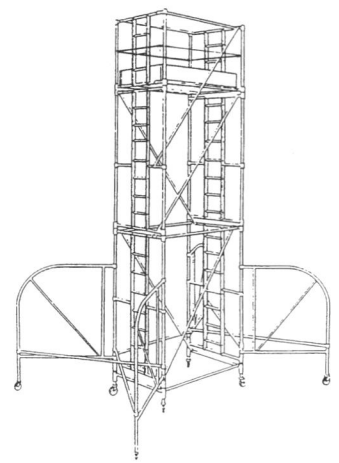
Ladder Section integral with 'Span-Type' frame member.

Figure C9-9: Tower scaffolds.

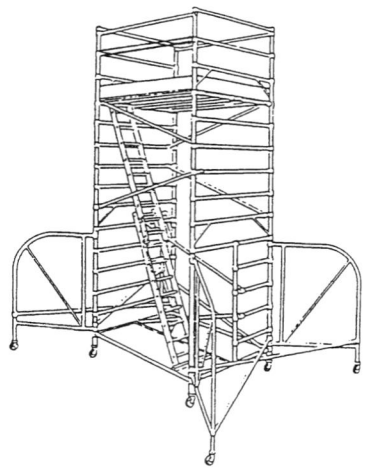
Inclined ladder for 'Span-Type' tower scaffold.

Source: Ambiguous.

The requirements for the erection, use and dismantling of scaffolds and falsework

SCAFFOLDS

Scaffold should be designed, erected, altered and dismantled by competent people, with all scaffolding work under the supervision of a 'competent person'.

Scaffold erectors must erect and dismantle scaffold in a way that minimises the risk of falling of people or materials. Where practicable scaffold erectors should erect intermediate platforms, with guard rails and toe boards, to enable them to build the next scaffold 'lift' safely.

If a platform is not practicable falls must be prevented (or their effects minimised) by other means, such as the use of a safety harness or similar fall arrest equipment.

Scaffolds must be inspected by a competent person:

- Before first use.
- After substantial alteration.
- After any event likely to have affected their stability, for example, following a collision, exposed to strong winds.
- At regular intervals not exceeding seven days.

To ensure safe use of scaffolds, workers must:

- Not take up boards.
- Move handrails or remove ties to gain access for work.
- Not modify the design.
- Not work from platforms that are not fully boarded.
- Not overload scaffolds.
- Store materials so the load is spread evenly.
- Ensure there is suitable stair and ladder access onto the working platform.

FALSEWORK

Falsework is any temporary structure used to support a permanent structure while it is not self-supporting, either in new construction or refurbishment. All falsework should be designed for the purpose of its use. The extent of the design will vary from the use of simple standard solution tables and graphs, to site-specific design and supporting drawings.

Before erection begins a risk assessment should be carried out and a safe system of work developed. A method statement that includes how all the hazards are to be managed should be prepared. This should be read and understood by those doing the work.

Erectors should understand:

- The method statement.
- When checks or permits are required.
- The correct materials to be used.
- They must not use unapproved substitutes.

Figure C9-10: Falsework. *Source: BMA Construction Engineers Inc.*

Once complete, all falsework should be inspected and certified as ready for use, including loading, which should be appropriate for the task (a written permit-to-load procedure should be considered). The frequency of subsequent inspections will depend on the nature of the temporary works. They should be carried out frequently enough to enable any faults to be rectified promptly.

The temporary works co-ordinator should agree the time of striking (removal) for each section of the falsework and a written permit-to-strike procedure should be used. A sequence for dismantling should be agreed and detailed. During dismantling, it is important to ensure that workers can work safely and cannot be injured by falling objects.

Inspection of working platforms above 2 metres

Regulation 12 of the Work at Height Regulations (WAH) 2005 sets out the requirements for inspection of working platforms above 2 metres. Those in control of workplaces must ensure inspections of working platforms above 2 metes are carried out by a competent person. All employers and people in control of construction work should make sure that places of work are safe before they allow their workers to use them for the first time or stop work if the inspection shows it is not safe to continue.

GENERAL

The general requirements for inspections are:

- The inspection report should be completed by a competent person before the end of the relevant working period.
- The person who prepares the report should, within 24 hours, provide either the report or a copy to the person on whose behalf the inspection was carried out.
- The report should be kept on site until work is complete. It should then be retained for three months at an office of the person for whom the inspection was carried out.

WORKING PLATFORMS ONLY

The general requirements for inspection of working platforms above 2 metres are:

- Any inspection is only required where a person is liable to fall more than two metres from a place of work.
- Any employer or any other person who controls the activities of people using a scaffold shall ensure that it is stable and of sound construction and that the relevant safeguards are in place before their employees or people under their control first use the scaffold.
- No report is required following the inspection of any mobile tower scaffold which remains in the same place for less than seven days.
- A report is required where an inspection of a working platform or part thereof or any personal suspension equipment is carried out:
  i) Before it is taken into use for the first time.
  ii) After any substantial addition, dismantling or other alteration.

A report is not needed following every inspection, but is required where:

- A tower scaffold if it stays in the same place for seven days or more.
- An inspection of a working platform or any personal suspension equipment is carried out:
  - Before being used for the first time.
  - After any substantial addition, dismantling or other alteration.

Not more than one report is required for any 24 hour period.

The report must include the following information:
1) Name and address of person for whom the inspection is carried out.
2) Location of the work equipment.
3) Description of the work equipment.
4) Date and time of inspection.
5) Details of any matter identified that could give rise to a risk to the health and safety of any person.
6) Details of any action taken as a result of 5 above.
7) Details of any further action considered necessary.
8) Name and position of the person making the report.

Hazards associated with falling materials and appropriate precautionary measures

HAZARDS

The hazards associated with falling materials include part of a structure being constructed or demolished falling from a height while being fitted or removed, tools in use being dropped, materials and tools being knocked from a working platform. The hazards also include materials and equipment deliberately dropped from a height to remove them from the building or as part of the dismantling process, for example, parts of a scaffold that are no longer required. A further hazard may arise due to weather conditions, where materials are blown off part of a structure.

PRECAUTIONS

The Work at Height Regulations (WAH) 2005, Regulation 10, specifies the following requirements to avoid injury from falling objects:

"Every employer shall, where necessary to prevent injury to any person, take suitable and sufficient steps to prevent, so far as is reasonably practicable, the fall of any material or object.

Where it is not reasonably practicable to comply with the requirements of paragraph (1), every employer shall take suitable and sufficient steps to prevent any person being struck by any falling material or object which is liable to cause personal injury.

Figure C9-11: Hazards associated with falling materials.
Source: RMS.

Every employer shall ensure that no material or object is thrown or tipped from height in circumstances where it is liable to cause injury to any person.

Every employer shall ensure that materials and objects are stored in such a way as to prevent risk to any person arising from the collapse, overturning or unintended movement of such materials or objects".

In order to prevent harm from falling objects care should be taken to avoid leaving materials on the roof when the site is closed, especially at weekends and during holiday periods. If materials are left on the roof ensure that they are secured so that they cannot be blown off the roof by windy weather.

Toe boards should be placed around the roof perimeter. Control other trades' access to areas underneath roofing work, unless protection such as debris netting is provided, which ensures protection for anyone working underneath.

Figure C9-12: Chute for falling materials.
Source: Midland Power Hoists.

In addition, methods provided should prevent materials or other objects rolling, or being kicked, off the edges of platforms. This may be done with solid barriers, brick guards, or similar at open edges. If working in a public place, nets, fans or covered walkways may be needed to give extra protection for people who may be passing below.

High-visibility barrier netting is not suitable for use as a fall prevention device. Materials such as old slates, tiles etc should not be thrown from the roof or scaffold - passers-by may be at risk of being injured. Enclosed debris chutes should be used or debris lowered in containers.

Safe methods of roof work

Fragile roofs

On any fragile or angled roof (greater than 30°) or on any roof which is considered hazardous because of its condition or because of the weather, suitable crawling boards must be used. They must be correctly positioned and secure. If it is obvious that the job requires a progression along the roof, extra crawling boards must be provided and no fewer than two such boards shall be taken on any job.

Flat roofs

Work on a flat roof is high risk. People can fall:

- From the edge of a completed roof.
- From the edge where work is being carried out.
- Through openings or gaps.

Edge protection for flat roofs

Unless the roof parapet provides equivalent safety, temporary edge protection will be required during most work on flat roofs. Both the roof edge and any openings in it need to be protected. It will often be more appropriate to securely cover openings rather than put edge protection around them. Any protection should be:

- In place from start to finish of the work.
- Strong enough to withstand people and materials falling against it.

Where possible the edge protection should be supported at ground level, for example, by scaffold standards, so that there is no obstruction on the roof. If the building is too high for this, the roof edge up-stand can support the edge protection provided it is strong enough. Edge protection can also be supported by frames, counterweights or scaffolding on the roof. The protection should be in place at all times. Guarding systems are widely available that enable roof repair work to carry on without removing any guard rails.

Short-duration work on flat roofs

Short-duration means a matter of minutes rather than hours. It includes such jobs as brief inspections or adjusting a television aerial. Work on a flat roof is dangerous even if it only lasts a short time. Appropriate safety measures are essential. It may not be reasonably practicable to provide edge protection during short-duration work. In such cases anyone working nearer than 2 metre to any unguarded edge should be using a safety harness. Where safety harnesses are used they need to be:

- Appropriate for the user and in good condition - full harnesses are essential, safety belts are not sufficient.
- Securely attached to an anchorage point of sufficient strength.
- Fitted with as short a lanyard as possible that enables wearers to do their work (significant management discipline is needed to ensure this).

Demarcating safe areas

Full edge protection may not be necessary if limited work on a larger roof involves nobody going any closer than 2 metres to an open edge. In such cases demarcated areas can be set up to limit the area where work can be conducted safely.

Demarcated areas should be:

- Limited to areas from which nobody can fall.
- Indicated by an obvious physical barrier (full edge protection is not necessary but a painted line or bunting is not sufficient).
- Subject to a high level of supervision to make sure that nobody strays outside them (demarcation areas are unacceptable if this standard is not achieved).

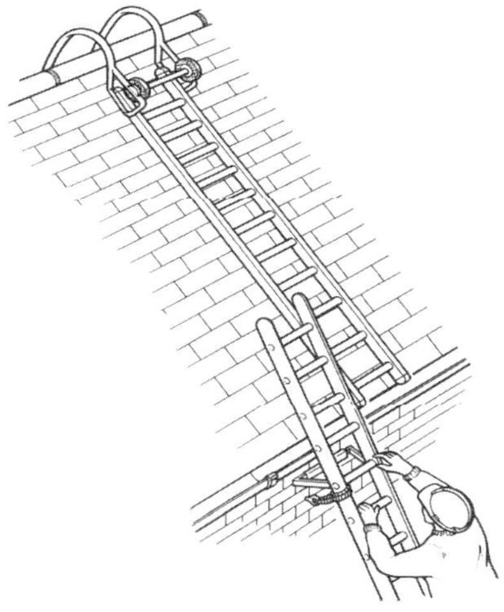

Sloping roofs

Figure C9-13: Use of roof ladders. *Source: HSG150, HSE.*

On traditional pitched roofs most people fall:

- From eaves.
- By slipping down the roof and then over the eaves.
- Through the roof internally, for example during roof truss erection.
- From gable ends.

ELEMENT C9 - CONSTRUCTION HAZARDS AND CONTROLS

Edge protection for sloping roofs

Full edge protection at eaves level will normally be required for work on sloping roofs. The edge protection needs to be strong enough to withstand a person falling against it.

The longer the slope and the steeper the pitch the stronger the edge protection needs to be.

A properly designed and installed independent scaffold platform at eaves level will usually be enough.

Less substantial scaffolding barriers (rather than platforms) may not be strong enough for work on larger or steeper roofs, especially slopes in excess of 30°. On some larger roofs, the consequences of sliding down the whole roof and hitting the eaves edge protection may be such that intermediate platforms at the work site are needed to prevent this happening. If the work requires access within 2 metres of gable ends, edge protection will be needed there as well as at the eaves. Powered access platforms can provide good access as an alternative to fixed edge protection. They can be particularly useful in short-duration work.

Figure C9-14: Access system for roof work.   *Source: HSE, HSG284.*

Means of temporary access types and safety features

CRADLES

Before use

- Equipment is installed, modified and dismantled only by competent specialists.
- There is a current report of thorough examination for the equipment.
- A handover certificate is provided by the installer. The certificate should cover how to deal with emergencies, operate, check and maintain the equipment, and state its safe working load.
- Areas of the site where people may be struck by the cradle or falling materials have been fenced off or similar. Debris fans or covered walkways may also be required.
- Systems are in place to prevent people within the building being struck by the cradle as it rises or descends and prevent the cradle coming into contact with open windows or similar obstructions which could cause it to tip.

Figure C9-15: Cradle.   *Source: www.apollocradles.co.uk.*

- Supports are protected from damage (for example, by being struck by passing vehicles or by interference from vandals).
- Check the shift report for warnings of malfunction.
- Should not be used in adverse weather. High winds will create instability. Establish a maximum safe wind speed for operation. Storms, snow falls and ice accumulation can also damage platforms, so they should be inspected before use after severe weather.
- Only trained personnel are to operate.

At the end of each day

- All power has been switched off and, where appropriate, power cables have been secured and made dead.
- The equipment is secured where it will not be accessible to vandals or trespassers.
- Notices are attached to the equipment warning that it is out of service and must not be used.
- Report and log any defects or malfunctions.

BOATSWAINS' CHAIRS

Boatswains' chairs and seats can be used for light, short-term work. The chair is distinguished from a climbing harness by the inclusion of a rigid seat, providing more comfort than padded straps for long-term use.

The boatswains chair does not allow the freedom of movement necessary for climbing, and the occupant is generally hoisted or lowered into place using the rope alone. They should only be used where it is not practicable to provide a working platform.

Before use

- Installation and use of boatswain's chair to be supervised by trained, experienced and competent person.
- Chair and associated equipment carefully examined for defects.
- Confirm test/examination certificates are valid. Establish safe working load.
- Check that user is both trained and competent in the use of the chair.
- Warning notice displayed and notification of intention to carry out work given.
- Prohibit access to the area below the chair in case materials fall.

In use

- Free of material or articles which could interfere with user's hand-hold.
- The fall rope must be properly tied off in use and always under or around a cleat to act as a brake.

Figure C9-16: Boatswains chair. *Source: Photo, Pete Verdon.*

After use

Chairs and rope should be left in a safe condition:

- Top rope secured.
- Chair and rope secured to prevent swing.
- Raised when out of use or for overnight storage.
- Inspected for defects.
- Ropes (and chair, if timber) dried before storage.

ROPE ACCESS AND POSITIONING SYSTEMS

Rope access

Rope access use a form of personal suspension equipment and is often known as abseiling. This technique is usually used for inspection and cleaning work rather than construction work. Like a boatswain's chair, it should only be used when a working platform cannot be provided. If rope access is necessary, then ensure that:

- A competent person has installed the equipment.
- The user is fully trained.
- There is more than one point securing the equipment.
- Tools and equipment are securely attached and the area below cordoned off.
- The main rope and safety rope are attached to separate points.

Figure C9-17: Personal suspension equipment. *Source: RMS.*

Positioning systems

Terms such as 'safety belts' and 'lanyards' have been replaced with references to 'personal fall arrest', 'personal fall restraint' or 'positioning systems' or 'personal fall protection systems'.

The Work at Height Regulations (WAH) 2005, schedule 5, part 3, 'Additional requirements for rope access and positioning techniques' state that:

A rope access or positioning technique shall be used only if:

- It involves a system comprising of at least two separately anchored lines, of which one ("the working line") is used as a means of access, egress and support and the other is the safety line.
- The user is provided with a suitable harness and is connected by it to the working line and the safety line.
- The working line is equipped with safe means of ascent and descent and has a self-locking system to prevent the user falling should he lose control of his movements.
- The safety line is equipped with a mobile fall protection system which is connected to and travels with the user of the system.

The system may comprise a single rope where a risk assessment has demonstrated that the use of a second line would entail higher risk to persons and appropriate measures have been taken to ensure the safety of the user.

ELEMENT C9 - CONSTRUCTION HAZARDS AND CONTROLS

The use, application, selection and precautions in use of personal and collective fall arrest devices

The Work at Height Regulations (WAH) 2005, Schedule 4, 'Requirements for collective safeguards for arresting falls' requires that:

"A safeguard shall only be used if a risk assessment has demonstrated its effectiveness and it is not reasonably practicable to use other safer work equipment and a sufficient number of persons have received adequate training in its use, including rescue procedures. In the event of a fall the safeguard does not itself cause injury to that person.

A safeguard shall be of suitable and sufficient strength to arrest the fall of any person safely and if it is designed to be attached, be securely attached to all the required anchors. In the case of an airbag, landing mat or similar, be stable in use; and in the case of a safeguard which distorts, in arresting a fall, for example, a safety net, afford sufficient clearance to prevent injury by its distortion".

SAFETY NETS

Safety nets are used in a variety of applications where other forms of protection are reasonably impracticable - such as steel erecting and roof work where site personnel are at risk of falling through fragile roofs onto solid surfaces or structures (steel work) below.

Safety nets will arrest the fall of an individual preventing an impact that may cause injury or death. Safety nets must be installed beneath the work area, as a minimum, and consideration should be given to an extension of the protection to allow for people working outside the planned area.

Safety nets should only to be installed under supervision by competent installers and should be inspected weekly and checked daily as the build height progresses.

Figure C9-18: Safety nets. Source: RMS.

Relocation of the nets will be necessary if the build height increases to keep the fall distance to a minimum.

It should be remembered that some nets are used to collect debris that may fall. These may be rigged to take a lesser weight than that for protection of people. It is important to identify which type of net is in use in a workplace as reliance on the wrong type may have fatal consequences.

AIR BAGS

Airbags are shock absorption devices that can be employed to protect against the effects of falls from a height. They are made of a toughened nylon, or similar man-made material, and are usually inflated using a powered fan device.

They are designed so that should a person fall onto one, a volume of air is forced out of the bag creating a cushioning effect that does not bounce or deflect the person in another direction. This equipment must be matched to correspond to the fall height and as such must only be put into use by a competent person.

SOFT FALL BEANBAGS

Soft fall bean bags use a soft polymer bean to reduce the effect of a fall from up to two metres. The system is used in both traditional building and timber frame constructions.

Figure C9-19: Soft fall arrest system.
Source: www.sitesafetysolutions.co.uk.

Figure C9-20: Soft fall arrest system.
Source: www.sitesafetysolutions.co.uk.

334 © RMS

The bags are lightweight (approximately weighing 6-7 kg per bag) and can be used in two layers to reduce the potential fall height. They are simple to install, low cost and maintenance free, and can be easily moved around the site and onto the next project. The size of each interlocking unit is typically 2.5 metres x 550 mm x 550 mm.

BELTS AND HARNESSES

There may be circumstances in which it is not practicable for guard rails etc to be provided, for example, where guard rails are taken down for short periods to land materials. In this situation if people approach an open edge from which they would be liable to fall two metres or more, a suitably attached harness and temporary horizontal lifeline could allow safe working. When using harnesses and temporary horizontal lifelines, ensure:

- An emergency rescue system must be in place before a harness and lanyard is used to protect against a fall. The rescue team must be trained to carry out the rescue procedure and in how to deal with a person who is possibly unconscious. The rescue will need to be initiated rapidly (for example, within 15 minutes) to reduce the risk of suspension trauma, a postural hypertension which occurs when the blood pressure drops significantly (the trauma is primarily caused by gravity-induced blood pooling in the lower extremities, which in turn reduces venous return i.e. blood back to the heart, resulting in decreased cardiac output and subsequent lowering of arterial pressure).
- The harness and lanyards are made of man-made fibres and as such are prone to degradation by sunlight, chemicals etc. It is important to carry out tactile pre-use checks daily, in good light, before taking harnesses and lanyards into use. A suspect defective harness or lanyard should not be used. Defects can include discolouration, minor tears, nicks and grittiness to touch.
- A harness will not prevent a fall - it can only minimise the injury if there is a fall. The person who falls may be injured by the impact load to the body when the line goes tight or when they strike against parts of the structure during the fall. An energy absorber fitted to the energy-absorbing lanyard can reduce the risk of injury from impact loads.
- Where possible the energy-absorbing lanyard should be attached above the wearer to reduce the fall distance. Extra free movement can be provided by running temporary horizontal lifelines or inertia reels. Any attachment point must be capable of withstanding the impact load in the event of a fall. Consider how to recover anyone who does fall.
- Anyone who needs to attach themselves should be able to do so from a safe position. They need to be able to attach themselves before they move into a position where they are relying on the protection provided by the harness.
- To ensure that there is an adequate fall height to allow the system to operate and arrest the fall.
- A twin lanyard may be necessary in some cases where the wearer needs to move about. A twin lanyard allows the wearer to clip on one lanyard in a different position before unclipping the other lanyard.
- Installation of equipment to which harnesses will be fixed, for example a suitable anchor, must be inspected regularly.
- Everyone who uses a harness must be instructed in how to check, wear and adjust it before use and how to connect themselves to the structure or safety line as appropriate.
- They should be thoroughly examined at intervals of no more than every six months.

Retractable type fall arresters tested against EN360 are tested with a 100 Kg mass and have to produce an arrest force of less than 6 kN. Therefore users greater than 100 Kg (15 stone 10 lbs.) should refer to the manufacturer's instruction for use and if not covered within the instruction should contact the manufacturer for information for users weighing greater than 100 Kg.

C9.4 - Demolition work

Main techniques in demolition of buildings and the associated hazards and safe working practices

MAIN TECHNIQUES FOR DEMOLITION OF BUILDINGS

Balling machines

Considerable skill is necessary in the use of a demolition ball. The ball is a large steel, pear-shaped device, which is suspended from the jib of an appliance.

The demolition ball can be used in three main ways:

- Raised to a height and allowed to fall vertically onto the structure.
- Swung forward into the structure in line with the jib of the appliance.
- Swung sideways by slewing the jib of the appliance.

Cranes should only be used for the vertical drop method. Crane jibs are not designed to withstand the stresses created by sideways drag or forward swinging. Excavators which can be converted into a 'crane' for drag line operations are more suited to the task.

ELEMENT C9 - CONSTRUCTION HAZARDS AND CONTROLS

Piecemeal

Piecemeal demolition is done by hand using hand held tools and is sometimes a preliminary to other methods. It can be completed or begun by machines. For example, when demolishing a tall chimney with occupied buildings in close proximity, the job may commence by dismantling by hand - brick by brick. When the structure has been reduced to about 10 metres, conventional heavy equipment can then be used.

Controlled collapse and pre-weakening

Deliberate controlled collapse involves the pre-weakening of the structure or building. This involves removing key structural members so the remaining structure collapses under its own weight.

There are several problems associated with this method of demolition:

- The structure may collapse to a greater extent than was anticipated.
- The planned collapse may only be a partial collapse and could leave the structure hazardous and insecure.
- The resultant debris may be projected over a wider area than anticipated.
- The pile of debris that is left after the collapse of the structure may be in a dangerous condition, presenting a serious risk to those who remove it.

One method of removing the key structural members is overturning by wire rope pulling. Wires are attached to the main supports, which are pulled away using a heavy tracked vehicle or a winch to provide the motive power. The area must be cleared of workers for this operation and there must be enough clearance for the vehicle to move the distance required to pull out the structural supports.

Problems associated with this method arise when the wire becomes overstressed. If it breaks, then whiplash can occur which can have the force to slice through the human body. The forces applied may be enough to overturn the winch or the tracked vehicle. Another problem can occur when the action of pulling has begun and there is inadequate power to complete it.

Use of explosives

The use of explosives requires the expertise of an experienced explosives engineer. Also, the HSE should be consulted to ensure compliance with the Control of Explosives Regulations (COER) 1991 (as amended by the Manufacture and Storage of Explosives Regulations 2005). There are a number of factors to be considered for safe demolition with the use of explosives, which include:

- The local and structural conditions must be considered when fixing the size of the charges. The structure to be blasted can be divided into a number of sections and suitable charges applied to each section.
- Shot holes should be drilled electrically. Drilling pneumatically could cause vibration which could result in premature collapse.
- Charges should not be placed near cast iron as it easily shatters into shrapnel (scattered metal fragments).
- The area around the structure being demolished and the firing point should be barricaded and unauthorised persons not allowed to enter.
- The demolition engineer must be satisfied that no dangerous situation or condition has been left or created.
- The danger zone must be barricaded until rendered safe.

Figure C9-21: Hydraulic demolition jaws. *Source: RMS.*

Figure C9-22: Hydraulic demolition grapple. *Source: RMS.*

TYPICAL HAZARDS

Demolition is probably the most hazardous operation undertaken in the construction industry. The principal hazards are:

- Falls of men, falls of materials, flying materials, dust and debris, resulting in a wide range of injuries and conditions, some of which are of a fatal nature.
- Premature collapse of a building or structure, either deliberately or unplanned.

CONSTRUCTION HAZARDS AND CONTROLS - ELEMENT C9

- Overloading of floors or the structure with debris, resulting in floor and/or building collapse.
- Explosions in tanks or other confined spaces.
- The presence of live electric cable or gas mains.
- The presence of dusty, corrosive and poisonous materials and/or atmospheres.
- Projecting nails in timber etc., broken glass and cast iron fragments which can penetrate the hands, feet and parts of the body.

SAFE WORKING PRACTICES

Falling materials

Protective screens and where appropriate fans should be set up around scaffolds around buildings undergoing demolition, to prevent debris falling on to passers-by. Fans are scaffold boards fixed on scaffold tubes set at an upward angle out from a scaffold in order to catch debris that may fall from the scaffold. They may be provided at the entrances to buildings to protect persons entering and leaving the building that the scaffold is erected against.

They are also used where a scaffold is erected alongside a pedestrian walkway where there is a need to have an increased confidence that materials that might fall cannot contact people below. In some cases it may be necessary for horizontal barriers to be erected to direct pedestrians under the fan.

Figure C9-23: Fans. *Source: RMS.*

In some cases it may be necessary for horizontal barriers to be erected to direct pedestrians under the fan. In addition, brick guards, debris nets and sheeting will help to contain falling materials and prevent them falling outside the framework of a scaffold erected as part of the demolition process.

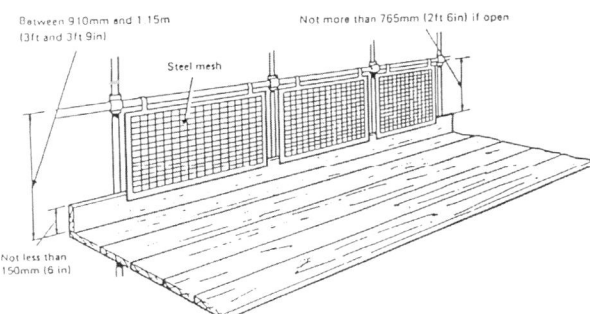

There must be a clearly demarcated area where workers can tell that the specific area of the structure is being worked on and that the work in that area has a risk from falling materials. This includes buildings being demolished by hand, where a safe access route to the work place must be maintained. Warning of planned demolition stages by use of audible and visual warnings will assist in removing people from the hazards area at this time. Head protection is an essential last line of defence for workers in this environment.

Figure C9-24: Brick guards. *Source: HSG150 Safety in Construction.*

Premature collapse of buildings

The technical advances in mechanical plant have considerably reduced the risk to demolition workers of working at a height. Modern machines can be fitted with scissor jaws that can break down a wall in small pieces. Another benefit of scissor jaws is that there is less likelihood of major structural damage or premature collapse. The likelihood of premature collapse remains a consideration when using the ball and chain method or carrying out partial demolition.

Figure C9-25: Protection of public. *Source: RMS.*

In some cases the façade of a building may be left intact for renovation and the rest of the structure removed. In these circumstances great care must be taken to avoid freestanding walls and to provide adequate support to the structure.

Materials of construction

The materials of construction may present a direct hazard during demolition in that they may be sharp, toxic, flammable or heavy.

- The presence of asbestos should be determined because its removal will require specialist treatment. The workers must have appropriate clothing and respirators.
- Special hazards during demolition will need to be identified, for example, reinforced concrete, pre-stressed members, arches, structural steelwork, etc.

- It is important to know the previous use of the buildings. They may still contain toxic or flammable materials or even radioactive materials or sources.

Planning, structural surveys and surveys for hazardous substances

Before any work begins and usually before the contract is signed, a survey is carried out to ensure that the demolition can go ahead safely and that property surrounding the site is protected from the demolition work as it progresses.

Items that are usually dealt with in the survey include the following:

- Details and location of all the public services must be known and shown on a large-scale plan. Most of these will be buried services: gas pipes, electrical cables, water pipes, sewerage, etc., and could present serious risk if damaged. It is necessary to state which of these will need to be cut off and which will need further protection. It should be made absolutely clear who is responsible for each to be sure that nothing gets overlooked.
- The structural design should be examined to identify the supporting members and structures.
- Basements, cellars, wells or storage tanks need to be identified. Workers may fall through into these underground areas, while tanks pose a special risk if they have held or still hold toxic or flammable materials.
- The suitability of the ground for scaffolds, cranes, excavators and other plant needs to be determined.
- Access to the site should enable the large plant and appliances to be taken or driven there safely. It may be necessary to get permission to close roads or pathways for the duration of the work.
- The recommended means of disposal of rubbish should be considered, according to the requirements of current environmental legislation and local authority provisions.
- Special requirements will necessarily arise out of the survey. Drains may need to be sealed to prevent toxic and flammable gases escaping to the site and to prevent infestation of rats. The special precautions, for example, respiratory protection or for entry into confined spaces, should be written into the contract. Other requirements, such as the removal of glass from all windows, should also be written into the contract.

Safe working methods

The following precautions are necessary during the demolition process and should be planned for:

- Demolition should be carried out in the reverse order of erection of the building.
- No freestanding wall should be left on its own unless judged to be secure by a competent person.
- Scaffold working platforms should be used.
- Entrances, passages, stairs and ladder runs should be kept clear of all material.
- Disturbed staircases, particularly stone staircases, should not be used.
- Timber with protruding nails should have the nails removed.
- Glass in partitions, doors, roofs and windows should be removed separately.
- Adequate and suitable lighting should be provided.

Provision of working places and means of access/egress

Working places are ever changing on demolition sites and it is important to constantly monitor the situation. Work on the structure being demolished needs careful planning to ensure that unplanned collapse does not occur. Scaffolds are used as working platforms and rely on the structure being demolished for their stability. Constant inspection is needed to ensure the scaffold does not collapse with the building.

Lighting is important for safe working and to make sure there are no hidden tripping hazards or dark areas where holes in flooring, for example, cannot be seen.

It is difficult to maintain safe access and egress because of the nature of demolition work. Because conditions are ever changing the safety systems should be constantly reviewed and updated. Housekeeping must be maintained to a very high standard by keeping walkways free of rubble. Where scaffolds are used, platforms and gangways must be kept clear of debris and any tripping hazards. Scaffolds must be constantly checked to ensure they have sufficient ties into the building.

Where there is a chance of falling debris, there must be some way of protecting the workers and the public. Protective fans can be set up, but they must be kept clear of any debris that does fall on them, as they are not designed to carry heavy weights.

Care must be taken with the use of ladders as the structure is demolished to ensure they are secured correctly on repositioning.

Use of method statements and permits to work

Health and safety method statements are an effective management tool for high risk work such as demolition. The method statement draws together the information concerning the hazards associated with the job and the controls that will be necessary. It takes into account the results of the assessments that have been carried out, including general risk, hazardous substances, manual handling, etc. This information will help in the planning of the job and highlight the resources that are needed for it.

The method statement will also provide information for other contractors working on the site about any effects the work will have on them. With demolition, the statement will need to be revised regularly as the circumstances and conditions constantly change.

The method statement is also a useful and effective way of giving employees information about how a particular task should be carried out and what precautions are necessary. The inclusion of simple diagrams is useful as they can make it clear how a task should be carried out. It is necessary to monitor the method statements to check that what is required is put into action.

Permits to work are used for particularly hazardous tasks such as hot work, work in confined spaces, using explosives, etc. They are a formal way of setting out what must be done to help minimise the risks involved. The competent person must sign to say everything necessary has been done according to the permit and allowing the work to go ahead. Boundaries may have to be set up to exclude personnel and warning notices posted. When the work is completed the permit must be signed off to enable routine work to continue.

Security of site boundaries and protection of the public

The boundaries of the demolition site need to be fenced off to exclude persons not involved with the work. These could be children, who are attracted to such sites, perceiving them as playgrounds; itinerant persons who may be seeking temporary shelter; those looking to salvage materials as well as those who are just passing by. The very nature of a demolition site suggests both attraction and danger. Some form of fencing or boarding about 2.5 metres high should be used, with warning notices set up around it. Where boarding is used the provision of viewing panels both at adult and children's height should be provided to satisfy those who may be curious about the work and might otherwise put themselves at risk by gaining access to the site. Protective screens and fans should be set up around scaffolds to prevent debris falling on to passers-by.

Plant and appliances should be secured and never left with the keys in the ignition. Serious accidents have been caused by children trying to drive or operate site vehicles.

Protection from noise

Demolition must take into account the public and neighbour interface. Simple controls for reducing the impact of noise on others include limiting the work hours/days to those more socially acceptable. The choice of equipment and where it might be sited may be used to limit the effects of noise, for example, by locating noisy plant away from boundaries shared with those affected.

Control and protection from dust

Dust can be both a nuisance and a risk to health to those exposed; this may not only affect the site personnel but neighbours and members of the public. The closure of roads and pathways is a good precaution to keep people and vehicles away from the site, but this is not always possible. Dust may contain fungal and bacterial matter (for example, demolition of empty buildings infested with vermin, pigeons etc.) that may be pathogenic to humans. Dust can be damped down with water to keep it to a minimum, but care must be taken to control any run-off of water that might contaminate neighbouring ground or water courses. Prevailing winds will need to be considered in order to decide the approach and order of the demolition; it may be possible to plan to use the un-demolished parts of the structure, to act as a shield, to reduce dust liberated from the site during the initial demolition phase.

Protection of the environment

Where vehicles are being used to transport the demolition waste material to a disposal site, then provision should be made for wheel washes and the cleaning of the highway by a road sweeper. Waste substances, such as oils, must not be allowed to leak away into the soil and must be disposed of in a controlled manner. During demolition sewers may become exposed and be at risk of contamination from substances, and care should be taken to identify and protect them from entry of such materials. In the same way, it may be necessary to establish interceptor pits to control water run off into water courses.

C9.5 - Excavations

Hazards and controls associated with excavation work

Work in excavations and trenches, basements, underground tanks, sewers, manholes etc., can involve high risks and each year construction workers are killed with some buried alive or asphyxiated.

The consequences of even a minor collapse can be very serious. A minor fall of earth can happen at high speed and bring with it anything (plant and machinery) that may be at the edge. Even if the arms and head of a person are not trapped in the soil, the material pressing on the person can lead to severe crush injuries to the lower body and asphyxiation due to restriction of movement of the chest.

Excavations that are carried out within close proximity to existing buildings or structures may result in their foundations becoming undermined and create the potential for significant settling damage to occur or collapse. Consideration should be given to the effects that excavation work might have on foundations of neighbouring buildings or structures, and control measures implemented to ensure that foundations are not disturbed or undermined.

Building foundations that are at a distance of less than twice the excavation depth from the face of the excavation are more likely to be affected by ground movement; underpinning or shoring of such structures may be required to prevent structural damage.

CONTROLS FOR SPECIFIC HAZARDS

Collapse

Often, the soil and earth that make up the sides of the excavation cannot be relied upon to support their own weight, leading to the possibility of collapse. The collapse may be sudden and unexpected providing many tonnes of earth to crush or constrict the movement of those working in the trench. Risk increases if:

- The soil structure is loose or made unstable by water logging.
- Heavy plant or materials are too close to the edge of the excavation.
- Machinery or vehicles cause vibration.
- There is inadequate support for the sides, for example shoring and cross-bracing - *see later in this section for detail on control of collapse by shoring*.
- Excavation occurs below the level of the shoring provided.

Figure C9-26: Excavation hazards. Source: RMS.

Access

The absence of planned proper access into, out of, around and across excavations presents the combined hazards of slips, trips and falls. Workers may be tempted to improvise and use cut away sections of earth to get in and out; however these do not tend to last long (particularly after rain has fallen) and quickly decline in condition till they become a slide. Ladders, when provided, may present a hazard due to becoming slippery or workers may fall from them after getting tired if they are too long and have insufficient resting places. An improvised crossing point, without proper edge protection represents a high risk of falling to the user. Ladders are the usual means of access and egress to excavations. They must be properly secured, in good condition and inspected regularly. The ladder should extend about one metre or three rungs above ground level to give a good handhold.

Falls of persons, objects and vehicles

Fall of persons and objects

When people are working below ground in excavations, the problems are very similar to those faced when people are working at a height - falls of people and falling objects, such as tools or pieces of equipment, for example, wheel barrows. Particular problems arise when:

- Materials, including spoil, are stored too close to the edge of the excavation.
- The excavation is close to another building and the foundations may be undermined.
- The edge of the excavation is not clear, especially if the excavation is in a public area.
- Absence of barriers or lighting.
- Poor positioning or the absence of access ladders allowing people to fall.
- Absence of organised crossing points.
- Badly constructed ramps for vehicle access which can cause the vehicle to topple.
- No stop blocks for back filling.
- Routing of vehicles too close to the excavation.

Where people, objects or materials can fall a distance of more than two metres, edge protection must be provided. Shallow trenches should be covered when they are left unattended. Guardrails must meet the same standards as those provided for working platforms.

Vehicles

Concrete or wooden blocks (usually old railway sleepers) are placed some distance from the edge to prevent vehicles from getting too close, particularly when the excavation is being 'back filled', where they provide a stop block.

Signs that comply with the Health and Safety (Signs and Signals) Regulations (SSSR) 1996 should be displayed to warn people of the excavation and any special measures to be taken. If working on a public highway, the police or the local authority must be consulted over the positioning of traffic lights. Appropriate lighting should be provided; it must provide sufficient illumination for those at work but should not create glare or other distractions for passers by, especially motorists, the works should be adequately fenced. Battery operated headlamps (to avoid trailing cables) may be considered for individual use. If excavations are present in dark conditions they must be suitably lit to prevent vehicles or people colliding or falling into them.

Vehicles passing close to or over an excavation represents a hazard in a number of ways. In the first instance it creates an additional loading on the sides of the trench and may cause it to collapse.

In addition, its close proximity to the edge of the excavation, perhaps for back filling (filling in the trench after use), could lead to the vehicle falling into the trench.

Two further hazards exist in that vehicles may collide with equipment in use around the trench or its barriers, particularly when it is badly identified. To prevent objects falling into excavations, the following precautions should be taken:

- Spoil and building materials must not be stacked near to the edge.
- The weight of stacks should not be enough to cause the sides to collapse.
- Designated operating areas for vehicles and machinery must be routed away from the excavation.
- Where vehicles have to approach, stop blocks must be provided to prevent overrunning.

Flooding

Unless a major watercourse is breached, leading to a massive ingress of water, drowning is not likely to be an issue. However, heavy rainfall, breaking into drains and digging below the natural water table can all lead to flooding. In deep excavations, where access is not readily available, the combined effect of water and mud could lead to difficulty in escape and the risk of drowning. In addition, this can lead to the sides of the trench becoming soft and the integrity of the supports can be undermined.

Consideration must be given to the likelihood of water entering the excavation and the measures to be implemented in order to control water levels within the excavation. Usually water is abstracted from excavations and pumped to sumps for settlement from where it can be pumped out for disposal. When an excavation is liable to water ingress the stability of walls can be undermined; this will influence the choice of shoring, for example, close boarded shoring *(see figure ref C9-34)* rather than open sheeting *(see figure ref C9-35)*.

When works are within close proximity to a watercourse, within 10 metres, then advice should be sought on the disposal of groundwater and a 'Consent for Works Affecting Watercourses' should be obtained from the Environment Agency.

Substances

Contaminated ground

Digging may uncover buried materials that have the potential to be hazardous to health. The history of the site should be examined to try to identify if substances have been buried on the site during its previous use. Sites that once were used as steel works may contain arsenic and cyanide dating back many years; farmyards may have been used as graves for animals and to dispose of pesticides and organo-phosphates. There is always the presence of vermin to consider - this can increase the risk of diseases such as leptospirosis.

Toxic and asphyxiating atmospheres

Excavations can, under different circumstances, be subject to toxic, asphyxiating or explosive atmospheres. Chalk or limestone deposits when in contact with acidic groundwater can release carbon dioxide, and gases such as methane or hydrogen sulphide can seep into excavations from contaminated ground or damaged services in built-up areas. These atmospheres can accumulate at the bottom of an excavation and result in asphyxiation, poisoning, explosion or potential fatalities.

Figure C9-27: Buried services.   *Source: RMS.*

Figure C9-28: Excavation hazards.   *Source: RMS.*

Buried services

The various types of buried services include electricity cable, gas pipes, water mains, drains, sewers, oil and other substance pipelines and communication cabling. It is very easy for buried services to become damaged when excavations are being dug. The impact equipment involved in digging excavations, for example excavators, pneumatic drills and picks, can easily damage the services.

ELEMENT C9 - CONSTRUCTION HAZARDS AND CONTROLS

If an electrical cable is damaged it may discharge large amounts of electrical energy leading to a flash, burns and possible electric shock for those in the area. Although electricity cables provide the most obvious risk, gas pipes, water mains, drains and sewers can all release dangerous substances. Gas is particularly dangerous if there is a potential ignition source close by. Fibre-optic cables may not produce a health and safety risk but are very expensive to repair.

Buried services (electricity, gas, water, etc) are not obvious upon site survey and so the likelihood of striking a service when excavating, drilling or piling is increased. The results of striking an underground service are varied, and the potential to cause injury or fatality is high. As with overhead power lines, any underground service should be treated as live until confirmed dead by an authority. Incidents can include shock, electrocution, explosion and burns from power cables, explosion, burns or unconsciousness from gas or power cables, impact injury from dislodged stones or flooding from ruptured water mains.

Plans and drawings

Excavation operations should not begin until all available service location information has been identified and thoroughly examined. Record, plans and location drawings should not be considered as completely accurate, but serve only as an indication of the likelihood of the presence of services, their location and depth. It is possible for the position of an electricity supply cable to alter if previous work has been carried out in the location, due to the flexibility of the cable and movement of surrounding features since the original installation of the cable. In addition, plans often show a proposed position for the services that does not translate to the ground, such that services are placed in position only approximately where the plan says.

Figure C9-29: Marking of services. Source: RMS.

Service location tools

It is important that 'service location devices' such as a cable avoidance tool (CAT and Genny) are used by competent, trained operatives to assist in the identification and marking of the actual location and position of buried services. When identified it is essential that physical markings be placed on the ground to show where these services are located.

Safe digging methods

Safe digging methods should be implemented within 0.5 metres of a buried service. This involves the use of insulated hand tools such as a spade or shovel with curved edges (to be used with light force and not sudden blows). Mechanical, probing or piercing tools and equipment such as excavators, forks, picks or drills should not be used when in the vicinity of buried services, as these may cause damage to any service if they strike it. Careful hand digging using a spade or shovel should be used instead.

NEED FOR TEMPORARY SHORING (DRAG BOXES, PILING)

Methods of supporting excavations

> *"Suitable and sufficient steps shall be taken to prevent any person, work equipment, or any accumulation of material from falling into any excavation".*

Figure C9-30: Methods of supporting excavations. Source: CDM 2007 Regulation 31.

Precautions must be taken to prevent collapse. The methods of supporting (shoring) the sides of excavations vary widely in design depending on:

- The nature of the subsoil - for example, wet may require close shoring with sheets.
- Projected life of the excavation - a trench box may give ready made access where it is only needed for short duration.
- Work to be undertaken, including equipment used - for example, the use of a drag (trench) box for shoring where pipe joints are made.
- The possibility of flooding from ground water and heavy rain - close shoring would be required.
- The depth of the excavation - a shallow excavation may use battering instead of shoring, particularly where shoring may impede access.
- The number of people using the excavation at any one time - a lot of space may be required so cantilever sheet piling may be preferred.

In order to ensure satisfactory support for excavations:

- Prevent trench collapse by battering the sides to a safe angle or supporting them with sheeting or proprietary support systems.
- Use experienced people for the erection and dismantling of timbering and other supports.

- Adequate material must be used to prevent danger from falls or falling objects.

Drag boxes

Drag boxes are large protective sheets separated by struts. The box is lowered into the trench and allows workers to lay pipes within a protected area. The equipment is normally supplied with fixed width struts that firmly resist trench collapse. As an excavation progresses, the drag box is pulled along the trench line by the excavator to allow a continuous pipe laying operation to proceed safely. The box can be raised when being moved, in order to avoid services that cross the trench. Drag boxes are best suited to open field situations, with reasonable ground conditions and where there is no requirement for active support of trench sites.

Figure C9-31: Battering.   Source: RMS.

Figure C9-32: Drag (trench) box.   Source: SRV Construction.

Piling

Piling (sheets) may be used to provide temporary support for a trench, a deep cofferdam or a riverside retaining wall.

The steel sheet piling provides a means to retain material of an excavated area behind a structure and prevent collapse.

The sheet may be loose fitted and braced with adjustable struts to prevent collapse or driven into the ground to an amount that resists collapse by means of a cantilever action.

The use of wood for shoring provides an alternative to the use of steel sheeting, though it is used less often in construction operations.

Figure C9-33: Open sheeting.   Source: Trench Control Ltd.

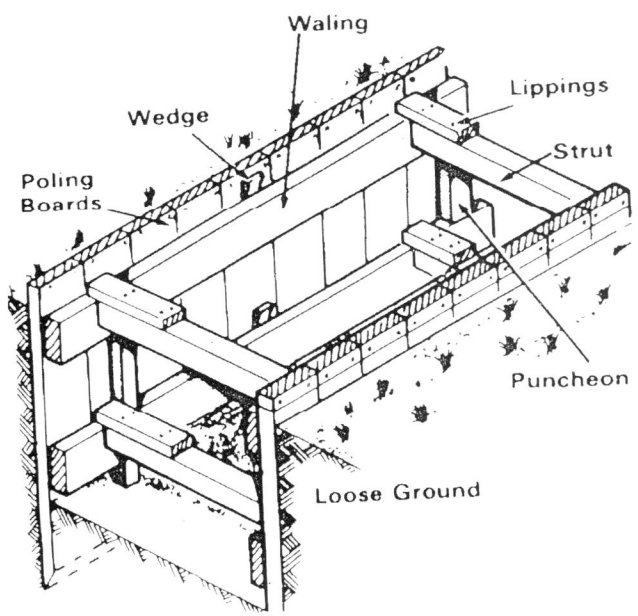

Figure C9-34: Close boarded excavation.   Source: BS6031.

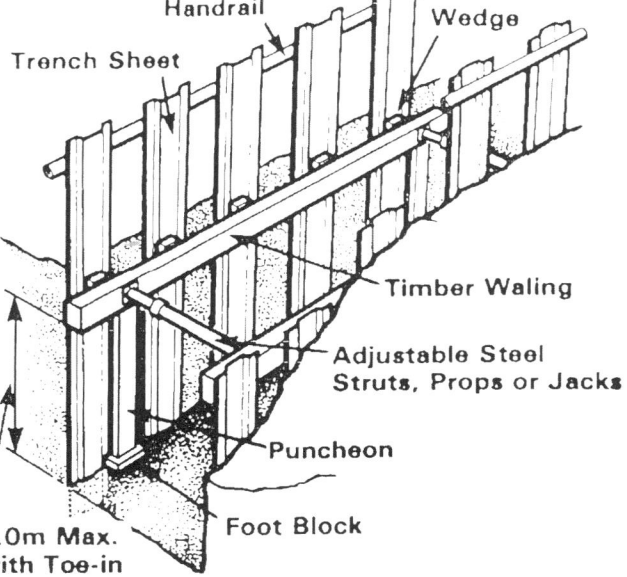

Figure C9-35: Open sheeting.   Source: BS6031.

ELEMENT C9 - CONSTRUCTION HAZARDS AND CONTROLS

Figure C9-36: Close sheeting.   Source: RMS.

Figure C9-37: Open sheeting.   Source: RMS.

USE OF 360° EXCAVATORS

360° excavators consist of a heavy duty chassis, with a fully rotating body and digging gear (jib arms and bucket), on either large diameter wheels and deep tread, pneumatic traction tyres or caterpillar track system.

Specific hazards associated with excavators are impact with pedestrians or vehicles by swinging jibs and booms, trap and crush beneath the excavator bucket as it digs into the ground or discharges its contents, falling objects from the bucket, high pressure hydraulic lines and tipping over on unstable ground or into excavations.

Other hazards include noise, chemicals and fumes produced by the running of the equipment.

Figure C9-38: Excavator.   Source: RMS.

Excavation equipment is generally adapted and used for a variety of different purposes that it may not specifically be designed for, including towing/shunting, lifting, loading/unloading/transport of articles and equipment. The fact that these are improvised activities increases the risk of injury.

Control measures should include:

- Trained and authorised users.
- Not overloading the bucket; maintenance and inspection.
- Segregation of pedestrians to a safe distance by the provision of suitable barriers and signs advising of the dangers of operating plant.
- Good visibility, with the assistance of mirrors where necessary.
- High visibility clothing for those working nearby.
- Seat restraints for the user, who should be enclosed in a protective cage that can also act as a guard against contact with moving machinery, falling materials and the effects of overturning.

The requirements for statutory inspections of excavations

Inspection of an excavation must be carried out under the requirements of Regulation 31 of CDM 2007.

A competent person must inspect excavations:

- At the start of each shift before work begins.
- After any event likely to have affected the strength or stability of the excavation.
- After any accidental fall of rock, earth or other material.

The competent person must stop the work if the inspection shows the excavation to be unsafe.

A written report should be made after the inspection under the requirements of Regulation 33 of CDM 2007.

The notes that follow the inspection report outline which places of work require inspection. They also specify the timing and frequency of those inspections.

The competent person must:

- Complete the inspection report before the end of the working period.
- Provide the report or a copy to the person for whom the inspection was carried out within 24 hours.
- A copy of the reports must be kept on site until the work is complete. Reports should then be kept for three months at an office of the person for whom the inspections were carried out.

Where the person carrying out the inspection is not satisfied that it is safe to work in the excavation they must inform the person who they are doing the inspection for and work must not continue until the matters identified by the inspection have been remedied.

The inspection record must include the following information as stated in Schedule 3 of CDM 2007:

- Name and address of person on whose behalf the inspection was carried out.
- Location of the workplace inspected.
- Description of workplace or part of workplace inspected (including any plant and equipment and materials).
- Date and time of inspection.
- Details of any matter identified that could lead to a risk to the health and safety of anyone.
- Details of any action taken as a result of any matter identified in the last point.
- Details of any more action considered necessary.
- The name and position of the person making the report.

ELEMENT C9 - CONSTRUCTION HAZARDS AND CONTROLS

Example of a permit to dig

PERMIT TO DIG

Contract: .... Contract No: ....

Principal contractor: .... Sub Contractor: ....

Permit No: .... Date: ....

1. Location: ....

2. Size, detail and depth of excavation: ....
   ....

3. Are Service Plans on site ? YES / NO
   Comments: ....

4. Has cable locating equipment been used to identify services ? YES / NO
   Comments: ....

5. Are all known services marked out ? (site inspection by relevant statutory bodies) YES / NO
   Comments: ....

6. Are trial holes required ? YES / NO
   Comments: ....

7. Have precautions been taken to prevent contact if overhead lines are in the vicinity of the operation or near the approach to the operation? YES / NO

8. Additional precautions, i.e. Shoring/Fencing/Access/Storage/Fumes/Record of setting out points to re-establish services routes
   Comments: ....

9. Sketch details or attach copy of plans

10. Date and time of excavation: ....

    Signed: .... Accepted by: ....
    For and on behalf of issuing party (Work shall not commence unless all persons involved are aware of the safe systems of work)

    A new permit will be required for any further excavations. This permit is for guidance only. Persons carrying out work must take reasonable precautions when working around services.

Figure C9-39: Permit to dig. *Source: Reproduced by kind permission of Lincsafe.*

Element C10

Workplace transport and driving for work

Learning outcomes

The intended learning outcomes are that the student will be able to:

C10.1 Explain the hazards, risks and control measures for safe workplace transport operations.

C10.2 Outline the factors associated with driving at work that increases the risk of an incident and the control measures to reduce work-related driving risks.

Contents

C10.1 - Hazards, risks and control measures for workplace transport operations 349
    Typical hazards..349
    Non-movement related hazards 350
    Conditions and environments in which each hazard may arise 352
    Control measures for safe workplace transport operations...352
C10.2 - Driving at work..358
    Extent of work-related road injuries and fatalities..358
    Factors that increase risks of a road traffic incident 358
    Managing work-related road risk 359

ELEMENT C10 - WORKPLACE TRANSPORT AND DRIVING FOR WORK

Relevant statutory provisions

The Provision and Use of Work Equipment Regulations (PUWER) 1998 - Part III in particular
The Health and Safety (Safety Signs and Signals) Regulations (SSSR) 1996

Tutor references

Workplace transport safety - An employers' guide (HSG 136) HSE Books, ISBN: 978-0-71766-154-1
Driving at work, managing work-related road safety, HSE INDG382

C10.1 - Hazards, risks and control measures for workplace transport operations

Typical hazards

There are five main kinds of accidents associated with vehicles used in the workplace, which often result from loss of control of the vehicle, overturning vehicles, and collision with other vehicles, pedestrians and fixed objects. They form a significant part of the accidents that occur in workplace transport operations:

- Being struck by a moving vehicle.
- Injury caused by a vehicle collapse or overturn.
- Falling from a vehicle.
- Being hit by a load (materials) falling from a vehicle.
- Being hit against a fixed or moving item whilst travelling in a vehicle.

Statistics provided by the Health and Safety Executive for 2008/09 show:

		Fatal injury	*Major injury*	*Over 3 day injury*
1	Struck by	25	605	1547
2	Collapse	9	46	25
3	Fall from	2	861	1205
4	Materials	5	172	342
5	Hit against	4	146	883
	Total	45	1830	4002

Figure C10-1: Workplace accident statistics 2008/09. *Source: HSE.*

Figures reported for 2009/10 show that, as in 2008/09, there were 45 fatal injuries during the period. The hazards relating to workplace vehicles are also discussed as part of mobile work equipment in element C7.

LOSS OF CONTROL

Hazards that can lead to loss of control of workplace vehicles include:

- Slippery surfaces due to contamination of the surface by materials such as oil and dusts, leading to poor traction when steering or braking. Weather conditions such as ice and water can also affect control of the vehicle.
- Potholes and other fracturing of the road surface, along with sudden changes of level, obstructions or kerbs. Contact with these may wrench the steering device from the hand of the driver or suddenly knock the steering in an unintended direction.
- Overloading of vehicles, which can influence their manoeuvrability and braking performance. A counterbalance vehicle, such as a fork lift truck may be overloaded to such an extent that the steering wheels are not sufficiently in contact with the ground. The overloading of vehicles can cause the vehicle to require unusually long braking time or cause it to overbalance on cornering.
- Excessive speed will also affect the performance of brakes and the ability of the driver to manoeuvre the vehicle, leading to loss of control.
- Failure of one of the vehicle controls or critical items can lead to poor or loss of control of the vehicle. A sudden puncture in a pneumatic tyre could make the vehicle difficult to steer. If the conditions of brakes and steering deteriorate, they will perform badly and may cause the vehicle to move suddenly in an unintended direction.

OVERTURNING OF VEHICLES

Various circumstances may cause a workplace vehicle to overturn including insecure and unstable loads, manoeuvring with the load elevated, colliding with kerbs and other obstructions, cornering at speed, braking harshly, driving on uneven or soft ground, driving across a slope, under inflated tyres, and mechanical failure.

Possible causes of a dumper truck overturning

- Overloading or uneven loading of the bucket.
- Cornering at excessive speed.
- Hitting obstructions.
- Driving too close to the edges of embankments or excavations.
- Mechanical defects that occur because of lack of maintenance.

Figure C10-2: Vehicle overturned. *Source: Lincsafe.*

ELEMENT C10 - WORKPLACE TRANSPORT AND DRIVING FOR WORK

- Inappropriate or unequal tyre pressures.
- Driving across slopes.

Possible causes of a fork lift truck overturning

- Driving too fast.
- Sudden braking.
- Driving across slopes.
- Driving over debris.
- Under-inflated tyres.
- Driving over holes in the floor, such as drains.
- Driving with the load elevated.
- Driving with the load incorrectly positioned on the forks.
- Overloading - exceeding maximum capacity.
- Collisions with buildings or other vehicles.

COLLISIONS WITH OTHER VEHICLES, PEDESTRIANS OR FIXED OBJECTS

It is common in workplace transport operations that a number of vehicles work together in the same workplace. This can lead to the hazard of collision between vehicles, particularly where the vision of the drivers is obstructed, for example, where they pass round corners, between racking, manoeuvre around vehicles or enter and exit buildings.

The hazard of collision is increased where vehicles are reversed as this may limit the driver's ability to see other vehicles and cause the vehicle to move in a direction not expected by other vehicles. There is a risk that vehicles may be reversed a short distance without the driver looking behind the vehicle, increasing the risk of collision between vehicles. In addition, sudden changes of light level may result in the driver not being able to see clearly enough to avoid a collision, as it can take time for the driver's eyesight to adjust to the change.

Workers involved in the workplace transport operations may need to share the workplace with vehicles as pedestrians in order to supervise work, organise movements and to clean spills or debris. This could place them in close proximity with the vehicles and present a hazard of the vehicles colliding with the workers. Other pedestrians at risk of collision are those that move between workplaces while vehicles are in operation, for example, pedestrians crossing a depot yard to get from the entrance to offices or workers moving through a vehicle operating area to get to rest facilities.

People may unexpectedly appear from a part of a building into a vehicle operating area, because the route they are taking is a shorter one or they are conducting maintenance work that takes them behind a racking or similar structure.

Collision of vehicles with fixed objects is more likely where the vehicles have to manoeuvre in limited space, particularly when reversing. Large vehicles could be at risk of collision with plant or buildings as they turn sharp corners and tall vehicles may collide with pipework or other services that cross a roadway. Fork lift trucks are at risk of collision with the frames of doorways or other overhead obstructions, particularly if the driver fails to lower the mast sufficiently.

Non-movement related hazards

LOADING AND UN-LOADING

There is a risk of material falling on a vehicle driver where the vehicle is used to provide materials at a height or to remove materials from delivery vehicles. In addition, when vehicles are being unloaded by hand there is a possibility that the load has shifted and become unstable during transportation. This could mean that the load collapses onto the person unloading the vehicle when a quantity of it is removed and this could lead to serious injury or death.

Some loading and unloading tasks cause people to work at height, which creates the risk that people may fall from a vehicle. People loading or unloading vehicles may loose awareness of the edge of the load/vehicle when they are paying particular attention to the task they are doing. Falls from vehicles may be more likely if the work is done in poor weather conditions, the load or vehicle surface is slippery or where there is no organised means of access to the vehicle.

Regulation 37 of the Construction (Design and Management) Regulations (CDM) 2007 states that:

> "No person shall remain or be required or permitted to remain on any vehicle during the loading or unloading of any loose material unless a safe place of work is provided and maintained for such person".

Figure C10-3: Regulation 37 of CDM 2007. *Source: Construction (Design and Management) Regulations (CDM) 2007.*

SECURING LOADS

The hazards relating to securing loads are work at height, slippery surfaces, weather conditions, and manual handling hazards. There is the additional hazard of a badly secured load shifting at some stage in the transport operation.

Tasks to secure loads may cause the person to go onto the vehicle in order to fix straps and tighten devices to hold the load. This will present them with the risk of falling from the vehicle or from the load onto the vehicle.

The vehicle may be contaminated with dirt, dust, oil or materials spilt from previous loads, which presents a risk of slipping. Load securing equipment will usually have to be placed in position and tightened by the person securing the load; this could expose them to manual handling hazards related to moving things and over-exertion.

SHEETING

Sheeting is the covering of a load with a sheet or net to secure it. This prevents parts of the load being disrupted by wind/air movement while being transported and protects the load from the weather. Though it may be possible to sheet some vehicles from the ground it is common for the person sheeting to have to gain access to the top of the vehicle and sometimes the top of the load.

If sheeting is not a mechanised process, it involves the manually unrolling of the sheet over the load and the sides of the vehicle, As sheets are designed to be robust they are also quite heavy and it takes a considerable amount of exertion to pull sheets over the load, leading to risk of strains and back injury. In manual sheeting processes the hazards of height, slips and manual handling usually exist.

COUPLING

The task of coupling a tractor unit to a trailer requires that the tractor unit is reversed towards the front trailer. The '5th wheel' is the connection between the tractor and the trailer. If the 5th wheel jaws are not located properly, this can lead to unexpected movement of the trailer.

Though most accidents during coupling involve drivers or other people being run over, hit or crushed by moving vehicles, a number of non-movement based hazards exist.

For example, there is a significant risk of falling during coupling, especially in the dark, as the person coupling may be less able to see slippery surfaces, obstructions or steps.

A particular hazard that may be encountered during coupling or uncoupling is that the vehicle trailer could move or overturn.

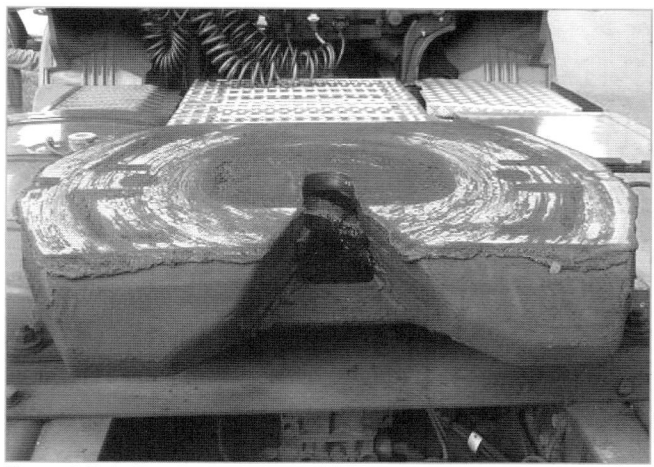

Figure C10-4: Coupling. Source: Wikipedia.

Though the ground may look flat it may be sufficient to cause the trailer to become unstable or move under its own weight. In addition, during uncoupling the trailer goes from being supported to bearing its own weight, and this can cause the trailer to sink into the ground and overturn.

VEHICLE MAINTENANCE WORK

There are a number of non-movement related hazards associated with vehicle maintenance work, including work with open pits, access gantries, oils and greases and manual handling issues that may be experienced when fitting large replacement parts.

One of the particular hazards associated with large vehicle maintenance work is the hazard of being crushed by a falling cab that was tilted to gain access to parts of the vehicle for maintenance.

Similar hazards exist at the rear of the vehicle if the vehicle has a tipping facility.

Hydraulic ramps and hoists that are used to raise vehicles and gain access to their underneath parts can create crush hazards as they are lowered to the ground or if there is a sudden failure of the hydraulic or mechanical system.

Figure C10-5: Synchronised vehicle lifting system. Source: Rotala.

There is an additional hazard that a vehicle or equipment could fall from a lift system, particularly if not located correctly or if the lift system is not raised uniformly.

ELEMENT C10 - WORKPLACE TRANSPORT AND DRIVING FOR WORK

There are many manual handling and posture hazards associated with vehicle maintenance work, from leaning over to reach parts to the movement of large vehicle wheels.

The presence of flammable liquids, in the form of fuels, oils and paints present a hazard of fire and explosion.

Electrical hazards are present as portable electric equipment may be used, some operating at mains (230 volt) voltage. Where pneumatic equipment is used it presents the hazard of noise, flying particles and possible injection of air into the body.

It may be necessary to work on part of the vehicle at height, for example, to repair the top of a tanker trailer or to refill refrigerant for a chilled foods vehicle. This work can present falling hazards that can lead to major injury or death. The hazards are accentuated when working on vehicles that come straight from use and are wet and slippery.

Figure C10-6: Tilted LGV cab and prop. *Source: HSE.*

Conditions and environments in which each hazard may arise

Factors that make conditions and environments in which workplace transport operating hazards may arise are:

- Inadequate lighting and direction signs.
- Inadequate signs or signals to identify the presence of vehicles.
- Drivers unfamiliar with site.
- Need to reverse.
- Poor visibility for example, sharp bends, mirror/windscreen misted up.
- Poor identification of fixed objects for example, overhead pipes, doorways, storage tanks, corners of buildings.
- Lack of safe crossing points on roads and vehicle routes.
- Lack of separate entrance/exit for vehicles and pedestrians.
- Lack of separation of pedestrians and vehicles.
- Pedestrians using doors provided for vehicle only use.
- Lack of barriers to prevent pedestrians suddenly stepping from an exit/entrance into a vehicle's path.
- Poor maintenance of vehicles for example, tyres or brakes.
- Excessive speed of vehicles.
- Lack of vehicle management for example, use of traffic control, 'banksman' (appointed individuals who control or direct plant).
- Environmental conditions for example, poor lighting, rain, snow or ice.

Figure C10-7: Poor maintenance of vehicle tyres. *Source: RMS.*   Figure C10-8: Reduced risk of collision - people/vehicles. *Source: RMS.*

Control measures for safe workplace transport operations

The employer, through its managers, needs to carry out an assessment of risk with regard to the safe movement of vehicles and their loads as part of the overall health and safety policy. This includes the use of vehicles such as dumper trucks, lift trucks, and those used for delivery. Consideration should be given to the following specific control measures.

SUITABILITY AND SUFFICIENCY OF TRAFFIC ROUTES

Suitability and sufficiency of traffic routes should consider the needs of the range of vehicles likely to use them. This will mean consideration of the needs of fork lift trucks to ensure they are able to negotiate speed retarding humps, put in place to control large road vehicles that come on to site, and provision of cycle lanes on large sites where cycles move around with larger vehicles. In addition, the following factors should be considered:

- The purpose of the routes, the types of vehicle using the routes.
- The likely volume of traffic, the layout of the area.
- Traffic routes should be clearly marked and signed. These should incorporate speed limits, one way systems, priorities and other factors normal to public roads. Vehicles that are visiting the premises should be made aware of any local rules and conditions.
- Attention should be paid to areas where the traffic routes meet other traffic, for example the entrance to the site.
- Consideration should be given to adequate lighting on routes and particularly in loading/unloading and operating areas.
- Separate routes, designated crossing places and suitable barriers should be provided for pedestrians at recognised danger spots. As far as is practicable pedestrians should be kept clear of vehicle operating areas and/or a notice displayed warning pedestrians that they are entering an operating area.
- Clear direction signs and marking of storage areas and buildings can help to avoid unnecessary movement, such as reversing.
- Sharp bends and overhead obstructions should be avoided where possible. Hazards that cannot be removed should be clearly marked with black and yellow diagonal stripes, for example, loading bay edges, and pits. If reasonably practicable barriers should be installed. The large turning circle required by some vehicles should be taken into account. The positioning of street furniture, such as lights should be considered to ensure they do not present an unnecessary obstruction to manoeuvring vehicles.
- The width of traffic routes should be sufficient to account for the vehicles using them; particular attention should be paid to where vehicles have to pass each other in two way traffic conditions. Markings on the traffic route should indicate where vehicles should position themselves to pass each other. The necessary width should be maintained by controlling where vehicles and other goods are allowed to be parked and unloaded in order that they do not become an obstruction.
- Consideration should be made to vehicle weight and height restriction on routes, signs, barriers and weight checks may be necessary.
- Adequacy of road surfaces and, if necessary, provision for adverse weather, for example, provision of salt bins.

MANAGEMENT OF VEHICLE MOVEMENTS

Many sites are complex in nature and require the careful management of vehicles in order to ensure that they are brought onto, move around and leave the site safely. Where materials are brought to site it may be necessary to manage deliveries to prevent too many vehicles arriving at the site at the same time causing them to back up into the public highway. Site security arrangements play a significant part in the management of vehicles on site and will assist with controlling vehicles so that they are routed correctly and safely. It is not uncommon for vehicles to be sent to a site that are too big or too heavy to access the roadways. Site security staff should be trained to identify these to prevent them accessing the site and causing harm.

Visiting drivers must be carefully managed. They must not be allowed to bring unauthorised passengers (for example, children during school holidays) onto the site.

In addition, the following factors should be considered:

- Appoint someone on site to be responsible for vehicle movements.
- Drivers must be properly trained.
- Ensure unauthorised people are not allowed to drive.
- Keep keys secure when vehicles are not in use.
- Check vehicles daily and have faults rectified promptly.
- Avoid reversing where possible.
- If vehicles have to reverse, use a banksman to guide the vehicle's movement and maintain pedestrian segregation.
- Ensure vehicles are parked, loaded and unloaded in a suitable place.
- Make sure visiting drivers are aware of site rules.
- Separate vehicles and pedestrians where practicable.
- Ensure the use of horns or other warning methods before entering doorways or at blind corners.
- Speed limits of 10 or 15 mph are usually considered appropriate, although 5 mph may be necessary in certain situations.

LOADING, UN-LOADING SHEETING AND COUPLING

Whenever possible loading and un-loading should be carried out with the aid of a fork lift truck (FLT) and a competent driver. When vehicles are being unloaded by hand the load should be carefully inspected to determine whether the load has shifted and become unstable during transportation. Care should be taken to adopt the correct posture and avoid overreaching, in order to prevent manual handling injuries. Appropriate footwear should be worn to avoid slips, the type required depends on the vehicle decking materials (decking could be steel plate, wood or synthetic). Remove spillages after each load has been removed to prevent slips trips or falls, particular care should be taken with spillages of oil or similar liquids. Avoid loading and unloading tasks at height in poor weather conditions or where there is no organised means of access to the vehicle.

ELEMENT C10 - WORKPLACE TRANSPORT AND DRIVING FOR WORK

Ensure the load is correctly placed before load securing equipment is positioned and tightened. When using sheeting a mechanised process should be used whenever possible. If the sheeting has to be fitted manually safe access to the vehicle should be provided, and work at a height should be avoided whenever possible. An appropriate manual sheeting technique should be used to avoid manual handling injuries during sheeting, for example, opening the sheeting progressively, attaching the sheeting as soon as possible, adopting good posture and avoiding overreaching.

Ensure the vehicle is correctly positioned on flat firm ground, ideally designed to take the weight of the trailer without sinking when uncoupled. Brakes should be locked securely when coupling or de-coupling. Particular care will be necessary in the hours of darkness to avoid slips or falls. Before the vehicle is moved it will be necessary to ensure the area is clear of pedestrians or obstructions.

ENVIRONMENTAL CONSIDERATIONS

Where vehicles operate, environmental conditions such as lighting and adverse weather will make a significant impact on their safe operation by affecting *visibility*. Where reasonably practicable a suitable standard of lighting must be maintained so that operators of vehicles can see to drive their vehicle and can be seen by others.

It is important to avoid areas of glare or shadow that could mask the presence of a person or vehicle. Similarly, if vehicles travel from within buildings to the outside it is important that the light level is maintained at a roughly even level in order to give the driver's eyes time to adjust to the change in light. Fixed structure hazards should be made as visible as possible with additional lighting and/or reflective strips.

Gradients and changes in ground level, such as ramps, represent a specific hazard to plant and vehicle operation. Vehicles have a limit of stability dependent on loading and their wheelbase. These conditions could put them at risk of overturning or cause damage to articulated vehicle couplings. Any gradient in a vehicle operating area should be kept as gentle as possible and traffic routes organised so that vehicles do not have to drive across steep slopes.

Where *changes in level* are at an edge that a vehicle might approach, and there is risk of falling, it must be provided with a robust barrier or similar means to demarcate the edge. Particular care must be taken at points where loading and unloading are conducted.

In some workplaces, such as factories or chemical plants, process products may contaminate the *surface condition* of the road, making it difficult for vehicles to brake effectively. It is important to have a programme that anticipates this, that includes regular cleaning or scarifying of the surface as well as means of dealing with spills. The floor surface should be in good condition, free of litter and obstructions.

Excessive ambient noise levels can mask the sound of vehicles working in the area; additional visual warning, for example, flashing lights should be used.

MAINTENANCE OF VEHICLES

All vehicles should be well maintained and 'roadworthy', with a formal system of checks and maintenance in place to ensure this. A vehicle, such as one used for moving trailers in a transport yard, that does not usually go on the public highway would be expected to have critical items, such as tyres and brakes, kept to the same good standard as one that was used on the public highway.

Vehicle maintenance should be planned to take place at regular intervals and vehicles taken out of use if critical items are not at an acceptable standard. In addition, it is important to conduct a pre-use check of the vehicle. This is usually done by the driver as part of their taking the vehicle over for a period of use, such as at the start of a work shift or day. This would identify the condition of critical items and provide a formal system to identify and consider problems that may affect the safety of the vehicle.

If there is no nominated driver and the vehicle is for general use someone should be nominated to make these pre-use checks. A record book or card should be used to record the checks and the findings.

DRIVER PROTECTION AND RESTRAINT SYSTEMS

In many work vehicle accidents the driver is injured because the vehicle does not offer protection when it rolls over or it does not restrain the driver to prevent them falling out of the vehicle and being injured by the fall or the vehicle falling on them.

Vehicles such as dumper trucks, road rollers and forklift trucks are examples of equipment that may present this risk. PUWER 1998 Part 3 recognises the importance of this and sets out requirements for equipment to be adapted, where practicable, to provide this protection. PUWER 1998 requires that new equipment provided by the employer, including hire equipment, must be fitted with roll over protection and restraint systems, where relevant.

SEGREGATING OF PEDESTRIANS AND VEHICLES

When establishing collective measures to control the risks relating to workplace transport operations it is important to establish, where possible, the segregation of pedestrians and vehicles.

> "Every workplace shall be organised in such a way that pedestrians and vehicles can circulate in a safe manner".

Figure C10-9: Means of segregation. Source: Regulation 17(1) of WHSWR 1992.

Segregation of pedestrians and vehicles will include the use of the following control measures:

- Separate gates should be provided for vehicle and pedestrian entry to the workplace.
- Clearly defined, marked and signposted routes should be provided for vehicles and pedestrians.
- Where pedestrians and vehicle routes cross each other, appropriate crossing points should be provided and used.
- Where necessary, barriers or rails should be provided to prevent pedestrians crossing at particularly dangerous points and to guide them to designated crossing places.
- At crossing points there should be adequate visibility and open space for the pedestrian to wait to cross.
- At crossing places where volumes of traffic are particularly heavy, the provision of suitable bridges or subways should be considered.
- In buildings where vehicles operate, separate doors and walkways should be provided for pedestrians.
- Meshed handrails and barriers should be used to channel people into pedestrian routes and to maintain segregation of vehicles from pedestrians.
- Where it is not possible to have a pedestrian route with a safe clearance from vehicle movement, because of building and plant design, then a raised pedestrian walkway could be considered to help establish segregation.
- Prevention of pedestrian access to vehicle areas when they are manoeuvring.

Figure C10-10: Crossing point.   Source: HSE, HSG76.   Figure C10-11: Segregating pedestrians and vehicles.   Source: RMS.

MEASURES TO BE TAKEN WHEN SEGREGATION IS NOT PRACTICABLE

Where segregation of pedestrians and vehicles is not possible the use of the following control measures should be considered:

- Where it is unavoidable that pedestrians will come into proximity with transport, they should be reminded of the hazards by briefings, site induction and signs, so they are aware at all times.
- Any traffic route that is used by both pedestrians and vehicles should be wide enough to enable any vehicle likely to use the route to pass pedestrians safely.
- In loading bays or similar areas where vehicles reverse to a loading point it should be possible for pedestrians to move to a safe point or use a refuge if there is a risk of them being trapped by the vehicle.
- One-way systems should be adopted to avoid vehicles reversing where pedestrians may be present.
- Reversing of large vehicles with restricted visibility should be strictly controlled and a banksman used to control the vehicle and pedestrians that might access the area.
- In buildings, lines should be drawn on the floor to indicate routes followed by vehicles such as fork lift trucks.
- Where segregation is not practicable and vehicles share the same workplace as pedestrians, for example, in order to deliver materials to workers, it is important to mark the work areas as being separate from vehicle routes; this will warn drivers to adjust their driving and be more aware of pedestrians.
- On routes used by automatic, driverless vehicles that are also used by pedestrians, steps should be taken to ensure that vehicles do not trap pedestrians. The vehicles should be fitted with safeguards to minimise the risk of injury, sufficient clearance should be provided between the vehicles and pedestrians, and care should be taken that fixtures along the route do not create trapping hazards.
- Blind spots, where the vision of the vehicle driver or pedestrian is restricted, should be improved by the careful positioning of mirrors on walls, plant or storage.
- Good lighting should be provided, particularly at crossing points, entrances and blind spots.
- Audible and visual warnings of the presence of the vehicle will assist pedestrians in avoiding them.
- Provision of high visibility clothing should be made to increase the ability to see the pedestrian.
- Speeds of vehicles should be carefully controlled to ensure safe operation where pedestrians are present. Where this will always be the case vehicles may be fitted with limiters to establish a safe maximum speed.

ELEMENT C10 - WORKPLACE TRANSPORT AND DRIVING FOR WORK

Figure C10-12: No segregation - high visibility clothing. *Source: RMS.*

Figure C10-13: Control of vehicle movement. *Source: RMS.*

PROTECTIVE MEASURES FOR PEOPLE AND STRUCTURES

Barriers

Moving vehicles, and in particular large plant, have high impact energy when they are in contact with structures or people. It is essential that vehicles be separated from vulnerable people and structures. Because of the high energy involved the barrier used must reflect the type of thing in contact with it. If it is only people that might contact it a simple portable barrier may be adequate, but if it is heavy vehicles robust barriers, including concrete structures, may need to be considered. It is important to identify vulnerable locations that warrant protection, for example, storage tanks, bund walls and where people exit buildings near to vehicle traffic routes.

Markings

Any structure that represents a height or width restriction should be readily identified for people and vehicle drivers. This will include low beams or doorways, pipe bridges, protruding scaffolds and edges where a risk of falling exists. These markings may be by means of attaching hazard tape or painting the structure to highlight the hazard.

Signs

Signs should be used to provide information, such as height restrictions, and to warn of the presence of vulnerable structures and people. Signs may be used to direct vehicles at a safe distance around workers.

Figure C10-14: Barriers and markings. *Source: RMS.*

Figure C10-15: Visual warning on a dumper truck. *Source: RMS.*

Warnings of vehicle approach and reversing

Warnings may be audible or visual or a combination of each. They are used to warn that the vehicle is operating in the area, such as a flashing light on the top of a fork lift truck or to warn of a specific movement, such as an audible warning that a large vehicle is reversing. These are designed to alert people in the area in order that they can place themselves in a position of safety. They do not provide the driver with authority to reverse the vehicle or to proceed in a work area without caution.

SITE RULES

It is important to establish clear and well understood site rules regarding vehicle operations and pedestrian movement. These may have to be communicated to drivers by security staff at the time they visit the site. They would often stipulate where the driver should be whilst vehicles are being loaded, where the keys to the vehicle should be, not reversing without permission and what access they have to areas of the site for such things as refreshment.

Pedestrians should also know what the site rules are in order to keep themselves safe. This may be communicated during worker or visitor induction. Site rules for pedestrians might include such things as using pedestrian exits/entrances or crossing points, not entering hazardous areas, the need to wear high visibility clothing in hazardous areas and not walking behind a reversing vehicle.

Where segregation of pedestrians from vehicles cannot be achieved it is important to identify who has priority - the vehicle or the pedestrian. Site rules may clarify that once the site boundary or building entrance is crossed the pedestrian has priority not the vehicle; this has to be clear to all parties. The site rules may be reinforced by the provision of additional signs to clarify the nature of the priority and provide information on speed limits.

SELECTION AND TRAINING OF DRIVERS

Only people that have been selected, trained and authorised to operate vehicles, or are undergoing properly organised formal training under competent supervision, should be permitted to do so.

Selection

The safe usage of vehicles calls for a reasonable degree of both physical and mental fitness. The selection procedure should be devised to identify people who have been shown to be reliable and mature enough to perform their work responsibly and carefully. To avoid wasteful training of workers who lack co-ordination and ability to learn, selection tests should be used.

Consideration must be given to any legal age restrictions that apply to vehicles that operate on the public highway. A similar approach may be adopted for the same vehicles used on site, though the law is not specific on age limitations in such cases.

Potential drivers should be medically examined prior to employment/training in order to assess the individual's physical ability to cope with this type of work.

They should also be medically examined every five years from middle age and after sickness or accident. Points to be considered are:

- General - normal agility, having full movement of trunk, neck and limbs.
- Vision - good eyesight in both eyes, corrected by spectacles if necessary, is important as drivers are required to have good judgement of space and distance.
- Hearing - the ability to hear instructions and warning signals with each ear is important.

Training

It is essential that the immediate supervisor of vehicle drivers receives training in the safe operation of vehicles and that senior management appreciates the risks resulting from the interaction of vehicles and pedestrians in the workplace.

For the driver, safety must constitute an integral part of the skill-training programme and not be treated as a separate subject. The driver should be trained to a level consistent with efficient operation and care for the safety of themselves and other persons. On completion of training they should be issued with a company authority to drive. A record of all basic training, refresher training and tests should be maintained in the individual's personal documents file.

Certification of training by other organisations must be checked to ensure it is appropriate for the needs of the organisation and the activities they conduct. It may be necessary to supplement general certified training with specific local training that relates to their tasks in their workplace and the associated risks involved.

MANAGEMENT SYSTEMS FOR ASSURING DRIVER COMPETENCE

The trained driver

It should not be assumed that employees who join as trained drivers have received adequate training to operate safely in their new organisation. The management must ensure that they have the basic skills and receive training in methods that relate to the tasks the organisation does and procedures *(local codes of practice)* for the type of work they are to undertake. They should be examined and tested before the issue of the organisation's driving authority.

A copy of the site rules and any local codes of practice must be given to all internal drivers and to external visiting drivers, such as delivery drivers, preferably before they arrive at the site.

Testing and refresher training

On completion of training, the driver should be examined and tested to ensure that they have achieved the required standard. It is recommended that at set intervals, when there is indication of the driver not working to required standards or following an accident, formal competence confirmation tests be introduced.

If high standards are to be maintained, periodic refresher training and testing should be considered.

Driver identification

Many organisations operate local codes of practice and take great care to confirm the authority they have given to drivers by the provision of a licence for that vehicle and sometimes a visible badge to confirm this. Access to vehicles should be supervised and authority checked carefully to confirm that the actual class of vehicle driven is within the authority given to the driver. This is important with such things as reach lift trucks that operate differently to a standard counterbalance truck. It is essential that access to keys for vehicles is restricted to those that are competent to drive them. This is not just a practical point, but also enables compliance with PUWER 1998.

C10.2 - Driving at work

The true cost of accidents to any organisation is nearly always higher than just the costs of repairs and insurance claims. This can include personal costs such as ill-health, time in hospital, stress on family members and possible penalty points being imposed on the driver's licences following an incident. There is also the potential for the driver to lose their licence. Therefore the benefits of managing driving activities through the introduction of policies, risk assessments and developing safe systems for work related driving is essential. This will ensure compliance with the Health and Safety at Work etc. Act (HASAWA) 1974 and the Management of Health and Safety at Work Regulations (MHSWR) 1999. The Health and Safety Executive (HSE) provides guidance to assist management in managing driving risk in the form of the document "Driving at work - Managing work-related road safety".

Extent of work-related road injuries and fatalities

The HSE estimates that up to a third of all road traffic accidents involved somebody who was at work at the time. This may account for over 20 fatalities and 250 serious injuries per week.

> "It has been estimated that between 800 and 1,000 road deaths a year are in some way work-related. Many bosses have ignored this problem in the past, but the Health and Safety Executive has now made it clear that employers have duties under health and safety law to manage the risks faced by their workers on the road".

Figure C10-16: Size of the road risk problem. Source: RoSPA.

> For the majority of people, the most dangerous thing they do while at work is drive on the public highway.

Figure C10-17: Road risk. Source: HSE 1996.

Factors that increase risks of a road traffic incident

DISTANCE

When assessing risk of any kind, an important consideration is the extent of exposure to hazards. It is logical then that the greater the journey distance (i.e. the greater the extent of exposure to the hazards of driving) the greater the risk of a road traffic incident occurring. Even an alert and experienced driver is at increased risk of being involved in a road traffic accident the greater the distance they travel.

The effects of the distance driven on risk are complicated by other factors. Whilst a driver driving longer distances under the same conditions is exposed to a higher risk. Drivers driving the same distance under different road conditions will be at a different level of risk. Road conditions have improved over the years, which have allowed greater travel distances in shorter periods of time, particularly by using the motorway network. Evidence tends to support that motorways are a lower risk than smaller standard roads. This could mean that drivers that are travelling long distances on motorways may not be exposed to as high a risk as those that travel long distances on standard roads. However, the fatigue encountered by all drivers that cover long distances often increases due to the poor performance of other drivers. This can lead to errors that could result in a road traffic incident.

It is possible that careful scheduling of routes may reduce the distance that has to be travelled and therefore affect the level of risk significantly.

DRIVING HOURS

Similar to the distance driven the driving hours can have a direct effect on the level of risk of being involved in a road traffic incident. The longer the driving hours of the journey (i.e. the greater the duration of exposure to the hazards of driving) the greater the risk of a road traffic incident occurring. Similarly, even an alert and experienced driver is at increased risk of being involved in a road traffic accident the longer hours they are travelling.

In addition, if driving hours are excessive the driver is likely to become fatigued, their attention and reaction levels will fall and they are at increased risk of making errors. The hours driven may be excessive because the driver has been driving too long without a break, their cumulative hours in a day have become too much or their rest period between days has become too little. For some drivers the driving hours they do is in addition to other work hours, for example, the driving hours done when someone is travelling to a meeting. These cumulative hours can have a significant effect on fatigue.

Most commercial vehicles will be fitted with tachometers, which record the time spent by the driver when driving. These driving hours are limited by legislation, driving hours of goods vehicles over 3.5 tonnes and some passenger vehicles are regulated by European Community rules that the UK has adopted.

These set limits on driver's hours:
- Daily driving limit: 9 hours.
- Maximum driving limit: 4 ½ hours.
- Daily rest period: 11 hours.
- Weekly driving limit: 56 hours.
- Fortnightly driving limit: 90 hours.
- Weekly rest period: 45 consecutive hours.

However, company car drivers do not have these specific legal limits and monitoring imposed on them. Therefore, safe systems of work and appropriate training should be given to all drivers; this should include the hazards and risks associated with excessive driving hours. It is important that cumulative hours are monitored and controlled and that breaks are taken at intervals on longer journeys. The Highway Code recommends that drivers should take a 15 minute break every two hours. The responsibility for monitoring hours and taking breaks is a shared responsibility of both the driver and the employer.

WORK SCHEDULES

Work schedules that are badly organised can put increased pressure on drivers to be in a particular place by a given time. This can lead to them being tempted to increase speed and take abrupt action to change lanes to improve their progress. This risky action can lead to higher risk of collision and reduced stopping distances, making the likelihood of being involved in a road traffic incident higher.

Work schedules should take account of periods when drivers are most likely to feel sleepy. The high risk times are 2am to 6am and 2pm to 4pm. Employers should provide drivers with the means to stop and take a break if they feel sleepy, without the fear of recrimination. Where possible, schedules should be organised so that breaks can naturally and easily be taken, with agreed break points if travel is going as planned or if it is not. Driving to and from the place of employment does not form part of the working day, but may be an accident causation factor if travelling home follows a long working day or heavy work schedule driving.

STRESS DUE TO TRAFFIC

Nearly one in three UK drivers report feeling stressed whilst behind the wheel. Driving-related stress is likely to be experienced when the demands of the road/traffic environment exceed the driver's ability to cope with or control that environment.

Sometimes driving stress can show itself as a 'road rage'. That is an irrational human mechanism that is activated to protect the sufferer from what they perceive to be actual or potential danger. A person may often resort to irrational behaviour in order to avoid certain situations or events. Others may perceive the circumstances which aggravate the 'road rage' as being either insignificant or trivial, but to the individual concerned they are 'very real' and 'very relevant'.

This increased stress can inhibit correct perception of hazards and influence reaction time. This coupled with the erratic driving pattern of the driver and others influenced by the stress of traffic conditions, can lead to an increased risk of being involved in a road traffic incident.

WEATHER CONDITIONS

Weather conditions have a significant impact on the risks of driving and the likelihood of being involved in a road traffic incident. Sudden rainfall or snow and fog can lead to poor visibility and sudden breaking. Snow and surface water conditions can increase stopping distances.

Even good weather can have a negative effect as glare from the sun can limit visibility. This is particularly the case in early morning or evening and is most significant during the winter when the sun is lower in the sky for longer.

Managing work-related road risk

POLICY

A road risk policy should be incorporated into the health and safety policy. Whether employers provide vehicles or expect employees to drive their own for work purposes, all employers should have a policy to address the issues.

As part of any driving at work policy, employers should include:
- A requirement that the employee must maintain their vehicle in a roadworthy condition if they are to use their own vehicle for work.
- A requirement that if the vehicle is over three years old, it has a valid MOT certificate.
- A requirement that the employee has a current driving licence.
- A requirement that the employee has appropriate insurance (the employee should present copies of certificates annually for inspection).
- A requirement that the employee informs their line manager of any changes in circumstances such as penalty points, changes in insurer or vehicle used or use of any prescription medication or changes to health that affect their ability to drive safely.
- Assessment of risks.

ELEMENT C10 - WORKPLACE TRANSPORT AND DRIVING FOR WORK

- Management strategies to plan, organise, control, monitor and review work-related road risk.
- Driver training and competence.
- Taking breaks.
- Breakdown of the vehicle.
- Reporting problems and delays.
- Weather conditions.

SYSTEMS TO MANAGE WORK-RELATED ROAD RISK

Systems of work to manage work-related road risk should be formally established and consider the main factors, the people, equipment, materials, and environment involved. Consideration of these factors, and how they interact with each other, can help to establish complete and effective systems of work that significantly influence work-related road risk.

Competent staff should be trained to manage and implement the work-related road risk policy. These should be developed using the guidance provided by professional organisations that have many years of experience and expertise around this subject for example, the Automobile Association (AA), the RAC or ROSPA.

Many employers carry out internal assessments of driving skills in addition to the minimum legal requirements. This can be done in-house or carried out by an external assessor. If drivers are being asked to drive minibuses, etc. then employers can require additional qualifications, as proof of abilities. Some employers offer specific training in safe driving techniques for their employees.

It is important that systems are put in place to organise that driving distances are kept to a minimum, driving hours are controlled and work schedules are organised to reduce pressure on drivers to meet challenging times and in turn reduce undue road risk. Organisations should have systems in place to respond to inclement weather and enable drivers to take safe decisions about the effects of weather on their driving or journey.

SELECTION AND MANAGEMENT OF FLEET

Selection

When selecting work-related road vehicles it is important to consider whether the vehicle is suitable for the intended purpose, the working conditions it will be exposed to and what risks may arise from its use. This will require a range of factors, including:

- Size, weight and capacity of the vehicle.
- Loading and unloading methods.
- Availability and training needs of drivers.
- Means to control use, for example, keys, electronic fobs or key pads.
- Driver access to the driving position.
- Driver having good all-round visibility.
- Ergonomic aspects of its use.
- Risks the vehicle may create, noise, vibration and fumes.
- Need to use it in specific circumstances, for example, at night, indoors or in flammable atmospheres.
- Safeguards to prevent people coming into contact with dangerous parts of the vehicle, such as power take-offs, chain drives, exposed hot exhaust pipes.
- Seat belts and restraints.
- Roll over protection.
- Protection from falling objects, weather, extremes of temperature, dirt, dust and fumes.
- Suitability and effectiveness of braking systems for the intended use.
- Visibility of the vehicle, colour and lighting.
- Warning systems, such as horns and lights.

It should be remembered that vehicles for use on the public highway must conform to the Road Vehicles (Construction and Use) Regulations and similar vehicles used in the workplace should conform to these standards, as a minimum.

Fleet management

Fleet management will involve activities like:

- Establishing a work related driving policy.
- Matching drivers to vehicles and the tasks they do, ensuring that they can be achieved safely. If this involves driving for extended periods this will mean consideration on limits for driving hours.
- Making sure drivers are provided with health and safety information, including vehicle checks and loads.
- Maintaining vehicles and driver competence.
- Ensuring driver fitness requirements are met.
- Planning journeys to minimise risk by considering distances, timing, fatigue and weather.

MONITORING PERFORMANCE

The Management of Health and Safety at Work Regulations (MHSWR) 1999 establishes a legal requirement to monitor health and safety systems to ensure the policy is effective.

Information that should be monitored includes:
- Compliance with legal responsibilities.
- Effectiveness of the organisational structure.
- Competence of drivers.
- Driving hours.
- Reporting of work-related road safety incidents.

INCIDENT REPORTING

Certain road traffic incidents are reportable under the Reporting of Injuries, Diseases and Dangerous Occurrences Regulations (RIDDOR) 1995. Employers should also monitor minor work-related road incidents resulting in damage to vehicles.

Drivers must be required to record information about all incidents, whether minor or serious, for all journeys. A similar reporting procedure should be in place for reporting significant "near misses", supported by training that emphasises how to recognise, analyse and learn from such events.

The data provided should be analysed and any changes or improvements noted. These changes or improvements should be communicated to those concerned and the policy or procedures updated.

ORGANISATION AND STRUCTURE

In a large organisation it is likely that various departments within the organisation will have different responsibilities that influence drivers at work. The despatch department will be responsible for planning journeys; the training department is responsible for driver competence; the human resources department could be responsible for driver selection and checking the validity of driving licences.

The maintenance department is responsible for the upkeep of vehicles and ensuring the roadworthiness of vehicles and the occupational health department is responsible for carrying routine health surveillance of large goods vehicle (LGV) drivers.

It is therefore essential that the structure of the organisation ensures that these activities are carried out in an effective manner. The responsibilities of different parts of the organisation should be defined, including the responsibility to co-operate and provide information to each other.

Legal responsibilities of individuals on public roads

Vehicle condition
- Ensure the vehicle and trailer complies with the full requirements of the Road Vehicles (Construction and Use) Regulations (CUR) 1986 and Road Vehicles Lighting Regulations (RVLR) 1989.

Fitness to drive
- Drivers must report to the Driver and Vehicle Licensing Agency (DVLA) any health condition likely to affect their driving.
- Do not begin a journey if tired.

Vision
- Must be able to read (with the aid of vision corrected lenses) a vehicle number plate, in good daylight, from a distance of 20 metres (or 20.5 metres where the old style number plate is used).
- Slow down, and if necessary stop, if dazzled by bright sunlight.
- At night or in poor visibility, do not use tinted glasses, lenses or visors if they restrict vision.

Alcohol and drugs
- Do not drink and drive in excess of the legal limit for alcohol.
- Do not drive under the influence of drugs or medicine.

General
- Drivers must ensure they use all due care and attention for others when in charge of a vehicle.
- Divers must not tow more than their licence permits. Those who passed a car test after 1 January 1997 are restricted on the weight of trailer they can tow.
- Do not overload the vehicle or trailer.
- Secure the load and ensure it does not protrude out dangerously.
- Drivers and other passengers must wear a seat belt or suitable restraining device for babies or small children in cars, vans and other goods vehicles if one is fitted (exemptions are allowed for the holders of medical exemption certificates and those making deliveries or collections in goods vehicles when travelling less than 50 metres (approx 162 feet).

For detailed information refer to the Road Traffic Act (RTA) 1991 and the 'new' Highway Code, for related legislation refer to www.direct.gov.uk.

RISK ASSESSMENT

Risk assessments for work-related driving activities should follow the same principles as risk assessments for any other work activity. They should be carried out by a competent person with practical knowledge, qualifications and training relating to the work activity being assessed.

ELEMENT C10 - WORKPLACE TRANSPORT AND DRIVING FOR WORK

Step 1 - Identify the hazards

Hazards will fall into the following categories:

The driver Competence, training, qualifications, fitness and health, alcohol and drug use, etc.

The vehicle Suitability, condition, safety equipment, ergonomic considerations, the load, security, etc.

The journey Route planning, scheduling, time, distance, driving hours, weather conditions, stress, volume of traffic, weather conditions, passengers, etc.

Step 2 - Decide who might be harmed

The driver would be a category of person that might be harmed, but this might include any passengers, other road users and/or pedestrians. Consideration should also be given to other groups who may be particularly at risk, such as young or newly qualified drivers and those driving long distances.

Step 3 - Evaluate the risk and decided on precautions

Risks may vary depending on whether driving is done at night or in the day, the type of vehicle or driving conditions. Decide the likelihood of the harm and severity (consequence) of any outcome. Consider risk factors such as distance travelled, driving hours, work schedules, traffic levels and weather conditions. Decide on appropriate precautions and once this has been established, decide whether the residual risk is acceptable.

Step 4 - Record the findings and implement them

Significant findings need to be recorded and risk assessment findings should be made available to all drivers.

Step 5 - Review the assessment and update it if necessary

Monitoring and reviewing the assessments should take place to ensure these risks are suitably controlled. Systems should be put into place to gather, monitor, record and analyse incidents that might affect these risk assessments. The vehicle and driver's history should also be recorded. Any changes in the route, new equipment and changes in the vehicle specifications should be reviewed and recorded. This will ensure the continued effectiveness of controlling the risks.

EVALUATING THE RISKS

The driver

The level of work-related road risk is particularly affected by the driver's **competency**. If someone is new to driving their skill may be adequate to provide them with a national driving licence, but their experience of driving will be low.

Drivers that only drive intermittently also present a high risk as any competence they may have may decay over the time between driving. The driver's competence has to be appropriate to the driving being expected of them. An inexperienced driver driving in heavy traffic in complicated driving settings at night in the winter will present a particularly high risk. Similarly, a person that is reasonably experienced in driving their small car may have difficulty when first driving a larger or faster accelerating vehicle. In the same way, some drivers will need to adjust to driving slower vehicles and ones with a different centre of gravity.

Driver **fitness** may influence their ability to see well when driving at night, their ability to travel distances without breaks and may put them in a high risk category for heart attack or other type of seizure. Pre-existing **health** conditions such as back injuries and late term pregnancy could influence the driver's ability to concentrate on road conditions.

The level of **training** that the driver has received may affect risk in that if no training is given a driver may have developed bad driving habits and not be aware of them. Refresher driver training may help to reduce risk.

The vehicle

The size, weight, centre of gravity and power of a vehicle will all influence the functioning of the vehicle and therefore the risk that may arise from its use. It is important that the vehicle is **suitable** for the task and the driver. A large, powerful, fast acceleration car may be suitable for a specific task, but very unsuitable for an inexperienced driver. The **condition** of the vehicle will have a significant effect on the level of risk. Vehicles that have poor brakes, lights, do not steer well and have poor suspension will represent a high risk in any driving situation. Vehicles with broken or missing mirrors will mean that the driver will not be able to see other road users adequately and will increase the risk when changing lanes.

Much of the **safety equipment** to prevent accidents, such as active braking systems (ABS), should be built into most modern vehicles. Other items may be optional, such as run-flat tyres, but may be useful in reducing certain road risks. Other safety equipment is designed to reduce the consequences of accidents and can therefore reduce risk, such as airbags, escape kits, warning triangles and high-visibility vests.

Consideration has to be made of the **safety critical information** related to the vehicle, including its height, width, length, weight and load carrying/towing capacity. The absence of this information can have an immediate and significant effect on the level of risk.

Ergonomic considerations have an effect on both comfort and ability to control the vehicle effectively. The comfort issues can increase fatigue and ergonomic considerations like seat height adjustment can significantly affect the ability of the driver to see out of the vehicle properly.

The journey

When evaluating the risk related to journeys it is important to take into account such factors as:

- The *route* being taken - motorways are safer than smaller roads; routes using motorways will be lower in risk.
- *Scheduling* - if the journey is to be made early in the morning there might be an increased level of risk due to tiredness, but this may be offset by the reduced level of traffic.
- *Time* allowed for travel - if not enough time is allowed for the journey and normal delays the risk will be higher.
- *Weather* conditions - can rapidly increase risks, conditions such as ice and snow will have a significant effect.

CONTROL MEASURES TO REDUCE WORK-RELATED DRIVING RISKS

When establishing control measures to reduce work-related driving risk elimination of as many driving activities as possible should be the first consideration. This will involve consideration of whether the road journey is necessary, perhaps telephone/video conference could be used instead of driving or goods could be sent by rail/air freight instead of by road.

The driver

It is the employer's duty to ensure that drivers are competent, fit, in good health and capable of doing their work in a way that is safe. Employers must **check drivers' licences and documentation**, including requiring them to produce evidence that they have a current licence to drive their vehicle. Without a current licence and/or test certificate the employer's/driver's insurance will be invalid. Regular assessment of driver competence and monitoring the validity of documentation, such as insurance and driving licence, should be carried out. Large goods vehicle (LGV) drivers and passenger carrying vehicle (PCV) drivers have to maintain a certificate of professional competence by undertaking 35 hours of *driver training* every 5 years.

The vehicle

It is the employer's responsibility to ensure that the vehicle fits the purpose for which it is used. It is important that the vehicle is safe, in a fit condition and suitable for the task to be carried out. This will include the proper fitting and maintenance of any safety equipment that is required. This will usually require planned periodic *vehicle checks* to ensure its suitability and condition. Any safety critical information should be displayed within the cab for example, height or width of the vehicle.

Ergonomics, such as the driver's seat should also be considered, it may require additional support for example, lumbar cushions. Whole body vibration should be considered and air-suspension seats may be required as a precaution.

Ensure safety equipment is fitted and used, for example:

- Seat belts, air bags are installed, maintained and used correctly.
- Two-wheeled vehicle riders should use appropriate safety helmets and protective clothing.
- Ensure vehicles do not exceed speed limits by fitting trackers to monitor the speed limits.

The journey

Journey planning and scheduling is essential in ensuring the safety of employees who drive for work. Investing time in ensuring that journey planning is implemented as a component of the work-related road risk policy will ensure that, where possible, routes are planned thoroughly, schedules are realistic, and sufficient time is allocated to complete journeys safely. It may be required to plan overnight stopovers (provide hotel accommodation) if the journey time extends due to bad weather or traffic conditions. Delivery schedules should be adjusted so that unrealistic targets are not set. This will reduce the stress to drivers and will not encourage them to drive too fast for the conditions, or exceed speed limits.

This page is intentionally blank

Pressure system hazards and controls

Element C11

Learning outcomes

The intended learning outcomes are that the student will be able to:

C11.1 Outline the principles of operation of liquefied gas storage; refrigeration systems; and heating systems.
C11.2 Outline the key features and safety requirements for 'simple' unfired pressure systems.
C11.3 Outline the key features and safety requirements for process pressure systems.
C11.4 Outline the likely causes of the failure of pressure systems and the testing and prevention strategies that can be used.

Content

C11.1 - Principles	367
The hazards of steam	367
Mechanism of a steam explosion	368
Corus Blast Furnace, 2001	368
Properties of liquefied petroleum gas	370
Storage in spheres vs. torpedoes	371
Bulk storage under pressure and refrigeration	372
The operation of a basic steam heating system	373
Meaning of pressure, positive pressure and negative pressure	373
C11.2 - Simple pressure systems	374
Meaning of terms related to simple pressure systems	374
Essential safety requirements	376
Examination of simple pressure systems	377
C11.3 - Pressure systems	378
Definitions	378
The key components and safety features of pressure systems	379
C11.4 - Failure of pressure systems	381
The hazards of over pressure and over temperature in pressure systems	381
The mechanisms of mechanical failure that lead to a loss of containment	381
Prevention strategy	385

Relevant statutory provisions

Pressure Equipment Regulations (PER) 1999
Pressure Systems Safety Regulations (PSSR) 2000
Simple Pressure Vessels (Safety) Regulations (SPVSR) 1991

PRESSURE SYSTEM HAZARDS AND CONTROLS - ELEMENT C11

C11.1 - Principles

When water is heated above its boiling point 100°C the volume change at atmospheric pressure is in the order of 1:1650. This volume change with phase change, from liquid to vapour, was put to significant use with the invention of the steam engine, where relatively small amounts of water produce large volumes of steam to operate the pistons that supply the drive force to the engine.

The hazards of steam

The principal hazards associated with steam are that of explosion and scalding. This often results from failure of a pressure system, such as a steam main (see mechanisms of a steam explosion), or where water used to cool a high temperature process enters the process by error or failure of the coolers resulting in water/steam phase change and pressure change *(see also - Corus Blast Furnace, 2001 later in this element)*.

Consider a vertical cylinder closed by a piston on which there is a weight. The weight acting down under gravity on a piston of fixed size ensures that the fluid in the cylinder is always subject to the same pressure. Cylinder (A) contains only water at ambient temperature.

Initially the water at ambient temperature is sub-cooled. When heat is added its temperature rises steadily until it reaches the saturation temperature corresponding with the pressure in the cylinder. The volume of the water hardly changes during this process.

At this point the water is saturated (B). When more heat is added, steam is generated and the volume increases dramatically since the steam occupies a greater space than the water from which it was generated (C). The temperature however remains the same until all the water has been converted into steam.

At this point the steam is saturated (D). When additional heat is added the temperature of the steam increases, but at a faster rate than when the water only was being heated. The volume of the steam also increases. Steam at temperatures above the saturation temperature is called superheated steam (E).

WATER AND STEAM CHARACTERISTICS

Heating water and steam at constant pressure.

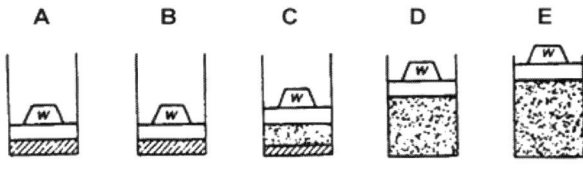

- **A** Subcooled Water
- **B** Saturated Water Only
- **C** Water and Steam Mixture
- **D** Saturated Steam Only
- **E** Superheated Steam

Figure C11-1: Water steam characteristics.   *Source: Ambiguous.*

The temperature of the boiling water and saturated steam within the same system is the same, but the heat energy per unit mass is much greater in the saturated steam.

At atmospheric pressure the saturation temperature is 100°C. However, if the pressure is increased, this will allow the addition of more heat and an increase in temperature without a change of phase.

The relationship between the saturation temperature and the change in pressure is known as the steam saturation curve *(see figure ref C11-2)*.

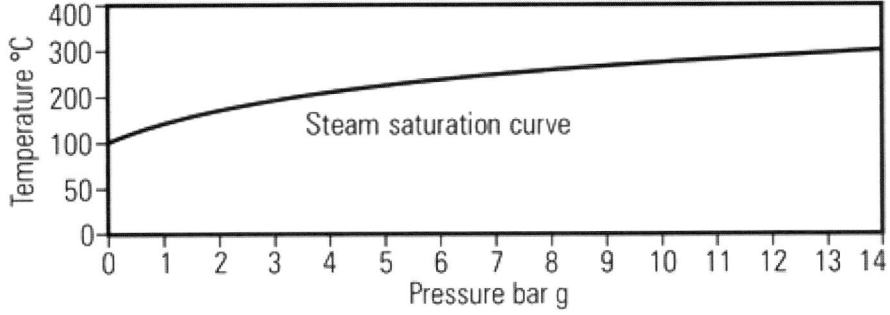

Figure C11-2: Steam saturation curve.   *Source: Spirax-sarco Ltd.*

Steam at a condition above the saturation curve is known as superheated steam. This property is used in high pressure steam mains that are used in urban heating or industrial process plant systems to transfer greater energy per unit mass than would be possible with water alone.

Mechanism of a steam explosion

Water hammer in steam pipes is caused by moving water (condensed from the steam, i.e. 'condensate'). Condensate creates a pocket of water at lower temperature than the steam, which is propelled by steam until it impacts on closed valves or filters producing the characteristic water hammer sound. The sound is released energy as the water pocket hits the obstruction and transfers its kinetic energy into force per unit area.

Normally the system is designed to minimise the effect of damage by such occurrences, but there is one type of water hammer, 'condensation induced water hammer' (CIWH), that can occur with devastating results to the system if the circumstances are as follows:

- Condensate collects at a low point in the steam main due to failure of a steam trap (a condensate drainage device).
- Condensate cools to below the saturated steam temperature by a minimum of 30°C.
- A triggering event, such as a steam valve is opened allowing condensate to drain from the line and allowing steam to re-enter the line containing the sub cooled condensate.
- The entering steam gives up heat rapidly to the sub-cooled condensate and pipe walls; it condenses (causing a pressure drop) and draws in more steam to replace the condensing steam.
- The induced steam flowing over the condensate, if rapid enough, results in the creation of waves on the surface of the condensate.

If the wave front is high enough to fill the pipe so that it cuts off steam inflow into the condensate pocket, condensation in the now isolated pocket will drop the pressure of the pocket, resulting in rapid heat transfer between the saturated steam and the sub-cooled condensate and pipe walls.

At this point, the pressure drop can be instantaneous, milliseconds. Condensate formed from the steam occupies less than one hundredth to one thousandth of the steam it replaces.

The pressure differential between the disappearing condensate pocket and the full system steam pressure outside the pocket accelerates the condensate until it crashes into stationary water or a valve, abruptly halting and converting its kinetic energy into high pressure. In a typical steam main at 100 psi (7 bar) steam pressure water can be accelerated at 40 fps (12.2 mps) if there is a sufficient sized steam void, causing a transient water hammer pressure up to 2000 psi (140 bar).

Figure C11-3: Steel pipe blown open at a tee junction by water hammer.
Source: Kirsner Consulting Engineering, Inc.

Typically the pressure required to fracture an 18 inch (44 mm) standard weight pipe with a continuously welded seam can be as low as 1,100 psi (76 bar).

Sourced and adapted from chapter 10 Water in Steam Lines - Kirsner Consulting Engineering, Inc. for BP.

Corus Blast Furnace, 2001

At the time of the incident, Port Talbot was an integrated steelworks, manufacturing flat steel products for a very extensive range of industries. Iron was produced on site from basic raw materials in two blast furnaces (designated no. 4 and no. 5) and then converted into steel. The two furnaces at Port Talbot at the time of the explosion were fundamentally different. Number 5 was to a 1950s design, although modified over the intervening years, number 4 was constructed in the early 1990s to a Japanese design.

THE IRON MAKING PROCESS

The purpose of a blast furnace is to produce iron by chemical reactions on iron oxides (iron ores) and convert them into liquid iron. This is achieved by 'charging' iron ore, coke, sinter (a product of iron ore fines and coke), and limestone into the top of the furnace and subjecting these materials to a series of complex chemical reactions within the furnace.

The charge materials (or 'burden') gradually work down the furnace vessel, reacting chemically and thermally as they travel. At any given time the furnace burden could amount to around 1,800 - 2,000 tonnes of materials. Preheated air or 'hot blast' was blown into the furnace via nozzles known as 'tuyères'. This blast air is an essential part of the process - typically it would be heated up to 1,100°C.

The raw materials introduced into the top of the furnace took some six to eight hours to descend to the bottom of the furnace where their conversion into liquid iron and slag (i.e. molten waste material from the furnace) was completed. The liquid iron and slag was then drained or 'tapped off' at regular intervals from the furnace.

PRESSURE SYSTEM HAZARDS AND CONTROLS - ELEMENT C11

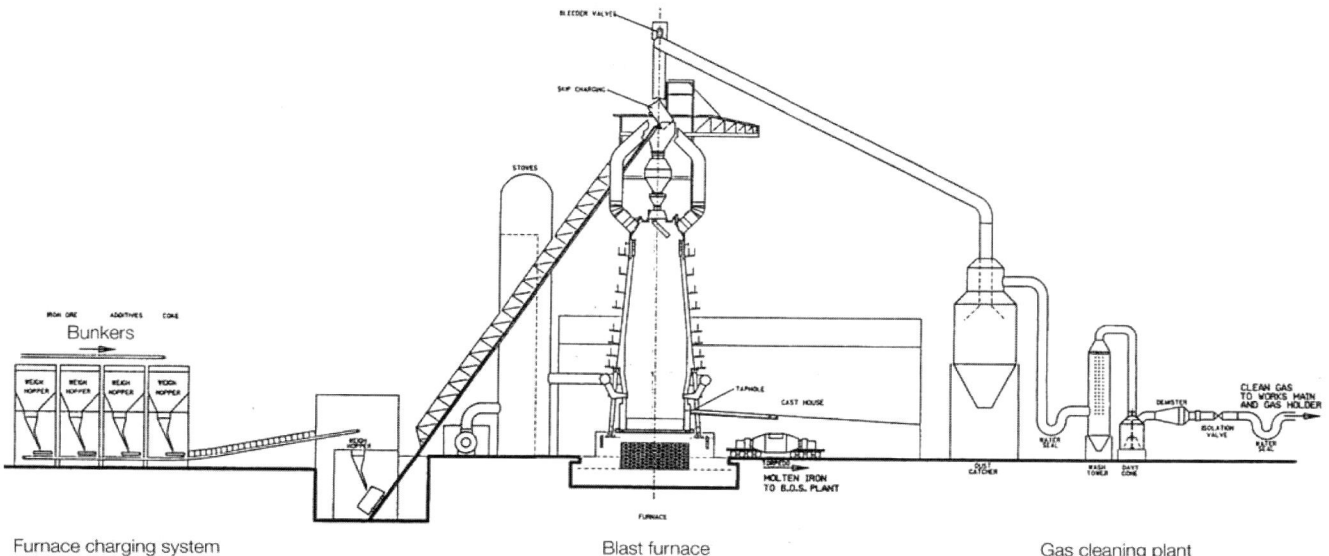

Figure C11-4: Diagrammatic arrangement of No. 5 Blast furnace. *Source: HSE.*

The process of iron production is extremely exothermic, generating temperatures of over 2,000°C within the furnace, and the provision and maintenance of adequate supplies of cooling water was essential. The normal requirement on the Corus No. 5 blast furnace cooling system was for approximately 80 - 90 thousand litres of cooling water per minute.

The majority of the coolers in No. 5 blast furnace were 'flat' or 'plate' coolers.

At various locations within the furnace other specialised coolers, again usually cast iron, but on occasion copper, were fitted to the furnace.

These included:

- Tuyère coolers - copper cooling elements at the end of the tuyères (tuyères supply hot air to the furnace).
- Stave coolers - these were large coolers made of cast iron.
- 'Big coolers' - these were copper cooling elements fitted around the tuyère cooler and fixed into the hearth jacket.
- Tap-hole staves - cast-iron cooling elements around the tap holes where molten metal and slag is drawn off.

Figure ref C11-5 shows a section of dismantled furnace shell (minus the refractory lining). The darker lozenge-shaped coolers are plate coolers.

Figure C11-5: Section of dismantled furnace shell. *Source: HSE.*

When the supply of water to a cooler is interrupted any residual water within the coolers would boil and evaporate. This in turn rapidly caused the cooler to melt or 'burn out'. Copper has a melting point of approximately 1,083°C, much less than the temperatures encountered in parts of the furnace and quickly melted in these conditions. The gas pressure within the operating furnace was less than the water delivery pressures within the coolers. When the water supply to a failed cooler was subsequently restored, there was the potential for a serious water leak into the furnace.

The immediate cause of the explosion was a chain of events as follows:

- On the 7th November there was a period of time, approximately 12 minutes, when the water supply to the coolers of blast furnace number 5 was reduced by 45%. This was because a switch of transformers governing the flow of electricity to one of the two pumps that were in use for pumping water to the cooling system caused the pump to trip. Within seconds the back-up pump also tripped.
- The reduction in water supply to the coolers caused a number of them to overheat, burn out and leak substantial quantities of water into the furnace.
- Due to the complex array of water supply pipes covering the furnace exterior, it took a very long time (over ten hours) for the leaking coolers to be detected and isolated. The switch of transformers took place at 08.45 and the leaking coolers were not detected until about 19.00. In that time about 50 to 60 tonnes of water, possibly more, leaked into the furnace.

ELEMENT C11 - PRESSURE SYSTEM HAZARDS AND CONTROLS

- The water ingress into the furnace caused its cooling. This led to a solidifying of the molten materials in the furnace.
- Efforts were made during the night of the 7th/8th and during the day of 8th November to extract molten metal, but with very limited success.
- On 8th November there was a further substantial leak of water into the furnace.
- The interaction of water and hot molten materials in the furnace caused the explosion.

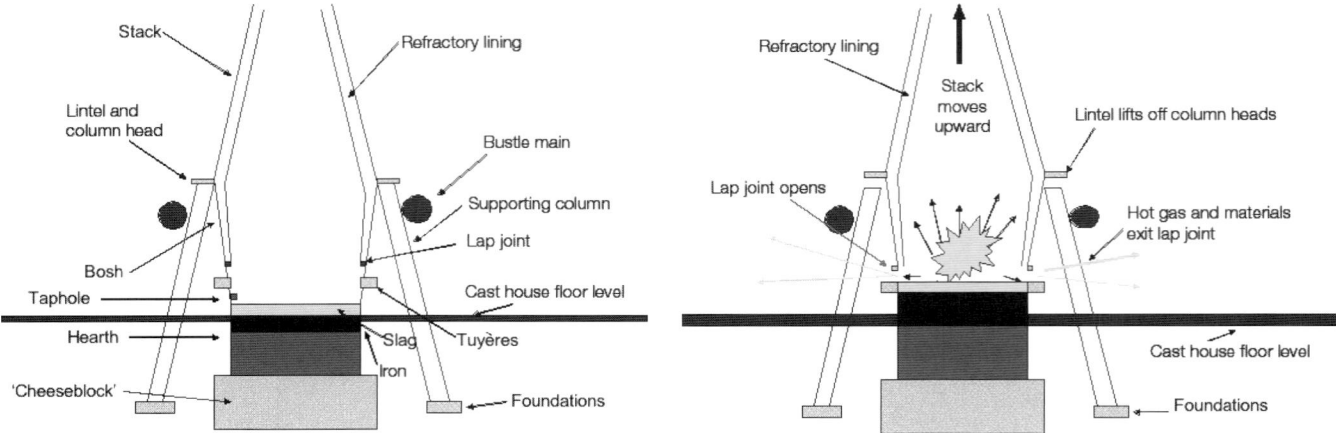

Figure C11-6: Prior to event. *Source: HSE.*

Figure C11-7: Furnace movement (5,000 tonnes 0.75 metres vertical) during explosion. *Source: HSE.*

The precise mechanism of the events within number 5 blast furnace on 8 November 2001 was not definitively determined, despite considerable analysis by a number of experts, both from within the industry and the Health and Safety Executive (HSE). The one feature that all the investigators agreed upon is that the explosion was without doubt brought about in some fashion by the interaction of water and hot molten materials in the lower reaches of the furnace.

CAUSATIVE FACTORS

- There were a series of serious pumping problems in the weeks before 7th November.
- The two main pumps (Sulzer 1 and Turbo T2) that failed on 7th November were set to operate unduly close to their tripping criteria. The safety margins were thereby reduced significantly.
- Total lack of written procedures for reliability-sensitive maintenance work.
- Training and supervision of key energy personnel was inadequate.
- The communication arrangements between energy supply and production were not sufficiently robust.
- No. 5 water cooling systems review, scheduled in 1994/5 and planned to secure their reliability to the end of the extended life of the furnace, was not carried out.
- The water cooling system as a whole was not seen as safety critical.
- No safety professional, reliability or risk assessment experts were members of the blast furnace number 5 extended use committee, nor were any involved in the work.
- No effective maintenance of the column head/lintel base securing bolts had been carried out.

Properties of liquefied petroleum gas

Liquefied petroleum gas (LPG) is a generic term used to describe two flammable gases, butane and propane; or mixtures of the two.

Properties	Butane	Propane
Appearance	Colourless gas	Colourless gas
Boiling point	-0.5°C	-42°C
Flash point	-60°C	-104°C
Auto-ignition temperature	500°C	540°C
Explosive limits	1.8 - 8.4 %	2.4 - 9.5 %
Critical temperature	152°C	97°C
Critical pressure	3.8 MPa (37.96 bar)	4.2 MPa (41.8 bar)

Figure C11-8: Properties of liquefied petroleum gas. *Source: Various.*

LPG will evaporate at normal temperatures and pressures and is supplied in pressurised steel cylinders. The containers are filled to between 80% and 85% of their capacity to allow for thermal expansion of the contained liquid. The mixtures of the two gases are adjusted seasonally; butane will not evaporate readily at temperatures below its boiling point of -0.5°C, so more propane in the mixture is used in colder climates to maintain an adequate supply pressure.

If the temperature of a cylinder of LPG is increased progressively then the vapour pressure will rise. The rising vapour pressure corresponds to the greater number of molecules in the limited volume of the vapour phase above the liquid, i.e. the vapour becomes considerably denser. Eventually a temperature will be reached at which the density of the vapour becomes the same as that of the liquid. Since liquids are usually distinguished from gases on the basis of density, at this point both have become identical. The temperature at which this occurs is called the critical temperature, i.e. the temperature above which a gas cannot be liquefied, regardless of the pressure applied. If the temperature continues to rise, the now incompressible volume in the cylinder will cause the cylinder to fracture catastrophically.

The critical temperature for both pure butane and propane is well above ambient temperature, LPG can be stored at relatively low pressure (of the order of 1 MPa or 10 bar) and this enables it to be readily transportable as a pressurised gas. Because the LPG is highly flammable, precautions have to be taken to provide adequate vent systems to pressurised bulk storage vessels (and ideally reflective coatings) that may be at risk of intense heat in a fire situation.

See also - C2.1 Properties of flammable and explosive materials and the mechanisms by which they ignite: boiling liquid exploding vapour explosions.

A release of LPG that was contained in a vessel under pressure will provide a large amount of gas as the liquid vaporises under ambient pressure. LPG gas is heavier than air and, if released from containment, will flow along floors and tend to settle in low points, such as drains and cellars, with the associated potential for ignition and suffocation hazards. LPG is used as a fuel for many domestic and agricultural heating systems; to power depot equipment, such as fork lift trucks, and more recently as a fuel for road vehicles. LPG is used as an aerosol propellant (usually butane) in spray containers and as a refrigerant in the replacement of chlorofluorocarbons, to reduce damage to the ozone layer.

Storage in spheres vs. torpedoes

Pressure vessels may theoretically be almost any shape, but shapes made of sections of spheres, torpedoes (i.e. cylinders), and cones are usually employed. A common design is a cylinder with end caps called heads. Many pressure vessels are made of chemically stable steel with good tensile properties and high impact resistance, particularly where vessels are used at low temperatures.

In applications where carbon steel would suffer corrosion, special corrosion resistant material or linings are used; they may be lined with various metals, ceramics, or polymers to prevent leaking and protect the structure of the vessel from its contents. This liner may also carry a significant portion of the pressure load.

The design pressure of a vessel depends on the product it contains and takes into account the vapour pressure of the product at the maximum temperature within the vessel. This is particularly important in hot countries where heat from solar radiation can cause the liquid within the vessel to expand, exerting greater pressure. In cases where the ambient temperature can fall below the atmospheric boiling point of the fluid, for example, n-butane at -1°C, the vessel must also be designed for vacuum conditions.

SPHERES

Theoretically, a sphere would be the best shape for a pressure vessel as the pressure in a spherical vessel is divided equally across the surface. A spherical vessel is the most expensive vessel shape to manufacture and, as a result is normally only used if no other type will meet the pressure requirements. The maximum capacity of pressurised spheres is limited by the maximum plate thickness that can be welded, typically 50 - 60mm. The capacity is also limited by the grade of steel. Due to several major accidents/explosions involving LPG spheres they are now rarely installed in Europe due to the planning permission required. The spheres have to be surrounded by a concrete enclosure to prevent damage to and impact from external fires if they fail.

Figure C11-9: High pressure storage spheres.   *Source: VTV.*

Figure C11-10: Steel pressure vessel with heads on skid mount.
Source: Gizelle; Mbeychok.

ELEMENT C11 - PRESSURE SYSTEM HAZARDS AND CONTROLS

TORPEDOES

Torpedo shaped containers are used for lower pressure applications than a sphere. Their simplified design enables them to be to be manufactured more easily and at a lower cost than a sphere. Generally torpedoes in use are smaller than spheres, but significant sizes of torpedoes, over 3,500m3 capacities, have been constructed. Most pressure vessels in use are cylindrical with two semi-elliptical heads or end caps at each end. Skid mounts are now common enabling the vessel to be readily secured to the ground or if required for transportation to be loaded onto a flat based transport heavy goods vehicle or rail carriage.

Mounded pressurised torpedoes offer a safer option than vessels left in the open and eliminate the possibility of a BLEVE. The torpedoes are embedded in sand and encased within a masonry structure with only the inlet and outlet controls exposed. The catastrophic failure mode of a cylindrical vessel is also such that it can be directed away from any processing or occupied areas.

The cover of the mound protects the vessel from fire engulfment, radiation from a fire in close proximity and acts of sabotage, terrorism or vandalism.

Figure C11-11: Mounded LPG storage tanks.   Source: GR.

Figure C11-12: Concrete encased moulded storage tanks. Source: GR.

Bulk storage under pressure and refrigeration

LIQUEFACTION OF GASES

Liquefaction of gases is the process by which a gas is converted into a liquid. Liquefaction is an important process commercially, because substances in the liquid state take up much less room than they do in their gaseous state. The molecules of any gas are relatively far apart from each other. The distance between gas molecules can be reduced by increasing the pressure on the gas and/or by lowering the temperature of the gas. The ease with which a gas can be liquefied is dependent upon its critical temperature and critical pressure.

The critical temperature of a gas is the temperature at or above which increased pressure will not cause the gas to liquefy. The minimum pressure required to liquefy the gas at the critical temperature is called the critical pressure.

For example, the critical temperature of ammonia is 133°C, which is above ambient temperature and this property enables it to be liquefied relatively easily. By comparison, the critical temperature of nitrogen gas is minus 147°C, well below ambient temperature. Liquefying gases at such low critical temperatures as nitrogen is more complex than with ammonia.

The most common practical applications of liquefied gases are the compact storage and transportation of combustible fuels used for heating, cooking, or powering motor vehicles. Liquefied petroleum gas (LPG) is widely used commercially for such purposes. In a similar way, compression of gases, which leads to liquefaction, is used in the design of a closed circuit refrigeration unit.

CLOSED CIRCUIT REFRIGERATION

Closed circuit refrigeration is used in the manufacture of refrigerators. The coolant in the refrigerator, for example ammonia, is first converted from a gas to a liquid by the use of a compressor.

The process of compression results in heat loss when the gas turns into a liquid through the condenser.

Liquid ammonia then passes through a series of tubes (volume expanders) within the refrigerator unit, the evaporator, where the liquid ammonia takes up heat from the contents of the refrigerator as it expands into a gas, chilling the contents of the freezer unit.

The cycle of compression and evaporation continues until the desired temperature of the storage unit of the refrigerator is reached.

PRESSURE SYSTEM HAZARDS AND CONTROLS - ELEMENT C11

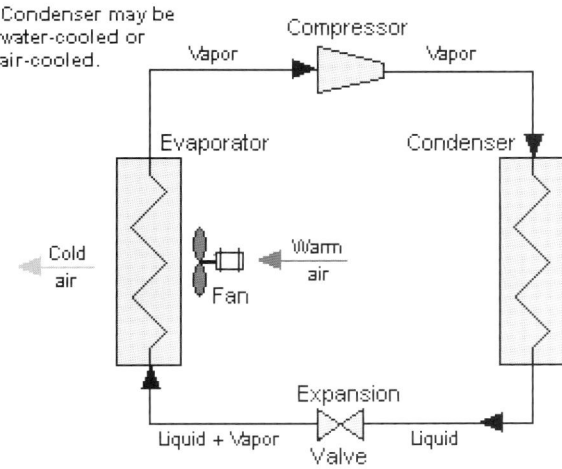

Figure C11-13: Typical single-stage vapour compression refrigeration. Source: Ambiguous.

The operation of a basic steam heating system

In a two pipe steam heating system, supply to the radiators and condensate return from the radiators is through separate pipes. Air accumulated in piping and from radiators discharges from the system through the open vent on the condensate pump receiver.

Piping and radiators must be installed with the correct pitch to provide gravity flow of all condensate to the pump receiver. Float and thermostatic trap (FandT Trap) controls steam flow and continuously discharges condensate and air accumulations into the returns main.

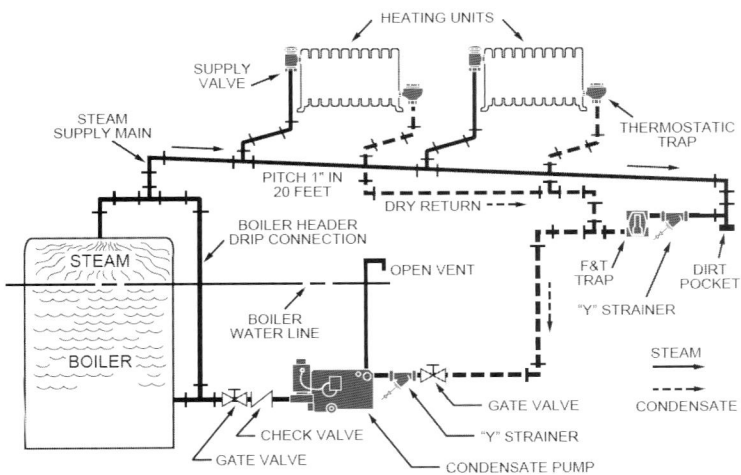

Figure C11-14: Two-pipe steam heating system. Source: ITT Corporation.

Meaning of pressure, positive pressure and negative pressure

PRESSURE

Pressure is the force per unit area applied in a direction perpendicular to the surface of an object.

The SI unit for pressure is the Pascal (Pa), equal to one Newton per square meter (Nm-2).

A system under pressure has the potential to perform work on its surroundings. Pressure is a measure of potential energy stored per unit volume measured in Joules per square metre (Jm-3).

POSITIVE PRESSURE

Positive pressure is a pressure within a system that is greater than the environment that surrounds that system and usually refers to pressures higher than atmospheric pressure. Consequently if there is any leak from within the positively pressurised system the leak will egress into the surrounding environment. Use is made of positive pressure to ensure there is no ingress of the environment into a supposed closed system:

- Use of a habitat on oil rigs to prevent the ingress of gases from the operation.
- Hospital rooms with patients with compromised immune systems to be kept away from any airborne micro-organisms (for example, bacteria) that may infect the patient.
- Manufacture of computer processors and electronic equipment to keep dust out.

NEGATIVE PRESSURE

Negative pressure is a pressure within a system that is less than the environment that surrounds that system and usually refers to pressures lower than atmospheric pressure, approaching that of a total vacuum. Any leakage to the system will draw in air from the outside. Negative pressure is used in the design of:

- Biological research laboratories to prevent air born micro-organisms from escaping into the general atmosphere.
- Equipment that utilises suction, such as vacuum cleaners, lifting equipment and money cartridge transfer systems.

C11.2 - Simple pressure systems

Meaning of terms related to simple pressure systems

The Simple Pressure Vessels (Safety) Regulations (SPVSR) 1991, as amended, Regulation 2 defines the principal terms for vessel, maximum working pressure, minimum working pressure and maximum working temperature.

VESSELS

For the purposes of the Pressure Systems Safety Regulations 2000, a pressure vessel may be regarded as a vessel used, or intended to be used, to contain a relevant fluid.

Figure C11-15: The term vessel explained in ACOP to PSSR 2000. Source: HSE.

UNFIRED

Unfired means not intended to be exposed to flame or heat.

CONTENTS

The vessel is intended to contain air or nitrogen at a gauge pressure >0.5 bar (0.05 MPa), but less than or equal to 30 bar (3.0 MPa). With a maximum working pressure (PS), of not more than 30 bar (3.0 MPa), and a PS.V (the product of PS and the vessel's capacity expressed in litres) of not more than 10,000 bar.litres (1.000 MPa.litres). With a minimum working temperature of not lower than -50°C, and the maximum working temperature is not >300°C for steel vessels and not >100°C for aluminium or aluminium alloy vessels.

SHAPE

The vessel consists of either a cylindrical component, with circular cross-section closed at each end, each end either outwardly dished or flat and also co-axial with the cylindrical component; or of two co-axial outwardly dished ends.

CONSTRUCTION AND MATERIALS

The vessel is made of welded non-alloy steel or non-alloy aluminium construction or non-age hardening aluminium alloy. Manufactured in series, i.e. more than one vessel of the same type is manufactured during a given period by the same continuous manufacturing processes, in accordance with a common design.

Maximum working pressure

The maximum working pressure is the maximum gauge pressure that may be exerted under normal conditions of use.

Minimum working temperature

The minimum working temperature is the lowest stabilised temperature in the wall of the vessel under normal conditions of use.

Figure C11-16: Carbon steel vessel. Source: Calor Gas.

Maximum working temperature

The maximum working temperature is the highest stabilised temperature in the wall of the vessel under normal conditions of use.

ABSOLUTE, ATMOSPHERIC AND GAUGE PRESSURE

Absolute pressure

The absolute pressure p_{abs} is measured relative to the absolute zero pressure - the pressure that would occur at absolute vacuum. All calculations involving the gas laws require pressure (and temperature) to be in absolute units.

Atmospheric pressure

Atmospheric pressure is pressure in the surrounding air at or close to the surface of the earth. The atmospheric pressure varies with temperature and altitude above sea level.

Gauge pressure

A gauge is often used to measure the pressure difference between a system and the surrounding atmosphere. This pressure is often called the gauge pressure and can be expressed as:

$p_g = p_s - p_{atm}$

Where:

p_g = gauge pressure

p_s = system pressure

p_{atm} = atmospheric pressure

Standard atmospheric pressure (atm) is used as a reference for gas densities and volumes. The standard atmospheric pressure is defined at sea-level at 273oK (0oC) and is 1.01325 bar or 101,325 Pa (absolute). The temperature of 293oK (20oC) is also used.

In imperial units the Standard Atmospheric Pressure is 14.696 psi.

1 atm = 1.01325 bar = 101.3 kPa = 14.696 psi (lbf/in2), where kPa = 1 kiloPascal

Many applications of pressure are not so much dependent on the absolute value of a pressure as the difference between it and the pressure of the atmosphere. A punctured car tyre is said to have 'no air in it' and a connected tyre pressure gauge would read 'zero' whilst obviously still containing atmospheric air. Such gauges are designed to measure pressure values that are expressed with respect to atmospheric pressure and thus indicate zero when the measurement port 'merely' contains molecules at atmospheric pressure. These measurements are known as gauge pressure measurements. Thus the difference between an absolute pressure value and a gauge pressure value is the variable value of atmospheric pressure:

Absolute pressure = gauge pressure + atmospheric pressure.

Therefore 100 psi gauge pressure would be equivalent to approximately 14.7 + 100 psi = 114.7 psi absolute.

In some cases, for example, when measuring the pressure reduction in an engine manifold, it is the value of the pressure reduction below the external 'reference' atmospheric pressure that is required, rather than the absolute value of the pressure. This is sometimes known as a negative gauge pressure measurement, but it should be appreciated that the concept of a negative absolute pressure is meaningless.

Where knowledge of the pressure difference between two places or systems is needed the reference pressure may not necessarily be either zero or atmospheric pressure, but some other value. These are known as differential pressures. For example, the flow of gas along a pipeline depends on the pressure difference between the ends of the pipe and in practice both ends are usually at comparatively high pressures.

If serious errors are to be avoided, it is important when making pressure measurements to be clear which mode of measurement is being employed - absolute, gauge (positive or negative) or differential.

Pressure modes are illustrated in *figure ref C11-17*; note that the reference line for gauge-mode measurements is not straight, illustrating the changeable nature of atmospheric pressure.

Sourced and adapted from the 'Guide to the Measurement of Pressure and Vacuum'.

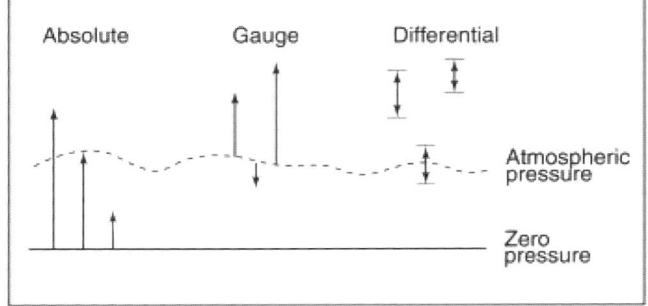

Figure C11-17: Comparison of pressures.   Source: Ambiguous.

OPERATING CONDITIONS

The Pressure Equipment Regulations (PER) 1999 concerns the manufacture of items such as vessels, pressure storage containers, heat exchanger etc. For pressure equipment not covered by the PER 1999, the more general requirements of the Pressure Systems Safety Regulations (PSSR) 2000 apply:

Reg. 3 of PSSR 2000, states that the primary purpose of the Regulations is to secure the **safety of people at work.** The Regulations therefore apply to pressure systems used, or intended to be used, at work. The duties imposed relate to activities at work. They also cover the self-employed, for example, a self-employed installer of a pressure system, or a self-employed competent person. The regulation also places duties on designers, manufacturers and any person who supplies equipment or a component intended to be part of a pressure system to ensure that it is fit for purpose, so as to prevent danger.

Reg. 4 of PSSR 2000 follows on from Section 6 of the Health and Safety at Work etc. Act (HASAWA) 1974 and states that the designer, manufacturer, importer or supplier should consider and take due account of the following factors, including the operating conditions, where applicable:

- The expected working life (the design life) of the system.

ELEMENT C11 - PRESSURE SYSTEM HAZARDS AND CONTROLS

- The properties of the contained fluid.
- All extreme operating conditions including start-up, shutdown and reasonably foreseeable fault or emergency conditions.
- The need for system examination to ensure continued integrity throughout the design life.
- Any foreseeable changes to the design conditions.
- Conditions for standby operation.
- Protection against system failure, using suitable measuring, control and protective devices as appropriate.
- Suitable materials for each component part.
- The external forces expected to be exerted on the system including thermal loads and wind loading.
- Safe access for operation, maintenance and examination, including the fitting of access (for example, door) safety devices or suitable guards, as appropriate.

Stress calculations for pressure vessels must be performed to demonstrate that at least minimum requirements of the relevant harmonised European Standard (BS EN 286-1:1998 + A2:2005 - "Simple unfired pressure vessels designed to contain air or nitrogen. Pressure vessels for general purposes") have been met during manufacture.

Significant improvements in vessel performance and component life can be gained at low expense if simple design principles are observed, such as the influence of stress concentrations and expansion constraints; the importance of using the proper weld seam; the influence of manufacture-based stress concentrations such as undercuts, edge displacements and surface influences.

At the design stage, operating conditions of the vessel will have to be taken into account as part of the design stage risk assessment required as part of the essential health and safety requirements (EHSR) in the EU Pressure Equipment Directive.

TRANSPORTABLE GAS CONTAINERS

PSSR 2000 define transportable as "designed to be transportable for the purpose of refilling"; which means that the container so described should be designed so that it can be removed from its appliance when it is empty and transported to another place where it can be filled.

Transportable cryogenic (deeply refrigerated) gas containers and chlorine gas containers, come within the definition of "transportable gas container" because the containers are for a relevant fluid; and the containers are designed to be transported for the purposes of refilling. The fact that they may occasionally be used for static storage is irrelevant.

Essential safety requirements

The Simple Pressure Vessels (Safety) Regulations (SPVSR) 1991, Schedule 1, set out the essential safety requirements for:

- Pressurised components, with particular emphasis on the materials being suitable.
- Steel vessels, with particular emphasis on the steel being suitable.
- Aluminium vessels, with particular emphasis on the aluminium being suitable.
- Welding materials - compatibility with materials to be welded.
- Accessories contributing to the strength of the vessel - made of material with similar characteristics to the vessel that they are fitted to.
- Non-pressurised components.

PRESSURISED COMPONENTS

The non-alloy quality steel, non-alloy aluminium or non-age hardening aluminium alloy used to manufacture the pressurised components must:

- Be capable of being welded.
- Be ductile and tough, so that a rupture at the minimum working temperature does not give rise to either fragmentation or brittle-type fracture.
- Not be adversely affected by ageing.

STEEL VESSELS

In addition to that required for pressurised components, non-alloy quality steels must be non-effervescent and be supplied after normalisation treatment, or in an equivalent state.

The content per product of carbon must be less than 0.25% and that of sulphur and phosphorus must each be less than 0.05%. Steel supplied must meet the specified mechanical test requirements described in the schedule to the regulations.

ALUMINIUM VESSELS

Non-alloy aluminium must have an aluminium content of at least 99.5% and non-age hardening aluminium alloys must display adequate resistance to inter-crystalline corrosion at the maximum working temperature. Materials must be supplied in the annealed state and meet the specified mechanical test requirements described in the schedule to the regulations.

NON-PRESSURISED COMPONENTS

All welded non-pressurised components must be of a material which is compatible with that of the parts to which they are welded.

Examination of simple pressure systems

Whilst there is no specific requirement to carry out inspections of simple pressure systems under pressure systems regulations, it is in keeping with the Provision and Use of Work Equipment Regulations (PUWER) 1998, Regulation 6, requirement to include such systems:

"Every employer shall ensure that work equipment exposed to conditions causing deterioration which is liable to result in dangerous situations is inspected:

(a) At suitable intervals.

(b) Each time that exceptional circumstances which are liable to jeopardise the safety of the work equipment have occurred, to ensure that health and safety conditions are maintained and that any deterioration can be detected and remedied in good time.

Every employer shall ensure that the result of an inspection made under this regulation is recorded and kept until the next inspection under this regulation is recorded".

TYPES OF INSPECTION

User checks

The type of inspection required to satisfy this requirement may include user checks of the equipment to identify obvious damage that may threaten the integrity of the system and to determine that protective devices are in place and in working order.

Maintenance

Scheduled maintenance inspections will be required to determine the condition of the pressure system and any action necessary to keep the pressure system and protective devices in working order. This may identify underlying deterioration, but will be limited by the competence of the person conducting the maintenance inspection.

Competent Person

An inspection during an examination by a competent person working to a written scheme of examination would be expected to be detailed and may involve non-destructive testing in order to identify conditions that could lead to danger of the failure of the pressure system.

STATUTORY BASIS FOR EXAMINATION OF PRESSURE SYSTEMS

Regulation 8 of PSSR 2000 requires that the user of an installed pressure system and owner of a mobile pressure system not operate the system unless a written scheme of periodic examination, by a competent person, has been drawn up (or certified as being suitable) by a competent person.

Exclusions for simple pressure systems

Part II of Schedule 1 to the PSSR 2000 exempts specific, simpler pressure systems that represent lower risk from having a written scheme of examination.

"Regulations 5(4), 8 to 10 and 14 shall not apply to a pressure system containing a relevant fluid (other than steam) if the product of the pressure in bar and internal volume in litres of its pressure vessels is in each case less than 250 bar litres".

The ACOP to PSSR 2000 suggests that the following are unlikely to need a written scheme of examination.

- An office hot water urn (for tea making).
- A machine tool hydraulic system.
- Portable oxy-fuel gas welding sets.
- An atmospheric oil storage tank.

Competent person

Regulation 9 of PSSR 2000 requires that examinations in accordance with the written scheme be carried out by a competent person.

Frequencies of examination

Neither PUWER 1998 nor PSSR 2000 specify intervals for examination of pressure systems, this is a matter for a competent person acting on behalf of the user or owner to decide. Frequencies of examination relating to some common pressure systems, based on earlier more prescriptive legislation, are shown in *figure ref C11-17*; however the actual frequency of examination will depend on a number of factors, including the conditions of use of the pressure system.

See also 'C11.4 - Failure of Pressure Systems' - Prevention strategy for more information on written schemes of examination.

ELEMENT C11 - PRESSURE SYSTEM HAZARDS AND CONTROLS

Pressure system type	Frequency in months
Air pressure plant	26
Hot water boiler over 100°C	14
Steam boilers and steam ovens	14
Steam pressure vessels	26
Refrigeration and air conditioning plant	26
Other pressure systems	26

Figure C11-18: Frequencies of examination based on earlier prescriptive legislation, as examples only not as a basis of written schemes. *Source: RMS.*

Regulation 9 of PSSR 2000 sets out the requirement to carry out examinations in accordance with the written scheme. The user of installed systems must ensure that the examinations are carried out by a competent person as laid down in the written scheme, before it is put into use and ongoing in accordance with the scheme. A competent person may be:

- A company's own in-house inspection department.
- An individual person (for example, a self-employed person).
- An organisation providing independent inspection services.

C11.3 - Pressure systems

Definitions

RELEVANT FLUIDS

The term 'relevant fluid' as defined in PSSR 2000, Regulation 2, "Interpretation" means:

(a) Steam;

(b) Any fluid or mixture of fluids which is at a pressure greater than 0.5 bar above atmospheric pressure, and which fluid or mixture of fluids is:

  (i) A gas, or

  (ii) A liquid which would have a vapour pressure greater than 0.5 bar above atmospheric pressure when in equilibrium with its vapour at either the actual temperature of the liquid or 17.5 degrees Celsius; or

(c) A gas dissolved under pressure in a solvent contained in a porous substance at ambient temperature and which could be released from the solvent without the application of heat.

The definition includes pressurised hot water above 110°C, steam at any pressure; a compressed gas (for example, nitrogen, oxygen and ammonia) including air (a mixture of gases) or liquefied gas (for example, propane) at a pressure greater than 0.5 bar (approximately 7 psi (0.7MPa) above atmospheric pressure.

Practical examples of the use of fluids include a hydraulic fluid in a hydraulic press or vehicle hoist, air used to operate a pneumatic drill and ammonia used in refrigeration units.

The term relevant fluid also includes a gas dissolved under pressure in a solvent contained in a porous substance at ambient temperature and that could be released from the solvent without the application of heat, for example, acetylene contained in an acetylene cylinder. An acetylene cylinder has a different design from most other gas cylinders. It consists of a steel shell containing a porous mass. The porous mass is a cellular structure which completely fills the cylinder. The acetylene gas in the cylinder is dissolved in acetone which is absorbed by the porous mass.

SCOPE OF WHAT CONSTITUTES A PRESSURE SYSTEM

Regulation PSSR 2000 defines the term pressure system as:

"(a) A system comprising one or more pressure vessels of rigid construction, any associated pipework and protective devices;

(b) The pipework with its protective devices to which a transportable pressure receptacle is, or is intended to be, connected; or

(c) A pipeline and its protective devices which contains or is liable to contain a relevant fluid, but does not include a transportable pressure receptacle".

The four main types of pressure vessel are steam boilers, steam receivers, steam container and air receivers: they each may form part of a pressure system.

A steam boiler consists of any closed vessel used for any purpose where steam is generated under a pressure greater than atmospheric and includes any economiser used to heat water being fed to any such vessel, and any super-heater used for heating steam. The purpose of the steam boiler is to generate steam under pressure. This is achieved by using fuel, air and water. The fuel is burnt and its potential heat transmits this energy which heats the water into water vapour, which also stores heat in the form of sensible and latent heat. There are 2 common types of boiler - horizontal and vertical.

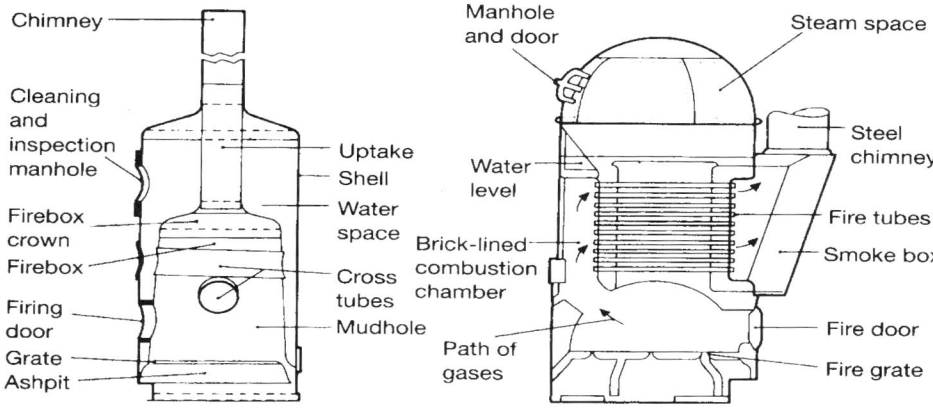

Figure C11-19: Pressure systems. *Source: J Stranks; Health and Safety in Practice (Safety Technology); Pitman Publishing; 1996.*

A steam receiver consists of any vessel or apparatus, other than a steam boiler, steam container, steam pipe or coil, or part of a prime mover, used for containing steam under pressure greater than atmospheric pressure.

A steam container consists of any vessel, other than a steam pipe or coil, constructed with a permanent outlet to atmosphere or into a space where pressure does not exceed atmospheric pressure, and through which steam is passed at atmospheric pressure, or at approximately that pressure, for the purpose of heating, boiling, drying, evaporating or other similar purpose.

An air receiver consists of any vessel or apparatus used for containing air under pressure greater than atmospheric pressure.

Pipe work and protective devices include:

- Valves, steam traps and filters.
- Rigid pipe and flexible hoses.
- Pressure gauges and level indicators.

Examples of pressure systems and equipment are:

- Boilers and steam heating systems.
- Pressurised process plant and piping.
- Compressed air systems (fixed and portable).
- Pressure cookers, autoclaves and retorts.
- Heat exchangers and refrigeration plant.

STEAM AT ANY PRESSURE

Steam at any pressure greater than 0.5 bar (0.05 MPa) above atmospheric pressure, for example, a pressurised water system at 110°C (0.5 bar, 0.05 MPa) through to a high pressure steam main in excess of 220°C (in excess of 7 bar, 0.7 MPa).

The key components and safety features of pressure systems

The key components and safety features of pressure systems include both protective and functional devices. The PSSR 2000, Regulation 2, defines protective devices as:

"Devices designed to protect the pressure system against system failure and devices designed to give warning that system failure might occur, and include bursting discs".

This legal definition of protective devices includes such protective devices as pressure relief valves and warning devices like temperature gauges, which indicate that system failure might occur if the maximum temperature is exceeded. Functional devices include devices like drain valves that enable water or sludge to be removed from the vessel.

BOILERS

Common devices fitted to boilers include:

Device	Protective device	Description
Temperature gauge	Yes	Fitted to indicate and warn of overheating, they must be connected to a cut off device to prevent overheating.
Pressure gauge	Yes	Fitted at all stages of pressure generation to show the working pressure in the line. This should have a range that includes 1.5 - 2 times the design pressure of the system.
Water level gauge	Yes	This indicates the amount of water in a system or boiler. The bottom of the gauge should be fitted at least 50 mm above the uppermost heating surface in the boiler. Can have remote systems fitted with probes indicating levels by lighting red or green lights as appropriate. These should be tested once a shift or day as appropriate.

ELEMENT C11 - PRESSURE SYSTEM HAZARDS AND CONTROLS

Device	Protective device	Description
Pressure relief valve	Yes	This is usually a spring loaded valve that is designed to lift at a predetermined pressure value to relieve excess pressure. These values should never be set at a higher value than the permissible working pressure or design pressure of the boiler.
Fuel cut off	Yes	To isolate the supply of energy to the boiler.
Bursting discs	Yes	To prevent catastrophic system failure when the pressure relief fails or is unable to cope with the rise in pressure above the safe working design pressure.
Water level replenishment controls	Yes	Two of these should be fitted to each boiler. They have a dual function: ■ To control the water at the correct operating level, i.e. water replenishment. ■ To shut down the burner in the event of a low water level warning. These should be tested once per shift or day as appropriate.
Water treatment	No	To prevent scale, corrosion, fouling and foaming and maintain the heat transfer efficiency.
Blow down valve	No	This is situated at the bottom of the boiler and is used to discharge water/sludge from the boiler.
Feed check valves	No	Used to control feed water being pumped into the boiler. There are two valves, the first is a screw down valve, the second a non-return valve which prevents water flowing back through the pump when it stops.
Main stop valve	No	Used to control the discharge of steam into the steam mains. The main stop valve is situated on top of the boiler.

Figure C11-20: Description of steam systems devices. Source: RMS.

AIR SYSTEMS

In an air system air is generated under pressure, normally by the use of a compressor or similar device. Common devices fitted to air systems are as follows:

Device	Protective device	Description
Pressure gauge	Yes	Fitted at all stages of pressure generation to show the working pressure in the line. This should have a range that includes 1.5 - 2 times the design pressure of the system.
Pressure sensing and cut off device	Yes	Operates to stop the compressor operating when the working pressure has been reached.
Safety valves	Yes	Operation is the same as for steam systems and is fitted at various points of the system.
Automatic temperature sensor and cut out	Yes	Oil flooded compressors should have an automatic shutdown device to prevent the temperature of the compressor oil or air from exceeding safe limits.
Inter coolers and after coolers	Yes	Used to cool the air in the system at various stages; when generated the air becomes very hot. These devices are a form of heat exchangers.

Figure C11-21: Description of air systems devices. Source: RMS.

AIR RECEIVERS

These have similar devices fitted as those required for air systems; however they do have additional devices.

Device	Protective device	Description
Drain valve	No	Fitted to the bottom of the receiver, used to drain moisture from the receiver. Should be regularly and frequently used to prevent the build up of moisture and/or emulsified oil.
Stop valve	Yes	Used to control the air outlet from the receiver.

Figure C11-22: Description of air receiver devices. Source: RMS.

See also - Pressure Systems Safety Regulations (PSSR) 2000 in relevant statutory provisions.

C11.4 - Failure of pressure systems

The hazards of over pressure and over temperature in pressure systems

Two of the most common causes of failure with pressure systems, in particular boilers, are:

- Over pressurisation of systems, which can occur if temperature controls and pressure relief valves fail because they have not been tested or maintained or inappropriate controls have been fitted.
- Over temperature is usually caused by low boiler water levels, which can occur if temperature controls have not been tested or maintained or inappropriate controls have been fitted, loss of water supply, build up of scale caused by inadequate water treatment may also cause localised overheating.

Both can lead to pressure system, in particular boiler, failure or catastrophic explosion due to fracture under pressure.

The main hazards from failure of pressure systems while they are under pressure are:

- Impact from the blast of an explosion or release of compressed liquid or gas.
- Impact from parts of equipment that fail or any flying debris.
- Contact with the released liquid or gas, such as steam.
- Fire resulting from the escape of flammable liquids or gases.

The mechanisms of mechanical failure that lead to a loss of containment

The pressure in a boiler or other pressure vessels results in longitudinal and circumferential tensile stresses. Other stresses may also be present, such as residual stresses resulting from welding, thermal stresses from heating/cooling and restraint stresses from fixings holding the vessel in place.

EXCESSIVE STRESS

Ductility is the amount a material will stretch before fracture. The atoms in a material slide over one another, rather than splitting, as they would do in a brittle failure. A pressure system could fail if the materials used in its manufacture were not capable of withstanding the normal operating stresses, this pressure may create excessive stress, beyond the capability of the material. This could also occur in situations where the thickness of the material has reduced, perhaps through corrosion or erosion, and it can no longer withstand the stress it is exposed to. A failure of this nature may affect part or the whole of the system and could lead to complete loss of containment.

ABNORMAL EXTERNAL LOADING

Failure of a pressure system due to abnormal external loading may be due to factors such as being struck by a fork lift truck or fuel delivery vehicle. This could create concentrated additional stresses from the impact that may be beyond the tensile strength of the pressure system. Where an accidental explosion, such as a dust explosion was to occur this too could provide abnormal stresses. If the vessel is restrained in such a way that it is not evenly held in place the additional stress created when it is secured may be sufficient to cause failure. This could occur where mounting bolts have been fixed to the floor out of alignment with the fixing holes.

OVERPRESSURE

Over pressurisation of systems can occur if pressure relief valves fail coupled with other devices failing. This will lead to the pressure level rising beyond safe working and design limits, which normally leads to catastrophic results. A pressure system could failure as a result of a single over pressure that creates enough excessive stress to lead to ductile failure. This could lead to complete loss of containment of the fluid under pressure. A copper hot water cistern can balloon due to excessive pressure; this would be an example of ductile failure.

OVERHEATING

Overheating can occur if alarms and controls fitted to prevent this have not been tested or maintained or inappropriate controls have been fitted originally. The overheating can lead to pressure in the system that rises beyond safe working and design limits, which can lead to catastrophic results.

Although pressure vessels are usually manufactured to withstand 3 times their safe working pressure, corrosion, erosion and fatigue can soon become a problem.

MECHANICAL FATIGUE AND SHOCK

Pressure within a system will cause tensile stresses in all directions. If the stresses are greater than the materials can cope with it will lead to ductile or brittle failure. Mechanical fatigue is the phenomenon leading to fracture under repeated or fluctuating stress.

These types of fatigue stresses can occur in pressure systems that have fluctuating levels of pressure. For example, a compressed air system is raised to a working pressure and the pressure in the system falls when air is used; this is subsequently raised again to the working pressure. The pressure in the system will fluctuate between the working pressure and the pressure set for the compressor to build pressure back up again. There will be an accompanying cycle of stress arising from the pressure rise and fall.

ELEMENT C11 - PRESSURE SYSTEM HAZARDS AND CONTROLS

The effects of fatigue stress is usually progressive, starting with minute cracks and grows under the action of fluctuating stress. Pressure system fatigue failure is often triggered by some surface interruption.

In engineering components, these surface faults could include sharp changes in direction, threads, oxide inclusions, grinding marks, weld defects, gauge mounts and seal mounts. All these surface faults constitute what is known as a 'stress raiser'. The stress applied to the component is concentrated in the area of a stress raiser and may exceed its capability, leading to the development of a crack.

Mechanical shock arises with a sudden increase or decrease in applied stresses. This may be due to a too abrupt build up of pressure in the system, which may not give the material that the system is made from enough time to respond in an elastic way, leading to sudden failure.

RELEVANT CASE STUDIES - FATIGUE FAILURE

On May 25, 2003 the cruise liner SS Norway with over 3,000 passengers and crew on board arrived at the Port of Miami. Within an hour of docking a massive explosion ripped through the ship as one of the vessels four steam boilers ruptured, sending superheated steam and oil, through the engineering spaces, fatally injuring four crew members in the boiler room, as well as four other crew who were in their living quarters. As the steam expanded and rose through the boiler room, it broke through the bulkheads on two further decks breaching the crew accommodation areas and seriously burning a further six crew members.

An investigation into the boiler failure was carried out by the National Transportation Safety Board (NTSB), who on examining the failed boiler (No 23), discovered that a large section of the waterwall header had fractured and broken away.

The water-wall header had been manufactured by longitudinally welding together two half-cylinder components - the tube sheet, so called because it contains openings for the waterwall tubes, and a thinner sheet called the wrapper sheet.

The entire waterwall header, including the caps ("dished heads"), was about 16.5 feet (5m) long.

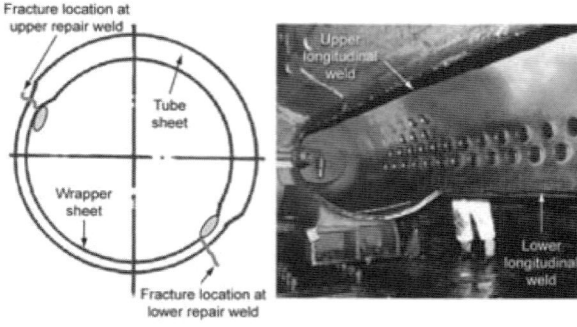

Figure C11-23: Waterwall header.   Source: NTSB.

The fracture along the upper longitudinal weld extended about 11 feet (3.35m), and the fracture along the lower longitudinal weld extended about 8 feet (2.44m). Metallurgical tests showed that the boiler header ruptured because of extensive fatigue cracking and that a number of factors contributed to the initiation and propagation of the cracking:

- Cracks were detected at original welds beginning in the 1970s.
- From 1990 to 2003, it appears that no non-destructive testing or appropriate internal visual inspections were carried out on the weld seams of boiler 23, even though the history of cracking was well documented and cracking was rediscovered on the weld seams of two of the ship's other boilers in 1996.
- Additional cracks were observed on later occasions and ground away until the minimum allowable wall thickness was reached, at which time weld repairs were made to build up the material thickness.
- The cracks initiated at the base of corrosion pits at the original longitudinal welds when the boiler was exposed to excessive cycling (thermal and mechanical loading), with severe transients (rates of temperature change) from start-up to cool down and constraint from fixed support feet (bolted solid restricting movement).
- The pitting most likely resulted from improper water chemistry (oxygen pitting) during lay-up periods. In 1987 and 1990, weld repairs were performed when the cracks extended below the minimum allowable grinding thickness.
- Cracking began again a few years later.
- The width and length of the weld repairs probably accelerated the pitting and cracking because of residual stresses in the weld repairs.
- The cracks then grew to critical size, causing the boiler to fail.

Figure C11-24: View of matching fracture halves. Source: NTSB.

Metallurgical examination also discovered large, isolated copper nuggets on the fracture surfaces near the surface of the header.

Analysis of the nuggets revealed that the material was pure copper as found in copper tubing. The copper had been worked into the cracks after they were largely formed in what appears to have been an attempt to hide the cracks from inspectors. *Figure ref C11-24* shows a view of matching fracture halves and enlarged image of copper nuggets at the edge of the fracture. Arrow points to area of enlarged image.

THERMAL FATIGUE AND SHOCK

Thermal shock is a situation where a hot fluid, for example, water in a boiler, is suddenly displaced by fluid with substantially different temperatures.

This causes rapid expansion or contraction of tubes, pressure vessel plate, pipes, valves and fittings, resulting in stresses to the boiler or piping system. If this change in temperature is smaller, but becomes a frequent event, this can result in fatigue, leading to such things as leaking tubes, cracked pressure vessels, and cracked cast iron sections.

BRITTLE FRACTURE

This type of failure has a tendency to fracture without deformation. Brittle materials may be incredibly strong, but lack resistance to the propagation of cracks. Brittle failure is promoted by factors such as high tensile and residual stresses; impact loading; high/low temperatures; thick plated vessels (> 100mm) and welded joints. It must be understood that a normally ductile material can fail in a brittle manner when complex stress fields exist.

CREEP

When a material is under constant load or stress, it may undergo progressive plastic (permanent) deformation over a period of time. This time dependent deformation is called 'creep'. The creep of materials used for pressure systems is very important, especially those pressure systems that operate at elevated temperatures. For such systems, creep may be the limiting factor with respect to the operating temperature. For some materials, such as lead, creep can occur at room temperature.

HYDROGEN ATTACK

This occurs when hydrogen seeps into gaps in the molecular framework of the metal and causes stresses from within the framework causing hydrogen embrittlement. Hydrogen attack can occur as a result of the cathode reaction during corrosion. Hydrogen can also be introduced during melting and entrapped during solidification. It can also occur during heat treatment, electroplating, acid pickling or welding. Systems are most susceptible at room temperature and as little as 0.0001% of hydrogen by weight can cause cracking in steel.

CORROSIVE FAILURE

Corrosion is the deterioration of a material through chemical or electro-chemical attack by atmosphere, moisture or other agents. In pressure systems, corrosion can thin the material causing it to lose strength. Corrosion occurs where levels of oxygen or carbon dioxide are high, where pH values are low or high, where contact occurs between dissimilar metals and in damp or corrosive atmospheres. The conditions for corrosion exist in air receivers that contain water in the air, where water is present in boilers and where different oxygen levels exist in boiler water. For this reason, any modification to the environment that makes it less aggressive will be beneficial.

RELEVANT CASE STUDIES - CORROSIVE FAILURE

Explosion of a natural gas transmission line

On 19 August 2000, a 30-inch-diameter natural gas transmission pipeline operated by El Paso Natural Gas Co. (Carlsbad, New Mexico) ruptured next to the Pecos River near Carlsbad. The gas ignited and burned for 55 minutes. Twelve people camping under a concrete-decked steel bridge that supported the pipeline across the river perished in the blast, and three vehicles were destroyed. Two nearby steel suspension bridges for gas pipelines crossing the river also suffered extensive damage.

During the investigation, investigators found the rupture was a result of severe internal corrosion that caused a reduction in pipe wall thickness to the point that the remaining metal could no longer contain the pressure within the pipe. According to the report, the corrosion was likely to have occurred within the pipeline by the combination of microbes and such contaminants as moisture, chlorides, oxygen, carbon dioxide, and hydrogen sulphide.

One of the major factors identified during the investigation concerned the failure to use cleaning "pigs". A pig is a mechanical device that cleans the pipeline. These devices, which may include scrapers or brushes on the pig body, are inserted into a pipeline and travel downstream with the gas flow.

Periodic use of cleaning pigs could remove water and other liquid and solid contaminants that may cause corrosion in a pipeline, according to the report. However, because the section of pipeline that ruptured could not accommodate pigs, the company did not run them through this section.

Recommendations

- Internal corrosion control programs to address the role of water and other contaminants in the corrosion process should be developed and implemented.
- The Office of Pipeline Safety's pipeline operator inspection program, which resulted in the failure of the inspectors to identify the inadequacies in El Paso's internal corrosion control programme, should be reviewed.

Explosion of a power plant's steam generating boiler

On November 6, 2007, the Dominion Energy New England's Salem Harbour Massachusetts, Generating Station Unit 3, a power plant's steam-generating boiler, a 1957 vintage 120-MW coal-fired radiant power boiler, exploded and three men died.

The Department of Public Safety's Incident Report investigation determined that the primary cause of explosion was extensive corrosion of boiler tubes in the division wall at the east furnace lower slope dead air space.

Three operators, who were working directly below the furnace on a pulveriser seal air fan, died of burns and related complications when the explosion occurred. The boiler was operating at 1,900 psi at the time of the failure, caused by accumulated ash and water from boiler washing, coming into contact with external surface of the tubes.

The alkaline mixture caused corrosion which resulted in excessive tube metal thickness loss.

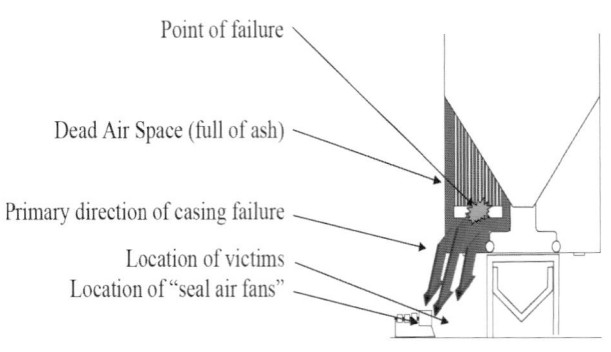

Figure C11-25: Failure point of boiler.   Source: Garry J Bases.

Because the plant had operated as a cycling unit for the 10 years prior to the explosion, planned outages were so reduced in length that the required maintenance activities were not completed.

The report also noted that the dead air space had not been opened or inspected in at least 10 years and was full of ash at the time of the explosion. At the time of the accident, approximately 2,500 maintenance work orders were outstanding. The report held the chief engineer and the outside boiler inspector directly responsible for the explosion because they failed to perform a comprehensive inspection as required by Massachusetts law.

CONTRIBUTORY FACTORS INFLUENCING FAILURE OF PRESSURE SYSTEMS

Design considerations

Design extends beyond the calculation of thickness and includes an assessment of materials to be used, together with manufacturing and welding processes to be employed. Service conditions should be carefully reviewed to ensure the design parameters are appropriate. Failures are usually associated with the influence of some element not envisaged or catered for at the design stage. Overload due to excessive pressures can be catered for by fitting adequate relief devices. The most common form of failure is fatigue and this is perhaps the least appreciated. It is important to assess the anticipated range and frequency of load cycling and to pay close attention to detailed design to minimise stress concentration effects.

Scale

Scale is an extremely hard substance created when mineral salts come out of solution as their solubility drops with a rise in water temperature. Scale forming salts adhere directly to heating surfaces, forming layers of insulation on the metal; substantially decreasing its heat transfer efficiency, 1.5 mm of scale in a boiler will increase fuel consumption by 12.5%. Scale results in metal fatigue/failure causing overheating, energy waste, high maintenance costs and unnecessary safety risks.

Fouling

This is very similar to scaling; fouling occurs when restriction develops in piping and equipment passages, creating inefficient water flow. The major consequences of fouling to boiler room equipment are energy waste and increased operating/maintenance costs.

Foaming

This is a condition in which concentrations of soluble salts (aggravated by grease, suspended solids or organic metal) create frothy bubbles (resembling the foam in a beer mug) in the steam space of a boiler. Foaming can cause priming, in which the bubbles break and create liquid that combines to form slugs of water that are carried over into the steam system. Pressure from the steam can create velocities as high as 80 -100 miles per hour for slugs of water discharges into the steam lines. These slugs can cause severe damage to the devices and piping downstream of the boiler (a similar version of this phenomenon is 'water hammer' where entrapped air causes a similar effect).

Low water level

If this is not properly sensed and the burners do not shutdown the boiler will overheat due to the exposure of metal surfaces that are no longer cooled by being contact with the fluid. Overheated boilers will be permanently damaged. If the safety valve has not been serviced properly and does not relieve the pressure adequately, the boiler could explode violently and result in injury or death. Low water conditions are a significant cause of accidents involving pressure vessels.

Lamella tearing

This is a form of cracking that can occur in steel plates under large fillet welds. The cracking, which can destroy the integrity of the plate, can be difficult to detect as it may be entirely sub-surface. There is evidence that lamella tearing is caused by inclusions in the plate.

Wear

This is the loss of material through friction. The pressure vessel itself does not usually suffer thinning due to wear, but components in the system do, for example, pumps and motorised valves etc. The effects of wear can be accentuated by the absence of lubrication and the presence of foreign matter.

Seal failures

Smaller scale failures commonly occur when seals such as 'O' rings or 'H' seals fail at joins or couplings in the system pipeline. This can be due to the heat effects produced in air systems or incorrect fitting during installation. Failures can also be found in high pressure systems where parts of the system are isolated and a section of pipeline is then drained of pressure. When the line is then re-pressurised it may be carried out too quickly and the sudden pressurisation on the seal actually dislodges the seal from its seat in the coupling, producing a coupling seal failure and the system then leaks. Once this has occurred the seal is more susceptible to further damage.

Water hammer

Steam systems are very prone to water hammer, which can have disastrous effects. Pipe work should therefore be designed and constructed so that any water in the system only collects at suitable points where drains are provided.

Unsuitable material for pipes

Plastic pipes are often used on compressed air systems. Not all plastics are suitable for use where there is the possibility of their exposure to heat or becoming brittle. Care should therefore be taken that pipes are suitable for the intended use.

Prevention strategy

DESIGN AND CONSTRUCTION

The Pressure Systems Safety Regulations (PSSR) 2000, Regulation 4, requires any person who designs, manufactures, imports or supplies any pressure system or any article which is intended to be a component part of any pressure system must ensure that the pressure system:

- Be designed and properly constructed from suitable material, so as to prevent danger.
- Be designed and constructed so that examinations for preventing danger can be carried out.
- Any means of access to the pressure system's interior must be designed and constructed so that access can be gained without danger.
- Protective devices must be provided to prevent danger and any protective devices designed to release contents must do so safely.

Designers should work to a clear specification and take account of current safe practice. The specification should set out the necessary operating and safety requirements. In some cases it will be provided by the user, but in others the designer should draw up the specification. This information needs to be passed on by designers to clients and users.

Factors that the designer should consider and take account of are as follows:

- The expected life of the equipment.
- The need for the system to be examined.
- Adequately sized openings so as to permit thorough examination of the interior of the vessel.
- If interior examination is not possible, due to the small vessel size, the designer should consider what examinations are needed and provide means for carrying them out.
- The conditions of operation and performance requirements of the system, allowing for the most onerous combination of temperature, pressure, nature of the contents and any other factors which may affect the integrity of the vessel.
- Dealing with abnormal conditions which will exist during start-up and shut-down of the system.
- Appropriate controls and protective devices which will either prevent the unplanned conditions arising or enable the stored energy to be safely dissipated.
- Such devices should commence to operate at the set pressure, which shall not exceed the system design pressure and will reach full discharge capacity within a set limit of overpressure (accumulation).
- Additional features include warning devices to alert that the system failure may occur.
- Measuring devices should give adequate indications of relevant critical conditions within the system, for example, temperatures, pressures.
- Suitable control equipment should be provided to enable the system to be properly controlled within its safe operating limits, with allowance for likely fluctuations in the operating conditions.

ELEMENT C11 - PRESSURE SYSTEM HAZARDS AND CONTROLS

- The design should provide for corrosion allowances, if some corrosion is unavoidable and foreseeable.
- Pipework should be designed so as to allow for the forces due to thermal expansion and contraction, externally applied loads or any reasonably foreseeable vibration. Suitable expansion bends and/or joints should be incorporated in the pipework as necessary.
- Additionally where it is used for some gases and vapours which may accumulate as liquids or condensates, the design should minimise the number low points to prevent liquid accumulation; drainage pipework should be to a safe place.

It should be noted that the supply of pressure equipment is also governed by the Pressure Equipment Regulations (PER) 1999. These set out the general requirements relating to the placing on the market or putting into service of pressure equipment and assemblies by a responsible person (a person who manufactures the pressure equipment or assemblies for their own use or imports pressure equipment or assemblies from a third country, where it is in the course of business). Pressure equipment or assemblies must satisfy the relevant essential health and safety requirements (EHSR) and be safe with the appropriate conformity assessment procedure carried out (unless the equipment is to be used for experimentation). A declaration of conformity with the EHSR and any harmonised EU standards must be drawn up and CE marking affixed.

REPAIR AND MODIFICATION

PSSR 2000, Regulation 13, requires the employer of a person who modifies or repairs a pressure system at work to ensure that nothing about the way in which it is modified or repaired gives rise to danger or otherwise impairs the operation of any protective device or inspection facility.

When repairs or modifications to the pressurised parts of the system, whether temporary or otherwise, are carried out consideration should be given to:

- The original design specification.
- The duty for which the system is to be used after the repair or modification.
- Any change in relevant fluid.
- The effects any such work may have on the integrity of the pressure system.
- As to whether the protective equipment is still adequate.

INFORMATION AND MARKING

PSSR 2000, Regulation 5, requires anyone who designs for another or supplies any pressure system or any article that is intended to be a component part of a pressure system must provide sufficient written information concerning its design, construction, examination, operation and maintenance as may reasonably foreseeable be needed. The information should be provided:

- With the design.
- When the system or article is supplied to the user.
- After the modification or repair to the user of the system immediately.

Adequate information should include:

- Safe operating limits.
- Scheme of examination.
- Design standards and constructional materials.
- Certificates of conformity.
- Design pressures and temperatures.
- Intended contents, flow rates, capacities, etc.

PSSR 2000, Schedule 3, requires manufactures of pressure vessels to ensure that before it is supplied to a user the information specified is marked on the vessel, or on a plate attached to it, in a visible, legible and indelible form. The PSSR 2000 prohibits anyone from importing a pressure vessel unless it is marked as specified. The information required is:

- Manufacturers name.
- Serial number of vessel.
- Date of manufacture.
- Standard to which the vessel was built.
- Maximum allowable pressure.
- Minimum allowable pressure, where it is other than atmospheric.
- Design temperature.

In addition, the Pressure Equipment Regulations (PER) 1999, Regulation 16, requires a CE marking is affixed to the pressure vessel.

PSSR 2000, Regulation 5, prevents the removal of any mark or plate containing any of the information specified in Schedule 3 from a pressure vessel. It also prohibits anyone from 'falsifying' any mark on a pressure system, or on a plate attached to it, relating to its design, construction, test or operation.

SAFE OPERATING LIMITS

Safe operating limits must be known to those that operate a pressure system and the system must only be operated within these limits. Clear marking on the system of the limits will help to communicate the safe operating limits and assist with compliance with the limits. Care will need to be taken to ensure that pressure relief valves are functional in order to respond to accidental over pressure. They must be periodically inspected to ensure they have not been tampered with such that they operate at pressures greater than the safe operating limit or that they are not corroded or stuck closed.

The provision of a well placed, legible gauge that identifies the safe working pressure will assist with compliance to the safe operating limits.

Anyone operating a pressure system must be given adequate and suitable instructions for its safe operation and emergency action.

This instruction should form part of the operating instructions for the pressure system and should include information on start-up, shutdown, normal operation, functions of controls, emergency procedures, etc.

The Pressure Systems Safety Regulations (PSSR) 2000, Regulation 7, requires the user of an installed system and owner of a mobile system not to operate the system or allow it to be operated unless they have established the safe operating limits of that system.

The owner of a mobile system must, if they are not also the user of it:

- Supply the user with a written statement specifying the safe operating limits of that system.
- Ensure that the system is legibly and durably marked with the safe operating limits and that the mark is clearly visible.

Figure C11-26: Mobile Air compressor. *Source: Speedy Hire plc.*

WRITTEN SCHEME OF EXAMINATION

Regulation 8 of PSSR 2000 requires that the user of an installed system and owner of a mobile system not operate the system unless a written scheme of periodic examination, by a competent person, has been drawn up (or certified as being suitable) by a competent person. However, Part II of Schedule 1 to the PSSR 2000 exempts specific, simpler pressure systems that represent lower risk, for example a hot water urn, from having a written scheme of examination. The types of pressurised systems that are likely to require a written scheme of examination are indicated in the ACOP to the PSSR 2000 and include:

- Steam sterilising autoclave.
- Steam boiler.
- Pressure cooker.
- Portable hot water/steam-cleaning unit fitted with a pressure vessel.
- Vapour compression refrigeration system where the installed power exceeds 25 kW.
- The components of self-contained breathing apparatus sets (excluding the transportable pressure receptacle.)
- Fixed LPG storage system supplying fuel for heating in a workplace.

The written scheme of examination must be drawn up by a competent person and should include:

- Pressure vessels.
- Pipe work and valves.
- Protective devices.
- Pumps and compressors.

The written scheme of examination must cover:

- The nature and frequency of examinations.
- Any measures that may be needed to prepare a system for a safe examination.

For fired (heated) pressure systems, such as steam boilers, the written scheme should include an examination of the system when it is cold and stripped down and when it is running under normal conditions.

Regulation 2 of PSSR 2000 clarifies the term examination and defines it as:

"A careful and critical scrutiny of a pressure system or part of a pressure system, in or out of service as appropriate, using suitable techniques, including testing where appropriate, to assess -

(a) Its actual condition; and

(b) Whether, for the period up to the next examination, it will not cause danger when properly used if normal maintenance is carried out, and for this purpose "normal maintenance" means such maintenance as it is reasonable to expect the user (in the case of an installed system) or owner (in the case of a mobile system) to ensure is carried out independently of any advice from the competent person making the examination".

Examination requires the use of a range of suitable techniques, including visual examination, non-destructive testing and performance testing where appropriate.

Examination frequencies should be specified, though these may be different for different parts of the system, so that deterioration, etc. can be detected before danger arises. An initial examination should be done before use. Any repairs or modifications should be controlled.

ELEMENT C11 - PRESSURE SYSTEM HAZARDS AND CONTROLS

Factors to be taken into account when deciding upon the frequency of examination will include:

- Previous intervals and system records.
- Standards of supervision and routine checks.
- Type and quality of fluids in the system.
- The likelihood of creep, fatigue, etc. failures.
- Corrosion potential and effect.
- Presence of heat sources etc.

Examinations must be carried out in accordance with the written scheme and the pressure system adequately assessed for fitness for continued use. Appropriate preparations for and precautions during examination should be arranged for by the user. A report with any conditions or limitations on use should be prepared on completion of the examination.

Where the competent person's examination identifies imminent danger then a report must be made to the user, who should ensure the pressure system is not used further and a report is sent to the relevant enforcing authority.

Adequate records of examinations, repairs, modifications etc., should be kept at the premises where the system is used.

MAINTENANCE AND RECORD KEEPING

Maintenance

There is a general duty to maintain equipment set out in Regulation 5 of PUWER 1998; this requires the equipment to be maintained in an "efficient state, in effective working order and in good repair". In addition, the Pressure Systems Safety Regulations (PSSR) 2000, Regulation 12, requires that the user of an installed system and the owner of a mobile system must ensure that the system is properly maintained in good repair, so as to prevent danger.

The type and frequency of maintenance of the pressure system should be assessed and a maintenance programme planned. The ACOP to the PSSR 2000 suggest that the following should be taken into account when preparing the maintenance programme:

- Age of the system.
- Operating/process conditions.
- Working environment.
- Manufacturer's/supplier's instructions.
- Previous maintenance history.
- Reports of examinations carried out.
- Results of other relevant inspections.
- Repairs or modifications to the system.
- Risks to health and safety from failure or deterioration.

Routine and regular maintenance should be carried out including periodic checks, inspections, repair and replacement of important parts or protective devices.

Record keeping

The PSSR 2000, Regulation 14, contains specific requirements to maintain record keeping. Records retained should assist the competent person in the examination under the written scheme. Also, records of examinations in accordance with the written scheme must be kept for the last examination and any previous ones that contain material information relating to the system's safe operation, details of repairs or modifications. In addition, the user/owner must keep any instructions provided by the manufacturer or supplier related to the pressure system. Records would usually be kept at the premises where the system is used, or the base for mobile systems.

COMPETENT PERSONS

The PSSR 2000 defines the term competent person as a competent individual person (other than an employee) or a competent body of persons. There are 3 distinct functions of the competent person:

- Advising the user on the scope of the written scheme of examination.
- Drawing up or certifying schemes of examination.
- Carrying out examinations under the scheme.

It is the responsibility of all users/owners to select a competent person who is capable of carrying out the duties in a proper manner. The competent person should have relevant knowledge and experience of the system. For complex systems the competent person may be a number of such people covering different parts of the system.

The competent person should be capable of conducting examinations that are impartial and objective, with the safety considerations and use of the system in mind.

Relevant statutory provisions

Content

Building Regulations (BR) 2010, Approved Document B...390
Chemicals (Hazard Information and Packaging for Supply) Regulations (CHIP 4) 2009 391
Confined Spaces Regulations (CSR) 1997 393
Construction (Design and Management) Regulations (CDM) 2007...393
Construction (Head Protection) Regulations (CHPR) 1989..402
Control of Major Accident Hazard Regulations (COMAH) 1999 (as amended 2009).....................................403
Carriage of Dangerous Goods and Use of Transportable Pressure Equipment Regulations (CDGUTPER) 2009.....404
Dangerous Substances (Notification and Marking of Sites) Regulations (NOMAS) 1990 405
Dangerous Substances and Explosive Atmospheres Regulations (DSEAR) 2002 405
Electricity at Work Regulations (EWR) 1989 407
European Agreement concerning the International Carriage of Dangerous Goods by Road (ADR) 2009 (as amended 2011) 409
Fire Safety (Scotland) Regulations (FSSR) 2006...409
Fire (Scotland) Act (FSA) 2005...410
Health and Safety (Safety Signs and Signals) Regulations (SSSR) 1996...412
Health and Safety at Work etc. Act (HASAWA) 1974 412
IET Wiring Regulations 17th Edition (BS 7671: 2008)..416
Lifting Operations and Lifting Equipment Regulations (LOLER) 1998 417
Management of Health and Safety at Work Regulations (MHSWR) 1999 418
New Roads and Street Works Act (NRSWA) 1991..421
Notification of Conventional Tower Cranes Regulations (NCTC) 2010 422
Notification of Installations Handling Hazardous Substances Regulations (NIHHS) 1982 (as amended)....422
Pressure Equipment Regulations (PER) 1999 423
Pressure Systems Safety Regulations (PSSR) 2000...425
Provision and Use of Work Equipment Regulations (PUWER) 1998 426
Registration, Evaluation, Authorisation and Restriction of Chemicals (REACH Regulation, EC 1907/2006)...............428
Regulatory Reform (Fire Safety) Order (RRFSO) 2005...429
Simple Pressure Vessels (Safety) Regulations (SPVSR) 1991 (as amended) 430
Supply of Machinery (Safety) Regulations (SMSR) 2008 432
Work at Height Regulations (WAH) 2005 434
Workplace (Health, Safety and Welfare) Regulations (WHSWR) 1992...436

RELEVANT STATUTORY PROVISIONS

Building Regulations (BR) 2010, Approved Document B

Law considered in context/more depth in Element C2 and C3.

Outline of main points

Approved Document B is a fire safety document that provides practical guidance on meeting the fire safety requirements of Schedule 1 to and Regulation 4 of the Building Regulations 2010 for England and Wales.

The areas covered by the Approved Document B are as follows:

- B1   Means of warning and escape.
- B2   Internal fire spread (linings).
- B3   Internal fire spread (structure).
- B4   External fire spread.
- B5   Access and facilities for the Fire Service.

The current Approved Document was updated in 2006, with two separate volumes being issued, one that covers dwelling houses and the main document that covers buildings other than dwelling houses. In the commercial world, it is the second document that is relevant.

The document is one of several Approved Documents issued by the Secretary of State that are intended to provide guidance for some of the more common building situations. However, there may well be alternative ways (e.g. BS 9999) of achieving compliance with the requirements.

Thus, there is no obligation to adopt any particular solution contained in an Approved Document if you prefer to meet the relevant requirement in some other way.

MAIN CHANGES IN THE 2006 EDITION

The main changes are:

GENERAL

- Approved document B has been split into two volumes. Volume 1 deals with dwelling houses and volume 2 deals with buildings other than dwelling houses.
- Fire safety information: a new regulation (16B) has been introduced to ensure that sufficient information is recorded to assist owner/occupier/employer to meet duties under Regulatory Reform (Fire Safety) Order 2005.

INTRODUCTION

- Management of premises: New guidance on need to ensure management regimes are realistic.
- Certification schemes: Acceptance of suitable schemes as evidence of compliance.
- Residential sprinklers: Use of sprinklers to BS 9251:2005 is recognised.
- Alternative approaches: HTM 05 for hospitals and similar premises. BB 100 used for design of schools.

B1

- Fire alarms in flats: Guidance amended so that BS 5839 Part 6 should be used. Commentary on standard given so that there is no need to purchase standard. All smoke alarms to have standby power supply.
- Fire alarms: Guidance for buildings other than dwellings updated to take account of BS 5839 Part 1-2002.
- Means of escape:
    - Child locks and safety stays allowed on escape windows.
    - New guidance on galleries and inner rooms in flats.
    - Sprinkler protection options for flats.
    - Guidance on air circulation systems in flats.
    - Smoke control in common areas of flats has changed.
    - Guidance on means of escape for open spatial planning included.
    - Calculation method included for final exit widths for merging escape routes at ground floor level.
    - Guidance on provision of cavity barriers in sub divided corridors.
    - Guidance for small premises included.
    - Guidance on design of residential care homes given including use of sprinklers and/or free swing door closers. Greater flexibility given if sprinklers provided.
    - Guidance on means of escape for disabled included in general means of escape.
    - Tall buildings with phased evacuation, consideration given to interaction of fire fighters entering whilst people evacuating.
    - More detailed guidance on protection of ventilation systems.

B3

- Compartment walls: Predicted deflection of floor to be accommodated in design of compartment wall.
- Sprinkler protection in flats: Sprinklers to be provided in flats over 30m in height.
- Warehouses: Maximum compartment size introduced for unsprinklered single storey warehouse buildings.
- Concealed spaces: Whole section reconstructed with information on openings, floor voids and cavity barriers.
- Fire dampers: Guidance on specification and installation of fire dampers.
- Car parks. Information on structure and fire resistance.

RELEVANT STATUTORY PROVISIONS

The following sets out the scope of the two volumes.

DWELLING HOUSES - VOLUME 1	BUILDINGS OTHER THAN DWELLING HOUSES - VOLUME 2
B1 MEANS OF WARNING AND ESCAPE *Guidance* *Section 1:* Fire detection and fire alarm systems. *Section 2:* Means of escape. **B2 INTERNAL FIRE SPREAD (LININGS)** *Guidance* *Section 3:* Wall and ceiling linings. **B3 INTERNAL FIRE SPREAD (STRUCTURE)** *Guidance* *Section 4:* Load bearing elements of structure. *Section 5:* Compartmentation. *Section 6:* Concealed spaces (cavities). *Section 7:* Protection of openings and fire stopping. **B4 EXTERNAL FIRE SPREAD** *Guidance* *Section 8:* Construction of external walls. *Section 9:* Space separation. *Section 10:* Roof coverings. **B5 ACCESS AND FACILITIES FOR THE FIRE AND RESCUE SERVICE** *Guidance* *Section 11:* Vehicle access. **APPENDICES** *Appendix A:* Performance of materials, products and structures. *Appendix B:* Fire doors. *Appendix C:* Methods of measurement. *Appendix D:* Purpose groups. *Appendix E:* Definitions. *Appendix F:* Standards and other publications referred to.	**B1 MEANS OF WARNING AND ESCAPE** *Guidance* *Section 1:* Fire alarm and fire detection systems. *Section 2:* Means of escape from flats. *Section 3:* Design for horizontal escape - buildings other than flats. *Section 4:* Design for vertical escape. *Section 5:* General provisions. **B2 INTERNAL FIRE SPREAD (LININGS)** *Guidance* *Section 6:* Wall and ceiling linings. **B3 INTERNAL FIRE SPREAD (STRUCTURE)** *Guidance* *Section 7:* Load bearing elements of structure. *Section 8:* Compartmentation. *Section 9:* Concealed spaces (cavities). *Section 10:* Protection of openings and fire stopping. *Section 11:* Special provisions for car parks and shopping complexes. **B4 EXTERNAL FIRE SPREAD** *Guidance* *Section 12:* Construction of external walls. *Section 13:* Space separation. *Section 14:* Roof coverings. **B5 ACCESS AND FACILITIES FOR THE FIRE SERVICE** *Guidance* *Section 15:* Fire Mains. *Section 16:* Vehicle access. *Section 17:* Access to buildings for fire fighting personnel. *Section 18:* Venting of heat and smoke from basements. **APPENDICES** *Appendix A:* Performance of materials, products and structures. *Appendix B:* Fire doors. *Appendix C:* Methods of measurement. *Appendix D:* Purpose groups. *Appendix E:* Definitions. *Appendix F:* Fire behaviour of insulating core panels used for internal structures. *Appendix G:* Fire safety information. *Appendix H:* Standards and other publications referred to.

Chemicals (Hazard Information and Packaging for Supply) Regulations (CHIP 4) 2009

Law considered in context/more depth in Element C4.

Arrangement of Regulations

PART 1 - INTRODUCTION

1. Citation, commencement and extent
2. Interpretation
3. Application

PART 2 - GENERAL REQUIREMENTS

4. Classification of dangerous substances and dangerous preparations
5. Safety data sheets for substances and preparations
6. Packaging of dangerous substances, dangerous preparations and certain specified preparations

RELEVANT STATUTORY PROVISIONS

7. Labelling of dangerous substances and dangerous preparations
8. Labelling of single receptacles and receptacles in outer packagings
9. Particular labelling requirements for certain preparations
10. Methods of marking or labelling packages
11. Child resistant fastenings, tactile warning devices and other consumer protection measures
12. Retention of data for dangerous preparations
13. Transitional provisions for dangerous substances, dangerous preparations and certain specified preparations

PART 3 - MISCELLANEOUS

14. Enforcement
15. Defence
16. Extension outside Great Britain
17. Revocations and amendments

SCHEDULES

Schedule 1 - Classification of dangerous substances and dangerous preparations

Schedule 2 - Indications of danger and symbols for dangerous substances and dangerous preparations

Schedule 3 - Provisions for classifying dangerous preparations

Part 1 - General provisions

Part 2 - Concentration limits to be used in the evaluation of health hazards

Part 3 - Concentration limits to be used for the evaluation of environment hazards

Schedule 4 - Labelling particulars for dangerous substances, dangerous preparations and for certain other preparations

Part 1 - General provisions relating to labels

Part 2 - Particular provisions concerning certain preparations

Schedule 5 - British and international standards relating to child resistant fastenings and tactile warning devices

Schedule 6 - Amendments

Schedule 7 - Revocations

Outline of main points

CHIP refers to the Chemicals (Hazard Information and Packaging for Supply) Regulations 2009, which came into force on 06th April 2009. These regulations are also known as CHIP 4, their application does not extend to Northern Ireland.

CHIP is the law that applies to suppliers of dangerous chemicals. Its purpose is to protect people and the environment from the effects of those chemicals by requiring suppliers to provide information about the dangers and to package them safely.

CHIP requires the supplier of a dangerous chemical to:

- Identify the hazards (dangers) of the chemical. This is known as 'classification'.
- Give information about the hazards to their customers. Suppliers usually provide this information on the package itself (e.g. a label).
- Package the chemical safely.

'Supply' means making a chemical available to another person. Manufacturers, importers, distributors, wholesalers and retailers are all examples of suppliers.

CHIP applies to most chemicals but not all. The details of the scope are set out in the regulations.

Some chemicals, such as cosmetics and medicines, are outside the scope and have their own specific laws.

The revision to the regulations relating to CHIP 4 arises from the need to align national legislation with the new European regulation on the Classification, Labelling and Packaging of Substances and Mixtures, known as the CLP Regulation, which will directly apply in all member states of the European Union and gradually replace CHIP 4.

CHIP 4 will also put in place the necessary legal provisions to allow regulators in Great Britain to enforce the CLP Regulation.

Safety data sheets (SDS) are no longer covered by the CHIP regulations. The laws that require a SDS to be provided have been transferred to the European Union Registration, Evaluation, Authorisation and Restriction of Chemicals (REACH) Regulation.

REACH

REACH is a European Union regulation concerning the registration, evaluation, authorisation and restriction of chemicals. It came into force on 1st June 2007 and replaces a number of European Directives and Regulations with a single system to gather hazard information, assess risks, classify, label, and restrict the marketing and use of individual chemicals and mixtures. This is known as the REACH system:

R egistration of basic information of substances to be submitted by companies, to a central database.
E valuation of the registered information to determine hazards and risks.
A uthorisation requirements imposed on the use of high-concern substances.
CH emicals.

REACH covers both "new" and "existing" substances and puts the onus on Industry to prove that chemicals it uses are safe. REACH only applies to chemicals manufactured in or imported into the EU. It does not apply to the use of chemicals in finished products. So a product like a television, or computer or shampoo made outside the EU could contain chemicals that are not registered under REACH - providing they are not banned under specific safety regulations (such as lead).

Confined Spaces Regulations (CSR) 1997

Law considered in context/more depth in Element C1.

Arrangement of Regulations

1) Citation, commencement and interpretation.
2) Disapplication of Regulations.
3) Duties.
4) Work in confined spaces.
5) Emergency arrangements.
6) Exemption certificates.
7) Defence in proceedings.
8) Extension outside Great Britain.
9) Repeal and revocations.

Outline of main points

The Confined Spaces Regulations (CSR) 1997, define a confined space as any place, including any chamber, tank, vat, silo, pit, pipe, sewer, flue, well, or other similar space, in which, by virtue of its enclosed nature, there is a foreseeable risk of a 'specified occurrence'.

A failure to appreciate the dangers associated with confined spaces has led not only to the deaths of many workers, but also to the demise of some of those who have attempted to rescue them. A confined space is not only a space that is small and difficult to enter, exit or work in; it can also be a large space, but with limited/restricted access. It can also be a space which is badly ventilated for example, a tank or a large tunnel.

The regulations prohibit entry to confined spaces to carry out work unless a system of work "renders the work safe and without risks". The only exception to this requirement is where it is as a result of an emergency. The regulations emphasise the need to make suitable arrangements for emergencies, which do not put those carrying out the arrangements unnecessarily at risk. When making emergency arrangements consideration should be made to the need for resuscitation. There are arrangements in the regulations that allow the Health and Safety Executive (HSE) to exempt certain classes of person or confined space from the requirements of the regulations.

Construction (Design and Management) Regulations (CDM) 2007

Law considered in context/more depth in Element C9.

The simplified version of the CDM Regulations revised and brought together the existing CDM 1994 and the Construction (Health Safety and Welfare) (CHSWR) Regulations 1996 into a single regulatory package. The Construction (Design and Management) (CDM) Regulations (2007) are supported by an Approved Code of Practice (ACoP) and industry-approved guidance.

Arrangement of Regulations

PART 1 - INTRODUCTION

1. Citation and commencement.
2. Interpretation.
3. Application.

PART 2 - GENERAL MANAGEMENT DUTIES APPLYING TO CONSTRUCTION PROJECTS

4. Competence.
5. Co-operation.
6. Co-ordination.
7. General principles of prevention.
8. Election by clients.
9. The client's duty in relation to arrangements for managing projects.
10. Client's duty in relation to information.
11. Duties of designers.
12. Designs prepared or modified outside Great Britain.
13. Duties of contractors.

PART 3 - ADDITIONAL DUTIES WHERE PROJECT IS NOTIFIABLE

14. Appointments by the client.
15. Client's duty in relation to information.
16. The client's duty in relation to the start of construction phase.
17. The client's duty in relation to the health and safety file.
18. Additional duties of designers.
19. Additional duties of contractors.
20. General duties of CDM co-ordinators.

RELEVANT STATUTORY PROVISIONS

21. Notification of project by CDM co-ordinator.
22. Duties of the principal contractor.
23. Principal contractor's duties in relation to the construction phase plan.
24. Principal contractor's duties in relation to co-operation and consultation with workers.

PART 4 - DUTIES RELATING TO HEALTH AND SAFETY ON CONSTRUCTION SITES

25. Application of regulations 26-44.
26. Safe places of work.
27. Good order and site security.
28. Stability of structures.
29. Demolition or dismantling.
30. Explosives.
31. Excavations.
32. Cofferdams and caissons.
33. Reports of inspections.
34. Energy distribution installations.
35. Prevention of drowning.
36. Traffic routes.
37. Vehicles.
38. Prevention of risk from fire etc.
39. Emergency procedures.
40. Emergency routes and exits.
41. Fire detection and fire-fighting.
42. Fresh air.
43. Temperature and weather protection.
44. Lighting.

PART 5 - GENERAL

45. Civil liability.
46. Enforcement in respect of fire.
47. Transitional provision.
48. Revocation and amendments.

SCHEDULES

Schedule 1 (regulation 21(1), (2) and (4)) - Particulars to be notified to the Executive

Schedule 2 (regulation 11, 16(l)(b) and 19(4)) - Welfare facilities

1. Sanitary conveniences.
2. Washing facilities.
3. Drinking water.
4. Changing rooms and lockers.
5. Facilities for rest.

Schedule 3 (regulation 33(1)(b)) - Particulars to be included in a report of inspection

Schedule 4 (regulation 48(1)) - Revocation of instruments

Schedule 5 (regulation 48(2)) - Amendments

Outline of main points

PART 2 - GENERAL MANAGEMENT DUTIES

Competence

4(1) No person on whom these regulations place a duty shall:

    (a) Appoint or engage a co-ordinator, designer, principal contractor or contractor unless he has taken reasonable steps to ensure that he is competent.

    (b) Accept such appointment or engagement unless he is competent.

    (c) Arrange for or instruct a worker to carry out or manage design or construction work unless he is -

        (i) Competent.

        (ii) Under the supervision of a competent person.

Co-operation

5(1) Every person concerned in a project on whom a duty is placed by these regulations, including paragraph (2), shall:

    (a) Co-operate with any other person concerned in any project involving construction work at the same or an adjoining site so far as is necessary to enable the latter to perform any duty or function under these regulations.

    (b) Seek the co-operation of any other person concerned in any project involving construction work at the same or an adjoining site so far as is necessary to enable the former to perform any duty or function under these regulations.

(2) Every person concerned in a project who is working under the control of another person shall report to him anything which he is aware is likely to endanger the health or safety of himself or others.

Co-ordination

6 All persons shall coordinate their activities with one another in a manner which ensures, so far as is reasonably practicable, the health and safety of persons affected by the work.

General principles of prevention

7 Every person on whom a duty is placed by these regulations in relation to the design, planning and preparation of a project shall take account of the general principles of prevention in the performance of those duties during all the stages of the project.

Election by clients

8. If, in relation to a project, one or more clients elect in writing to be treated for the purposes of these regulations as the only clients, other clients who have agreed in writing to such election shall not be subject to any duty owed by a client under these regulations after such election and consent, save the duties in regulations 5(1)(a), 10(1) so far as it relates to information in his possession, and 12(1).

The client's arrangements for managing projects

9(1) The client shall take reasonable steps to ensure that arrangements are made, and maintained throughout the project, for managing it which are suitable to ensure:

(a) that:

(i) the construction work can be carried out; and

(ii) any structure to which the construction work relates, and which is designed for use as a place of work, can be used,

without risk to health or safety; and

(b) the welfare of the persons carrying out the construction work.

(2) The arrangements referred to in paragraph (1) shall include:

    (a) the allocation of resources (including time) to:

        (i) the design of a structure;

        (ii) planning and preparation for construction work; and

        (iii) the construction work itself,

which are, so far as the client in question can reasonably determine, adequate; and

(b) arrangements for:

(i) review and revision of the arrangements;

(ii) review of the suitability and compatibility of designs and for any modification;

(iii) ensuring that persons arc appointed under regulation 8 or engaged as designers or contractors in a suitable sequence and in good time;

(iv) the planning for and monitoring of construction work; (v) ensuring that the duties in regulations 5 and 16 are performed; and

(vi) communication.

Client's duty in relation to information

10(1) The client shall ensure that the persons specified in regulation 13(l)(f)(i) to (iii) are promptly provided by the co-ordinator with all the information in the client's possession, or prepared by the co-ordinator, or which is reasonably obtainable (or with such of the information as is relevant to the person to whom the co-ordinator provides it), including:

    (a) any such information in a health and safety file;

    (b) any such further information about or affecting the site or the construction work;

    (c) information provided by a designer under regulation 14(5);

RELEVANT STATUTORY PROVISIONS

  (d) the minimum notice which will be allowed to the principal contractor, and the contractors directly appointed by the client, for planning and preparation for construction work, which is relevant to the purposes specified in paragraph (2).

(2) The purposes referred to in paragraph (1) are:

  (a) to secure so far as is reasonably practicable the health, safety of persons engaged in the construction work and the health and safety of persons liable to be affected by the way in which it is carried out;

  (b) without prejudice to sub-paragraph (a), to assist the persons to whom information is provided under this regulation

    (i) to perform their duties and functions under these regulations; and

    (ii) to determine the adequacy of the resources referred to in regulation 7(2) to be allocated by them.

Duties of designers

11 No designer shall commence work in relation to a project unless any client for the project is aware of his duties under these regulations.

Every designer shall in preparing or modifying a design which may be used in construction work in Great Britain avoid foreseeable risks to the health and safety of any person liable to be affected by such construction work;

In discharging these duties, the designer shall -

- Eliminate hazards which may give rise to risks.
- Reduce risks from any remaining hazards, and in so doing shall give collective measures priority over individual measures.

In designing any structure for use as a workplace the designer shall take account of the provisions of the Workplace (Health, Safety and Welfare) Regulations 1992 which relate to the design of, and materials used in, the structure.

The designer shall take all reasonable steps to provide with his design sufficient information about aspects of the design of the structure or its construction or maintenance as will adequately assist -

- Clients.
- Other designers.
- Contractors.

to comply with their duties under these Regulations.

Designs prepared or modified outside Great Britain

12. Where a design is prepared or modified outside Great Britain for use in construction work to which these Regulations apply:

  (a) the person who commissions it, if he is established within Great Britain; or

  (b) if that person is not so established, the client, shall ensure that Regulation 14 is complied with.

Duties of contractors

13 No contractor shall carry out construction work in relation to a project unless any client for the project is aware of his duties under these Regulations.

Every contractor shall ensure that any contractor whom he appoints or engages in his turn in connection with a project is informed of the minimum amount of time which will be allowed to him for planning and preparation before he begins construction work

Every contractor shall provide every worker carrying out the construction work under his control with any information and training which he needs for the particular work to be carried out safely and without risk to health.

No contractor shall begin work on a construction site unless reasonable steps have been taken to prevent access by unauthorised persons to that site.

PART 3 - ADDITIONAL DUTIES FOR NOTIFIABLE PROJECTS

Appointments by the client

14(1) The client shall:

  (a) appoint a person ("the co-ordinator"), before design work, or planning or other preparation for construction work is begun, to perform the functions specified in regulation 13(1); and

  (b) ensure so far as is reasonably practicable that the functions are performed.

(2) The client shall appoint one person (in these Regulations called "the principal contractor") as soon as is practicable after the client knows enough about the project to be able to select a suitable person for such appointment, to perform the functions specified in regulations 16 to 18.

(3) The client shall ensure that appointments under paragraphs (1) and (2) are changed or renewed as necessary to ensure that there are at all times until the end of the construction phase -

  (a) a co-ordinator; and

  (b) a principal contractor, filling them.

(4) The client shall:

(a) be deemed for the purposes of these Regulations, save paragraphs (1) and (2) and regulations 14(l)(b) and 19(1)(b), to have been appointed as the co-ordinator or principal contractor for any period for which no person (including himself) has been so appointed; and

(b) accordingly be subject to the duty imposed by regulation 13(2) on a co-ordinator or, as the case may be, the duties imposed by regulations 16 to 18 on a principal contractor.

(5) Any reference in this regulation to appointment is to appointment in writing.

Client's duty in relation to information where a project is notifiable

15. Where the project is notifiable, the client shall provide the CDM co-ordinator with pre-construction information consisting of -
    - Any information about or affecting the site or the construction work.
    - Any information concerning the proposed use of the structure as a workplace.
    - The minimum amount of time before the construction phase which will be allowed to the contractors appointed by the client for planning and preparation for construction work.
    - Any information in any existing health and safety file.

The client's duty in relation to the start of construction phase

16. The client shall ensure that the construction phase does not start unless:

    (a) the principal contractor has prepared a construction phase plan which is sufficient to enable the construction work to start without undue risk to health or safety; and

    (b) the requirements of Schedule 2 are complied with.

The client's duty in relation to the health and safety file

17(1) The client shall ensure that the co-ordinator is provided with all the health and safety information likely to be needed during any subsequent works for inclusion in a record ("the health and safety file").

(1) Where a single health and safety file relates to more than one project, site or structure, or where it includes other related information the client shall ensure that the information relating to each site or structure can be easily identified.

(2) The client shall take reasonable steps to ensure that after the construction phase the information in the health and safety file:

   (a) is kept available for inspection by any person who may need it to comply with the relevant statutory provisions; and

   (b) is revised as often as may be appropriate to incorporate any relevant new information, including information specified in regulation 4(9)(c) of the Control of Asbestos at Work Regulations 2002(d) *(see S.I. 2002/2675.)*

(3) It shall be sufficient compliance with paragraph (3)(a) by a client who disposes of his entire interest in the site if he delivers the health and safety file to the person who acquires his interest in it and ensures that he is aware of the nature and purpose of the file.

Additional duties of designers

18(1) No designer shall commence work in relation to a project unless:

   (a) the client is aware of his duties under these Regulations;

   (b) a co-ordinator has been appointed for the project; and

   (c) notice of the project has been given to the Executive under regulation 9.

(2) The duties in paragraphs (3) and (4) shall be performed so far as is reasonably practicable, taking due account of other relevant design considerations.

(3) Every designer shall in preparing or modifying a design which may be used in construction work in the United Kingdom avoid risks to the health and safety of any person:

   (a) carrying out construction work;

   (b) cleaning or maintaining the permanent fixtures and fittings of a structure;

   (c) using a structure designed as a place of work; or

   (d) liable to be affected by such construction work.

(4) In discharging the duty in paragraph (3), the designer shall:

   (a) eliminate hazards which may give rise to risks; and

   (b) reduce risks from any remaining hazards, and in doing so shall give collective measures priority over individual measures.

(5) The designer shall provide with the design sufficient information about aspects of the design of a structure or its construction or maintenance as will adequately assist:

   (a) other designers to comply with their duties under this regulation;

   (b) contractors to comply with their duties under regulation 19.

RELEVANT STATUTORY PROVISIONS

Additional duties of contractors

19 *Where a project is notifiable,* no contractor shall carry out construction work in relation to the project unless -
- He has been provided with the names of the CDM co-ordinator and principal contractor.
- He has been given access to such part of the construction phase plan as is relevant to the work to be performed by him, containing sufficient detail in relation to such work.
- Notice of the project has been given to the Executive.

Every contractor shall -
- Provide the principal contractor with any information (including any relevant part of any risk assessment in his possession or control) which -
- Might affect the health or safety of any person carrying out the construction work or of any person who may be affected by it.
- Might justify a review of the construction phase plan.
- Which has been identified for inclusion in the health and safety file in pursuance of regulation 22(1)(j).
- Identify any contractor whom he appoints or engages in his turn in connection with the project to the principal contractor.
- Comply with -
- Any directions of the principal contractor given to him under regulation 22(1)(e).
- Any site rules.
- Provide the principal contractor with the information in relation to any death, injury, condition or dangerous occurrence which the contractor is required to notify or report under the Reporting of Injuries, Diseases and Dangerous Occurrences Regulations 1995.

Every contractor shall -
- Take all reasonable steps to ensure that the construction work is carried out in accordance with the construction phase plan.
- Notify the principal contractor of any significant finding which requires the construction phase plan to be altered or added to.

General duties of CDM co-ordinators

20(1) The functions of a co-ordinator, referred to in regulation 8(l)(a), are to:

(a) advise and assist the client in undertaking the measures he needs to take to comply with these Regulations (including in particular, in assisting the client in complying with regulations 9 and 16);

(b) identify and extract the information specified in regulation 10;

(c) advise on the suitability and compatibility of designs and on any need for modification;

(d) co-ordinate design work, planning and other preparation;

(e) liaise with the principal contractor in relation to any design or change to a design requiring a review of the construction phase plan, during the construction phase;

(f) promptly provide, in a convenient form, to:

(i) every person designing the structure;

(ii) the principal contractor; and

(iii) every contractor who has been or is likely to be appointed by the client, the information specified in regulation 10 (or such of it as is relevant to him);

(g) prepare, where none exists, and otherwise review and update the health and safety file;

(h) at the end of the construction phase, pass the health and safety file to the client.

(2) A co-ordinator shall so far as is reasonably practicable perform any function specified in paragraph (1) for which he is appointed.

Notification of the project by the CDM co-ordinator

21 The CDM co-ordinator shall as soon as is practicable after his appointment ensure that notice is given to the Executive containing such of the particulars specified in Schedule 1 as are available.

Duties of the principal contractor

22 The principal contractor for a project shall -
- Plan, manage and monitor the construction phase in a way which ensures that, so far as is reasonably practicable, it is carried out without risks to health or safety, including facilitating -
  (i) Co-operation and co-ordination between persons concerned in the project in pursuance of regulations 5 and 6; and
  (ii) The application of the general principles of prevention in pursuance of regulation 7.
- Liaise with the CDM co-ordinator in performing his duties in regulation 20(2)(d) during the construction phase in relation to any design or change to a design.
- Ensure that sufficient welfare facilities are provided.
- Draw up rules which are appropriate to the construction site and the activities on it.

- Give reasonable directions to any contractor.
- Ensure that every contractor is informed of the minimum amount of time which will be allowed to him.
- Consult a contractor before finalising such part of the construction phase plan as is relevant to the work to be performed by him.
- Ensure that every contractor is given, access to such part of the construction phase plan as is relevant to the work to be performed by him.
- Ensure that every contractor is given, such further information as he needs to carry out the work to be performed by him without risk.
- Identify to each contractor the information relating to the contractor's activity which is likely to be required by the CDM co-ordinator for inclusion in the health and safety file.
- Ensure that the particulars required to be in the notice are displayed in a readable condition in a position where they can be read by any worker.
- Take reasonable steps to prevent access by unauthorised persons to the construction site.

The principal contractor shall take all reasonable steps to ensure that every worker carrying out the construction work is provided with -

- A suitable site induction.
- Any further information and training which he needs for the particular work to be carried out without undue risk to health or safety.

The principal contractor's duty in relation to the construction phase plan

The principal contractor shall -

- Prepare a construction phase plan.
- Update, review, revise and refine the construction phase plan.
- Arrange for the construction phase plan to be implemented in a way which will ensure so far as is reasonably practicable the health and safety of all persons carrying out construction work and all persons who may be affected by the work.

The principal contractor's duty in relation to co-operation and consultation with workers

The principal contractor shall -

- Consult those workers or their representatives on matters connected with the project which may affect their health, safety or welfare.
- Ensure that such workers or their representatives can inspect and take copies of any information except any information—
  - The disclosure of which would be against the interests of national security.
  - Which he could not disclose without contravening a prohibition imposed by or under an enactment.
  - Relating specifically to an individual, unless he has consented to its being disclosed.
  - The disclosure of which would, for reasons other than its effect on health, safety or welfare at work, cause substantial injury to his undertaking or, where the information was supplied to him by some other person, to the undertaking of that other person.
  - Obtained by him for the purpose of bringing, prosecuting or defending any legal proceedings.

Principal contractor's duties in relation to the construction phase plan

23(1) The principal contractor shall

(a) before the start of the construction phase, prepare a sufficient health and safety plan to allow the construction phase to start, so far as is reasonably practicable, without risk to health and safety

(b) review, update, revise and refine the plan as necessary

(c) arrange for the construction phase to be implemented in such a way as to ensure, so far as is reasonably practicable, the health and safety of people carrying out the construction work

(2) Take reasonable steps to ensure that the construction phase plan identifies all the risks arising from the construction phase.

Principal contractor's duties in relation to co-operation and consultation with workers

24 The principal contractor shall

(a) make and maintain arrangements to ensure that workers co-operate in promoting and developing measures to ensure the health, safety and welfare of workers.

(b) consult with workers or their representatives in good time on matters that may affect their health, safety or welfare.

(c) ensure that relevant information is available to workers except any information which is specified in the Health and Safety (Consultation with Employees) Regulations 1996.

PART 4 - DUTIES RELATING TO HEALTH AND SAFETY ON CONSTRUCTION SITES

Safe place of work (regulations 26)

A general duty to ensure a safe place of work and safe means of access to and from that place of work, this regulation sets out a general requirement that applies to all construction work. It applies equally to places of work in the ground, at ground level and at height. In essence, it requires that 'reasonably practicable' steps should be taken to provide for safety and to ensure risks to health are minimised. This means that action to be taken should be proportionate to the risk involved.

Work on structures (regulations 28, 29 and 30)

- Prevent accidental collapse of new or existing structures or those under construction.

RELEVANT STATUTORY PROVISIONS

- Make sure any dismantling or demolition of any structure is planned and carried out in a safe manner under the supervision of a competent person.
- Only fire explosive charges after steps have been taken to ensure that no one is exposed to risk or injury from the explosion.

Every year there are structural collapses which have the potential to cause serious accidents. The regulations set a high standard to prevent collapses, which involves taking into account the hazard during the planning stage. Demolition or dismantling are recognised as high risk activities. In any cases where this work presents a risk of danger to anyone, it should be planned and carried out under the direct supervision of a competent person.

Excavations, cofferdams and caissons (regulations 31 and 32)

- Prevent collapse of ground both in and above excavations.
- Identify and prevent risk from underground cables and other services.
- Ensure cofferdams and caissons are properly designed, constructed and maintained.

From the outset, and as work progresses, any excavation which has the potential to collapse unless supported, should have suitable equipment immediately available to provide such support. Underground cables and services can also be a source of danger. These should be identified before work starts and positive action taken to prevent injury.

Energy distribution installations (regulation 34)

- Where necessary to prevent danger, energy distribution installations shall be suitably located, checked and clearly indicated.
- Where there is a risk from electric power cables: they shall be directed away from the area of risk; or the power shall be cut off; or if it is not reasonably practicable to comply with these requirements:
  - Suitable warning notices.
  - Barriers suitable for excluding work equipment which is not needed.
  - Where vehicles need to pass beneath the cables, suspended protections.
  - In either case, measures providing an equivalent level of safety, shall be provided or (in the case of measures) taken.
- No construction work which is liable to create a risk to health or safety from an underground service, or from damage to or disturbance of it, shall be carried out unless suitable and sufficient steps (including any steps required by this regulation) have been taken to prevent such risk, so far as is reasonably practicable.

Prevention or avoidance of drowning (regulation 35)

- Take steps to prevent people from falling into water or other liquid so far as is reasonably practicable.
- Ensure that personal protective and rescue equipment is immediately available for use and maintained, in the event of a fall.
- Make sure safe transport by water is under the control of a competent person.

Traffic routes and vehicles (regulations 36 and 37)

- Ensure construction sites are organised so that pedestrians and vehicles can both move safely and without risks to health.
- Make sure routes are suitable and sufficient for the people or vehicles using them.
- Prevent or control the unintended movement of any vehicle.
- Make arrangements for giving a warning of any possible dangerous movement, e.g. reversing vehicles.
- Ensure safe operation of vehicles including prohibition of riding or remaining in unsafe positions.
- Make sure doors and gates which could present danger, e.g. trapping risk of powered doors, have suitable safeguards.

Prevention and control of emergencies (regulations 38, 39, 40 and 41)

- Prevent risk from fire, explosion, flooding and asphyxiation.
- Provide emergency routes and exits.
- Make arrangements for dealing with emergencies, including procedures for evacuating the site.
- Where necessary, provide fire-fighting equipment, fire detectors and alarm systems.

These Regulations require the prevention of risk as far as it is reasonably practicable to achieve. However, there are times when emergencies do arise and planning is needed to ensure, for example, that emergency routes are provided and evacuation procedures are in place. These particular Regulations (as well as those on traffic routes, welfare, cleanliness and signing of sites) apply to construction work which is carried out on construction sites. However, the rest of the Regulations apply to all construction work.

The HSE continues to be responsible for inspection of means of escape and fire-fighting for most sites. However, fire authorities have enforcement responsibility in many premises which remain in normal use during construction work. This continues the sensible arrangement which ensures that the most appropriate advice is given.

Site-wide issues (regulations 27, 42, 43, and 44)

- Ensure sufficient fresh or purified air is available at every workplace, and associated plant is capable of giving visible or audible warning of failure.
- Make sure a reasonable working temperature is maintained at indoor work places during working hours.
- Provide facilities for protection against adverse weather conditions.
- Make sure suitable and sufficient emergency lighting is available.
- Make sure suitable and sufficient lighting is available, including providing secondary lighting where there would be a risk to health or safety if primary or artificial lighting failed.
- Keep construction sites in good order and in a reasonable state of cleanliness.
- Ensure the perimeter of a construction site to which people, other than those working on the site could gain access, is marked by suitable signs so that its extent can be easily identified.

Reports of inspections (regulation 33)

- The person who carries out an inspection under regulations 31 or 32 must:
  - Inform the person for whom the inspection was carried out if he is not satisfied that the construction work can be carried out safely at the place inspected.
  - Prepare a report which includes the particulars set out in Schedule 3 and within 24 hours of completion of the inspection, to which the report relates, provide a copy to the person for whom the inspection was carried out.
- The inspector's employer, or the person under whose control he works, shall ensure that the inspector performs his duty.
- The person for whom the inspection was carried out must keep the report or a copy of it available for inspection at the site of the place of work until that work is completed, and after that for 3 months, and send out extracts from or copies of it as required by an inspector appointed under section 19 of The Health and Safety at Work etc. Act 1974.
- No further inspection reports required within a 7 day period.

SCHEDULE 2 (REGULATIONS 9(1)(B), 13(7) AND 22(1)(C)) WELFARE FACILITIES

SANITARY CONVENIENCES

1. Suitable and sufficient sanitary conveniences shall be provided or made available at readily accessible places. So far as is reasonably practicable, rooms containing sanitary conveniences shall be adequately ventilated and lit.

2. So far as is reasonably practicable, sanitary conveniences and the rooms containing them shall be kept in a clean and orderly condition.

3. Separate rooms containing sanitary conveniences shall be provided for men and women, except where and so far as each convenience is in a separate room the door of which is capable of being secured from the inside.

Washing facilities

4. Suitable and sufficient washing facilities, including showers if required by the nature of the work or for health reasons, shall so far as is reasonably practicable be provided or made available at readily accessible places.

5. Washing facilities shall be provided:
   (a) in the immediate vicinity of every sanitary convenience, whether or not provided elsewhere; and
   (b) in the vicinity of any changing rooms required by paragraph 15 whether or not provided elsewhere.

6. Washing facilities shall include:
   (a) a supply of clean hot and cold, or warm, water (which shall be running water so far as is reasonably practicable); and
   (b) soap or other suitable means of cleaning; and
   (c) towels or other suitable means of drying.

7. Rooms containing washing facilities shall be sufficiently ventilated and lit.

8. Washing facilities and the rooms containing them shall be kept in a clean and orderly condition.

9. Subject to paragraph 10 below, separate washing facilities shall be provided for men and women, except where and so far as they are provided in a room the door of which is capable of being secured from inside and the facilities in each such room arc intended to be used by only one person at a time.

10. Paragraph 9 above shall not apply to facilities which are provided for washing hands, forearms and face only.

Drinking water

11. An adequate supply of wholesome drinking water shall be provided or made available at readily accessible and suitable places.

12. Every supply of drinking water shall be conspicuously marked by an appropriate sign where necessary for reasons of health and safety.

13. Where a supply of drinking water is provided, there shall also be provided a sufficient number of suitable cups or other drinking vessels unless the supply of drinking water is in a jet from which persons can drink easily.

Changing rooms and lockers

14(1) Suitable and sufficient changing rooms shall be provided or made available at readily accessible places if:
   (a) a worker has to wear special clothing for the purposes of his work; and
   (b) he cannot, for reasons of health or propriety, be expected to change elsewhere, being separate rooms for, or separate use of rooms by, men and women where necessary for reasons of propriety.

(2) Changing rooms shall:
   (a) be provided with seating;
   (b) include, where necessary, facilities to enable a person to dry any such special clothing and his own clothing and personal effects.

RELEVANT STATUTORY PROVISIONS

(3) Suitable and sufficient facilities shall, where necessary, be provided or made available at readily accessible places to enable persons to lock away:

- (a) any such special clothing which is not taken home;
- (b) their own clothing which is not worn during working hours; and
- (c) their personal effects.

Facilities for rest

15(1) Suitable and sufficient rest rooms or rest areas shall be provided or made available at readily accessible places.

(1) Rest rooms and rest areas shall:

- (a) include suitable arrangements to protect non-smokers from discomfort caused by tobacco smoke;
- (b) be equipped with an adequate number of tables and adequate seating with backs for the number of persons at work likely to use them at any one time;
- (c) where necessary, include suitable facilities for any person at work who is a pregnant woman or nursing mother to rest lying down;
- (d) include suitable arrangements to ensure that meals can be prepared and eaten; and
- (e) include the means for boiling water.

Construction (Head Protection) Regulations (CHPR) 1989

Law considered in context/more depth in Element C9.

Arrangement of Regulations

1) Citation, commencement and interpretation.
2) Application of these Regulations.
3) Provision, maintenance and replacement of suitable head protection.
4) Ensuring suitable head protection is worn.
5) Rules and directions.
6) Wearing of suitable head protection.
7) Reporting the loss of, or defect in, suitable head protection.
8) Extension outside Great Britain.
9) Exemption certificates.

Outline of main points

ENSURING SUITABLE HEAD PROTECTION IS WORN

Reg. 4(1) Every employer shall ensure so far as is reasonably practicable that each of his employees who is at work on operations or works to which these Regulations apply wears suitable head protection, unless there is no foreseeable risk to injury to his head other than by his falling.

4(2) Every employer, self-employed person or employee who has control over any other person who is at work on operations or works to which these Regulations apply shall ensure so far as is reasonably practicable that each such other person wears suitable head protection, unless there is no foreseeable risk of injury to that other person's head other than by his falling.

RULES AND DIRECTIONS

Reg.5(1) The person for the time being having control of a site where operations or works to which these Regulations apply are being carried out may, so far as is necessary to comply with regulation 4 of these Regulations, make rules regulating the wearing of suitable head protection on that site by persons at work on those operations or works.

5(2) Rules made in accordance with paragraph (1) of this regulation shall be in writing and shall be brought to the notice of persons who may be affected by them.

5(3) An employer may, so far as is necessary to comply with regulation 4(1) of these Regulations, give directions requiring his employees to wear suitable head protection.

5(4) An employer, self-employed person or employee who has control over any other self-employed person may, so far as is necessary to comply with regulation 4(2) of these Regulations, give directions requiring each such other self-employed person to wear suitable head protection.

WEARING OF SUITABLE HEAD PROTECTION

Reg.6(1) Every employee who has been provided with suitable head protection shall wear that head protection when required to do so by rules made or directions given under regulation 5 of these Regulations.

6(2) Every self-employed person shall wear suitable head protection when required to do so by rules made or directions given under regulation 5 of these Regulations.

RELEVANT STATUTORY PROVISIONS

6(3)	Every self-employed person who is at work on operations or works to which these Regulations apply, but who is not under the control of another employer or self-employed person or of an employee, shall wear suitable head protection unless there is no foreseeable risk of injury to his head other than by his falling.
6(4)	Every employee or self-employed person who is required to wear suitable head protection by or under these Regulations shall do so properly.

REPORTING THE LOSS OF, OR DEFECT IN, SUITABLE HEAD PROTECTION

Reg. 7	Every employee who has been provided with suitable head protection by his employer shall take reasonable care of it and shall forthwith report to his employer any loss of, or obvious defect in, that head protection.

Control of Major Accident Hazard Regulations (COMAH) 1999 (as amended 2009)

Law considered in context/more depth in Elements C4.

Arrangement of Regulations

PART 1 - INTRODUCTION
1) Citation and commencement.
2) Interpretation.
3) Application.

PART 2 - GENERAL
4) General duty.
5) Major accident prevention policy.
6) Notifications.

PART 3 - SAFETY REPORTS
7) Safety report.
8) Review and revision of safety report.

PART 4 - EMERGENCY PLANS
9) On-site emergency plan.
10) Off-site emergency plan.
11) Review and testing of emergency plans.
12) Implementing emergency plans.
13) Charge for preparation, review and testing of off-site emergency plan.

PART 5 - PROVISION OF INFORMATION BY OPERATOR
14) Provision of information to the public.
15) Provision of information to the competent authority (the Agency).
16) Provision of information to other establishments.

PART 6 - FUNCTIONS OF COMPETENT AUTHORITY
17) Functions of competent authority in relation to the safety report.
18) Prohibition of use.
19) Inspections and investigations.
20) Enforcement.
21) Provision of information by competent authority (the agency).
22) Fee payable by operator (amendment to provide power to the HSE to recover cost form certain establishments).

PART 7 - AMENDMENTS, REVOCATIONS, SAVINGS AND TRANSITIONAL PROVISIONS
23) Amendments.
24) Revocations and savings.
25) Transitional provisions.

SCHEDULES

Schedule 1	Dangerous substances to which the regulations apply.
Schedule 2	Principles to be taken into account when preparing major accident prevention policy document.
Schedule 3	Information to be included in a notification.
Schedule 4	Purpose and contents of safety reports.
Schedule 5	Emergency Plans.
Schedule 6	Information to be supplied to the public.
Schedule 7	Criteria for notification of a major accident to the European Commission and information to be notified.

RELEVANT STATUTORY PROVISIONS

Schedule 8   Provision of information by competent authority.

Outline of main points

The Control of Major Accident Hazards Regulations 1999 (COMAH) implemented the Seveso II Directive (except for the land use planning requirements), and replaced the Control of Industrial Major Accident Hazards Regulations 1984 (CIMAH).

The Regulations were amended from 30 June 2005 to reflect changes to Seveso II, and from the 1st July 2009 to enable the HSE to recover their cost from certain establishments.

COMAH applies mainly to the chemical industry, but also to some storage activities, explosives and nuclear sites, and other industries where threshold quantities of dangerous substances identified in the Regulations are kept or used.

The main aim of COMAH is to prevent and mitigate the effects of a major accident involving dangerous substances, such as chlorine, LPG, explosives and arsenic pentoxide which can cause serious damage/harm to people and/or the environment. COMAH treats risks to environment as seriously as those to people.

The main duty is to prepare a safety report which will include:

- A policy on how to prevent and mitigate major accidents.
- A management system for implementing that policy.
- An effective method for identifying any Major Accidents that may occur.
- Measures (safe plant and procedures) to prevent and mitigate major accidents.
- Information on safety precautions built into the plant when designed and constructed.
- Details of measures (fire fighting, relief systems, filters, etc) to limit the consequences of any accident.
- Information about the emergency plan for the site, this is used by the Local Authority for their off site plan.

These amendment Regulations:

- Provide for the sending of notifications by electronic means.
- Modify the exclusions relating to mines, quarries, boreholes and waste land-fill sites.
- Introduce a time limit for the preparation of a major accident prevention policy and for notification.
- Require the notification of certain modifications to the establishment.
- Notification when a safety report is revised or when a review of a report does not lead to revision.
- Modify the requirement to consult persons working in the establishment on the preparation of the plan.
- Environment/Scottish Environment Protection Agency consultees on the off-site emergency plan.
- Require the local authority to consult the public when the off-site emergency plan is reviewed.
- Require that schools, hospitals and other such establishments are supplied with safety information.
- Amend the quantities and classification of dangerous substances to which COMAH apply.
- Require specific training in planning for emergencies for all persons working in the establishment.
- Require that a notification in respect of the quantity and physical form of petroleum products.
- Require the use of maps, images or equivalent descriptions to support the assessment of the extent and severity of the consequences of identified major accidents, and require the safety report to include the names of organisations involved in drawing up the report.
- Competent authority to include, in the register of information any notification it receives.
- Operator to provide an amended safety report if information is excluded from the register.

Carriage of Dangerous Goods and Use of Transportable Pressure Equipment Regulations (CDGUTPER) 2009

Law considered in context/more depth in Element C4.

Arrangement of Regulations

Part 1 - Introductory provisions.

Part 2 - Prohibitions and requirements.

Part 3 - Exemptions.

Part 4 - Transportable pressure equipment.

Part 5 - Radiological emergencies.

Part 6 - GB competent authority functions.

Part 7 - Miscellaneous.

SCHEDULES

Schedule 1   Placards, marks and plate markings for national carriage.

Schedule 2   Radiological emergencies.

Schedule 3   Appointments.

Outline of main points

The Carriage of Dangerous Goods and Use of Transportable Pressure Equipment Regulations (CDGUTPER) 2009, came into force on 1st July 2009 and replace the 2007 regulations. The Regulations implement the European agreement know as ADR 2009, concerning the International Carriage of Dangerous Goods by Road, (with a number of exceptions). The main duties are now covered by a single regulation, namely Regulation 5, which comes under Part 2 of CDGUTPER 2009.

The purpose of the regulations is to protect everyone, either directly involved (such as consignors or carriers) or those who might become involved in an emergency. Dangerous goods are assigned to various classifications depending on their fundamental hazard.

Dangerous Substances (Notification and Marking of Sites) Regulations (NOMAS) 1990

Law considered in context/more depth in Element C4.

Arrangement of Regulations

1) Citation and commencement.
2) Interpretation.
3) Exceptions.
4) Notification.
5) Access Marking.
6) Location marking.
7) Signs to be kept clean, etc.
8) Enforcing authority.
9) Exemption certificates.
10) Transitional provisions.
11) Repeals.

Schedule 1	Exceptions.
Schedule 2	Matters to be notified.
	Part I - Particulars to be notified under regulation 4(1).
	Part II - Changes to be notified under regulation 4(2).
Schedule 3	Table of classifications and hazard warnings.
Schedule 4	Repeals and enabling powers.

Outline of main points

These regulations establish duties for persons who control sites where hazardous substances that are dangerous for conveyance are stored. If there is a total quantity of 25 tonnes or more of a hazardous substance, the person in control must notify in writing the fire authority and the enforcing authority; for regulations 5 - 7 this will be HSE.

Safety notices must be displayed with specific direction and location to warn fire fighters who may come on site in an emergency. The safety notices must bear the hazard-warning symbol and be of the standard colour and shape. The signs must be kept clean and free from obstruction.

Dangerous Substances and Explosive Atmospheres Regulations (DSEAR) 2002

Law considered in context/more depth in Element C4.

Arrangement of Regulations

1) Citation and commencement.
2) Interpretation.
3) Application.
4) Duties under these Regulations.
5) Risk assessment.
6) Elimination or reduction of risks from dangerous substances.
7) Places where explosive atmospheres may occur.
8) Arrangements to deal with accidents, incidents and emergencies.
9) Information, instruction and training.
10) Identification of hazardous contents of containers and pipes.
11) Duty of co-ordination.
12) Extension outside Great Britain.
13) Exemption certificates.
14) Exemptions for Ministry of Defence etc.
15) Amendments.
16) Repeals and revocations.
17) Transitional provisions.

Schedule 1.	General safety measures.
Schedule 2.	Classification of places where explosive atmospheres may occur.
Schedule 3.	Criteria for the selection of equipment and protective systems.

RELEVANT STATUTORY PROVISIONS

Schedule 4.   Warning sign for places where explosive atmospheres may occur.
Schedule 5.   Legislation concerned with the marking of containers and pipes.
Schedule 6.   Amendments.
Schedule 7.   Repeal and revocation.

Outline of main points

These regulations aim to protect against risks from fire, explosion and similar events arising from dangerous substances that are present in the workplace.

DANGEROUS SUBSTANCES

These are any substances or preparations that due to their properties or the way in which they are being used could cause harm to people from fires and explosions. They may include petrol, liquefied petroleum gases, paints, varnishes, solvents and dusts.

APPLICATION

DSEAR 2002 applies in most workplaces where a dangerous substance is present. There are a few exceptions where only certain parts of the regulations apply, for example:

- Ships.
- Medical treatment areas.
- Explosives/chemically unstable substances.
- Mines.
- Quarries.
- Boreholes.
- Offshore installations.
- Means of transport.

MAIN REQUIREMENTS

You must:

- Conduct a risk assessment of work activities involving dangerous substances.
- Provide measures to eliminate or reduce risks.
- Provide equipment and procedures to deal with accidents and emergencies.
- Provide information and training for employees.
- Classify places into zones and mark zones where appropriate.

The risk assessment should include:

- The hazardous properties of substance.
- The way they are used or stored.
- Possibility of hazardous explosive atmosphere occurring.
- Potential ignition sources.
- Details of zoned areas (July 2003).
- Co-ordination between employers (July 2003).

SAFETY MEASURES

Where possible eliminate safety risks from dangerous substances or, if not reasonably practicable to do this, control risks and reduce the harmful effects of any fire, explosion or similar event.

Substitution - Replace with totally safe or safer substance (best solution).

Control measures - If risk cannot be eliminated apply the following control measures in the following order:

- Reduce quantity.
- Avoid or minimise releases.
- Control releases at source.
- Prevent formation of explosive atmosphere.
- Collect, contain and remove any release to a safe place e.g. ventilation.
- Avoid ignition sources.
- Avoid adverse conditions e.g. exceeding temperature limits.
- Keep incompatible substances apart.

Mitigation measures - Apply measures to mitigate the effects of any situation.

- Prevent fire and explosions from spreading to other plant, equipment or other parts of the workplace.
- Reduce number of employees exposed.
- Provide process plant that can contain or suppress an explosion, or vent it to a safe place.

ZONED AREAS

In workplaces where explosive atmospheres may occur, areas should be classified into zones based on the likelihood of an explosive atmosphere occurring. Any equipment in these areas should ideally meet the requirements of the Equipment and Protective Systems Intended for Use in Potentially Explosive Atmospheres Regulations (EPS) 1996. However equipment in use before July 2003 can continue to be used providing that the risk assessment says that it is safe to do so. Areas may need to be marked with an 'Ex' warning sign at their entry points. Employees may need to be provided with appropriate clothing for example, anti static overalls. Before use for the first time, a person competent in the field of explosion protection must confirm hazardous areas as being safe.

ACCIDENTS, INCIDENTS AND EMERGENCIES

DSEAR 2002 builds on existing requirements for emergency procedures, which are contained in other regulations. These may need to be supplemented if you assess that a fire, explosion or significant spillage could occur, due to the quantities of dangerous substances present in the workplace. You may need to arrange for:

- Suitable warning systems.
- Escape facilities.
- Emergency procedures.
- Equipment and clothing for essential personnel who may need to deal with the situation.
- Practice drills.
- Make information, instruction and training available to employees and if necessary liaise with the emergency services.

Electricity at Work Regulations (EWR) 1989

Law considered in context/more depth in Element C8.

Arrangement of Regulations

PART I - INTRODUCTION

1) Citation and commencement.
2) Interpretation.
3) Persons on whom duties are imposed by these Regulations.

PART II - GENERAL

4) Systems, work activities and protective equipment.
5) Strength and capability of electrical equipment.
6) Adverse or hazardous environments.
7) Insulation, protection and placing of conductors.
8) Earthing or other suitable precautions.
9) Integrity of referenced conductors.
10) Connections.
11) Means for protecting from excess of current.
12) Means for cutting off the supply and for isolation.
13) Precautions for work on equipment made dead.
14) Work on or near live conductors.
15) Working space, access and lighting.
16) Persons to be competent to prevent danger and injury.

PART III - REGULATIONS APPLYING TO MINES ONLY

17) Provisions applying to mines only.
18) Introduction of electrical equipment.
19) Restriction of equipment in certain zones below ground.
20) Cutting off electricity or making safe where firedamp is found either below ground or at the surface.
21) Approval of certain equipment for use in safety-lamp mines.
22) Means of cutting off electricity to circuits below ground.
23) Oil-filled equipment.
24) Records and information.
25) Electric shock notices.
26) Introduction of battery-powered locomotives and vehicles into safety-lamp mines.
27) Storage, charging and transfer of electrical storage batteries.
28) Disapplication of section 157 of the Mines and Quarries Act 1954.

PART IV - MISCELLANEOUS AND GENERAL

29) Defence.
30) Exemption certificates.
31) Extension outside Great Britain.
32) Disapplication of duties.
33) Revocations and modifications.

Schedule 1   Provisions applying to mines only and having effect in particular in relation to the use below ground in coal mines of film lighting circuits.
Schedule 2   Revocations and modifications.

RELEVANT STATUTORY PROVISIONS

Outline of main points

SYSTEMS, WORK ACTIVITIES AND PROTECTIVE EQUIPMENT (REGULATION 4)

The system and the equipment comprising it must be designed and installed to take account of all reasonably foreseeable conditions of use.

- The system must be maintained so as to prevent danger.
- All work activities must be carried out in such a manner as to not give rise to danger.
- Equipment provided to protect people working on live equipment must be suitable and maintained.

STRENGTH AND CAPABILITY OF ELECTRICAL EQUIPMENT (REGULATION 5)

Strength and capability refers to the equipment's ability to withstand the effects of its load current and any transient overloads or pulses of current.

ADVERSE OR HAZARDOUS ENVIRONMENTS (REGULATION 6)

This regulation requires that electrical equipment is suitable for the environment and conditions that might be reasonably foreseen. In particular, attention should be paid to:

- Mechanical damage caused by for example; vehicles, people, vibration, etc.
- Weather, natural hazards, temperature or pressure. Ice, snow, lightning, bird droppings, etc.
- Wet, dirty, dusty or corrosive conditions. Conductors, moving parts, insulators and other materials may be affected by the corrosive nature of water, chemicals and solvents. The presence of explosive dusts must be given special consideration.
- Flammable or explosive substances. Electrical equipment may be a source of ignition for liquids, gases, vapours etc.

INSULATION, PROTECTION AND PLACING OF CONDUCTORS (REGULATION 7)

The purpose of this regulation is to prevent danger from direct contact. Therefore, if none exists, no action is needed. Conductors though will normally need to be insulated and also have some other protection to prevent mechanical damage.

EARTHING OR OTHER SUITABLE PRECAUTIONS (REGULATION 8)

The purpose of this regulation is to prevent danger from indirect contact. Conductors such as metal casings may become live through fault conditions. The likelihood of danger arising from these circumstances must be prevented by using the techniques described earlier in this section i.e. earthing, double insulation, reduced voltages etc.

INTEGRITY OF REFERENCED CONDUCTORS (REGULATION 9)

In many circumstances the reference point is earthed because the majority of power distribution installations are referenced by a deliberate connection to earth at the generators or distribution transformers. The purpose of this regulation is to ensure that electrical continuity is never broken.

CONNECTIONS (REGULATION 10)

As well as having suitable insulation and conductance, connections must have adequate mechanical protection and strength. Plugs and sockets must conform to recognised standards as must connections between cables. Special attention should be paid to the quality of connections on portable appliances.

MEANS FOR PROTECTING FROM EXCESS CURRENT (REGULATION 11)

Faults or overloads can occur in electrical systems and protection must be provided against their effects. The type of protection depends on several factors but usually rests between fuses and circuit breakers.

MEANS FOR CUTTING OFF THE SUPPLY AND FOR ISOLATION (REGULATION 12)

Means must be provided to switch off electrical supplies together with a means of isolation so as to prevent inadvertent reconnection.

PRECAUTIONS FOR WORK ON EQUIPMENT MADE DEAD (REGULATION 13)

Working dead should be the norm. This regulation requires that precautions be taken to ensure that the system remains dead and to protect those at work on the system. Any or all of the following steps should be considered:

- Identify the circuit. Never assume that the labelling is correct.
- Disconnection and isolation. These are the most common methods: isolation switches, fuse removal and plug removal.
- Notices and barriers.
- Proving dead. The test device itself must also be tested before and after testing.
- Earthing.
- Permits to work.

WORK ON OR NEAR LIVE CONDUCTORS (REGULATION 14)

This regulation prevents working on or near live conductors where danger may arise, unless it is unreasonable for them to be dead, and it is reasonable to work on or near to them while live, and suitable precautions are taken to prevent injury.

Precautions include:

- Competent staff (see reg. 16).
- Adequate information.
- Suitable tools: insulated tools; protective clothing.
- Barriers or screens.
- Instruments and test probes to identify what is live and what is dead.
- Accompaniment.
- Designated test areas.

WORKING SPACE, ACCESS AND LIGHTING (REGULATION 15)

Space. Where there are dangerous live exposed conductors, space should be adequate to:
- Allow persons to pull back from the hazard.
- Allow persons to pass each other.

Lighting. The first preference is for natural lighting then for permanent artificial lighting.

PERSONS TO BE COMPETENT TO PREVENT DANGER AND INJURY (REGULATION 16)

The object of this regulation is to 'ensure that persons are not placed at risk due to a lack of skills on the part of themselves or others in dealing with electrical equipment'.

In order to meet the requirements of this regulation a competent person would need:

- An understanding of the concepts of electricity and the risks involved in work associated with it.
- Knowledge of electrical work and some suitable qualification in electrical principles.
- Experience of the type of system to be worked on with an understanding of the hazards and risks involved.
- Knowledge of the systems of work to be employed and the ability to recognise hazards and risks.
- Physical attributes to be able to recognise elements of the system e.g. colour blindness and wiring.

Advice and queries regarding qualifications and training can be directed to the IEE - Institute of Electrical Engineers, London.

DEFENCE (REGULATION 29)

In any regulation where the absolute duty applies, a defence in any criminal proceedings shall exist where a person can show that: *"He took all reasonable steps and exercised due diligence to avoid the commission of the offence".*

Any defence should consider whether there was a prepared procedure (steps), the procedure was being followed (diligence) and there are records or witnesses to prove it retrospectively.

European Agreement concerning the International Carriage of Dangerous Goods by Road (ADR) 2009 (as amended 2011)

Considered in context/more depth in Element C4.

Arrangement of agreement

ANNEX A: GENERAL PROVISIONS AND PROVISIONS CONCERNING DANGEROUS ARTICLES AND SUBSTANCES

Part 1   General provisions
Part 2   Classification
Part 3   Dangerous goods list, special provisions and exemptions related to limited and excepted quantities
Part 4   Packing and tank provisions
Part 5   Consignment procedures
Part 6   Requirements for the construction and testing of packagings, intermediate bulk containers (IBCs), large packagings and tanks
Part 7   Provisions concerning the conditions of carriage, loading, unloading and handling

ANNEX B: PROVISIONS CONCERNING TRANSPORT EQUIPMENT AND TRANSPORT OPERATIONS

Part 8   Requirements for vehicle crews, equipment, operation and documentation
Part 9   Requirements concerning the construction and approval of vehicles

Outline of main points

Moving dangerous goods by road is governed by international regulations and is strictly policed. Most European countries are signed up to the European Agreement concerning the International Carriage of Dangerous Goods by Road, known as ADR (Accord Européen Relatif au Transport International des Marchandises Dangereuses par Route). Each country which adheres to ADR implements specific safety measures through its own national legislation. The purpose of ADR is to ensure that dangerous goods - including clinical and other dangerous waste - being carried by road are able to cross international borders freely, as long as goods, vehicles and drivers comply with its provisions. ADR has been in force since 1968 and is administered by the United Nations Economic Commission for Europe (UNECE). It is updated every two years to take account of technological advances. On 1 January 2011, ADR 2011 replaced ADR 2009, with any changes applying as of July 2011. ADR sets out the requirements for classifying, packaging, labelling and certifying ***dangerous goods***. These requirements are set out in Annex A to ADR. ***Vehicles carrying dangerous goods*** must comply with the provisions of Annex B to ADR, which includes vehicle and tank specifications and other operational requirements. The drivers of all vehicles (including those with a gross vehicle weight of 3.5 tonnes or less) carrying dangerous goods must have an ADR training certificate. There are exemptions for drivers carrying small loads below the threshold limits, drivers carrying dangerous goods packed in limited quantities, and drivers carrying dangerous goods packed in accepted quantities. Find more information in our guide on ***transporting dangerous goods in limited quantities***.

Source: Business Link.

RELEVANT STATUTORY PROVISIONS

Fire Safety (Scotland) Regulations (FSSR) 2006

Law considered in context/more depth in Elements C3.

Arrangement of regulations

PART 1 - PRELIMINARY
1. Citation and commencement
2. Interpretation

PART 2 - ASSESSMENTS
3. Duty to review
4. Duty in respect of young persons
5. Assessment and review duty in respect of young persons
6. Assessment and review duty in respect of dangerous substances
7. New work activities where dangerous substances are present
8. Duty to record information
9. Specified information

PART 3 - FIRE SAFETY
10. Fire safety arrangements
11. Elimination or reduction of risks from dangerous substances
12. Means for fighting fire and means for giving warning in the event of fire
13. Means of escape
14. Procedures for serious and imminent danger from fire and for danger areas
15. Additional emergency measures in respect of dangerous substances
16. Maintenance
17. Safety assistance
18. Provision of information to employees
19. Provision of information to employers and the self-employed from outside undertakings
20. Training
21. Co-operation and co-ordination
22. Duties of employees

PART 4 - MISCELLANEOUS
23. Maintenance of measures provided in relevant premises for protection of fire fighters
24. Maintenance of measures provided in the common areas of private dwellings for protection of fire-fighters
25. Arrangements with the Office of Rail Regulation
26. Nominated person's act or omission not to afford employer defence
27. Service of documents: further provision
28. Disapplication of certain provisions

SCHEDULE - MEASURES TO BE TAKEN IN RESPECT OF DANGEROUS SUBSTANCES

Outline of main points

The Fire Safety (Scotland) Regulations (FSSR) 2006 are regulations that were made by Scottish Ministers under the powers contained in the Fire (Scotland) Act (FSA) 2005, and further build upon the requirements of that act. Reference to the Regulatory Reform (Fire Safety) Order (RRFSO) 2005 should be made for the equivalent legislation for England and Wales.

The FSSR2006 builds on the primary duty to conduct a fire risk assessment set out in the Fire (Scotland) Act (FSA) 2005 and requires consideration of young people affected and dangerous substances. The FSSR 2006 establish a duty to put in place safety measures that are found necessary as a result of the fire risk assessment, including comprehensive arrangements for planning, organisation, control, monitoring and review; as well as means of escape, information and training. The FSSR 2006 includes requirements to maintain measures for the protection of fire fighters and contains a schedule of measures that relate specifically to dangerous substances, including control of quantities and measures to minimise the propagation of fires or explosions.

Fire (Scotland) Act (FSA) 2005

Considered in context in Element C3.

Arrangement of Act

PART 1 - FIRE AND RESCUE AUTHORITIES
- Fire and rescue authorities.
- Joint fire and rescue boards.
- Meaning of "relevant authority".

PART 2 - FIRE AND RESCUE SERVICES

Chapter 1	Appointment of chief officer.
Chapter 2	Principal fire and rescue functions.
Chapter 3	Ancillary functions.
Chapter 4	Water supply.
Chapter 5	Powers of employees and constables.
Chapter 6	Mutual assistance etc.
Chapter 7	Assaulting or impeding employees and others.
Chapter 8	Central supervision and support.
Chapter 9	Employment.
Chapter 10	Interpretation.

PART 3 - FIRE SAFETY

Chapter 1	Fire safety duties.
Chapter 2	Enforcement.
Chapter 3	Miscellaneous.
Chapter 4	Offences.
Chapter 5	General.

PART 4 - MISCELLANEOUS

- Inquiries.
- Consultation requirements.
- Pre-commencement consultation.
- Advisory bodies.
- Payments in respect of advisory bodies.
- Abolition of Scottish Central Fire Brigades Advisory Council.
- False alarms.
- Disposal of land.

PART 5 - GENERAL

- Ancillary provision.
- Orders and regulations.
- Minor and consequential amendments and repeals.
- Commencement.
- Short title.

Schedule 1	Joint fire and rescue boards: supplementary provision.
Schedule 2	Fire safety measures.
Schedule 3	Minor and consequential amendments.
Schedule 4	Repeals.

Outline of main points

The FSA 2005 establishes a framework for the provision of fire and rescue services and structure for fire legislation relating to workplaces in Scotland. The FSA 2006 provides for the implementation of subordinate legislation to establish specific duties, particularly in respect of workplace fire safety, and lead to the creation of the Fire Safety (Scotland) Regulations 2006, which reflected the Regulatory Reform (Fire Safety) Order 2005 relating to England and Wales. The FSA 2005 is targeted at reducing the number of workplace fires by imposing far reaching responsibilities on all employers, as well as those who have control to any extent of non-domestic premises, to assess and reduce the risks from fire.

Fire certificates were abolished in Scotland under the FSA 2005 and have been replaced by a fire safety regime that is based upon the principles of risk assessment and the requirement to take steps to mitigate the detrimental effects of a fire on relevant premises. The regime applies to all employers as well as to anyone who has control of non-domestic premises to any extent including building owners, tenants, occupiers and factors.

The overriding duty is to ensure, so far as is reasonably practicable, safety in respect of harm caused by fire in the workplace. Schedule 1 establishes a general duty to implement specified fire safety measures:

- To reduce risk of fires occurring and spreading.
- Means of escape.
- Fire fighting.
- Detection of fire and warnings of fire.
- Action to be taken in the event of a fire, particularly instruction and training of employees and mitigation of the effects of fire.

The Schedule 1 clarifies that the measures required do not extend to requirements for process fire safety precautions.

RELEVANT STATUTORY PROVISIONS

Health and Safety (Safety Signs and Signals) Regulations (SSSR) 1996

Law considered in context/more depth in Elements C1, C3 and C4.

Arrangement of Regulations

1) Citation and commencement.
2) Interpretation.
3) Application.
4) Provision and maintenance of safety signs.
5) Information, instruction and training.
6) Transitional provisions.
7) Enforcement.
8) Revocations and amendments.

Outline of main points

The Regulations require employers to provide specific safety signs whenever there is a risk which has not been avoided or controlled by other means, for example, by engineering controls and safe systems of work. Where a safety sign would not help to reduce that risk, or where the sign is not significant, there is no need to provide a sign.

They require, where necessary, the use of road traffic signs within workplaces to regulate road traffic.

They also require employers to:

- Maintain the safety signs which are provided by them.
- Explain unfamiliar signs to their employees and tell them what they need to do when they see a safety sign.

Regs cover 4 main areas of signs:

1) **Prohibition** - circular signs, prime colours red and white, e.g. no pedestrian access.
2) **Warning** - triangular signs, prime colours black on yellow, e.g. overhead electrics.
3) **Mandatory** - circular signs, prime colours blue and white, e.g. safety helmets must be worn.
4) **Safe condition** - oblong/square signs, prime colours green and white e.g. fire exit, first aid etc.

Supplementary signs provide additional information.

Supplementary signs with yellow/black or red/white diagonal stripes can be used to highlight a hazard, but must not substitute for signs as defined above.

Fire fighting, rescue equipment and emergency exit signs have to comply with a separate British Standard.

Health and Safety at Work etc. Act (HASAWA) 1974

Law considered in context/more depth in Element C5.

Arrangement of Act

PRELIMINARY

1) Preliminary.

GENERAL DUTIES

2) General duties of employers to the employees.
3) General duties of employers and self-employed to persons other than their employees.
4) General duties of persons concerned with premises to persons other than their employees.
5) [repealed].
6) General duties of manufacturers etc. as regards articles and substances for use at work.
7) General duties of employees at work.
8) Duty not to interfere with or misuse things provided pursuant to certain provisions.
9) Duty not to charge employees for things done or provided pursuant to certain specific requirements.

THE HEALTH AND SAFETY COMMISSION AND THE HEALTH AND SAFETY EXECUTIVE

10) Establishment of the Commission and the Executive (amended to reflect Executive now includes role of Commission).
11) General functions of the Commission and the Executive.
12) Control of the Commission by the Secretary of State.
13) Other powers of the Commission.
14) Power of the Commission to direct investigations and Inquiries.

HEALTH AND SAFETY REGULATIONS AND APPROVED CODES OF PRACTICE

15) Health and safety regulations.
16) Approval of codes of practice by the Commission.

RELEVANT STATUTORY PROVISIONS

17) Use of approved codes of practice in criminal proceedings.

ENFORCEMENT

18) Authorities responsible for enforcement of the relevant statutory provisions.
19) Appointment of inspectors.
20) Powers of inspectors.
21) Improvement notices.
22) Prohibition notices.
23) Provisions supplementary toss. 21 and 22.
24) Appeal against improvement or prohibition notice.
25) Power to deal with cause of imminent danger.
26) Power of enforcing authorities to indemnify their inspectors.

OBTAINING AND DISCLOSURE OF INFORMATION

27) Obtaining of information by the Commission, the Executive, enforcing authorities etc.
28) Restrictions on disclosure of information.

SPECIAL PROVISIONS RELATING TO AGRICULTURE

29-32) [repealed].

PROVISIONS AS TO OFFENCES

33) Offences.
34) Extension of time for bringing summary proceedings.
35) Venue.
36) Offences due to fault of other person.
37) Offences by bodies corporate.
38) Restriction on institution of proceedings in England and Wales.
39) Prosecutions by inspectors.
40) Onus of proving limits of what is practicable etc.
41) Evidence.
42) Power of court to order cause of offence to be remedied or, in certain cases, forfeiture.

FINANCIAL PROVISION

43) Financial provisions.

MISCELLANEOUS AND SUPPLEMENTARY

44) Appeals in connection with licensing provisions in the relevant statutory provisions.
45) Default powers.
46) Service of notices.
47) Civil liability.
48) Application to Crown.
49) Adaptation of enactments to metric units or appropriate metric units.
50) Regulations under the relevant statutory provisions.
51) Exclusion of application to domestic employment.
52) Meaning of work and at work.
53) General interpretation of Part I.
54) Application of Part I to Isles of Scilly.

Outline of main points

AIMS

1) To protect people.
2) To protect the public from risks which may arise from work activities.

THE MAIN PROVISIONS - SECTION 1

a) Securing the health, safety and welfare of people at work.
b) Protecting others against risks arising from workplace activities.
c) Controlling the obtaining, keeping, and use of explosive and highly flammable substances.
d) Controlling emissions into the atmosphere of noxious or offensive substances.

Duties imposed on:

a) The employer.
b) The self employed.

RELEVANT STATUTORY PROVISIONS

c) Employees.
d) Contractors and subcontractors.
e) Designers, manufacturers, suppliers, importers and installers.
f) Specialists - architects, surveyors, engineers, personnel managers, health and safety specialists, and many more.

EMPLOYER'S DUTIES - [TO EMPLOYEES]

Section 2(1)

To ensure, so far as *reasonably practicable*, the health, safety and welfare at work of employees.

Section 2(2)

Ensuring health, safety and welfare at work through:
a) Safe plant and systems of work e.g. provision of guards on machines.
b) Safe use, handling, storage and transport of goods and materials e.g. good manual handling of boxes.
c) Provision of information, instruction, training and supervision e.g. provision of induction training.
d) Safe place of work including means of access and egress e.g. aisles kept clear.
e) Safe and healthy working environment e.g. good lighting.

Further duties are placed on the employer by:

Section 2(3)

Prepare and keep up to date a written safety policy supported by information on the organisation and arrangements for carrying out the policy. The safety policy has to be brought to the notice of employees. If there are fewer than five employees, this section does not apply.

Section 2(4)

Recognised Trade Unions have the right to appoint safety representatives to represent the employees in consultations with the employer about health and safety matters.

Section 2(6)

Employers must consult with any safety representatives appointed by recognised Trade Unions.

Section 2(7)

To establish a safety committee if requested by two or more safety representatives.

EMPLOYER'S DUTIES - [TO PERSONS NOT HIS EMPLOYEES]

Section 3

a) Not to expose them to risk to their heath and safety e.g. contractor work barriered off.
b) To give information about risks which may affect them e.g. location induction for contractors.

SELF EMPLOYED DUTIES

Section 3

a) Not to expose themselves to risks to their health and safety e.g. wear personal protection.
b) Not to expose other persons to risks to their health and safety e.g. keep shared work area tidy.

Some of the practical steps that an organisation might take in order to ensure the safety of visitors to its premises are:
- Identify visitors by signing in, badges etc.
- Provide information regarding the risks present and the site rules and procedures to be followed, particularly in emergencies.
- Provide escorts to supervise visitors throughout the site.
- Restrict access to certain areas.

Figure RSP-1: Risks from road side work. *Source: RMS.*

Figure RSP-2: Risks from street light repair or tree felling. *Source: RMS.*

PEOPLE IN CONTROL OF PREMISES

Section 4

This section places duties on anyone who has control to any extent of non-domestic premises used by people who are not their employees. The duty extends to the provision of safe premises, plant and substances, e.g. maintenance of a boiler in rented out property.

MANUFACTURERS, DESIGNERS, SUPPLIERS, IMPORTERS, INSTALLERS

Section 6

This section places specific duties on those who can ensure that articles and substances are as safe and without risks as is reasonably practicable. The section covers:

- Safe design, installation and testing of equipment (including fairground equipment).
- Safe substances tested for risks.
- Provision of information on safe use and conditions essential to health and safety.
- Research to minimise risks.

EMPLOYEES' DUTIES

Section 7

a) To take reasonable care for themselves and others that may be affected by their acts/omissions e.g. wear eye protection, not obstruct a fire exit.

b) To co-operate with the employer or other to enable them to carry out their duty and/or statutory requirements e.g. report hazards or defects in controls, attend training, provide medical samples.

Additional duties created by the Management of Health and Safety at Work Regulations employees' duties:

- Every employee shall use any equipment, material or substance provided to them in accordance with any training and instruction.
- Every employee shall inform (via supervisory staff) their employer of any (a) risk situation or (b) shortcoming in the employer's protection arrangements.

OTHER DUTIES

Section 8

No person to interfere with or misuse anything provided to secure health and safety - e.g. wedge fire door open, remove first aid equipment without authority, breach lock off systems.

Section 9

Employees cannot be charged for anything done or provided to comply with a specific legal obligation e.g. personal protective equipment, health surveillance or welfare facilities.

OFFENCES COMMITTED BY OTHER PERSONS

Section 36

- Where the commission by any person of the breach of legislation is due to the act or default of some other person, that other person shall be guilty of the offence and may be charged with and convicted of the offence whether or not proceedings are taken against the first mentioned person.
- Case law indicates that 'other person' refers to persons lower down the corporate tree than mentioned in section 37, e.g. middle managers, safety advisors, training officers; and may extend to people working on contract e.g. architects, consultants or a planning supervisor.

OFFENCES COMMITTED BY THE BODY CORPORATE

Section 37

- Where there has been a breach of legislation on the part of a body corporate (limited company or local authority) and the offence can be proved to have been committed with the consent or connivance of or to be attributable to any neglect on the part of any director, manager, secretary or similar officer of the body corporate, he, as well as the body corporate, can be found guilty and punished accordingly.

ONUS OF PROOF

Section 40

In any proceedings for an offence under any of the relevant statutory involving a failure to comply with a duty or requirement:

- To do something so far as is practicable.
- To do something so far as is reasonably practicable.
- It shall be for the accused to prove that the requirements were met rather than for the prosecution to prove that the requirements were not met.

RELEVANT STATUTORY PROVISIONS

IET Wiring Regulations 17th Edition (BS 7671: 2008)

Considered in context/more depth in Element C8.

Arrangements of Regulations

INTRODUCTION TO BS 7671:2008

NOTES ON THE PLAN OF THE 17TH EDITION

PART 1 - SCOPE, OBJECT AND FUNDAMENTAL PRINCIPLES

Chapter 11: Scope
Chapter 12: Object and effects
Chapter 13: Fundamental principles

PART 2 - DEFINITIONS

PART 3 - ASSESSMENT OF GENERAL CHARACTERISTICS

Chapter 31: Purpose, supplies and structure
Chapter 32: Classification of external influences
Chapter 33: Compatibility
Chapter 34: Maintainability
Chapter 35: Safety services
Chapter 36: Continuity of service

PART 4 - PROTECTION FOR SAFETY

Chapter 41: Protection against electric shock
Chapter 42: Protection against thermal effects
Chapter 43: Protection against overcurrent
Chapter 44: Protection against voltage disturbances and electromagnetic disturbances

PART 5 - SELECTION AND ERECTION OF EQUIPMENT

Chapter 51: Common rules
Chapter 52: Selection and erection of wiring systems
Chapter 53: Protection, isolation, switching, control and monitoring
Chapter 54: Earthing arrangements and protective conductors
Chapter 55: Other equipment
Chapter 56: Safety services

PART 6 - INSPECTION AND TESTING

Chapter 61: Initial verification
Chapter 62: Periodic inspection and testing
Chapter 63: Certification and reporting

PART 7 - SPECIAL INSTALLATIONS OR LOCATIONS

Section 700: General
Section 701: Locations containing a bath or shower
Section 702: Swimming pools and other basins
Section 703: Rooms and cabins containing sauna heaters
Section 704: Construction and demolition site installations
Section 705: Agricultural and horticultural premises
Section 706: Conducting locations with restricted movement
Section 708: Electrical installations in caravan/camping parks and similar locations
Section 709: Marinas and similar locations
Section 711: Exhibitions, shows and stands
Section 712: Solar photovoltaic (PV) power supply systems
Section 717: Mobile or transportable units
Section 721: Electrical installations in caravans and motor caravans
Section 740: Temporary electrical installations for structures, amusement devices and booths at fairgrounds, amusement parks and circuses
Section 753: Floor and ceiling heating systems

APPENDICES

1) British Standards to which reference is made in the Regulations

RELEVANT STATUTORY PROVISIONS

2) Statutory regulations and associated memoranda
3) Time/current characteristics of overcurrent protective devices and rcds
4) Current-carrying capacity and voltage drop for cables and flexible cords
5) Classification of external influences
6) Model forms for certification and reporting
7) Harmonized cable core colours
8) Current-carrying capacity and voltage drop for busbar trunking and powertrack systems
9) Definitions - multiple source, d.c. and other systems
10) Protection of conductors in parallel against overcurrent
11) Effect of harmonic currents on balanced three-phase systems
12) Voltage drop in consumers' installations
13) Methods for measuring the insulation resistance/impedance of floors and walls to Earth or to the protective conductor system
14) Measurement of earth fault loop impedance: consideration of the increase of the resistance of conductors with increase of temperature
15) Ring and radial final circuit arrangements, Regulation 433.1

Source: IET.

Outline of main points

The IET has co-operated with the British Standards Institute to establish a code of working that both satisfies the IET's need for regulation of members and the national need to establish formal standards. This collaboration has resulted in the codification of the IEE Wiring Regulations in to the UK standard BS 7671:2008 Requirements for Electrical Installations.

The revised standard applies to the design, erection and verification of electrical installations, also additions and alternations to existing installations. BS 7671: 2008 includes changes necessary to maintain technical alignment with CENELEC, the European Committee for Electrotechnical Standardisation and The International Electrotechnical Commission (IEC) harmonisation documents.

Compliance with IEE Wiring Regulations and BS 7671 is not a statutory requirement.

Lifting Operations and Lifting Equipment Regulations (LOLER) 1998

Law considered in context/more depth in Elements C7 and C9.

Arrangements of Regulations

1) Citation and commencement.
2) Interpretation.
3) Application.
4) Strength and stability.
5) Lifting equipment for lifting persons.
6) Positioning and installation.
7) Marking of lifting equipment.
8) Organisation of lifting operations.
9) Thorough examination and inspection.
10) Reports and defects.
11) Keeping of information.
12) Exemption for the armed forces.
13) Amendment of the Shipbuilding and Ship-repairing Regulations 1960.
14) Amendment of the Docks Regulation 1988.
15) Repeal of provisions of the Factories Act 1961.
16) Repeal of section 85 of the Mines and Quarries Act 1954.
17) Revocation of instruments.

Schedule 1   Information to be contained in a report of a thorough examination.
Schedule 2   Revocation of instruments.

Outline of main points

The Lifting Operations and Lifting Equipment Regulations (LOLER) 1998 impose health and safety requirements with respect to lifting equipment (as defined in regulation 2(1)). They are not industry specific and apply to almost all lifting operations. The regulations place duties on employers, the self-employed, and certain persons having control of lifting equipment (of persons at work who use or supervise or manage its use, or of the way it is used, to the extent of their control (regulation 3(3) to (5)).

RELEVANT STATUTORY PROVISIONS

The regulations make provision with respect to:

- The strength and stability of lifting equipment (regulation 4).
- The safety of lifting equipment for lifting persons (regulation 5).
- The way lifting equipment is positioned and installed (regulation 6).
- The marking of machinery and accessories for lifting, and lifting equipment which is designed for lifting persons or which might so be used in error (regulation 7).
- The organisation of lifting operations (regulation 8).
- The thorough examination (defined in (regulation 2(1)) and inspection of lifting equipment in specified circumstances, (regulation 9(1) to (3)).
- The evidence of examination to accompany it outside the undertaking (regulation 9(4)).
- The exception for winding apparatus at mines from regulation 9 (regulation 9(5)).
- Transitional arrangements relating to regulation 9 (regulation 9(6) and (7)).
- The making of reports of thorough examinations and records of inspections (regulation 10 and Schedule 1).
- The keeping of information in the reports and records (regulation 11).

Management of Health and Safety at Work Regulations (MHSWR) 1999

Law considered in context/more depth in Elements C1, C3 and C4.

Arrangement of Regulations

1) Citation, commencement and interpretation.
2) Disapplication of these Regulations.
3) Risk assessment.
4) Principles of prevention to be applied.
5) Health and safety arrangements.
6) Health surveillance.
7) Health and safety assistance.
8) Procedures for serious and imminent danger and for danger areas.
9) Contacts with external services.
10) Information for employees.
11) Co-operation and co-ordination.
12) Persons working in host employers' or self-employed persons' undertakings.
13) Capabilities and training.
14) Employees' duties.
15) Temporary workers.
16) Risk assessment in respect of new or expectant mothers.
17) Certificate from a registered medical practitioner in respect of new or expectant mothers.
18) Notification by new or expectant mothers.
19) Protection of young persons.
20) Exemption certificates.
21) Provisions as to liability.
22) Exclusion of civil liability.
23) Extension outside Great Britain.
24) Amendment of the Health and Safety (First-Aid) Regulations 1981.
25) Amendment of the Offshore Installations and Pipeline Works (First-Aid) Regulations 1989.
26) Amendment of the Mines Miscellaneous Health and Safety Provisions Regulations 1995.
27) Amendment of the Construction (Health, Safety and Welfare) Regulations 1996.
28) Regulations to have effect as health and safety regulations.
29) Revocations and consequential amendments.
30) Transitional provision.

Schedule 1   General principles of prevention.
Schedule 2   Consequential amendments.

Outline of main points

The Management of Health and Safety at Work Regulations (MHSWR) 1999 (and as amended 2003) set out some broad general duties which apply to almost all kinds of work. They are aimed mainly at improving health and safety management and can be seen as a way of fleshing out what is already in the HASAWA 1974. The principal regulations are discussed below.

RISK ASSESSMENT (REGULATION 3)

The regulations require employers (and the self-employed) to assess the risk to the health and safety of their employees and to anyone else who may be affected by their work activity. This is necessary to ensure that the preventive and protective steps can be identified to control hazards in the workplace.

A *hazard* is defined as something with the potential to cause harm and may include machinery, substances or a work practice.

A *risk* is defined as the likelihood that a particular hazard will cause harm. Consideration must be given to the population, i.e. the number of persons who might be exposed to harm and the consequence of such exposure.

Where an employer is employing or about to employ young persons (under 18 years of age) he must carry out a risk assessment which takes particular account of:

- The inexperience, lack of awareness of risks and immaturity of young persons.
- The layout of the workplace and workstations.
- Exposure to physical, biological and chemical agents.
- Work equipment and the way in which it is handled.
- The extent of health and safety training to be provided.
- Risks from agents, processes and work listed in the Annex to Council Directive 94/33/EC on the protection of young people at work.

Where 5 or more employees are employed, the significant findings of risk assessments must be recorded in writing (the same threshold that is used in respect of having a written safety policy). This record must include details of any employees being identified as being especially at risk.

PRINCIPLES OF PREVENTION TO BE APPLIED (REGULATION 4)

Regulation 4 requires an employer to implement preventive and protective measures on the basis of general principles of prevention specified in Schedule 1 to the MHSWR 1999. These are:

1) Avoiding risks.
2) Evaluating the risks which cannot be avoided.
3) Combating the risks at source.
4) Adapting the work to the individual, especially as regards the design of workplaces, the choice of work equipment and the choice of working and production methods, with a view, in particular, to alleviating monotonous work and work at a predetermined work-rate and to reducing their effect on health.
5) Adapting to technical progress.
6) Replacing the dangerous by the non-dangerous or the less dangerous.
7) Developing a coherent overall prevention policy which covers technology, organisation of work, working conditions, social relationships and the influence of factors relating to the working environment.
8) Giving collective protective measures priority over individual protective measures.
9) Giving appropriate instructions to employees.

HEALTH AND SAFETY ARRANGEMENTS (REGULATION 5)

Appropriate arrangements must be made for the effective planning, organisation, control, monitoring and review of preventative and protective measures (in other words, for the management of health and safety). Again, employers with five or more employees must have their arrangements in writing.

HEALTH SURVEILLANCE (REGULATION 6)

In addition to the requirements of specific regulations such as Control of Substances Hazardous to Health (COSHH) and Asbestos regulations, consideration must be given to carry out health surveillance of employees where there is a disease or adverse health condition identified in risk assessments.

HEALTH AND SAFETY ASSISTANCE (REGULATION 7)

The employer must appoint one or more competent persons to assist him in complying with the legal obligations imposed on the undertaking. The number of persons appointed should reflect the number of employees and the type of hazards in the workplace.

If more than one competent person is appointed, then arrangements must be made for ensuring adequate co-operation between them. The competent person(s) must be given the necessary time and resources to fulfil their functions. This will depend on the size the undertaking, the risks to which employees are exposed and the distribution of those risks throughout the undertaking.

The employer must ensure that competent person(s) who are not employees are informed of the factors known (or suspected) to affect the health and safety of anyone affected by business activities.

Competent people are defined as those who have sufficient training and experience or knowledge and other qualities to enable them to perform their functions.

Persons may be selected from among existing employees or from outside. Where there is a suitable person in the employer's employment, that person shall be appointed as the 'competent person' in preference to a non-employee.

PROCEDURES FOR SERIOUS AND IMMINENT DANGER AND FOR DANGER AREAS (REGULATION 8)

Employers are required to set up emergency procedures and appoint **competent persons** to ensure compliance with identified arrangements, to devise control strategies as appropriate and to limit access to areas of risk to ensure that only those persons with adequate health and safety knowledge and instruction are admitted.

The factors to be considered when preparing a procedure to deal with workplace emergencies such as fire, explosion, bomb scare, chemical leakage or other dangerous occurrence should include:

- The identification and training requirements of persons with specific responsibilities.
- The layout of the premises in relation to escape routes etc.
- The number of persons affected.
- Assessment of special needs (disabled persons, children etc.).

RELEVANT STATUTORY PROVISIONS

- Warning systems.
- Emergency lighting.
- Location of shut-off valves, isolation switches, hydrants etc.
- Equipment required to deal with the emergency.
- Location of assembly points.
- Communication with emergency services.
- Training and/or information to be given to employees, visitors, local residents and anyone else who might be affected.

CONTACTS WITH EXTERNAL SERVICES (REGULATION 9)

Employers must ensure that, where necessary, contacts are made with external services. This particularly applies with regard to first-aid, emergency medical care and rescue work.

INFORMATION FOR EMPLOYEES (REGULATION 10)

Employees must be provided with relevant information about hazards to their health and safety arising from risks identified by the assessments. Clear instruction must be provided concerning any preventative or protective control measures including those relating to serious and imminent danger and fire assessments. Details of any competent persons nominated to discharge specific duties in accordance with the regulations must also be communicated as should risks arising from contact with other employer's activities (see Regulation 11).

Before employing a child (a person who is not over compulsory school age) the employer must provide those with parental responsibility for the child with information on the risks that have been identified and preventative and protective measures to be taken.

CO-OPERATION AND CO-ORDINATION (REGULATION 11)

Employers who work together in a common workplace have a duty to co-operate to discharge their duties under relevant statutory provisions. They must also take all reasonable steps to inform their respective employees of risks to their health or safety which may arise out of their work. Specific arrangements must be made to ensure compliance with fire legislation.

PERSONS WORKING IN HOST EMPLOYERS' OR SELF EMPLOYED PERSONS' UNDERTAKINGS (REGULATION 12)

This regulation extends the requirements of regulation 11 to include employees working as sole occupiers of a workplace under the control of another employer. Such employees would include those working under a service of contract and employees in temporary employment businesses under the control of the first employer.

CAPABILITIES AND TRAINING (REGULATION 13)

Employers need to take into account the capabilities of their employees before entrusting tasks. This is necessary to ensure that they have adequate health and safety training and are capable enough at their jobs to avoid risk. To this end consideration must be given to recruitment including job orientation when transferring between jobs and work departments. Training must also be provided when other factors such as the introduction of new technology and new systems of work or work equipment arise.

Training must:

- Be repeated periodically where appropriate.
- Be adapted to take account of any new or changed risks to the health and safety of the employees concerned.
- Take place during working hours.

EMPLOYEES' DUTIES (REGULATION 14)

Employees are required to use machinery, substances, transport, means of production and safety devices in accordance with the instructions and training that they have received.

They must also inform their employer (and other employees with responsibility for health and safety) of any serous and imminent dangers or shortcoming in the health and safety arrangements that affects the employee or arises out of work activities of the employee.

TEMPORARY WORKERS (REGULATION 15)

Consideration is given to the special needs of temporary workers. In particular to the provision of particular health and safety information such as qualifications required to perform the task safely or any special arrangements such as the need to provide health screening.

RISKS ASSESSMENT IN RESPECT OF NEW OR EXPECTANT MOTHERS (REGULATION 16)

Where the work is of a kind which would involve risk to a new or expectant mother or her baby, then the assessment required by regulation 3 should take this into account.

If the risk cannot be avoided, then the employer should take reasonable steps to:

- Adjust the hours worked.
- Offer alternative work.
- Give paid leave for as long as is necessary.

CERTIFICATE FROM A REGISTERED MEDICAL PRACTITIONER IN RESPECT OF NEW OR EXPECTANT MOTHERS (REGULATION 17)

Where the woman is a night shift worker and has a medical certificate identifying night shift work as a risk then the employer must put her on day shift or give paid leave for as long as is necessary.

NOTIFICATION BY NEW OR EXPECTANT MOTHERS (REGULATION 18)

The employer need take no action until he is notified in writing by the woman that she is pregnant, has given birth in the last six months, or is breastfeeding.

PROTECTION OF YOUNG PERSONS (REGULATION 19)

Employers of young persons shall ensure that they are not exposed to risk as a consequence of their lack of experience, lack of awareness or lack of maturity.

No employer shall employ young people for work which:

- Is beyond his physical or psychological capacity.
- Involves exposure to agents which chronically affect human health.
- Involves harmful exposure to radiation.
- Involves a risk to health from extremes of temperature, noise or vibration.
- Involves risks which could not be reasonably foreseen by young persons.

This regulation does not prevent the employment of a young person who is no longer a child for work:

- Where it is necessary for his training.
- Where the young person will be supervised by a competent person.
- Where any risk will be reduced to the lowest level that is reasonably practicable.

EXEMPTION CERTIFICATES (REGULATION 20)

The Secretary of State for Defence may, in the interests of national security, by a certificate in writing exempt the armed forces, any visiting force or any headquarters from certain obligations imposed by the Regulations.

PROVISIONS AS TO LIABILITY (REGULATION 21)

Employers cannot submit a defence in criminal proceedings that contravention was caused by the act or default either of an employee or the competent person appointed under Regulation 7.

EXCLUSION OF CIVIL LIABILITY (REGULATION 22)

The 2006 amendment to the Management of Health and Safety at Work Regulations 1999 removes the right to civil action proceedings by a third party against an employer for breach of statutory duty relating to the regulations and similarly employees for any failure in their duties under regulation 14. Employees retain the right to sue employers and other employees for breach of their statutory duty under MHSWR 1999.

New Roads and Street Works Act (NRSWA) 1991

Law considered in context/more depth in Element C9.

Arrangement of Regulations

Part I - New Roads in England and Wales

- Concession agreements.
- Toll orders.
- Further provisions with respect to tolls.
- Annual Report.
- Miscellaneous.
- General.

Part II - New Roads in Scotland

- Toll roads.
- Further provision with respect to tolls.
- Report.
- Supplementary provisions.

Part III - Street works in England and Wales

- Introductory provisions.
- The street works register.
- Notice and co-ordination of works.
- Street subject to special controls.
- General requirements as to execution of street works.
- Reinstatement.
- Charges, fees and contributions payable by undertakers.
- Duties and liabilities of undertakers with respect to apparatus.
- Apparatus affected by highway, bridge or transport works.
- Provisions with respect to particular authorities and undertakings.
- Power of street authority or district council to undertake street works.
- Supplementary provisions.

Part IV - Road works in Scotland

- Introductory provisions.
- The road work register.
- Notice and co-ordination of works.
- Roads subject to special controls.
- General requirements as to execution of road works.
- Reinstatement.
- Charges, fees and contributions payable by undertakers.

RELEVANT STATUTORY PROVISIONS

- Duties and liabilities of undertakers with respect to apparatus.
- Apparatus affected by road, bridge or transport works.
- Provisions with respect to particular authorities and undertakings.
- Power of road works authority or district council to undertake road works.
- Supplementary provisions.

Part V - General

SCHEDULES

Schedule 1	Supplementary provisions as to termination of concession.
Schedule 2	Procedure in Connection with Toll Orders.
Schedule 3	Street works licences.
Schedule 4	Streets with special engineering difficulties.
Schedule 5	Procedure for making certain orders under Part III.
Schedule 6	Roads with special engineering difficulties.
Schedule 7	Procedure for making certain orders under Part IV.
Schedule 8	Minor and consequential amendments.
Schedule 9	Repeals

Outline of main points

The New Roads and Street Works Act 1991 (NRSWA) provides a legislative framework for street works activities by undertakers (including public utilities). The efficient co-ordination of street works is one of the most important aspects of street works legislation, benefiting street authorities, undertakers and road users alike. The main objectives of NRSWA 1991 are to:

- Ensure safety.
- To minimise inconvenience to people using a street, including a specific reference to people with a disability.
- To protect the structure of the street and the apparatus in it.

Guidance is available on specific aspects of the NRSWA 1991, for example guidance for operatives in how to sign, light and guard street works safely - "Safety at Street Works and Road Works Code of Practice (also known as the Red Book)" as well as non-statutory guidance on safety at street works - "Chapter 8 of the Traffic Signs Manual".

Notification of Conventional Tower Cranes Regulations (NCTC) 2010

Law considered in context/more depth in Element C9.

Arrangement of Regulations

1) Citation and commencement.
2) Interpretation.
3) Application.
4) Notification of conventional tower cranes on construction sites.
5) Exemptions.
6) Conventional tower cranes installed prior to the commencement of these Regulations.

Schedule - Information which is required to be notified to the Executive.

Outline of main points

The Notification of Conventional Tower Cranes Regulations 2010 came into force on 6 April 2010. The Regulations require certain information about conventional tower cranes used on construction sites to be notified to the Health and Safety Executive (HSE). Since 2000 there have been a number of high profile incidents and deaths involving tower cranes. These have led to public concern over tower crane safety and in 2008 the Work and Pensions Select Committee, inquiring into the work of the HSE, called on HSE to bring forward proposals for a national register. The UK's lifting regulations, the 1998 Lifting Operations and Lifting Equipment Regulations (LOLER) require that tower cranes are thoroughly examined by a competent person when they are erected, and then at least every 6 or 12 months (depending on whether they are used for personnel lifts). The new tower crane registration scheme builds on this requirement. The register is aimed at conventional tower cranes, not self erectors or truck mounted towers. Under NCTC 2010 employers (typically the lead contractor on the site where the crane is erected) need to notify the HSE within 14 days of performing the thorough examination (TE) required under LOLER. The HSE needs to be notified of the address where the crane is erected, the name and address of the crane's owners, the details needed to identify the crane, the date of its TE, the details of the employer for whom the TE was performed, and whether any defects posing a risk of serious injury were identified.

Notification of Installations Handling Hazardous Substances Regulations (NIHHS) 1982 (as amended)

Law considered in context/more depth in Element C4.

Arrangement of Regulations

1) Citation and commencement.
2) Interpretation.

RELEVANT STATUTORY PROVISIONS

3) Notification of installations handling hazardous substances.
4) Updating of the notification following changes in the notifiable activity.
5) Re-notification where the quantity of a substance is increased to 3 times that already notified.
6) Exemption certificates.
7) Enforcing authority.
8) Transitional provision.

Schedule 1   Part I   Named substances.
                  Part II   Classes of substances not specifically named in Part I.
Schedule 2   Part I   Particulars to be included in the notification of a site.
                  Part II   Particulars to be included in a notification relating to a pipeline.

Outline of main points

These regulations specify hazardous substances and the quantities that trigger **obligations to notify the HSE of their use 3 months before such use commences**. The list of notifiable hazardous substances is divided into specifically named substances and classes of substances not specifically named; the related notifiable quantities of such substances are also listed in Schedule 1.

SCHEDULE 1 - LIST OF HAZARDOUS SUBSTANCES - EXAMPLES

Named substances		Classes of substances not specifically named	
Substance	**Notifiable quantity (tonnes)**	**Substance**	**Notifiable quantity (tonnes)**
Phosgene	2	1. Gas or any mixture which is flammable in air and is held in the installation as a gas.	15
Sulphur dioxide	20		
Ammonium nitrate and mixtures of ammonium nitrate where the nitrogen content derived from the ammonium nitrate exceeds 15.75%* of the mixture by weight other than - (a) mixtures to which the Explosives Act 1975 applies; or (b) ammonium nitrate based products manufactured chemically for use as fertiliser which comply with the Council Directive 80/876/EEC. * (Formerly 28% before these regulations were amended).	150		

Figure RSP-3: Schedule 1 examples.   *Source: Notification of Installations Handling Hazardous Substances Regulations 1982 (as amended).*

Note: the **Notification of Installations Handling Hazardous Substances (Amendment) Regulations 2002 (into force 30th December 2002)**, amended the original regulations with regard to **ammonium nitrate**. For example, quantities of ammonium nitrate trigger an obligation to notify the HSE of its use at least **4 weeks** before such use commences; also, the **notifiable quantity** was amended from 500 to **150 tonnes**.

Pressure Equipment Regulations (PER) 1999

Law considered in context/more depth in Element C11.

Arrangement of Regulations

PART I - PRELIMINARY
1) Citation and commencement
2) Interpretation

PART II - APPLICATION
3) Pressure equipment and assemblies
4) Excluded pressure equipment and assemblies
5) Pressure equipment and assemblies placed on the market before 29th November 1999
6) Exclusion until 30th May 2002 of pressure equipment and assemblies complying with provisions in force on 28th November 1999

PART III - GENERAL REQUIREMENTS
7) General duty relating to the placing on the market or putting into service of pressure equipment
8) General duty relating to the placing on the market or putting into service of assemblies
9) Requirement for pressure equipment or assemblies to comply with sound engineering practice
10) General duty relating to the supply of pressure equipment or assemblies

© RMS   423

RELEVANT STATUTORY PROVISIONS

11) Exceptions to placing on the market or supply in respect of certain pressure equipment and assemblies
12) Classification of pressure equipment
13) Conformity assessment procedures for pressure equipment
14) Conformity assessment procedure for assemblies
15) Exclusion for pressure equipment and assemblies for use for experimentation
16) CE marking
17) European approval for materials
18) Notified bodies
19) Recognised third-party organisations
20) Notified bodies and recognised third-party organisations appointed by the Secretary of State
21) Fees
22) User inspectorates
23) Conditions for pressure equipment and assemblies being taken to conform with the provisions of these Regulations

PART IV - ENFORCEMENT

24) Application of Schedule 8
25) Offences
26) Penalties
27) Defence of due diligence
28) Liability of persons other than the principal offender
29) Consequential amendments

SCHEDULES

Schedule 1   Excluded pressure equipment and assemblies
Schedule 2   Essential safety requirements (Annex I to the Pressure Equipment Directive)
Schedule 3   Conformity assessment tables (Annex II to the Pressure Equipment Directive)
Schedule 4   Conformity assessment procedures (Annex III to the Pressure Equipment Directive)
Schedule 5   CE marking (Annex VI to the Pressure Equipment Directive)
Schedule 6   EC declaration of conformity (Annex VII to the Pressure Equipment Directive)
Schedule 7   European approval for materials
Schedule 8   Enforcement

Outline of main points

These regulations set out the general requirements relating to the placing on the market or putting into service of pressure equipment and assemblies by a **responsible person** (a person who manufactures the pressure equipment or assemblies for his own use or imports pressure equipment or assemblies from a third party, where it is in the course of business). Pressure equipment or assemblies must satisfy the relevant essential requirements and be safe with the appropriate conformity assessment procedure carried out (unless the equipment is to be used for experimentation). A declaration of conformity must be drawn up and a CE mark affixed.

Where pressure equipment or assemblies fall below the limits prescribed in the Pressure Equipment Regulations, it must be designed and manufactured in accordance with sound engineering practice, be accompanied by adequate instructions for use, bear markings to permit identification of the manufacturer or his authorised representative established within the EU, and be safe.

PRESSURE EQUIPMENT (AMENDMENT) REGULATIONS 2002

The *Pressure Equipment (Amendment) Regulations 2002* amended the Pressure Equipment Regulations 1999 as follows:

After regulation 2(3) there shall be inserted the following paragraph:

(4) "For the purposes of these Regulations, an item of pressure equipment or an assembly which is made available for the first time in the Community whether for reward or free of charge shall not be regarded as having been placed on the market where: -

 (a) it has been manufactured within the Community or imported from a country or territory outside the Community; and

 (b) prior to its being made so available it has been used otherwise than in the course of business at all times since its manufacture or import".

For regulation 26(1) there shall be substituted the following:

26(1) " A person guilty of an offence under regulation 25(a) shall be liable -

 (a) on summary conviction, to a fine not exceeding the statutory maximum or to imprisonment not exceeding three months or to both;

 (b) on conviction on indictment, to a fine or to imprisonment for a term not exceeding two years or to both".

In Schedule 8, sub-paragraph 2(d), for the reference to sub-paragraph "(b)" there shall be substituted a reference to sub-paragraph "(c)".

Pressure Systems Safety Regulations (PSSR) 2000

Law considered in context/more depth in Element C11.

Arrangement of Regulations

PART I - INTRODUCTION

1) Citation and commencement.
2) Interpretation.
3) Application and duties.

PART II - GENERAL

4) Design and construction.
5) Provision of information and marking.
6) Installation.
7) Safe operating limits.
8) Written scheme of examination.
9) Examination in accordance with the written scheme.
10) Action in case of imminent danger.
11) Operation.
12) Maintenance.
13) Modification and repair.
14) Keeping of records, etc.
15) Precautions to prevent pressurisation of certain vessels.

PART III - MISCELLANEOUS

16) Defence.
17) Power to grant exemptions.
18) Repeals and revocations.
19) Transitional provision.

SCHEDULES

Schedule 1   Exceptions to the Regulations.
Schedule 2   Modification of duties in cases where pressure systems are supplied by way of lease, hire or other arrangements.
Schedule 3   Marking of pressure vessels.

Outline of main points

PRESSURE SYSTEMS SAFETY REGULATIONS 2000

The Pressure Systems Safety Regulations (PSSR) 2000 are primarily concerned with matters affecting the mechanical integrity of pressure-containing parts. As in the HASAWA 1974 the duties imposed by the PSSR 2000 are shared between a number of persons, for example, designers, manufacturers, suppliers, importers, installers, users, maintainers and repairers. It should be noted therefore that the overall intention of the PSSR 2000 is to prevent the risk of serious injury from stored energy as a result of the failure of a pressure system or unintended releases of gas or fluid from pressure systems.

The PSSR 2000 reflects much of the revoked Pressure Systems and Transportable Gas Containers Regulations (PSTGCR) 1989. As with the PSTGCR 1989, safety requirements are imposed with respect to pressure systems that are used or intended to be used at work. They also impose safety requirements to prevent certain vessels from becoming pressurised.

The PSSR 2000 are concerned with steam, gases under pressure or fluids that are artificially kept under pressure and become gases on release to the atmosphere. The regulations do not apply to purely hydraulic systems, systems containing traces of dissolved gas or to liquids in storage tanks that exert a static pressure. The regulations thus apply to steam systems and systems in which gases exert a pressure in excess of half a bar above atmospheric pressure (0.5 bar). 1 bar = 14.5038 psi (pounds per square inch).

A pressure system is defined in the Regulations as:

- A system comprising one or more pressure vessels of rigid construction, any associated pipework and protective devices.
- The pipework with its protective devices to which a transportable gas container is, or intended to be connected.
- A pipeline and its protective devices; which contains or is liable to contain a relevant fluid.

The definition does not include a transportable pressure receptacle. The Regulations apply to pressure systems if there is a relevant fluid in the system (i.e. a compressed or liquefied gases including air) above 0.5 bar or steam, the pressure volume (PV) product of the largest rigid pressure vessel in the system is grater than 250 bar litres and there is no exemption under Schedule 1 then Regulations 7 and 8 apply.

A competent person is required to draw up or certify written schemes of examination and to carry out examinations. The level of competence, access to specialist services and organisational requirements varies according to the category of the system.

RELEVANT STATUTORY PROVISIONS

Designers, manufacturers, importers or suppliers of any pressure system or any article which is intended to be a component part of any pressure system must ensure that the pressure system or article is:

- Properly designed and properly constructed from suitable material so as to prevent danger.
- Designed and constructed so that all necessary examinations for preventing danger can be carried out.
- Provided with the necessary protective devices for preventing danger.
- Ensuring that any such device designed to release contents shall do so safely.

In addition, where the pressure system has any means of access to its interior, it must be designed and constructed as to ensure, so far as practicable, that access can be gained without danger.

In practical terms, safety equipment includes:

- Control equipment to enable safe operation.
- Protective devices to limit or relieve pressure.
- Measuring devices to indicate conditions of operation.
- Access door safety devices to ensure interlocking for regularly used doors, etc.

Installers are to ensure installation does not cause danger. This might include controlling any welding work during installation, ensuring adequate foundations are provided, ensuring no obstruction of access, protection from vehicle impacts etc.

Adequate information about the pressure system must be passed on to the user. This should include:

- Safe operating limits.
- Scheme of examination.
- Design standards and constructional materials.
- Certificates of conformity.
- Design pressures and temperatures.
- Intended contents, flow rates, capacities, etc.

System users must use the information provided by the designer to ensure safe operation and proper maintenance. The extent of duty depends upon the system type. Anyone operating a pressure system must be given adequate and suitable instructions for safe operation and emergency action. This instruction should form part of the operating instructions for the plant and should include information on start-up, shutdown, normal operation, functions of controls, emergency procedures, etc. Doors providing routine access should be dealt with by specific instructions covering interlocking checks, opening and closing precautions, failure signs, etc. Precautions must be taken to prevent unintentional pressurisation of parts of any system not designed for pressure. Routine and regular maintenance should be carried out including periodic checks and inspections of important parts or components.

A written scheme of examination must be available before any system is used. This should be drawn up by a competent person and should include:

- Pressure vessels.
- Pipework and valves.
- Protective devices.
- Pumps and compressors.

Examination intervals should be specified, though these may be different for different parts of the system, so that deterioration, etc. can be detected before danger arises. An initial examination should be done before use. Any repairs or modifications should be controlled. Factors to be taken into account when deciding upon the frequency of examination will include:

- Previous intervals and system records.
- Standards of supervision and routine checks.
- Type and quality of fluids in the system.
- The likelihood of creep, fatigue, etc. failures.
- Corrosion potential and effect.
- Presence of heat sources etc.

The type of examination should also be specified. Examinations must be carried out in accordance with the written scheme and the system adequately assessed for fitness for continued use. Appropriate preparations for and precautions during examination should be arranged for by the user. A report with any conditions or limitations on use should be prepared on completion of the examination.

Where the competent person's examination identifies imminent danger then a report must be made to the user who should ensure the system is not used further and a report sent to the relevant enforcing authority. Adequate records of examinations, repairs, modifications etc., should be kept at the premises where the system is used.

The PSSR 2000 modify and extend provision for sending, keeping and passing on in electronic form reports of examinations. It also provides that references to anything "in writing" or "written" includes it being in a form in which it is capable of being reproduced as a written copy. The regulations no longer requires a report to be signed; and requires information to be kept and passed on, whether or not it has been supplied as a document. This is in keeping with the trend towards allowing the use of computer software systems to store and transmit statutory documents.

Provision and Use of Work Equipment Regulations (PUWER) 1998

Law considered in context/more depth in Elements C5 and C7.

Arrangement of Regulations

PART I - INTRODUCTION

1) Citation and commencement.
2) Interpretation.
3) Application.

PART II - GENERAL
4) Suitability of work equipment.
5) Maintenance.
6) Inspection.
7) Specific risks.
8) Information and instructions.
9) Training.
10) Conformity with Community requirements.
11) Dangerous parts of machinery.
12) Protection against specified hazards.
13) High or very low temperature.
14) Controls for starting or making a significant change in operating conditions.
15) Stop controls.
16) Emergency stop controls.
17) Controls.
18) Control systems.
19) Isolation from sources of energy.
20) Stability.
21) Lighting.
22) Maintenance operations.
23) Markings.
24) Warnings.

PART III - MOBILE WORK EQUIPMENT
25) Employees carried on mobile work equipment.
26) Rolling over of mobile work equipment.
27) Overturning of fork-lift trucks.
28) Self-propelled work equipment.
29) Remote-controlled self-propelled work equipment.
30) Drive shafts.

PART IV - POWER PRESSES
31) Power presses to which Part IV does not apply.
32) Thorough examination of power presses, guards and protection devices.
33) Inspection of guards and protection devices.
34) Reports.
35) Keeping of information.

PART V - MISCELLANEOUS
36) Exemption for the armed forces.
37) Transitional provision.
38) Repeal of enactment.
39) Revocation of instruments.
Schedule 1   Instruments which give effect to Community directives concerning the safety of products.
Schedule 2   Power presses to which regulations 32 to 35 do not apply.
Schedule 3   Information to be contained in a report of a thorough examination of a power press, guard or protection device.
Schedule 4   Revocation of instruments.

Outline of main points

These regulations impose health and safety requirements with respect to the provision and use of work equipment, which is defined as 'any machinery, appliance, apparatus, tool or installation for use at work (whether exclusively or not)'. These regulations:
- Place general duties on employers.
- Certain persons having control of work equipment, of persons at work who use or supervise or manage its use or of the way it is used, to the extent of their control.
- List minimum requirements for work equipment to deal with selected hazards whatever the industry.

'Use' includes any activity involving work equipment and includes starting, stopping, programming, setting, transporting, repairing, modifying, maintaining, servicing and cleaning. The general duties require you to:
- Make sure that equipment is suitable for the use that will be made of it.
- Take into account the working conditions and hazards in the workplace when selecting equipment.
- Ensure equipment is used only for operations for which, and under conditions for which, it is suitable.

RELEVANT STATUTORY PROVISIONS

- Ensure that equipment is maintained in an efficient state, in efficient working order and in good repair.
- Ensure the inspection of work equipment in specified circumstances by a competent person; keep a record of the result for specified periods; and ensure that evidence of the last inspection accompany work equipment used outside the undertaking.
- Give adequate information, instruction and training.
- Provide equipment that conforms with EU product safety directives.

SPECIFIC REQUIREMENTS COVER

- Guarding of dangerous parts of machinery.
- Protection against specified hazards i.e. falling/ejected articles and substances, rupture/disintegration of work equipment parts, equipment catching fire or overheating, unintended or premature discharge of articles and substances, explosion.
- Work equipment parts and substances at high or very low temperatures.
- Control systems and control devices.
- Isolation of equipment from sources of energy.
- Stability of equipment.
- Lighting.
- Maintenance operations.
- Warnings and markings.

MOBILE WORK EQUIPMENT

Mobile work equipment must have provision as to:

- Its suitability for carrying persons and its safety features.
- Means to minimise the risk to safety from its rolling over.
- Means to reduce the risk to safety from the rolling over of a fork-lift truck.
- The safety of self-propelled work equipment and remote-controlled self propelled work equipment.
- The drive shafts of mobile work equipment.

POWER PRESSES

The regulations provide for:

- The thorough examination (defined in regulation 2(1)) of power presses and their guards and protection devices (regulation 32).
- Their inspection after setting, re-setting or adjustment of their tools, and every working period (regulation 33).
- The making (regulation 34 and Schedule 3) and keeping (regulation 35) of reports.
- The regulations implement an EC directive aimed at the protection of workers. There are other directives setting out conditions which much new equipment (especially machinery) will have to satisfy before it can be sold in EC member states.

Registration, Evaluation, Authorisation and Restriction of Chemicals (REACH Regulation, EC 1907/2006)

Law considered in context/more depth in Elements C4.

The Registration, Evaluation, Authorisation and Restriction of Chemicals (REACH) Regulation is a new European Union regulation concerning the registration, evaluation, authorisation and restriction of chemicals. It came into force on 1st June 2007 and replaces a number of European Directives and Regulations (see table below for details) with a single system to gather hazard information, assess risks, classify, label, and restrict the marketing and use of individual chemicals and mixtures. This is known as the REACH system:

R egistration of basic information of substances to be submitted by companies, to a central database.
E valuation of the registered information to determine hazards and risks.
A uthorisation requirements imposed on the use of high-concern substances.
CH emicals.

REACH covers both "new" and "existing" substances and puts the onus on Industry to prove that chemicals it uses are safe.

REACH only applies to chemicals manufactured in or imported into the EU. It does not apply to the use of chemicals in finished products. So a product like a television, or computer or shampoo made outside the EU could contain chemicals that are not registered under REACH - providing they are not banned under specific safety regulations (such as lead).

REACH entered into force on 1st June 2007. The pre-registration period for eligible chemicals was 1st June - 1st December 2008, and chemicals that were pre-registered benefit from phased registration deadlines up to June 2018.

The new regime creates the European Chemicals Agency (ECHA) with a central coordination and implementation role in the overall process. *(See http://reach.jrc.it/guidance for more information)*. Industry will be able to use "substances of very high concern" only if they have authorisation from ECHA. Authorisation will be granted under specific conditions, and will have to be regularly renewed, encouraging companies to seek safer alternatives. "Substances of very high concern" are defined by REACH, these are chemicals that:

- Cause cancer or mutation or interfere with the body's reproductive function (CMRs).
- Take a long time to break down, accumulate in the body and are toxic (PBTs).
- Take a very long time to break down and accumulate in the body (vPvBs).
- Have serious and irreversible effects on humans and the environment, for example substances that disturb the body's hormone system.

However, polymers, a group of chemicals that includes plastics, will be exempted. But monomers - the basic building block of an individual polymer do have to be registered and evaluated. All manufacturers and importers of chemicals must identify and manage risks linked to the substances they manufacture and market. For substances produced or imported in quantities of 1 tonne or more per year per company, manufacturers and importers need to demonstrate that they have appropriately done so by means of a registration dossier, which shall be submitted to the Agency.

Once the registration dossier has been received, the Agency may check that it is compliant with the Regulation and shall evaluate testing proposals to ensure that the assessment of the chemical substances will not result in unnecessary testing, especially on animals. Where appropriate, authorities may also select substances for a broader substance evaluation to further investigate substances of concern. Manufacturers and importers must provide their downstream users with the risk information they need to use the substance safely. This will be done via the classification and labelling system and Safety Data Sheets (SDS), where needed.

ENFORCEMENT

REACH requires each Member State to appoint a Competent Authority (CA) and maintain an appropriate control system with respect to enforcement. The authorities given enforcement responsibility by the REACH Enforcement Regulations 2008 are those with existing remits to protect human health, consumer safety, and the environment:

- The Health and Safety Executive (HSE).
- The Health and Safety Executive for Northern Ireland (HSENI).
- The Environment Agency (EA).
- The Scottish Environment Protection Agency (SEPA).
- The Northern Ireland Environment Agency (NIEA).
- The Department of Energy and Climate Change (DECC).
- Local Authorities (LAs), as regards health and safety and consumer protection (trading standards).

Regulation 3 and Schedule 1 of the REACH Enforcement Regulations 2008 sets out which enforcing authority is responsible for enforcing the listed REACH provisions, though broadly speaking:

- HSE, in its capacity as UK REACH CA, will enforce those duties in REACH concerning registration.
- HSE in Great Britain and HSENI in Northern Ireland will enforce supply chain related duties up to the point of retail sale, and for retail sale local authority trading standards departments are responsible.
- A wide range of enforcing authorities will enforce use related duties, as per existing arrangements for enforcing health, safety and environmental legislation. HSE will enforce use-related duties relating to occupational safety and health in Great Britain.

TABLE OF AMENDMENTS

Citation	Extent of revocation
The Notification of New Substances (Amendment) Regulations 2001.	The whole instrument.
The Chemicals (Hazard Information and Packaging for Supply) Regulations 2002.	In regulation 8, paragraphs (4), (5) and (6). Regulation 12(1)(d). Schedule 4.
The Control of Substances Hazardous to Health Regulations 2002.	Regulation 4(4). In Schedule 2, entries numbered 11, 12 and 13. Regulation 2(g).
The Chemicals (Hazard Information and Packaging for Supply) (Amendment) Regulations 2005.	Regulation 2(3).
The Control of Asbestos Regulations 2006.	Regulations 25(3), 27, 28, 29 and 32(2).

Main sources: www.hse.gov.uk/reach and http://reach.jrc.it/about_reach_en.htm.

Regulatory Reform (Fire Safety) Order (RRFSO) 2005

Law considered in context/more depth in Element C3.

Arrangement of Order

This is a new, all encompassing, fire safety order, which came into force 01 October 2006.

The order is split into 5 parts:

- Part 1 - General.
- Part 2 - Fire Safety Duties.
- Part 3 - Enforcement.
- Part 4 - Offences and appeals.
- Part 5 - Miscellaneous.

Each part is then subdivided into the individual points or articles as they are called in the order.

Outline of main points

INTRODUCTION

The amount of legislation covering the risk of fire has grown considerably over time. The situation was identified as unwieldy with many different regulations, often with conflicting definitions and requirements. In order to simply this and remove confusion the Regulatory Reform (Fire Safety) Order 2005 has been introduced. There were 4 principal pieces of legislation that covered fire safety in the workplace that have been affected by the RRFSO:

- Fire Precautions Act (FPA) - Repealed.
- Fire Precautions (Workplace) Regulations (FPWR) - Repealed.
- Management of Health and Safety at Work Regulations (MHSWR).
- Dangerous Substances & Explosive Atmosphere Regulations (DSEAR).

RELEVANT STATUTORY PROVISIONS

Fire Precautions Act
This legislation is has been repealed by the RRFSO 2005.

Fire Precautions Workplace Regulations
This regulation outlined the fire safety measures that need to be achieved via the risk assessment of fire and management of fire safety within a workplace. These regulations have been repealed by the implementation of the RRFSO; however they have been incorporated within the RRFSO 2005.

Management of Health and Safety at Work Regulations
It is this regulation that makes the legal requirement for risk assessments. In addition, it made various requirements for the management of fire safety within workplaces. This regulation will continue as a stand alone health and safety regulation as the relevant fire aspects of this regulation have been incorporated within the RRFSO 2005.

Dangerous Substances & Explosive Atmosphere Regulations
This regulation outlines the safety and control measures that need to be taken if dangerous or flammable / explosive substances are present. This regulation will continue as a stand alone health and safety regulation. Again the relevant fire aspects of this regulation have been incorporated within the RRFSO 2005.

REGULATORY REFORM (FIRE SAFETY) ORDER 2005

Part 1 - General
This part covers various issues such as the interpretation of terminology used, definition of responsible person, definition of general fire precautions, duties under the order, and its application.

Part 2 - Fire Safety Duties
This part imposes a duty on the responsible person to carry out a fire risk assessment to identify what the necessary general fire precautions should be. It also outlines the principles of prevention that should be applied and the necessary arrangements for the management of fire safety. The following areas are also covered:

- Fire-fighting and fire detection.
- Emergency routes and exits.
- Procedures for serious and imminent danger and for danger areas.
- Additional emergency measures re dangerous substances.
- Maintenance.
- Safety assistance.
- Provision of information to employees, employers and self employed.
- Capabilities and training.
- Co-operation and co-ordination.
- General duties of employees.

Part 3 - Enforcement
This part details who the enforcing authority is, (which in the main is the Fire Authority), and it states they must enforce the order. It also details the powers of inspectors. It also details the different types of enforcement that can be taken:

- Alterations notice.
- Enforcement notice.
- Prohibition notice.

Part 4 - Offences and appeals
This part details the 13 offences that may occur and the subsequent punishments and appeals procedure. It also explains that the legal onus for proving that an offence was not committed is on the accused. A new disputes procedure is also outlined within this part.

Part 5 - Miscellaneous
Various matters are covered within this part the principal points being:

- 'Fire-fighters switches' for luminous tube signs etc.
- Maintenance of measures provided for the protection of fire-fighters.
- Civil liability.
- Duty to consult employees.
- Special provisions for licensed premises.
- Application to crown premises.

There is then a schedule that covers the risk assessment process.

Simple Pressure Vessels (Safety) Regulations (SPVSR) 1991 (as amended)

Law considered in context/more depth in Element C11.

Arrangement of Regulations

1) Citation and commencement.
2) Interpretation.
3) Application (now amended to 'Interpretation of the principle Regulations').

4) Safety requirements (now amended to 'Implementation of the CE Marking Directive').
5) Obligations of manufacturers, suppliers and importers.
6) Transitional and other exceptions.
7) Approved bodies.
8) Fees.
9) Safety clearance.
10) EC certificate of adequacy.
11) EC type-examination certificate.
12) EC verification certificate (now amended to 'EC verification').
13) EC certificate of conformity.
14) The EC mark (now amended to 'CE mark').
15) Retention of documentation.
16) Special provisions applying to vessels in Category A.2.
17) Functions of approved bodies in course of EC surveillance.
18) Report by United Kingdom approved body concerning contraventions.
19) Enforcement.
20) Offences.
21) Power of the court to require matter to be remedied.
22) Defence of due diligence.
23) Liability of persons other than the principal offender.
24) Consequential amendment of United Kingdom law.

Outline of main points

The *Simple Pressure Vessels (Safety) (Amendment) Regulations 1994 (into force 1st January 1995)* amended the Simple Pressure Vessels (Safety) Regulations 1991. The SPVSR 1991 apply to the following:

- Simple pressure vessels i.e. welded vessels made of certain types of steel or aluminium, which are intended to contain air or nitrogen under pressure and are manufactured in series.
- Relevant assemblies, i.e. any assembly incorporating a pressure vessel.

Important definitions relating to these regulations are:

Vessel - this means a simple pressure vessel that has been welded and is intended for the storage of nitrogen or air at a gauge pressure greater than 0.5 Bar but not exceeding 30 Bar.

Series manufacture - this is where more than one vessel of the same type are produced during a given period by the same continuous process. The regulations only apply to series manufactured vessels.

The regulations do not apply to:

- Fire Extinguishers.
- Vessels intended for use in the propulsive systems of ships, aircraft.
- Vessels intended for nuclear use where if a failure occurs, a release of radioactivity would occur.

CATEGORISATION OF VESSELS

The regulations specifically categorise vessels into 2 classes:

Category A	A.1 3000 - 10,000	Bar litres
	A.2 200 - 30000	Bar litres
	A.3 50 - 200	Bar litres
Category B	50 Bar litres or less	

PRINCIPAL REQUIREMENTS

A vessel with a stored energy in excess of 50 Bar litres must, if supplied in the UK:

- Ensure that materials used in its construction must meet relevant safety requirements.
- Be certified safe for use by an appropriate body.
- Bear the CE mark and any other relevant inscriptions.
- Follow the CE mark by the identification number of the approved body responsible for EC verifications or EC surveillance.
- Must bear at least the following information -
  - the maximum working pressure (PS in bar);
  - the maximum working temperature (Tmax in °C);
  - the minimum working temperature (Tmin in °C);
  - the capacity of the vessel (V in litres);
  - the name or mark of the manufacturer;
  - the type and serial or batch identification of the vessel; and
  - the last two digits of the year in which the CE marking was affixed.

RELEVANT STATUTORY PROVISIONS

(If a data plate is used, it must be so designed that it cannot be re-used and must include a vacant space to enable other information to be provided).
- Have a set of manufacturers work instructions and guidance.
- Be safe as defined by the regulations.

A vessel with a stored energy up to 50 Bar litres must, if supplied in the UK:
- Be safe as defined by the regulations.
- Bear specific inscriptions but not the CE mark.
- Be engineered and manufactured to a recognised suitable standard within the Community Country.

Exports

The regulations do not apply to any vessel supplied outside of the European Community.

Prosecution

Failure to comply with these regulations will result in the following:
- Fine of up to £2,000.00 and/or imprisonment of up to three months.
- The vessels cannot be sold legally.

Approved bodies

These are designated by the Secretary for Trade and Industry and the bodies are given certain rights of power with regard to surveillance of vessels. These powers include:

Powers of entry

- To take samples.
- To acquire information.
- To compile reports on surveillance operations.
- To report to the secretary of state cases of wrongful application, and failures by manufacturers in respect of their legal duties.

Supply of Machinery (Safety) Regulations (SMSR) 2008

Law considered in context/more depth in Element C6 and C7.

Arrangement of Regulations

PART 1 - PRELIMINARY

1) Citation, commencement and revocation.
2) Interpretation.
3) Placing on the market and putting into service; supplies outside the EEA and showing at trade fairs not covered.

PART 2 - APPLICATION

4) Products to which Regulations apply; definition of "machinery".
5) Disapplication where more specific Community safety rules apply.
6) Partly completed machinery.

PART 3 - GENERAL PROHIBITIONS AND OBLIGATIONS

7) Supply of machinery: general obligations and prohibition.
8) Supply of partly completed machinery: general obligations and prohibition.
9) Putting machinery into service.

Conformity assessment procedures

10) Machinery not referred to in Annex IV.
11) Annex IV machinery manufactured fully in accordance with published harmonised standards and fully covered by such standards.
12) Annex IV machinery not manufactured fully in accordance with published harmonised standards or not fully covered by such standards.

PART 4 - CE MARKING

13) CE-marked machinery to be taken to comply with Regulations.
14) Machinery covered by more than one Directive.
15) Protection of CE marking.

PART 5 - NOTIFIED BODIES

16) Designation and monitoring of UK notified bodies.
17) Duration, variation and termination of designations.
18) Functions of UK notified bodies.
19) Fees.

PART 6 - ENFORCEMENT

20) General duties and powers of enforcement authorities.

21) Non-compliance with CE marking requirements.
22) Offences and penalties.
23) Defence of due diligence.
24) Liability of persons other than the principal offender.

PART 7 - MISCELLANEOUS

25) Amendment of Lifts Regulations 1987.
26) Other amendments.
27) Consequential disapplication of domestic health and safety law.
28) Time-limited derogation for impact machinery.

SCHEDULES

Schedule 1	Regulations revoked.
Schedule 2	Annexes to the directive.
Schedule 3	Products to which the regulations do not apply.
Schedule 4	Appeals against notified body decisions.
Schedule 5	Enforcement.
Schedule 6	Amendments to the Lifts Regulations 1997.
Schedule 7	Other amendments.

Outline of main points

Previously the Supply of Machinery (Safety) Regulations 1992 as amended by the Supply of Machinery (Safety) (Amendment) Regulations 1994 and the Supply of Machinery (Safety) (Amendment) Regulations 2005.

The SMSR 2008 imposes duties upon those who place machinery and safety components onto the market, or put them into service (this includes second-hand machinery which is "new" to Europe). They set out the essential requirements which must be met before machinery or safety components may be placed on the market or put into service in the UK. They implement the latest version of the Machinery Directive 2006/42/EC and came into force on 29 December 2009, replacing the previous Supply of Machinery (Safety) Regulations 1992, as amended in 1994 and 2005.

MEETING THE REQUIREMENTS

The duty to meet the requirements mainly falls to the 'responsible person' who is defined as the manufacturer or the manufacturer's representative. If the manufacturer is not established in the EEA, the person who first supplies the machinery in the EEA may be the responsible person, which can be a user who manufactures or imports a machine for their own use.

Conformity assessment

The responsible person should ensure that machinery and safety components satisfy the **Essential Health and Safety Requirements (EHSRs)**, see Schedule 2, Part 1 of the Regulations, and that appropriate conformity assessment procedures have been carried out. These requirements are intended to ensure that all machinery throughout the EC is constructed to the same safety standards. In addition, the responsible person must draw up a technical file (see below).

For certain classes of dangerous machine and safety component, a more rigorous procedure is required.

The new SMSR place even greater emphasis on the EHSR requirements. However, still extant are the requirements of primary legislation by way of the Health and Safety at Work Act 1974 (HASAWA), which makes a specific reference to the duties of manufacturers and suppliers of workplace machinery (including second hand machinery).

Section 6 of HASAWA (general duties of manufacturers) states:
"It shall be the duty of any person who designs, manufactures, imports or supplies any article for use at work....
(a) To ensure, so far as is reasonably practicable, that the article is so designed and constructed that it will be safe and without risks to health at all times when it is being set, used, cleaned or maintained by a person at work".

HASAWA is reinforced by the duties under Part 3 of SMSR 2008 (general prohibitions and obligations), which states:
"No responsible person shall place machinery on the market or put it into service unless it is safe; and "before machinery is placed on the market or put into service, the responsible person must-
(a) Ensure that the applicable essential health and safety requirements are satisfied in respect of it...".

Declaration procedure

The responsible person must issue one of two forms of declaration.

Declaration of conformity

This declaration should be issued with the finished product so that it is available to the user. It will contain various details such as the manufacturer's address, the machinery type and serial number, and Harmonised European or other Standards used in design.

Declaration of Incorporation

Where machinery is intended for incorporation into other machinery, the responsible person can draw up a declaration of incorporation. This should state that the machinery must not be put into service until the machinery into which it is to be incorporated has been given a Declaration of Conformity. A CE mark is not affixed at this intermediate stage.

Marking

When the first two steps have been satisfactorily completed, the responsible person or the person assembling the final product should affix the CE mark.

RELEVANT STATUTORY PROVISIONS

ENFORCEMENT

In the UK the Health and Safety Executive is responsible for enforcing these Regulations in relation to machinery and safety components designed for use at work. Trading Standards Officers are responsible for enforcing these Regulations in relation to consumer goods.

DETAILED ADVICE FOR THE DESIGNER AND MANUFACTURER

Technical file contents

The responsible person (defined above) is required to draw up a technical file for all machinery and safety components covered by these Regulations. The file or documents should comprise:

a) An overall drawing of the product together with the drawings of the control circuits.
b) Full detailed drawings, accompanied by any calculation notes, test results etc. required to check the conformity of the product with the essential health and safety requirements.
c) A list of the essential health and safety requirements, transposed harmonised standards, national standards and other technical specifications which were used when the product was designed.
d) A description of methods adopted to eliminate hazards presented by the machinery or safety component.
e) If the responsible person so desires, any technical report or certificate obtained from a component body or laboratory.
f) If the responsible person declares conformity with a transposed harmonised standard, any technical report giving the results of tests.
g) A copy of the instructions for the product.

For series manufacture, the responsible person must also have available documentation on the necessary administrative measures that the manufacturer will take to ensure that the product meets requirements.

Technical file procedure

The technical file document need not be on a permanent file, but it should be possible to assemble and make them available to an enforcement authority. The technical file documents should be retained and kept available for at least ten years following the date of manufacture of the product or of the last unit produced, in the case of a series manufacture. If the technical file documents are drawn up in the United Kingdom, they should be in English unless they are to be submitted to an Approved/Notified Body in another Member State, in which case they should be in a language acceptable to that approved Body. In all cases the instructions for the machinery should be in accordance with the language requirements of the EHSRs.

Work at Height Regulations (WAH) 2005

Law considered in context/more depth in Elements C1, C7 and C9.
See also - PUWER 1998 and WHSWR 1992.

Arrangement of Regulations

1) Citation and commencement.
2) Interpretation.
3) Application.
4) Organisation and planning.
5) Competence.
6) Avoidance of risks from work at height.
7) Selection of work equipment for work at height.
8) Requirements for particular work equipment.
9) Fragile surfaces.
10) Falling objects.
11) Danger areas.
12) Inspection of work equipment.
13) Inspection of places of work at height.
14) Duties of persons at work.
15) Exemption by the Health and Safety Executive.
16) Exemption for the Armed Forces.
17) Amendment to the Provision and Use of Work Equipment Regulations 1998.
18) Repeal of section 24 of the Factories Act 1961.
19) Revocation of instruments.

SCHEDULES

Schedule 1	Requirements for existing places of work and means of access or egress at height.
Schedule 2	Requirements for guard-rails, toe-boards, barriers and similar collective means of protection.
Schedule 3	Requirements for working platforms.
	Part 1 Requirements for all working platforms.
	Part 2 Additional requirements for scaffolding.
Schedule 4	Requirements for collective safeguards for arresting falls.

Schedule 5   Requirements for personal fall protection systems.
                Part 1   Requirements for all personal fall protection systems.
                Part 2   Additional requirements for work positioning systems.
                Part 3   Additional requirements for rope access and positioning techniques.
                Part 4   Additional requirements for fall arrest systems.
                Part 5   Additional requirements for work restraint systems.
Schedule 6   Requirements for ladders.
Schedule 7   Particulars to be included in a report of inspection.
Schedule 8   Revocation of instruments.

Outline of main points

Falls from height at work are the most common cause of fatality and the second most common cause of major injury to workers and during the period between 2001/2002 resulted in 68 fatalities and approximately 4,000 serious injuries.

The final version of the regulations, designated the **Work at Height Regulations (WAH) 2005** came into force 6th April 2005. Under these regulations the interpretation of 'work at height' includes any place of work at ground level, above or below ground level that a person could fall a distance liable to cause personal injury and includes places for obtaining access or egress, except by staircase in a permanent workplace.

AMENDMENTS TO OTHER REGULATIONS AS A RESULT OF THE WORK AT HEIGHT REGULATIONS 2005

WAH 2005 makes an amendment to the Provision and Use of Work Equipment Regulations 1998; they also replace certain regulations in the Workplace (Health and Safety) Regulations; and amend definitions in the Construction (Health, Safety and Welfare) Regulations:

Regulation 17 - amendment of the Provision and Use of Work Equipment Regulations 1998. There shall be added to regulation 6(5) of the Provision and Use of Work Equipment Regulations 1998 the following sub-paragraph -

(f)   "Work equipment to which regulation 12 of the Work at Height Regulations 2005 applies".

Schedule 8 - revocation of instruments

Workplace (Health and Safety) Regulations 1992 - extent of revocation: regulation 13(1) to (4).

Construction (Health, Safety and Welfare) Regulations 1996 - extent of revocation: in regulation 2(1), the definitions of "fragile material", "personal suspension equipment" and "working platform"; regulations 6 to 8; in regulation 29(2) the word "scaffold" in both instances; regulation 30(5) and (6)(a); Schedules 1 to 5; and the entry first mentioned in columns 1 and 2 of Schedule 7.

WORK AT HEIGHT (AMENDMENT) REGULATIONS 2007

These regulations amended WAH 2005 to remove the dis-application of WAH 2005 to certain work concerning the provision of instruction or leadership to people engaged in caving or climbing by way of sport, recreation, team building or similar activities. They introduce a new duty under Regulation 14A that takes into account the special circumstances of work at height in caving and climbing.

Under these regulations the interpretation of 'work at height' includes any place of work at ground level, above or below ground level that a person could fall a distance liable to cause personal injury and includes places for obtaining access or egress, except by staircase in a permanent workplace.

Regulation 4 states that all work at height must be properly planned, supervised and be carried out so far as is reasonably practicable safe. Planning must include the selection of suitable equipment, take account of emergencies and give consideration to weather conditions impacting on safety.

Regulation 5 states that those engaged in any activity in relation to work at height must be competent; and, if under training, are supervised by a competent person.

Regulation 6 states that work at height must only be carried out when it is not reasonably practicable to carry out the work otherwise. If work at height does take place, suitable and sufficient measures must be taken to prevent a fall of any distance, to minimise the distance and the consequences of any fall liable to cause injury. Employers must also make a risk assessment, as required by regulation 3 of the Management of Health and Safety at Work Regulations.

Regulation 7 states that when selecting equipment for use in work at height the employer shall take account of working conditions and any risk to persons in connection with the place where the equipment is to be used. The selection of work equipment must have regard in particular to the purposes specified in regulation 6.

Regulation 8 sets out requirements for particular equipment to conform to standards expressed in schedules to the regulations. It includes guard-rails, toe-boards, working platforms, nets, airbags, personal fall arrest equipment rope access and ladders.

Regulation 9 states that every employer shall ensure that suitable and sufficient steps are taken to prevent any person at work falling through any fragile surface; and that no work may pass across or near, or work on, from or near, fragile surfaces when it is reasonably practicable to carry out work without doing so. If work has to be from a fragile roof then suitable and sufficient means of support must be provided that can sustain foreseeable loads. No person at work should be allowed to pass or work near a fragile surface unless suitable and sufficient guard rails and other means of fall protection is in place. Signs must be situated at a prominent place at or near to works involving fragile surfaces, or persons are made aware of the fragile roof by other means.

Regulation 10 states that every employer shall take reasonably practicable steps to prevent injury to any person from the fall of any material or object; and where it is not reasonably practicable to do so, to take similar steps to prevent any person being struck by any falling material or object which is liable to cause personal injury. Also, that no material is thrown or tipped from height in circumstances where it is liable to cause injury to any person. Materials and objects must be stored in such a way as to prevent risk to any person arising from the collapse, overturning or unintended movement of the materials or objects.

RELEVANT STATUTORY PROVISIONS

Regulation 11 states that every employer shall ensure that where an area presents a risk of falling from height or being struck from an item falling at height that the area is equipped with devices preventing unauthorised persons from entering such areas and the area is clearly indicated.

Regulation 12 states that every employer shall ensure that, where the safety of work equipment depends on how it is installed or assembled, it is not used after installation or assembly in any position unless it has been inspected in that position.

Also, that work equipment is inspected at suitable intervals and each time that exceptional circumstances which are liable to jeopardise the safety of the work equipment occur. Specific requirements exist for periodic (every 7 days) inspection of a working platform where someone could fall 2 metres or more.

Regulation 13 states that every employer shall ensure that fall protection measures of every place of work at height are visually inspected before use.

Regulation 14 states the duties of persons at work to report defects and use equipment in accordance with training/instruction.

Workplace (Health, Safety and Welfare) Regulations (WHSWR) 1992

Law considered in context/more depth in Elements C1, and C6 and C7.

Arrangement of Regulations

1) Citation and commencement.
2) Interpretation.
3) Application of these Regulations.
4) Requirements under these Regulations.
5) Maintenance of workplace, and of equipment, devices and systems.
6) Ventilation.
7) Temperature in indoor workplaces.
8) Lighting.
9) Cleanliness and waste materials.
10) Room dimensions and space.
11) Workstations and seating.
12) Condition of floors and traffic routes.
13) Falls or falling objects *(revoked in part by WAH 2005)*.
14) Windows, and transparent or translucent doors, gates and walls.
15) Windows, skylights and ventilators.
16) Ability to clean windows etc. safely.
17) Organisation etc. of traffic routes.
18) Doors and gates.
19) Escalators and moving walkways.
20) Sanitary conveniences.
21) Washing facilities.
22) Drinking water.
23) Accommodation for clothing.
24) Facilities for changing clothing.
25) Facilities for rest and to eat meals.
26) Exemption certificates.
27) Repeals, saving and revocations.

Schedule 1   Provisions applicable to factories which are not new workplaces, extensions or conversions.
Schedule 2   Repeals and revocations.

Outline of main points

SUMMARY

The main requirements of the Workplace (Health, Safety and Welfare) Regs 1992 are:

1) **Maintenance** of the workplace and equipment.
2) **Safety** of those carrying out maintenance work and others who might be at risk (e.g. segregation of pedestrians and vehicles, prevention of falls and falling objects etc.).
3) Provision of **welfare** facilities (e.g. rest rooms, changing rooms etc.).
4) Provision of a safe **environment** (e.g. lighting, ventilation etc.).

ENVIRONMENT

Reg 1   New workplaces, extensions and modifications must comply.

Reg 4   Requires employers, persons in control of premises and occupiers of factories to comply with the regulations.

Reg 6	Ventilation - enclosed workplaces should be ventilated with a sufficient quantity of fresh or purified air (5 to 8 litres per second per occupant).
Reg 7	Temperature indoors - This needs to be reasonable and the heating device must not cause injurious fumes. Thermometers must be provided. Temperature should be a minimum of 16oC or 13oC if there is physical effort.
Reg 8	Lighting - must be suitable and sufficient. Natural light if possible. Emergency lighting should be provided if danger exists.
Reg 10	Room dimensions and space - every room where persons work shall have sufficient floor area, height and unoccupied space (min 11 cu.m per person).
Reg 11	Workstations and seating have to be suitable for the person and the work being done.

SAFETY

Reg 12	Floors and traffic routes must be of suitable construction. This includes absence of holes, slope, uneven or slippery surface. Drainage where necessary. Handrails and guards to be provided on slopes and staircases.
Reg 13	Tanks and pits containing dangerous substances to be covered or fenced where people could fall into them and traffic routes fenced.
Reg 14	Windows and transparent doors, where necessary for health and safety, must be of safety material and be marked to make it apparent.
Reg 15	Windows, skylights and ventilators must be capable of opening without putting anyone at risk.
Reg 17	Traffic routes for pedestrians and vehicles must be organised in such a way that they can move safely.
Reg 18	Doors and gates must be suitably constructed and fitted with any necessary safety devices.
Reg 19	Escalators and moving walkways shall function safely, be equipped with any necessary safety devices and be fitted with emergency stop.

HOUSEKEEPING

Reg 5	Workplace and equipment, devices and systems must be maintained in efficient working order and good repair.
Reg 9	Cleanliness and waste materials - workplaces must be kept sufficiently clean. Floors, walls and ceilings must be capable of being kept sufficiently clean. Waste materials shall not be allowed to accumulate, except in suitable receptacles.
Reg 16	Windows etc. must be designed so that they can be cleaned safety.

FACILITIES

Reg 20	Sanitary conveniences must be suitable and sufficient and in readily accessible places. They must be adequately ventilated, kept clean and there must be separate provision for men and women.
Reg 21	Washing facilities must be suitable and sufficient. Showers if required (a table gives minimum numbers of toilets and washing facilities).
Reg 22	Drinking water - an adequate supply of wholesome drinking water must be provided.
Reg 23	Accommodation for clothing must be suitable and sufficient.
Reg 24	Facilities for changing clothes must be suitable and sufficient, where a person has to use special clothing for work.
Reg 25	Facilities for rest and eating meals must be suitable and sufficient.

The WHSWR 1992 were amended by the Health and Safety (Miscellaneous Amendments) Regulations 2002 to establish specific requirements that rest rooms be equipped with:

- An adequate number of tables and adequate seating with backs for the number of persons at work likely to use them at any one time.
- Seating which is adequate for the number of disabled persons at work and suitable for them.

In addition, WHSWR 1992 were amended to take account of disability arrangements. Where necessary, those parts of the workplace used or occupied directly by disabled persons at work, including in particular doors, passageways, stairs, showers, washbasins, lavatories and workstations, must be organised to take account of such persons.

RELEVANT STATUTORY PROVISIONS

This page is intentionally blank

Index

360° excavators, 344

A

Abnormal external loading, 381
Abrasion, 197, 200
Abrasive wheels, 176, 197
Absolute pressure, 374
Access, 3, 338, 340
    boards, 27
    controls, 279
    equipment, 324
    hazards, 278
    machinery, 183
    temporary, 332
Action in event of fire, 114
Adaptation of work equipment, 157
Adjustable guards, 229
Adverse weather conditions, 20
Agricultural tractors, 253
Air
    bags, 334
    receivers, 380
    systems, 380
Alarm
    staff controlled evacuation, 114
    systems, 85
Albright and Wilson, 3 October 1996, 135
Allied Colloids Ltd, 1992, 67
Alterations
    construction, 315
    fire, 82
    notice, 71
    structural members, 21
Alternating current, 285
Aluminium vessels, 376
Annex IV machinery, 193
Anthropometric, 159, 221
Appeal against fire notices, 71
Appointment of relevant parties (CDM), 320
Appropriate footwear for cleaning floors, 7
Approved codes of practice and guidance, 75
Arcing, 39
Arrangements for emergency, 19
Arrest systems, 334
Assembly point, 114
Assessment of risk
    confined spaces, 15
    fire, 77
    machinery, 182
ATEX, 143
Atmospheres
    confined spaces, 16
    corrosive, 21
    hot, 21
    testing, 16
Atmospheric pressure, 375
Atomisation, 42
Attachments used on lift trucks, 259
Authorisation, 167
Authorised persons, 306
Auto-ignition temperature, 35
Automatic
    alarm systems, 89
    doors and gates, 197
    guards, 226
    sprinkler systems, 93
Avoiding working at height, 25

B

Balling machines, 335
Barriers, 161, 222, 356
Battery powered equipment, 256
Beanbags, 334
Behaviour
    building contents in a fire, 54, 57
    buildings in a fire, 54
    fabrics in a fire, 57
    paper-based materials in a fire, 57
    plastics in a fire, 57
    structural materials in a fire, 54
Belts and harnesses, 335
Bending moment, 201
BLEVES, 46
Boatswains' chairs, 332
Boilers, 379
Boiling liquid expanding vapour explosions (BLEVES), 46
Boundaries, 339
Breakdown
    maintenance, 170
    of insulation, 289
Breaking stress, 202
Brent Cross, 20 June 1964, 207
Brick guards, 337
British Standards Institute, 302
Brittle
    failure, 204
    fracture, 383
Brush discharge, 290
BS 7671:2008, 'Requirements for Electrical Installations', 302
Buckling, 205
Building
    behaviour in a fire, 54
    boards, 55
    contents and fire Spread, 57
    materials deterioration, 22
    regulations, 76, 390
    unauthorised modifications, 22
    works, 315
Building regulations, 76
    Approved Document B, 390
Bulk storage, 129
Bulk storage pressure and refrigeration, 372
Buncefield, 2005, 43, 58, 135
Bunding, 133
Buried services, 341
Bursting discs, 65

C

Caisson, 15
Call points, 85, 89
Capability, 292
Captive key system, 224
Carbon dioxide, 91, 97
Carriage of Dangerous Goods and Use of Transportable Pressure Equipment Regs. 2009, 404
Case sling, 276
Case studies
    corrosive failure, 383
    fatigue failure, 382
Categories
    fire alarm and detection, 83
    safety Signs, 9
Causes of failure
    materials, 200
    structural alterations, 22
Causes of fire, 288
CCTV, 262
CDM
    construction phase plan, 320
    co-ordinator, 319
    duties, 318
    pre-construction information, 320
    projects, 320
    relevant parties, 320
CE marking, 184
Certification, 167
Chain slings, 274
Chain saws, 175
Changes
    systems of work, 174
    workplace, 317
Channel Tunnel fire, 2008, 58
Chemical
    processes, 121
    reaction, 121
Chemicals (Hazard Information and Packaging for Supply) Regs. 2009, 391
Chlorine, 123
Circuit breakers, 294

INDEX

Circular saws, 196
Civil engineering, 315
Classification
    fires, 90
    hazardous area zoning, 64, 144
    sprinkler systems, 93
Cleaning, 317
    footwear, 7
    machine, 7
    wet, 7
Client
    duties, 318
    time pressures, 317
Close boarded excavation, 343
Closed circuit refrigeration, 372
CNC machines, 198
Coefficient of friction (CoF), 4
    between surfaces, 6
    effects of contamination, 6
Cofferdam, 15
Collapse
    buildings, 337
    controlled, 336
    excavations, 340
Collective fall arrest devices, 334
Collisions, 255, 350
Combustible, 64
Combustible material, 289
Combustion
    definition, 40
    stages of, 41
Common
    law duty of employer, 3
    mode failures, 243
    safety signs, 9
Compartmentation, 60
Competence, 174, 357
    availability, 171
    relevant parties (CDM), 320
Competent person, 301, 305, 306, 377, 388
    meaning of, 305
Compliance issues, 10
Compressive stress, 201
Concrete, 55
Condition based maintenance, 169
Conductors, 292
Confined space, 14
    conditions, 14
    definition, 14
    egress, 16
    examples, 15
    safe access, 16
    training, 19
Confined Spaces Regulations 1997, 393
Confined vapour cloud explosions
    examples, 47
    mechanisms, 41
Conformity
    assessments, 185, 188
    declaration, 194
    relevant standards, 157
Consequences
    falls, 28
    minimisation, 150
Construction, 315, 385, 374
    activities, 316
    issues, 317
    materials, 337
    meaning, 291
    phase plan, 321
    statistics, 315
    types of work, 315
    work, 315
Construction (Design and Management) Regs. 2007, 318, 393
Construction (Head Protection) Regs. 1989, 402
Contact
    services, 24
    structures, 24
Containers, 136
Contaminant, 6, 133
    explosion, 66
Contaminated ground, 341
Contractors, 319
Control
    panel, 85
    pressure, 124
    substances, 158
    temperature, 124
Control hierarchy
    work at height, 25
    work equipment, 164
Control interlocking, 222

Control measures
    access, 279
    coupling, 353
    crane operations, 265
    driving at work, 363
    environmental, 354
    excavations, 340
    explosion, 42, 60
    flammable atmospheres, 20
    gin wheel hoist, 266
    hierarchy, 25, 164
    hoists, 266
    lifting equipment, 269
    lifting operations, 265, 271
    lifts, 266
    loading, 353
    maintenance of vehicles, 354
    mobile elevating work platforms (MEWP), 268
    mobile work equipment, 251
    scissor lifts, 267
    un-loading, 353
    vapour phase explosions, 49
    vehicle inspection lifts, 267
    work at height, 25, 279
    work equipment, 165
    workplace transport, 352
Control of energy, 158
Control of Major Accident Hazard Regs. 1999, 147, 403
Controlled collapse, 336
Controls
    speed, 261
    two-handed, 230
Corns blast furnace, 2001, 368
Corrosion, 143, 205
Corrosive
    atmospheres, 21
    failure, case studies, 383
Counterbalance lift trucks, 251
Coupling
    control measures, 353
    hazards, 351
Cradles, 332
Crane operations, 265
Cranes, 263
Creep, 207, 383
Critical
    pressure, 37
    temperature, 37
Crushing, 197, 199
Current, 283
    alternating, 285
    direct, 285
    effects on the body, 287
    fault, 293
    protection, 293
Cutting, 196, 199
Cutting off electric supply, 295

D

Damage
    causes of, 20
    impact, 21
    structure of buildings, 20
Dangerous goods safety advisers, 140
Dangerous substances, 126
    assessment of risk, 128
    definitions, 127
    handling, 135
    hazards, 128
    packaging, 140
    storage methods, 128
    transport, 138
Dangerous Substances and Explosive Atmospheres Regs. 2002, 405
Dangerous Substances (Notification and Marking of Sites) Regs. 1990, 405
Dangers of electricity in hazardous areas, 138
Declaration
    conformity, 194
    incorporation, 194
Decoration, 317
Defective apparatus, 311
Definition
    combustion, 40
    confined space, 14
    dangerous substances, 127
    disaster, 145
    explosion, 41
    means of escape, 105
    pressure systems, 378
Demarcating safe areas, 331
Demolition, 316, 335
    access / egress, 338

INDEX

Demolition - Cont'd
    explosives, 336
    hazardous substances, 338
    hazards, 336
    method statements / permit to work, 338
    safe working practices, 337
    security, 339
Density
    effects of gases and vapours, 36
    effects of liquids, 36
    relative, 35
    vapour, 35
Design, 385
    alarm systems, 85
    considerations, 384
    fixed fire fighting systems, 92
    hazards, 321
    plant and process controls, 60
    safe working practices, 18
    surfaces, 4
Designer, 318
Detection
    fire, 80, 83, 87
    flame and thermal, 87
Deterioration
    building materials, 22
    equipment, 163
Development of emergency plans, 150
Devices
    safeguarding, 219
    trip, 226
Diesel powered equipment, 257
Direct
    current, 285
    shock, 288
Directional signs, 111
Disabled people, 115
Disc sanders, 197
Dismantling, 316
Dismantling scaffolds and falsework, 328
Dispensing of flammable liquids, 136
Disposal of flammable liquids, 136
Distance from danger, 160
Diversity, 245
Dominion energy, 384
Doors, 109, 197
Double insulation, 299
Drag boxes, 343
Drawing-in, 196, 199
Drencher systems, 96
Drills, 196
Driver
    competence, 357
    identification, 357
    protection systems, 354
    refresher training, 357
    restraint systems, 354
    selection, 357
    training, 140, 357
Driving at work, 358
    control measures, 363
    evaluating risks, 362
    risk assessment, 362
Driving hours, 358
Drum
    sling, 276
    storage, 129
Dry powder
    extinguishing media, 91
Dry powder, fixed installations, 98
Dual enforcement, 73
Ductile failure, 204
Dumper truck 349
Duration
    effects on the body, 287
    exposure, 183
Dust
    control, 339
    explosions, 50
    hazardous area zoning, 64
    protection of equipment -, 141
Duties
    CDM co-ordinator, 319
    client, 318
    contractors, 319
    designer, 318
    principal contractor, 319
'Duty holders', 290
Dye penetrant inspection, 216

E

Earth free zones, 299
Earthing, 285
EC type examination, 190
Eddy current testing, 217
Edge protection, 332
Effect
    atomisation, 42
    catalysts, 122
    hydrodynamic, 7
    oxygen, 42
    pressure, 121
    temperature, 121
Egress, 3
    confined spaces, 16
El Paso Natural Gas Co., 383
Elasticity, 202
Electric
    arcs, 289
    shock, 286
Electrical
    causes of fire, 288
    circuitry, 284
Electrical equipment
    ATEX, 143
    capability, 292
    flammable atmospheres, 143
    inspection, 299, 312
    maintenance, 299, 303
    overheating, 288
    selection and suitability, 296
    strength, 292
Electricity at Work Regulations 1989, 302, 407
Electricity in hazardous areas, 138
Electromagnetic radiation, 285
Electrostatic discharge, 39
Eliminating risks, 164
Emergency
    arrangements, 19
    controls for work equipment, 159
    controls, 159
    evacuation plans, 118
    lighting, 110
    lone workers, 31
    planning, 145
    resuscitation, 305
    stop controls, 238
Employer's
    common law duty, 3
    statutory duty, 3
Emptying containers, 136
Endothermic reactions, 122
Enforcement
    dual, 73
    notice, 71
Engineering construction, 315
English language, 12
    non-English speaking workers, 318
Entanglement, 196, 199
Enthalpy, 123
Environment, 339
    changes of level, 354
    fire water runoff, 104
    gradients, 354
    hazardous, 141
    protection, 339
    restrictions, 321
    surface conditions, 354
    visibility, 354
Equipment
    fire detection, 83
    inspection, 24
    protection from environments, 141
Erection of scaffold and falsework, 328
Ergonomic, 159, 238
Essential health and safety requirements, 185, 386
European Agreement concerning the International Carriage of Dangerous Goods by Road 2009 (as amended 2011), 409
Evacuation
    disabled people, 115
    horizontal, 114
    plans, 118
    procedures, 113
    single stage, 114
    stair, 115
    two stage, 115
Evaluation of risk, 79
    driving at work, 36
Examination
    frequency, 377
    lifting equipment, 270
    plant and equipment, 247

INDEX

Examination – cont'd
    simple pressure systems, 377
    written scheme, 387
Excavations, 22, 316, 339
    360° excavators, 344
    access, 340
    buried services, 341
    collapse, 340
    controls, 340
    falls, 340
    flooding, 341
    hazards, 339
    plans and drawings, 342
    safe digging methods, 342
    service location tools, 342
    statutory inspection, 344
    substances, 341
    supporting methods, 344
Excavators, 344
Exceptional circumstances, 164
Excessive stress, 381
Exclusion of ignition sources, 65
Exits, 111
Exothermic reactions, 123
Explosions
    amount of material, 49
    containment, 66
    controls 60
    definition, 41
    dust, 50
    examples, 43, 46, 47, 50, 52
    failure of control measures, 42
    hazardous area zoning, 64
    how they occur, 40
    ignition sources, 49
    limits, 20, 36
    maximum pressure, 37
    mechanisms of, 40
    natural gas transmission line, 383
    panels, 65
    prevention of release, 49
    primary, 51
    rate of pressure rise, 37
    relief, 65
    secondary, 51
    sensing of vapour, 49
    steam, 368
    steam generating boiler, 384
    suppression, 66
    terms, 35
    vapour cloud, 41
Explosives, 336
Exposure, 183
Extinguishers, 99
Extinguishing media, 90
Eyebolts, 276

F

Fabrication, 317
Fabrics, 57
Factor of safety, 214
Factors
    assessing risk, 15
    safe working practices, 18
Failure
    causes, 200
    common mode, 243
    explosion control measures, 42
    modes of structures, 22, 200
    pressure systems, 381, 384
    prevention strategies, 213
    to danger, 245
Fall arrest
    devices, 334
    systems, 28
Falling
    materials, 24, 330, 337
    objects, 256, 260
Falls
    consequences, 28
    mitigating distance, 28
    persons, objects and vehicles, 340
Falsework, 329
Familiarisation training, 263
Fans, 337
Fatalities, 358
Fatigue
    failure case studies, 382
    mechanical, 381
    metal, 203
Fault current, 293
FD20/20 and FD30/20, 110

Fencing, 26
Fibre rope slings, 275
Fighting fire, 80
Filling and transfer, 135
Fire
    action instructions, 114
    alarm, 83
    alterations to buildings 82
    assembly point, 114
    authority powers, 71
    detection and warning, 80
    disabled people, 115
    drills, 117
    extinguishers, 99
    extinguishing media, 90
    fighting, 80
    hazards, 76
    how it occurs, 40
    maintenance and testing, 80
    marshal system, 115
    means of escape, 80, 104
    notices, 71
    plan, 81
    point, 35
    procedures, 80
    properties of materials and structures, 54
    refuges, 115
    regulations, 75, 410
    risk assessment, 77
    roll call system, 115
    signs 10
    single stage, 86
    spread, 40, 57
    terms, 35
    training, 80
    triangle, 38
    two stage, 86
    wardens, 118
    water runoff, 104
    zones, 86
Fire Safety (Scotland) Regulations 2006, 410
Fire (Scotland) Act 2005, 410
First aid, 305
Five steps to fire risk assessment, 77
Fixed
    distance guards, 221
    enclosed guards, 221
    objects and collisions, 350
Flame detectors, 87
Flameproof equipment (Ex d), 144
Flammability limits, 36
Flammable, 64
Flammable atmospheres, 19
    control measures when entering, 20
    electrical equipment, 143
    explosion limits (LEL), 20
    how arise, 19
Flammable liquids, 136
Flammable materials storage, 62
Flammable vapour, 289
Flash point, 35
Flat roofs, 331
Fleet
Flixborough 1974, 45, 135
Flooding
    excavations, 341
    gas, 96
Flow through pipelines, 136
Foam
    extinguishing media, 91
    fixed installations, 98
Foaming, 384
Footwear, 5
Footwear, for cleaning, 7
Footwear related to Surfaces, 5
Forensic examination, 215
Forklift truck, 350
Fouling, 384
Fragile
    roofs, 331
    surfaces, 24
Frequency
    effects on the body, 287
    examination, 377
    use, 171
Fresnel lens, 261
Friction, coefficient of (CoF), 4
Fuel, 256
Functional testing, 173
Fuses, 293, 296

INDEX

G
Gases
- containers, 376
- density effects, 36
- flooding, 96
- liquefaction, 372
- properties, 35

Gates and doors, 197
Gauge pressure, 375
GEEP, 118
General Foods, Banbury 1981, 52
Generators, 312
Generic emergency evacuation plan (GEEP), 118
Gin wheel hoist, 266
Glove work, 309
Good housekeeping, 8
Grangemouth, 1987, 67
Guardrails, 26
Guards, 221
- adjustable, 229
- anthropometrics, 221
- automatic, 226
- construction, 221
- fixed distance, 221
- fixed enclosed, 221
- interlocked, 222
- self-adjusting, 229

Guillotines, 196

H
Hand signals, 12
Handling of dangerous substances, 135
'Hardware' (physical) measures, 165
Harmonised standards, 185
Harnesses, 335
Hazardous
- environments, 141
- substances, 338

Hazardous area
- classification, 144
- electricity, 138
- zoning, 64

Hazards
- access, 278
- crane operations, 265
- dangerous substances, 128
- demolition, 336
- excavations, 339
- falling materials, 330
- fire, 39, 76
- gin wheel hoist, 266
- hoists, 266
- lifting operations, 265
- lifts, 266
- lone workers, 31
- machinery, 196
- mechanical, 198
- maintenance of work equipment, 168
- mobile elevating work platforms (MEWP), 268
- mobile work equipment -, 251
- non-mechanical, 200
- non-movement related, 350
- over pressure in pressure systems, 381
- over temperature in pressure systems, 381
- scissor lifts, 267
- steam, 367
- vehicle inspection lifts, 267
- vehicle maintenance, 351
- working at height, 22, 278, 324
- workplace transport operations, 349

Health and Safety at Work etc. Act 1974, 412
Health and Safety (Safety Signs and Signals) Regs. 1996, 14, 412
Health and safety file, 321
Heat
- detection equipment, 84
- of reaction, 122

Height
- barriers, 161
- cables, 312
- work at, 23

Hickson and Welch, 1992, 47
Hierarchy
- control measures, 25
- controls for work equipment, 164
- work at height, 25

High voltage, 283
- glove work, 309
- systems, 305

Hoists, 264, 266
Holistic approaches, 240
Horizontal evacuation, 114

Hosereels, 92, 98
Hot
- atmospheres, 21
- gases, 76
- objects, 76

Housekeeping, 8
Human
- error, 247
- reliability, 159
- reliability analysis, 243

Hydrant systems, 95
Hydraulic and mechanical presses, 197
Hydrodynamic effect, 7
Hydrogen attack, 383

I
Identifying, 357
- dangerous substances, 127
- fire hazards, 78
- people at risk from fire, 79

IET Wiring Regulations 17th Edition (BS 7671: 2008), 416
Ignition
- exclusion, 65
- sources, 39

Immobile access equipment, 324
Impact, 197, 199
- damage, 21

Impedance, 284
Imperial Sugar, Georgia USA, 2008, 52
Incidents of dust explosions, 52
Incompatible materials, 64
- storage and segregation, 131

Independent scaffold, 326
Index of protection, 141
Indirect shock, 288
Inerting, 65
Information, 166, 386
- CDM 322
- machinery, 234
- pre-construction, 320

Injection, 200
Injury, 182
Inspection
- electrical equipment, 299
- equipment, 24
- excavations, 344
- lifting equipment, 270
- methods, 173
- simple pressure systems, 377
- work equipment, 172
- working platforms, 329

Installation
- services, 317
- work equipment, 163

Institution of Engineering and Technology (IET), 302
Instruction, 166
- fire, 114, 117
- machinery, 235
- working at heights, 29

Insulated core panels, 56
Insulation, 292
- conductors, 292
- double, 299

Integration
- of safety, 179
- work equipment, 185

Integrity, 155, 163
Interlocked guards, 222
Interlocking
- control, 222
- power, 222

Intermediate storage, 129
Intrinsically safe equipment (Ex i), 144
Intumescent strip, 110
Iron making process, 368
Isolation, 295
- electrical, 297
- maintenance, 232
- methods, 233

J
Jigs, 231

L
Labelling of vehicles, 140
Ladders, 27, 324
Lamella tearing, 384
Landscaping, 317
Lathes, 197
Layout, 257
Leaking containment, 133

© RMS

443

INDEX

Legal requirements, 71
    CDM projects, 320
    egress, 3
    individuals on public roads, 361
    non-CDM projects, 320
    safe means of access, 3
    safe place of work, 3
Lift trucks, 251
    attachments, 259
    selection of operators, 262
    training, 263
    use to move people, 259
Lifting
    accessories, 274
    hooks, 276
    operations, 265
    spreader beam, 276
Lifting equipment
    controls, 269
    examination, 270
    inspection, 270
    integrity, 269
    maintenance, 270
    safe working load, 269
Lifting Operations and Lifting Equipment Regulations 1998, 417
Lifts, 264
Lighting, 110
Limits of flammability, 36
Liquefaction of gases, 372
Liquefied petroleum gas (LPG), 370
Liquids, 35
Littlebrook D power station, 09 January 1978, 209
Live line overhead working, 310
Loading, 316
    control measures, 353
    hazards, 350
Location, 163
Log books, 117
Lone workers
    emergency procedures, 31
    hazards, 31
    lifting heavy objects, 31
    medical conditions, 30
    monitoring, 31
    problems, 30
    supervision, 31
    training, 30
Loss
    of containment, 381
    of control, 349
Low
    voltage, 283
    water level, 384
Lower
    explosion limits (LEL), 20, 36
    flammable limit, 36
    tier sites, 148
LPG powered equipment, 257

M

Machinery
    annex IV, 193
    CNC, 198
    conformity assessment, 185, 188
    control systems, 236
    essential health and safety requirements, 185
    hazards, 196, 198
    information, 234
    instructions, 235
    risk assessment, 179
    unguarded, 232
    use, 234
Magnetic particle testing, 217
Maintenance, 231, 377, 388
    breakdown, 170
    condition based, 169
    control measures, 354
    electrical equipment, 299, 303
    emergency plans, 152
    existing premises, 315
    fire extinguishers, 103
    hazards, 168, 351
    hosereels, 99
    isolation, 232
    lifting equipment, 270
    management strategies, 169
    permits, 231
    personnel, 156
    planned preventative, 169
    preventive, 246
    safe atmospheres, 16
    safe systems of work, 231
    services, 317
    sprinklers, 99
    work equipment, 156, 168
Maintenance and testing, 80
Major accidents, 66
Major accident prevention policy (MAPP), 148
Major incidents, 207
Management of Health and Safety at Work Regulations 1999, 418
Managing
    fleet, 360
    work-related road risk, 359
Manual alarm systems, 89
Markham Colliery, 30 July 1973, 211
Markings, 235, 356, 386
Materials
    behaviour in a fire, 54
    construction, 337
    fall of, 24
    fire properties, 54
    handlers, 252
    incompatible, 64
Maximum
    explosion pressure, 374
    working pressure, 374
    working temperature, 374
Meaning of
    competent person, 305
    construction, 291, 374
    construction work, 315
    contents, 374
    duty holders, 290
    materials, 374
    negative pressure, 374
    positive pressure, 373
    pressure, 373
    shape, 374
    unfired, 374
Means of escape, 80, 104
Mechanical
    damage, 141
    failure of containment, 381
    fatigue and shock, 381
    hazards, 198
    presses, 197
    restraints, 230
Mechanisms
    confined vapour cloud explosions, 41
    dust explosions, 50
    explosions, 40
    fire Spread, 40
    steam explosion, 368
    unconfined vapour cloud explosions, 41
Medical conditions, 30
Metal fatigue, 203
Metals, 54
Method statements, 338
MEWP, 22, 26, 28, 268, 277
Mexico City 1984, 47, 135
Minimising failures to danger, 245
Minimum working temperature, 374
Mitigating distance of falls, 28
Mitigation measures, 62
Mixed systems, 242
Mobile elevating work platforms (MEWP), 22, 26, 28, 268, 277
Mobile work equipment
    applications, 251
    control measures, 251
    hazards, 254
    pre-operational checks, 258
    remotely controlled, 253
    safe operation, 257
Modes
    action of extinguishing media, 90
    failure, 200
Modification, 386
    buildings, 22
Monitoring
    emergency plans, 152
    lone workers, 31
    road risk performance, 360

N

Naked flame, 39
Need for access, 183
    reducing the, 160
Negative pressure, 374
Nets, 334
New Roads and Street Works Act 1991, 421
New technology, 174
Noise protection, 339
Non-CDM projects, 320
Non-destructive testing, 215

INDEX

Non-English speaking workers, 318
Non-mechanical hazards, 200
Non-movement related hazards, 350
Non-pressurised components, 377
Notification of Conventional Tower Cranes Regulations 2010, 422
Notification of Installations Handling Hazardous Substances Regs 1982, 422
Notification of projects, 320

O

Occupied premises, 315
Off-site
    emergency plans, 152
    risks, 321
Ohm's law, 284
Openings, 60
Operating
    conditions, 375
    procedures, 18, 183
Operators, 15
Overbalancing, 255
Overhead power lines, 307
Overheating, 381
    electrical equipment, 288
Overloading of structures, 21
Overpressure, 381
Overrun of speed, 256
Overturning, 254
    vehicles, 349
Oxidisation, 43
Oxygen, 42

P

Packaging of dangerous substances, 140
Paper, 57
    shredders, 196
Parallel
    redundancy, 245
    systems, 241
Particle size, 42, 50
Passageways, 108
Pedestal drills, 196
Pedestrians
    collisions, 350
    mobile work equipment, 257
PEEPS, 118
Pendulum test value (PTV), 5
People hoists, 264
Permit to dig, 346
Permit to work, 18, 144, 338
    demolition, 338
    electrical, 307
    maintenance, 231
Personal
    emergency evacuation plans (PEEPS), 118
    fall arrest devices, 334
    fall protection systems, 29
    suspension systems, 333
Persons at risk, 17, 182, 340
Phased evacuation, 115
Photocopiers, 196
Photosynthesis, 122
Piecemeal, 336
Piling, 343
Pipelines, 136
Piper Alpha, 6 July 1988, 66
Pipes, 384
Placing of conductors, 292
Plans, 342
    construction phase, 320
    fire, 81
Planned preventative maintenance, 169, 246
Planning
    emergency, 145
    hazardous substances, 338
    working at heights, 23
Plasticity, 202
Plastics, 57
Plate clamp, 276
Poor literacy, 318
Port Ramsgate, September 1994, 212
Portable electrical equipment, 302, 310
Portable fire fighting equipment, 99
Portable power tools, 197
Positioning systems, 333
Positive pressure, 373
Post-incident recovery, 151
Potential difference, 283
Powder, 91
Power
    interlocking, 222
    presses, 176
    tools, 197
Powers
    fire authority, 71
    inspectors, 71
Practical considerations
    egress, 3
    safe means of access, 3
    safe place of work, 3
Precautionary measures
    falling materials, 330
    maintenance of work equipment, 168
    working at heights, 23
Pre-construction information, 320
Premature collapse of buildings, 337
Pre-operational checks, 258
Presses, 197
Pressure, 373
    absolute, 374
    atmospheric, 375
    bulk storage, 372
    control, 124
    critical, 37
    gauge, 375
    maximum explosion level, 37
    rate of rise, 38
    steam, 379
Pressure Equipment Regulations 1999, 375, 386, 423
Pressure systems, 378
    competent persons, 388
    construction, 385
    definitions, 378
    design, 385
    failure prevention, 385
    failures, 381, 384
    hazards, 381
    information, 386
    key components, 379
    maintenance, 388
    marking, 386
    meaning of terms, 374
    modification, 386
    principles, 367
    record keeping, 388
    relevant fluids, 378
    repair, 386
    safe operating limits, 386
    safety features, 379
    statutory examination, 377
    written scheme of examination, 387
Pressure Systems Safety Regulations 2000, 387, 425
Pressurisation, 144
Pressurised components, 376
Preventative maintenance, 169
Prevention
    falls, 26
    of danger, 306
Preventive maintenance, 246
Pre-weakening, 336
Principal contractor, 319
Principles of safety integration, 179
Probability of injury, 182
Problems facing lone workers, 30
Procedures
    evacuation, 113
    fire, 80
    operating machinery, 183
Process controls, 61
Prohibition
    notice, 72
    signs 9
Project notification, 320
Properties
    gases, 35
    liquids, 35
    solids, 35
Prosecution, 72
Protection
    conductors, 292
    equipment, 141
    falling object, 260
    fire risk, 79
    index, 141
    public, the, 339
    roll-over, 260
Provision and Use of Work Equipment Regulations 1998, 155, 165, 377, 426
Provision of information, 322
Public
    protection, 339
    roads, 361
Purging, 20, 144
Push sticks, 231

INDEX

Q
Quality assurance
    conformity assessment, 191
    manufacture and installation, 214
    reliability, 245
Quartzoid glass bulb, 89, 95

R
Radial arm drills, 196
Radiography, 218
Rate
    of chemical reaction, 121, 124
    of pressure rise, 38
Rated capacity, 251
Registration, Evaluation, Authorisation and Restriction of Chemicals Regs. EC1907/2006, 428
Reach lift trucks, 251
Reaction, 121
Record keeping, 388
Reduced voltage systems, 296
Reducing need for access, 160
Reductionist approaches, 240
Redundancy, 245
Refresher training, 174, 357
Refrigeration
    bulk storage, 372
    closed circuit, 372
Refuges, 115
Regulations
    building, 76
    fire safety, 75
Regulatory Reform (Fire Safety) Order 2005, 429
Re-installation of work equipment, 163
Relative density, 35
Relevant fluids, 378
Reliability of safeguards, 17, 183
Remotely controlled mobile equipment, 253
Renovation, 315
Repair, 386
Residual current devices (RCDs), 298
Resistance, 283
    effects on the body, 287
Respiratory protective equipment (RPE), 17
Restraining systems, 261, 354
Restraints
    driver, 260
    mechanical, 230
Resuscitation, 305
Reveal tie, 327
Risk assessment
    driving at work, 361
    fire, 77
    machinery, 179
    review 81
    use, 162
Risk control hierarchy
    work at height, 25
    work equipment, 164
Risk evaluation, 79
Risks
    road, 358
    work at heights, 23
    work equipment, 163
Road
    distance driven, 358
    driving hours, 358
    incident reporting, 361
    injuries, 358
    managing risk, 359
    monitoring risk performance, 361
    policy, 359
    risks, 358
    stress due to traffic, 359
    weather conditions, 359
    work schedules, 359
Robotics, 198
Role of fire wardens, 118
Roll call system, 115
Roll-over, 254
    protection, 260
Roof
    ladders, 331
    work, 331
Rope access and positioning systems, 333
Rough terrain lift trucks, 251
Roughness (Rz), 6
Runaway reactions, 123

S
Safe
    access, 16
    atmospheres, 16
    condition signs 9
    digging methods, 342
    means of access and egress, 3
    methods of roof work, 331
    place of work, 3
    working load, 269
Safe operating
    limits, 386
    mobile work equipment, 257
    platform, 256
    station, 256
Safe systems of work
    demolition, 335, 337
    electrical 307
    installations made dead, 304
    live working, 304
    maintenance, 231
Safeguarding, 17, 219
    devices, 219
    reliability, 17, 183
Safety
    factor, 214
    features of pressure systems, 379
    integration, 179
    nets, 334
    related parts, 173
    report, 149
    requirements of simple pressure vessels, 376
    signs, 9
Sandwich panels, 56
Scaffolds, 326, 328
    independent, 326
    tower, 327
Scale, 384
Scissor lifts, 267, 278
Seal failures, 384
Securing loads, 350
Security, 339
Segregating, 62
    incompatible materials, 131
    pedestrians and vehicles, 354
Selection
    drivers, 357
    electrical equipment, 296
    fleet, 360
    lift truck operators, 262
    suitable equipment, 155
    work equipment, 185
Self-adjusting guards, 229
Separated Extra Low Voltage (SELV), 293
Series systems, 241
Services
    contact, 24
    location tools, 342
Severity of possible injury, 182
Shackles, 276
Shear, 196, 199
    stress, 201
Sheeting, 343
    hazards, 351
Shock, 286, 292
Short-duration work, 331
Side loading lift trucks, 252
Signals, 12
    fire, 86
Signs, 356
    directional for fire, 111
    safety, 9
Simple pressure
    systems, 374
    vessels, 376
Simple Pressure Vessels (Safety) Regulations 1991, 374, 376, 430
Single stage
    evacuation, 114
    fire alarm, 86
Site
    boundaries, 339
    clearance, 316
    movements, 316
    rules, 356
    security, 339
Siting of fire extinguishers, 103
Size of openings, 160
Slings, 274
Slipping, 4
    potential, classification, 5
    resistance testing, 5
Sloping roofs, 331, 332

INDEX

Smoke
    detection equipment, 84
    seals, 110
Sodium, 123
Soft fall beanbags, 334
'Software' measures, 165
Solids - properties, 35
Sources of ignition, 39
Sparking, 39, 289
Speed control systems, 261
Spheres, 371
Spillage containment, 133
Spraying of flammable liquids, 136
Sprinklers, 99
Stabbing and puncture, 196, 200
Stability, 272
Staff alarm controlled evacuation, 114
Staged fire alarm, 86
Stages of combustion, 41
Stairs, 108
Standards, 185, 192
Standby systems, 245
Static electricity, 289
Statistics, 315
Statutory duty
    means of access and egress, 3
    place of work, 3
Statutory examination
    lifting equipment, 270
    plant and equipment, 247
    pressure systems, 377
Statutory requirement
    certification and authorisation, 167
    inspection, 172
    inspections of excavations, 344
    maintenance of work equipment, 171
Statutory restrictions, 167
Steam
    at any pressure, 379
    explosions, 368
    hazards, 367
    heating system, 373
    receiver, 379
    saturation, 367
Steel
    vessels, 376
    wire rope, 274
Storage, 62
    dangerous substances, 130
    flammable materials, 62
    incompatible materials, 131
    materials, 316
    spheres vs. torpedoes, 371
Strain, 200
Strength, 292
Stress, 200
    due to traffic, 359
Structural
    members, 21
    protection, 59
Structures
    causes of damage, 20
    overloading, 21
Subsidence, 21
Substations, 309
Sufficiency of traffic routes, 352
Suitability
    traffic routes, 352
    work equipment, 157
Summit tunnel fire, 1984, 59
Supervision of vehicles, 140
Supervisors, 174
    lone workers, 31
Supplier information, 171
Supply of Machinery (Safety) Regulations 2008, 179, 432
Supporting excavations, 342
Suppression, 66
Surfaces, 4, 5
Surveys, 338
Suspension equipment, 333
Systematic analysis, 240
System
    failure analysis, 240
    failures, 239
    meaning, 239
    permit to work, 18
    reliability, 239, 244
    standby, 245
    types, 241

T

Task, material and equipment, 17
Technical file, 193
Telescopic materials handlers, 252
Temperature
    control, 124
    critical, 37
Temporary
    access, 332
    construction activities, 317
    immobile access equipment, 324
    shoring, 342
Tensile stress, 201
Terms
    auto-ignition temperature, 35
    explosion, 35
    fire point, 35
    fire, 35
    flash point, 35
    relative density, 35
    vapour density, 35
Testing, 173
    alarm system, 86
    drivers, 357
    manufacture and installation, 214
    non-destructive, 215
Thermal
    detectors, 88
    fatigue, 383
    radiation, 77
    shock, 383
Through tie, 327
Time pressures from clients, 317
Toe boards, 26
Top-tier sites, 149
Torpedoes, 372
Tower scaffold, 327
Toxic
    atmospheres, 341
    gases and smoke, 76
Traffic routes
    sufficiency, 352
    suitability, 352
Training
    driver, 140, 357
    familiarisation, 263
    fire extinguishers, 104
    fire, 80
    hosereels, 99
    lift truck operators, 263
    lone workers, 30
    sprinklers, 99
    work equipment, 166, 174
    work in confined spaces, 19
    working at heights, 29
Transfer and filling, 135
Transitory nature of workers, 317
Transport
    control measures, 352
    coupling, 351
    dangerous substances, 138
    hazards, 349
    loading and un-loading, 350
    operations, 349
    securing loads, 350
    sheeting, 351
    vehicle maintenance work, 351
Transportable gas containers, 376
Trapped key system, 224
Travel distances, 108
Trench box, 343
Trestles, 325
Trip devices, 226
Two-hand controls, 230
Two stage
    evacuation, 115
    fire alarm, 86
Type
    'e' equipment, 145
    'N' equipment, 145
    of equipment, 173
    of inspection, 377

U

Ultimate tensile strength, 202
Ultrasonic testing, 219
Unauthorised
    modifications to buildings, 22
    start-up, 255
Unconfined vapour cloud explosions, 41
Underground cables, 308

INDEX

Unfired, 374
Unguarded machinery, 232
Unloading, 316
    control measures, 353
    hazards, 350
Unoccupied premises, 315
Upper explosive limit, 36
Upper flammable limit, 36
User checks, 377

V

Vaporising liquids, 91
Vapour
    cloud explosions, 41
    density, 35
    hazardous area zoning, 64
Vehicle
    collisions, 350
    inspection lifts, 267
    labelling, 140
    maintenance work, 351
    management of movements, 353
    overturning, 349
    segregating, 354
    supervision, 140
    warnings, 356
Venting, 65
Verbal signals, 12
Vessels, 374, 376
Vibration, 21
VICES, 64
Voids, 60
Voltage, 283
    effects on the body, 286
Vulnerable persons, 175

W

Wardens, 118
Warnings, 235
    fire, 80
    signs, 9
    vehicle approach and reversing, 356
Water
    extinguishing media, 90
    hammer, 384
    mist systems, 97
    runoff, 104
    saturation, 367
Wear, 206, 384
Weather conditions, 317, 359
    adverse, 20
    avoidance, 24
Welding, 312
Wet
    cleaning, 7
    Coefficient of Friction (CoF), 4
    environments, 143
Wilson and Clyde Coal Co. v English (1938), 3
Windsor Castle fire, 1992, 58
Windsor Tower fire (Madrid), 2005, 58
Wood, 55
Woodworking machines, 175
Work at Height Regulations 2005, 25, 329, 330, 434
Work at height, 324
    alternatives, 23
    avoiding, 25
    controls, 279
    existing safe place of work, 25
    hazards, 23, 278, 324
    hierarchy, 25
    instruction, 29
    main precautions, 23
    means of temporary access, 332
    organisation and planning, 23
    risks, 23
    safe working procedures, 23
    training, 29
Work equipment
    access, 324
    control measures, 165
    controls, 159
    deterioration, 163
    hazards, 168
    information, 166
    inspection, 172
    installation, 163
    maintenance, 155, 168
    mobile, 251
    precautions, 168
    preventing falls, 26
    risk control hierarchy, 164
    risks, 163
    selection, 155, 185
    statutory restrictions, 167
    suitability, 157
    training, 166, 172
Work schedules, 359
Workers
    non-English speaking, 318
    poor literacy and numeracy, 318
    transitory nature, 317
Working
    adverse weather conditions, 24
    load limit, 214
    platforms, 26, 329
    pressure, 374
    temperature, 374
Workplace
    changing, 317
    inspection, 24
    transport, 349
Workplace (Health, Safety and Welfare) Regulations 1992, 8, 436
Work-related road risk, 358
    distance driven, 358
    driving hours, 358
    incident reporting, 361
    injuries and fatalities, 358
    managing, 359
    monitoring risk performance, 361
    policy, 359
    stress due to traffic, 359
    weather conditions, 359
    work schedules, 359
Written scheme of examination, 387

Y

Yield point, 202
Young people, 175
Young's modulus, 202

Z

Zones
    fire alarm, 86
    hazardous area, 64

NOTES

NOTES